CICERO, *DE HARUSPICUM RESPONSIS*

Cicero,
De haruspicum responsis

Introduction, Text, Translation, and Commentary

ANTHONY CORBEILL

Great Clarendon Street, Oxford, OX2 6DP,
United Kingdom

Oxford University Press is a department of the University of Oxford.
It furthers the University's objective of excellence in research, scholarship,
and education by publishing worldwide. Oxford is a registered trade mark of
Oxford University Press in the UK and in certain other countries

© Anthony Corbeill 2023

The moral rights of the author have been asserted

All rights reserved. No part of this publication may be reproduced, stored in
a retrieval system, or transmitted, in any form or by any means, without the
prior permission in writing of Oxford University Press, or as expressly permitted
by law, by licence or under terms agreed with the appropriate reprographics
rights organization. Enquiries concerning reproduction outside the scope of the
above should be sent to the Rights Department, Oxford University Press, at the
address above

You must not circulate this work in any other form
and you must impose this same condition on any acquirer

Published in the United States of America by Oxford University Press
198 Madison Avenue, New York, NY 10016, United States of America

British Library Cataloguing in Publication Data
Data available

Library of Congress Control Number: 2023933550

ISBN 978–0–19–286895–4

Printed and bound by
CPI Group (UK) Ltd, Croydon, CR0 4YY

Links to third party websites are provided by Oxford in good faith and
for information only. Oxford disclaims any responsibility for the materials
contained in any third party website referenced in this work.

Acknowledgments

Two decades ago, at a cafe in Austin, Texas, Andrew Riggsby and I decided to team up to write a commentary on Cicero's *De haruspicum responsis*. After Andrew wrote a draft of the notes for sections 5–9 (which still bear his stamp), other commitments forced him to drop the project. I would have been incapable of soldiering on alone were it not for several generous institutions. My home universities—Kansas *quondam* and Virginia *nunc*—provided much-needed internal funding, while external support from All Souls and Corpus Christi Colleges (Oxford University) and the Institute of Classical Studies (University of London, where I was Dorothy Tarrant Fellow) provided time and excellent library facilities for completing a first draft. I must single out in particular the generosity of Stephen Harrison at Corpus for letting me use his office while he was on leave. Human resources were equally valuable, with the following scholars responding to specific queries or offering ideas in areas that lay far outside my expertise. William Altman, Andreas Bendlin, Christer Bruun, Orazio Cappello, Jeffrey Easton, Tom Hillard, Astrid Khoo, Francho Pina Polo, Catherine Steel, Phil Stinson, Kathryn Tempest, Lewis Webb, and George Woudhuysen were all generous and encouraging, as were those who provided comments after lectures; here I single out in particular Coulter George, Fiachra Mac Góráin, Roland Mayer, Tobias Reinhardt, and Tony Woodman. Graduate students have endured reading and analyzing this speech with me at the Universities of both Kansas and Virginia and throughout the commentary they should recognize their contributions; I am grateful especially to Christine Boltsi, Jovan Cvjetičanin, Michael Fons, Rubén García Fernández, Kara Kopchinski, Holly Maggiore, Rachel Morrison, and Michael Woo. Among classicists, Ciceronians make up a truly generous *factio*; the following kindly offered suggestions after reading through large chunks of the commentary's penultimate version—Wes Hanson, Thomas Keeline, Gesine Manuwald, Andrew Riggsby, and Brian Walters—while Chris van den Berg critiqued the introduction and Stan Lombardo the translation. The Basil L. Gildersleeve Professorship at the University of Virginia provided funding for travel and books but most importantly for an excellent proofreader and copyeditor in the person of Will Nichols. Finally, at Oxford University Press Charlotte Loveridge has been supportive and patient throughout the publication progress, as has Juliet Gardner during the copyediting.

The dust jacket of this book illustrates my conception of the situation informing this speech. The upper image, made by Hans W. Schmidt in the early twentieth century, depicts Cicero delivering the first oration against Catiline in 63 BCE. But if we squint, we can imagine the stooping figure right of center to be Clodius, reacting to the steady stream of invective coming from Cicero's mouth. One can also imagine Cicero holding in his right hand the response of the *haruspices*, for which he offers a sentence-by-sentence, even a word-by-word, interpretation in order to incriminate Clodius before his fellow senators. But unlike the situation with Catiline, where it was left to the senate alone to render a decision—one with disastrous consequences for Cicero—there intrudes upon these proceedings from below a *haruspex*, a foreign seer from Etruria whose independent contribution to this Roman problem allows a potential means of resolution.

To close with a final expression of gratitude: my greatest regret for the delayed appearance of this volume is that it appeared too late for two great Latinists, and two great friends, to read my words of thanks. Nicholas Horsfall and Jim Adams, each in their uniquely penetrating way, provided invaluable counsel and criticism throughout the time span of researching and writing. With an acute awareness of its flaws and shortcomings I dedicate this commentary to their memory.

Contents

Abbreviations	ix
Introduction	xi
A. Historical background	xii
1. Cicero and Clodius	xii
2. Cicero's exile and return	xiii
B. Cicero's oratory upon his return	xiv
1. Rhetorical strategies in the *post reditum* orations	xiv
2. Clodius's lost speech *De haruspicum responsis*	xv
3. Cicero's strategy in *De haruspicum responsis*	xvii
C. Style	xix
1. General remarks	xix
2. Language and figures of speech	xx
3. Sound as sense: grammatical gender, sonic effects, and prose rhythm	xxii
D. Authenticity of the speeches *post reditum*	xxv
E. The speech *De haruspicum responsis*	xxvii
1. Title	xxvii
2. Date	xxix
F. Religious background: Roman prodigies and Etruscan *haruspices*	xxxi
1. The Roman prodigy process	xxxi
2. The Etruscan *haruspices*	xxxiv
a. Composition and training	xxxiv
b. Role in the Roman prodigy process	xxxvi
G. The haruspical response: text, style, and content	xxxix
1. Latin text	xxxix
2. Archaic features	xl
a. Lexical elements	xli
b. Word order	xlii
H. Note on the Latin text	xlii
I. A note on the translation	xliv
Text and translation	1
M. Tulli Ciceronis oratio de haruspicum responsis	2
Commentary	47
Bibliography	331
Index of Latin Terms	355
General Index	357

Abbreviations

AG	J. B. Greenough *et al.* eds. 1903. *Allen and Greenough's New Latin Grammar*. Boston.
BNP	M. Beard, J. North, and S. Price. 1998. *Religions of Rome: A History*. Cambridge. 2 vols.
DS	C. Daremberg and E. Saglio. 1873–1919. *Dictionnaire des antiquités grecques et romaines, d'après les textes et les monuments*. Paris. 5 vols.
FRHist	T. J. Cornell ed. 2013. *The Fragments of the Roman Historians*. Oxford. 3 vols.
IGR	R. Cagnat *et al.* eds. 1911–1927. *Inscriptiones Graecae ad res Romanas pertinentes*. Paris. 4 vols.
ILLRP	A. Degrassi ed. 1972. *Inscriptiones latinae liberae rei publicae*. Florence. 2 vols.
KS	*Ausführliche Grammatik der lateinischen Sprache*. Vol. 1 ed. R. Kühner and F. Holzweissig (1912; 2nd ed.), vol. 2 ed. R. Kühner and C. Stegmann (1976; 5th ed. rev. A. Thierfelder). Hannover. 2 vols. in 3 parts.
LHS	M. Leumann, J. B. Hofmann, and A. Szantyr. 1972–1979. *Lateinische Grammatik*. Handbuch der Altertumswissenschaft 2: 2. Rev. ed. Munich. 2 vols.
LIMC	H. C. Ackermann and J.-R. Gisler eds. 1981–1999. *Lexicon iconographicum mythologiae classicae*. Zurich. 8 vols.
LPPR	G. Rotondi. 1912. *Leges publicae populi Romani: elenco cronologico con una introduzione sull'attività legislativa dei comizi romani*. Milan.
LS	C. Lewis and C. Short eds. 1879. *A Latin Dictionary*. Oxford.
LTUR	E. Steinby ed. 1993–2000. *Lexicon topographicum urbis Romae*. Rome. 6 vols.
MRR	T. R. S. Broughton. 1951–1952. *The Magistrates of the Roman Republic*. New York. 3 vols.
OCD	S. Hornblower and A. Spawforth eds. 2009. *The Oxford Classical Dictionary*. 3rd ed. rev. Oxford.
OLD	P. G. W. Glare ed. 1968. *Oxford Latin Dictionary*. Oxford.
OLS	H. Pinkster. 2015, 2021. *The Oxford Latin Syntax*. 2 vols.

PHI	Packard Humanities Institute Classical Latin Texts (latin.packhum.org).
RE	A. Pauly, G. Wissowa, *et al.* eds. 1894–1980. *Realencyclopädie der classischen Altertumswissenschaft*. Stuttgart.
Roscher	W. H. Roscher ed. 1884–1937. *Ausführliches Lexikon der griechischen und römischen Mythologie*. Leipzig. 6 vols. + 4 suppl.
ThesCRA	*Thesaurus cultus et rituum antiquorum*. 2004–2014. Los Angeles. 9 vols.
ThLL	*Thesaurus linguae Latinae*. 1900–present. Leipzig *et al*.
TLRR	M. Alexander. 1990. *Trials in the Late Roman Republic, 149 B.C. to 50 B.C.* Toronto. Phoenix suppl. 26.
TRF	O. Ribbeck. 1897. *Tragicorum Romanorum fragmenta*. 3rd ed. Leipzig.
TrRF	*Tragicorum Romanorum fragmenta*. 2012. Vol. 1 ed. M. Schauer (*Livius Andronicus, Naevius, Tragici minores, fragmenta adespota*), vol. 2 ed. G. Manuwald (*Ennius*). Göttingen.
WH	A. Walde and J. B. Hofmann. 1938–1956. *Lateinisches etymologisches Wörterbuch*. 3rd ed. Heidelberg. 3 vols.

Introduction

In spring 56 BCE, in the countryside about a dozen miles north of Rome, mysterious rumblings emanated from the earth. This event in the world of nature would produce major aftershocks in the world of politics during the late Roman Republic. Most importantly, it would once again pit two key political players against one another in an interpretive struggle over what this disruption could mean. But how does one interpret an earthquake? The Roman senate, the ultimate arbiter, convened to discuss how best to resolve this confusion of the natural, the divine, and the political. Our sole surviving witness to this senate meeting is Cicero's oration *De haruspicum responsis*.

The speech involves three main actors: Marcus Tullius Cicero, Rome's greatest orator, who had recently returned from an exile imposed for his part in executing the followers of Catiline more than six years earlier; Publius Clodius Pulcher, Cicero's political archnemesis, who had engineered that exile in 58 BCE while tribune of the people; and the *haruspices*, a group of Etruscan priests, called in for their expertise in interpreting odd occurrences in nature. In late summer of 57, in what he came to regard as a major moral victory, Cicero had returned from exile after being recalled by votes of the senate and the Roman people. While Cicero was in the East, Clodius seized his property on Rome's Palatine Hill, tore down his house, and consecrated on the site a shrine to Liberty (*Libertas*). The symbolism of the goddess Liberty is obvious: Rome was now free of the tyrannical Cicero. More devious were the consequences of the shrine. When Cicero returned from exile, he could not immediately reclaim his property since it was now sanctified ground. This issue was soon resolved, in fall 57, when a panel of Roman priests—the *pontifices*—declared Clodius's consecration invalid (as retailed in Cicero's speech *De domo sua*). Cicero seemed well on his way to regaining the political stature that he had had before exile when, in late spring 56, the earth's trembling signaled a prodigy that required consideration at the highest levels of government. The history of the Roman Republic is filled with reports of prodigies, particularly in times of political crisis. And yet, despite countless mentions in ancient authors and records, only *De haruspicum responsis* offers unique insight into the actual workings by which the senate analyzed, assessed, and resolved a prodigy. As a result, this speech provides one of our best introductions to the intersection of politics and religion during this period.

A. HISTORICAL BACKGROUND

1. Cicero and Clodius

Born into a prominent branch of the *gens Claudia* in approximately 92 BCE, Clodius began his political career in a way typical for a young man of his station. Upon returning to Rome after military service in the East, he underwent training in both oratory and politics, which included an additional term of service in Gaul on the staff of Lucius Licinius Murena, future consul of 62. Cicero's resumé of this part of Clodius's life offers a predictably biased perspective, but there is no reason to dispute the basic facts.[1] During this period, Plutarch writes, the two men were on friendly terms, a situation that was to change abruptly in the aftermath of an unfortunate and rash action on Clodius's part in 62 BCE.[2] The conflict resulting from this event initiated Clodius's lifelong hatred of Cicero and in turn fueled Ciceronian invective that was to continue even after Clodius's death ten years later.[3]

It was in December of 62 that Clodius, dressed as a woman, penetrated mysteries in honor of the goddess Bona Dea, mysteries that males were forbidden to attend.[4] Adding to the scandal was the fact that Clodius had allegedly arranged an assignation with the matron at whose house the ceremony was being celebrated—Pompeia, wife of the *pontifex maximus* Julius Caesar.[5] In a letter written soon after the event, Cicero tells us that Clodius escaped capture through the assistance of a slave-girl.[6] The senate subsequently referred the investigation of Clodius's actions to the *pontifices* and Vestals, who declared that his behavior violated divine law (*nefas*).[7] In the ensuing trial, Cicero gave evidence that contradicted Clodius's alibi, namely that he was not in Rome on the night of the rituals.[8] Despite this testimony, a jury acquitted Clodius of all charges by a vote of 31–25, a verdict that Cicero duly attributes to large-scale bribery.[9]

---

[1] Details in notes to 42; Tatum 1999: 43–61 offers a balanced assessment.
[2] Plut. *Cic.* 29.1 with Lintott 2013: 172–173.   [3] 4n.
[4] For these rituals see notes on 4, 37.
[5] Brouwer 1989 provides a full conspectus of sources on Bona Dea, treating the case of Clodius on 363–370. For the immense bibliography on this incident see in particular Moreau 1982, Tatum 1999: 62–86, and the relevant notes in this commentary.
[6] 44n.
[7] *Att.* 1.13.3=SB 13: *rem ex senatus consulto ad virgines atque ad pontifices relatam idque ab iis nefas esse decretum.*
[8] Schol. Bob. p. 85.28–32 Stangl; cf. *Att.* 1.16.2=SB 16, 2.1.5=SB 21, *dom.* 80.
[9] 36n.

A. *Historical background* xiii

2. Cicero's exile and return

Clodius did not realize his ultimate revenge for Cicero's incriminating testimony until nearly five years later, after his adoption into a plebeian family and election as tribune of the plebs for 58.[10] In December 63, Cicero had ordered the execution of the Catilinarian conspirators, basing his actions on the authority of an emergency decree of the senate (*senatus consultum ultimum*). The open-ended ambiguity of such decrees enabled Cicero's enemies to interpret his actions as violating the *lex Sempronia de capite civium* of 123 BCE, which outlawed executing citizens without appropriate legal proceedings. Taking advantage of the ill-will toward Cicero that had grown over the intervening period, Clodius passed two pieces of legislation in order to effect Cicero's departure from Rome. In February 58, he proposed a law to prosecute anyone who had taken the life of a Roman citizen without trial. Rather than opposing this move through either debate or arms, Cicero chose to leave the city voluntarily on the morning of the law's eventual passage, later claiming that he did so to avoid the slaughter that would have ensued if he had resisted.[11] Soon after Cicero's departure, perhaps even on the same day, Clodius's gangs pillaged his home on the Palatine and burned it to the ground.[12] Clodius then passed an additional piece of legislation explicitly exiling Cicero, confiscating his property, and outlawing any discussion of his restoration. It was at this point that Clodius erected the shrine to *Libertas*, celebrating the departure of the alleged "tyrant" Cicero.[13]

Although Cicero's supporters, including Pompey, began working for his recall within a couple of months of his departure, Clodius took steps to curtail any such attempts both through his actions as tribune and by private threats of violence. As a result, moves to recall the orator were postponed until the newly elected officials for 57 took office. Even then several attempts to restore Cicero were forestalled by the intervention of the new tribunes or violence in the streets, until in August the *comitia centuriata* finally voted for recall by a unanimous vote. Cicero celebrated his triumphal return in the first two speeches delivered when back in Rome, one to the senate and one to the people.

---

[10] On the adoption see notes on 44, 57. The following accounts, drawn from a variety of perspectives, underlie my brief description of the complex series of event leading to Cicero's exile and recall: Gelzer 1939: 916–926; Mitchell 1991: 98–143 (full listing of primary sources); Tatum 1999: 150–185 (from the perspective of Clodius); Kaster 2006: 1–14 (especially on Cicero's credibility as a source), 395–405; Kelly 2006: 110–125, 225–237 (in context of exile); Manuwald 2021: xi–xix (with recent bibliography).

[11] E.g., *p. red. in sen.* 33–34, with Manuwald 2021: 208–211 for other references.

[12] E.g., *Sest.* 53–54, with Kaster 2006: 242.

[13] Weinstock 1971: 133–145 surveys the divine personification of *Libertas* and its associations in the late Republic.

B. CICERO'S ORATORY UPON HIS RETURN

1. Rhetorical strategies in the *post reditum* orations

Three distinct groupings of speeches have received from modern scholars the designation *post reditum* ("after his return"): the fourteen extant speeches dating from Cicero's return to his Caesarian orations of 46–45; the two orations delivered immediately upon his arrival in Rome; and the four speeches from late 57 and the first half of 56 that treat most directly Cicero's exile and its implications and in which consequently Clodius occupies prominent place.[14] Riggsby has identified certain themes that recur throughout the first group, such as an increased use of historical exempla, excurses on Cicero's definition of what constitutes "exile," and a self-conscious reticence to avoid offending any of his contemporaries, for example by acknowledging the existence of the so-called First Triumvirate. Cicero touches on all these topics in *De haruspicum responsis*.[15] Related to the final topic is one particularly relevant to our speech, namely the manner in which Cicero stresses, both directly and indirectly, that there exists a consensus of values and goals among the elite and that the response to the prodigy indicates, through its warning about potential discord (40: OPTIMATIVM DISCORDIAM DISSENSIONEMQVE), the fragility of this consensus.[16] The ultimate goal is to prove that Clodius is the cause of that discord.

Clodius, predictably, adopts an opposing oratorical strategy during this period: Cicero's recall was a mistake, and one with major repercussions for peace and stability. His first major attempt to assert this in direct opposition to Cicero came less than a month after the orator was back in Rome. As noted above, in late September 57 Cicero successfully argued before the *pontifices* in the speech *De domo sua* that Clodius's consecration of his property was invalid.[17] Although Clodius's counterargument does not survive, Cicero quotes from it sufficiently to give a reasonable idea of his main points. The bulk of these involved technical legal arguments for the validity of the consecration.[18] When it came to the less technical aspect of character assassination, however, Clodius relied on the sustained envy of the politically powerful for Cicero's treatment of the Catilinarian conspirators, an envy fueled in no small part by the common sentiment that Cicero, as a *novus homo*, did not belong to the

---

[14] Riggsby 2002 concentrates on the first group, Manuwald 2021 the second. The third group comprises *p. red. in sen.*, *p. red. ad Quir.*, *dom.*, and *har. resp.*
[15] For exempla see, e.g., notes on 16, 51, 54, and particularly section 41 (Riggsby 2002: 160–167); on the definition of exile see 49n; and on the "hidden present" see Riggsby 2002: 172–179, with notes on 45, 47, 48.
[16] More at Riggsby 2002: 182–184.
[17] Nisbet 1939 offers a commentary, Stroh 2004 a detailed legal and rhetorical analysis.
[18] Stroh 2004: 332–338 provides a plausible reconstruction of Clodius's main points.

B. Cicero's oratory upon his return

traditional elite.[19] Analogously, by stressing Cicero's support for giving Pompey a five-year appointment as grain commissioner, Clodius attempted to portray his opponent as a popular politician, opposed to traditional senatorial values.[20] Cicero's recounting also indicates that Clodius leveled accusations of cruelty, despotism, and vanity, elements that would come to pervade negative perceptions of Cicero throughout antiquity and traces of which appear in *De haruspicum responsis*.[21]

2. Clodius's lost speech *De haruspicum responsis*

The situation treated in *De haruspicum responsis* did not entail the legal intricacies of the speech *De domo sua*, and so for their next major confrontation each speaker needed to adapt his strategy from that used the previous fall. The objective for both in this case is straightforward: to prove that the previous actions of his opponent have aroused the displeasure of the gods and that therefore they must be the source of the tremors in Latium. Clodius, as a former tribune and a favorite of the urban populace, chose to address his remarks to the larger audience of people assembled in a *contio* rather than at a meeting of the senate.[22] Given the urgency of needing to resolve the prodigy as soon as possible, I assume that Clodius's meeting had occurred a day or two before Cicero's speech.[23] Regardless of when it was delivered, however, Cicero notes that he possessed what seems to have been a written copy of Clodius's remarks on that occasion, and presumably other members of his audience were aware of the main points that Clodius had made.[24] Fortunately, Cicero refers to, and even claims to quote, his opponent's remarks with enough frequency and apparent specificity that, relying upon these allusions and an awareness of the two men's history, the outline of Clodius's argument may be reconstructed with a fair degree of probability.[25] Furthermore, Clodius seems to have attended the senate meeting at which Cicero spoke, which would impose at least some limitation on Cicero's distortion of Clodius's arguments.[26]

---

[19] For this invective topos see 17n.

[20] *Dom.* 3–4 with Nisbet 1939: 69–70, Stroh 2004: 332–334; for the commission see Seager 2002: 107–109 and notes at 31.

[21] Stroh 2004: 337, citing Zielinski 1912: 280–288. Cruelty: e.g., 3n; despotism: 58n; conceit: 17n.

[22] Clodius's rank entitled him to speak in the senate (as *har. resp.* 1 makes clear); Ryan 1998: 368–369 lists instances from 57 BCE.

[23] 8n.   [24] 8n.

[25] For the following reconstruction, including a hypothetical version of Clodius's speech (in English), see Corbeill 2018.

[26] Clodius had attended the previous day's meeting and is addressed throughout *har. resp.* in the second person. Furthermore, it is unlikely that Clodius, who had attended the session rescinding Cicero's exile in which he was the lone dissenting vote, would have been deterred from attendance on this occasion (*red. in sen.* 26, *red. ad Quir.* 15).

Even a cursory reading of the response of the *haruspices* as compiled from the excerpts quoted by Cicero will reveal a number of clauses that could be applied to the returned exile (see section F below for a full reconstruction of the response itself). Further complicating Cicero's case at this time was Clodius's position as a member of the *quindecimviri sacris faciundis*, the group supervising the Sibylline books, which constitute the major source of prophecy directly controlled by Romans. Such a position would have endowed him with special authority in the treatment of portents, and it is even possible that he had by dint of this office some control over the conduct of the *haruspices* themselves.[27] Hence when Cicero sarcastically mocks Clodius as a "most scrupulous priest" (*religiosissimus sacerdos*), he may very well be providing a characterization that Clodius would have embraced as legitimate and that he would have noted in his *contio*.[28]

There is no reason to doubt that Clodius will have employed some of the same general invective topoi that he had in *De domo sua*, such as mocking Cicero for his undistinguished ancestry.[29] As with Cicero, however, the bulk of his time would have been spent in a selective reading of the various portions of the response, which Cicero tells us that he had read aloud to those assembled (*har. resp.* 9: *responsum haruspicum hoc recens de fremitu in contione recitavit*). Among the most damning for Cicero's case is the reference to the profanation of sacred spaces (*har. resp.* 9: LOCA SACRA ET RELIGOSA PROFANA HABERI). The obvious interpretation of this divine statement in spring 56 would have been that the *pontifices* were mistaken in restoring to Cicero his property, which would have involved desecrating the shrine to Liberty; indeed, Cicero spends roughly one-fourth of his own speech defending himself from this possible interpretation.[30] A second clause that seems to point directly to Cicero's activity is that describing the murder of ambassadors (*har. resp.* 34: ORATORES CONTRA IVS FASQVE INTERFECTOS). Since Cicero had successfully defended P. Asicius of this charge in late 57 or early 56 and referred more recently to the innocence of others in the matter, Clodius must have included this portion of the response in order to show the gods commenting on the injustice of Cicero's views.[31] A final clause that it seems Clodius treated involves Cicero's position as procurator of the cult of the agricultural deity Tellus. Since she receives mention as one of the gods due reparations in light of

---

[27] For Clodius as *XVvir* see 26n. MacBain 1982: 57–59 assesses the evidence for the extent of the supervisory role that the *X(V)viri* played over the *haruspices*; cf. Rawson 1978: 140. A possible indication of their mutual independence is that when the *X(V)viri* and *haruspices* are consulted simultaneously, a division of duties is normally maintained between interpretation by the *haruspices* and expiation recommended by the *X(V)viri* (Boyce 1938: 170).
[28] 9n. [29] Notes on 17, 26.
[30] Notes on 9; Cicero treats this clause explicitly at *har. resp.* 9–18, 30–33, 37–39.
[31] 34n.

the prodigy, and since Rome was facing a grain crisis, it requires little imagination to see how Clodius would have exploited Cicero's connections.[32]

In addition to showing the several ways in which Cicero could be implicated in the impieties decried in the response, Clodius surely also would have spent time preempting any portion of it that Cicero could apply to him. Among the possibilities, it can hardly be doubted that foremost would be the Bona Dea scandal. And indeed, Cicero does note Clodius making public reference to the Bona Dea, although he does not specify that it was in this *contio*.[33] Regardless of the source of this remark, however, Clodius could have predicted that Cicero would—as indeed he did—place emphasis on this incident in the context of the clause regarding the violation of ancient religious rites.[34] Furthermore, Clodius would have known that his current position as curule aedile, part of whose duties is the administration of festivals, made him a likely candidate for the charge of negligence in conducting games (*har. resp.* 21: LVDOS MINVS DILIGENTER FACTOS POLLVTOSQVE). The only evidence of any disruption, however, is Cicero's own convoluted account about the Megalesia that had taken place the previous month, an incident that, scholars agree, Cicero created or at least exaggerated to make this point.[35] Finally, Clodius's emphasis in the *contio* that he had recently reconciled with Pompey anticipated the likelihood that Cicero would attribute to him the source of the elite discord that the haruspical report predicted would lead to general slaughter.[36] With the evidence of the response seemingly so weighted against him, and with Clodius able to provide a convincing defense, Cicero needed to develop a strong case.

3. Cicero's strategy in *De haruspicum responsis*

We are of course in a much better position to assess Cicero's strategy on this occasion. The first thing to notice is how Cicero selects from among the types of speech traditionally available to him: epideictic, deliberative, or forensic.[37] He ultimately chooses all three at different points. Normally a senator speaking in the curia about a weighty issue adopts the deliberative form, arguing for a future course of action from which he wishes to elicit the help of the audience. This is certainly how *De haruspicum responsis* closes, where Cicero pleads with his fellow senators that concord in the state can be achieved only through

---

[32] Notes on 31. The reference to men who have been "rejected" could also have given Clodius the opportunity to apply this to Cicero in exile (56n).

[33] 37n.

[34] See notes on *har. resp.* 37 (SACRIFICIA VETVSTA OCCVLTAQVE MINVS DILIGENTER FACTA POLLVTAQVE).

[35] Wiseman 1974: 160–162, 166; Tatum 1999: 211–212.

[36] *har. resp.* 40: PER OPTIMATIVM DISCORDIAM DISSENSIONEMQVE PATRIBVS PRINCIPIBVSQVE CAEDES PERICVLAQVE CREENTVR; see 51n.

[37] Lausberg 1998: 62–111 offers a schematic treatment, with full citation of ancient sources.

mutual cooperation and the reconciliation of differences among the elite. The oration's beginning, however, upsets any expectations of calm deliberation. In fact, the speech's explicit subject matter, the haruspical response, is not introduced at the outset, receiving its first mention only when the speech is already one-eighth complete. Instead, in the opening eight sections Cicero adopts an epideictic mode consisting of blame (*vituperatio*), with a concentrated invective on Clodius (and, to a lesser extent, Piso and Gabinius) that introduces the oration's leitmotifs: Clodius's sacrilegious past, stupidity, inchastity, and above all his unbridled madness.[38] Immediately afterward, however, once Cicero begins his reading of the haruspical response he adopts a forensic approach, establishing facts about past events in order to establish (Clodius's) guilt and (his own) innocence regarding the origins of the earthquake prodigy.[39] Cicero's analysis of each clause, and the arguments that he offers based on supporting evidence, occupies the bulk of the speech, and he adopts the same mode of argumentation that Clodius, as outlined in the previous section, employed in making his own case.

Cicero launches an attack against Clodius throughout the speech not (merely) for its shock and entertainment value: the topics of invective, such as physical appearance and movement, derive persuasive force from their appeal to fundamental ethical biases in Roman society.[40] Cicero was later to write in the moral treatise *De officiis* that the experienced orator should refrain from taking part in judicial prosecutions, since relentless attacks on other citizens risk damaging a speaker's reputation. Among the three exceptions to this practice that he mentions, he stresses most the situation when the attack occurs in defense of the state.[41] As a result, in the vituperative opening of *De haruspicum responsis*, Cicero emphasizes that his attacks on Clodius arise not from hatred but from a need to protect the state from Clodius and his associates, and so he proceeds to situate his resentment in a broader historical context.[42] By identifying himself with the state, Cicero promises that he intends his prosecution not to deepen his and Clodius's mutual hatred but to result in the peaceful resolution of a tense historical moment. In other words, his attack will serve to heal, rather than exacerbate, the political discord identified by the *haruspices*.

The particular context of *De haruspicum responsis*, however, provides an added dimension to Cicero's public attack on Clodius's private activities. Cicero mentions early on Clodius's illicit admission to the Bona Dea rites of December

---

[38] For blame as an integral feature of Roman epideictic, see *Rhet. Her.* 3.10, Cic. *inv.* 1.7; Corbeill 2002.

[39] For a possible forensic element in lexical choice see 11n.

[40] Corbeill 1996; cf. Leach 2001: 346: "Certainly Cicero is at his rhetorical best in this oration, yet the thematic control of cultural semiotics with which he defends his status and property should not obscure the psychological appeal inherent in the imagistic particulars of the situation."

[41] *Off.* 2.50: *hoc quidem non est saepe faciendum, nec umquam nisi...reipublicae causa.*

[42] Sections 3–5.

62. The dual nature of the transgression—both religious and sexual—provides Cicero with two separate and seemingly incompatible topoi in his attack on Clodius. First, he consistently assails the sacrilegious nature of a man who would disrupt a women's ritual in order to engage in sexual congress with a woman.[43] But toward the end of the speech, Cicero focuses on how the act of cross-dressing on that same occasion impugns Clodius's masculine status.[44] Each type of attack serves a specific rhetorical purpose. Characterizing Clodius as a hypermasculine violator of religious propriety allows Cicero to identify his actions as the source of displeasure that the gods have indicated through the earth tremors. At the same time, Cicero's characterization of Clodius as a sexual deviant allows the orator to mark him as a prodigy that transgresses the natural world, just as the unpredictable earthquake had that spring.[45]

C. STYLE

1. General remarks

There are numerous studies of Cicero's style, none of which can be completely satisfactory if only because of the immense size of Cicero's extant corpus and the range of genres contained therein. Among more recent works, von Albrecht 2003 surveys the entire range of Cicero's prose works and is especially good on stylistic developments, but of necessity must rely upon generalizations without full consideration of context; more satisfactory in terms of details are the relevant chapters in von Albrecht 1989. A shorter general survey is offered by Powell 2013. Gotoff 1979 consists of a valuable word-by-word analysis of one speech, *Pro Archia*, which is stimulating and suggestive even at points where the reader may disagree.[46] There are also numerous studies on individual technical matters, particularly in French and German, many of which I cite in the notes in the commentary. Craig 2002: 524–531 and Powell 2013: 71–72 offer additional bibliographical discussion.

For the *post reditum* speeches in particular, scholars have noted how Cicero displays a wide variety of styles, in which rounded periods alternate with shorter, hypotactic sentences.[47] Certain elements of this increasingly variable

---

[43] Notes on 4, 33.   [44] E.g., notes on 42, 44.
[45] Leach 2001 discusses in detail this apparently inconsistent treatment, while Dyck 2001 treats more broadly Cicero's treatment of dress as a mode of characterization. For Cicero labeling Clodius (and other opponents) as a deviant prodigy see Corbeill 2008.
[46] For other treatments of the style of individual speeches see Gotoff 1993, Keeline 2021: 26–34, and especially Landgraf 1914.
[47] Albrecht 2003: 103–105; Grillo 2015: 38–41, who applies the term *post reditum* to the larger corpus of fourteen speeches; Manuwald xxxvi–lx, concentrating on the first two speeches.

style may be influenced by his interest in poetry during this period.[48] In any case, it seems clear that Cicero is attempting with this more fluid and varied style to reestablish himself after exile as Rome's supreme orator. I offer in the following paragraphs a selection of some of the more prominent devices on display in *De haruspicum responsis*, with reference to places in the commentary where they are discussed.

2. Language and figures of speech

Cicero avoids archaisms in his oratory.[49] In support of this claim, the four most likely candidates for archaic language in the speech occur not in Cicero's voice but either in alleged quotations of Clodius or in the wording of the haruspical response.[50] Similarly, in only a few places does he seem to adopt a more colloquial syntax.[51] Another clear case in which Cicero hews to expected oratorical practice is in his use of *geminatio*, that is, the repetition of a word in an identical form in close proximity so as to stress a particular point—e.g., <u>tum</u>, inquam, <u>tum</u> vidi. Of the five separate occasions on which Cicero employs this figure, all their types but one characterize oratorical and prose texts and are either never or rarely attested in poetic texts.[52]

On the positive side, Cicero fully exhibits in *De haruspicum responsis* his predilection for the tricolon. The author of the rhetorical treatise *Ad Herennium* characterizes the tricolon as the neatest and fullest way of expressing a complete idea, particularly when the number of syllables increases in each successive portion, as in "life, liberty, and the pursuit of happiness."[53] In Cicero's speeches, the construction creates a swift but at the same time a considered pace. I note numerous examples in the commentary but here I wish to survey briefly the ways in which Cicero introduces variety to prevent the device—occurring well over thirty times—from becoming predictable and tedious. To begin with, alongside the tendency of having a growing number of syllables—the so-called *tricolon crescens*—the syllable count also occasionally decreases; perhaps not coincidentally this deviation from the norm tends to occur in the context of describing Clodius or his activities.[54] There also occurs grammatical variation in the element that is repeated, from a single word (*neglegi, violari, pollui*), to a prepositional phrase (*sine suo voltu, sine colore, sine voce*), to an

---

[48] E.g., notes on 3, 10.   [49] Albrecht 2003: 11–12.
[50] Clodius: 8n (*senati*); response: 40n (*creentur*), 34n (*oratores*).
[51] E.g., 7n (hypotaxis); 51 (anticipatory *quod*).
[52] See notes on 4 (*tum*), 22 (*te*), 49 (*illum*), 37 (*non*); the sole exception is 22 (*tua*).
[53] *Rhet. Her.* 4.26: [*exornatio*] *commodissima et absolutissima est quae ex tribus constat*; LHS 2: 722–726; Wilkinson 1963: 174–178. The rising tricolon constitutes the majority of instances in our speech.
[54] E.g., notes on 2, 25, 27; cf. 16. This tendency has not, to my knowledge, been investigated in detail for Ciceronian oratory more generally.

C. Style

ablative absolute (*causa cognita, duobus locis dicta, maxima frequentia...adstante*), to entire sentences (*primum...deinde...postea*).[55] The tricolon can be further enhanced by anaphora of the opening element. In a particularly complex example Cicero closes one sentence with two juxtaposed tricola in anaphora, with the final colon of each containing the largest number of syllables: *id <u>semper</u> populo Romano, <u>semper</u> senatui, <u>semper</u> ipsis dis immortalibus **satis** sanctum, **satis** augustum, **satis** religiosum esse visum est.*[56] Finally, Cicero can manipulate the expectation of a tricolon by adding a fourth element, thereby drawing special attention to this final clause: *de sacris publicis, de ludis maximis, de deorum penatium Vestaeque matris caerimoniis, <u>de illo ipso sacrificio quod</u>* etc.[57] Throughout the commentary I discuss other common devices by which Cicero reinforces meaning, such as asyndeton, polysyndeton, and chiasmus.[58]

The most prominent figure of speech in *De haruspicum responsis*, as in the *post reditum* speeches generally, is metaphor.[59] In the discussion of this device in the treatise *De oratore*, written a year later, the speaker Crassus advises apologizing for an adventurous metaphor by adding some sort of proviso. To say, for example, that the senate became an orphan when Cato died is too extreme; better to say that it became "an orphan, as it were."[60] Cicero follows this advice only twice in the speech, when he cautiously ascribes "divine" authority to Servilius and when he refers to Piso and Gabinius as "nearly a plague."[61] When it comes to Clodius, however, the virtual synonym of *haec lues impura* (24: "this impure pestilence") and the equally vivid *labes* (46: "ruin") are applied without qualification, as are a number of other vivid single-word descriptors, such that tenor and vehicle are made to cohere without hesitation.[62] Beyond these straightforward comparisons, moreover, Cicero engages with the high emotional content of the speech by applying allegory to describe Clodius, a mode that, as Crassus notes, lends special adornment to a speech in its reliance upon not a single word but a string of related words.[63] Three

---

[55] My selections are drawn from sections eight (single word), two (prepositional phrase), twelve (ablative absolute), and eleven (sentence).

[56] For the entire sentence see 12n. See too the regularity of the *tricolon crescens* at 14, in which each portion consists of anaphora of *aut*, followed by a verb in the future tense and a relative clause.

[57] 12. The following sentence exhibits the opposite phenomenon; here the third element in a sequence of clauses, with *quod* in anaphora, does not in fact constitute the final part of a tricolon.

[58] See, e.g., 11n, 22n, 42n, 53n (asyndeton); 27n, 57n (polysyndeton); 19n, 21n, 40n (chiasmus).

[59] Fantham 1972: 115–136 analyzes metaphorical imagery in speeches from the period 57–56, most especially *p. red. in sen., p. red. ad Quir., Sest.*, and *Balb*. She notes not simply the abundance of the figure, but also how application differs depending upon the specific occasion (125).

[60] *De orat.* 3.165: "*ut ita dicam, pupillum*", *aliquanto mitius*.

[61] Notes on 2 and 4.

[62] E.g., *gladiator* (1), *hostia* (6), *vipera* (50).

[63] *De orat.* 3.166–167. For *allegoria*, see Leeman *et al.* 1989: 285.

particular allegorical readings of Clodius recur throughout the speech. Cicero introduces the first early on: Clodius as an untamed and unshackled beast who must be hunted down and subdued.[64] The second type of narrative allegory figures Clodius as associated with the storm that threatens to capsize the metaphorical ship of state, if he is not indeed imagined to embody the storm itself.[65] *De haruspicum responsis* contains a particularly vivid extension of this common allegory when Cicero compares in detail Clodius with the mythical monsters Scylla and Charybdis as he attacks the "rostra" of the ship of state. In this instance, Ciceronian rhetoric violates the standards of decorum that he would soon recommend in his own *De oratore*.[66] Finally, the most consistent and striking allegory running throughout the speech depicts Clodius and his associates as earthly representatives of the Furies, the mythical beings charged with avenging crimes within the household. Cicero utilizes this imagery throughout his career but develops it in particular with the speeches *post reditum*, where Clodius and his cohort seem to be imagined as committing crimes in the household that is Rome while simultaneously embodying these crazed agents of vengeance.[67] This recurring motif facilitates Cicero's depiction of Clodius's rage as a symptom of insanity, and his gangs as a horde circulating throughout Rome wielding torches, setting fires, and creating terror—imagery that climaxes with the striking metaphor of Cicero bursting into flames after willingly accepting into his own body a flame that has been cast against the republic.[68] The conclusion of Fantham regarding the abundance of imagery in *Pro Sestio* applies equally well to Cicero's use of allegory in our speech: it "allows imagery to assume functions beyond mere local ornament, and creates relationships between metaphors, and between systems of metaphor."[69]

3. Sound as sense: grammatical gender, sonic effects, and prose rhythm

I have reserved for last a stylistic feature that plays an especially unique role in *De haruspicum responsis*: the use of the forms and sounds of words to mirror sense. While most scholars since antiquity have agreed that Cicero is a master of rhetorical persuasion and Latin style, his sensitivity to wordplay in the orations tends to be undervalued.[70] I touch here upon three particular effects, all

---

[64] Notes on 4 (*vulnerati*), 5, 6, 7, 57; cf. 2 (*ecfrenato*), 8 (*confixum*), 39 (*figuntur*), and generally Fantham 1972: 132–133.
[65] 4n; cf. 19, 48.   [66] *De orat.* 3.163, quoted at 59n.
[67] Berno 2007 traces Cicero's references to the Furies throughout his corpus; for *har. resp.* see 4n, where the term first appears to describe Piso and Gabinius.
[68] See section 45; for related imagery see, e.g., 2, 4.
[69] Fantham 1972: 136.
[70] Woodman 1998 (esp. 218–229) has demonstrated convincingly that similar sorts of wordplay in Tacitus involve more than mere frivolity.

of which receive further attention in the commentary: play with grammatical gender, sound effects, and prose rhythm.

Roman poets could exploit the relationship between grammatical gender and biological sex in order to achieve various literary goals.[71] Cicero as orator also takes advantage of this relationship at several points in *De haruspicum responsis*. I will restrict myself to where this play first occurs, in a remarkably prescient remark that Cicero makes about Clodius being offered as a sacrificial victim to his future murderer, Titus Annius Milo: *exspectatione omnium fortissimo et clarissimo viro, Tito Annio, devota et constituta ista hostia esse videtur* (6: "Everyone expects that [Clodius] is destined to be sacrificed as a victim to the famously brave man Titus Annius"). The series of contrasting grammatical genders is unusual simply by their quantity: five instances of *vir* and its attendant masculine adjectives, all ending in long [o], describe Milo; in direct juxtaposition Cicero places four feminine noun and adjectives, ending in long [a], to describe Clodius. Rhetorical handbooks warn about repeating sounds in this way, but when this does happen scholars of Cicero claim that the intended effect is to emphasize an underlying idea.[72] I would concur with this assessment by suggesting that the emphasis here lies in contrasting the masculine *vir* Milo with the passively effeminate Clodius.[73]

Sound expresses sense in ways paralleled outside this particular speech, such as in Cicero's use of an alliterative sequence of sibilants as a way of expressing exasperation.[74] The device is especially marked, however, in the portion of the haruspical response that describes the prodigy: AVDITVS EST STREPITVS CVM FREMITV (20: "a rumbling, accompanied by a trembling, was heard"). The rare juxtaposition of the consonant cluster [st], the hiatus resulting from this combination, and the threefold repetition of [itu] seem unmistakably intended to echo the sound and appearance of the earth tremor it describes.[75] The resulting intrusion of the sound of the prodigy into senatorial proceedings mirrors the relationship upon which the speech centers—the intrusion of the natural world into political decision-making.

Writers on Greek and Roman rhetoric have treated since at least the fifth century BCE the notion that literary prose should have its own metrical rhythms, with Aristotle's *Rhetoric* providing our earliest extant discussion.[76] While these ancient discussions are both complex and often frustratingly inconsistent with practice, the general principle remains clear: writers of prose utilize their own

---

[71] Discussion and examples in Corbeill 2015: 1–103.
[72] E.g., *Rhet. Her.* 4.32; Laurand 1936–1940: 131–135; Gotoff 1979: 230–231.
[73] See also notes on 6, 24, 37, 42, 45, 46, 50, 59.
[74] 32n; for a different alliterative effect see 23n.
[75] For details see 20n.
[76] *Rhet.* 3.8. Oberhelman 2003 offers a thorough account of the study of Latin prose rhythm from antiquity through the twenty-first century, while Wilkinson 1963: 135–164 remains a succinct and readable survey; their statistics on Ciceronian and other Latin authors' clausulae have, however, been superseded by those in Keeline and Kirby 2019.

rhythms, using sequences of long and short syllables that distinguish them from the commonest meters employed by poets. In this discussion and in the notes I will concentrate in particular on the clausulae of Cicero, that is, the rhythms he employs at the close of his sentences or cola. It remains controversial the extent to which Cicero may have consciously preferred certain rhythms at other points in the sentence.[77]

Since the groundbreaking research of Zielinski 1904, who catalogued 17,902 of the various rhythmical clausulae in Cicero by dividing them into the categories of those favored and those avoided, considerations of prose rhythm have played a crucial role in the study of Cicero, and Zielinski's work has initiated numerous investigations into other aspects of the topic.[78] Among the most reliable areas in which rhythm has proven to be a helpful tool is as an aid in determining authorship or as an ancillary indication that a reading in a text may require emendation.[79] More recently, the computer-based analyses of Keeline and Kirby 2019 have corrected and refined Zielinski's data, covering the rhythms favored by Cicero and other major prose authors up through the second century CE. I reproduce here their data for the orations generally and *De haruspicum responsis* and *Pro Sestio* in particular:[80]

	Cretic-trochee	Double cretic / molossus cretic	Double trochee	Spondaic	Heroic
har. resp.	35.41	19.45	28.68	8.98	2.74
Sest.	33.22	16.09	28.97	11.38	2.30
All orations	28.42	23.78	26.24	8.80	1.86

The basic rhythms represented in this table are as follows:[81]

Cretic-trochee	- ˘ - - x
Double cretic or molossus cretic	- ˘ - - ˘ x or - - - - ˘ x
Double trochee	- ˘ - x
Spondaic	- - - x (no resolutions permitted)
Heroic	- ˘ ˘ - x (no resolutions permitted)

A glance at this table provides confirmation, if such were needed, of the Ciceronian authorship of *De haruspicum responsis*. The close correspondence

---

[77] Particularly valuable here are the contributions of Fraenkel 1968 and Nisbet 1990; cf. notes on 1, 37.
[78] Oberhelman 2003: 90–106 summarizes and critiques Zielinski's methods; see too Berry 1996b: 48–61.
[79] Authorship: Berry 1996b provides a thorough discussion; for its use in *har. resp.* see 39n and, for its relevance to Ciceronian authorship of the speech, below in this section. Notes on 16 and 30 discuss possible limitations in using rhythm for emendation.
[80] Keeline and Kirby 2019: 173–176.
[81] Resolutions of a long syllable for two shorts were allowed in certain instances; for discussion see Keeline and Kirby 2019: 163–165.

between the relative use of clausulae in that speech and in *Pro Sestio*, delivered two months previously, virtually guarantees that both speeches were written by the same hand.

If one may take Cicero at his word in his treatises, rhythm in his oratory went beyond simple aesthetics. In his rhetorical tract *Orator*, he introduces his lengthiest account of prose rhythm with a dogmatic assertion about the essential and inherent humanity of euphony: "if someone does not feel [the aptness of certain rhythms], then I don't know what kind of ears they have or what among them even resembles a human being" (*orat.* 168: *quod qui non sentiunt, quas auris habeant aut quid in his hominis simile sit, nescio*). In other words, appreciation of specific rhythms constitutes not simply an aesthetic preference but is tied into the nature of what defines our humanity. I cite a number of examples in the speech where a particularly rousing argument is capped by one of the orator's preferred rhythms.[82] Conversely, one particular passage demonstrates that not sounding good can be precisely the point, much as in the extract from the haruspical description discussed above, where the cacophonous nature of the Latin matches the disruptive nature of the earth tremors. I examine in the commentary how the use of a heroic clausula of dactyl + spondee, a prose rhythm that since Aristotle has met with unequivocal disapproval in rhetorical treatises, is used by Cicero to make a particular rhetorical point.[83] In all the cases discussed in this section, as well as elsewhere in the commentary, the form, sound, and rhythm of words work to advance Cicero's persuasive goals.

D. AUTHENTICITY OF THE SPEECHES *POST REDITUM*

The four *post reditum* speeches that treat most explicitly the theme of Cicero's exile—those addressed to the senate and people immediately after his return to Rome, that on the recovery of his home, and *De haruspicum responsis*—have only recently received sustained attention as literary works of persuasion.[84] A number of factors contribute to this neglect: the often obscure subject matter, particularly on issues concerning the sanctity of Cicero's house; the egoism that the orator unashamedly puts on display; or the often bombastic nature of the rhetoric. Equally significant, however, is the weight of scholarly tradition. In 1745, the British classics scholar Jeremiah Markland argued in an appendix to a larger work on the authenticity of Cicero's correspondence with Brutus that these speeches were not written by Cicero but were produced in Roman schools

---

[82] E.g., notes on 2, 3, 9, 19.   [83] 16n.
[84] The excellent commentary on *De domo sua* by Nisbet 1939 constitutes a notable exception. More recently have appeared commentaries by Bohl 2019 (*p. red. in sen.*) and Manuwald 2021 (*p. red. in sen., p. red. ad Quir.*); a full-scale commentary on *dom.* is in the works.

of declamation during the century after his death.[85] His arguments often suffer from circularity: if a construction or idiom occurs that is not elsewhere attested in Cicero, it is branded as the inept addition of a forger; if, on the other hand, some turn of phrase is well attested, this points to the blind imitation of an unoriginal declaimer.[86]

Markland's hypothesis would likely have been forgotten had it not been for the efforts fifty years later of the preeminent German classicist of his day, Friedrich Wolf. Wolf is well known among classicists for his *Prolegomena to Homer* of 1795, in which he was the first scholar to argue systematically that the Homeric epics were composed orally and only committed to writing several centuries later. Six years after publishing this masterwork, Wolf devoted his energy to producing a set of commentaries on Cicero designed exclusively to supporting in detail Markland's points about these speeches, including *De haruspicum responsis*, being forgeries.[87] Despite Wolf's efforts, however, the discovery of better manuscripts and the study of Ciceronian prose rhythm have vitiated the majority of Markland's and Wolf's arguments, and no Ciceronian scholar today doubts these speeches' authenticity. As a result of this scholarly consensus, I do not intend to defend them again here.[88]

From the perspective of a modern scholar of Roman culture, armed with concordances, databases, and detailed lexica and grammars, these attempts seem misguided and at times even comical in their zeal—"Could *Cicero* return from his Grave, and see such things as these imposed upon the world for his Writings, what Grief and Indignation would it occasion him!"[89] Yet these scholars not infrequently present reasons for skepticism that highlight real peculiarities of Ciceronian diction.[90] As a result, their efforts have inspired me to consider issues in the oration that may otherwise have escaped notice. These can include something as apparently minor as Wolf's dissatisfaction with the use of the imperfect tense by his "fickle declaimer" on the grounds that it points to an inconsistency in the narrative.[91] Their comments can also help refine our understanding of religious procedure, as in Markland's remark on the appropriate verb used to describe the consultation of the Sibylline books.[92] Elsewhere, Markland cogently remarks on the peculiarity of the verb *stuprare* ("to rape")

---

[85] Markland 1745.

[86] The tendency reaches its nadir with Long 1856, who "imports peculiar and even outrageous misinterpretations, and then blames the author for stupidity" (Nisbet 1939: xxxiii–xxxiv).

[87] Wolf 1801, prompted particularly by the cogent counterarguments in support of authenticity by Gessner 1753. The treatise of van Meerdervort 1850, devoted exclusively to impugning *har. resp.*, contains little of value.

[88] Nicholson 1992: 1–18 offers a lively and detailed survey of the scholarly debates from Markland onward. Further discussion is provided by Nisbet 1939: xxix–xxxiv; Lenaghan 1969: 38–41; Manuwald 2021: xx–xxii.

[89] Markland 1745: 348.

[90] In addition to the instances mentioned here see, e.g., notes on 3, 6, 20, 33.

[91] Wolf 1801: 311 with 3n.   [92] Markland 1745: 347 and 26n.

E. *The speech* De haruspicum responsis

having an inanimate item as its direct object, which prompts Gesner to justify the usage by pointing out that the metaphorical use of this verb occurs elsewhere in Cicero, but only in conjunction with the activity of Clodius.[93] The criticisms of Markland and Wolf have also assisted later editors in identifying passages in need of textual emendation.[94]

E. THE SPEECH *DE HARUSPICUM RESPONSIS*

1. Title

Cicero refers to orations delivered by himself and others with phrases that we anachronistically call "titles." Although variations occur, these names tend to follow a regular pattern for forensic speeches, the speech "spoken on behalf of (*pro*) X" or "against (*in*) X."[95] Cicero also conceived of groups of his speeches as part of a coherent collection, such as those delivered during his consulship, or the fourteen *Philippics*.[96] At the same time, the descriptions that Cicero gives of his own orations can vary widely from those offered by the manuscript tradition, as with the speech arguing for the passage of the *lex Manilia* in 66.[97] In the majority of cases, however, the shorthand by which Cicero's speeches have been designated from antiquity to the present remains inconsequential and would seem to be simply of antiquarian interest. I intend to show in this section that the precise title of Cicero's speech on the haruspical response, by contrast, can aid in understanding how the *haruspices* treated the appearance of a prodigy.

The only two texts from antiquity that refer to our speech supply alternative designations. Asconius twice refers to a passage *in ea [oratione] ... de (h)aruspicum responso*, while Quintilian refers in the plural form to *liber de (h)aruspicum responsis*.[98] The manuscripts of the speech agree with Quintilian in offering the plural form *responsis*, as does at least one witness to the *Florilegium Gallicum*

---

[93] Markland 1745: 349 and Gesner 1753: 278, with my notes on 8 and 33. For other instances where Markland correctly identifies a peculiar lexical usage see notes on 38 and 42.

[94] Of many examples, see Markland 1745: 353–354 on 49, 357–358 on 62; Wolf 1801: 373–374 on 49.

[95] Of numerous examples, see *Brut.* 312 *causa ... pro Sex. Roscio dicta*; Quint. *inst.* 4.2.19: *in Verrem de Proserpina*.

[96] Consular speeches: Cic. *Att.* 2.1.3=SB 21. *Philippics*: Cic. *ad Brut.* 2.3.4=SB 2, 2.4.2=SB 4; Plut. *Cic.* 48.6; La Bua 2019: 74–75.

[97] Cic. *orat.* 102 (*in Manilia lege*) vs. Fortun. *rhet.* p. 114.15–16, Iul. Vict. *rhet.* p. 438.27, and Empor. *rhet.* p. 572.17 (*de imperio Gn. Pompei*); further examples in Rouse and Reeve 1983: 55. Manuwald 2021: xx compiles variations for the titles of the first two speeches *post reditum*. La Bua 2019: 16–99 surveys early editions of the speeches from Cicero onward.

[98] Ascon. *Corn.* p. 70.2–3, 20 Clark (with variant readings unimportant for this discussion); Quint. *inst.* 5.11.42.

(39n), although they differ in other aspects of the title.[99] Finally, in a passage clearly indebted to the oration, Arnobius refers to the *haruspicum... responsis*.[100] This distinction between whether Cicero is treating in his speech a single response offered by the *haruspices*, as Asconius would imply, or a number of individual responses touches on what precisely it was thought that the *haruspices* were doing in creating a document for the senate. That is, did their text result from a single consultation of the Etruscan books or was it compiled from multiple responses found at different places in their source text?

The evidence within the speech itself would seem to offer a striking contrast to these witnesses, where all but Asconius use the plural. Of the nine instances of the noun *responsum*, Cicero uses the plural form three times in comparison with six instances of the singular. Most instances of the singular, however, can be understood either as referring to the specific, single clause under discussion (11n), or as a collective singular that allows Cicero to stress the unity of the haruspical text (10, 18).[101] In the passages containing the plural, by contrast, Cicero seems unambiguously to conceive of the text under discussion as created from a series of separate responses. Although Cicero can use the plural of a substantive to give a sense of grandeur, this most certainly is not the case here.[102] At 29, he speaks of the "first" part of the "responses" and at 34 of the "remaining responses," while at 61 the plural form follows a reference to "all the pronouncements of the *haruspices*" (*sententiae quidem omnes haruspicum*). Cicero also uses the plural elsewhere to refer to what was presumably a single document of the *haruspices* produced in 65 BCE (*Catil.* 3.20, *div.* 2.45; cf. *Catil.* 3.9). In sum, evidence from the speech itself, ancient testimonia, and the manuscripts indicates that Cicero perceived of himself as speaking "about the responses of the *haruspices*" (*de haruspicum responsis*).

How precisely the *haruspices* compiled these multiple responses is unclear. According to Roman sources, Etruscan doctrine—the *disciplina Etrusca*—was based on written texts that had been dictated by a mysterious being called Tages.[103] These writings are classed by Cicero into three groups that apparently treated, respectively, the inspection of entrails, the interpretation of thunder and lightning, and various rituals and ceremonies.[104] It is this third set that included prescriptions for the treatment of prodigies.[105] Different modes were

---

[99] PE: *de aruspicu(m) responsis*; H: *de responsis aruspicum*; G: *pro responsis aruspicum*; similarly, the *subscriptiones* of PH (omitted in GE). For the independent tradition of the *Florilegium Gallicum*, see Ullman 1932: 32 (*de responsis auruspicii*).

[100] Arnob. *nat.* 7.38.3 (context quoted at 21n).

[101] There are textual issues in the remaining two passages; see notes at 37, 60.

[102] Lebreton 1901: 37–38.

[103] For Tages see 20n; Thulin 1906b: 3–6 contains all testimonia.

[104] Cic. *div.* 1.72: *et haruspicini et fulgurales et rituales libri*; Rawson 1985: 303–306. Capdeville 1997 and Turfa 2012: 20–36 survey the Etruscan context of written religious texts, the most complete extant example being the brontoscopic calendar which is the subject of Turfa's book.

[105] Thulin 1905–1909: 3.76–77 discusses the few surviving fragments, all from Latin sources.

E. *The speech* De haruspicum responsis

used in consultation, depending on the type of ritual: one determined the significance of thunder in part according to the date on which it occurred, whereas the bronze liver from Piacenza depicts which specific god corresponds to the various portions of a sacrificial animal's liver.[106] In the case of haruspical responses to prodigies, it appears that these were originally presented orally by the priests to the senate, after which the text was written down for study and consultation by individual members.[107] This assumption receives support from parallels with the Greek Sibylline books, where the text would have been compiled first in the original language and then translated into Latin for broader official consideration.[108] References from throughout antiquity indicate that the *haruspices* too would have consulted the *libri Etrusci* in the original Etruscan language.[109] Ancient sources do not record the manner in which the books were consulted, but the typical topics discussed by the senators indicate that the *haruspices* considered the category of prodigy that had occurred, its provenance, the time of occurrence, and any important attendant circumstances.[110] In other words, unlike the consultation of the lightning books, determining the circumstances surrounding a prodigy required multiple modes and occasions for consultation, thereby producing a single report that consists of several *responsa*. Such a model best accounts for the way Cicero seems to visualize the situation at 29: "but to get back to these responses (*responsa*) of the *haruspices*, the first of which concerns the games: who would not admit that as a whole (*totum*) the prediction and response was entirely directed toward his games?" (*sed ut ad haec haruspicum responsa redeam, ex quibus est primum [responsum] de ludis, quis est qui id non totum in istius ludos praedictum et responsum esse fateatur?*). In other words, the single *responsum* about the disrupted games constituted the first part of a larger set of *responsa*.

2. Date

Once the issue of Ciceronian authorship had been settled (C above), the bulk of scholarship on *De haruspicum responsis* has centered on establishing the date of delivery.[111] Progress has been made, but a consensus has still to be reached. To begin with, it is clear from the references to the consulships of Gnaeus Cornelius Lentulus Marcellinus and Lucius Marcius Philippus, as well as to Clodius's

---

[106] Thunder: Wissowa 1912: 545, Turfa 2012; Piacenza liver: van der Meer 1987.
[107] Cic. *nat. deor.* 2.10, Liv. 32.1.14, App. *BC* 4.4; Wissowa 1912: 545. Beard 1991: 51–53 notes the importance of written texts among the Romans for communication with the divine.
[108] Dio 39.16.1; 20n.
[109] Capdeville 1997: 501–504.
[110] Wissowa 1912: 547. We are similarly in the dark about how the Sibylline books were consulted (Parke 1988: 191) but see 26n.
[111] Meyer 2003 offers the most recent thorough assessment of the evidence, with full bibliography.

position as curule aedile, that the speech was delivered in 56 BCE.[112] Cicero's account of the Megalesia, sponsored by Clodius as aedile, further indicates that the speech's delivery must have occurred after these games concluded on April 9.[113] Since Cicero writes to his brother Quintus that he planned to be away from Rome between April 8 and May 6, this final date gives us a possible *terminus post quem*, although we do not know if Cicero stuck to this schedule and it is hardly inconceivable that he would have cut his trip short if events in Rome demanded his return.[114] More tenuous attempts at dating aim to correlate with known and datable events Cicero's allusions to the contemporary political atmosphere. In particular, scholars have frequently tried to find evidence that the speech betrays knowledge of the conference at Luca in April between Caesar, Crassus, and Pompey, but no agreement has been reached over this issue.[115] These arguments are in particular hampered by the fact that they frequently rely upon the wording of the haruspical response, with the unverifiable—and to me, misguided—assumption that someone concealed contemporary political references in a text ostensibly produced from an ancient, and Etruscan, source.[116]

Better precision may be found in Cicero's worry that Clodius would attack his house during his absence in mid-April. Courtney 1963 hypothesizes that this sudden concern was prompted by news of the (otherwise undatable) prodigy in the *ager Latiniensis*, in which Clodius saw an opportunity to prove that the restoration of Cicero's house, and therefore his recall, had been a mistake that roused the gods' disapproval and so he proceeded to attack his property.[117] Even if some time after mid-April is not accepted, it is nevertheless possible to narrow the date even further. Lentulus served as the presiding consul in the senate in odd-numbered months (*fam.* 1.1.2=SB 12). Since he seems to have occupied that role when our speech was delivered (2n), we can conjecture May as the most plausible month for the speech. A later odd-numbered month is less likely considering that Cicero's invective in the speech against the proconsular administration of Gabinius does not include the denial of a *supplicatio* to him by the senate on May 15; the silence is particularly marked since he mentions this refusal in other speeches of the period.[118]

---

[112] Consuls: 2n; Clodius's aedileship: MRR 2: 208.
[113] See 22n.
[114] *ad Q. fr.* 2.6.4=SB 10.
[115] Gelzer 1937 surveys early attempts at dating, from mid-April to September, following Stein 1930: 97–100 in opting for the later date; see too Kumaniecki 1959: 135. Meyer 2003: 103–108 argues convincingly against this possibility. Beard 2012: 24 expresses skepticism over fixing any date with precision.
[116] See, e.g., 55n; van den Bruwaene 1948 offers a particularly extreme example of this tendency.
[117] *Att.* 4.7.3=SB 77, Dio 39.20.3. Meyer 2003: 100 n. 19 offers counterarguments.
[118] Wuilleumier and Tupet 1966: 9; Lenaghan 1969: 27. See *prov. cons.* 14 and 25, *Pis.* 45, and for the date *ad. Q. fr.* 2.7.1=SB 11. The counterclaim of Meyer 2003: 101 n. 19, and her dating to

F. Religious background   xxxi

If this reasonable argument from silence is accepted, potential dates become restricted to the first two weeks of May, a span that can, if Cicero indeed returned to Rome on the date planned, be reduced more precisely to May 6–14. Kaster points out that since the senate had also met the day before the delivery of the speech, possible dates become further restricted to May 8, 9, or 14.[119] Lenaghan expresses a slight preference for May 8, but on the basis of a more subjective reading of Clodius's reconciliation with Pompey and Cicero's allegedly "cool" attitude toward Caesar.[120] Wiseman posits May 14 on the grounds that the senate was in recess in early May.[121] In the end, however, one must be content with Kaster's conjecture that the senate heard Cicero's speech on either May 8, 9, or 14.

F. RELIGIOUS BACKGROUND: ROMAN PRODIGIES AND ETRUSCAN *HARUSPICES*

1. The Roman prodigy process

The Roman senate considered of paramount importance the expiation of potential prodigies, with consultation about them regularly constituting one of the first subjects to be considered at the beginning of each year. On these occasions this deliberation could precede seemingly more weighty matters such as preparations for war.[122] References to the procedure, however, tend to be restricted in our texts to short descriptions of the types of prodigies reported, to the choice of which priestly bodies were chosen to provide recommendations, or to the mode of expiation adopted. They rarely give details about how the senate reached these decisions. Cicero's speech *De haruspicum responsis* is the only text from antiquity to offer a contemporary account that allows us to reconstruct how the Roman senate analyzed, discussed, and treated these important events.

The steps involved in recognizing and treating prodigies during the Republic can be reconstructed with reliable accuracy from the many references to the procedure in Greek and Latin texts.[123] Unlike oracles, prodigies in Roman

---

July, is unconvincing. Goar 1972: 59–69 does not consider this argument from silence in opting for a date in late May.

[119] Kaster 2006: Appendix 1 n. 40.
[120] Lenaghan 1969: 26; for a critique see Meyer 2003: 100–101 n. 190.
[121] Wiseman 1974: 161 n. 18, an argument anticipated and rebutted by Lenaghan 1969: 27.
[122] Mommsen 1887–1888: 3.1059–1060, who cites multiple instances from Livy (see, e.g., Liv. 32.9, 24.11.1); cf. Gell. 14.7.9 (Varro).
[123] This section relies principally on Wissowa 1912: 391–396, Rosenberger 1998: 17–90 (with abundant bibliography), and Rasmussen 2003: 35–116 (with listing of all attested prodigies), and includes material from Corbeill 2010b: 83–86.

religion were not essentially predictive. In other words, they did not normally provide warnings about some specific future event.[124] Rather, the occurrence of a prodigy, and its acceptance by the state, signaled an awareness of an unspecific rupture of order in the natural world. This order is marked in Latin by the term *pax deorum*, which refers to the process of reestablishing proper relations between gods and mortals during a period of moral or political crisis.[125] Contrary to the normal practice in Greek religion, where an oracle predicts a future event that cannot be avoided, the type of rupture indicated by a prodigy in the Roman world can be countered through timely and appropriate human ritual activity.[126] A common approach in the prodigy process is to identify the source of disruption—be it a hermaphrodite or an unchaste Vestal virgin or a lightning bolt that has struck the earth—and to isolate that source from the community. In the cases cited, this could take the form of, respectively, banishment to the sea for the androgyne, burial alive for the Vestal, or the creation of a small sepulchral monument around the place where lightning has struck.

Although we have no evidence outside the speech, one can reconstruct from parallels the plausible sequence of events that would have prompted the senate to consider as a prodigy the earth tremors of spring 56. The following schematic representation concisely summarizes the steps involved in the prodigy process.

The life of a prodigy

A. Possible prodigy occurs.
B. Reported to magistrate.
C. Reported to **senate** >>> **Senate** rejects report. Process ends.
D. Confirmed by **senate** as possible prodigy.
E. Forwarded to priestly body (*pontifices, X(V)viri sacris faciundis, haruspices*).
F. Priestly body makes recommendation to **senate** >>> **Senate** rejects report and process ends.
G. **Senate** decides upon means of expiation.

To begin with steps **A** and **B**: when a possible prodigy is observed during the Republican period, the witness or witnesses report its occurrence to a magistrate who, in our extant examples, is normally a praetor or consul. If the magistrate judges the incident to have potential significance, the process continues with step **C**, in which a report is brought before the senate for consideration.

---

[124] This remains true despite Cicero's apparent claims to the contrary, where he seems to be misled by the ancient etymology of *prodigium* as deriving from *praedico* (*nat. deor.* 2.7, *div.* 1.93; see too *Phil.* 4.10).

[125] See the convincing reassessment of the term in Santangelo 2011a: 162–168.

[126] Bloch 1964 concisely outlines this and other unique features of Roman divination; North 1990: 60 provides cases in which prophecy is an element—although not an essential one—of Roman divination more generally.

F. Religious background

The role of the senate should not be underestimated; as mentioned above, the expiation of prodigies was sometimes, and perhaps always, first on the senate's agenda, preceding even pressing issues of war. Should the senate deem the reported event unimportant, the incident is forgotten. If, however, the senators accept the occurrence as a possible prodigy, their own report is forwarded to one of three religious bodies for an expert opinion—the *pontifices*, the *Xviri* (later *XVviri*) *sacris faciundis*, or the *haruspices*. This referral constitutes steps D and E (cf. 61n). It is not known precisely what criteria determined the particular priestly body to be consulted and occasionally a prodigy could be brought before more than one of these groups simultaneously. At step F, the priestly body chosen then submits a report back to the senate concerning the meaning of the prodigy and recommends a method by which it should be expiated. At this point, step G, the senate has the final say on whether and to what extent it should accept these recommendations, and it may even choose, after all this trouble, to ignore the event altogether. If, however, the recommendations of the priests are accepted, the three most common forms of expiation, often used in combination, include real or symbolic banishment of the prodigy (or the related act of containment), a *lectisternium* or festival honoring the gods, and a lustration of the city walls.

One point emerges clearly from this brief summary. The senate as a group is constantly involved throughout the process of assessing a prodigy, and the popular assemblies are never consulted.[127] Domination of the process by the elite becomes especially marked when one considers that for the *pontifices* and *X(V)viri*, that is, for two of the three bodies potentially consulted during the process, the majority of members hold senatorial rank.[128] The third body of *haruspices*, on the contrary, constitutes a group seemingly divorced from urban politics.

The procedure for treating a prodigy is therefore quite clear. What our sources have not preserved is a precise set of criteria that the Romans would have applied in deciding what could constitute the prodigy itself.[129] Certain events make up a clear majority of the attestations recorded in the extant material—lightning strikes dominate, for example, followed by eclipses and odd births of human beings and animals. Still, the surviving sources hardly constitute an all-inclusive list. It would be hazardous if not impossible to say with certainty whether the senate would have judged this or that given event a prodigy.[130] The extant lists, in fact, offer several unique examples that we would have perhaps hesitated to label as prodigies if ancient authors had not so clearly

---

[127] Rosenberger 1998: 23–24.   [128] Rosenberger 1998: 49.
[129] North 1990: 54 is inaccurate in claiming that "We know what events were counted as prodigies."
[130] Wülker 1903: 6–25 categorizes our extant examples; Rosenberger 1998: 91–126 attempts a structural analysis of the kinds of categories represented, such as the transgression of liminality or fears of infertility.

xxxiv *Introduction*

labeled them as such. For example, Julius Obsequens notes that in the year 42 BCE the praetor Publius Titius ejected his colleague from office due to differences of opinion. This phenomenon of human politics would seem divorced from divine will, a fact that prompts Obsequens to add that the act is classified as a prodigy since history shows that, whenever a Roman magistrate removes a colleague, he dies within the year.[131] A second example dates to the early stages of the Second Punic War, when Valerius Maximus records that a wave of sexual license among both married and unmarried women was officially recognized as an event with direct bearing on the state, one that needed to be expiated by offering a statue to Venus Verticordia (8.15.12; cf. Plin. *nat.* 7.120). These two examples indicate that the best we can say is that the senate knew a prodigy when it saw one—or wanted to see one.

2. The Etruscan *haruspices*

a. Composition and training

In using the term *haruspices* in this commentary, I do not include those independent entrepreneurs who offered their divinatory services for hire throughout the Roman world. Although the Romans also called these persons *haruspices*, their sphere of activity evidently does not correspond with that of the body consulted by the senate in 56 BCE. First entering the historical record in the second century, the professional worked abroad with provincial governors and military commanders or traveled as a freelance *haruspex* around Italy and practiced predominantly, if not entirely, a different type of divination, namely, extispicy or the examination of entrails.[132] Furthermore, ancient texts depict this class of diviners as possessing largely negative reputations among the elite, as conveyed by the Elder Cato's quip that "he was amazed that *haruspices* didn't laugh when they saw each other."[133]

By contrast, the *haruspices* of our speech belong to an exclusive set of highly respected men, trained in what the emperor (and Etruscologist) Claudius referred to as "the oldest discipline in Italy."[134] This class originates from the religious elite of Etruscan society, and the Roman senate made an effort both to benefit from and to nurture these expert diviners. Following the conquest of

---

[131] Obseq. 70; Dio 46.49.1–2 correctly refers the incident to Titius's tribunate of 43 (*MRR* 2: 340).
[132] Commanders: Plut. *Sull.* 9.3, 27.4 (Sulla); *div.* 2.36–37 (Caesar); *div.* 2.53 (Pompey); further examples in Rawson 1978: 140–146. Freelance practitioners: Cato *agr.* 5.4, with Haack 2003: 44–57, Corbeill 2012: 245–247. Haack 2003: 1–84 provides a full discussion of the range of haruspical activity in Rome from the earliest times to the end of the Republic.
[133] Cic. *div.* 2.51: *mirari se aiebat quod non rideret haruspex haruspicem cum vidisset* (cf. *nat.* 1.71, *fam.* 6.18.1=SB 218). Haack 2006 contains a prosopography of all known *haruspices*.
[134] Tac. *ann.* 11.15: *vetustissima Italiae disciplina*. The following discussion derives from Corbeill 2012: 247–252.

F. *Religious background*

the city-states of Etruria, training in the so-called "Etruscan doctrine" (*Etrusca disciplina*) suffered from neglect, dependent as it was upon familiarity with a rapidly dying Etruscan language and the use of that society's sacred books. Several Latin texts refer to the senate's efforts in the third or second centuries BCE to revive education in this area.[135] Cicero provides the fullest account: "Etruria uses its deep learning to observe lightning bolts and to interpret what is meant concerning various signs and portents. It is for this reason that, when the state was at a peak in the time of our ancestors (*cum florebat imperium*), the senate wisely decreed that ten sons of the elite from each of the Etruscan peoples be given training so that such a great art should not, because of this group's poverty, be withdrawn from religious action in order to turn a profit."[136]

With most recent commentators, I assume that the "sons of the elite" refer here to children of Etruscan ancestry.[137] Three points make this inference likely. First, if the senate were to revive a religious practice from an alien culture, it is intuitively likely that they would retain those persons for whom such practices form a significant portion of their ancestral heritage. This likelihood receives further support from a letter in which Cicero refers to how training in divination had been passed down to a friend by a father of Etruscan lineage.[138] Second, during a later period when the *haruspices* were suffering from neglect, Tacitus records that the emperor Claudius referred to this Republican action as a precedent for his own measures. He notes unambiguously that in the Roman past it was "members of the Etruscan elite, either of their own accord or at the instigation of the senate, who retained their knowledge and passed it on to their families."[139] Third, in his treatise *De legibus*, Cicero includes the following provision among the foundational sacral legislation of his ideal Roman state: "When the senate orders, let prodigies and portents be reported to the Etruscan *haruspices*, and let Etruria teach this art to the elite" (*leg.* 2.21: *prodigia portenta ad Etruscos et haruspices, si senatus iussit, deferunto. Etruriaque principes disciplinam doceto*). Syntax indicates that the "elite" (*principes*) in the final clause refers to the upper ranks of Etruscan, not Roman, society. Other linguistic considerations further support this reading. The most natural way of construing the epexegetic *et* in the clause *Etruscos et haruspices* is as an emphatic identification of the art of haruspicy with the race of the Etruscans (in other words,

---

[135] The date of this move is disputed, resting largely on the interpretation of Cicero's imprecise *cum florebat imperium* (quoted in next note); Wardle 2006: 325 reviews various possible dates.
[136] Cic. *div.* 1.92: *Etruria autem de caelo tacta scientissime animaduertit eademque interpretatur, quid quibusque ostendatur monstris atque portentis. quocirca bene apud maiores nostros senatus tum, cum florebat imperium, decreuit ut de principum filiis decem ex singulis Etruriae populis in disciplinam traderentur, ne ars tanta propter tenuitatem hominum a religionis auctoritate abduceretur ad mercedem atque quaestum.* I accept the conjecture *decem ex* (sc. *X ex*) for *sex* of the codices; see Thulin 1905–1909: 3.143 n. 2.
[137] Rawson 1978: 139–140.   [138] Cic. *fam.* 6.6.3=SB 234.   [139] Tac. *ann.* 11.15.1.

a literal translation would yield "let prodigies and portents be reported to the Etruscans, that is, to the *haruspices*").[140]

If we accept, therefore, that a senatorial decree of the middle Republic aimed to restore the art of divination among the very ranks of the Etruscans, we may now consider motivations. The practice of Etruscan divination had fallen into neglect, Cicero writes, "because of this group's poverty" (*propter tenuitatem hominum*). In response, the Roman senate took steps to alleviate the situation it had created among its former enemies. The second motivation that Cicero ascribes to the senate points up the basic contrast, stressed above, between private and public *haruspices*. The decree explicitly addresses concerns that the elite *haruspices* may come to disregard their important function as a public religious authority "in order to turn a profit." The clear intention of the senate, therefore, is not only to encourage the continued training of Etruscan youths but also to provide the material means for them to do so.

That the integration of Etruscan practice into Roman society was not generally perceived as problematic is clearly indicated by Livy's narrative of the year 186 BCE. The Roman authorities had just succeeded in suppressing an outbreak of Bacchic frenzy on the Italian peninsula. In response to fears from the populace that this suppression could invite divine reprisals, Livy portrays the consul, Spurius Postumius, attempting to calm them with the following words: "Fear enters our hearts that in punishing human misdeeds we may be violating some divine right that is intertwined with those misdeeds. It is from scruples such as these that you are freed by countless decrees of the pontifices, by resolutions of the senate, and by responses of the *haruspices*."[141] Here the ability of the *haruspices* to respond to and to interpret how divine will manifests itself in the natural world is equated with the sacred decisions of the *pontifices* and the rational deliberations of the senate. What causes even more surprise is that these *haruspices* are being marshaled as a defense against the encroachment of the "foreign rites" of Bacchus (39.16.8: *sacra externa... externo ritu*). With no trace of self-irony, the Roman consul views Etruscan learning as a fixed part of traditional state religion.

b. Role in the Roman prodigy process

After their first historically attested appearance in 278 BCE, the public *haruspices* quickly occupy a central role in the process by which the Roman senate assessed and expiated prodigies.[142] As noted in the table above, when the

---

[140] See Dyck 2004a: 311 in defense of retaining the *et* of the transmitted text. On epexegetic *et*, see *ThLL* V, 2 874.35–53 (J. B. Hofmann).

[141] Liv. 39.16.7.

[142] MacBain 1982: 45–49; Haack 2003: 39 suggests that the phrase *haruspices ex Etruria acciti* ("*haruspices* summoned from Etruria"; Liv. 27.37.6, Gell. 4.5.2) was a stock phrase preserved in the writings of the pontifices.

F. Religious background

senate of the late Republic decided that a prodigy deserved serious consideration, it consulted one, sometimes two, and on one known occasion all of three priestly bodies: the *pontifices*, the *X(V)viri sacris faciundis*, and the *haruspices*.[143] The sources do not explain how the choice among these three groups was made in any particular instance, but patterns can be detected. The *haruspices* appear with special frequency in the context of the lightning prodigies that are an Etruscan specialty; in this area, they are consulted in ten of the thirteen attested cases—that is, nearly 80 percent of the time.[144] For prodigies in general, the Roman college of the *X(V)viri* tends to be consulted more frequently up until the 140s BCE; thereupon the tendency is reversed until the end of the Republic, with the *haruspices* being summoned more than twice as often, particularly in the decade of the 90s.[145] Clearly, their foreignness did not trouble the senate when confronted by enigmas in nature. Quite the contrary; by 56 BCE we find Cicero praising the Roman ancestors for their prescient wisdom in including the *haruspices* as one of the four groups responsible for the maintenance of religious ritual at the state level (18n). By this date the interpretation of prodigies has become identified as the chief function for the public *haruspices*.

In the case of the Latian rumblings of 56, multiple factors make it possible to reconstruct a plausible scenario for why the *haruspices* were chosen for consultation. First, geographical considerations likely played a role: the region of northern Latium would have had long historical associations with the Etruscans and, as MacBain has shown in detail, since the third century BCE it seems to have been considered natural, and at times even politically expedient, that the *haruspices* be in charge of phenomena that arise in regions of former Etruscan dominance.[146] Second, our extant record of prodigy types indicates a slight preference for consulting the *haruspices* when the phenomenon involves rumblings under the earth.[147] A third and final point to be considered involves circumstances that have direct relevance to politics within the city of Rome in 56. As already noted, the portion of the response most damning to Cicero's case is the reference to the profanation of sacred spaces (*LOCA SACRA ET RELIGIOSA PROFANA HABERI*; 9n). Clodius's reading is an obvious one: the clause refers to the consecration of a portion of Cicero's house during his exile and to the subsequent restoration of the property to Cicero—and hence its profanation—upon his return. The most convincing refutation to Clodius's claim offered by the orator is that the house had already been "released from every religious

---

[143] Rosenberger 1998: 50–56; for *pontifices* in particular see Wissowa 1912: 514–515.
[144] MacBain 1982: 50.
[145] MacBain 1982: 106. Thulin 1912: 2433 gives the proportion for consultation of *decemviri* to *haruspices* after the Second Punic War as sixteen to twenty-two, whereas by the first century *haruspices* are favored by a ratio of twelve to five.
[146] MacBain 1982: esp. 60–79; for the location of the prodigy of 56 see 20n.
[147] MacBain 1982: 119.

sanction through every authority" (11). In support of this claim, Cicero places considerable emphasis in this portion of the speech on the verdict of the college of *pontifices*, who had sided with the argument that Cicero offers in the extant *De domo sua*, that Cicero may rightfully regain his house since the ceremony consecrating the site was performed improperly. Because of this pontifical verdict from the autumn of 57, it makes sense that the senate, in choosing for the recent prodigy the appropriate priestly body, would not choose the *pontifices* since they had recently made a judgment on this related issue.[148] The senate also had two important reasons to doubt that the *XVviri* could render an impartial verdict: first, the majority of this college would have been senators and the senate had already reaffirmed the earlier verdict of the *pontifices* through a written edict; and second, it is surely relevant that by 56 P. Clodius was himself a *quindecimvir*.[149] By process of elimination, only the *haruspices* remain.

This combination of factors makes it nearly certain that in 56 the *haruspices* were intended, through their response, to craft an objective document from which the senate could in turn claim to produce a reasoned decision, endorsed by the divine, about the conflict between Cicero and Clodius. Such a scenario makes better sense than that the *haruspices* were somehow manipulated to produce a response aimed at incriminating major political players of the time. Indeed, introducing the *haruspices* as an independent supplement meant to resolve a seemingly irresolvable conflict has parallels in other aspects of the political system. For example, Taylor has hypothesized that the use of divinely sanctioned auspices increased in the late Republic as an alternative to the veto because the veto had become subject to human manipulation and would often lead to violence.[150] In an analogous fashion, the Romans used divination to resolve legal controversies: "by delegating the solution of a legal controversy to a divinatory procedure divine support is sought and the outcome of the process is fully legitimised."[151] At the same time, it is important to keep in mind that the response of the *haruspices* receives its meaning from the senate, which is able to control a foreign element that could potentially advise moves harmful to the state.[152]

One final element of the Roman constitution that performs a similar function needs to be considered: exile. By relegating a controversial citizen to a location far from the city, the Romans prevent the potential, and at times

---

[148] This change of tactic is reflected in the difference between *dom.* 1, where the intersection of politicians and religious figures in Rome is praised, and the addition of the *haruspices* to this list at *har. resp.* 18.

[149] On the senate confirmation see Cic. *Att.* 4.2.3–4=SB 74, *har. resp.* 14; for Clodius as *quindecimvir* see 26n.

[150] Taylor 1949: 82.

[151] Santangelo 2011b: 34.

[152] Orlin 1997: 113–115 offers an analogous interpretation of Rome's use of the Sibylline books.

G. The haruspical response xxxix

seemingly inevitable, escalation of violence.[153] In the case of the conflict between Clodius and Cicero, exile had provided only a one-year stopgap. Soon after Cicero's return, the next attempt to prevent open street violence was the decision of the *pontifices* in September 57 recorded in *De domo sua*. The external intervention of the *haruspices* provided what would be yet another way of introducing internal concord. History does not record the outcome of this debate, although it would seem that Cicero won the day since he continued possession of his property. What is clear is that the decision did not curb late Republican violence and political conflict. But that is a sad story that has often been told.

G. THE HARUSPICAL RESPONSE: TEXT, STYLE, AND CONTENT

1. Latin text

As discussed in E.1 above, the *haruspices* excerpted their responses from Etruscan sacred writings, after which the completed document was translated into Latin and handed over to the senate for consideration. The text as quoted by Cicero shares features of structure and tone with the haruspical response produced during the Catilinarian conspiracy and preserved in verse form in Cicero's treatise on divination.[154] In *De haruspicum responsis*, although he quotes the response only in pieces, interspersing his own interpretation of each section, it is nevertheless a straightforward task to reconstruct the sequence of the original. I reproduce below a probable reconstruction, accompanied by an English translation; numbers in square brackets indicate the section of the speech from which each clause was drawn:[155]

Prodigy and recommended expiation:
¹*QVOD IN AGRO LATINIENSI AVDITVS EST STREPITVS CVM FREMITV,* [20]
²*POSTILIONES ESSE IOVI SATVRNO NEPTVNO TELLVRI DIS CAELESTIBVS;* [20]

Causes of divine anger:
³*LVDOS MINVS DILIGENTER FACTOS POLLVTOSQVE,* [21]
⁴*LOCA SACRA ET RELIGIOSA PROFANA HABERI,* [9]
⁵*ORATORES CONTRA IVS FASQVE INTERFECTOS,* [34]

---
[153] Kelly 2006: 13.
[154] *Div.* 1.17=*carm. frg.* 3.47–59 (*De consulato suo*).
[155] I follow the order adopted by Wissowa 1912: 545 n. 4, using the text of Maslowski 1981 with my own proposed emendations for the eighth clause, for which see the various notes on section 40. These emendations do not affect the discussion here. Details on the order of clauses are discussed in the notes on 29, 30, 34, 36 (twice), 37, 40, 56, 60.

xl *Introduction*

⁶*FIDEM IVSQVE IVRANDVM NEGLECTVM,* [36]
⁷*SACRIFICIA VETVSTA OCCVLTAQVE MINVS DILIGENTER FACTA POLLVTAQVE;* [37]

Potential dangers:
⁸*NE PER OPTIMATIVM DISCORDIAM DISSENSIONEMQVE PATRIBVS PRINCIPIBVSQVE CAEDES PERICVLAQVE CREENTVR AVXILIOQVE DIVINITVS DEFICIANTVR, QVA RE AD VNVM IMPERIVM PECVNIAE REDEANT EXERCITVSQVE PVLSVS DOMINATIOQVE ACCEDAT,* [40]
⁹*NE OCCVLTIS CONSILIIS RES PVBLICA LAEDATVR,* [55]
¹⁰*NE DETERIORIBVS REPVLSISQVE HONOS AVGEATVR,* [56]
¹¹*NE REIPVBLICAE STATVS COMMVTETVR.* [60]

¹Since a rumbling, accompanied by a trembling, was heard in the *ager Latiniensis*,
²reparations are owed to Jupiter, Saturn, Neptune, Tellus, the heavenly gods.
[The gods are angered]
³that games have been conducted less carefully and polluted;
⁴that sacred and hallowed places have been desecrated;
⁵that *oratores* have been killed contrary to human and divine law;
⁶that trust and oath-taking have been neglected;
⁷that ancient and secret rites have been conducted less carefully and polluted.
[One must take care]
⁸that through discord and disagreement of the best men there not arise death and danger for the fathers and leading men, and that they not require help from a divine source, because of which circumstance wealth would revert to a single ruler and there would occur the driving away of the army and despotism [*text uncertain*];
⁹that the republic not be harmed by secret plans;
¹⁰that baser men, and those rejected, not receive an increase in honor;
¹¹that the constitution of the republic not be subverted.

Cicero makes clear that the senators had access to a written copy of this text, as seems to have been the customary procedure for haruspical responses.[156] He also indicates that Clodius read this same text aloud at his *contio* before offering his own interpretation; Clodius perhaps also had it displayed for public consultation over the course of several days.[157]

2. Archaic features

The translator of the response into Latin scattered throughout the text a number of archaic elements. It is impossible to know whether these features were intended to reflect the language of the presumed Etruscan original. Regardless, however, it is probable that the translator has inserted these elements in order to defamiliarize the contents of the response, to add an air of mystique. Powell

---

[156] 9n; cf. 9 (*scriptum etiam illud est*), 20 (*de ea re scriptum est*); Thulin 1905: 78.
[157] 9n.

G. The haruspical response

has demonstrated how Cicero adopts an analogous practice in composing his imaginary law code in *De legibus*, a code that includes religious legislation: while the basic register of that text belongs to contemporary legal language, Cicero intersperses archaic elements throughout to create a tone of greater authority and authenticity.[158] The following archaic features occur in the response.

a. Lexical elements

In two places the response uses a common word with what would seem an archaic meaning. Included among the positive outcomes of expiating the prodigy is the clause "that death and danger not arise" (*NE...CAEDES PERICVLAQVE CREENTVR*), where the unusual sense of the verb *creo* seems to belong to an older speech register; the same archaizing tendency holds true for the use of *ORATORES* to refer to international ambassadors rather than political orators.[159]

The lexical choice that stands out most in this context, however, is the predominance of the conjunction *-que*, "the connective *par excellence*" in archaic Latin.[160] In contrast with a single appearance in this text of the commonest Latin conjunction *et*, which Adams denotes here as "an isolated modernism," the enclitic form *-que* occurs eleven times within a text of roughly ninety-six words.[161] In eight of those eleven cases the word is used to join pairs of nouns or adjectives, a feature that characterizes "high religious language."[162] A similar avoidance of *et* can be found in the Latin version of the alleged Etruscan prophecy of Vegoia. There *et* again appears only once, in contrast with nine occurrences of *-que* and *atque*. Adams believes that this and other unusual features of the Latin of the Vegoia prophecy constitute an attempt not to capture some flavor of the original Etruscan but to create a Latin text with literary pretensions.[163]

In contrast with the numerous conjunctions, the response contains only a single instance of asyndeton, in a catalogue of divine names (20: *IOVI SATVRNO NEPTVNO TELLVRI DIS CAELESTIBVS*). This manner of grouping deities seems also to constitute an archaic feature.[164]

---

[158] Powell 2005: 124–137.   [159] 40n; 34n.
[160] Penney 2005: 41, with abundant testimony. LHS 2: 473–476 provides a diachronic summary of its use in different genres and authors.
[161] Adams 2021: 245. I include separately in this total the occurrences of the enclitics *-ve* and *-que*.
[162] Adams 2016: 77.
[163] Adams 2003: 179–182, who concludes that there is no evidence in this case for positing an Etruscan original.
[164] Penney 2005: 38–40.

b. Word order

In noun-adjective pairings archaic Latin tends to follow the order substantive + adjective, with the largest class of exceptions being those cases in which the descriptor signifies size or quantity or for adjectives that express a personal judgment (such as *bonus, iustus,* or *improbus*).[165] Six instances in the response follow this order of substantive + adjective (included in this number are two cases of *res publica*). Of the other two examples, in one case the adjective denotes quantity (*unum imperium*; the text is uncertain), while the remaining instance appears to constitute a real exception (*occultis consiliis*). In addition, the response follows the tendency of consistently placing verbs in final position: after the introductory *quod* clause giving the reason for the response, all eleven verbs occur at clause end. This placement of the verb also characterizes archaic style.[166]

Finally, it is well known that word pairs in early Latin tend to follow the pattern by which a shorter word precedes a longer (of the type *aurum argentum*).[167] Lindholm notes that this sequence holds true in particular for sacral language, regardless of whether the words are substantives or adjectives.[168] The construction certainly characterizes the response, with four instances of adjective pairs (including participles) and five of substantive pairs. In fact, there is only one instance of a pair of words in which the second member contains fewer syllables than the first (*DETERIORIBVS REPVLSISQVE*). Furthermore, two of the examples in section 40 have the additional archaic characteristic of constituting alliterative pairs (*DISCORDIAM DISSENSIONEMQVE; PATRIBVS PRINCIPIBVSQVE*). Each of these nine groups also contains synonyms or near synonyms, an additional characteristic of the prolix archaic style, where the combination is intended to cover all possible permutations of a single idea.[169]

Each of these features makes it clear that the translator of the haruspical response into Latin intended either to preserve or to manufacture an archaic tone.

H. NOTE ON THE LATIN TEXT

The transmission of the text of *De haruspicum responsis* consists of three main branches.[170] The oldest surviving witness, and the closest to the hypothetical

---

[165] Adams 1976: 88–90.
[166] Adams 1976: 91–92; for evidence that this order may be artificial see Clackson and Horrocks 2007: 26–31.
[167] Lindholm 1931 offers a full analysis of the combination for the archaic and classical periods.
[168] Lindholm 1931: 57–60; represented in Habinek 1985: 178 (Table 3).
[169] Löfstedt 1956: 2.314–316; cf. Powell 2005: 129 on this feature in Cicero's fictional laws in *De legibus*.
[170] This section derives largely from Maslowski 1981: v–xxxv (with important updates in Maslowski and Rouse 1984), and Rouse and Reeve 1983: 57–61. Clark 1912: 266–280 remains worth consulting.

H. Note on the Latin text

archetype (**A**), is the codex **P**, written in France in the mid-ninth century. It contains nine speeches of Cicero dating to the period after his return from exile along with the pseudo-Ciceronian *Pridie quam in exilium iret* ("On the day before he went into exile").[171] The first corrector of this manuscript (**P²**), roughly contemporary with the creation of the text, has improved **P** considerably by consultation of the y branch of the tradition. This branch produced the hyparchetype **m**, which is represented by the extant manuscripts **G** (first half of eleventh century) and **E** (second quarter of twelfth century). Codex **H**, from the second half of the twelfth century, offers a third independent line of descent.[172] Finally, the twelfth-century anthology known as the *Florilegium Gallicum* contains two quotations of *har. resp.* that are independent of these three branches but offer limited value in reconstructing its text (see notes on 39 and 54). I provide here a simplified stemma of the tradition; for further details see Maslowski 1981: xxxiii:

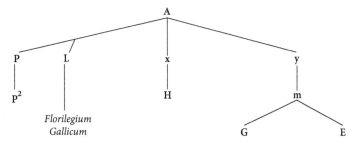

I have based my Latin text on Maslowski's 1981 Teubner and adopted his sigla in reporting manuscript readings. For a full record of important variations, the interested reader should check that edition. In compiling these notes I have regularly consulted digital versions of **P**, **G**, and **H**, as well as earlier critical editions listed in the bibliography. For orthography I also follow Maslowski, who primarily adopts the conventions of **P**.[173] In lieu of an apparatus I discuss all important textual issues in the commentary, where they are preceded by a double asterisk (**). My text differs from Maslowski in the following places (I omit minor changes in punctuation and paragraphing):

	This edition	*Maslowski*
1	P. Tullio Nisyro	P. Tullioni Syro
4	tum, tum, inquam	tum, inquam, tum
4	mobilis	nobilis
5	sensit	sentit
7	tacenti stans	stanti tacens

---

[171] For this product of the declamation schools see Manuwald 2021: xl–xliii, who also offers text, translation, and commentary.

[172] Maslowski 1981: xxv–xxix discusses the complexities of H as a reliable witness.

[173] Maslowski 1981: xxxiv–xxxv.

8	sacris, caerimoniis		sacris et caerimoniis
8	Publius, inquam		P., inquam
11	scrupulus		scripulus
14	quid ergo? ii		quid ergo ii
15	aedibus		sedibus
24	loquar? quos		loquar quos
25	pollueret		polluerit
25	in alteram caveam		in alteram scaenam
30	fuisse ⟨et⟩ aras		fuisse [aras]
30	referri ad nos		referri ad vos
37	in haruspicum responso		in haruspicum responsum
40	iam a dis immortalibus		a dis iam immortalibus
40	† QVA RE AD VNVM IMPERIVM PECVNIAE REDEANT		QVA RE AD VNIVS IMPERIVM RES REDEAT
40	PVLSVS DOMINATIOQVE ACCEDAT		† APVLSVS DIMINVTIOQVE ACCEDAT †
41	ubertas		brevitas
43	patria		patrum
46	inter eos		in eos
48	quod caecus		quam caecus
49	vero est elatus		vero elatus
54	dominatus et regnum		dominatus ac regnum
54	C. Mario		Mario
54	Fortuna		fortuna
56	monemur		monent
62	multis quibusdam		quibusdam †multis†

I. A NOTE ON THE TRANSLATION

To render Cicero literally is to risk incomprehension, and in his post-exilic speeches in particular he not infrequently pushes his rhetoric and syntax to extremes in order to regain his status as Rome's master orator. In my translation I have tried to maintain the variety for which Cicero is famous, such as his manner of alternating long periods with short punchy attacks, or the abruptness with which he can move from the expression of serious concerns regarding the relationship between gods and humans to a scurrilous and often witty attack on one of his opponents. In this way, I hope that the translation will supplement comprehension of the accompanying Latin text in ways complementary to the more philological issues treated in the notes. I do not, however,

I. A note on the translation

make any attempt to be consistent in rendering Latin words with a single English equivalent; in some cases, as with *religio*, such consistency is impossible (see 8n). In places where I may seem to have taken liberties with the text, for example by rendering two nouns in hendiadys with a noun-adjective pairing, my notes frequently explicate and justify the translation; in contrast, such apparently free translation has made me sensitive to places where Cicero is making special distinctions (e.g., notes on 22, 25).

Text and translation

Text

M. Tulli Ciceronis
oratio de haruspicum responsis

1 Hesterno die, patres conscripti, cum me et vestra dignitas et frequentia equitum Romanorum praesentium, quibus senatus dabatur, magnopere commosset, putavi mihi reprimendam esse P. Clodi impudicam impudentiam, cum is publicanorum causam stultissimis interrogationibus impediret, P. Tullio Nisyro navaret operam atque ei se, cui totus venierat, etiam vobis inspectantibus venditaret. itaque hominem furentem exsultantemque continui simul ac periculum iudici intendi; duobus inceptis verbis omnem impetum gladiatoris ferociamque compressi. 2 ac tamen ignarus ille qui consules essent, exsanguis atque aestuans se ex curia repente proripuit, cum quibusdam fractis iam atque inanibus minis et cum illius Pisoniani temporis Gabinianique terroribus. quem cum egredientem insequi coepissem, cepi equidem fructum maximum et ex consurrectione omnium vestrum et ex comitatu publicanorum. sed vaecors repente sine suo voltu, sine colore, sine voce constitit; deinde respexit et, simul atque Cn. Lentulum consulem aspexit, concidit in curiae paene limine, recordatione, credo, Gabini sui desiderioque Pisonis. cuius ego de ecfrenato et praecipiti furore quid dicam? an potest gravioribus a me verbis volnerari quam est statim in facto ipso a gravissimo viro, P. Servilio, confectus ac trucidatus? cuius si iam vim et gravitatem illam singularem ac paene divinam adsequi possem, tamen non dubito quin ea tela quae coniecerit inimicus, quam ea quae collega patris emisit, leviora atque hebetiora esse videantur.

3 Sed tamen mei facti rationem exponere illis volo qui hesterno die dolore me elatum et iracundia longius prope progressum arbitrabantur quam sapientis hominis cogitata ratio postulasset. nihil feci iratus, nihil impotenti animo, nihil non diu consideratum ac multo ante meditatum. ego enim me, patres conscripti, inimicum semper esse professus sum duobus, qui me, qui rem publicam cum defendere deberent, servare possent, cumque ad consulare officium ipsis insignibus illius imperi, ad meam salutem non solum auctoritate sed etiam precibus vestris vocarentur, primo reliquerunt, deinde prodiderunt, postremo oppugnarunt praemiisque nefariae pactionis funditus una cum re publica oppressum exstinctumque voluerunt; qui quae suo ductu et imperio cruento illo atque funesto supplicia neque a sociorum moenibus prohibere neque

Translation

Speech of Marcus Tullius Cicero on the Responses of the *Haruspices*, Delivered in the Senate against Publius Clodius

1 Yesterday, senators, greatly inspired not only by your own eminence but by the presence of the many Roman knights who had received permission to attend the senate, I decided that I had to check the unchaste scurrility of Publius Clodius. He kept disrupting with the most inane questions the debate over tax collection, devoting himself to the cause of Publius Tullius Nisyrus and selling his favors, even while all of you were watching, to this man who had already bought him wholesale. So I checked him in the midst of his riotous madness by threatening to take him to court: with barely two words begun I entirely shut down the gladiator's vicious attack. **2** But even so, unaware of who this year's consuls were, pale and seething, he suddenly burst out of the senate house, taking with him some of those now ineffectual threats and fearmongering from the Pisogabinian age. As I began to follow him out, I felt a great deal of satisfaction because not only did all of you rise up, but the tax-collectors joined us as well. Suddenly the lunatic stopped—with a blank expression, pale and silent. He then looked behind him and, once he spotted the consul Gnaeus Lentulus, collapsed nearly at the threshold of the senate house—remembering with longing, I imagine, his dear Gabinius and Piso.

What can I say about his unbridled, headlong madness? Do you think I have the power to wound him with words more authoritative than those of that ultimate authority, Publius Servilius, who straightaway cut him down and snuffed him out? Even if I were now able to rival that man's singularly forceful, almost divine, authority, I still don't doubt that the weapons cast by a personal enemy would be more ineffectual and blunt than those hurled by his father's colleague.

3 All the same, I want to explain the reason for my own behavior to those who thought that I had been carried away by grievous indignation yesterday to an extent almost greater than the disciplined reason of a wise man should have desired. There was nothing that I did in anger, nothing in a reckless temper, nothing that I had not pondered at length and been planning long before. For you see, senators, I have always expressed my opposition to two men in particular. When they should have been defending—and could have been saving—me and the republic, and when they were being called upon to do their duty as consuls through the very insignia of that office and to protect me in response to both your authority and pleading, their first act was to abandon us, then betray us, and finally attack us. Enjoying the rewards of a wicked alliance, they wanted me, along with the republic, utterly overwhelmed and destroyed.

hostium urbibus inferre potuerunt, excisionem, inflammationem, eversionem, depopulationem, vastitatem, ea sua cum praeda meis omnibus tectis atque agris intulerunt. 4 cum his furiis et facibus, cum his, inquam, exitiosis prodigiis ac paene huius imperi pestibus bellum mihi inexpiabile dico esse susceptum, neque id tamen ipsum tantum quantum meus ac meorum, sed tantum quantum vester atque omnium bonorum dolor postulavit. in Clodium vero non est hodie meum maius odium quam illo die fuit cum illum ambustum religiosissimis ignibus cognovi muliebri ornatu ex incesto stupro atque ex domo pontificis maximi emissum. tum, tum, inquam, vidi ac multo ante prospexi quanta tempestas excitaretur, quanta impenderet procella rei publicae. videbam illud scelus tam importunum, audaciam tam immanem adulescentis furentis, mobilis, volnerati non posse arceri oti finibus; erupturum illud malum aliquando, si impunitum fuisset, ad perniciem civitatis. 5 non multum mihi sane post ad odium accessit. nihil enim contra me fecit odio mei, sed odio severitatis, odio dignitatis, odio rei publicae. non me magis violavit quam senatum, quam equites Romanos, quam omnes bonos, quam Italiam cunctam; non denique in me sceleratior fuit quam in ipsos deos immortales. etenim illos eo scelere violavit quo nemo antea; in me fuit eodem animo quo etiam eius familiaris Catilina, si vicisset, fuisset. itaque eum numquam a me esse accusandum putavi, non plus quam stipitem illum qui quorum hominum esset nesciremus, nisi se Ligurem ipse esse diceret. quid enim hunc persequar, pecudem ac beluam, pabulo inimicorum meorum et glande corruptum? qui si sensit quo se scelere devinxerit, non dubito quin sit miserrimus; sin autem id non videt, periculum est ne se stuporis excusatione defendat.

6 Accedit etiam quod exspectatione omnium fortissimo et clarissimo viro, T. Annio, devota et constituta ista hostia esse videtur. cui me praeripere desponsam iam et destinatam laudem, cum ipse eius opera et dignitatem et salutem reciperarim, valde est iniquum. etenim ut P. ille Scipio natus mihi videtur ad interitum exitiumque Carthaginis, qui illam a multis imperatoribus obsessam, oppugnatam, labefactam, paene captam aliquando quasi fatali adventu solus evertit, sic T. Annius ad illam pestem comprimendam, exstinguendam, funditus delendam natus esse videtur et quasi divino munere

De haruspicum responsis 4–6

And the sufferings that their powerful leadership, bloody and deadly as it was, could neither keep from the walls of our allies nor bring upon enemy cities—we're talking about creating a desert through demolition, fires, rampage, and general destruction—they have instead, along with their looting, inflicted on my entire property. 4 I declare that it is against these torch-wielding Furies—no, against these dreaded prodigies, a virtual plague on this country—that I have been waging an inexpiable war. And I am required to do this not so much because of my own indignation and that of my family as because of your own and that of our fellow elite. As for Clodius, my odium toward him today is no greater than it was on that notorious day when I learned that, wearing women's clothes and scorched by sacred flames, he was thrown out of a sacrilegious orgy at the home of the *pontifex maximus*. It was precisely then that I foresaw well in advance the great storm that was rising up and the hurricane winds that would be threatening the state. I understood that such a wildly criminal act of boldness, perpetrated by a crazed, fickle, and damaged young man, could not be kept within peaceful limits. I saw that that evil, if it had remained unpunished, would eventually burst forth to destroy the state.

5 Afterward hatred, at least on my part, did not increase much, since he opposed me not because he hated me, but because he hated anything serious or honorable; he hated the state. And he did no more violence to me than to the senate, to the Roman knights, to all right-thinking men, and to the whole of Italy. Most of all, he was no more wicked to me than to the very immortal gods, since he violated them with such a crime as no one has committed before. He felt the same way toward me as his friend Catiline would have if he had come out on top. As a result, I didn't think that I ever had to bring charges against him any more than against that blockhead who claims to be a Ligurian (if he hadn't, we'd have no idea to what class of human beings he belongs). But why should I bring charges against Clodius? He's an animal—from the farm and from the wild—perverted by the fodder and nuts of my enemies. If he has realized the wickedness he's gotten mixed up in then I've no doubt he's the most wretched person alive. But if he doesn't see this, then there is the risk that he may plead stupidity.

6 And on top of all this, everyone expects that Clodius is destined to be sacrificed as a victim to the famously brave Titus Annius Milo. So it is very wrong that I, who recovered my dignity and well-being through his efforts, should snatch from him this praise that is vowed and long overdue. Milo is like the great Scipio, who seemed born to raze Carthage; as if sent by fate, he overturned that city by himself, after many military leaders had besieged, attacked, undermined, and at one point nearly captured it. In the same way, Milo seems born to choke, stifle, and utterly destroy that pest, as if he were given as a gift to the

donatus rei publicae. solus ille cognovit quem ad modum armatum civem, qui lapidibus, qui ferro alios fugaret, alios domi contineret, qui urbem totam, qui curiam, qui forum, qui templa omnia caede incendiisque terreret, non modo vinci verum etiam vinciri oporteret. 7 huic ego et tali et ita de me ac de patria merito viro numquam mea voluntate praeripiam eum praesertim reum cuius ille inimicitias non solum suscepit propter salutem meam, verum etiam adpetivit. sed si etiam nunc inlaqueatus iam omnium legum periculis, inretitus odio bonorum omnium, exspectatione supplici iam non diuturna implicatus feretur tamen haesitans et in me impetum impeditus facere conabitur, resistam et aut concedente aut etiam adiuvante Milone eius conatum refutabo, velut hesterno die cum mihi tacenti stans minaretur, voce tantum attigi legum initium et iudici. consedit ille, conticui. diem dixisset, ut iecerat, fecissem ut ei statim tertius a praetore dies diceretur. atque hoc sic moderetur et cogitet, si contentus sit iis sceleribus quae commisit, esse se iam consecratum Miloni; si quod in me telum intenderit, statim me esse arrepturum arma iudiciorum atque legum.

8 Atque paulo ante, patres conscripti, contionem habuit quae est ad me tota delata. cuius contionis primum universum argumentum sententiamque audite; cum riseritis impudentiam hominis, tum a me de tota contione audietis. de religionibus, sacris, caerimoniis est contionatus, patres conscripti, Clodius; Publius, inquam, Clodius sacra et religiones neglegi, violari, pollui questus est! non mirum si hoc vobis ridiculum videtur; etiam sua contio risit hominem, quo modo ipse gloriari solet, ducentis confixum senati consultis, quae sunt omnia contra illum pro religionibus facta, hominemque eum qui pulvinaribus Bonae Deae stuprum intulerit eaque sacra quae viri oculis ne imprudentis quidem aspici fas est non solum aspectu virili sed flagitio stuproque violarit, in contione de religionibus neglectis conqueri. 9 itaque nunc proxima contio eius exspectatur de pudicitia. quid enim interest utrum ab altaribus religiosissimis fugatus de sacris et religionibus conqueratur, an ex sororum cubiculo egressus pudorem pudicitiamque defendat?

republic by divine dispensation. He is the only person who recognized how necessary it was not only to defeat but even to fetter a fully armed citizen of Rome, one who was using stones and knives to put to flight some, to trap at home others, and to terrify the entire city—senate house, forum, and all the temples—with threats of carnage and conflagration. **7** I would never willingly snatch from a man such as this, a benefactor both to me and to the state, the opportunity to prosecute Clodius in court, especially since in protecting me he not only took on my enemies but he even sought them out. Yet even now, if Clodius, although ensnared in every kind of legal threat, entangled in a net of hatred toward all good citizens, and caught up in the expectation of imminent punishment, will nevertheless come forward haltingly and attempt to make an attack on me despite his being hampered, I will resist his attempt and, with Milo allowing me or even helping, I will reject it. Yesterday, for example: when he was standing there threatening me as I remained silent, I used my voice to just touch upon the onset of legal proceedings. He sank down; I fell silent. Had he set up a day in court as he had threatened, I would have encouraged that the summons from the praetor be announced no later than the second day. And yet this is how he should guide his thinking: if he is content with the crimes that he has committed, then he has already been given over to Milo; and if he aims one of his spears at me, right away I will shield myself behind the justice of the courts.

8 And so just a little while ago, senators, he held a meeting of the people, the contents of which were brought to me in full. Listen first to the gist of the meeting's argument; then, after you have laughed at this man's lack of shame, you will hear about his entire speech. Addressing the people about religious scruples, rites, and ceremonies, my fellow senators, was Clodius. That's right, *Publius* Clodius has lamented that the proper observation of ritual has been neglected, violated, and polluted. It's no surprise if you find this ridiculous. Even those in his own meeting laughed at him, a person—as he is himself accustomed to boast—pierced by two hundred decrees of the senate (each of which was made against him in defense of religious practice), and who engaged in sex on the couches of the Bona Dea. That goddess's rites, which it is sacrilegious for a man to see even by accident, he violated not only with his male gaze but with sexual violence. This is the person who in a public assembly complained about the violation of religious rites. **9** So now we await his next public meeting, on sexual purity. For is there any difference between a man who complains about religious rites after taking flight from a most sacred altar and one who, after leaving his sisters' bedroom, speaks in defense of chastity and physical purity?

Responsum haruspicum hoc recens de fremitu in contione recitavit, in quo cum aliis multis scriptum etiam illud est, id quod audistis, LOCA SACRA ET RELIGIOSA PROFANA HABERI. in ea causa esse dixit domum meam a religiosissimo sacerdote, P. Clodio, consecratam. 10 gaudeo mihi de toto hoc ostento, quod haud scio an gravissimum multis his annis huic ordini nuntiatum sit, datam non modo iustam sed etiam necessariam causam esse dicendi; reperietis enim ex hoc toto prodigio atque responso nos de istius scelere ac furore ac de impendentibus periculis maximis prope iam voce Iovis Optimi Maximi praemoneri. 11 sed primum expiabo religionem aedium mearum, si id facere vere ac sine cuiusquam dubitatione potero; sin scrupulus tenuissimus residere alicui videbitur, non modo patienti sed etiam libenti animo portentis deorum immortalium religionique parebo.

Sed quae tandem est in hac urbe tanta domus ab ista suspicione religionis tam vacua atque pura? quamquam vestrae domus, patres conscripti, ceterorumque civium multo maxima ex parte sunt liberae religione, tamen una mea domus iudiciis omnibus liberata in hac urbe sola est. te enim appello, Lentule, et te, Philippe. ex hoc haruspicum responso decrevit senatus ut de locis sacris, religiosis ad hunc ordinem referretis. potestisne referre de mea domo? quae, ut dixi, sola in hac urbe omni religione omnibus iudiciis liberata est; quam primum inimicus ipse in illa tempestate ac nocte rei publicae, cum cetera scelera stilo illo impuro Sex. Cloeli ore tincto conscripsisset, ne una quidem attigit littera religionis. deinde eandem domum populus Romanus, cuius est summa potestas omnium rerum, comitiis centuriatis, omnium aetatum ordinumque suffragiis eodem iure esse iussit quo fuisset. postea vos, patres conscripti, non quo dubia res esset, sed ut huic furiae, si diutius in hac urbe quam delere cuperet maneret, vox interdiceretur, decrevistis ut de mearum aedium religione ad pontificum collegium referretur. 12 quae tanta religio est qua non in nostris dubitationibus atque in maximis superstitionibus unius P. Servili aut M. Luculli responso ac verbo liberemur? de sacris publicis, de ludis maximis, de deorum penatium Vestaeque matris caerimoniis, de illo ipso sacrificio quod fit pro salute populi Romani, quod post Romam conditam huius unius casti tutoris religionum scelere violatum est, quod tres pontifices statuissent, id semper populo Romano, semper senatui, semper ipsis dis immortalibus satis sanctum, satis augustum, satis religiosum esse visum est. at vero meam domum

He read aloud at the public meeting this recent haruspical response about a rumbling noise. Among the many other things written there is what you have already heard, that SACRED AND HALLOWED PLACES HAVE BEEN DESECRATED. In this context he claimed that my home had been made sacred by a most sanctified priest—Publius Clodius. 10 I am delighted to be given the opportunity, one not simply appropriate but even necessary, of speaking about this entire portent, which is probably the most serious to come before this body in the past several years. For you will discover that this entire prodigy and its response warns us, as if through the voice of Jupiter Optimus Maximus, about the crazed criminality of this man and about the threat of unparalleled dangers. 11 First, though, I shall free my home from any religious restrictions, if I can do so truthfully and without anyone expressing doubt. And yet if a single person feels even the tiniest bit of uneasiness, I will heed the portents and scruples of the immortal gods not just with patience but even with pleasure.

But in the end, which home in such an immense city as this stands so free and clear of any suspicion of religious restrictions? Granted that your own homes, fellow senators, and those of all other citizens are almost entirely free of religious sanction, still, in this city mine alone has been made free by every possible authority. And so I call on you, Lentulus, and you, Philippus: on account of the haruspical response before us the senate has decreed that you make a motion to this body about sacred places that are bound by religion. Do you have the power to make a motion about my home? As I have said, it is the only one in Rome that has been released from every religious sanction by every authority. To begin with: in that stormy night of the republic my own enemy touched on it with not one single letter concerning religious purity, although he had scrupulously written out all his remaining crimes with a pen made wet by Sextus Cloelius's notoriously disgusting mouth. Secondly, the Roman people, endowed with the highest authority in all things, ordered through the centuriate assembly, with votes taken from every age and class, that this same house exist with the same rights that it had always had. Finally, not because the affair was in doubt, but so that this Fury would be silenced if he should remain any longer in the city that he wanted to destroy, you senators decreed that the matter of my house's religious status be referred to the college of pontiffs. 12 What sacred obligation is so great that a verbal response of Publius Servilius alone, or of Marcus Lucullus, does not set us free despite our own doubts and extreme religious uncertainty? The decision of three pontiffs has always been deemed sacred, venerable, and scrupulous enough for the people, the senate, and the immortal gods when it concerns a matter of public rites, the most prestigious games, the rituals of the Penates and Mother Vesta, and the very ceremony that takes place on behalf of the safety of the Roman people, a ceremony that, since Rome's founding, has been violated only by the criminal action of this upright guardian of religion. But as it is, my home has been liberated from every religious liability by the unanimous decision of Publius Lentulus, consul and

P. Lentulus, consul et pontifex, P. Servilius, M. Lucullus, Q. Metellus, M'. Glabrio, M. Messalla, L. Lentulus flamen Martialis, P. Galba, Q. Metellus Scipio, C. Fannius, M. Lepidus, L. Claudius rex sacrorum, M. Scaurus, M. Crassus, C. Curio, Sex. Caesar flamen Quirinalis, Q. Cornelius, P. Albinovanus, Q. Terentius pontifices minores causa cognita, duobus locis dicta, maxima frequentia amplissimorum ac sapientissimorum civium adstante, omni religione una mente omnes liberaverunt. **13** nego umquam post sacra constituta, quorum eadem est antiquitas quae ipsius urbis, ulla de re, ne de capite quidem virginum Vestalium, tam frequens collegium iudicasse. quamquam ad facinoris disquisitionem interest adesse quam plurimos—ita est enim interpretatio illa pontificum ut eidem potestatem habeant iudicum—religionis explanatio vel ab uno pontifice perito recte fieri potest—quod idem in iudicio capitis durum atque iniquum est—tamen sic reperietis, frequentiores pontifices de mea domo quam umquam de caerimoniis virginum iudicasse. postero die frequentissimus senatus te consule designato, Lentule, sententiae principe, P. Lentulo et Q. Metello consulibus referentibus statuit, cum omnes pontifices qui erant huius ordinis adessent, cumque alii qui honoribus populi Romani antecedebant multa de collegi iudicio verba fecissent omnesque idem scribendo adessent, domum meam iudicio pontificum religione liberatam videri.

14 De hoc igitur loco sacro potissimum videntur haruspices dicere, qui locus solus ex privatis locis omnibus hoc praecipue iuris habet ut ab ipsis qui sacris praesunt sacer non esse iudicatus sit? verum referte, quod ex senatus consulto facere debetis. aut vobis cognitio dabitur, qui primi de hac domo sententiam dixistis et eam religione omni liberastis, aut senatus ipse iudicabit, qui uno illo solo antistite sacrorum dissentiente frequentissimus antea iudicavit, aut—id quod certe fiet—ad pontifices reicietur, quorum auctoritati, fidei, prudentiae maiores nostri sacra religionesque et privatas et publicas commendarunt. quid ergo? ii possunt aliud iudicare ac iudicaverunt? multae sunt domus in hac urbe, patres conscripti, atque haud scio an paene cunctae iure optimo, sed tamen iure privato, iure hereditario, iure auctoritatis, iure mancipi, iure nexi; nego esse ullam domum aliam privato eodem quo quae optima lege, publico vero omni praecipuo et humano et divino iure munitam. **15** quae primum aedificatur ex

pontiff, Publius Servilius, Marcus Lucullus, Quintus Metellus, Manius Glabrio, Marcus Messalla, Lucius Lentulus the flamen of Mars, Publius Galba, Quintus Metellus Scipio, Gaius Fannius, Marcus Lepidus, the *rex sacrorum* Lucius Claudius, Marcus Scaurus, Marcus Crassus, Gaius Curio, Sextus Caesar the flamen of Quirinus, as well as the lesser pontiffs Quintus Cornelius, Publius Albinovanus, and Quintus Terentius. The case was heard in two places before a huge crowd of esteemed and brilliant citizens. **13** Ever since the establishment of the city's sacred rites—whose antiquity matches that of Rome itself—I assert that the college has never passed a judgment in such numbers about any matter, not even about the capital punishment of Vestal Virgins. Whereas it is important in investigating a misdeed that there be present as many people as possible (the assessment process of *pontifices* is such that these men also have authority as judges), the elucidation of a matter of religion can be rightly made by even one *pontifex* with experience—a situation that is harsh and unfair in a capital case. Nevertheless, you will learn that a greater number of *pontifices* has rendered a decision regarding my house than they ever had done concerning the rites of the Vestals. On the next day, after the consuls Publius Lentulus and Quintus Metellus introduced the matter, you, Lentulus, our consul designate, were the first to put forward the motion to the packed senate house. Since all the *pontifices* of senatorial rank were present, and since others who held high office from the Roman people had offered many words about the college's decision and were all present to act as witness to the drafting of a document, the senate decided that my home, through a pontifical decision, was deemed to have been freed from religious taint.

14 So could this be the "sacred" place that the *haruspices* seem especially to be talking about, the only place of all private property that possesses the special status of being judged *not* to be sacred by the very ones who are in charge of sacred affairs? In any case, introduce the issue as you should, in accordance with the senatorial decree. Either the two of you will be assigned to investigate the matter, you who were the first to render a decision about my house, freeing it of all scruple, or the senators themselves will make a judgment, who have already done so at a packed meeting in which there was only one dissenter, our sacred high priest, or (and this surely will happen) it will be referred to the *pontifices*, to whose trusted authority and wisdom our ancestors have assigned the sacred rites, both public and private. What then? Can those men decide anything other than what they already have? This city has many houses, senators, and nearly all of them, I suppose, exist with an unobjectionable title; and yet it is with a title granted through private law—either hereditary, or based on authority, or based on property transfer through sale or debt. I assert that not one other home is protected by the same private title as those homes that are protected by the best laws; but it is also protected by every outstanding public title, both human and divine. **15** First off, on senatorial authorization it is

auctoritate senatus pecunia publica, deinde contra vim nefariam huius gladiatoris tot senati consultis munita atque saepta est. primum negotium isdem magistratibus est datum anno superiore, ut curarent ut sine vi aedificare mihi liceret, quibus in maximis periculis universa res publica commendari solet; deinde, cum ille saxis et ignibus et ferro vastitatem meis aedibus intulisset, decrevit senatus eos qui id fecissent lege de vi, quae esset in eos qui universam rem publicam oppugnassent, teneri. vobis vero referentibus, o post hominum memoriam fortissimi atque optimi consules, decrevit idem senatus frequentissimus, qui meam domum violasset, contra rem publicam esse facturum.

16 Nego ullo de opere publico, de monumento, de templo tot senatus exstare consulta quot de mea domo, quam senatus unam post hanc urbem constitutam ex aerario aedificandam, a pontificibus liberandam, a magistratibus defendendam, a iudicibus poeniendam putarit. P. Valerio pro maximis in rem publicam beneficiis data domus est in Velia publice, at mihi in Palatio restituta; illi locus, at mihi etiam parietes atque tectum; illi quam ipse privato iure tueretur, mihi quam publice magistratus omnes defenderent. quae quidem ego si aut per me aut ab aliis haberem, non praedicarem apud vos, ne nimis gloriari viderer; sed cum sint mihi data a vobis, cum ea adtemptentur eius lingua cuius ante manu eversa vos mihi et liberis meis manibus vestris reddidistis, non ego de meis sed de vestris factis loquor, nec vereor ne haec mea vestrorum beneficiorum praedicatio non grata potius quam adrogans videatur. **17** quamquam si me tantis laboribus pro communi salute perfunctum ecferret aliquando ad gloriam in refutandis maledictis hominum improborum animi quidam dolor, quis non ignosceret? vidi enim hesterno die quendam murmurantem, quem aiebant negare ferre me posse, quia, cum ab hoc eodem impurissimo parricida rogarer cuius essem civitatis, respondi me probantibus et vobis et equitibus Romanis eius esse quae carere me non potuisset. ille, ut opinor, ingemuit. quid igitur responderem?—quaero ex eo ipso qui ferre me non potest—me civem esse Romanum? litterate respondissem. An tacuissem? desertum negotium. potest quisquam vir in rebus magnis cum invidia versatus satis graviter inimici contumeliis sine sua laude respondere? at ipse non modo respondet quidquid potest, cum est lacessitus, sed etiam gaudet se ab amicis quid respondeat admoneri.

18 Sed quoniam mea causa expedita est, videamus nunc quid haruspices dicant. ego enim fateor me et magnitudine ostenti et gravitate responsi et una atque constanti haruspicum ⟨voce⟩ vehementer esse commotum; neque is sum

being rebuilt at public expense and, second, so many decrees of the senate protect it, closing it off against the execrable violence of this gladiator here. To begin with, the same magistrates to whom the entire state is usually entrusted during its most dire emergencies were last year assigned the task of ensuring that I could build without incurring violence; then, after he had assailed my home with stones, fire, and sword, the senate decreed that any who had acted in this way were under the jurisdiction of the law on violence that exists for those who had attacked the entire commonwealth. It's true: in response to the motion made by you, the bravest and best consuls in human memory, this same senate decreed in a full session that whoever had violated my home would be acting against the state.

16 I maintain that no public structure, monument, or temple has been the subject of as many senatorial decrees as has my house. Since the founding of this city the senate has deemed that it alone should be rebuilt from the treasury, be set free of religious taint by the *pontifices*, be defended by the magistrates, and be avenged by a panel of judges. Publius Valerius, in recognition of his distinguished service to the state, was provided a home at public expense on the Velia, whereas mine was restored on the Palatine; he was given a site, but I was given both walls and a roof; his home was such that it was protected by private law, mine defended by all magistrates at public expense. If I possessed these things either through my own actions or from anyone else, I would not declare it in your presence— I wouldn't want to seem to brag excessively. But since you granted them to me while they were being assailed by the tongue of the man whose hand had overturned them and since with your own hands you have restored them to me and my children, I am speaking not about my actions but yours, and I have no fear that this boasting that I make about your kindnesses may seem arrogant rather than grateful. **17** And yet who would not pardon me, a man who has endured immense labors for the common good, if a kind of mental anguish were sometimes to lead me to boast while refuting the slanders of evil men? In fact, just yesterday I saw someone muttering, apparently saying that he couldn't tolerate me because, when this same filthy traitor asked me to what state I belonged I answered (with both you and the Roman *equites* voicing your approval) that I belonged to the state that had been unable to continue without me. He groaned, I'm guessing. So how should I have answered? I am asking the very person who cannot tolerate me. That I am a Roman citizen? What a clever answer! Or should I have stayed silent? But then the case is closed. Can any man who is engaged in important affairs and who has envy as his companion answer the abuse of an enemy with sufficient gravity without praising himself? And yet Clodius not only responds in whatever way he can when he has been attacked; he is even happy to be prompted for a response from his friends.

18 And so, since I have provided the details for my own case, let's now consider what the *haruspices* are saying. I admit it; I have been deeply disturbed by the consequential nature of the portent, by the gravity of the response, and by

qui, si cui forte videor plus quam ceteri qui aeque atque ego sunt occupati versari in studio litterarum, his delecter aut utar omnino litteris quae nostros animos deterrent atque avocant a religione. ego vero primum habeo auctores ac magistros religionum colendarum maiores nostros, quorum mihi tanta fuisse sapientia videtur ut satis superque prudentes sint qui illorum prudentiam non dicam adsequi, sed quanta fuerit perspicere possint, qui statas sollemnisque caerimonias pontificatu, rerum bene gerundarum auctoritates augurio, fatorum veteres praedictiones Apollinis vatum libris, portentorum expiationes Etruscorum disciplina contineri putaverunt; quae quidem tanta est ut nostra memoria primum Italici belli funesta illa principia, post Sullani Cinnanique temporis extremum paene discrimen, tum hanc recentem urbis inflammandae delendique imperi coniurationem non obscure nobis paulo ante praedixerint. **19** deinde, si quid habui oti, etiam cognovi multa homines doctos sapientisque et dixisse et scripta ⟨de⟩ deorum immortalium numine reliquisse. quae quamquam divinitus perscripta video, tamen eius modi sunt ut ea maiores nostri docuisse illos, non ab illis didicisse videantur. etenim quis est tam vaecors qui aut, cum suspexit in caelum, deos esse non sentiat, et ea quae tanta mente fiunt, ut vix quisquam arte ulla ordinem rerum ac necessitudinem persequi possit, casu fieri putet, aut, cum deos esse intellexerit, non intellegat eorum numine hoc tantum imperium esse natum et auctum et retentum? quam volumus licet, patres conscripti, ipsi nos amemus, tamen nec numero Hispanos nec robore Gallos nec calliditate Poenos nec artibus Graecos nec denique hoc ipso huius gentis ac terrae domestico nativoque sensu Italos ipsos ac Latinos, sed pietate ac religione atque hac una sapientia, quod deorum numine omnia regi gubernarique perspeximus, omnis gentis nationesque superavimus.

20 Qua re, ne plura de re minime loquar dubia, adhibete animos et mentes vestras, non solum auris, ad haruspicum vocem admovete: QVOD IN AGRO LATINIENSI AVDITVS EST STREPITVS CVM FREMITV. mitto haruspices, mitto illam veterem ab ipsis dis immortalibus, ut hominum fama est, Etruriae traditam disciplinam; nos nonne haruspices esse possumus? exauditus in agro propinquo et suburbano est strepitus quidam reconditus et horribilis fremitus armorum. quis est ex gigantibus illis, quos poetae ferunt bellum dis immortalibus intulisse, tam impius qui hoc tam novo tantoque motu non magnum

the single unanimous voice of the *haruspices*. If I may seem to some to be more involved in the study of the written word than others who are just as busy, I am in fact not the kind of person who enjoys—or makes use of at all—those writings that frighten our minds and distract them from religious considerations. To begin with, I assure you that I consider our ancestors to be the authoritative teachers of religious procedure. I regard their wisdom to have been so profound that those people are more than sufficiently wise who can—I won't say achieve their wisdom—but who can fully comprehend how great that wisdom was. They assigned the fixed and regular ceremonial rites to the *pontifices*, the authority for successfully conducting state affairs to the augurs, the ancient oracles of our destiny to the books of Apollo's prophets, and the expiation of prodigies to the learning of the Etruscans. That learning is in fact so great that, just in recent memory, they have in no uncertain terms warned us a little beforehand not only about the deadly onset of the Social War and the nearly fatal crisis of the Sullan and Cinnan era but also about that recent conspiracy to set the city aflame and destroy the state. **19** As for my second point: whenever I have had any free time, I have also discovered that learned and wise scholars have both said and left behind in writing many things about the power of the immortal gods. Although I understand that these works were brilliantly composed, they still consist of the sorts of things that our ancestors would seem to have taught them, not to have learned from them. For in the end, who is so devoid of sense that, whenever he looks to the heavens, he does not sense the existence of the gods, or believes that there arise by chance the things that have been created by a mind so awesome that scarcely anyone with any skill can trace the order and bonds of nature; or who, alternatively, although he has understood that the gods exist, does not understand that it is through their will that this great empire of ours was born, increased, and maintained? Although it is fine, senators, that we hold ourselves in high esteem, nevertheless the Hispani are more numerous, the Gauls stronger, the Carthaginians shrewder, the Greeks better in the arts, and in particular the Italians and Latins superior in the local, inherent sense of this people and land. It is instead in our outward respect toward the gods, in our internal awe, and in this one piece of wisdom—our realization that everything is guided and controlled by divine will—that we have vanquished all peoples and tribes.

20 With this in mind, so as not to say more about a matter that is hardly in doubt, pay attention, turning your minds and not just your ears to the words of the *haruspices*: SINCE A RUMBLING, ACCOMPANIED BY A TREMBLING, WAS HEARD IN THE *AGER LATINIENSIS*. I dismiss the *haruspices*, I dismiss that ancient learning transmitted to Etruria by, as people say, the immortal gods themselves. Surely can't we ourselves be *haruspices*? In a nearby district outside the city was heard some sort of mysterious rumbling and a frightful trembling of weapons. The poets say that giants waged war with the immortal

aliquid deos populo Romano praemonstrare et praecinere fateatur? de ea re scriptum est: POSTILIONES ESSE IOVI, SATVRNO, NEPTVNO, TELLVRI, DIS CAELESTIBVS. 21 audio quibus dis violatis expiatio debeatur, sed hominum quae ob delicta quaero. LVDOS MINVS DILIGENTER FACTOS POLLVTOSQVE. quos ludos? te appello, Lentule—tui sacerdoti sunt tensae, curricula, praecentio, ludi, libationes epulaeque ludorum—vosque, pontifices, ad quos epulones Iovis Optimi Maximi si quid est praetermissum aut commissum adferunt, quorum de sententia illa eadem renovata atque instaurata celebrantur. qui sunt ludi "minus diligenter facti", quando aut quo scelere "polluti"? respondebis et pro te et pro collegis tuis, etiam pro pontificum collegio, nihil cuiusquam aut neglegentia contemptum aut scelere esse pollutum, omnia sollemnia ac iusta ludorum omnibus rebus observatis summa cum caerimonia esse servata.

22 Quos igitur haruspices "ludos minus diligenter factos pollutosque" esse dicunt? eos quorum ipsi di immortales atque illa mater Idaea te, te, Cn. Lentule, cuius abavi manibus esset accepta, spectatorem esse voluit. quod ni tu Megalesia illo die spectare voluisses, haud scio an vivere nobis atque his de rebus iam queri ⟨non⟩ liceret. vis enim innumerabilis incitata, ex omnibus vicis collecta servorum ab hoc aedile religioso repente ⟨e⟩ fornicibus ostiisque omnibus in scaenam signo dato immissa inrupit. Tua tum, tua, Cn. Lentule, eadem virtus fuit quae in privato quondam tuo proavo; te, nomen, imperium, vocem, aspectum, impetum tuum stans senatus equitesque Romani et omnes boni sequebantur, cum ille servorum eludentium multitudini senatum populumque Romanum vinctum ipso consessu et constrictum spectaculis atque impeditum turba et angustiis tradidisset. 23 an si ludius constitit aut tibicen repente conticuit, aut puer ille patrimus et matrimus si tensam non tenuit, si lorum omisit, aut si aedilis verbo aut simpuio aberravit, ludi sunt non rite facti, eaque errata expiantur et mentes deorum immortalium ludorum instauratione placantur; si ludi ab laetitia ad metum traducti, si non intermissi sed perempti atque sublati sunt, si civitati universae scelere eius qui ludos ad luctum conferre voluit

gods—which of those giants is so irreverent as not to admit that, through this strange and awesome disturbance, the gods are prophetically pointing to something momentous for the Roman people? It has been pronounced about this event that REPARATIONS ARE OWED TO JUPITER, SATURN, NEPTUNE, TELLUS, THE HEAVENLY GODS. **21** I can hear which gods are due expiatory rites for being violated, but I ask what human faults are the cause. THAT GAMES HAVE BEEN CONDUCTED LESS CAREFULLY AND POLLUTED. Which games? I call on you, Lentulus—your priesthood controls the sacred wagons, chariot racing, musical preludes, games, and the libations and feasting proper to the games—and I call on you, *pontifices*, since the priests in charge of the banquets for Jupiter Optimus Maximus report to you when there has been an error of omission or commission, and it is you who decide whether those events are to be repeated and celebrated anew: what are the games that have been "conducted less carefully," and when or because of what fault have they been "polluted"? You will respond on behalf of yourself and your colleagues, as well as the college of *pontifices*, that nothing has been slighted by anyone's negligence or polluted by anyone's fault and that, with eyes watchful for everything, all the traditional components of the games were preserved with the greatest attention to ceremony.

22 What then are the games that the *haruspices* say "have been conducted less carefully and polluted"? The ones at which the immortal gods, and in particular the Idaean mother goddess, wanted you, Gnaeus Lentulus, to be in the audience, since it was at the hands of your ancestor that she had been received in Rome. But if on that day you had not wanted to be a spectator at the Megalesian games, we would probably not be allowed to live, and to complain now about what happened. For an excited mass of countless slaves, gathered from every neighborhood by our holy aedile here and emerging at a prearranged signal, suddenly burst onto the stage from every arch and doorway. At that point you, Gnaeus Lentulus, displayed the same virtue as your great-grandfather once had when he was a private citizen. The senate and Roman *equites* and all good men rose up and followed you—your authority and power, your voice and look, your energetic attack—when that man had given over to a mob of jeering slaves the senate and Roman people as they sat cramped in their seats, checked by the audience, and fettered by the tightness of the crowd.

23 Now, if a dancer has stood still, or a flute-player suddenly gone silent, or a boy whose mother and father are still alive has failed to hold onto the sacred wagon and dropped the reins, or if the aedile has erred in prayer or in libation, then the games have not been performed properly. These errors are expiated and the minds of the immortal gods are appeased by a re-performance of the games. But if the games have passed from joy to fear, if they have been not interrupted but utterly destroyed, if for the entire citizenry those days turned out not fun but almost funereal because of the criminal behavior of the person who wanted to bring the games to grimness,

exstiterunt dies illi pro festis paene funesti, dubitabimus quos ille fremitus nuntiet ludos esse pollutos? **24** ac si volumus ea quae de quoque deo nobis tradita sunt recordari, hanc Matrem Magnam, cuius ludi violati, polluti, paene ad caedem et ad funus civitatis conversi sunt, hanc, inquam, accepimus agros et nemora cum quodam strepitu fremituque peragrare. haec igitur vobis, haec populo Romano et scelerum indicia ostendit et periculorum signa patefecit. nam quid ego de illis ludis loquar? quos in Palatio nostri maiores ante templum in ipso Matris Magnae conspectu Megalesibus fieri celebrarique voluerunt, qui sunt more institutisque maxime casti, sollemnes, religiosi, quibus ludis primum ante populi consessum senatui locum P. Africanus iterum consul ille maior dedit, ut eos ludos haec lues impura pollueret? quo si qui liber aut spectandi aut etiam religionis causa accesserat, manus adferebantur, quo matrona nulla adiit propter vim consessumque servorum. ita ludos eos quorum religio tanta est, ut ex ultimis terris arcessita in hac urbe consederit, qui uni ludi ne verbo quidem appellantur Latino, ut vocabulo ipso et adpetita religio externa et Matris Magnae nomine suscepta declaretur—hos ludos servi fecerunt, servi spectaverunt, tota denique hoc aedile servorum Megalesia fuerunt. **25** pro di immortales! qui magis nobiscum loqui possetis, si essetis versareminique nobiscum? ludos esse pollutos significastis ac plane dicitis. quid magis inquinatum deformatum, perversum conturbatum dici potest quam omne servitium permissu magistratus liberatum in alteram caveam immissum, alteri praepositum, ut alter consessus potestati servorum obiceretur, alter servorum totus esset? si examen apium ludis in scaenam caveam⟨ve⟩ venisset, haruspices acciendos ex Etruria putaremus; videmus universi repente examina tanta servorum immissa in populum Romanum saeptum atque inclusum et non commovemur? atque in apium fortasse examine nos ex Etruscorum scriptis haruspices ut a servitio caveremus monerent. **26** quod igitur ex aliquo diiuncto diversoque monstro significatum caveremus, id cum ipsum sibi monstrum est, et cum in eo ipso periculum est ex quo periculum portenditur, non pertimescemus? istius modi Megalesia fecit pater tuus, istius modi patruus? is mihi etiam generis sui mentionem facit, cum Athenionis aut Spartaci exemplo ludos facere maluerit quam C. aut Appi Claudiorum. illi cum ludos facerent, servos de cavea exire iubebant; tu in alteram servos immisisti, ex altera liberos

then will we doubt what are the games that this earthly rumbling proclaims to be polluted? **24** And if we wish to recall what has been passed down to us concerning each particular deity, we have heard that the Mater Magna here, the violation and pollution of whose games nearly led to the death and destruction of the state, that this Mater Magna has been roaming through our fields and groves with a kind of rumbling and trembling. Consequently she has not only revealed both to you and to the Roman people the evidence for criminality, but she has also made clear the premonitions of danger. Now what should I say about those games? Our ancestors intended to establish their celebration at the Megalesia, in front of her temple on the Palatine—in the very sight of the Mater Magna. By custom and practice they are thoroughly chaste, regular, and reverent. At these games, when consul for the second time, did Publius Africanus the Elder first give the senate a seating section in front of the people so that the impure pestilence of Clodius could pollute the games? If any free citizen had arrived there either to watch or because of a religious obligation, then hands were laid upon him. No Roman matron approached there due to the violent slaves sitting everywhere. And so those games, whose holiness was such that it settled in this city after being summoned from the ends of the earth—the only games not even given a Latin name so that by their very designation it would be clear that this worship had been both sought from a foreign source and undertaken in the name of the Mater Magna—these games were conducted by slaves, watched by slaves—in short, the entire Megalesia consisted of slaves when this man was aedile.

25 Oh immortal gods! Could you speak with us more clearly if you were present here among us? You have given signals, and now are saying clearly, that the games have been polluted. What can be uttered more stained and misshapen, perverted and completely disturbed, than that the entire slave population, set free by a magistrate's authority, was sent into one section of the theater and put in charge of a second, so that one part of the audience might be subjected to the power of slaves, while the other consisted entirely of slaves? If a swarm of bees had come onto the stage or into the stands during the games, we would think that the *haruspices* had to be summoned from Etruria. But we do see, all of us, that great swarms of slaves were suddenly set upon the Roman people, who were hemmed in and surrounded—and we are not moved? As a matter of fact, in the hypothetical case of a swarm of bees the *haruspices* would consult the texts of the Etruscans and warn us to watch out for the slave population. **26** So shall we not be thoroughly afraid when that very thing which we would watch out for when signified by some unconnected and separate warning is in fact a warning of itself, and when danger resides in the very thing from which danger is predicted? Is this the type of Megalesian festival that your father organized, or your paternal uncle? I understand that this man mentions even his ancestry, although in exhibiting his games he preferred to follow the example of Athenion and Spartacus rather than that of Gaius and Appius Claudius. When those men had their games, they ordered slaves to leave the seating area; but you sent slaves into one area and kicked free men out of the other. As a result, those who

eiecisti. itaque qui antea voce praeconis a liberis semovebantur, tuis ludis non voce sed manu liberos a se segregabant. ne hoc quidem tibi in mentem veniebat, Sibyllino sacerdoti, haec sacra maiores nostros ex vestris libris expetisse? si illi sunt vestri quos tu impia mente conquiris, violatis oculis legis, contaminatis manibus adtrectas. 27 hac igitur vate suadente quondam defessa Italia Punico bello atque ⟨ab⟩ Hannibale vexata sacra ista nostri maiores adscita ex Phrygia Romae conlocarunt. quae vir is accepit qui est optimus populi Romani iudicatus, P. Scipio, femina autem quae matronarum castissima putabatur, Quinta Claudia, cuius priscam illam severitatem [sacrificii] mirifice tua soror existimatur imitata. nihil te igitur neque maiores tui coniuncti cum his religionibus neque sacerdotium ipsum, quo est haec tota religio constituta, neque curulis aedilitas, quae maxime hanc tueri religionem solet, permovit quo minus castissimos ludos omni flagitio pollueres, dedecore maculares, scelere obligares?

28 Sed quid ego id admiror? qui accepta pecunia Pessinuntem ipsum, sedem domiciliumque Matris deorum, vastaris et Brogitaro Gallograeco, impuro homini ac nefario, cuius legati te tribuno dividere in aede Castoris tuis operis nummos solebant, totum illum locum fanumque vendideris, sacerdotem ab ipsis aris pulvinaribusque detraxeris, omnia illa quae vetustas, quae Persae, quae Syri, quae reges omnes qui Europam Asiamque tenuerunt semper summa religione coluerunt, perverteris, quae denique nostri maiores tam sancta duxerunt ut, cum refertam urbem atque Italiam fanorum haberemus, tamen nostri imperatores maximis et periculosissimis bellis huic deae vota facerent eaque in ipso Pessinunte ad illam ipsam principem aram et in illo loco fanoque persolverent. 29 quod cum Deiotarus religione sua castissime tueretur, quem unum habemus in orbe terrarum fidelissimum huic imperio atque amantissimum nostri nominis, Brogitaro, ut ante dixi, addictum pecunia tradidisti. atque hunc tamen Deiotarum saepe a senatu regali nomine dignum existimatum, clarissimorum imperatorum testimoniis ornatum, tu etiam regem appellari cum Brogitaro iubes. sed alter est rex iudicio senatus per nos, pecunia Brogitarus per te appellatus *** alterum putabo regem, si habuerit unde tibi solvat quod ei per syngrapham credidisti. nam cum multa regia sunt in Deiotaro, tum illa maxime, quod tibi nummum nullum dedit, quod eam partem legis tuae quae congruebat cum iudicio senatus, ut ipse rex esset, non repudiavit, quod Pessinuntem per scelus a te violatum et sacerdote sacrisque spoliatum recuperavit, ut in pristina religione servaret, quod caerimonias ab

in the past were separated from free men at the cry of the herald, at your games were setting free men apart from themselves not with their voice but by force. Did it not even occur to you, as a priest of the Sibyl, that our ancestors sought out these sacred rites from the books of your priesthood? If in fact they do belong to you, when you gather them with impious intention, read them with blinded eyes, and handle them with contaminated hands. **27** It was this Sibyl who once persuaded our ancestors to bring those sacred rites from Phrygia to Rome when Italy had been worn down by the Punic Wars and harassed by Hannibal. The man who was judged the best among the Romans—Publius Scipio—received them, along with the married woman believed to be most chaste, Quinta Claudia, whose time-honored austerity your sister is considered to have done a wonderful job of imitating. This being the case, did neither your ancestors, who were involved with these rituals, nor your own priesthood, through which this entire cult was established, nor the curule aedileship, which normally takes the greatest care for this cult—did none of these things prevent you from polluting these purest games with every disgrace, staining them with every dishonor, and encumbering them with every wickedness?

28 But why am I surprised at this? You are the person who took a bribe to destroy Pessinus, the original seat of the Mother of the gods, and to sell the entire place, including the sanctuary, to the Galatian Brogitarus, a wickedly impure man whose ambassadors used to distribute money to your gangs in the temple of Castor while you were tribune. You dragged the priest from the very altar and sacred couches, overturning everything that men of old and the Persians and the Syrians and all the kings of Europe and Asia have always worshipped with the greatest scruples. In short, these are the items that our ancestors considered so sacred that even though Rome and Italy were crammed with shrines our generals still made vows to this goddess in the midst of their greatest and fiercest wars, making them in Pessinus itself at her principal altar, at the very site of her shrine. **29** Deiotarus protected this place with the utmost purity in accordance with his own scruples, a man we consider the single most loyal person in the world to our rule and the most devoted to our reputation. But as I said earlier, you handed it over to Brogitarus, assigned it to him for a price. And despite all this it is Deiotarus—although often deemed worthy by the senate of the title "king" and glorified by the testimony of our most glorious generals—that you decide must share also this title "king" with Brogitarus. But the one is in fact a king through us, by judgment of the senate, while the other, Brogitarus, is called a king through you, because of a bribe. *** This other one I'll consider a king if he has had the means to pay you what you loaned him through a bond. For while Deiotarus has many kingly characteristics, these are the worthiest: that he has never given you a penny; that he did not reject that part of your legislation that corresponded with the judgment of the senate, namely, that he should be king; that he recovered Pessinus in order to preserve its former sanctity after it had been violated by you through crime and deprived

omni vetustate acceptas a Brogitaro pollui non sinit, mavoltque generum suum munere tuo quam illud fanum antiquitate religionis carere. sed ut ad haec haruspicum responsa redeam, ex quibus est primum de ludis, quis est qui id non totum in istius ludos praedictum et responsum esse fateatur?

30 Sequitur de locis sacris, religiosis. o impudentiam miram! de mea domo dicere audes? committe vel consulibus vel senatui vel collegio pontificum tuam. ac mea quidem his tribus omnibus iudiciis, ut dixi antea, liberata est; at in iis aedibus quas tu Quinto Seio, equite Romano, viro optimo, per te apertissime interfecto tenes, sacellum dico fuisse ⟨et⟩ aras. tabulis hoc censoriis, memoria multorum firmabo ac docebo. agatur modo haec res, quod ex eo senatus consulto quod nuper est factum referri ad nos necesse est, habeo quae de locis religiosis velim dicere. **31** cum de domo tua dixero, in qua tamen ita est inaedificatum sacellum ut alius fecerit, tibi tantum modo sit demoliendum, tum videbo num mihi necesse sit de aliis etiam aliquid dicere. putant enim ad me non nulli pertinere magmentarium Telluris aperire. nuper id patuisse dicunt, et ego recordor. nunc sanctissimam partem ac sedem maximae religionis privato dicunt vestibulo contineri. multa me movent: quod aedes Telluris est curationis meae, quod is qui illud magmentarium sustulit mea domo pontificum iudicio liberata secundum fratrem suum iudicatum esse dicebat; movet me etiam in hac caritate annonae, sterilitate agrorum, inopia frugum religio Telluris, et eo magis quod eodem ostento Telluri postilio deberi dicitur. **32** vetera fortasse loquimur; quamquam hoc si minus civili iure perscriptum est, lege tamen naturae, communi iure gentium sanctum est ut nihil mortales a dis immortalibus usu capere possint. verum tamen antiqua neglegimus; etiamne ea neglegemus quae fiunt cum maxime, quae videmus? L. Pisonem quis nescit his temporibus ipsis maximum et sanctissimum Dianae sacellum in Caeliculo sustulisse? adsunt vicini eius loci; multi sunt etiam in hoc ordine qui sacrificia gentilicia illo ipso in sacello stato loco anniversaria factitarint. et quaerimus di immortales quae loca desiderent, quid significent, de quo loquantur? a Sexto

of its priest and holy objects; that he does not allow the rites that have been welcomed by all the ancients to be polluted by Brogitarus, preferring that his son-in-law be without your gift rather than that that shrine be without its ancient sanctity. But to get back to these responses of the *haruspices*, the first of which concerns the games: who would not admit that the prediction and response were entirely directed toward *his* games?

30 Next comes the part about "sacred" and "hallowed" places. What unbelievable impudence! You dare mention my home? Entrust a decision about your own to the consuls, or to the senate, or to the college of *pontifices*. Although mine has been acquitted, as I said before, by all three decision-making bodies, I contend that there was a shrine, as well as altars, in the house that you own after having Quintus Seius, a Roman *eques* and a fine man, openly murdered. I will confirm and elaborate on this by citing the records of the censors and appealing to the memory of many. Provided that we attend to this affair—which has to be referred to us in accordance with the recent senatorial decree—I have things that I would like to say about hallowed places. **31** After I have spoken about your house—where a shrine has been built over in such a way that someone else has been doing the overbuilding, and you only have to destroy it—then I will consider whether I should also say something about others. For some consider it my responsibility to render accessible the *magmentarium* of Tellus. They say that it recently lay open, and I do recall this. Now they are saying that the most sacred part, the seat of the greatest religious sanctity, is contained within the forecourt of a private home. Many things concern me: that I am the caretaker of the temple of Tellus; that the person who removed that *magmentarium* said, after my house had been acquitted by the decision of the *pontifices*, that the judgment had been made in favor of his brother. The cult of Tellus also concerns me during this period of expensive grain, sterile fields, and scarcity of crops, all the more so because this same prodigy tells us that reparations are owed to Tellus.

32 Maybe I'm talking about things that are out of date. In fact, if it hasn't been written explicitly in civil law, it has nonetheless been consecrated by the law of nature, by the shared law of peoples, that mortals cannot acquire anything from the immortal gods through uninterrupted possession. But still, we are neglecting events of the past; shall we also neglect those things that we see are happening at this very moment? Take Lucius Piso: who is unaware that in our own time he destroyed a most important and sacred shrine of Diana on the Caelian? Neighbors of that spot are present here; there are even many in this senatorial order who have conducted in that very chapel, at the appointed place, the annual rites for their families. And are we investigating what places the immortal gods are expressing longing for, what they mean and what they are talking

Serrano sanctissima sacella suffossa, inaedificata, oppressa, summa denique turpitudine foedata esse nescimus? **33** tu meam domum religiosam facere potuisti? qua mente? quam amiseras. qua manu? qua disturbaras. qua voce? qua incendi iusseras. qua lege? quam ne in illa quidem impunitate tua scripseras. quo pulvinari? quod stupraras. quo simulacro? quod ereptum ex meretricis sepulcro ⟨in⟩ imperatoris monumento conlocaras. quid habet mea domus religiosi nisi quod impuri et sacrilegi parietem tangit? itaque ne quis meorum imprudens introspicere tuam domum possit ac te sacra illa tua facientem videre, tollam altius tectum, non ut ego te despiciam, sed tu ne aspicias urbem eam quam delere voluisti.

34 Sed iam haruspicum reliqua responsa videamus. ORATORES CONTRA IVS FASQVE INTERFECTOS. quid est hoc? de Alexandrinis esse video sermonem; quem ego non refuto. sic enim sentio, ius legatorum cum hominum praesidio munitum sit, tum etiam divino iure esse vallatum. sed quaero ab illo qui omnis indices tribunus e carcere in forum effudit, cuius arbitrio sicae nunc omnes atque omnia venena tractantur, qui cum Hermarcho Chio syngraphas fecit, ecquid sciat unum acerrimum adversarium Hermarchi, Theodosium, legatum ad senatum a civitate libera missum sica percussum, quod non minus quam de Alexandrinis indignum dis immortalibus esse visum certo scio. **35** nec confero nunc in te unum omnia. spes maior esset salutis, si praeter te nemo esset impurus; plures sunt; hoc et tu tibi confidis magis et nos prope iure diffidimus. quis Platorem ex Orestide, quae pars Macedoniae libera est, hominem in illis locis clarum ac nobilem, legatum Thessalonicam ad nostrum, ut se ipse appellavit, "imperatorem" venisse nescit? quem ille propter pecuniam, quam ab eo extorquere non poterat, in vincla coniecit et medicum intromisit suum, qui legato, socio, amico, libero foedissime et crudelissime venas incideret. secures suas cruentari scelere noluit; nomen quidem populi Romani tanto scelere contaminavit ut id nulla re possit nisi ipsius supplicio expiari. quales hunc carnifices putamus habere, qui etiam medicis suis non ad salutem sed ad necem utatur?

36 Sed recitemus quid sequatur. FIDEM IVSQVE IVRANDVM NEGLECTVM. hoc quid sit per se ipsum non facile interpretor, sed ex eo quod sequitur suspicor de tuorum iudicum manifesto periurio dici, quibus olim erepti essent nummi nisi a

about? Are we ignorant that Sextus Serranus has undermined, built over, and blocked access to very sacred shrines, ultimately defiling them with the greatest disgrace? **33** As for you: were you able to make my house a site of religious pollution? With what mind? The one you had lost. With what hand? The one with which you had demolished it. With what voice? The one with which you had ordered it burned. Through what law? The one you hadn't even written during that time when you would have been unpunished for doing so. With what sacred couch? The one you had debauched. With what image? The one you had stolen from the tomb of a whore and erected in the monument of a general. What religious pollution does my house have other than that it shares a party wall with someone impure and sacrilegious? And so, in order that none of my family may be able to glimpse inside your house unknowingly and see you going through your own rites, I will raise my roof higher—not that I may look down upon you but so that you may not look out on the city that you wanted to destroy.

34 So now let's consider the remaining responses of the *haruspices*: ORATORES HAVE BEEN KILLED CONTRARY TO HUMAN AND DIVINE LAW. What does this mean? I see that people are talking about the Alexandrians. I am not going to refute this, since I understand that the rights of embassies have been not only fortified by the safeguards of human beings but also protected by the ramparts of divine law. Still, I have a question for the person who, while tribune, released from prison into the forum all his spies, and at whose whim these men wield all sorts of daggers and every poison, and who signed promissory notes with Hermarchus of Chios: is he aware that Theodosius, a very bitter enemy of Hermarchus, was struck down by a dagger after being sent to the senate as an ambassador from a free state? I know for a fact that this seemed to the immortal gods no less unworthy than the business about the Alexandrians. **35** And yet I am not now attributing everything to you alone. There would surely be a greater sense of security if you were the only unsavory character, but there are several. For this reason not only do you have more confidence in yourself but we are almost justified in our lack of it. Everyone knows that in Thessalonica there came to our "imperator" (that's how he styled himself) a legate from Orestis, a free part of Macedon—Plator, a well-known and noble man in those parts. That man threw Plator in chains because he was unable to extort money from him. He then sent in his own doctor to sever in a most cruel and foul fashion the veins of an ambassador, an ally, a friend, a freeborn man. He didn't want his axes bloodied from this crime but in fact he stained the reputation of the Roman people with a crime so great that nothing except his own punishment could expiate it. What sort of assassins do we think this man has when he employs even his own doctors not to cure but to kill?

36 But let me read out what comes next: CREDIBILITY AND OATH-TAKING HAVE BEEN NEGLECTED. It isn't easy for me to explain what this means by itself, but from what follows I imagine that it is about the open perjury of your

senatu praesidium postulassent. qua re autem de iis dici suspicer haec causa est, quod sic statuo et illud in hac civitate esse maxime inlustre atque insigne periurium et te ipsum tamen in crimen ab iis quibuscum coniurasti non vocari.

37 Et video in haruspicum responso haec esse subiuncta: SACRIFICIA VETVSTA OCCVLTAQVE MINVS DILIGENTER FACTA POLLVTAQVE. haruspices haec loquuntur an patrii penatesque di? multi enim sunt, credo, in quos huius malefici suspicio cadat. quis praeter hunc unum? obscure dicitur quae sacra polluta sint? quid planius, quid religiosius, quid gravius dici potest? VETVSTA OCCVLTAQVE. nego ulla verba Lentulum, gravem oratorem ac disertum, saepius, cum te accusaret, usurpasse quam haec quae nunc ex Etruscis libris in te conversa atque interpretata dicuntur. etenim quod sacrificium tam vetustum est quam hoc quod a regibus aequale huius urbis accepimus? quod autem tam occultum quam id quod non solum curiosos oculos excludit sed etiam errantis, quo non modo improbitas sed ne imprudentia quidem possit intrare? quod quidem sacrificium nemo ante P. Clodium omni memoria violavit, nemo umquam adiit, nemo neglexit, nemo vir aspicere non horruit, quod fit per virgines Vestales, fit pro populo Romano, fit in ea domo quae est in imperio, fit incredibili caerimonia, fit ei deae cuius ne nomen quidem viros scire fas est, quam iste idcirco Bonam dicit quod in tanto sibi scelere ignoverit. non ignovit, mihi crede, non: nisi forte tibi esse ignotum putas, quod te iudices emiserunt excussum et exhaustum, suo iudicio absolutum, omnium condemnatum, aut quod oculos, ut opinio illius religionis est, non perdidisti. **38** quis enim ante te sacra illa vir sciens viderat, ut quisquam poenam quae sequeretur id scelus scire posset? an tibi luminis obesset caecitas plus quam libidinis? ne id quidem sentis, coniventes illos oculos abavi tui magis optandos fuisse quam hos flagrantis sororis? tibi vero, si diligenter attendes, intelleges hominum poenas deesse adhuc, non deorum. homines te in re foedissima defenderunt, homines turpissimum nocentissimumque laudarunt, homines prope confitentem iudicio liberaverunt, hominibus iniuria tui stupri inlata in ipsos dolori non fuit, homines tibi arma alii in me, alii post in illum invictum civem dederunt, hominum beneficia prorsus concedo tibi iam maiora non esse quaerenda.

jurors, who at one time would have had their money stolen back if they hadn't demanded from the senate a bodyguard. Here is the reason why I imagine it is about these men: because I am convinced both that that was the single most notorious and distinctive case of perjury in this state and that, in spite of this, no charge was brought against you by your fellow conspirators.

37 And I see that the following has been appended to the haruspical response: ANCIENT AND SECRET RITES HAVE BEEN CONDUCTED LESS CAREFULLY AND POLLUTED. Are the *haruspices* saying this or are the gods of our city and homes? Sure, I'd imagine that there are many people upon whom suspicion may fall for this kind of offense—who other than this one man here? Are these words obscure about what rites have been polluted? What can be uttered with more clarity, with more consideration for religion, with more gravity? ANCIENT AND SECRET. I assert that Lentulus, a serious and skilled speaker, used no words more often when he prosecuted you than these which are spoken now, interpreted and redirected from the Etruscan books against you. For what rite is so ancient as this one, inherited from the kings as coeval with this city? And which rite is as secret as the one that excludes not only inquisitive eyes but even wandering eyes, where not only impudence but even imprudence cannot enter? Until Publius Clodius, no one in human memory has violated this rite, no one has ever approached it, no one (who is male) has not dreaded to look upon it. It is conducted through the Vestal Virgins, on behalf of the Roman people, in a house that has magisterial authority, with unbelievable ceremony, and for that goddess whose name it is sacrilege for men even to know. That man says that this goddess is "good" because she forgave him such a horrid crime. No; she didn't forgive, believe me. Or maybe you think you've been forgiven because the jurors set you loose, emptied out and drained dry, innocent by their own verdict but guilty by everyone else's? Or is it because you didn't lose your eyes, as is the general belief regarding that cult? **38** For what man before you had knowingly witnessed those rites, with the result that someone could know the punishment attendant upon that crime? Would blindness in your eyes hinder you more than blindness in your passions? You don't even realize that you should have chosen those dull eyes of your great-great-grandfather over the passionate eyes of your sister. In fact, if you pay attention carefully you will understand that up until this point you have avoided punishment from human beings but not from the gods. People have defended you in the ugliest affair; people have praised you, though disgusting and utterly guilty; people have freed you in court when you had practically confessed; people were not aggrieved at the injustice of your libidinous activity even against themselves; some people provided you with weapons against me, later others did so against our unconquerable fellow citizen; from people, I fully admit, you should not seek greater favors.

39 A dis quidem immortalibus quae potest homini maior esse poena furore atque dementia? nisi forte in tragoediis quos vulnere ac dolore corporis cruciari et consumi vides, graviores deorum immortalium iras subire quam illos qui furentes inducuntur putas. non sunt illi eiulatus et gemitus Philoctetae tam miseri, quamquam sunt acerbi, quam illa exsultatio Athamantis et quam senium matricidarum. tu cum furiales in contionibus voces mittis, cum domos civium evertis, cum lapidibus optimos viros foro pellis, cum ardentis faces in vicinorum tecta iactas, cum aedes sacras inflammas, cum servos concitas, cum sacra ludosque conturbas, cum uxorem sororemque non discernis, cum quod ineas cubile non sentis, tum baccharis, tum furis, tum das eas poenas quae solae sunt hominum sceleri a dis immortalibus constitutae. nam corporis quidem nostri infirmitas multos subit casus per se, denique ipsum corpus tenuissima de causa saepe conficitur; "deorum tela in impiorum mentibus figuntur". qua re miserior es cum in omnem fraudem raperis oculis quam si omnino oculos non haberes.

40 Sed quoniam de his omnibus quae haruspices commissa esse dicunt satis est dictum, videamus quid idem haruspices iam a dis immortalibus dicant moneri. monent NE PER OPTIMATIVM DISCORDIAM DISSENSIONEMQVE PATRIBVS PRINCIPIBVSQVE CAEDES PERICVLAQVE CREENTVR AVXILIOQVE DIVINITVS DEFICIANTVR, † QVA RE AD VNVM IMPERIVM PECVNIAE REDEANT EXERCITVSQVE PVLSVS DOMINATIOQVE ACCEDAT †. haruspicum verba sunt haec omnia, nihil addo de meo. quis igitur hanc optimatium discordiam molitur? idem iste, nec ulla vi ingeni aut consili sui, sed quodam errore nostro; quem quidem ille, quod obscurus non erat, facile perspexit. hoc enim etiam turpius adflictatur res publica quod ne ab eo quidem vexatur, ut tamquam fortis in pugna vir acceptis a forti adversario vulneribus adversis honeste cadere videatur. **41** Ti. Gracchus convellit statum civitatis, qua gravitate vir, qua eloquentia, qua dignitate! nihil ut a patris avique Africani praestabili insignique virtute, praeterquam quod a senatu desciverat, deflexisset. secutus est C. Gracchus, quo ingenio, qua eloquentia, quanta vi, quanta gravitate dicendi! ut dolerent boni non illa tanta ornamenta ad meliorem mentem voluntatemque esse conversa. ipse L. Saturninus ita fuit effrenatus et paene demens ut actor esset egregius et ad animos imperitorum excitandos inflammandosque perfectus. nam quid ego de P. Sulpicio loquar? cuius tanta in dicendo gravitas, tanta iucunditas, tanta ubertas fuit ut posset vel ut prudentes errarent vel ut boni minus bene sentirent perficere

39 But what of the immortal gods? What greater punishment can they give a person than raging madness? Unless perhaps you think that the characters in tragedy that you see tortured and consumed by wounds and physical pain experience worse anger from the immortal gods than those who are led onstage raging mad. Those familiar shrieks and groans of Philoctetes, bitter as they are, are not so wretched as the raving of Athamas and the dark moods of the matricides. As for you, whenever you utter crazed words at public assemblies, overturn the homes of citizens, drive from the forum with stones our finest men, toss burning torches onto the roofs of your neighbors, set aflame sacred temples, stir up slaves, disrupt rites and games, cannot tell your wife from your sister, are unaware what bedroom you are entering—that's when you rave like one possessed, exhibit fury, and pay the only penalty that the immortal gods have established for human wickedness. The frailty of our body experiences many misfortunes on its own. In fact, the body is itself done in from the slenderest cause; but "the spears of the gods are fixed in the minds of the impious." For this reason, whenever you are cast into every sort of crime because of your eyes you are more wretched than if you had no eyes at all.

40 Since we have spoken enough about all the things that the *haruspices* say have been perpetrated, let's consider what these same *haruspices* say is now being warned by the immortal gods. They warn THAT THROUGH DISCORD AND DISAGREEMENT OF THE BEST MEN THERE NOT ARISE DEATH AND DANGER FOR THE FATHERS AND LEADING MEN, AND THAT THEY NOT BE WITHOUT HELP FROM A DIVINE SOURCE, † BECAUSE OF WHICH CIRCUMSTANCE WEALTH WOULD REVERT TO A SINGLE RULER AND THERE WOULD OCCUR THE DRIVING AWAY OF THE ARMY AND DESPOTISM †. These are all the words of the *haruspices*; I add nothing of my own. So who is contriving this discord among the best men? That same man: and not by virtue of his genius or planning, but because of a mistake on our part, a mistake that he recognized easily since it was not hidden. For the state is endangered all the worse because it is being stirred up not even by such a person that may lend the appearance of its falling honorably, like a brave man in battle after receiving direct wounds from a brave opponent. **41** Tiberius Gracchus uprooted the state constitution—a man of such seriousness, eloquence, and reputation! He would not have strayed from the remarkably distinguished virtue of his father and of Africanus his grandfather, were it not for the fact that he had turned away from the senate. He was followed by Gaius Gracchus—what natural talent and eloquence, such force and seriousness in speech! As a result, good men grieved that these outstanding qualities were not directed toward better purposes and intentions. Lucius Saturninus, for his part, was so unrestrained—almost mad—that he was an exceptional public speaker, perfect for rousing to extremes the passions of the naive. And what can I say about Publius Sulpicius? The seriousness, agreeability, and richness of his oratory was so great that by speaking he could cause the prudent

dicendo. cum his conflictari et pro salute patriae cotidie dimicare erat omnino illis qui tum rem publicam gubernabant molestum; sed habebat ea molestia quandam tamen dignitatem. 42 hic vero de quo ego ipse tam multa nunc dico, pro di immortales! quid est, quid valet, quid adfert, ut tanta civitas, si cadet,— quod di omen obruant!—a viro tamen confecta videatur? qui post patris mortem primam illam aetatulam suam ad scurrarum locupletium libidines detulit, quorum intemperantia expleta in domesticis est germanitatis stupris volutatus; deinde iam robustus provinciae se ac rei militari dedit, atque ibi piratarum contumelias perpessus etiam Cilicum libidines barbarorumque satiavit; post exercitu L. Luculli sollicitato per nefandum scelus fugit illim Romaeque recenti adventu suo cum propinquis suis decidit ne reos faceret, a Catilina pecuniam accepit ut turpissime praevaricaretur. inde cum Murena se in Galliam contulit, in qua provincia mortuorum testamenta conscripsit, pupillos necavit, nefarias cum multis scelerum pactiones societatesque conflavit. unde ut rediit, quaestum illum maxime fecundum uberemque campestrem totum ad se ita redegit ut homo popularis fraudaret improbissime populum, idemque vir clemens divisores omnium tribuum domi ipse suae crudelissima morte mactaret. 43 exorta est illa rei publicae, sacris, religionibus, auctoritati vestrae, iudiciis publicis funesta quaestura, in qua idem iste deos hominesque, pudorem, pudicitiam, senatus auctoritatem, ius, fas, leges, iudicia violavit. atque hic ei gradus—o misera tempora stultasque nostras discordias!—P. Clodio gradus ad rem publicam hic primus ⟨fuit⟩ et aditus ad popularem iactationem atque ascensus. nam Ti. Graccho invidia Numantini foederis, cui feriendo, quaestor C. Mancini consulis cum esset, interfuerat, et in eo foedere improbando senatus severitas dolori et timori fuit, eaque res illum fortem et clarum virum a gravitate patria desciscere coegit. C. autem Gracchum mors fraterna, pietas, dolor, magnitudo animi ad expetendas domestici sanguinis poenas excitavit. Saturninum, quod in annonae caritate quaestorem a sua frumentaria procuratione senatus amovit eique rei M. Scaurum praefecit, scimus dolore factum esse popularem. Sulpicium ab optima causa profectum Gaioque Iulio consulatum contra leges petenti resistentem longius quam voluit popularis aura provexit.

to err, or the honorable to think less honorably. The struggles with these men and the daily battles on behalf of our country's welfare was immensely troublesome to those who governed the state at the time. But it was nonetheless the kind of trouble that entailed a certain dignity.

42 But this person here, about whom I now have so much to say—by the immortal gods! what sort of thing is he, what power does he have, what force is he applying so that our great state, should it fall—and may the gods avert this omen!—would at least seem to have been destroyed by a real man? After his father's death he offered up the notorious beginnings of his tender youth to the lusts of wealthy flâneurs. When their intemperate desires were sated he played around at home having sex with siblings. Once he was fully grown he gave himself over to military affairs in the provinces and while there endured abuse from pirates, satiating even the lusts of Cilician barbarians. Then, after stirring up Lucius Lucullus's troops through an unspeakable crime, he took flight and, freshly arrived in Rome, he came to an agreement with his relatives not to prosecute them and took money from Catiline to collude in a disgraceful acquittal. From there he departed for Gaul with Murena, where he wrote the wills of those already dead, murdered young heirs, and forged with many people wickedly criminal pacts and alliances. Upon his return he redirected entirely to himself such an eminently rich and fertile profit from the electoral field that this "popular" politician ended up most wickedly defrauding the people, and this same gentle man most cruelly executed in his own home the paymasters of all the tribes.

43 Then it happened: the quaestorship deadly to the state, to its sacred rites and religious scruples, to your authority, and to the public courts. During that time this same man violated gods and men, shame and chastity, senatorial authority, human and divine justice, the laws and courts. This was his first entrée—oh these are wretched times and our disagreements are stupid!—this was Publius Clodius's first entrée into the republic, his first upward ascent toward the flaunting of his popular credentials. Tiberius Gracchus, since he was present at the crafting of an invidious treaty with the Numantines while quaestor to the consul Gaius Mancinus, suffered distress and fear on account of the senate's stern disapproval of that treaty. It was this affair that drove such a brave and renowned man to turn away from the severity of his father. Gaius Gracchus was roused by loyalty and grief at his brother's death, as well as by a noble spirit, to seek vengeance for bloodshed within his family. As for Saturninus, we know that it was grief that made him a popular politician since, during a period of high prices, the senate removed him while quaestor from the administration of grain and put Marcus Scaurus in charge. The winds of popularity carried away Sulpicius further than he had intended when, starting with the best intentions, he resisted Gaius Julius's illegal pursuit of the consulship.

44 fuit in his omnibus causa, etsi non iusta,—nulla enim potest cuiquam male de re publica merendi iusta esse causa,—gravis tamen et cum aliquo animi [et] virilis dolore coniuncta: P. Clodius a crocota, a mitra, a muliebribus soleis purpureisque fasceolis, a strophio, a psalterio, ⟨a⟩ flagitio, a stupro est factus repente popularis. nisi eum mulieres exornatum ita deprendissent, nisi ex eo loco quo eum adire fas non fuerat ancillarum beneficio emissus esset, populari homine populus Romanus, res publica cive tali careret.

Hanc ob amentiam in discordiis nostris, de quibus ipsis his prodigiis recentibus a dis immortalibus admonemur, arreptus est unus ex patriciis cui tribuno plebis fieri non liceret. **45** quod anno ante frater Metellus et concors etiam tum senatus, principe Cn. Pompeio sententiam dicente, excluserat acerrimeque una voce ac mente restiterat, id post discidium optimatium, de quo ipso nunc monemur, ita perturbatum itaque permutatum est ut, quod frater consul ne fieret obstiterat, quod adfinis et sodalis, clarissimus vir, qui illum reum non laudarat, excluserat, id is consul efficeret in discordiis principum qui illi unus inimicissimus esse debuerat, eo fecisse auctore se diceret cuius auctoritatis neminem posset paenitere. iniecta fax est foeda ac luctuosa rei publicae; petita est auctoritas vestra, gravitas amplissimorum ordinum, consensio bonorum omnium, totus denique civitatis status. haec enim certe petebantur, cum in me cognitorem harum omnium rerum illa flamma illorum temporum coniciebatur. excepi et pro patria solus exarsi, sic tamen ut vos isdem ignibus circumsaepti me primum ictum pro vobis et fumantem videretis. **46** non sedabantur discordiae, sed etiam crescebat inter eos odium a quibus nos defendi putabamur. ecce isdem auctoribus, Pompeio principe, qui cupientem Italiam, flagitantis vos, populum Romanum desiderantem non auctoritate sua solum sed etiam precibus ad meam salutem excitavit, restituti sumus. sit discordiarum finis aliquando, a diuturnis dissensionibus conquiescamus. non sinit eadem ista labes; eas habet contiones, ea miscet ac turbat ut ⟨modo his se⟩, modo vendat illis, nec tamen ita ut se quisquam, si ab isto laudatus sit, laudatiorem putet, sed ut eos quos non amant ab eodem gaudeant vituperari. atque ego hunc non miror—quid enim faciat aliud?—illos homines sapientissimos gravissimosque miror, primum quod quemquam clarum hominem atque optime de re publica saepe meritum impurissimi voce hominis violari facile patiuntur, deinde si existimant perditi hominis profligatique maledictis posse, id quod minime conducit ipsis, cuiusquam gloriam dignitatemque violari,

44 Each of these men had a cause; while it was not just—since no one can have just cause for behaving badly toward the state—nevertheless it was serious, and bound up with the grief of a manly spirit. Publius Clodius? Changing from a saffron robe, a headdress, women's slippers and purple veils, a breastband, a lute, his disgraceful sexual behavior, he suddenly became a popular politician. If women had not caught him dressed up in this way, and if maidservants had not helped send him out of a place that it was sacrilege to enter, the Roman people would now be deprived of a man of the people, the republic of so distinguished a citizen.

During our own disagreements, which the immortal gods warn us about through these recent prodigies, it was his insane behavior that allowed him to be the only man snatched from the ranks of the patricians, one who could not lawfully become a tribune of the people. **45** A year earlier his cousin Metellus and the senate—still then in agreement—had dismissed and unanimously resisted most keenly this action, with Gnaeus Pompey being the first to state his opinion. But after a division among the elite, the very one about which we are now being warned, there was so much turmoil and disarray that the very thing that his relative the consul had refused to let happen, that his brilliant relation and comrade (who had not praised him when on trial) had blocked, was now being put into effect amidst the discord of the leaders by that consul who ought to have been his single greatest enemy but claimed that he had acted at the instigation of someone whose authority no one could possibly regret. A torch was cast, foul and sorrowful for the republic. An assault was made on your authority, on the stability of the upper classes, on the agreement of all good men, in short on the state's entire constitution. For all these things were surely under assault when there was hurled against me, their defender, the firebrand of those times. I was the only person to intercept it, and to be set ablaze for my country. Although surrounded by these same fires, you nevertheless looked on as I, the first to be struck down, went up in smoke on your behalf.

46 Discord did not abate; instead, hatred grew even stronger among those who were thought to be defending me. Then look what happened: these same men restored me from exile, with Pompey leading the way, who used not only his authority but even personal entreaties to rouse up for my salvation an Italy that wanted me, you who demanded me, and the Roman populace who longed for me. May there be an end at last to discord, may we find rest from our long-standing disagreements. But this very same instrument of ruin here prevents it, holding public assemblies and stirring up confusion in such a way that he offers himself for sale to different people at different times; and yet he does not do this so that each person may believe himself worthy of praise if he has been praised by Clodius but so that they may take delight when he attacks people that they don't like. Still, I'm not surprised by him—what else could he do?—but I am surprised by those men who are very wise and serious: first, because without compunction they allow any well-known person, even a great benefactor to the state, to be attacked by the words of this disgusting creature; next, that they consider that someone's fame and stature can be harmed by the slander of a ruined and dissolute person, an opinion that hardly benefits them; and, finally,

postremo quod non sentiunt, id quod tamen mihi iam suspicari videntur, illius furentis ac volaticos impetus in se ipsos posse converti. **47** atque ex hac nimia non nullorum alienatione a quibusdam haerent ea tela in re publica quae, quam diu haerebant in uno me, graviter equidem, sed aliquanto levius ferebam. an iste nisi primo se dedisset iis quorum animos a vestra auctoritate seiunctos esse arbitrabatur, nisi eos in caelum suis laudibus praeclarus auctor extolleret, nisi exercitum ⟨C.⟩ Caesaris—in quo fallebat, sed eum nemo redarguebat—nisi eum, inquam, exercitum signis infestis in curiam se immissurum minitaretur, nisi se Cn. Pompeio adiutore, M. Crasso auctore, quae faciebat facere clamaret, nisi consules causam coniunxisse secum, in quo uno non mentiebatur, confirmaret, tam crudelis mei, tam sceleratus rei publicae vexator esse potuisset? **48** idem postea quam respirare vos a metu caedis, emergere auctoritatem vestram e fluctibus illis servitutis, reviviscere memoriam ac desiderium mei vidit, vobis se coepit subito fallacissime venditare. tum leges Iulias contra auspicia latas et hic et in contionibus dicere, in quibus legibus inerat curiata illa lex quae totum eius tribunatum continebat, quod caecus amentia non videbat. producebat fortissimum virum, M. Bibulum; quaerebat ex eo, C. Caesare leges ferente de caelo semperne servasset. semper se ille servasse dicebat. augures interrogabat, quae ita lata essent rectene lata essent. illi vitio lata esse dicebant. ferebant in oculis hominem quidam boni viri et de me optime meriti, sed illius, ut ego arbitror, furoris ignari. longius processit; in ipsum Cn. Pompeium, auctorem, ut praedicare est solitus, consiliorum suorum, invehi coepit; inibat gratiam a non nullis. **49** tum vero est elatus spe posse se, quoniam togatum domestici belli exstinctorem nefario scelere foedasset, illum etiam, illum externorum bellorum hostiumque victorem adfligere; tum est illa in templo Castoris scelerata et paene deletrix huius imperi sica deprensa; tum ille cui nulla hostium diutius urbs umquam fuit clausa, qui omnis angustias, omnis altitudines moenium obiectas semper vi ac virtute perfregit, obsessus ipse est domi meque non nulla imperitorum vituperatione timiditatis meae consilio et facto suo liberavit. nam si Cn. Pompeio, viro uni omnium fortissimo quicumque nati sunt, miserum magis fuit quam turpe, quam diu ille tribunus plebis fuit, lucem non aspicere, carere publico, minas eius perferre, cum in contionibus diceret velle se in Carinis aedificare alteram porticum, quae Palatio responderet, certe mihi exire domo mea ad privatum dolorem fuit luctuosum, ad rationem rei publicae gloriosum.

because they do not consider (although I believe they have suspicions) that his insanely fickle attacks could be turned back upon themselves. **47** And so, as a result of this wholesale alienation of not a few people from certain individuals, there now clings to the republic the weapons that I bore with great difficulty, but a little more easily so long as they clung only to me. What about this man? If from the first he hadn't given himself over to those who he thought had been hostile to your leadership, if this renowned authority were not praising them to high heaven, if he weren't threatening to send Gaius Caesar's army—he was mistaken here, but no one contradicted him—to send Caesar's army, I say, into the senate house ready for battle, if he were not proclaiming that he was doing what he did with the help of Pompey and at the instigation of Crassus, if he weren't asserting that the consuls had made common cause with him—the only instance where he wasn't lying—could he have been such a cruel tormentor of me, and such a wicked one of the republic? **48** But after he saw that you were recovering your breath from the fear of slaughter, that your authority was resurfacing from the billows of servitude, and that the yearning memory of me was coming back to life, this same man suddenly began to offer himself for sale to you with the greatest deception and then to say, both here and in public assemblies, that the laws of Julius Caesar had been passed contrary to the auspices, including that law passed by the curiate assembly which held in place his entire tribunate, a fact that he failed to recognize in his blind insanity. He used to bring forward the extraordinarily brave Marcus Bibulus and ask him whether he had continuously observed the auspices when Caesar was passing his legislation. He replied that he had. He used to ask the augurs whether anything that had been passed in such a fashion had been passed properly. They would say that such passage was faulty. Some good men who were my benefactors used to hold this man very dear, but I believe they were unaware of his raging madness.

He went further: he began to attack Gnaeus Pompey, whom he used to brag was the promoter of his own plans. This won him the approval of many. **49** It was then that he was swept away by the hope that, since he had disgraced with a wicked crime the man who had quelled civil war while still wearing a toga, he could also ruin that hero who had conquered our enemies in foreign wars; it was then that an accursed dagger, nearly fatal to our empire, was seized in the temple of Castor; it was then that that hero, to whom no enemy city was ever shut for long and who without fail used his strength and courage to break through every mountain pass and through every high city wall placed in his path, was besieged in his own home. His plan of action freed me from many of the charges of cowardice that I had received from the naive. Because for as long as that man was tribune of the plebs, if Gnaeus Pompey, the bravest man who ever lived, was more aggrieved than disgraced that he could not gaze at the light of day, that he kept out of the public eye, that he endured the threats of Clodius when he proclaimed in public assemblies his desire to build a second portico in the Carinae district that would face the Palatine,—then surely the fact that I left my own home was lamentable in respect to my private grief, but glorious when taking into account the republic.

50 Videtis igitur hominem per se ipsum iam pridem adflictum ac iacentem perniciosis optimatium discordiis excitari, cuius initia furoris dissensionibus eorum qui tum a vobis seiuncti videbantur sustentata sunt. reliqua iam praecipitantis tribunatus etiam post tribunatum obtrectatores eorum atque adversarii defenderunt; ne a re publica rei publicae pestis removeretur restiterunt, etiam ne causam diceret, etiam ne privatus esset. etiamne in sinu atque in deliciis quidam optimi viri viperam illam venenatam ac pestiferam habere potuerunt? quo tandem decepti munere? "volo" inquiunt "esse qui in contione detrahat de Pompeio." detrahat ille vituperando? velim sic hoc vir summus atque optime de mea salute meritus accipiat ut a me dicitur; dicam quidem certe quod sentio. mihi me dius fidius tum de illius amplissima dignitate detrahere cum illum maximis laudibus ecferebat videbatur. **51** utrum tandem C. Marius splendidior cum eum C. Glaucia laudabat an cum eundem iratus postea vituperabat? an ille demens et iam pridem ad poenam exitiumque praeceps foedior aut inquinatior in Cn. Pompeio accusando quam in universo senatu vituperando fuit? quod quidem miror, cum alterum gratum sit iratis, alterum esse tam bonis civibus non acerbum. sed ne id viros optimos diutius delectet, legant hanc eius contionem de qua loquor; in qua Pompeium ornat— an potius deformat? certe laudat, et unum esse in hac civitate dignum huius imperi gloria dicit et significat se illi esse amicissimum et reconciliationem esse gratiae factam. **52** quod ego quamquam quid sit nescio, tamen hoc statuo, hunc, si amicus esset Pompeio, laudaturum illum non fuisse. quid enim, si illi inimicissimus esset, amplius ad eius laudem minuendam facere potuisset? videant ii qui illum Pompeio inimicum esse gaudebant ob eamque causam in tot tantisque sceleribus conivebant et non numquam eius indomitos atque ecfrenatos furores plausu etiam suo prosequebantur, quam se cito inverterit. nunc enim iam laudat illum, in eos invehitur quibus se antea venditabat. quid existimatis eum, si reditus ei gratiae patuerit, esse facturum, qui tam libenter in opinionem gratiae inrepat?

50 And so you see that this man, lying low for a long time now from a self-inflicted wound, is being roused up by deadly discord among the optimates. The early stages of his madness were nurtured by disagreements with men who at the time seemed to have been estranged from you. The detractors and enemies of these men defended what was left of his tribunate when it was already in decline—and even afterward. They stood in the way of this pest of the republic being removed from the republic, of his pleading his case in court, even of his being a private citizen. Were some of our best citizens even able to hold that venomous and plague-bearing viper in their embrace and among their favorites? In the end, what gift lured them? They say: "I want there to be someone who can take down Pompey at a public assembly." Take him down through verbal attacks? I would like for this most important man, one to whom I am most grateful for my well-being, to hear what I have to say; I will certainly say what I think. I solemnly swear that I thought he was diminishing Pompey's magnificent importance at that time when he was extolling him with the highest praise. **51** Tell me, was Gaius Marius more resplendent when being praised by Gaius Glaucia or when he was later angrily abused by him? Or was that madman, already going headlong to punishment and destruction, more foul or defiled while accusing Pompey than while attacking the entire senate? This is the very thing that I marvel at, namely that while they are pleased with the former action when they are angry, the latter is not unpleasant to such loyal citizens. But don't let this delight our best citizens any longer: just let them read this contional speech of his that I am talking about. In it he glorifies Pompey—or does he defame him? Surely he praises him, saying that there is one man in this state worthy of the glory of this empire, and indicating that he is himself his very close friend and has been reconciled to his favor. **52** Although I don't know the meaning of this, I nevertheless am of this opinion: if he were Pompey's friend he would not have praised him, because if he were his greatest enemy what more could he have done to diminish his glory? As for those who were delighted that he was Pompey's enemy and for that reason turned a blind eye to his numerous serious crimes, even sometimes offering their own applause for his reckless, untamed madness—let them consider how swiftly he has changed. For right now he is praising Pompey but attacking those to whom he previously used to offer himself up for sale. What do you imagine he would do if he were allowed to return to Pompey's good graces, when he is now creeping so gladly into the expectation of them?

53 Quas ego alias optimatium discordias a dis immortalibus definiri putem? nam hoc quidem verbo neque P. Clodius neque quisquam de gregalibus eius aut de consiliariis designatur. habent Etrusci libri certa nomina quae in id genus civium cadere possint: DETERIORES, REPVLSOS, quod iam audietis, hos appellant quorum et mentes et res sunt perditae longeque a communi salute diiunctae. qua re cum di immortales monent de "optimatium" discordia, de clarissimorum et optime meritorum civium dissensione praedicunt; cum "principibus" periculum caedemque portendunt, in tuto conlocant Clodium, qui tantum abest a principibus quantum a puris, quantum ab religiosis. **54** vobis, o clarissimi atque optimi cives, et vestrae saluti consulendum et prospiciendum vident. caedes principum ostenditur; id quod interitum optimatium sequi necesse est adiungitur; ne in unius imperium res reccidat admonemur. ad quem metum si deorum monitis non duceremur, tamen ipsi nostro sensu coniecturaque raperemur. neque enim ullus alius discordiarum solet esse exitus inter claros ⟨et⟩ potentis viros nisi aut universus interitus aut victoris dominatus et regnum. dissensit cum C. Mario, clarissimo cive, consul nobilissimus et fortissimus, L. Sulla; horum uterque ita cecidit victus ut victor idem regnaverit. cum Octavio collega Cinna dissedit; utrique horum secunda Fortuna regnum est largita, adversa mortem. idem iterum Sulla superavit; tum sine dubio habuit regalem potestatem, quamquam rem publicam reciperarat. **55** inest hoc tempore haud obscurum odium, atque id insitum penitus et inustum animis hominum amplissimorum; dissident principes, captatur occasio. qui non tantum opibus valent nescio quam fortunam tamen ac tempus exspectant; qui sine controversia plus possunt, ei fortasse non numquam consilia ac sententias inimicorum suorum extimescunt. tollatur haec e civitate discordia: iam omnes isti qui portenduntur metus exstinguentur, iam ista serpens, quae tum hic delitiscit, tum se emergit et fertur illuc, compressa atque inlisa morietur.

Monent enim eidem NE OCCVLTIS CONSILIIS RES PVBLICA LAEDATVR. quae sunt occultiora quam eius qui in contione ausus est dicere iustitium edici oportere, iuris dictionem intermitti, claudi aerarium, iudicia tolli? nisi forte existimatis hanc tantam conluvionem illi tantamque eversionem civitatis in mentem subito in rostris cogitanti venire potuisse. est quidem ille plenus vini, stupri, somni plenusque inconsideratissimae ac dementissimae temeritatis; verum tamen nocturnis vigiliis, etiam coitione hominum iustitium illud concoctum atque meditatum est. mementote, patres conscripti, verbo illo nefario temptatas aures nostras et perniciosam viam audiendi consuetudine esse munitam.

53 What other instances of "discord among the best" should I consider the gods to be describing? This term, "the best," describes neither Publius Clodius nor anyone from his mob of advisors. The Etruscan books have fixed words to apply to that class of citizens: "the lowly, the rejects." You will hear about them soon; this is their word for men whose thoughts and affairs have become corrupted and far removed from the common welfare. That's why, when the immortal gods warn about discord "among the best," they pronounce on dissension among the most brilliant and meritorious citizens. When they predict danger and slaughter for the "leaders," they keep Clodius safe. He's as far from a leader as he is from the pure and the scrupulous. **54** They understand that it is up to you, my most brilliant and honorable fellow citizens, to plan for the protection of your well-being. The slaughter of leaders is being predicted; what is destined to follow the death of the best is appended: we are being warned not to let the state revert to the rule of one. If we weren't being led to fear this because of the gods' warnings, we would still be caught up in it due to our own feelings and reason. For normally there is no other outcome of discord among brilliant and powerful men than either universal destruction or a conqueror taking power and creating a kingdom. There was disagreement between Gaius Marius, a most brilliant citizen, and Lucius Sulla, a high-born, extremely powerful consul: each was defeated and fell; each then conquered and ruled like a king. Octavius quarreled with his colleague Cinna: favorable Fortune granted a kingdom to both, hostile Fortune death. Sulla conquered a second time, and there was no doubt that he had the power of a king even though he had restored the republic. **55** At the present time odium is in no way hidden; it is sown and seared deep in the minds of our most valuable citizens. Our leaders are in disagreement; opportunity is there for the taking. Those who do not have as many resources nevertheless wait for some chance opportunity, while those who are indisputably more powerful are perhaps sometimes afraid of what their enemies are planning and thinking. Just let this discord be removed from our state and soon all these fears that threaten will be extinguished. Soon that serpent, who at one time hides over here, then emerges to head off in another direction, will be caught, crushed, and die.

For these same ones warn THAT THE REPUBLIC NOT BE HARMED BY SECRET PLANS. And which are more secret than the plans of the man who dared say in a public assembly that a cessation of public business should be declared, the administration of justice interrupted, the treasury closed, and the courts adjourned? Or maybe you think that such turmoil in overturning the state could have come to his mind spontaneously, as he was cogitating on the rostra. In fact, he gorges on wine, sex, and sleep; he gorges on a crazed and unadvised recklessness. Despite all this that cessation of business was carefully cooked up and reflected upon in all-night sessions, even in meetings with co-conspirators. Remember, fellow senators, that our ears have been tested by that wicked concept and, since we are used to hearing about it, we have built a road to destruction.

56 Sequitur illud, NE DETERIORIBVS REPVLSISQVE HONOS AVGEATVR. repulsos videamus, nam deteriores qui sint, post docebo. sed tamen in eum cadere hoc verbum maxime, qui sit unus omnium mortalium sine ulla dubitatione deterrimus, concedendum est. qui sunt igitur repulsi? non, ut opinor, ii qui aliquando honorem vitio civitatis, non suo, non sunt adsecuti; nam id quidem multis saepe optimis civibus atque honestissimis viris accidit. repulsi sunt ii quos ad omnia progredientes, quos munera contra leges gladiatoria parantes, quos apertissime largientes non solum alieni sed etiam sui, vicini, tribules, urbani, rustici reppulerunt. hi ne honore augeantur monemur. debet esse gratum quod praedicunt, sed tamen huic malo populus Romanus ipse nullo haruspicum admonitu sua sponte prospexit. **57** deteriores cavete; quorum quidem est magna natio, sed tamen eorum omnium hic dux est atque princeps. etenim si unum hominem deterrimum poeta praestanti aliquis ingenio fictis conquisitisque vitiis deformatum vellet inducere, nullum profecto dedecus reperire posset quod in hoc non inesset, multaque in eo penitus defixa atque haerentia praeteriret.

Parentibus et dis immortalibus et patriae nos primum natura conciliat; eodem enim tempore et suscipimur in lucem et hoc caelesti spiritu augemur et certam in sedem civitatis ac libertatis adscribimur. iste parentum nomen, sacra, memoriam, gentem Fonteiano nomine obruit; deorum ignis, solia, mensas, abditos ac penetrales focos, occulta et maribus non invisa solum sed etiam inaudita sacra inexpiabili scelere pervertit, idemque earum templum inflammavit dearum quarum ope etiam aliis incendiis subvenitur. **58** quid de patria loquar? qui primum eum civem vi, ferro, periculis urbe, omnibus patriae praesidiis depulit quem vos patriae conservatorem esse saepissime iudicaritis, deinde everso senatus, ut ego semper dixi, comite, duce, ut ille dicebat, senatum ipsum, principem salutis mentisque publicae, vi, caede incendiisque pervertit, sustulit duas leges, Aeliam et Fufiam, maxime rei publicae salutares, censuram exstinxit, intercessionem removit, auspicia delevit, consules sceleris sui socios aerario, provinciis, exercitu armavit, reges qui erant vendidit, qui non erant appellavit, Cn. Pompeium ferro domum compulit, imperatorum monumenta evertit, inimicorum domos disturbavit, vestris monumentis suum nomen inscripsit. infinita sunt scelera quae ab illo in patriam sunt edita. quid? quae in

56 The clause that follows reads: THAT BASER MEN, AND THOSE REJECTED, NOT RECEIVE AN INCREASE IN HONOR. Let's consider these "rejected" men since I will explain later who are the "baser" ones (although it has to be admitted that this word fits very well the man who is beyond doubt the worst of all mortals). So who then are the "rejected"? In my opinion it is not those who, through the state's fault rather than their own, have not ever attained political office, since this very thing happens frequently to many of the best citizens and most honorable men. The rejected are in fact those who stoop to anything, staging illegal gladiatorial shows and dispensing bribes out in the open, and who have been rejected not only by strangers but even by their own family, neighbors, people belonging to the same tribe, and fellow-citizens in both the city and the country. We are warned that these are the men not to receive an increase in honor. These predictions should be welcomed, and yet the Roman people have of their own accord foreseen this evil without any warning from the *haruspices*. **57** As for the "baser men," beware! There is indeed a whole tribe of them, but this man here is the chief leader of them all. For if some outstandingly talented poet were to wish to bring on stage the single worst human being, misshapen by preciously contrived vices, he would be able to discover not a single disgrace that is not present in this man, and he would skip over many that cling to him, deeply fixed.

From the first, the condition of our being born commends us to our parents and the immortal gods and the fatherland, because we are simultaneously taken up into the light and increased through the divine spirit within us and enrolled in a fixed place of citizenship and liberty. That scoundrel has washed away the name, rites, memory, and family that belonged to his parents by adopting the name "Fonteius." When it comes to the gods, he has overturned with a crime that cannot be expiated their sacred fires, their thrones, their tables, their hidden inner hearths, and the secret rites that are not only not to be seen by men but not even to be spoken of; and he has also set aflame the temple of the very goddesses whose assistance is used for other fires. **58** What should I say about his fatherland? First, he used violence, weapons, and threats to drive from the city and from all the safeguards of this fatherland that man whom you repeatedly deemed the "the fatherland's savior"; then, after turning out this partner of the senate (that's what I've always said; Clodius was accustomed to speak of the senate's "leader"), he overturned the senate itself, the head of public safety and order, with violence, slaughter, and flames. He repealed two laws that were most beneficial to the republic, the *leges Aelia* and *Fufia*, eliminated the censorship, removed the tribunician veto, destroyed the auspices, armed the consuls, his partners in crime, with the treasury, provinces, and an army, sold royal rights that already existed and created those that did not, drove Pompey into his home with the sword, overturned monuments of generals, destroyed the homes of his enemies, and wrote his own name on monuments that belong to you. Countless are the crimes that he has committed against his fatherland. What else can I say? He committed crimes against

singulos civis quos necavit, socios quos diripuit, imperatores quos prodidit, exercitus quos temptavit? 59 quid vero? ea quanta sunt quae in ipsum se scelera, quae in suos edidit! quis minus umquam pepercit hostium castris quam ille omnibus corporis sui partibus? quae navis umquam in flumine publico tam vulgata omnibus quam istius aetas fuit? quis umquam nepos tam libere est cum scortis quam hic cum sororibus volutatus? quam denique tam immanem Charybdim poetae fingendo exprimere potuerunt, quae tantos exhaurire gurgites possit quantas iste Byzantiorum Brogitarorumque praedas exsorbuit? aut tam eminentibus canibus Scyllam tamque ieiunis quam quibus istum videtis, Gelliis, Cloeliis, Titiis, rostra ipsa mandentem?

60 Qua re, id quod extremum est in haruspicum responso, providete NE REI PVBLICAE STATVS COMMVTETVR; etenim vix haec, si undique fulciamus iam labefacta, vix, inquam, nixa in omnium nostrum umeris cohaerebunt. fuit quondam ita firma haec civitas et valens ut neglegentiam senatus vel etiam iniurias civium ferre posset. iam non potest. aerarium nullum est, vectigalibus non fruuntur qui redemerunt, auctoritas principum cecidit, consensus ordinum est divolsus, iudicia perierunt, suffragia descripta tenentur a paucis, bonorum animus ad nutum nostri ordinis expeditus iam non erit, civem qui se pro patriae salute opponat invidiae frustra posthac requiretis. 61 qua re hunc statum qui nunc est, qualiscumque est, nulla alia re nisi concordia retinere possumus; nam ut meliore simus loco ne optandum quidem est illo impunito; deteriore autem statu ut simus, unus est inferior gradus aut interitus aut servitutis; quo ne trudamur di immortales nos admonent, quoniam iam pridem humana consilia ceciderunt.

Atque ego hanc orationem, patres conscripti, tam tristem, tam gravem non suscepissem, non quin hanc personam et has partis, honoribus populi Romani, vestris plurimis ornamentis mihi tributis, deberem et possem sustinere, sed tamen facile tacentibus ceteris reticuissem; sed haec oratio omnis fuit non auctoritatis meae, sed publicae religionis. mea fuerunt verba fortasse plura, sententiae quidem omnes haruspicum, ad quos aut referri nuntiata ostenta non convenit aut eorum responsis commoveri necesse est. 62 quod si cetera magis pervulgata nos saepe et leviora moverunt, vox ipsa deorum immortalium non mentes omnium permovebit? nolite enim id putare accidere posse quod in

individual citizens (murdering them), allies (plundering them), generals (betraying them), and armies (tampering with them). **59** And what else? How great are the crimes that he committed against himself and his family! Did anyone ever show less mercy to an enemy camp than he has to every single part of his body? Was any ship in a public thoroughfare ever ridden less frequently by everyone than he was in his youth? What playboy ever rolled around with whores as freely as this man has with his sisters? And lastly, what kind of enormous Charybdis could poets describe in their fictions that could suck up whirlpools of the same size as the loot that Clodius has drained from the Byzantines and King Brogitarus? Or what kind of a Scylla, with dogs projecting out as famished as Clodius's henchmen—Gellius, Cloelius, Titius, and their ilk—as you watch him chomping away at the very *rostra*?

60 And so, give your attention to the last part of the haruspical response, that THE CONSTITUTION OF THE REPUBLIC NOT BE SUBVERTED. Even if we should prop up this city of ours on every side after it has already toppled, it will still just barely stay together, resting on all our shoulders. Once upon a time this state was so stable and strong that it could endure the negligence of the senate and even the unjust actions of its citizens. It can no longer. There is no treasury; those who have collected the taxes make no profit from them; the authority of our leaders has come to an end; harmony among the orders has been ripped apart; the courts have perished; the ballots, filled out in advance, are controlled by a few; the assistance of the elite will no longer be at our beck and call; as for the citizen who, for the sake of the country's well-being, would stand up to public indignation, in vain will you all long for him in the future. **61** As a result, we have the ability to preserve the current system—in whatever condition it is now—only through mutual harmony. We must not even have the hope of being in a better situation so long as that man remains unpunished. But for us to be in a worse position there is only one step down from here: that of annihilation or slavery. The immortal gods warn us not to be beaten down because human counsel has long since failed.

And so, members of the senate, I would not have undertaken such a melancholic and stern speech—not because I did not possess the duty and ability to adopt this character and play this part, inasmuch as the Roman people have given me political offices and you have given me so many honors. Still, with everyone else saying nothing I could easily have remained silent. And yet my entire speech is not to be credited to my authority, but to public religious sentiment. The majority of the words have perhaps been my own, but the judgments belong entirely to the *haruspices*. Either it was inappropriate to refer to them the portents that had been announced or it is necessary that we be deeply moved by their responses. **62** Accordingly, if we have often been disturbed by all these other signs that are more common and less serious, will not the very voice of the immortal gods rouse up the minds of us all? Do not think that what

fabulis saepe videtis fieri, ut deus aliqui delapsus de caelo coetus hominum adeat, versetur in terris, cum hominibus conloquatur. cogitate genus sonitus eius quem Latinienses nuntiarunt, recordamini illud etiam quod nondum est relatum, quod eodem fere tempore factus in agro Piceno Potentiae nuntiatur terrae motus horribilis cum multis quibusdam metuendisque rebus. haec eadem profecto quae prospicimus impendentia pertimescetis. **63** etenim haec deorum immortalium vox, haec paene oratio iudicanda est, cum ipse mundus, cum agri atque terrae motu quodam novo contremescunt et inusitato aliquid sono incredibilique praedicunt. in quo constituendae nobis quidem sunt procurationes et obsecratio, quem ad modum monemur. sed faciles sunt preces apud eos qui ultro nobis viam salutis ostendunt; nostrae nobis sunt inter nos irae discordiaeque placandae.

you often see happening in plays could possibly occur—no god will slip down from the sky to approach a human gathering, spend time on earth, and converse with people. Recall the type of sound that the Latinienses have reported and recall also what has not yet been brought before our body: there are reports that at almost the same time a horrible shaking of the earth, along with so many fearful events, took place at Potentia in the *ager Picenus*. These very same things that I foresee as a threat all of you will soon be dreading. **63** For this must be considered the voice of the immortal gods—almost their speech—when the world itself, the fields and lands, shake all over with a strange tremor, portending something through an unusual and extraordinary sound. In this instance it is we who must prepare for expiations and public prayer, just as we are warned. But prayers are easy in the presence of those gods who willingly show us the way to safety; our own anger and disagreements, felt among ourselves, must be reconciled by us.

Commentary

References to bare numbers without further specification are to the relevant sections of *De haruspicum responsis*. All texts cited without author refer to works of Cicero. Abbreviations for Latin writers follow the format of the *Index* of the *Thesaurus Linguae Latinae* (1990), with occasional expansion for clarity's sake; references to Greek authors follow the conventions of *LSJ*. Two asterisks (**) indicate that the following note discusses primarily textual issues.

1–7

The speech begins with a classic case of misdirection. The senatorial audience would have readily recognized that several elements of the response could be interpreted to incriminate Cicero, particularly in light of Clodius's recent *contio* (see Introduction B.2). As a result, rather than providing the expected prooemium to outline the points at issue, Cicero instead introduces Clodius as the insane disrupter of Roman politics, beginning with events of the preceding day and reaching back to the Bona Dea incident (see further Gildenhard 2011: 328–330). The senate will of course have known in advance what Cicero intended to speak on—this is a special session solely called for discussing the response—a circumstance that makes this misdirection especially crucial.

A reference to the actual subject of the speech does not occur until section 8, when a continuation of the anti-Clodian invective, in particular his inadequacies as a representative of religion, segues into an account of Clodius's recent public meeting at which he gave his own interpretation of the haruspical response.

1–2

Cicero describes an incident from the previous day when Clodius allegedly attempted to disrupt proceedings in the senate. In response, Cicero drove him out of the *curia* by threatening litigation.

1 *Hēstērnō dĭē*: Cicero deems the rhythm of the speech's opening colon, the dochmius (spondee + cretic), as appropriate for any position in a sentence, provided that it is not repeated (*orat.* 218: *quovis loco aptus est, dum semel ponatur*; Fraenkel 1968: 193–197). The phrase *hesterno die* occurs also at 3, 7, and 17; the sixteen remaining occurrences in the speeches normally occupy emphatic first position, as here. The alternative form *heri* occurs only twice in Cicero's oratory, in contexts of rebuke (*Phil.* 1.16, 2.110, where it follows *hodiernus dies*), but predominates in comic drama and is the exclusive choice in Cicero's correspondence (Kinsey 1971: 103). For words meaning "today" Cicero exhibits a slightly different tendency: *hodie* is common in all genres, but *hodierno die* occurs only in the speeches, with twenty-three appearances. Livian usage of *hesterno die* also resembles Cicero's so that, despite its use by characters in Petronius (131.2, 139.3), the phrase "probably indicates a certain formality in style" (Oakley 1997–2005: 2.343). The emphatic position, complemented by an attractive rhythm, is appropriate here since Cicero wishes to contrast Clodius's erratic behavior in the senate on the previous day with his own reasoned exposition that is to follow.

patres conscripti: This vocative is almost invariably used in addressing the members of the assembled senate (Dickey 2002: 284–286). Mommsen 1887–1888: 3.836–841 agrees with the many ancient sources that explain this collocation as referring to two groups—an original one of patricians and a later one enlisted from non-patricians (see esp. Fest. p. 254 M; Paul. Fest. p. 7 M; Plut. QR 58; for the asyndeton see Adams 2021: 252–254, who summarizes contrary views).

me et vestra dignitas et frequentia equitum: The juxtaposition of Cicero (*me*) with the senate and the *equites* serves to unite them in their common cause. The sense of unity between senators and *equites* is further reinforced by the use of *et... et* and the singular number of the accompanying verb (*commosset*; cf. OLS 1: 1252). Cicero often employs this type of juxtaposition, which proves to be particularly common in the speeches *post reditum*, as he seeks to re-establish a broad base of support after exile. I offer a small selection of examples; the first two, as here, are from the opening sentence: *p. red. in sen.* 1: *si, patres conscripti, pro vestris immortalibus in me fratremque meum liberosque nostros meritis parum vobis cumulate gratias egero*; *p. red. ad Quir.* 1: *me fortunasque meas pro vestra incolumitate otio concordiaque devovi, ut, si meas rationes umquam vestrae saluti anteposuissem...*; *dom.* 147: *si dis immortalibus, si senatui, si populo Romano, si cunctae Italiae, si provinciis, si exteris nationibus, si vobismet ipsis [sc. pontificibus]... gratum et iucundum meum reditum intellegitis esse, quaeso obtestorque vos, pontifices, ut me....* For a similar technique, by which Cicero unites himself with the Roman people, senate, and *pontifices* against Clodius, see 11n (*primum... deinde... postea*).

By using abstract nouns to describe people—or in this case groups of people (senators and *equites*, respectively)—Cicero allies himself not only with these persons, but also with their moral stature and enthusiasm (*dignitas, frequentia*). Lebreton 1901: 38–42 discusses many examples of this trope.

Although Cicero refers to himself in the opening sentence in oblique cases (*me; mihi*, where it acts as agent), both words occupy emphatic first position in their cola, and he appears as the subject of the main verb (*putavi*). The sentence then closes as it had opened, with a *cum* clause. In a grammatical contrast, however, this final subordinate clause introduces Clodius in first position in the nominative (*is*), and he becomes the grammatical subject of the last four verbs of the sentence (*impediret, navaret, venierat, venditaret*). The effect is to syntactically pit Cicero, the senate, and the *equites* against the actions of Clodius, with

Cicero's decisive action placed concisely in the center between these opposing camps (*putavi mihi reprimendam esse P. Clodi impudicam impudentiam*).

quibus senatus dabatur: This technical expression glosses the preceding *praesentium* by explaining how the *equites* could have attended the previous day's senatorial meeting, since non-senatorial members may not normally proceed farther into the curia than the *vestibulum* (e.g., Liv. 2.48.10, Val. Max. 2.1.9, Plin. *ep.* 8.14.5). The phrase *alicui senatum dare* is also regularly applied to extraordinary meetings held for generals holding *imperium* or for foreign legates (at the temple of Bellona; Fest. p. 519 M). If the proper noun *Syro* later in the sentence is an ethnic term rather than a cognomen, he may be a representative of a Syrian delegation (see note below). For parallels to the expression see *ad Q. fr.* 2.12.2 =SB 16; Sall. *Iug.* 13.9; ThLL V, 1 1680.24–26 (H. Rubenbauer). At least some of these *equites* belong to the *publicani* mentioned below. Cicero had a special relationship with the class of *equites*, to which his family belonged; see especially *Rab. Post.* 15 (with Siani-Davies 2001: 153–154); *Phil.* 6.13; Q. Cic. *pet.* 3, 50; Plin. *nat.* 33.34.

P. Clodi: For the reference to Clodius by *praenomen* + *nomen*, see 7n (*Milone*).

impudicam impudentiam: Just as he had done for both the senate (*dignitas*) and *equites* (*frequentia*), Cicero characterizes Clodius at his first appearance with an abstract noun, in this case accompanied by a descriptive adjective. As Wolf 1801: 307 observes, forms of *impudicus* tend to denote physical unchastity, those of *impudens* mental, so that the combination represents a form of syllepsis that can be rendered as something like "unchaste scurrility" (for this particular combination, cf. *Catil.* 2.25, where *pudor* contrasts with *petulantia*, *pudicitia* with *stuprum*; Wölfflin 1881: 273 catalogues the pairing throughout antiquity). The concepts of *impudentia* and *impudicitia* form a leitmotif of the speech (8, 30, 43 and in particular 9 [*pudorem pudicitiamque*]), and are a standard feature of Cicero's invective against Clodius (cf. *Sest.* 73, with another contrast of mental and physical manifestations: *illum amentissimum et profligatissimum hostem pudoris et pudicitiae*; *Mil.* 77; Langlands 2006: 298–305).

At 4, 22, and 37 Cicero again uses the negative prefix *in-/im-* to characterize Clodius's behavior as the negative of what is proper; in this instance Cicero represents Clodius as antithetical to *pudor*, an emotion that acts in Rome as a check on socially reprehensible behavior (Kaster 2005: 28–65). The concept of *pudor/pudicitia* has particular relevance for Cicero who, in contrast with other treatments, places special emphasis on the role of *pudicitia* in the lives of "politically active men rather than women or young people" (Langlands 2006: 281). The sexual connotations of the charge of *impudicitia*, indicating that Clodius's "masculine inviolability had been compromised" (Williams 2010: 191), are picked up at the close of the sentence.

publicanorum causam: The *publicani* were private individuals contracted by the senate to carry out various functions on behalf of the state, in this context to collect taxes in the provinces. The case referred to here likely involves Aulus Gabinius, a frequent target of Ciceronian invective (2n). As governor of Syria, he had a long-standing conflict with the *publicani* with whom Cicero had been involved around the same time as *har. resp.* (*prov. cons.* 10–12 with Grillo 2015: 135–136; *Pis.* 41; *ad Q. fr.* 2.12.2=SB 16, 3.2.2=SB 22; Dio 39.59.2). For Clodius's possible motivations in opposing the *publicani* on this occasion see Tatum 1999: 218–219.

stultissimis interrogationibus: As curule aedile, Clodius had a right to participate in cross-examination at a senate meeting (Mommsen 1887–1888: 3.942–944).

** *P. Tullio Nisyro*: The word divisions in the major manuscripts support the reading *P. Tullioni Syro* (tollioni **P¹**; siro **H**), but the form of the name is objectionable. Kajanto 1965: 203–205 includes no instance of the cognomen *Syrus* and records very few cognomina from demonyms of the Middle East. As a result Lenaghan 1969: 49 suggests that *Syrus* is not a cognomen but an ethnic referring to Syrian origins, with the epithet arising "as an insult merely because [Clodius] represented their interests." He cites as parallel Cicero's reference to Piso as a Syrian slave (*Pis.* 1; at *prov.* 10 Syrians are a "tribe born for servitude"; cf. 5n on Aelius Ligus). Further support that *Syrus* does not refer to ethnicity may be found in the fact that ancient sources specify that foreign legates could only meet with the senate outside the city walls (Willems 1885: 2.485; Mommsen 1887–1888: 3.959), whereas the previous day's meeting is explicitly said in the next section to have taken place in the *curia*. Shackleton Bailey 1991b: 44 counters less convincingly that the man is indeed Syrian and that *P. Tullioni* is corrupted from a Greek form such as *Pantoleoni*. Solin 1987: 521–522 concurs with Shackleton Bailey that "a gentile name *Tullio* would be a monster" and offers the reading adopted here, *Nisyrus* being an otherwise unattested cognomen deriving from the name of the Aegean island. Solin's suggestion, which relies simply on a different word division, offers the least objectionable solution.

navaret operam: "Devoting himself to the cause of (+ dative)." The verb *navo*, with *opera* as its direct object, is largely restricted to this idiom; *ThLL* IX, 1 245.74–246.38 (I. Hajdú).

totus venierat…venditaret: Cicero frequently accuses Clodius and other opponents of "selling" political favors for financial gain (46, 48, 52; *dom.* 24). The additional emphasis on his doing so "wholly" would seem to allude to the sexual misconduct implied in *impudicam impudentiam* (on possible sexual connotations of *totus* see Adams 1982: 151). For *vendito* used of prostitutes see *OLD* s.v. 1b and especially *Sest.* 18 (of Gabinius), where Cicero uses the verb to indicate both sexual and political corruption.

hominem furentem exsultantemque: The singular form of the noun *homo* can function as a demonstrative pronoun in early comedy (Lindsay 1907: 45), often with a derisive tone as in English "that guy" (*ThLL* VI, 3 2882.13–58

[C. O. Brink]). The pejorative connotations persist in Ciceronian oratory, where the noun *homo* is normally accompanied by adjectives denoting negative characteristics (*homo improbus*), the principal exception being those that mark birth (*homo novus, Romanus*); by contrast, adjectives describing positive characteristics, especially of statesmen, normally accompany *vir* (Landgraf 1914: 115; KS 2: 1.226–227; Santoro L'Hoir 1992: 10–12, 21–28; for exceptions see Adams 2021: 17–18). The noun *homo* describes Clodius three times in *har. resp.* 8 alone, and applications to him elsewhere are numerous (e.g., *Sest.* 89: *praestantissimus vir profligatissimo homini*; *Mil.* 89: *homo effeminatus fortissimum virum*; both in contrast with Milo). The adjective *furentem* begins the characterization of a crazed Clodius that receives elaboration in the next section; references to Clodius's madness will recur throughout the speech, climaxing in his personification as a tragic Fury (nn. on 2, 39). As noted above, in Cicero's use of noun and adjective pairs one word tends to be abstract, the other concrete. In this instance, the adjectives describe in hendiadys a mental (*furentem*) and physical (*exsultantem*; 39n) state ("riotous madness"); cf. the nouns immediately below—*impetum gladiatoris ferociamque*—in which *impetus* has greater physical associations, *ferocia* more emotional ("vicious attack").

continui…compressi: The preverbs associated with Cicero in this sentence echo *commosset*, underscoring the impression of Cicero as presenting a united front and being thorough in his actions (*OLD* s.v. *con-*). These forms contrast with the negative *im-* compounds with which Clodius is associated (*impudicam impudentiam*; *impediret*; *ignarus*; cf. *impetum*), whereas the only use of an *in-* prefix regarding Cicero describes his threats to prosecute Clodius (*intendi, inceptis*).

periculum iudici intendi: Literally, "I threatened the test of a trial" (*Mur.* 3: *periculum iudici praestare*). For the judicial sense of *intendere* see *ThLL* VII, 1 2115.68–82 (P. Nielsen). Clodius had been accused *de vi* by Milo twice in the previous year (7) and it is likely that this charge of Cicero's, which seems never to have been formally issued, would have been similar.

duobus inceptis verbis: Literally, "with two words begun." Cicero alludes to the previous day's exchange with Clodius no less cryptically at 7: *voce tantum attigi legum initium et iudici* ("I used my voice to just touch upon the onset of legal proceedings"; see too nn. in section 7 on *etiam nunc inlaqueatus iam omnium legum periculis* and *arma iudiciorum atque legum*, both of Clodius). These later mentions imply that the "two words" threatened litigation and hence initiated some type of legal action. But what are the precise two words that Cicero has begun to say that could so effectively silence the raging Clodius?

Before turning to possible legal meanings, it will be helpful to consider the phrase's syntax and semantics. The adjective *duo*, to begin with, must denote a specific two words, rather than an indeterminate number, as in English "a few" (for this, the adjective *tres* is conventionally used: Otto 1890: 366–367, Sutphen

1901: 385–386). Among the several cases listed by F. Vollmer where *duo* indicates an approximate number another value is always added, as in "two or three" or "two or more" (*ThLL* V, 1 2247.65–82). By contrast, and unsurprisingly, parallels exist for the phrase *duo verba* referring to precisely two words (Cic. *Quinct.* 53: *haec...duo verba...*: *"quid agis?"* and, in a legal metaphor, Ov. *am.* 3.14.49, where *duobus...verbis* refers to *"non feci"*). This lexicographical likelihood that *duo* means "two" is supported by the type of hyperbaton found in the ablative absolute phrase, by which the predicative *inceptis* intervenes between the attributive adjective and its noun (*duobus...verbis*). As a result, the word *duobus* receives focus (von Albrecht 1989: 62; Powell 2010: 176–177), thereby further affirming that *duobus* represents an exact number rather than a general approximation.

A second issue involves *inceptis*, which occurs only here in Cicero as an adjective: how does one "begin" two separate words? Markland 1745: 332 uses the phrase as evidence that our author is not Cicero, who "would rather have said, *duobus primis verbis*" (cf. *fam.* 9.19.1=SB 194). Since, however, Cicero is undoubtedly the author, the sense of *inceptis* must be confronted. Two possibilities suggest themselves. First, it could mean "after having begun to say two words," at which point Cicero stops from what would have been a longer remark; if this is the case, it would be sheer guesswork to recover the actual words spoken, or begun. An alternative is that the phrase means "having started to say *the* two words," that is, Cicero spoke a recognizable two-word formula. This possibility well explains the meaning of *inceptis*—you can "begin" to say a known two-word phrase, whereas the participle is less likely to be used for just any two words. The fact that Cicero specified that he spoke two words—no more, no less—further supports this hypothesis. If so, then three probable interpretations present themselves:

1. Cicero uttered a Roman name—presumably *praenomen* + *nomen*, and in this case a form of *Publius Clodius*—in the procedure known as *nominis delatio* (Lenaghan 1969: 49; cf. 72). Greenidge 1901a: 461 n. 2 collects all Ciceronian references to this procedure, which takes place before the praetor presiding at a trial, and concludes that it involves a formal step in an accusation. It is, however, not clear that the name of the accused plays a crucial role in this process. The sole indication that it involves the express mention of a name occurs at *Lig.* 1, where Cicero seems to quote, albeit sarcastically, the charge against Ligarius as "Quintus Ligarius was in Africa" (*novum crimen...Q. Tubero detulit, Q. Ligarium in Africa fuisse*). So while the name of the accused plays a role in bringing a case before the praetor, it is unclear how we are to imagine Clodius to have interpreted an intention on Cicero's part to commence litigation simply on the basis of hearing the orator utter his name, in particular since the *nominis delatio* does not occur until after the commencement of legal proceedings (*postulatio*).

2. A second possibility is that Cicero was threatening to initiate a prosecution before the *comitia centuriata*, probably *de vi* (Lenaghan 1969: 72, citing Greenidge 1901a: 330 n. 2 and Mommsen 1887–1888: 1.195 n. 4, 1899: 168 n. 5). In 57 Clodius had been accused twice, probably *de vi*, with neither case coming to court (7n). Gelzer 1939: 945, however, counters that Cicero's references to a *iudicium* and *leges* (1, 7) indicate that Cicero must be threatening prosecution in a *quaestio*, and not before the *comitia centuriata*.

3. I suggest a third option, namely that the *duo verba* represent a common legal formula, either *in ius* or something such as *in ius voco* (the latter if *in ius* constitutes one *verbum*; for ambiguous evidence from punctuation that a prepositional phrase could have constituted a single word group in classical antiquity, see Wingo 1972: 16, 32; Crawford 1996: 1.35; cf. other evidence from word placement with enclitics such as *-ne*, *-que*, and *-ve* cited by KS 2: 1.583–584). Such a hypothesis corresponds well with Cicero's later reference to this incident at 7 (*voce tantum attigi legum initium et iudici*), where *legum* would refer to actual legislation such as that found as early as the fifth-century Lex XII tab. 1.1: *si in ius vocat, ?ito* ("if a person is summoned to trial, he should go"; cf. Paul. *dig.* 2.4.1: *in ius vocare est iuris experiundi causa vocare*). Variations of the phrase *in ius vocare* occur or are alluded to frequently throughout Latin literature of the Republic (e.g., *Cael.* 1: *quem ipse in iudicium et vocet et vocarit*; Crawford 1996 2: 584–586; a fuller listing in *ThLL* VII, 2 696.32–48 [R. Teßmer]). Passages of special relevance to the context here include Plaut. *Asin.* 480, where in response to the threat "*in ius voco te*," a character responds "*non eo*" ("I am not going"); he is subsequently subjected to physical abuse, much as Cicero's verbal assault here causes Clodius to collapse. For the wide array of contexts in which the procedure of *in ius vocatio* is relevant, see Behrends 1974: 11–14 (11: "Es handelt sich um eine Schlüsselfigur...des gesamten römischen Rechtsganges," 14: "Insgesamt gewürdigt ergeben diese Beispiele, daß die *in ius vocatio* immer schon dann gerechtfertigt war, wenn sie einer der magistratischen Gerichtsbarkeit unterliegende Rechtsfrage betraf"; he counters Weinrib 1968a: 34–35, who believes the process is limited to civil cases).

A weighing of these three possibilities favors the third, namely that Cicero uttered *in ius (voco)* or some analogous formula in order to summon Clodius to legal action. Even if we grant this as probable, a final issue remains. As curule aedile, Clodius could apparently not be brought to trial—this is the clear inference drawn from the fact that Marcellinus, consul-designate, wanted to bring Clodius to trial *de vi* before the aedilician elections for 56 (*Att.* 4.3.3=SB 75) and that Milo used *obnuntiatio* to prevent these elections (Dio 39.7.3; Maslowski 1976: 24; cf. 50n). This immunity, however, does not appear to apply universally to lower magisterial holders of *imperium*, and Varro preserves information of a curule aedile being tried by a citizen in what appears to be a private action (Varro frg. Gell. 13.13.4; Weinrib 1968a: 34). Another possibility is that Clodius could have been forced to abrogate his magistracy in order to be prosecuted, as had Lentulus, praetor in 63, after the discovery of his involvement with Catiline (Weinrib 1968a: 46–51).

I would like to conclude by observing that, regardless of what exactly Cicero is doing here on a legal level, the recounting of this conflict at the speech's opening has a clear rhetorical function. Immediately before presenting an account of how to rationalize a prodigy, he introduces his audience of senators to his own method of argumentation. When reason and violence clash, reason will win out. In contrast with Clodius's irrationality, which rages like the tremors in the earth, Cicero evokes calm by alluding to a stable formulaic text from law, much as the bulk of his later argument rests on the stable religious text of the *haruspices*. Cicero can silence the *furor* of Clodius with just words—with just *two* words, to be precise.

impetum gladiatoris ferociamque: Cicero uses terms designating gladiators to describe Catiline, Clodius, and the Antonii, as well as Clodius's gang (for Clodius, see also 15, *dom.* 81, *Sest.* 55, *Pis.* 19 and 28; full catalogue in Opelt 1965: 136). Since gladiators were normally slaves who were trained to kill, the trope derives particular force from the Roman fear of slaves (22n). The metaphor mirrors the historical situation in the late Republic, when gladiators could be used as bodyguards, such as by Cicero's ally Milo (*off.* 2.58; Ascon. *Mil.* pp. 31.26–32.2 Clark; Lintott 1968: 83–85). For the tendency of Cicero to combine the concrete and abstract in hendiadys ("vicious attack"), see n. above on *hominem furentem exsultantemque*.

compressi: The verb likely has a sexual undertone that derives special irony here from Cicero's ability to silence a violent "gladiator." *Comprimo* "was probably a native Latin euphemism of the educated language" (Adams 1982: 182; *ThLL* III 2157.70–2158.2 [O. Hey]) and its use to describe male-on-male intercourse continues the motif of Clodius's effeminacy introduced by *impudicam impudentiam* (for the same *double entendre*, see, e.g., Plaut. *Cas.* 362, *Rud.* 1073).

2 ignarus qui consules essent: The construction of *ignarus* plus indirect question is first found in Cicero (*Verr.* 2.1.65), who seems to favor it (*ThLL* VII, 1 274.30–58 [C. F. Wiese]). In addition to the literal sense—Clodius is unaware that the current consuls are more severe than Piso and Gabinius had been during his tribunate—Cicero seem to be punning on the idea that Clodius is "unaware of what year it was," since the Romans marked years by consulships (for *consul* as a metonym for "year" see, e.g., Sen. *epist.* 4.4, describing a long life: *inter magna bona multos consules numerat*). Of the two consuls of 56, Gnaeus Cornelius Lentulus Marcellinus (*RE* 228) and Lucius Marcius Philippus (*RE* 76), Lentulus was a long-time ally of Cicero. During the trial against Verres in 70, Cicero describes Lentulus as a patron of the Sicilians by dint of his descent from the Marcelli (*div. in Caec.* 13; *Verr.* 2.2.103, 2.4.53; Ps. Ascon. *div. in Caec.* p. 190.22–24 Stangl). He was a long-standing opponent of Clodius, supporting the prosecutor L. Lentulus Crus in the Bona Dea trial (37n). Later, at the senate meeting of October 1, 57, he had actively backed Cicero's claim to recover his house (*Att.* 4.2.4=SB 74) and continued his opposition to Clodius throughout his consulship (*Att.* 4.3.3=SB 75; *Q. fr.* 2.1.2=SB 5). Perhaps as a result of these actions, Cicero is fulsome in praising Lentulus's oratorical abilities, in particular during his consulship (*pereloquens*; *Brut.* 247). The other consul, Philippus, publicly supported Cicero's causes but seems to have had a more ambivalent relationship with him. Before his consulship, along with his future colleague he supported eliminating obstacles to the prosecution of Clodius (*Q. fr.* 2.1.2=SB 5); at the same time, according to Macrobius, Cicero included Philippus among the luxurious Romans who envied him (Macr. *Sat.* 3.15.6: *piscinarii*; cf. *Att.* 1.19.6=SB 19, 1.20.3=SB 20). In addition to instances in this speech, Cicero publicly praises his consulship elsewhere (*Sest.* 110: *viro clarissimo atque optimo consule*; cf. *prov. cons.* 21, 39), although he qualifies this exuberance in his correspondence (*Q. fr.* 2.5.2=SB 9).

exsanguis atque aestuans se ex curia repente proripuit: The portrayal of Clodius as unaware of the year is continued here by attributing to him stereotypical features of madness—pallor and feverishness—traits elaborated in the next sentence (cf. *ad Q. fr.* 2.3.2=SB 7: *ille [sc. Clodius] furens et exsanguis*). The phrase *se ex curia repente proripuit* further underscores the violent activity of Clodius which ends, as the subsequent account makes clear, with his collapse at the door of the curia.

cum quibusdam fractis iam atque inanibus minis et cum illius Pisoniani temporis Gabinianique terroribus: The addition of two extended prepositional phrases introduced by *cum* breaks the periodicity of the sentence, as they describe Clodius attempting to flee from the senate house accompanied by his own fearful threats (cf. *Catil.* 1.33). The resulting word order creates an image of the threats following in his wake. A close parallel for construction, sense, and word order occurs at Cic. *Font.* 33 (in an extended invective against the Gauls): *vagantur… toto foro* cum quibusdam minis *et barbaro atque immani* terrore *verborum*. See too Sall. *Catil.* 14.1, where the metaphor is made more explicit: *[Catilina] omnium flagitiorum atque facinorum circum se tamquam stipatorum catervas habebat*. The combination of the plural nouns *minae* and *terrores* (as well as the verbs *minor* and *terreo*) occurs often in Latin, particularly in Cicero's speeches (Landgraf 1914: 78).

The adverb *iam* (to be construed with *fractis* and *inanibus*) indicates that Clodius's threats are now ineffectual, since he is no longer under the protection of the men who were consuls during his tribunate (cf. his not knowing the year, above).

illius Pisoniani temporis Gabinianique: Lucius Calpurnius Piso Caesoninus (*RE* 90) and Aulus Gabinius (*RE* 11) were consuls in 58, the year of Clodius's tribunate. In supporting, or at least not actively resisting, the Clodian legislation that effected Cicero's exile they were often the object of Ciceronian invective in the speeches *post reditum*. Their first appearance here is marked by mock-grand language and syntax. First one encounters the hyperbole of *ille*—"that famous" (*OLS* 1: 1099–1100)—which is picked up by *imperio... illo* at 3; the adjective also suggests a time no longer accessible (see *iam* in the previous note). The forms *Pisonianum* and *Gabinianum* have a similar tone. Radford 1902: 96 notes that such adjectival forms, in contrast with the plain genitive, "refer to some act or quality of a person which is assumed to be well-known or notorious, e. g., *Clodianus furor*" (see 57 below, *Fonteiano nomine*). For their history in early and colloquial Latin, see Wackernagel 1926–1928: 2.70–75=2009: 487–492, with the important additions of Löfstedt 1956: 1.107–124, who notes that generally the genitive denotes possession, the adjective the person credited with some achievement (e.g., the *portus Corneli*, built and owned by Cornelius, vs. *aqua Appia* or *colonia Augusta* or *lex Sempronia*). LHS 2: 60–61 offers a concise and balanced summary, noting that the adjectival form often appears "mit einer Nuance des Verehrungswürdigen" (60). The third component signaling sarcasm is the adjective-noun-adjective word order in place of the expected formula *L. Pisone A. Gabinio consulibus* (Caes. *Gall.* 1.6.4). In this particular example of conjunct hyperbaton (the "brave men and true" construction) the second element, *Gabiniani*, as part of a natural pair, is anticipated but postponed (*nat. deor.* 1.95: *et maris deos et feminas esse dicitis*; *fin.* 2.111: *summum pecudis bonum et hominis*; Adams 2021: 220–221). A Ciceronian parallel for the word order and effect occurs in the deliberate artifice of *Mario consule et Catulo* at *Arch.* 5, a speech where Cicero self-consciously employs grandiose rhetoric throughout (Gotoff 1979: 122; cf. *Brut.* 328).

The mocking tone of the passage is underscored by a parallel used later to mark a truly significant period of Roman history (18: *Sullani Cinnanique temporis*). This particular example of the formation is very common in Cicero: forms of *Sullanus* occur twenty-three times in the speeches, of *Cinnanus* five. Contrast the use, only here, of *Pisonianus* and *Gabinianus*, perhaps a humorous coinage of Cicero (*in iudicio Gabiniano* is unnecessarily conjectured at *Rab. Post.* 11; cf. *Rab. Post.* 34: *in iudicio Gabini*).

et ex <u>con</u>surrectione omnium vestrum et ex <u>com</u>itatu publicanorum: As Clodius attempts to flee the senate house, accompanied only by empty threats that trail behind (*cum... cum*), Cicero pursues him in company with the allies noted in the first sentence of the speech. The crazed Clodius is pitted against Cicero, the senate, and the *equites*. The parallel syntax, consisting of the unperiodic addition of two prepositional phrases, reinforces the contrast with the sentence describing Clodius's departure. For the emphatic prefixes (*con-, com-*) see section 1. *Consurrectio* occurs in classical Latin only here and at *Att.* 1.16.4, where again it expresses a group of men rising to support Cicero in opposition to Clodius.

vaecors repente sine suo voltu, sine colore, sine voce constitit: Having described Clodius's sole companions as "threats and terrors," Cicero proceeds to detail the qualities that Clodius lacks. Destitute of his senses (*vaecors*; 19n), Clodius stops his flight, literally as suddenly as it had begun (the first use of *repente* in this section describes his start, the second here his stop). For the transition from madness to a silent and sudden realization of guilt, compare *Catil.* 3.11: *tum ille [Lentulus] subito scelere demens quanta conscientiae vis esset ostendit*.

In a regularly descending tricolon of prepositional phrases in anaphora (6-5-4 syllables), Cicero isolates the three areas that he notes in his treatises as "impossible for us to feign: the face, the expression, the voice" (*de orat.* 1.127: *ea quae nobis non possumus fingere, facies, vultus, sonus*; cf. *fin.* 5.47). This "representation of psychology in terms of physiognomy" (von Albrecht 1989: 41) is characteristic of Ciceronian invective (Corbeill 1996: 14-56, 99-173). For the anaphora of *sine*, compare the description of Cloelius in the *peroratio* of *Cael.* (78: *hominem sine re, sine fide, sine spe, sine sede, sine fortunis*). The stereotypical features detailed here—madness, unusual facial expression, paleness, inability to speak—anticipate Vergil's maddened Sibyl (*Aen.* 6.47, 49-50: *non vultus, non color unus/...rabie fera corda tument.../ nec mortale sonans*; for *non...unus* in the sense "not the same as before" see Horsfall 2013: 104), and for its visibility to the viewer see Sallust's description of Catiline's "perceptible madness" (*Catil.* 15.5: *prorsus in facie voltuque vecordia inerat*), where *facies* denotes one's entire external appearance and mannerisms (Corbeill 2004: 20). Sallust's account also includes Catiline's pallor (*Catil.* 15.5: *colos exsanguis*; cf. *sine colore* here and *exsanguis* above, for which see *ThLL* V, 2 1825.51-1826.16 [P. Schmid]).

cōnstĭtĭt; **deinde re**spexit et, simul atque **Cn. Lentulum consulem a**spexit, cōncĭdit: The sight of his opponent, the current consul Lentulus (2n), returns Clodius to the moment. Lentulus appears to be singled out as the presiding consul, an assumption that assists in dating the speech (Introduction E.2). The description of Clodius's collapse is underscored by four trisyllabic verbs delivered in a quick ABBA sequence in which the related words recall each other through homoioteleuton and rhythm (with two cretics flanking). This closing scene recalls the end of a similarly heated exchange between Cicero and Clodius in the senate in July 61: *[Clodius] magnis clamoribus adflictus conticuit et concidit* (*Att.* 1.16.10=SB 16; cf. 1.16.5: *iudicum vocibus...fractus reus* [sc. Clodius] *et una patroni omnes conciderunt*). Note that in these two earlier passages *concido* describes a figurative collapse, unlike the literal one—*in curiae paene limine*—that Cicero describes here.

concidit in curiae paene limine: As Clodius's ranting was carrying him towards the exit "he collapsed nearly at the threshold of the senate house." The phrase *curiae limen* signifies the border beyond which occurs the private deliberation of the senate (e.g., Liv. 5.7.9; Val. Max. 2.2.1b; Talbert 1984: 154-155).

Despite the unusual hyperbaton, Shackleton Bailey 1991a: 104 takes *paene* as modifying *concidit* ("he almost collapsed"); for which one might compare the unusual postponement of the adverb at *Planc.* 65 (*concidi paene*). *ThLL* X, 1 47.55 (G. Thome), by contrast, correctly understands the adverb as modifying *in... limine*, while noting that *fam.* 7.1.4=SB 24 (*dirupi me paene*) is the only place in Cicero (of c. 300 examples) where postpositive *paene* is separated from the verb it modifies (see too Wolf 1801: 310, Watts 1923: 315, Wuilleumier and Tupet 1966: 33). For hyperbaton of *paene* before its verb, see Petron. 29.1: *paene resupinatus crura mea fregi*.

recordatione, credo, Gabini sui desiderioque Pisonis: For the frequently ironic tone of parenthetical *credo*, see Berry 1996a: 153: "by expressing hesitation and doubt, the word allows Cicero's real feelings to show through" (cf., e.g., *in Clod.* 24, *Vatin.* 25, *Sest.* 110; more generally, LHS 2: 837). Here the aside serves to underscore how powerless and crazed Cicero finds Clodius when not backed by the former consuls; note in particular the play on *vae<u>cors</u>... re<u>corda</u>tione*, implying that his sanity returned upon seeing the current consul, Lentulus. Gallo 1969: 62 notes the irony of *sui* being applied to Gabinius, with whom Clodius is currently in conflict (*dom.* 124; *Pis.* 27; Dio 38.30.2). As above, an unperiodic sentence ends with reference to the consuls of 58.

cuius ego de ecfrenato et praecipiti furore quid dicam?: Except for the verb *dicam*, the entirety of this question is fronted for emphasis before the interrogative pronoun *quid*. Having given a recent instance of Clodius's madness in the senate the day before, an event witnessed by most of his current audience of senators, Cicero pretends that he will expatiate on the topic further but instead simply describes the reaction of a venerable senator. The epithet *ecfrenatus* ("unbridled") originally has literal application to a horse but beginning with early Latin it occurs frequently as a dead metaphor to describe individual people and aspects of their character (*ThLL* V 200.83–202.11 [W. Bannier] has details). Cicero uses the participle in his philosophical treatises to describe madness (*Tusc.* 3.11: *exisse ex potestate <mentis> dicimus eos, qui ecfrenati feruntur aut libidine aut iracundia*) and, earlier in the spring, to characterize Clodius's sister Clodia in language similar to that here (*Cael.* 35: *mente nescio qua effrenata atque praecipiti*). Cicero returns to this imagery toward the speech's close (52).

The conception that a person can be crazed by *furor* and so incapable of self-control dates back as early as the fifth-century Twelve Tables, where a person declared mad (*furiosus*) is grouped with a spendthrift (*prodigus*) as someone who must be handed over to relatives for safekeeping: Lex *XII tab.* 5.7: *si furiosus ?prodigusve? ess⟨i⟩t agnatum gentiliumque in eo ⟨familiaque⟩ ?pecuniaque? eius potestas esto* (Crawford 1996: 2.643–646). Similarly, Cicero in his oratory contrasts *furor* with its opposite, reason (*Catil.* 1.22: *neque enim is es, Catilina, ut te... ratio a furore revocarit*) and in his *Tusculan Disputations* defines *furor* as a "complete blindness of the mind," as opposed to the loss of sanity marked by *insania*, which at least allows the victim to carry out the basic necessities of life (*Tusc.* 3.11; Taldone 1993: 3–4). This correspondence between Cicero's writings and Roman law would indicate that the invective associated with *furor* involves not simply empty verbiage, but could appeal to longstanding biases in Cicero's senatorial audience. *Furor* and its cognates indeed occur frequently in Roman invective, and their harsher connotations than those of apparent synonyms such as *insania/insanus*, *amentia/amens*, or *dementia/demens* lend them a greater political valence (Taldone 1993: 9), as evidenced by the fact that Cicero favors these terms to describe his fiercest opponents and their adherents, in particular Catiline (17 percent of uses) and Antonius (16 percent), but with the majority of occurrences applied to Clodius and the *Clodiani* (51 percent; figures from Achard 1981: 518, who does not include related words such as *furia*, *furialis*, *furibundus*, *furo*). The term particularly suits Clodius in this speech, with its leitmotif that the gods are invested in punishing through madness those guilty, like Clodius, of directly violating the gods (39n). For the related proper noun *furia*, see 4n.

** **an potest**: (*aut potest* **GEH**, omitted by **P** and Lambinus: *haud potest* recent codices). *An* is a conjecture of Peterson (adopted by Maslowski), who suggests haplography after the preceding -*am*. *An* frequently elaborates on a preceding initial question, as here (*ThLL* II, 4.67–83 [F. Vollmer]; see too 17, 38, 51). Lambinus 1566: 2.704=1830: 263 notes against *haud* of the later tradition that a question is rhetorically more effective than a statement.

an potest gravioribus a me verbis volnerari quam est…a gravissimo viro, P. Servilio, confectus ac trucidatus: When the particle *an* introduces a direct question, usually raised abruptly, a negative answer is expected (KS 2: 2.517–520). Cicero uses the metaphorical notion of wounding through invective again at 4 (*volnerati*) and elsewhere throughout his corpus: "people want criminals to be wounded with something stronger than a joke" (*de orat.* 2.237: *facinerosos maiore quadam vi quam ridiculi vulnerari volunt*; *nat. deor.* 3.91: *Archilochi versu volneratus*; *Catil.* 1.9; *ad Q. fr.* 3.2.2=SB 22). Dyck 2008: 84 conjectures that the metaphorical usage originates with Cicero. Note the brachylogy, by which the fuller and more logical expression *quam illis verbis quibus* is truncated ("do you think I am able to wound him with words more authoritative than [by those words by which] he was cut down and snuffed out by that ultimate authority, Publius Servilius?"). While brachylogy is a common rhetorical device and as natural here in English as in Latin, the effect in this instance is particularly dramatic, as the grammar undergoes a distinct shift from Clodius being possibly wounded by *words* spoken by Cicero to his being in fact slaughtered by Servilius himself. Servilius's sternness seems to have been the source of rumors at this time; jokes circulated that he had himself been flogged by his father (Quint. *inst.* 6.3.25, 48).

est statim in facto ipso: For the sequence -*st st*- see 20n (*AVDITVS EST STREPITVS CVM FREMITV*). The hiatus after *est* caused by the consonant combination highlights the already emphatic word *statim*. Clodius was verbally abused by Servilius the previous day after being caught "in the very act" (cf. *inv.* 2.16: *ex facto ipso*, 2.38; Tryph. *dig.* 50.16.225: *ipso facto fugae*), which Cicero portrays as more effective than his own attempts the next day. The position of the intensifying adjective *ipse* varies among authors, with post-positive placement rare in Caesar (3 vs. 39) but very common in Cicero (345 vs. 544; Marouzeau 1922: 186–187).

P. Servilio: As pontifex since 76, Publius Servilius Atia Isauricus (*RE* 93) would have witnessed Clodius's trial for sacrilege in 61 and been a judge in the matter of Cicero's house the previous September. At the time of this speech he was "perhaps the oldest consular, certainly the oldest active consular" (Lenaghan 1969: 56). Cicero links himself with Servilius through linguistic echoes, with the repeated stress on the "weight" of authority contrasting the unpredictable recklessness of Clodius (*gravioribus a me verbis* >< *a gravissimo viro…gravitatem*). Cicero depicts *gravitas* as a standard characteristic of Servilius (*Flacc.* frg. Schol. Cic. Bob. 8, *p. red. in sen.* 25, *p. red. ad Quir.* 17, *Sest.* 130, *prov. cons.* 22).

paene divinam: Although Cicero frequently uses *divinus* to describe a human being or human traits (*ThLL* V, 1 1624.11–1625.7 [A. Gudeman]; Cole 2013: esp. 18–62), he apologizes for both uses of the metaphor in *har. resp.*, here with the adverb *paene*, perhaps because of the divine circumstances underlying the speech (6: *quasi divino munere*; but cf. 19 *divinitus*). Intriguingly, all examples from the speeches in which Cicero apologizes for metaphorical *divinus* occur after exile (*p. red. ad Quir.* 2, *Marcell.* 1, *Phil.* 2.39, 9.10, with *paene*; *p. red. ad Quir.* 7, *p. red. in sen.* 25, *Mil.* 21, 44, *Phil.* 3.3, with forms of *quidam*), the sole exceptions being in *Arch.*, where it describes characteristics of poets (15 [*prope*], 18 [*quodam*]).

coniecerit inimicus: By using both a subjunctive of characteristic and a generalizing third-person verb ("the weapons that an enemy may have cast"), Cicero makes clear that he is not the only person opposing Clodius.

quae collega patris emisit: Clodius's father, Appius Claudius Pulcher, held the consulship with Servilius in 79 (26n). For the invective motif of members of the elite, and in particular Clodius, not living up to their ancestors, see 27, 38; Craig 2004: 190, 192, 200–201, 206. The reversion to the indicative form *emisit* where a subjunctive by attraction may be expected underscores the reality of Servilius's opposition (KS 2: 2.173–174).

ēssĕ vĭdĕāntūr: The favored clausula of resolved cretic + trochee brings to a close the strong and violent metaphorical language and affords a transition to the next part of the speech. The cretic + trochee clausula, including resolutions, comprises 28.42 percent of all clausulae in Cicero's speeches, and 35.41 percent of those in *har. resp.* (Keeline and Kirby 2019: 175–176). Of resolved forms, the one used here is by far the commonest, with Zielinski recording that it occurs throughout the speeches in 48.6 percent of this clausula type (772/1594;

Zielinski 1904: end table, n. p.). The sequence is not favored by other authors except Quintilian, which may help explain why Cicero's preference for this resolved form of his favored clausula became notorious among later writers. In Tacitus's *Dialogus* the interlocutor Aper remarks: "I don't want to make fun of [Cicero's] practice of ending every third sentence in all his orations with *esse videatur*" (23.1: *nolo inridere… illud tertio quoque sensu in omnibus orationibus… positum "esse videatur"*; cf. Quint. *inst.* 9.4.73, 10.2.18). Aper's claim is grossly hyperbolic; Keeline 2018: 256 n. 90 provides a reasonable explanation for this misperception.

3–5

The repetition of *hesterno die* from the speech's opening signals that the introductory narrative has come to an end. Cicero now turns from the events of the previous day to offer an impressionistic account of the historical reasons for his enmity toward Piso, Gabinius, and Clodius, all of whom present as great a danger to the state as they do to Cicero himself.

The section introduces an *anticipatio*, foreseeing possible objections to Cicero's current reasons for speaking (Lausberg 1998: §855). This technique, which later declaimers will employ to a fault (Quint. *inst.* 4.1.49–50), is particularly prominent in Cicero's speeches *post reditum*, as witnessed by the openings of *p. red. in sen.*, *Sest.*, *Cael.*, *prov. cons.*, and *Balb*. Here the technique differs slightly since, rather than countering a hypothetical objection, Cicero addresses those who found fault with his actions from the previous day, asserting that they were rational (*mei facti rationem*) when compared with Clodius's irrational behavior at the same time (2: *in facto ipso*).

The notion that a wise man (*sapientis hominis… ratio*) should be able to control his emotions of indignation or anger (*dolore… iracundia*) is a common trope in the later philosophical works of Cicero (e.g., *Tusc.* 4.34–57). In denying that he was carried away by *iracundia*, Cicero further recalls the notion that *iracundia* describes a constant condition or proclivity ("wrathfulness"), whereas *ira* denotes an outburst ("anger"); see *Tusc.* 4.27–28, Sen. *dial.* 4.4. In contrast with this philosophical ideal, the orator may display controlled anger in order to convince an audience of his sincerity, and it is this practice to which Cicero appeals here (cf. *de orat.* 2.189 [Antonius], *orat.* 132 [Crassus]; Kaster 2006: 118–119). How properly to control these emotions constitutes a recurrent motif in the *exordia* of other speeches delivered soon after exile, e.g., *Sest.* 4: *itaque si aut acrius egero aut liberius quam qui ante me dixerunt, peto a vobis ut tantum orationi meae concedatis quantum et pio dolori et iustae iracundiae concedendum putetis* etc.; *prov.* 2: *non parebo dolori meo, non iracundiae serviam* (of Piso and Gabinius); see further Narducci 1997: 55–66. In these passages, *iracundia* is paired, as here, with *dolor*, to which Cicero makes frequent appeal in *har. resp.* to denote the justified reaction to an injustice (see esp. nn. on 4, 43). In a similar passage at *dom.* 97, Cicero again mentions how his critics interpret his strong feelings of *dolor* as a lack of wisdom (*sapientia*). In a private letter (*Att.* 4.2.2=SB 74), he tells Atticus that it was in fact *dolor* that enhanced his eloquence when delivering that speech.

illis...qui hesterno die...arbitrabantur: Wolf 1801: 311 legitimately queries who these *illi* could be if in fact on the day before, as Cicero just claimed, the assembled senate and *equites* had joined him in his indignation (but see 17n). While such inconsistency could surely be paralleled in Cicero, the imperfect tense of *arbitrabantur*, to which Wolf also objects, may be intended to suggest that criticism of his behavior had been continuing since the close of the previous day's meeting up until the current session of the senate.

nihil feci iratus, nihil impotenti animo, nihil non diu consideratum ac multo ante meditatum: In a mannerism characteristic of his mature style, Cicero simultaneously suggests and violates parallelism. The familiar structure of a rising tricolon (6 + 8 + 17 syllables), here with anaphora of *nihil*, is varied by the use of three different grammatical constructions—a participle modifying Cicero, the subject of *feci* (*iratus*); a second modifier of Cicero, this time an ablative of manner (*impotenti animo*); a long participial phrase modifying *nihil*, the direct object of *feci*, but referring to Cicero's actions (the tricolon concludes with the favored clausula of resolved cretic + spondee—ā̆ntĕ mĕdĭtātūm). The inconcinnity between a *prima facie* clear rhetorical structure and a variable grammar allows Cicero to focus on his (non)actions without offering a rote and predictable list. At the same time, the careful crafting of the sentence underscores the meaning: then as now, nothing was reckless, but everything the result of careful planning. Gotoff 1979 offers a practical analysis of Cicero's stylistic *variatio* as it is employed throughout the course of an entire speech.

ego enim me, patres conscripti, inimicum semper esse professus sum duobus: The inferential particle *enim*, in its normal function of giving the grounds for a previous statement, introduces the expectation that Cicero will explain that he "was always an enemy" to Clodius. As a result the word *duobus*, already in an unexpected position at the end of the clause, comes as a surprise. The subsequent relative clause clarifies that Piso and Gabinius are meant (2n). For the use of *duo* to mean "those two" without an additional modifier see Shackleton Bailey 1979: 267.

qui me, qui rem publicam cum defendere deberent, servare possent: Syntax and word order provide a clear example of Cicero identifying himself with the state, as both he and the republic are the direct object of what the two consuls should and could have done, but did not. This identification is especially common in the post-exilic corpus (e.g., *p. red. in sen.* 34, 36; *dom.* 99; *Sest.* 15: *intentus est arcus in me unum..., re quidem vera in universam rem publicam*, 31; and note on 3 below [*primo...deinde...postremo*]; of the many secondary discussions of this trope see esp. May 1988: 93–105, with a generous selection at 190 n. 18; Nicholson 1992: 107–110; Kaster 2006: 27–31). Lenaghan 1969: 58

provides parallels from the *post reditum* speeches for "this motif of the consuls, who not only do not defend Cicero, but even actively work against him" (e.g., *p. red. in sen.* 10, 32–33; *p. red. ad Quir.* 21; *dom.* 2; *Sest.* 24–25, 42; *prov. cons.* 2; Kaster 2006: 171–172).

ipsis insignibus illius imperi: The material *insignia* signifying the authority of the consul include especially the *fasces*, as well as perhaps the *toga praetexta* and the twelve lictors who acted as bodyguard, but Cicero is probably considering immaterial qualities such as counsel and loyalty as well (see *Pis.* 23). Lenaghan 1969: 58 aptly notes the emphatic alliteration, which is typical of Cicero's prose writings of the late 50s, a feature perhaps attributable to his active interest in poetry at the time (von Albrecht 2003: 105).

primo...deinde...postremo: Following a tricolon of embedded *cum* clauses of varying length and containing three different finite verbs, the first three main verbs of the relative clause are given in three brief isocola (6/6/6) in homoioteleuton with the direct objects being *me* and *rem publicam*, as anticipated by the position of these nouns before the initial *cum*. Wolf 1801: 311 accuses his alleged forger of sloppy writing, noting that, although the object of these three verbs are both *me* and *rem publicam*, he seemingly forgot how the syntax of the clause began and so changed the object of the final verb to himself alone, accompanied by the state (*una cum re publica*). Such examples of anacolutha would seem natural for a text written as if spoken, but they in fact occur with surprising infrequency in Cicero's orations, and I have not discovered a parallel for this type, where a direct object of the verb is forgotten (for various other types, see 61n; *Verr.* 2.4.33; Nisbet 1939: 192–193; Berry 1996a: 259; Ramsey 2003: 136, 235–236, 309, with comments of Mayer 2005: 199–201; and, generally, LHS 2: 729–732, who note that anacolutha are most common in Cicero's philosophical treatises). In this instance, the allegedly mistaken change from *rem publicam* to *una cum re publica* allows Cicero to stress the underlying point of the sentence, that is, the equation of himself with the state.

praemiis nefariae pactionis: The ablative *praemiis* supplies the attendant circumstances that informed the actions of Piso and Gabinius ("enjoying the rewards of a wicked alliance"). Cicero refers dozens of times in his orations to how the awarding of the provinces of Macedonia and Cilicia (later Syria) to Piso and Gabinius, respectively, was facilitated by Clodius in exchange for their support of his actions while tribune (see 47, 58; *LPPR* 393–394; Tatum 1999: 152–156 provides context). Such extraordinary appointments were not unusual (Kaster 2006: 172–173); Cicero had himself argued for special provincial commands for Pompey in 66 (*Man.*) and for Caesar about a month after *har. resp.* (*prov. cons.*).

**pactionis is a certain conjecture of Naugerius for *factionis* of the codices (cf., e.g., *Sest.* 69: *provinciarum pactione*). *ThLL* X, 1 24.72–76 (F. Fröhlke) records other instances of manuscripts confusing the two words.

suo ductu et imperio cruento illo atque funesto: The phrase *ductu et imperio* provides another pairing of concrete + abstract in hendiadys ("powerful leadership"), and its appearance in encomiastic military contexts underscores the irony here (Plaut. *Amph.* 196; *CIL* 1.626; Liv. 40.52.5, quoting an inscription). Elsewhere in the speeches, *ductus* appears in this sense only at *Man.* 61, to describe Pompey's past military exploits. For more generous assessments of these two men's military careers as proconsul, see Nisbet 1961: 172–180 (Piso) and Sanford 1939: 80–88 (Gabinius).

Cicero normally avoids *atque* before a consonant; here and elsewhere in the speech its presence provides a desirable rhythm at colon-end: *ātquĕ fūnēstō* rather than the series of long syllables that would have been produced, with elision, by *et* or *ac* (Nisbet 1990: 355; Berry 1996a: 53–54, with bibliography; Hutchinson 1995, esp. 485–490; for an exception in *har. resp.* see 18n).

qui quae…supplicia neque a sociorum moenibus prohibere neque hostium urbibus inferre potuerunt, excisionem, inflammationem, eversionem, depopulationem, vastitatem, ea: The pronoun *qui*, while most easily construed as a connecting relative, nevertheless picks up a sequence from the previous sentence, where two clauses introduced by *qui* also describe the actions of the former consuls, and so this last clause in effect offers the longest part of a tricolon. Immediately following *qui* appears an adjectival relative clause, introduced by *quae* (the juxtaposition is common in Cicero; AG 308 f note). The syntax of this embedded clause is notable for four reasons. First, the noun that acts as "antecedent" to the relative pronoun *quae*, namely *supplicia*, is placed within the relative clause (the "relative-correlative" type described by Probert 2015: 142–144; the long-range hyperbaton *quae* here does not act as a focusing device [Powell 2010: 174–176]). Second, after the finite verb (*potuerunt*)—which normally ends relative clauses—a string of five abstract nouns in the accusative elaborates on the various types of punishments (*supplicia*) that Piso and Gabinius wielded inappropriately. Lengthy appositions that serve to describe a first term occur elsewhere in Cicero, though these sorts of lists of abstractions are more typical of his treatises (e.g., *off.* 1.69: *animi perturbatione, cum cupiditate et metu, tum etiam aegritudine et voluptate nimia et iracundia*; *de orat.* 2.36; *Tusc.* 3.7). Third, these appositional terms receive further emphasis from their ten-word separation from *supplicia*. Finally, the antecedent to *quae* in the main clause, *ea*, follows rather than precedes the relative pronoun, causing this preposed relative clause, detailing the "punishments" wrought by Piso and Gabinius, to receive still more emphasis (KS 2: 2.309–311; Pompei 2011: 519–522, 529–532 considers developmental arguments for the preposed clause as the earliest form of the Latin relative). Each of these syntactic features, which highlight the idea and nature of the *supplicia*, is underscored further by the abstract nouns used, the first four of which are uncommon in the speeches and echo one another in the homoioteleuton of their final three syllables, *-ionem* (*excisio*: two occurrences; *inflammatio*: here only; *eversio*: two occurrences outside *har. resp.*; *depopulatio*: six occurrences). The final noun in the list, *vastitas*, a relatively common word in the speeches (twenty-one occurrences), brings the instances of homoioteleuton to an end as it sums up the action implied in the previous four words: after "demolition, fires, rampage, and general destruction" Piso and Gabinius created a "desert" (*vastitas*) where once stood Cicero's property (cf. 5n).

sua cum praeda: "Along with their looting" (i.e., "and took their plunder"). There is no action noun that is cognate with *praeda* (*praedatio* is post-Augustan; *depraedatio* first attested in *Vetus Latina*), so *praeda* often has the sense of "looting" (*ThLL* X, 2 527.66–528.21 [P. Gatti]; cf. esp. *dom.* 146: *non me bonorum* **direptio**, *non tectorum* **excisio**, *non* **depopulatio** *praediorum, non* **praeda** *consulum…permovet*); the active sense may be helped by the noun's relationship with *pre(he)ndere* ("to take"; Vaan 2008: 487).

meis omnibus tectis atque agris: For the combination of "homes and fields" to denote the total real property of a person, see *nat. deor.* 2.150; cf. too *leg. agr.* 2.9, Verg. *Aen.* 7.812, Liv. 4.59.3. At *dom.* 60–62 Cicero recounts the destruction of his property by Piso and Gabinius, which included plundering items such as the marble columns from his home in Rome and even trees from his Tusculan villa (Manuwald 2021: 156 cites other testimony; for his sense of loss expressed privately see *Att.* 3.20.2=SB 65, *fam.* 14.2.3=SB 7).

4 cum his furiis et facibus: Following the complex series of relative clauses describing the military and consular failures of Piso and Gabinius, Cicero employs strong invective language to demonstrate how their actions have prompted him to "take up war" against them. With this first set of epithets, recalling the madness of Clodius with which the speech opened, Cicero begins his transition to the prolonged attack on Clodius that begins with the next sentence, *in Clodium*.

There is a long tradition in Greek and Roman literature of the Furies, armed with torches, haunting humanity's most notorious sinners against the household, most famously the matricides Orestes and Alcmaeon (Berno 2007, with full bibliography on 69; 39n). The characterization is particularly familiar from epic and tragedy, and in Roman culture from the works of the Neronian and Flavian eras. Cicero's own use of the Furies in his oratory has two particular functions. First, he is well aware of their mythical function as avengers. Although he doubts their reality in his prose treatises (*nat. deor.* 3.46), he adopts a more nuanced attitude in the speeches, as he posits a type of psychological existence for the Furies as the manifestation of a criminal's guilty conscience, a rhetorical topos that goes back at least as far as Aeschines (*Tim.* 190–191, with Berno 2007: 71–77; *S. Rosc.* 67, with Landgraf 1914: 140–141, Dufallo 2007: 38–44; *Sull.* 76; cf. *leg.* 1.40, *parad.* 27; Achard 1981: 240–242 argues that at least part of Cicero's audience would have been less skeptical of their existence). A second association of the Furies begins developing with the *post reditum* speeches, as the notion of the Furies becomes particularly applied to Clodius and his associates (Berno 2007: 83–87). The connection seems to be that, rather than committing crimes within a literal household, these *Clodiani* have committed crimes against the home that is Rome, and have as a result become so crazed by the gods that they come to embody the violent traits of the Furies (Berno 2007: 77–83 teases out the complexity of this characterization). The following includes the most direct references, using the noun *furia* or associated words (supplementing Opelt 1965: 141; Kaster 2006: 192–193): Clodius (*dom.* 99, 102; *Sest.* 33, 39; *Vatin.* 33, 40; *har. resp.* 11; *fam.* 1.9.15=SB 20; *ad Q. fr.* 3.1.11=SB 21; *parad.* 18; cf. *furialis vox* at *Sest.* 106; *har. resp.* 39; *Planc.* 86); Clodius's associates (*Sest.* 109, 112; *Pis.* 26), in particular Gabinius and/or Piso, as here (*Pis.* frg. 3, 8, 91). Finally, the term is used to characterize the followers of Vatinius, a tribune and sometime ally of Clodius (*Vatin.* 31, where the comparison seems due to the funerary context; cf. Tac. *ann.* 14.30.1). Later in his oratory, these adjectives describe Antonius (*Phil.* 2.1, described as *furiosior quam Clodius*; 13.16, 19, 39) and L. Antonius (*Phil.* 11.10). Significantly, at Liv. 21.10.11, when Hanno refers to Hannibal <u>tamquam</u> *furiam facemque huius belli*, Livy sees a need to apologize for the metaphor.

Piso and Gabinius are also described as *faces*, that is, literal "firebrands." The combination with *furia* describes Clodius elsewhere, as a minister to these two consuls (*dom.* 102: *fax ac furia patriae cum urbem Pisone et Gabinio ducibus cepisset, occupasset, teneret*), who are also depicted as supplying torches to Clodius and the Clodiani (*dom.* 63: *consulares faces iactae manibus tribuniciis*; *Pis.* 26: *ardentis faces furiis Clodianis paene ipse consul ministrabas*; cf. *Phil.* 2.48). The associations of the torch are dual. The surface allusion is to those torches traditionally carried by the Furies in the mythic tradition (Horsfall 2000: 306). Although another attribute of the Furies, such as the snake, would be more recognizable to his audience, Cicero chooses to focus on the torches in order to allude to the firebrands that Clodius and his associates wielded in contemporary Rome to set aflame the temple of the Nymphs (*har. resp.* 57; *Mil.* 73), Cicero's house (*dom.* 62), and to wreak general destruction (cf. *har. resp.* 6: *qui templa omnia caede incendiisque terreret*; 39: *ardentis faces in vicinorum tecta iactas*). The consistency of the terms of abuse *furia* and *fax* being applied by Cicero principally to Clodius and his associates, along with the dates of their use, suggests that perhaps the term *Furiae* was adopted by Clodius himself to describe his gang in the period following Cicero's exile. After all, since the role of the Furies was to avenge crimes within the household, one could imagine Clodius exploiting this mythical circumstance to describe his treatment of the traitor (*parricida*) Cicero, whom he succeeded in driving into exile like that paragon of parricides, Orestes (for the popularity of the Orestes story, see 39n). Clodius may also have exploited the fact that the Furies employed their torches not in general destruction, but as an instrument of just punishment. Cicero's insistence on the negative aspects of the Furies could, in other words, be viewed as the returned exile's attempt to distort his opponent's rhetoric for his own purposes.

cum his, inquam, exitiosis prodigiis ac paene huius imperi pestibus: Lenaghan 1969: 60 writes that Cicero employs both *inquam* and *paene* as a double "apology" for the metaphor. Rather, *inquam* emphasizes the demonstrative pronoun *his*, thereby emphatically asserting the identification of Piso and Gabinius as the referents (the use of *his* is not deictic since the consulars will have still been in their consular provinces at the time of this speech). Merguet 1877–1884: 2.713–715 offers numerous instances in which *inquam* emphasizes, as here, a repeated word (contrast 8n), a literary device that *Rhet. Her.* 4.38 calls *conduplicatio*: "*Nunc audes etiam venire in horum conspectum, proditor patriae? Proditor, inquam, patriae, venire audes in horum conspectum?*" (Wills 1996: 65–66); for the use of *inquam* with *hic* in particular, see *ThLL* VII, 1 1784.3–18 (A. Szantyr). It is, rather, the adverb *paene* alone that tones down the potentially harsh metaphor (2n). Note, however, that Cicero does not apologize in this sentence for his use of *fax*, *furia*, or *prodigia* (for reasons, see Introduction C.2; Dyck 2008: 17 notes a similar tendency in *Catil.*). The adverb *paene* here puts further emphasis on the fact of the metaphor, although *pestis* appears in Cicero's oratory elsewhere without any qualifications (several examples at Opelt 1965: 138, including the nearly synonymous *rei publicae pestis* at *har. resp.* 50).

This sentence contains the first mention of a prodigy (*prodigiis*) in a speech that centers on that very subject. It is peculiar, therefore, that the word refers not to literal prodigies but metaphorically to Cicero's opponents, here Piso and Gabinius and, only by association, Clodius. The metaphorical use underscores how the opponent is acting outside the normal bonds of nature in a way not signaled by hostile epithets that describe phenomena of the natural world, such as *pestis*, *pernicies*, or *belua* (Lévy 1998: 147). For the use of *prodigium* to make a political point, see Corbeill 2008 (Opelt 1965: 144, *passim* lists instances of this term and synonyms such as *monstrum*, *portentum* used in invective). In analogy with *furia* and its cognates, Cicero employs *prodigium* in a metaphorical sense in the *post reditum* speeches only to describe Clodius, Piso, and Gabinius, and primarily before an elite audience: Clodius (*Pis.* 9; cf. *in Clod. et Cur.* frg. 21), Piso/Gabinius (*Sest.* 38; *Vatin.* 36; *Pis.* frg. 1). See further the next note.

bellum...inexpiabile: The phrase *bellum inexpiabile* occurs twice in *Philippics* in reference to actual war (13.2, 14.8; other occurrences at *ThLL* VII, 1 1325.66–71 [A. Szantyr]). The recent mention of metaphorical *prodigia*, however, suggests that Cicero alludes here to the literal force of the adjective: the state faces prodigies that must be "expiated" (cf. 57n: *inexpiabili scelere*). On *(ex)piare* as official terminology regarding prodigies see Luterbacher 1904: 55.

neque id [bellum] tamen ipsum tantum quantum meus ac meorum, sed tantum quantum vester atque omnium bonorum dolor postulavit: Cicero concludes his digression on Piso and Gabinius as he had begun, with the theme of justified *dolor*. He once again unites his audience with him against the Clodian faction, as the two parallel constructions of *tantum quantum* equate his indignation with that of the senate (*vester*) and of all members of the elite (*omnium bonorum*). For the connotations of *boni* see 5n.

in Clodium vero non est hodie: With the phrase *in Clodium* Cicero shifts from Piso and Gabinius to introduces a new topic, Clodius. The stress on "today" (*hodie*) underlines a transition from the account of the previous day's activities in the senate with which the speech opened (*hesterno die*) to the current day's senate meeting. Before turning to the haruspical response, however, Cicero emphasizes that his concern about Clodius is long-standing, dating back to his violation of the Bona Dea rites (*illo die*; for the festival of the Bona Dea and the particular incident involving Clodius, see Introduction A.1). What would appear to be a digression, however, in fact contributes to the speech's overall argument since it is this alleged violation that will constitute Cicero's main proof that the *haruspices* refer to Clodius. Accordingly, allusions to this event recur throughout the speech. For the reference to Clodius by his *nomen* alone see 7n.

meum maius odium: The short-range hyperbaton here gives focus to *meum* (Powell 2010: 176–177), in contrast with the *dolor* felt by the senate and other members of the elite with which the previous sentence concluded. Cicero, under the influence of Greek philosophy, later comes to characterize *odium* as *ira inveterata* ("established anger"), which fits well the context here as he increases the stakes from accusations and feelings of *dolor* and *iracundia* to a frank confession of the *odium* that he has felt toward Clodius since the violation of the Bona Dea. The jingle of *Clodium*... *hodie*... *odium* underscores this connection (as does perhaps *illo die*; see Lausberg 1998: §§725–728 on normal conditions for homoioteleuton). For a survey of the development of *odium* and its cognates from indicating a physically adverse reaction (as normally in Plautus and frequently in poetry) to an ethical one (as here), see Skutsch 1910, esp. 231–234.

Lenaghan 1969: 60 cites *Att.* 1.13.3=SB 13 (*nosmet ipsi, qui Lycurgei a principio fuissemus, cottidie demitigamur*) to suggest that Cicero here exaggerates his hostile feelings toward Clodius at the time of the Bona Dea incident. Tatum 1999: 65, however, argues that regardless of how precisely we may characterize Cicero's tone in his correspondence at this time, he nevertheless "evinced sincere concern over the scandal from its very beginning."

illum ambustum religiosissimis ignibus: "Scorched by sacred flames"; a playfully violent metaphor. By Cicero's day, the etymological meaning of *amburo* ("burned on all sides," "scorched") had so developed that the verb could describe complete consumption by fire (*ThLL* I 1877, 31–35 [F. Vollmer]), such as in the cremation of a corpse (coincidentally at *Mil.* 86, for example, of Clodius's own "cremation" in the curia). The reference here is less harsh— Clodius was "scorched" by proximity to sacred fires, presumably those used by the Vestals, who were in charge of conducting a sacrifice during these proceedings (37: *sacrificium*... *quod fit per virgines Vestalis*; for burnt offerings cf. 57: *deorum ignis*... *pervertit* and Brouwer 1989: 349–350). Our own uncertainty over the reference likely matches that of the senators hearing the speech; as

Brouwer 1989: 360 notes, since all our sources for the rites are dependent upon written sources authored by men, "one should suspect conjecture rather than concrete information" when they mention details of the ritual. The reference to Clodius's "scorching," then, is probably best understood as hinting at improprieties about which no one had direct evidence.

This passage marks the first use in the speech of the adjective *religiosus*, which appears numerous times, both in a positive sense (9 [*bis*], 11, 12, 24, 30 [*bis*], 37, 53) and a negative (of Clodius: 9, 22; of Cicero's home 33 [*bis*]; for the double sense see Santangelo 2013: 41–44). The negative use of the adjective may have special resonance in regard to Clodius. Aelius Gallus (*RE* 58), a possible contemporary of Cicero, defined the word as "what it is improper for a human being to do so that, if he does it, he seems to act against the will of the gods" and gives as an example of *religiosus* behavior a man entering a shrine of Bona Dea (Fest. p. 278 M: *quo in genere sunt haec: in aedem Bonae Deae virum introire*).

muliebri ornatu: Clodius allegedly dressed in female attire to attend the Bona Dea festival, which was restricted to Vestal Virgins and elite women (Schol. Bob. p. 85.10–11 Stangl: *matronas honestissimas*). The vivid details of his adornment allow Cicero to imply that it adversely affects Clodius's masculinity (44n). Brouwer 1989: 255 catalogues the sources that indicate how at these rites "not only men are barred... but also all things male are excluded and representations of anything male are to be covered" (epigraphical evidence makes clear that, later at least, the prohibition was less strict; see Brouwer 1989: 258, 377, 384–385). Wiseman 1974: 130–134 provides an evocative reconstruction of the ceremony.

ex incesto stupro atque ex domo pontificis maximi emissum: Cicero employs an unexpected juxtaposition of abstract and concrete expressions to describe the place(s) from which Clodius is "ejected"—from a sacrilegious sexual act and from the home of the *pontifex maximus* (cf. 44: *a stupro*; for *emissum* see 44n). *Incestum stuprum* provides an accurate designation (cf. *Mil.* 13; *dom.* 105: *incesto flagitio et stupro*). According to ancient sources, the special court set up to try Clodius for violating the Bona Dea festival treated the charge of *incestum* (Ascon. *Mil.* p. 45.4–6 Clark; Schol. Bob. Cic. p. 89.23–24 Stangl: *patres conscribti* [sic] *decreverunt de ea re non aliter quam de incestu quaereretur*; for the relevance of *incestum* to this case see Greenidge 1901a: 376–380, 386–389; Tatum 1999: 74–75); because of the novelty of the charge, the way was open to the prosecutors to define the nature of that *incestum*, with *stuprum* here implying that sexual activity was a component (for the vagueness of *stuprum* see 8n). At the same time, the use here of the phrase *incesto stupro* suggests, inevitably, Clodius's incest with his sister(s), which is a common motif of Cicero's speeches *post reditum* (9n), and which we know was brought up at Clodius's trial (Moreau 1982: 168–174, esp. 172); note, however, that *ThLL* VII, 1 895, 51–62 (O. Prinz) cites Ps. Quint. *decl.* for the earliest use of *incestum* in reference to "incest."

The rites of the Bona Dea were held in the house not necessarily of the *pontifex maximus* but of a magistrate with *imperium*, in this case of Julius Caesar as praetor (cf. 37; Plut. *Caes.* 9.7 and Dio 37.45.1: house of consul or praetor; Plut. *Cic.* 19.5: Cicero's house when consul). It is unclear why Caesar's home was chosen. The consuls of 62, it seems, were still in Rome, so it was not simply a matter of choosing the highest-ranking holder of *imperium* (Linderski 1991: 534, *contra* Brouwer 1989: 364). Regardless of the reason, Cicero doubtless includes the detail that Caesar was *pontifex maximus* at the time, rather than a holder of *imperium*, in order to make the affair a more serious religious offense, in particular since Caesar's home, the *domus publica*, was supplied by the state (Lenaghan 1969: 62).

** **tum, tum, inquam**: For *inquam* see note above. Wills 1996: 109 notes the rarity of the gemination of *tum/tunc*. The codices agree in reading *tum, inquam, tum*, which was printed by all editors until Shackleton Bailey 1985: 146 suggested *tum, tum, inquam* with the simple note "Merguet's index, s.v. *inquam*, shows why." And indeed Merguet lists well over seventy examples of a word being repeated before *inquam* (including *prov. cons.* 7: *tum* ... [12 words] ... *tum, inquam*). By contrast, ThLL VII, 1 1782.52 (A. Szantyr) cites only two examples of the repeated word following *inquam*. One is late (Boeth. *c. Eut.* 4.96) and the other *Marcell.* 28: *illa, inquam, illa vita est tua*, where the strongly contrasting phrase **haec tua vita ducenda est** in the previous sentence may in part explain the anomaly (cf. Gotoff 1993: 79).

multo ante prospexi: What Cicero foresaw even before the incident of the Bona Dea is retailed in the following sentence, where *videbam* in emphatic first position picks up *vidi*, and the change in verb tense from perfect to imperfect underscores the expanse of time over which Cicero pondered these imminent dangers.

quanta tempestas excitaretur, quanta impenderet procella rei publicae: Cicero employs frequently in the orations the metaphor of the ship of state threatened by a storm; compare especially the extended metaphor at *dom.* 137, where as here the storm is associated with Clodius: *tu, procella patriae, turbo ac tempestas pacis atque oti, quod in naufragio rei publicae* etc. (cf. *Vatin.* 33: *tempestatem rei publicae, Clodium*; *Sest.* 25 [Piso and Gabinius as *duo rei publicae turbines*], with May 1980; *Pis.* 20–21; *Mil.* 5 [of *contiones*]; 48n). For storm imagery elsewhere in Cicero, see 11n; Fantham 1972: 23–26 (in correspondence), 126–128 (*Sest.*), 158–159 (*de oratore*); Mebane 2022 (orations); and in Greek and Roman antiquity generally Nisbet and Hubbard 1970: 178–179.

Two aspects of the word order deserve mention. First, the short-range hyperbaton *quanta impenderet procella*, a feature that tends to occur "at points of relatively high rhetorical tension," emphasizes "how great" the gusts were by focusing on the quantifier, as often (Powell 2010: 180, 176–177). For the second point, we may compare *Cael.* 59 (*quanta impenderet procella mihi, quanta tempestas civitati*), where in both clauses, as here with *rei publicae*, the expected dative complement is postponed to the end for emphasis. This order also secures the favored rhythm of a double cretic: *[pro]cēllă rēi pūblĭcæ*, with *rei* as monosyllable (LHS 1: 446) as opposed to the double spondee that would have resulted from ending with the expected verb, *impenderet*.

videbam illud scelus tam *importunum*, audaciam tam *immanem*: On *im*-words being associated with Clodius see 1n.

** ***mobilis***: All manuscripts read *nobilis* but there are two principal objections. First, it is normally a term with positive connotations in the speeches. An exception may be *S. Rosc.* 17, where Roscius Capito is described as *plurimarum palmarum vetus ac nobilis gladiator*, with clear intent to discredit him, but the sense of the adjective here is "well known." Clodius is described as *nobilis* at Quint. *inst.* 6.1.25 (of Milo, *qui a se virum **nobilem** interfectum…fateretur*) and by Schol. Bob. p. 111.29–30 Stangl (in preface to its commentary on *Mil.*: *adlato…cadavere **nobilissimi** senatoris et popularis viri*), with no apparent irony in either case. Second, one would not expect an asyndetic list like this to have a middle element with a strikingly different semantic connotation from its companions; as it is, the context does not signal an ironic use of the adjective (as reflected in the translation of Shackleton Bailey 1991a: 105: "a young man of reckless spirit, noble birth, with a hurt to avenge"); cf. *Mil.* 18, where the contrast with *equitem* makes the irony obvious, as does the well-known pun with *nota* at *Cael.* 31: *cum Clodia, muliere non solum nobili sed etiam nota*; see too the clear signals of irony at *Catil.* 2.4: *quos viros, quanto aere alieno, quam valentis, quam nobilis*.

Various attempts at emendation have been offered. Peterson prints in his apparatus "*mobilis* (Drechsler), *nebulonis* (K. Busche; *Rosc. Amer.* 128; *Phil.* 2.74)," to which Maslowski adds "*pleni bilis* (Walter[2] 4); sed cf. *dom.* 46 p. 52, 11." Of these, *mobilis* seems most promising. It is often confused with *nobilis* in codices (*ThLL* VIII 1197.38–39 [H. Wieland]), and Bentley conjectures it for *nobilium* at Lucan. 4.521: *sic cunctas sustulit ardor / **mobilium** mentes iuvenum* (comparing Verg. *georg.* 3.165; endorsed by Housman and Shackleton Bailey). Opelt, however, records *mobilis* as an invective term only for unfaithful male lovers in poetry (1965: 33–34, 200), while she has several references to *nebulo* (used by Cicero twice but as an isolated element, not in a list). A minor objection to the latter reading is that the loss of *nebulonis* is paleographically more difficult to account for than *mobilis*.

For *mobilis* in the speeches, see *Q. Rosc.* 49: *venit ad Cluvium. quem hominem?… **mobilem**? immo constantissimum* (cf. *fam.* 5.1.2=SB 1: Metellus angrily accuses Cicero of being *mobili…animo*; *de orat.* 2.256: *Nobiliorem mobiliorem*, perhaps from a speech [Leeman *et al.* 1989: 277]). In *Q. Rosc.*, however, the context is trustworthiness, which does not have as harsh a connotation as one might wish here. A little more seriously, *mobilitas* caps another tricolon as a disgraceful trait of those wishing to reconcile with Antonius, *Phil.* 7.9: *quid est inconstantia, levitate, **mobilitate** cum singulis hominibus, tum vero universo* *senatui turpius?* For a juxtaposition of strong passion and capriciousness, as here with the adjectives *furentis mobilis* see Sall. *Iug.* 113.1: *plerumque regiae voluntates ut vehementes, sic* **mobiles***, saepe ipsae sibi advorsae* or Sall. *Catil.* 49.4 on *mobilitas* of *equites* concerning whether to trust Caesar. On tribunes characterized by literally quick movement see Corbeill 2004: 107–139, although there are no examples of *mobilis* being used in this context (but note Horace's use of the adjective at *carm.* 1.1.7 to describe their constituency—*mobilium turba Quiritium*). A final consideration in favor of this reading is that the sequence of *furentis, mobilis* continues the metaphor from the previous sentence of Clodius as an unpredictable storm (cf. 46: *illius furentis ac volaticos impetus*); for the imagery, compare *nat. deor.* 2.30: *mundi... fervor... mobilior*, and for *furo/furor* of storms see *ThLL* VI, 1 1625.18–28, 1632.69–77, 1633. 53–57 (H. Rubenbauer), where it is largely poetic, and Plin. *nat.* 32.2, on the *furor* of *procellae*.

READ, hesitantly, *mobilis*.

volnerati: The reference is to the metaphorical wounding that Clodius receives from the words and actions of his opponents ; see nn. at 2 (*vulnerari*) and 8 (*confixum*). Gallo 1969: 66 aptly elaborates on the imagery: "like a beast, which is more dangerous when struck but still in a position to do harm" ("come una belva che, già ferita ma ancora in grado di nuocere, è piú pericolosa"). Cicero refers to his own "wounds" received from Piso and Gabinius, which could only be healed through his recall (*p. red in sen.* 9, 17, 24; *p. red ad Quir.* 15).

non posse arceri oti finibus: The natural interpretation of this phrase ("could not be kept *from* the limits of peace") would make little sense here. Rather, the verb is used in what seems to be its earliest sense to describe containment ("could not be kept *within* peaceful limits"; cf. *arx, arca*, with Vaan 2008: 57). Elsewhere in Cicero, context makes this meaning clear (e.g., *rep.* 6.17.2: *arcens et continens*; *nat. deor.* 2.136: *arcet... et continet*). Caerols Pérez 1995 suggests that Cicero is depicting Clodius as an *adulescens* in Roman comedy, and that *otium* refers not to "peace" but to the pleasures of youth, including the erotic, from which Clodius has emerged into the world of politics. For the construction with the ablative of means (*finibus*) the only parallels with this verb listed in *ThLL* are Fest. p. 334 M: *latebras... quibus arcuerit senem* and Hier. *epist.* 5.2: *ego arreptae solitudinis terminis arceor*.

The use of *otium* recalls Cicero's recent rallying cry of *cum dignitate otium* (*Sest.* 98), in which Clodius is depicted as the greatest threat to political tranquility (Wirszubski 1954, esp. 4–6). See too *dom.* 137, where Clodius is *turbo ac tempestas pacis atque oti*, and *Sest.* 15 *oti inimicus*. For the contracted genitive of second-declension nouns in *-ium* (*oti* rather than *otii*), see KS 1: 451 (inscriptional evidence for the uncontracted form occurs only from the age of Tiberius; 452–453 assesses the Ciceronian material; LHS 1: 424–425 gives the earliest poetic appearance of the uncontracted form, as determined by meter, in Lucretius for adjectives, in Vergil and Propertius for nouns). Later grammarians opt for the uncontracted form as the more regular (Char. *gramm.* p. 89.17 B; Mart. Cap. 3.295; Prisc. *gramm.* 2.296.8–20).

finibus: erupturum: After signaling the end of the sentence through a favored clausula (*[arc]ērī ōtī finĭbūs*=molossus + cretic), Cicero dramatically begins with a verb that proves his point by showing Clodius syntactically bursting outside the bounds of peace: "his crime and audacity could not be kept within peaceful limits. [It] would burst out."

si impunitum fuisset: This periphrastic verb represents in indirect statement an original *si impunitum fuerit*. Cicero relates what he had foreseen in the past.

5 *non multum mihi sane post ad odium accessit*: "Afterward hatred, at least on my part, did not increase much." Cicero rounds out the section with an emphatic initial negator (*non*) and verbal echoes (*odium*; emphatic *meum* answered by *mihi sane, non...maius* by *non multum*). He has portrayed his disdain for Clodius not as a recent development but as longstanding, beginning with the Bona Dea incident, when he foresaw what extremes Clodius could reach. The sentence provides a transition to the next section: the targets of Clodius's own *odium*.

In cataloguing Clodius's offenses at both the human and divine levels, Cicero adopts a sequence that successively allies him with increasingly important elements of Roman society, first the metaphorical values of the state (*severitas, dignitas, res publica*), then the human components of that state (*senatus, equites Romani, omnis bonos, Italiam cunctam*), and finally the *di immortales*, whose will Cicero has designed this speech to explain. The structure of the sequence warrants comment. The overall rhetorical form is a tricolon of descending members with each portion introduced by a negator (*nihil...non...non*) and whose third and concluding member is concisely expressed and clearly signaled (*denique*). Each limb has a slightly varied way of comparing Cicero's situation to others', beginning with a simple antithesis (*nihil...sed*), then progressing to a construction governed by a comparative adverb (*magis...quam*) and then by a comparative adjective (*sceleratior...quam*). Note too the varying ways in which Cicero refers to himself (*contra me...me...in me*). The entire sequence presents a set of key ideas expressed clearly but with elegant variation (cf. 3n).

*odio seve*ritatis, *odio dig*nitatis, *odio rei publicae*: Each member of the tricolon contains seven or eight syllables. Despite this balance, the homoioteleuton of the first two cola unites two key Roman concepts, while the third colon, describing Clodius's disdain for the personified state, combines the preceding two sentiments (cf. 3n above, on *vastitatem*). *Severitas* denotes seriousness accompanied by great moral rigor, an absence of which also characterizes Clodius's sister (27; Hellegouarc'h 1963: 281–282). For the Roman engaged in public life *dignitas* comprises a combination of personal deserts (cf. origin from *dignus*, "worthy"), the ability to wield influence (*auctoritas*), and serious comportment (*gravitas*); see esp. Hellegouarc'h 1963: 388–411 and more recent bibliography at Kaster 2006: 429. For the identification of attacks on Cicero as attacks on the republic, see 3n.

violavit: Cicero's use of this verb recalls Clodius's violation of the Bona Dea, in which context *violare* frequently appears: see 8 (twice), 12, 21, 26, 37 (of other religious violations at 24, 29, 43); *dom.* 112, 140; *Mil.* 59. The verb commonly describes the profanation of sacred objects (*OLD s.v.* 1), occurring three times in *CIL* I² 366, a *lex sacra* from the late third or early second century BCE, to describe violation of a sacred grove.

quam senatum, quam equites Romanos, quam omnis bonos, quam Italiam cunctam: For the list of groups that are progressively larger in size but lower in status, compare the (re)definition of *optimates* at *Sest.* 97 (Kaster 2006: 320; see too *Sest.* 36); a similar list occurs already at *Rab. perd.* 20, *Catil.* 4.15–16. This is not part of the "standard account" but a more pervasive phenomenon. Gunderson 1996: 123–126 notes how the seating in Roman amphitheaters served the ideological function of presenting to the Roman people (in the broadest sense of that term) a certain image of themselves, in which the elite classes (and males in general) were given both a (numerically) disproportionate share and a privileged position. Cicero's standard catalogues perform the same ideological function in verbal form.

Like *dignitas*, the designation *boni* ("all good men") has both a moral and political component, combining the finest qualities of a human being with an astute political mind (Hellegouarc'h 1963: 484–493). Not surprisingly, Cicero uses the term to describe those who have an outlook similar to his own. For his notion of a *consensus bonorum omnium* see Lapyrionok 2008.

sceleratior…scelere: The noun *scelus* and its derivatives have harsher connotations than the English "crime." Related words in PIE suggest that *scelus* derives from the literal sense of making a "false step" (Pokorny 1959: 1.928; Devoto 1933: 238–239 on possible connotations). Petersmann 1996: 672 points out that most words in Latin denoting ethical behavior originally had a concrete meaning and that, analogously, *scelus* originally referred to a literal "crookedness." He observes that from here the noun denoted an act associated with moral pollution and became contrasted with acts marked by *pietas* (cf. Verg. *Aen.* 3.42: "*parce pias scelerare manus*"). Fest. p. 334 M provides evidence for an association with pollution in his note on the portion of the city gate nicknamed the *scelerata porta*, so called because a large body of Romans left Rome through it and were subsequently killed by the Etruscan troops that they met in battle (Rocca 1994: 181–182 discusses similar associations with pollution for the *Campus* and *Vicus Sceleratus*). This resonance is further confirmed in Suetonius, where *sceleratus* is defined as *contaminatus* and *pollutus* (*frg.* p. 289.8–10: *sceleratus est suo aliquo scelere contaminatus vel aliqua contagione pollutus et infamis*; Lennon 2014: 39–41). If such connotations are felt here they would have particular applicability to Clodius, see, e.g., 12, 59; *Mil.* 85 (referring to various cults): *ille omni scelere polluerat… saepe omni nefario stupro et scelere macularat*.

familiaris Catilina: From a minor patrician family that had held high office in the fifth century (*MRR* 1: 58, 62), L. Sergius Catilina (*RE* 23) nonetheless became associated in his early career with major figures like Pompeius Strabo (*CIL* 6.37045=*ILLRP* 515) and Sulla (Sall. *hist.* 1.46). He rose to the praetorship of 68 and subsequent governorship in Africa (Ascon. *tog. cand.* p. 85.3–6 Clark). His career was dogged by prosecutions for *repetundae* and crimes during the Sullan proscriptions, and he was accused of other murders, incest, and *incestum* with a Vestal Virgin (Ascon. *tog. cand.* p. 91.19–23 Clark). Legal issues prevented his standing for consul in 65 (Sall. *Catil.* 18.3); he then ran unsuccessfully in 64 and 63. Following this failure, he apparently plotted a coup towards the end of 63; he was forced to flee and died early the next year in fighting between his supporters and government forces. Cicero suggests at points that there had been an earlier plot as well, but this is now generally disregarded (Seager 1964).

Usually, and probably more historically correctly, Cicero's comparisons of Clodius and Catiline are typological, or expressed in terms of their shared bases of supporters, or both (*Att.* 1.16.9=SB 16; *Sest.* 42; *Pis* 11, 15; *Planc.* 86; *Mil.* 37; *Phil.* 2.10; see Tatum 1999: 142–145, Kaster 2006: 217–218). Clodius prosecuted Catiline for *repetundae* in 65; Cicero later claims this was collusive, though there is no independent evidence, and in fact Cicero had considered joining the defense at the time, so it is hard to read any close tie here (42n). *Familiaris* by itself is, perhaps surprisingly, not a very serious charge, since it can describe in Cicero a wide assortment of interpersonal contacts; for a range of synonyms see *ThLL* VI, 1 252.46–61 (O. Hey). In cases of actual close affiliation, Cicero claims closer ties, such as his sexualization of Catiline's relationship with Gabinius (*p. red. in sen.* 10, 12; *dom.* 62).

a me esse accusandum: The construction of *ab* + ablative with gerundive instead of the expected dative serves to emphasize the agency; see KS 2: 1.730 Anm. 1 and compare 16 (*a iudicibus poeniendam*). Roby 1892: 2.lxxiv–lxxv, §1147, catalogues all instances in Cicero.

stipitem illum qui quorum hominum esset nesciremus, nisi se Ligurem ipse esse diceret: This is thought, generally and probably rightly, to refer to Aelius Ligus (*RE* 83), colleague and ally of Clodius in his tribunate of 58, who as tribune had vetoed a motion for Cicero's recall from exile in July 58 (*p. red. in sen.* 3; *Sest.* 68). Earlier in 56, Cicero had joked that Aelius "stole" his cognomen from the records of the "real" Aelii Ligures (*Sest.* 69). Here, however, the joke seems to lie in taking the name seriously in order to deliberately misread it as an ethnicon (literally "Ligurian"; more ironically at *Clu.* 72; for the type see Corbeill 1996: 82–83, 121), thereby attributing to our Aelius the purported stupidity of a Ligurian (*leg. agr.* 2.95; for Ligurian dishonesty see Cato, *FRHist* 5.34). This type of ethnic humor would have appealed to the prejudices of his elite audience of senators (Vasaly 1993: 191–243). The insult is reinforced by the abusive sense of *stipes*, "stick" or "blockhead," an invective term of lower register, characterized by a *senex* in Terence as a common word to describe a fool (Ter. *Haut.* 876–877: *quidvis harum rerum.../ quae sunt dicta in stulto:*

caudex stipes asinus plumbeus) and occurring in a freedman's speech in Petronius (43.5). Cicero also uses it against Piso (*p. red. in sen.* 14; *Pis.* 19; see further Otto 1890: 332). Lenaghan 1969: 66 states that Aelius was adopted into the Aelii Ligures, seemingly assuming that this is the same person as the Staienus accused of borrowing the cognomen *Ligus* at *Clu.* 72 and *Brut.* 241, but Staienus is a Paetus, not a Ligus.

In the context of the speech, this aside seems to have little point. It probably represents a joke designed to distract the senate from thinking too much about why Cicero, if he saw Clodius as such a threat to the state and gods, has hesitated bringing any of the formal charges that he had promised the previous day.

quorum hominum esset nesciremus: The insult resembles Clodius's gibe in the senate the day before about Cicero's own provincial origins (17: *rogarer cuius essem civitatis*: "I was asked what state I belonged to"). *Quorum hominum* ("to what class of human beings") makes Ligus even less civilized than was Cicero in Clodius's barb, since Clodius assumes that Cicero at least belongs to a state (*civitas*).

quid enim hunc persequar, pecudem ac beluam, pabulo inimicorum meorum et glande corruptum: The basic force of Cicero's insult is clear: "what's the difference between a human being becoming a beast and someone in human form taking on the savagery of a beast?" (*off.* 3.82: *quid enim interest utrum ex homine se convertat quis in beluam an hominis figura immanitatem gerat beluae?*; May 1996: 147–153). Cicero commonly uses the pejorative epithets *pecus* and *belua*, but the words occur in combination elsewhere only at *off.* 1.105, where they simply signify, respectively, domesticated versus wild animals. *Pecus*, "herd animal," is normally used, as here, in a dismissive way for unreasoning animals that seek physical gratification; *belua*, "beast," can have the same force (e.g., *off.* 1.11), but generally has more ferocious connotations (consider the common collocations with *immanis, ferus*, and *taeter*, adjectives never attached to *pecus*; Traina 1984: 117–119; Kaster 2006: 149, 416).

There is disagreement among commentators and translators over whether Cicero continues here discussing Ligus (Wuilleumier and Tupet 1966: 35; Courtney 1989: 50; Shackleton Bailey 1991a: 106) or turns his attention back to Clodius (Wolf 1801: 314; Watts 1923: 319; Lenaghan 1969: 67, adding however that "this description fits Ligus better"). The conception of someone too dull to grasp his own wrongdoing matches well the accusation of being a "blockhead" (*stipitem*) and fits other references to Ligus. Moreover, if this person is nourished by the *pabulo inimicorum meorum*, it suggests that he is not himself Clodius, one of Cicero's principal enemies, and the phrasing recalls Cicero's description of Ligus elsewhere as "a supplement to my enemies" (*Sest.* 68: *additamentum inimicorum meorum*). Nevertheless, this view has problems and, on balance, the sentence must signal a transition back to Clodius. First, the entire premise of the digression is that Clodius and Ligus have something in common (*non plus quam*), which makes it less remarkable that the content is not entirely standard for Clodius; in fact, the confusion may be part of the intent. Second, there is the distinction between the *illum* clearly used of Ligus in the previous sentence and the *hunc* here; also, *hunc* is used throughout the speech to indicate Clodius, who is present in the senate. Third, the use of *enim* follows logically from *itaque eum numquam a me esse accusandum putavi*: "I didn't think that I ever had to bring charges against him.... For why should I bring charges against him...?" (*ThLL* X, 1 1695.58 [F. Spoth] takes *persequar* here as referring to judicial prosecution). Finally, if the entire passage (*stipitem... defendat*) refers to Ligus, the digression is of limited relevance, ending rather limply and without any clear signal. In particular, the sentence beginning *accedit etiam* (6: "in addition to this"), which indisputably involves Clodius, is best understood as adding more points to some that have just been made (*OLD* s.v. *accedo*, 17). On balance, it is best to take this aside as a characterization of Clodius, with the reference to Ligus restricted to *stipitem illum qui quorum hominum esset nesciremus, nisi se Ligurem ipse esse diceret*. Imagery of Clodius as a beast continues throughout the speech (see nn. on 6, 7).

pabulo inimicorum meorum et glande corruptum: *Pabulum* is properly food for farm animals, and so corresponds with *pecudem*. Acorns (*glandes*) constitute, in technical manuals and literary texts, part of the stock diet for both domesticated and wild animals, as well as for extremely poor and/or primitive human beings (*ThLL* VI, 2 2032.47–81 and 2032.18–46 [G. Meyer]). The addition of these details seems otiose; it is possible that they may contain vague hints about Clodius's sexual deviance, which will constitute a leitmotif of the speech (see especially 42n). For *glans* as a metaphor for "penis," Adams 1982: 72 cites a pun on being "fed" on acorns (Mart. 12.75.3: *pastas glande natis habet Secundus*), while *corrumpere* can commonly denote sexual activity (Adams 1982: 199). If the precise force of the allusion cannot be reconstructed, the vagueness is part of the point (for Cicero's need for deniability in his invective see, e.g., 42n). Cicero has already used innuendo about Clodius's willingness to exchange sexual favors for political ends (1n). In this instance, the "enemies" who have corrupted Clodius are presumably Piso and Gabinius, whom Cicero has recently called his *inimici* (3). Both are characterized in Ciceronian invective by their sexual deviance (e.g., *p. red. in sen.* 10–14, with further references in Corbeill 1996: 171–172 [Piso], Kaster 2006: 156–157 [Gabinius]).

** **qui si sensit quo se scelere devinxerit, non dubito quin sit miserrimus**: Maslowski reads *sentit* here, following Lambinus; the codices vary between *sensit* (**PGH**; Mueller) and *senserit* (E). The normal rule for sequences of tenses favors *sentit*, but there are numerous examples in Cicero of an indirect question taking the perfect subjunctive (*devinxerit*) after a verb in an historical tense, particularly if it has a progressive sense (i.e., *sensit* as "he has come to realize"; examples in Lebreton 1901: 256–257). This is regularly the case for verbs that designate a persistent state, such as those that describe a current condition of knowing or understanding that is dependent on a past act (KS 2: 2.178–179;

cf. *ad Brut.* 5.1=SB 5: *quid melius fuerit magno dolore sensimus, magno periculo sentimus*; *fam.* 6.13.5=SB 227). In light of these parallels, the best option is to follow the majority of the codices in reading *sensit*.

si sensit quo se scelere devinxerit, non dubito quin sit miserrimus; sin autem id non videt, periculum est ne se stuporis excusatione defendat: Cicero employs the rhetorical technique of dilemma, by which he encourages his audience to decide between what he presents as two mutually exclusive alternatives (Lausberg 1998: §393); in either case, the notion that Clodius has committed a crime is assumed. There could of course be other explanations for Clodius's behavior—for example, that he is well aware of the consequences of his actions but believes that they are for the good of the state. Craig 1993: 175 aptly notes: "The regular pattern is to prove, or assume as fact, that the opponent's behavior has been wrongful or deficient, and then to propose in dilemma form alternate unflattering explanations for the opponent's action."

The reference to *scelus* recalls Clodius's escapade with the Bona Dea, and the possibility that Clodius acted at that time out of stupid ignorance (*stupor*) continues Cicero's characterization of him as a beast (cf. *Phil.* 2.30: *sed stuporem hominis vel dicam pecudis attendite*).

6–7

Cicero turns from Clodius to launch into an encomium of Milo. The verb *accedit* takes as its subject the *quod* clause, thereby supplying an additional reason why Cicero has not carried out legal proceedings against Clodius: not he but Milo is destined to be the person to bring Clodius to justice.

6 *T. Annio*: T. Annius Milo (*RE* 67) was tribune in 57 and praetor in 55 (*MRR* 2: 201, 215). Evidence for his career comes almost entirely from Cicero, derivative passages of Asconius, and Dio. He set himself in opposition to Clodius both in clashes between street gangs, particularly in the run-up to Cicero's recall in 57, and in ultimately unsuccessful prosecutions (7n). His bid for the consulship of 52 came to an abrupt end on January 18 of that year, when his entourage met that of Clodius outside Rome and Clodius died in the aftermath of a pitched (if accidental) brawl. After a trial under Pompey's martial law, in which he was defended by Cicero in a trial that produced *Pro Milone*, Milo was convicted and went into exile in southern Gaul.

devota et constituta ista hostia esse videtur: The metaphorical application of sacrificial language to human beings—here in reference to Clodius being condemned in court as if he were a sacrificial animal—is rare in non-poetic texts of the Republic (similarly for *immolare, mactare, victima*; cf. *consecratum*, used of Clodius at 7). When such language does occur (*Pis.* 16; *Flacc.* 95; *Phil.* 13.35), it more typically casts "good" Romans as the victims of their enemies, who add to other criminal activity the role of sacrilegious human-sacrificers (for the accusation, see *Vatin.* 14; Habinek 1998: 80–81). An apparent exception occurs in the *Catilinarians*, but there Jupiter himself, rather than Cicero, conducts the sacrifice (*Catil.* 1.33: *mactabis*). Cicero's choice of the participle *devota* recalls the legendary act of *devotio*, as best exemplified in the story of as many as three different generals named Decius Mus handing themselves over in self-sacrifice to the gods of the underworld in order to ensure the safety of their troops (Oakley 1997–2005: 2.477–480 evaluates the evidence). Throughout his corpus Cicero makes multiple references to these events. Accordingly, elsewhere in Cicero's speeches the actions described by *devoveo* and its associated noun imply voluntary sacrifice on behalf of the state; on two different occasions after his exile Cicero elaborately devotes himself to the gods (*p. red. ad Quir.* 1; *dom.* 145; cf. *Sest.* 49–50; at *Catil.* 1.16 Catiline is sardonically described as dedicating the dagger intended to assassinate Cicero). Outside of Cicero, Gaius Aurelius Cotta, consul of 75, offers himself up for *devotio* in a speech before the people assembled in a *contio* (Sall. *hist.* 2.47.9–12; Morstein-Marx 2004: 262). Dyck 2004b: 304–314 points out that this trope metaphorically makes the subject into a military leader; as a result, he suggests that Cicero stopped applying it to himself after the two examples from immediately after exile because he was *not* a general and, of course, did not die. The use of the participle *devota* here to describe a person, Clodius, not engaging in an act of self-sacrifice seems to be unique in Cicero. What then is the point? Versnel 1976: 375–383 has argued convincingly that the original form of the ritual of *devotio* consisted of the damning of enemy troops, and that it was only from this practice that the sacrifice of the commander developed (see esp. Macr. *Sat.* 3.9.9–13; Oakley 1997–2005: 2.480–484). Such an understanding here suits well the end of this passage, where Clodius is said to be "consecrated" to Milo (7: *consecratum Miloni*); compare the phrasing of Versnel 1976: 369: "every *votum*, after the fulfilment of the request, is redeemed by means of *consecratio*" (on the role of *consecratio* in *devotio hostium* see Macr. *Sat.* 3.9.10: *capita aetatesque eorum devotas consecratasque habeatis*; Versnel 1976: 379–383). Gildenhard 2011: 329 further notes how the act of *devotio* makes Milo an explicit agent of the gods. And indeed, four years later, Cicero uses as part of his defense that Milo was justified in killing Clodius the notion that Milo acted in accordance with divine will (*Mil.* 84). The idea that Clodius is destined to be punished by the gods becomes increasingly prominent as *har. resp.* develops (see esp. 39n).

Although Cicero refers to Clodius as Milo's "sacrificial victim" only in a metaphorical sense, it may seem unusually prescient in a speech delivered four years before Clodius's death (Wolf 1801: 315–317). But Cicero in fact could write frankly to Atticus about the possibility of Clodius's being murdered by Milo as early as November 57 (*Att.* 4.3.5=SB 75: *reum Publium, nisi ante occisus erit, fore a Milone puto, si se in turba ei iam obtulerit occisum iri ab ipso Milone video*).

ēssĕ vĭdētūr: Cicero normally avoids this sequence of dactyl + spondee at clause end, the so-called "heroic clausula," since it matches the final two feet of a line of dactylic hexameter (1.86 percent in all orations: Keeline and Kirby

2019: 176; 8.3 percent is expected: De Groot 1921: 106). Although Cicero not infrequently exploits the rarity of this rhythm, often to ironic or comic effect (E. Adams 2013; 16n), the occurrence here seems incidental (or could Cicero be alluding to Milo's "heroic" stature?); cf. 16n.

fortissim_o_ et clarissim_o_ vir_o_, Tit_o_ Anni_o_, devot_a_ et constitut_a_ ist_a_ hosti_a_…; me praeripere desponsam iam et destinatam laudem: Note the series of contrasting grammatical genders: *vir* and its attendant masculine adjectives describe Milo, in juxtaposition with a feminine noun and adjectives to describe Clodius, including the derogatory adjective *ista*. Rhetorical handbooks warn about creating homoioteleuton of this sort (*Rhet. Her.* 4.22.32; cf. Marouzeau 1946: 43, Guggenheimer 1972: 13–140), and the incidence here of five consecutive occurrences of long [o] and four of long [a] is indeed unusual in Cicero's later oratorical works. In the immediately following clause, furthermore, a listener expects Clodius to be the object of the infinitive *praeripere*, but instead another feminine noun appears: the praise that is promised and long overdue for Milo (*desponsam iam et destinatam laudem*). ThLL V, 1 750.46 (E. Lommatzsch) lists this passage as the first use of *despondeo* in its non-literal sense of a bride being promised in marriage to a man (for *praeripio* to describe the snatching of women, see ThLL X, 2 791.67–792.3 [M. Massaro]). The identification of Clodius with the feminine to mark him as having an unmanly character occurs throughout the speech (nn. on 6, 24, 42, 45, 46, 50, 59). For Roman sensitivity to identifying grammatical gender with biological sex, particularly in poetry, see Corbeill 2014.

P. ille Scipio: Publius Cornelius Scipio Aemilianus (*RE* 335; Astin 1967). Born to L. Aemilius Paullus, he was adopted as a youth by P. Cornelius Scipio, son of P. Cornelius Scipio Africanus, hero of the Second Punic War. After distinguished junior military service in Hispania, Macedonia, and Africa, Aemilianus was elected consul for 147 (after impediments to his eligibility were waived) and dispatched to take command in the ongoing Third Punic War. In the following year, he captured and destroyed Carthage. He went on to conquer Numantia, a similarly difficult enemy, in 132. Van der Blom 2010: 184–185 discusses Cicero's frequent exemplary use of the younger Scipio as both a great general and a statesman. Here the comparison between Aemilianus and Milo has two principal points of reference: divine destiny and the necessity of overcoming a formidable opponent.

The pronominal adjective *ille* commonly refers, usually positively, to someone neither physically present nor already mentioned in the discourse, but so well known as to be readily available to both speaker and audience (*OLS* 1: 1099–1100). Its clitic placement here between praenomen and nomen is fairly rare (*ThLL* VII, 1 361.75–79 [V. Bulhart]), but when it happens it customarily signals a following *qui* clause or similar succeeding element which specifies the aspect of the person that is relevant for the present case (*ThLL* VII, 1 347.83–348.27; LHS 2: 407).

natus mihi videtur ad... quasi fatali adventu: The suggestion that Scipio "seems to have been born" to destroy Carthage receives the cautious addition "as if sent by fate." The analogy with Milo is underscored by the repetition of language and sense in the second half of the comparison (*ad... natus esse videtur... quasi divino munere*—Milo "seems to have been born" to destroy Clodius "as if by divine dispensation"; Begemann 2012: 175–176). Cicero qualifies the possible transgression of attributing their actions to divine design by adding *quasi* in both instances (cf. 2n, on *paene*). The adjective *fatalis* is to be taken here in its literal sense, denoting an arrival (on earth) that has been predetermined by fate (cf. *p. red. ad Quir.* 19: *quasi aliqua fatali necessitate*). The noun *adventus* is especially associated with the arrival of generals or troops in advance of a battle, which may explain the choice of the word here (*ThLL* I 837.79–838.21 [O. Hey]).

ad ill<u>am</u> pestem comprimend<u>am</u>, exstinguend<u>am</u>, funditus delend<u>am</u>: Cicero continues to describe Clodius using feminine nouns and adjectives with clear feminine terminations, a description made emphatic by the rising tricolon of gerundives in homoioteleuton. For the common insult of calling an opponent a "plague," see 4n, index in Opelt 1965. The use of *delendam* at the end of the colon further equates Milo and Aemilianus, recalling as it does the elder Cato's injunction that "Carthage must be destroyed" (Plin. *nat.* 15.74: *cum [Cato] clamaret omni senatu Carthaginem **delendam***; Plut. *Cat. mai.* 27.1; *Vir. ill.* 47.8; Flor. *epit.* 1.31.4).

<u>natus</u> esse videtur et quasi divino munere do<u>natus</u> rei publicae: Coming after the apparent end of the clause (*videtur*), the unperiodic addition of *et quasi divino munere donatus rei publicae* receives special emphasis, as further underscored by the hyperbaton *munere... rei publicae* and partial rhyme (cf. *inv.* 1.84, of a horse: *neque do<u>natus</u> est neque domi <u>natus</u> est*).

solus ille: Although these words introduce a new sentence, their use to describe Aemilianus in the preceding comparison further serves to equate the two men.

qui lapidibus, qui ferro alios fugaret, alios domi contineret: For the ascending types of violence conveyed by stone-throwing and swords, compare *Sest.* 77: *lapidationes persaepe vidimus, non ita saepe, sed nimium tamen saepe gladios*. Who precisely Clodius is meant to have "put to flight" is not clear and the lack of specificity may be intentional (see 5n on "deniability"; Boll 2019: 118–119 discusses similarly vague lists). It may apply, for instance, to violence at *contiones* or *comitia* disrupted by Clodius's forces, such as the rioting that accompanied the meetings in early 57 involving Cicero's recall (Tatum 1999: 178–180), or may refer to Clodius's more recent involvement in destroying the property of his enemies (58n). The use of stones in rioting has a long history in Rome as a demonstration of popular justice inherited from the military (Lintott 1968: 6–8); Cicero comments on Clodius driving *boni viri* from the forum with stones during his tribunate (*Pis.* 23; cf. 39 below) and allegedly organizing a *lapidatio* by the people in response to a grain shortage in 57 (*dom.* 11–12; other general references involving Clodius include *dom.* 53, 54; *Sest.* 2, 27, 53; *Pis.* 28).

The allusion to those "trapped at home" by Clodius seems to refer to Pompey alone, whose retreat to his home receives explicit mention in five of the speeches *post reditum* (49n; *p. red. in sen.* 4, 29; *dom.* 67, 110; *Sest.* 69, 84; *Pis.* 16, 29; Riggsby 2002a: 176–177. Cf. *p. red. ad Quir.* 14). Using the generalizing plural *alios* allows Cicero to allude with delicacy to a potentially embarrassing time for Pompey. Since this retreat was in response to an assassination attempt, it would be natural to construe *ferro* with *domi contineret*, a common construction that separates out both the means at the beginning, then follows with both the results (Devine and Stephens 2006: 66).

qui urbem totam, qui curiam, qui forum, qui templa omnia caede incendisque terreret: Lenaghan 1969: 69 notes three occasions when Clodius and his associates disrupted meetings of the senate in the curia—Plut. *Cic.* 31.1 (March 58), *Sest.* 75 (January 57, when Cicero claims that several men were killed), and *ad Q. fr.* 2.1.3=SB 5 (December 57)—and a fourth when the senate met on the Capitol (*dom.* 5–6, 8, 10; cf. *Att.* 4.1.6 =SB 73). For assaults on temples, see 57n and Kaster 2006: 200–201 (temple of Castor).

The list of Clodius's targets resembles that given at *dom.* 5 (*obsessione templorum, occupatione fori, oppressione curiae*; cf. *p. red. in sen.* 7). Cicero probably concluded his list here with "all the temples" given the religious subject matter of this speech.

quem ad modum armatum civem...non modo vinci verum etiam vinciri oporteret: The *lex Cornelia de sicariis et veneficiis* prevented a private citizen from carrying a weapon with the intent of murder (Marcian. *dig.* 48.8.1; Ferrary 1991; Crawford 1996: 749–753; Riggsby 1999: 50–55; Ciceronian allusions at *Rab. perd.* 19, *Mil.* 11, *parad.* 31, *Phil.* 2.22). I have found only two other examples of the paronomasia *vincere/vincire*: *Rhet. Her.* 4.29: *hic quos homines alea vincit, eos ferro statim vincit* ("A man who beats others at dice, binds them straightaway in chains") and Paneg. 4.20.2: *aut virtute devincunt aut terrore devinciunt* ("They either overwhelm with virtue or bind down with fear"). It is worth noting that all three instances present the seemingly counterintuitive order "not only defeat but even fetter," which Wolf, following Garatoni 1786: 7.275, convincingly explains as continuing the imagery of Clodius as a wild beast, who must be overwhelmed before being put in chains (1801: 317: *nam ut [beluam] vincias, iam victam esse oportet*). Hunting imagery resumes at 7.

7 *praeripiam*: The repetition of a form of the verb *praeripere* from 6 (*praeripere*) signals the end of the digression, as it shifts from an encomium of Milo to justification for Cicero not having taken previous action against Clodius.

de me ac de patria merito viro: "A man who is a benefactor to me and to the state." This standard formulation derives from the notion that someone has through past services "earned" (*mereor*) respect and gratitude from (*de*) another (Hellegouarc'h 1963: 169–170).

eum praesertim reum cuius ille inimicitias non solum suscepit propter salutem meam, verum etiam adpetivit: *Inimicitiae*, normally in the plural as here, describes a relationship of hostility between individuals within a community, in contrast with an "enemy" of the entire state, as regularly designated by *hostis* (the fluidity between the terms is often rhetorical; see *ThLL* VI, 3 3057.79–3058.23 [W. Ehlers] and cf. *dom.* 101: *non ab inimico meo, sed ab hoste communi Clodio*). Like its opposite, *amicitia* ("friendship"), the term designates a relationship with both an affective and an action component, though the balance and intensity can vary widely. The action component might range from simply cutting off contact to interference with a rival's political or other plans, to prosecution, to violence (as here). While it was not a formal status in the Republic, the public announcement and renunciation of hostility were recognizable rituals (Epstein 1997: 3–11, *passim*). *Amicitia* and *inimicitiae* were fundamentally relationships between two individuals, though they created shareable interests that might bind ad hoc groups together. In his defense of Milo Cicero also uses *appetere* to describe his actions on behalf of Milo, the same verb that here describes Milo's actions on Cicero's behalf, a repetition that demonstrates well the reciprocal nature of their shared *inimicitiae* (*Mil.* 100: *ego **inimicitias** potentium pro te **appetivi**, ego meum saepe corpus et vitam obieci armis **inimicorum** tuorum* etc.; see further Epstein 1987: 47). Note that Cicero has already described himself as an *inimicus* (2, 3), a term designating an accepted social role provided that the feuds do not lead to actions that are discreditable on other grounds.

The term *reum* refers to Milo's unsuccessful attempt to prosecute Clodius *de vi* on two separate occasions during the previous year (*TLRR* nos. 261–262; Lintott 1968: 110 n. 2; Kaster 2006: 304–305, 316). Clodius retaliated by instituting proceedings against Milo in 56, for which the charges seem ultimately to have been dropped (details are uncertain; see *TLRR* no. 266; Tatum 1999: 201–204).

inlaqueatus iam omnium legum periculis, inretitus odio bonorum omnium, expectatione supplici iam non diuturna implicatus: Although there is probably no very specific reference here, Cicero seems to speak generally of Clodius's alleged violation of criminal statutes, which would expose him to prosecution before hostile jurors. Compare the similar metaphorical language, also used of Clodius, at *Sest.* 16 (*beluam, vinctam auspiciis, adligatam more maiorum, constrictam legum sacratarum catenis*), which treats the legal and religious considerations that had prevented him from holding the tribunate before his *transitio ad plebem*. The hunting imagery continues the references at 5 and 6, with the rare *inlaqueo* referring to snares (*laquei*), *inretio* to a net (*rete*), and *implico* general entanglement. Other examples describing Clodius include *Sest.* 88: *illum...legum...laqueis constringerent*; *Mil.* 40: *illam beluam, iudici laqueos declinantem, iam inretitam teneret*; Fantham 1972: 132.

The sentence contains a striking number of instances of the preverb *in/im*: *in*laqueatus...*in*retitus...*im*plicatus...*im*peditus, all participles describing a passive Clodius (cf. *in me impetum*), to which Cicero replies with his own actively resistant prefix (*resistam... refutabo*).

The ablative phrase *exspectatione supplici iam non diuturna* stresses that Clodius will not have long to wait: his punishment is imminent.

feretur tamen haesitans: A virtual oxymoron, as indicated by *tamen*, suggesting the final, futile resistance of a captured animal ("although hindered, he will nevertheless come forward"). For the passive of *fero* with a predicate adjective referring to being carried by one's own volition or internal turmoil cf. *Verr.* 2.5.121: *praeceps amentia ferebare, Planc.* 6; for the context cf. Nep. *Att.* 10.4: *[Antonius] odio ferebatur in Ciceronem*. *Haesito* refers not to any wariness on the part of Clodius—who has after all been characterized since the beginning of the oration as raging and maddened—but, like *impeditus*, to his motion impeded by imagined snares.

conabitur,... conatum refutabo: Cicero normally avoids this construction, by which a cognate participle resumes an idea expressed by a preceding verb. The combination, a type of *figura etymologica*, tends to be used in early Latin prose for the plain narration of sequential acts (Wills 1996: 312; e.g., Cato *orig.* 83 [Gell. 3.7.14]: *Romani milites circumveniuntur, circumventi repugnant*). Ovid was particularly enamored of the construction, using it over 125 times (Wills 1996: 323). By contrast, when Cicero uses an analogous construction, he modifies the expected pattern. Here, for example, he changes the subject of the verb and seems to employ the cognate noun *conatus* rather than the participle (see further Laughton 1964: 17–19).

Milone: Contrast *T. Annio* (6) and compare *Miloni* (7). A male Roman citizen's name at this period typically comprised three parts: the *praenomen* (an individual name, but one drawn from a very small stock), the *nomen* (inherited from the father by all interrelated members of the large *gentes* or "clans"), and the *cognomen* (a family name, often but not always inherited from the father as well; largely restricted at this period to members of the elite). The particular combination of these used for address or reference varied considerably with circumstance. The principal variables involve the degree of formality of the situation and the degree of respect and warmth intended by the namer (Adams 1978; Dickey 2002: 46–76). Secondarily, the form chosen can vary over the course of a single text as a reflection of information status. The more formal the situation, the more likely it is that a two-name address (*praenomen* plus *nomen* or *cognomen*) will be used. This is, for instance, the commonest form used in Cicero's speeches before the senate (Adams 1978: 146). Respect for a particularly notable person may be shown by extending this usage beyond its normal bounds; for instance, Cicero almost always gives Pompey his praenomen Gnaeus in any public context (Kaster 2006: 147). Conversely, Cicero generally denies his "villains" the two-name form (Catiline, Clodius, and often prosecutors in criminal cases; for the last, see below).

In his speeches, Cicero normally introduces (Roman, male) characters with *praenomen* and *nomen*, in accordance with the formality of the occasion. Once introduced, however, reference is typically reduced to the *nomen* alone, unless a character is reintroduced after a significant gap, in which case he is given the *praenomen* again. Adams 1978: 146 notes the fact without explanation and Dickey 2002: 51–52 suggests that later references in the same text are less formal. In fact, the pattern seems to involve information availability: entirely new information vs. presupposed information vs. reintroduced information (cf. the use of the definite article to reintroduce a topic in English discourse). The same pattern can be seen even more clearly in Caes. *Gall.*, where competing considerations (politeness, rhythm) do not really come into play: *praenomen, nomen* or *cognomen*, and rank at first appearance and after a gap; otherwise solely *nomen* or *cognomen*. This explanation may account for the rule above about prosecutors. Someone who is physically in court and has just spoken at great length may automatically be "present" enough that he never needs "introduction." The choice here of "Milo" rather than "Annius" to refer to Cicero's special ally is a gesture of solidarity with a lower-status figure, insofar as it recognizes his right to the (originally aristocratic) cognomen.

hesterno die: After repeating the first two words of the speech, Cicero returns to the subject of the opening, recounting in greater detail how on the previous day he had threatened Clodius with legal action (1n). The phrase also occurred at 3 to signal the end of the exordium; here it serves an analogous function by signaling the end of the introductory characterization of Clodius before finally turning at last in section 8 to the treatment of the haruspical response.

** tacenti stans: All codices read *stanti tacens*, and this is preserved by most editors despite the apparent problems it raises: how can Clodius threaten Cicero "in silence," in particular since the phrase alludes to the time when Cicero describes Clodius as raging (1: *furentem exsultantemque*), before rushing toward the door of the senate? One alternative is to attribute the inconsistency to lack of care on Cicero's part, but many scholars prefer to resort to emendation. Shackleton Bailey 1987: 275 proposes reading *stanti stans*, implying that the subsequent mention of Clodius sitting supports this (7: *consedit*). This indeed resolves the problems in the sentence, but no parallels are offered for why the change would have occurred and, more importantly, the sense of a "standoff" is weak. In addition, one loses the contrasting sequence of *stanti [Cicero] : tacens [Clodius] :: consedit [Clodius] : conticui [Cicero]*. Graevius 1696: 513–514 offers what seems a more attractive alternative: *tacenti stans*. For many examples of this type of corruption, by which two words in close proximity exchange morphological termination, see Housman 1909: 248; 1930: 22 (cited by Courtney 1960: 96, who thinks Graevius's emendation "involves fewer hypotheses"). The resultant chiastic sequence is also pleasing, with the silent Cicero embracing Clodius (*tacenti [Cicero] : stans [Clodius] :: consedit [Clodius] : conticui [Cicero]*). This sequence would seem marred by the fact that Cicero is in fact *not* silent, but immediately speaks, albeit briefly (7: *voce tantum attigi*); but here the emphatic position of *voce* can be understood as calling attention to this change: "as I remained silent, I used my voice to just touch upon...."

The decision is difficult, but given the advantages of the emendation, it seems best to emend to *tacenti stans*.

** legum ĭnĭtĭŭm et iŭdĭcī: Madvig conjectures *legum metum et iudici*, and is followed by Zielinski 1904: 206 ("besser," while *initium* is "nicht übel") and Shackleton Bailey 1987: 275. However, as Zielinski notes, the rhythm does not seem tremendously improved by the change (*pace* Shewring 1931: 15), with *metum* introducing a double cretic, while *initium* also produces a double cretic but with the first metron resolved (assuming elision). More significantly, the corresponding passage at 1, *duobus verbis <u>inceptis</u>* (also cited by Maslowski *ad loc.*), provides sufficient justification for retaining the reading of the codices; see further next note.

voce tantum attigi legum initium et iudici: "I used my voice to just touch upon the onset of legal proceedings." The phrasing reformulates the encounter narrated at 1: *periculum iudici intendi; duobus verbis inceptis* ("I threatened to take him to court; with barely two words…"). It is difficult to determine the precise sense of *voce*; translators take it as an alternative to *verbis* of the earlier passage (Watts 1923: 323: "I cowed him by my first syllables of reference"; Wuilleumier and Tupet 1966: 36: "j'ai seulement commencé à prononcer les mots"; Shackleton Bailey 1991a: 107: "I merely hinted"; for the meaning see *OLD* s.v. 7). In addition, the primary meaning ("voice") offers a pointed juxtaposition to Cicero's previous silence.

For the hendiadys *legum… et iudici* ("legal proceedings"), compare *dom.* 70 (*legum iudiciorumque*), and the apparent *asyndeton bimembre* at *dom.* 17 (*iudicia leges*; cf. Sall. *Iug.* 31.20: *leges iura iudicia*), with Adams 2021: 410: "*Iudicia leges* 'courts, laws' denotes the system of justice," with the two words combined expressing a single concept.

diem dixisset, ut iecerat, fecissem, ut ei statim tertius a praetore dies diceretur: The parataxis of two pluperfect subjunctives, rather than subordination of the first with the conjunction *si*, evokes a colloquial formulation (Hofmann 1980: 254–256, §103; LHS 2: 656–657; compare Plin. *epist.* 1.12.8: *dedisses huic animo par corpus, fecisset quod optabat*; cf. Cic. *off.* 3.75: *at dares hanc vim M. Crasso,… in foro, mihi crede, saltaret*).

The phrase *diem dicere* signals a denunciation on criminal charges before the praetor; it does not mean that the case was necessarily accepted (Landgraf 1914: 86; *ThLL* V, 1 1050.18–32 [K. Pflugbeil]). As made clear by the pluperfect subjunctive *dixisset* and the aside *ut iecerat*, Clodius's threat was not carried through. The granting of the *tertius dies* (=*[com]perindinus dies*) is the scheduling of a trial (under a variety of procedures) at a normal interval (the "third" day, i.e., the day after the next in Roman reckoning: Metzger 1997: 77–82). Greenidge 1901a: 329–330 (citing *inter alia* this passage) shows that a tribune seeking a capital penalty needed to hold the trial before the *comitia centuriata*, and therefore needed to appeal to the praetor for permission to do so. Cicero has already referred twice to threatening Clodius with prosecution and will again at the end of this section (*arma iudiciorum atque legum*). It seems generally accepted that *tertius a praetore dies diceretur* is yet another statement of the same threat, but that is not clear. Greenidge's discussion suggests that as a procedural matter it makes at least as much sense to take this clause as a further step in the proceedings initiated by Clodius with *diem dixisset*. Cicero will agree (demand, even) to proceed to trial immediately. That is, Cicero's response here is not, as elsewhere, a counteraccusation, but encouragement to "bring it on." The fact that the adjective *tertius* is doubly emphasized both by its unusual position after the adverb *statim* and the short-range hyperbaton from its noun *dies* further supports the idea that Cicero is meeting Clodius's idle threat with his own bravado (this interpretation is reflected in the translation).

Atque hoc sic moderetur et cogitet, si contentus sit iis sceleribus quae commisit, esse iam consecratum Miloni: The first part of the closing dilemma of this section of the speech may at first seem surprising: why would Clodius be content with any degree of misdeeds? The formulation, however, recalls the claim with which this encomium of Milo began: if Clodius does not persecute Cicero further, he will let Milo take care of him; but if Clodius continues with his attacks, Cicero will take matters into his own hands. For the sense of *commisit*, see 40n.

Further evidence of ring composition in this sentence is offered by *consecratum*, which recalls the sacrificial imagery employed at the beginning (6n).

** *esse iam consecratum*: *esse* omitted by H, *esse* ⟨*se*⟩ Baiter, Peterson. Although the omission of *se* is easily accounted for as haplography, Cicero and Caesar frequently omit the subject pronoun in indirect statement (Lebreton 1901: 376–378).

si quod in me telum intenderit, statim me esse arrepturum arma iudiciorum atque legum: Cicero refers to himself and Servilius hurling *tela* at Clodius at 2. Since *tela* properly denote offensive weapons, Cicero seems to be using *arma* here in the restricted sense of weapons of defense (*ThLL* II 591.43–77 [E. Bickel], with several examples of *arma* as synonym of *scutum*). Clodius casts wild charges, but Cicero shields himself with the legitimacy of the Roman courts (for the hendiadys *iudiciorum atque legum* see above). Such imagery is consistent with the characterization of Clodius as attacker and Cicero as rational victim.

Lenaghan 1969: 73 takes *intenderit* as a future perfect; more precisely, it is a perfect subjunctive in indirect statement (cf. *si contentus sit*) that represents a future perfect indicative in the implied direct statement.

8–9 (*defendat*)

At last Cicero transitions to the proper subject of the speech, as he turns to Clodius's recent public meeting on the haruspical response. Before treating the response proper, however, Cicero offers a series of jokes ridiculing Clodius's pretense at having the authority to pronounce on religious matters.

8 *Atque*: "And so"; contrast the adversative sense of the same conjunction that introduces the previous sentence (LS s.v. IV.8). Here, the sense of *atque* as a transitional particle to begin a new line of thought within an argument is reflected in its apparent etymology (*ad* "in addition" + *-que*: WH 1: 76; KS 2: 2.23; cf., e.g., *Catil.* 2.3, *off.* 3.27). Cicero's pronouncement of his willingness to defend himself from Clodius's attacks leads him to discuss the most recent instance at Clodius's *contio*.

paulo ante: The remark that this meeting had occurred "a little while ago" makes it unlikely that it can be dated to the second week of April as Wiseman 1974: 164 contends, since this would have been several weeks before the probable date of *har. resp.* (see Introduction E.2). The temporal imprecision would not have concerned the senatorial audience, which would of course have been well aware of when this *contio* had taken place. Although certainty is impossible, the urgency of discussing the response makes it likely that the *contio* had occurred on the previous day (Gallo 1969: 71), although it is also possible that the phrase *paulo ante* refers here not to a period "a little before" the current meeting, but before the previous day's disrupted senate meeting with which the speech opens.

contionem: For the content of Clodius's meeting, see Introduction B.2. A *contio* was an assembly called by a magistrate to convey information to the public (or whatever fraction of it showed up); the term can also refer to a speech given at such an assembly. In section 8 the noun has multiple meanings, referring to those attending the *contio* (*sua contio*) as well as to the content of the speech, as here; sometimes it seems to refer simultaneously to both the occasion and the content (e.g., *proxima contio*). Clodius presumably called this meeting in his capacity as aedile, as in fact the phrase *sua contio* implies (for a list of public officials possessing this authority see Pina Polo 1995: 206; full discussion in Pina Polo 1989: 43–51). The official might also summon others to speak, whether allies or political opponents to be interrogated, but there was no general debate. These meetings often preceded ballots on legislation but could also take on more general topics such as the one described here, or such as Cicero's speeches informing the people of the Catilinarian conspiracy or the oration giving thanks after his return from exile. *Contiones* were distinct from the *comitia*, in which public votes were taken. For the form and its implications for the structure of Republican politics, see Morstein-Marx 2004: 9: "The *contio* was, quite simply, center stage for the performance and observation of public, political acts in the Roman Republic" (his entire book demonstrates this claim). Forms of the word *contio* appear eight times in sections 8 and 9, perhaps to contrast Clodius's impromptu gathering of supporters with the more regularized meeting of the senate.

quae est ad me tota delata: The verb *deferre* is commonly used from Plautus onward to describe the transmission of written, copied texts (*ThLL* V, 1 314.21–76 [M. Lambertz]); see esp. Brut. Cic. *fam.* 11.13.3=SB 388, describing a copy of a military *contio* that Decimus Brutus had received (*contio eius ad me est adlata*). For other examples of texts of *contiones* being circulated soon after delivery see Mouritsen 2013: 63, 78–82, especially the close parallel at *Att.* 7.8.5=SB 131, where Cicero in Formiae receives within four days of its delivery a copy of a speech given by Antonius in Rome. For general evidence on copying texts as they were being delivered, see, e.g., 51n and Plut. *Cato Min.* 23.3, who notes that Cicero had clerks record in shorthand speeches delivered by others. It is to be expected that Cicero would have available a copy of the text of Clodius's *contio* so that he may refer to it as he delivers his own reply (cf. <u>universum</u> *argumentum sententiamque audite*). Corbeill 2018 offers an imaginative reconstruction of what Clodius's argument may have been.

** *de religionibus sacris caerimoniis*: Maslowski reports *de religionibus sacris et caerimoniis* as the reading of all codices. Courtney 1960: 97 (followed without acknowledgment by Shackleton Bailey 1991a: 230) proposed deleting *et*, thereby understanding *sacra* as a substantive in an asyndetic series rather than an adjective modifying *religiones* (Adams 2021: 14–16 notes that single-word tricola "often or usually" [687] occur without conjunctions). Three points make this deletion all but certain: first, the adjective *sacer* never modifies *religio* in pre-Christian Latin (Cèbe 1972–1999: 849); second, *dom.* 109 offers the same list in asyndeton (*hic* <u>sacra</u>, <u>religiones</u>, <u>caerimoniae</u> *continentur*; cf. *dom.* 33, *nat. deor.* 3.5; at *dom.* 121 *de religione, caerimoniis* occur as an *asyndeton bimembre*); third, the phrase *sacra et religiones* occurs in the next sentence, indicating that each word belongs in a separate category.

One apparently strong piece of evidence, however, supports retaining *et*: Arnob. *nat.* 4.31 uses the combination *religiones...sacras* in a passage summarizing *har. resp.* 23. Maslowski cites this in his *testimonia* to support retaining *et*. As noted above, however, since by Arnobius's day the combination *sacra religio* was acceptable, it seems likely that this would have affected both Arnobius's choice of expression and the manuscript tradition.

DELETE *et*.

de religionibus sacris caerimoniis: The tricolon encompasses three key aspects of the religious experience of an elite Roman of the Republican period, all of which Cicero claims that Clodius has violated. The term *religio* does not correspond with English "religion" in the sense of embodying a precise set of beliefs agreed upon by a discrete community. No single term or phrase in English can adequately encompass the concept of *religio*, which embraces the scrupulousness to be observed, often in a public context, in the relationship between human beings and the divine. When applied to a person, *religio* tends to describe actions that individuals choose to avoid rather than follow (*ThLL* XI, 2 903.55–58 [C. Wick and J. Blundell]); "religious scruples" is often offered as an admittedly inadequate shorthand for the idea. The diverse etymological speculation about *religio* offered by the ancients reflects the range of ideas that the word was thought to cover (Maltby 1991: 522–523 catalogues testimonia):

Cicero states that those filled with *religio* (*religiosi*) are so-called because they "retrace, so to speak" everything relating to divine worship (*re+legere, nat. deor.* 2.72), while his contemporary Servius Sulpicius understands the word's origin as describing something "remote and separated from us" (from *relinquo*: Macr. *Sat.* 3.3.8); Lactantius, by contrast, is one of several authors to derive the noun from *re+ligare* ("to bind"), on the grounds that we human beings "have been constrained and bound to god by fetters of piety" (*inst.* 4.28.3). Modern etymological studies are also inconclusive; contrast WH 1: 352–353 and *ThLL* XI, 2 902.30 (favoring *lego, -ere*) with Vaan 2008: 341 (*ligo, -are*). BNP 1: 214–219 provide a brief survey, with earlier bibliography, of the range of action and attitudes covered by the word *religio*, contrasting it with *superstitio* (12n). Of the many uses of the noun and its cognates in *har. resp.* see nn. on 11 (twice), 18, 29 (*religio*); 4, 9 (twice), 33, 53 (*religiosus*).

The Romans divided the rites designated as *sacra* into the *publica* and the *privata*, attributing to each realm specific sets of ritual behavior (Fest. p. 245 M; Wissowa 1912: 398–399). The context here would lead one to expect that Cicero refers solely to public ritual performed by magistrates and priests, but since in *De domo sua* of the previous fall he had made a point of how Clodius had neglected through his adoption the familial *sacra* of the Claudii, it is likely that recollection of this by his audience, which would have included most of the *pontifices* who judged the case *De domo sua* (12n), contributes to his sarcasm here when he repeats the term *sacra* in the next clause (*dom.* 34–35; for Cicero's treatment of the relationship between a family's *sacra* and the responsibility of heirs, see *leg.* 2.47–53). The term *caerimoniae* seems originally to have referred to "the secret ritual instructions that applied exclusively to the oldest religion" which, according to Wagenvoort, were the province of the *pontifices* (1937: 87). By the classical period, however, the word has become applicable to a broad range of rituals, including that of the Bona Dea (e.g., *dom.* 105, *har. resp.* 37, Suet. *Iul.* 6.2; generally, *ThLL* III 100.49–101.22 [W. Bannier]). Cicero uses a similar grouping at *dom.* 33, when he comments on the presumption of a person who is not a member of the pontifical college to speak *de religione, de rebus divinis, caerimoniis, sacris* (cf. 12 below, where the *pontifices* are authorities *de sacris publicis, de ludis maximis, de deorum penatium Vestaeque matris caerimoniis*).

Despite Cicero's evident sarcasm, it is possible that this phrase matches how Clodius described the *contio* since, as Cicero says in the next sentence, Clodius's speech covered entirely these areas. If so, Cicero's joke becomes even more pointed. The description does in fact suit well the subject matter, since it is clear from *har. resp.* that Clodius argued that, in reclaiming his property on the Palatine, Cicero violated a site consecrated to the divine *Libertas*. On *contiones* as one of the principal means by which the general Roman populace could learn of religious issues, see the general remarks of Bendlin 2000: 125–128 and, more specifically, Morstein-Marx 2004: 8–11.

patres conscripti, Clodius: The already emphatic position of the grammatical subject of the finite verb at clause end receives further emphasis through the single word being isolated following a vocative. As demonstrated in detail by Fraenkel 1965, vocatives in Greek and Latin tend to mark the end of a sentence constituent. Accordingly, this sentence consists of a series of three cola containing a descending number of syllables: *de religionibus sacris caerimoniis // est contionatus, patres conscripti, // Clodius.* The emphatic use of the proper name in a single-word colon underscores the irony of Clodius having the gall to speak publicly on religious matters.

Publius, inquam, Clodius: Pretending that the senate would be surprised at the identity of Clodius, Cicero further ironizes the joke by adding the praenomen as if clarity were needed. The parenthetical *inquam* emphasizes this "new" information by formulating with different words the entire previous sentence in another instance of *conduplicatio* (*Rhet. Her.* 4.38; compare *Verr.* 2.5.84: *habitare in ea parte urbis…Syracusanum neminem voluit; hodie, inquam, Syracusanum in ea parte habitare non licet*). As at 4, *inquam* stresses the repetition of an idea, although in that passage only a few words are repeated, not as here an entire sentence. For the effect of the delayed name compare Catull. 10.29–30, where the specification of the praenomen arises from the fact that the speaker is flustered rather than indignant: *"meus sodalis— / Cinna est Gaius—is sibi paravit"* (" 'My buddy Cinna—Gaius Cinna that is—*he* equipped it for himself' ").

** **Publius**: Maslowski print only the abbreviation *P.*, with no note in his apparatus. Of the three principal witnesses, the readings are *P* • [space of c. two letters] P, *P.* HG.

READ *Publius*. Maslowski's text does not record other abbreviations that occur throughout the codices, such as *p.c.* for *patres conscripti*. The only reason to retain the abbreviation is if we thought that Cicero would have said "P.," as beginning students of Latin often do (and which I do not consider outside the realm of possibility that the Romans themselves did).

sacra et religiones neglegi violari pollui: The tricolon of verbs in asyndeton has an archaic and in particular a sacral association (LHS 2: 830; Fraenkel 2007 [1922]: 379 n. 89), which we can imagine Cicero stressing as a way of mocking Clodius's hypocrisy. With clear irony, Cicero's representation of the complaining voice of Clodius includes the very charges that Cicero will raise against him throughout the speech. The senatorial audience would presumably recognize that the language echoes the words of the response regarding what has caused the disruption in Rome (*neglego*: 36; *polluo*: 21, 37; cf. *sacra et religiosa*: 9; Cicero uses *violo* in a close paraphrase of another part of the response at 24).

non mirum si hoc vobis ridiculum videtur: This aside acts as a type of stage direction, indicating to Cicero's reading audience the (presumed) jocular reaction of the senate to his sarcasm. *Catil.* 1.20–21 contains a well-known example of a similar type of cue, where Cicero describes and explains the senate's silent reaction to his demand that Catiline leave the city (*quid expectas auctoritatem loquentium, quorum voluntatem tacitorum perspicis?...cum tacent, clamant*); for an amusing occasion when such a strategy backfired for a tribune, see *ad Q. fr.* 2.1.1=SB 5.

sua...hominem: For the apparently illogical construction of *sua* see Lebreton 1901: 133–134; KS 2: 1.604.

risit: It is not clear that this verb governs an indirect statement until *conqueri* at sentence end (KS 2: 1.261 misconstrues *hominem* as sole direct object). The construction is rare with *ridere* and its compounds, apparently appearing only here in Cicero, and would have been even less expected since the same verb takes the simple accusative two sentences earlier—*cum riseritis impudentiam hominis*—which semantically is not so different from the initial two accusatives here (*hominem*; *hominemque eum*). It is likely that listeners would have begun to suspect *oratio obliqua* only deep into the sentence, at *in contione*, following which the vocabulary from the preceding sentence is repeated: *in contione* (cf. *contoniatus*) *de religionibus* (cf. *de religionibus, religiones*) *neglectis* (cf. *neglegi*) *conqueri* (capping *questus est*). Both the repetition and unexpectedness of this final clause serves to reinforce the ridiculousness of Clodius's complaint that proper religious procedure has been neglected. For another instance of Cicero claiming that the attendees of one of Clodius's *contiones* laughed at his remarks, see *Att.* 4.2.3=SB 74 (quoted at 31n).

quo modo ipse gloriari solet: This and closely similar phrases appear elsewhere in Cicero, generally in circumstances suggesting that, while the "boaster" may indeed have admitted to some underlying facts, he presumably would have disputed Cicero's (uniformly negative) interpretation of them; see, e.g., *Phil.* 2.5 (*victor qui tibi, ut tute gloriari solebas, detulerat ex latronibus suis principatum*), where Antonius presumably *did* glory in being Caesar's chief lieutenant without admitting to banditry, or *fam.* 2.16.3=SB 154, where Hortensius's customary "boast" of never being involved in civil war exposes him to accusations of idleness (*ignavia*; see too *Sest.* 135; *Pis.* frg. 9; *Phil.* 3.17, 4.15; *fam.* 10.32.2=SB 415). In the present instance, Cicero suggests at *parad.* 32 that Clodius actually had boasted about accessing the Bona Dea festival, though presumably not in a public setting.

ducentis confixum senati consultis: "Pierced by two hundred decrees of the senate." We do not know precisely which *senatus consulta* Clodius claims to boast about here (for some candidates, see *Att.* 1.13.3=SB 13 and 1.14.5=SB 14 with 15n; cf. *Att.* 4.3.3=SB 75, *ad Q. fr.* 2.3.5=SB 7; Tatum 1999: 72–73). Cicero presents the phrase as if it were a quotation, and indeed it would not be unusual for Clodius to represent himself in a *contio* as standing proudly in opposition to the senate (Tan 2008: 185–187, 2013: 125–126). Cicero does not, however, specify whether this utterance occurred at the recent *contio* or whether it represents a frequent boast made in other contexts, as *solet* implies. His subsequent discussion offers an indication that the exclamation was recent: Cicero adds that the senatorial decrees to which Clodius refers all treated instances when Clodius violated aspects of Roman religion, in particular those rites associated with the Bona Dea. Since Cicero immediately identifies these same profaned rites with those to which the haruspical response refers, it would appear that Clodius anticipated in his own *contio* any Ciceronian mention of the Bona Dea scandal (see 37n, discussed below). It seems likely, then, that the remark was made, or repeated, in the recent *contio*.

Three elements of the phrase, moreover, stand contrary to Cicero's normal oratorical practice and so further indicate Clodian authorship (the following derives from Corbeill 2018: 180–183). First, in the hyperbaton between the adjective *ducentis* and its noun *consultis*, the intervening word is a verb form (*confixum*), a sequence that Adams characterizes as "artistic rather than natural to ordinary speech" (Adams 1971: 1; cf. Powell 2010: 179, 184; *Rhet. Her.* 4.12 uses three instances of this comparatively unusual figure to illustrate "grand style"). Of the fifteen other instances in *har. resp.* of such "verbal hyperbaton," most of which occur at moments of high emotion, this is the only one where the inserted verb is a participle. In fact, the dramatic meaning of the participle— "pierced"—further distinguishes this particular type of hyperbaton, since "not only the enclosing noun phrase [here, *ducentis...consultis*] but also the intervening constituent [*confixum*] carries focus," with the result that "it could well be that this particular kind of hyperbaton was seen as characteristic of the grand, if not over-grand, rhetorical style. Instances in Cicero himself are not easy to find" (Powell 2010: 177, who does not discuss this example; Adams 1971: 4; for a close Ciceronian parallel, see *Clu.* 68: *Oppianicum...duobus iugulatum praeiudiciis*). The sole example from Ciceronian oratory cited by Powell supplies intriguing support for non-Ciceronian authorship here: a purported quotation of Marcus Antonius, also known for his exuberant oratory (Cic. *Phil.* 2.28: "*cruentum alte extollens Brutus pugionem*"; Powell 2010: 177–178; for Antonius's style, see Plut. *Ant.* 2.8 with Pelling 1988: 119–120). Furthermore, an allegedly verbatim fragment of Clodius from a *contio* delivered the year before *har. resp.* contains the same type of hyperbaton (*dom.* 127: "*dedicatio magnam habet religionem*"), where Stroh 2004: 363 comments on "the tone of voice of a pompous lecturer." On the semantic level as well the hyperbaton calls for attention. In all but two of the other fifteen examples from our speech the adjective beginning the hyperbaton is relatively colorless, the majority consisting of "preferential words" that tend to be attracted to this position, such as demonstrative adjectives and quantifiers (e.g., *quantus, unus, hic*; the exceptions are *priuato* and perhaps *melior*; for "preferential words," see Powell 2010: 174–175; Devine and Stephens 2006: 542–548). Contrast these instances with the use of *ducenti*, an adjective that often occurs, as here, to express large numbers hyperbolically (*ThLL* V, 1 2134.50–54 [F. Vollmer]). Moreover, this non-literal use of *ducenti* normally occurs in poetic contexts, with only one other instance in Ciceronian oratory, in an apparently humorous context (Wölfflin

1896: 188 on *Sest.* 135). These combined unCiceronian phenomena, then—an uncharacteristically hyperbolic adjective that is commonly registered as poetic being stressed both syntactically and semantically through a double-focus hyperbaton—support Clodian authorship.

Another non-Ciceronian feature involves the verb *configo*. The majority of instances of this verb occur in a military context, to describe someone or something as "pierced" by weapons (*ThLL* IV 211.10–66 [F. Burger]). Cicero employs the verb metaphorically only one other time in oratory, again in the context of Marcus Antonius (*Phil.* 12.18: *eius sententiis confixum Antonium*). This example is an indirect quotation, referring to a situation recalled by the *impii cives* who are Antonius's allies. A third instance represents the verb's literal use and indicates even more clearly that the verb does not originate with Cicero, since the formulation belongs to a proverb that describes piercing the eyes of crows (*Mur.* 25: *Cn. Flavius, qui cornicum oculos confixerit*; Otto 1890: 93). The existence of the verb *configo* only in a proverb and a quotation suggests further that here it does not represent Cicero's own word choice.

The third and most convincing argument for Clodian authorship concerns morphology. In all Cicero's speeches, the second-declension form of the genitive *senati*, accompanied by *consultum*, appears only here and at 15 (see too *Phil.* 3.38, with Manuwald 2007: 459); elsewhere, including in all codices of 14 and 16, Cicero uses the fourth-declension genitive form *senatus*. In his correspondence *senati* occurs twice, each time with *senatus* as a variant (*fam.* 2.7.4=SB 107, 5.2.9=SB 2). Outside Cicero, *ThLL* IV 587.42–49 (F. Burger) records *senati consultum* in, e.g., several inscriptions and Sisenna. In the two places in *har. resp.* that the *-i* form occurs the codices split, with better testimony for *senati*. The remaining example of this morphological peculiarity at 15 (*tot senati consultis*) is a clear reference back to this instance. It would seem that Cicero wished to characterize Clodius's speech in both places through this genitive form, which may be an archaism (Sihler 2014: 324) and is certainly embedded in a self-consciously dramatic phrase.

quae sunt omnia contra illum pro religionibus facta: The use of the indicative form *sunt facta* in a relative clause in indirect discourse stresses that Cicero is here detailing the fact of Clodius's boast (KS 2: 2.542–544), adding the essential detail that these "hundreds" of decrees were all sanctions concerning religious issues.

pulvinaribus Bonae Deae stuprum intulerit: Cf. *Pis.* 95: *cum stuprum Bonae Deae pulvinaribus intulisset* and 38 below: *iniuria tui stupri inlata*. For *inferre* to describe sexual violation, see *ThLL* VII, 1 1385.10–14 (J. B. Hofmann). Adams 1982: 201 comments on *stuprum* that "the range of sexual acts which might be described…was unlimited" and that violence is normally implied (e.g., *fin.* 2.66, 5.64, both of rape). This vagueness works to Cicero's advantage in leaving the precise act up to the listener's imagination.

Cicero frequently mentions the *pulvinar* in this connection (33: *quo pulvinari? quod stupraras*; *Pis.* 95; *Mil.* 72). Brouwer 1989: 160 n. 68 catalogues allusions to the goddess's *pulvinar* in both literary and epigraphic sources while Wissowa 1912: 422 discusses its function in Roman ritual more generally. Its multiple associations and ambiguities provide an ideal opportunity for Ciceronian invective (van den Berg 2008: 239–284, largely on *Phil.*), one which he exploits here in alluding to the couch as a site for sexual activity (for *pulvinar* as "marriage bed," see van den Berg 2008: 251–258).

ea sacra quae <u>viri oculis</u> ne imprudentis quidem aspici fas est <u>non solum aspectu virili sed flagitio stuproque</u> violarit: Cicero uses similar language at *dom.* 105 (*istius, qui <u>non solum aspectu sed</u> etiam incesto <u>flagitio et stupro</u> caerimonias polluit, poena omnis <u>oculorum</u> ad caecitatem mentis est conversa*), where Cicero contrasts Clodius's "mental blindness" with physical blindness (presumably of App. Claudius Caecus; see Nisbet 1939: 158 and 38n). Cicero likely plays on the literal meaning here of *imprudens*: Clodius's eyes are "not fore<u>see</u>ing" (*im+pro+videns*; for Cicero's awareness of this etymology see Non. pp. 41.28–42.4 M and 18n). He places particular emphasis on improper viewing in *har. resp.* because of its correspondence with the clause of the response that indicates that "hidden" rites have been violated, presumably by being witnessed (*occulta*, 37). For *fas* as denoting what is right in the religious sphere see 34n. The use of the conjunction *-que* in the phrase *flagitio stuproque* identifies the second term, denoting sexual violation, as specifying the nature of Clodius's *flagitium* (KS 2: 2.24–25).

The fact that even those who innocently violate religious rites receive punishment makes Clodius's crime particularly heinous since he performed his sacrilege consciously (cf. *leg.* 2.36 [also about Clodius]: *in sacrificium cogitatam libidinem intulit, quo* **ne imprudentiam quidem oculorum** *adici fas fuit?*). Cicero seems to allude to the popular myth of a man being punished for unwittingly stumbling upon a goddess, namely, that of Actaeon, attacked by his hunting dogs after glimpsing Diana at her bath (as famously recounted at Ov. *met.* 3.138–252; visual representations appear in the Roman world as early as the first century BCE [Guimond 1981]).

It is the violation of the rites of the Bona Dea that prompts Cicero to stress Clodius's status as a *vir*, since normally Cicero's invective prefers to play on his ambiguous gender (44 below; more generally, Leach 2001). Santoro L'Hoir 1992: 23 notes that "Clodius is always a *homo* unless Cicero can get mileage out of the *Bona Dea* Festival, the tribune's lack of fitness for the priesthood, or his supposed incest with Clodia. In each instance, Cicero uses *vir* in a trope designed to amplify Clodius' sacrilegious propensities." In the case of the Bona Dea, she adds, the noun "suggests sexual motives for Clodius' presence." This valence accounts for the apparent redundancy here of *viri…virili*, with which one can compare the triple occurrence of *vir* at 37.

Cicero testifies that syncopated forms such as *violarit* follow colloquial usage, although the fuller form *violaverit* is recognized as "correct" (*or.* 157: *quasi vero nesciamus…et plenum verbum recte dici et imminutum usitate*).

The shortened forms are phonologically regular, occurring as early as Plautus, and are frequent in the classical period (LHS 1: 598). Cicero shows a preference for the short forms, particularly in the letters, as do Caesar and Terence (as against roughly equal proportions in Plautus; Weiss 2009: 411–412).

de religionibus neglectis: For similar humorous sarcasm about Clodius's claims to religious authority see *dom.* 127 with Nisbet 1939: 175–176.

9 dē pŭdīcĭtĭā: After recounting how even his own followers laughed at the notion of Clodius as a representative of religious conservatism, Cicero caps this with his own joke, whose punch line is reserved for the last word and gives the favored clausula of cretic + (resolved) spondee. The mention of *pudicitia* (1n) then allows him to turn briefly from Clodius's public transgressions to the private.

quid enim interest utrum ab altaribus religiosissimis fugatus: The particle *enim* allows Cicero to pretend that he will explain the logic behind why he knows the subject matter of Clodius's next speech, when in fact the sentence allows him to compound his joke by adding some scurrilous details about incest among Clodius and his sisters. At the same time, however, with the introductory "is there any difference" (*quid… interest*) he does exploit a common Roman logic that connects sexual impurity with the violation of religious taboos: "Cicero presents himself as a crucial part of a traditional alliance between state, gods and virtues, and within this context the concept of *pudicitia* plays a leading role" (Langlands 2006: 282; see in particular 298–305, on Clodius).

The plural form *altaria* designates one altar, with the singular form *altare* occurring first only in the imperial period and becoming common in Christian writers. The word describes an altar at the same Bona Dea rites at *Planc.* 86, where religious violation is again paired with sexual misconduct (*furialis illa vox, nefariis stupris, religiosis altaribus effeminata*).

ex sororum cubiculo: Other ancient sources accuse Clodius of incest with multiple sisters (59, *Sest.* 16; *fam.* 1.9.15=SB 20 and Plut. *Cic.* 29.4–5 specify three). Kaster 2006: 409–411 offers a careful evaluation of which sister(s) seem to have been involved and is less skeptical of the truth content than other scholars (Kaster 2006: 411: "accusing a man of sibling-incest, even in the hardnosed discourse of Republican politics, was nearly as taboo as the act itself, an annihilating gesture made only against a deeply hated enemy"; the full discussion in Harders 2008: 234–248 is more circumspect). Corbeill 1996: 116–124 discusses how Cicero had thematized the subject in *dom.* of the previous September, while Hickson-Hahn 1998 conjectures about the impulses underlying incest humor in Catullus, Cicero, Martial, and Juvenal. See too nn. on 4, 38, 42, 59.

** *sororum*: The reading of all major codices is *suorum*; the reading *sororum* occurs only in the *recentiores*, presumably as a humanist emendation. Halm (in Orelli *et al.* 1856: 908) suggests *suarum sororum*, which does match a tendency of Cicero, who uses a form of *tuus* when addressing Clodius on the charge of incest; but, while it nicely accounts for the reading of the major *codices*, Halm's emendation does not seem necessary. One can, however, make a case for retaining the reading *suorum*, designating both his male and female siblings; see 42n. The decision is difficult, but Cicero's normal invective practice is to begin from well-known charges, progressing only later in the speech to more outlandish claims.

READ *sororum*.

pudorem pudicitiamque: For the jingle, and the combination of the concrete with the abstract, see nn. on 1 (*impudicam impudentiam*) and 43. The ring composition with the earlier pairing signals the close of the prefatory remarks on Clodius's impiety. The first two words of the next sentence at last turn to the response, the principal reason for the senate meeting and for Cicero's speech.

9 (*Responsum haruspicum*)-19

Cicero turns to the haruspical response, beginning with the portion most damaging to his own claims—that sacred and "religious" spaces have been desecrated. It now becomes clear that the previous parts of the speech were meant to remind the senate of Clodius's alleged profanation of the Bona Dea in order to predispose them into considering him the prime suspect for violating religious sanctity. It is also probably not accidental that one of Cicero's cleverest jokes in the speech—on Clodius's authority to address *pudicitia*—is given, and elaborated upon, immediately before he treats the response. Senators are surely still smiling as he shifts gears to his main, and eminently serious, subject.

Responsum haruspicum: See Introduction F.2 for the role of the Etruscan *haruspices* in Roman republican religion, and Introduction E.1 for suggestions about how the response was generated. Introduction G.1 offers a reconstruction of the probable original order of those portions of the response quoted by Cicero.

hoc recens: Cicero elsewhere uses the demonstrative *hic* to refer to the response (10, 11, 29), implying that, like Clodius the previous day (9n), he holds a copy in his hand or at least that there is one nearby to which he and his audience can refer (Corbeill 2010a). This impression is further reinforced by terms referring to "reading" or "looking at" the response: 9 (*recitavit*); 18 and 34 (*videamus*); 37 (*et video in haruspicum responso haec esse subiuncta*). This "presence" of the text, whether physical or merely mental, facilitates Cicero's major strategy in this speech, namely, to conduct a close philological reading of the response's contents in order to prove that it points conclusively to Clodius as the cause of disruption in the natural and, by extension, the political order.

de fremitu: The precise nature of the noise made is unclear; ancient etymologies consider the noun *fremitus* and the associated verb *fremo* onomatopoetic (Varro *ling.* 6.67; Dosith. *gramm.* 7.396.12; Char. *gramm.* p. 197.20 B). The text of the response describes it, with seeming redundancy, *strepitus cum fremitu* ("a rumbling, accompanied by a trembling"; see 20n), on which Cicero elaborates later: "some sort of mysterious rumbling and a frightful trembling of weapons" (20: *strepitus quidam reconditus et horribilis fremitus armorum*; cf. Obseq. 45: *fremitus armorum ex inferno* [prodigy of 100 BCE]). Cicero's final reference characterizes the prodigy simply as "a kind of sound" (62: *genus sonitus*).

Fremitus can refer to the noise generated by a number of natural phenomena—wind in the trees, rain, crashing waves, the murmur of the sea (*ThLL* VI 1280.62–1281.19 [F. Müller])—but parallels from other prodigies and its location in northern Latium (20n) indicate that these particular noises emanate from the earth (*div.* 1.35, 2.60; Obseq. 48: *Pisauri terrae fremitus auditus*, 53: *Faesulis fremitus terrae auditus*, 59: *fremitus inferni exauditi*; Turfa 2012: 32 states without argument that the noise was "heard in the heavens"). In *De divinatione* Cicero notes that Etruscans specialize in noises from the earth, which he distinguishes from tremors and which could predict serious dangers to the state (*div.* 1.35: *terrae saepe fremitus, saepe mugitus, saepe motus multa rei publicae...gravia et vera praedixerint*; Thulin 1905–1909: 3.86–87), while Obsequens records from 99 BCE that a noise extending from earth to sky portended want and famine (46: *fremitus ab inferno ad caelum ferri visus inopiam famemque portendit*). Wülker 1901: 18–19 compiles other instances of noises being considered prodigies.

According to Cicero's discussion, the *haruspices* restricted themselves to investigating this one event (he mentions at 62 a second that the senate had not yet considered). Dio, by contrast, catalogues a series of prodigies on this occasion—a shifting temple, a meteor (?; Ramsey 2006: 203–204), a wolf entering the city, an earthquake, citizens struck by lightning, and this rumbling in the *ager Latiniensis*—and implies that all were referred to the senate, thereby occasioning a conflict between Cicero and Clodius: τεράτων τέ τινων ἐν τούτῳ γενομένων (ἔν τε γὰρ τῷ Ἀλβανῷ νεὼς Ἥρας βραχὺς ἐπὶ τραπέζης τινὸς πρὸς ἀνατολῶν ἱδρυμένος πρὸς τὴν ἄρκτον μετεστράφη, καὶ λαμπὰς ἀπὸ τῆς μεσημβρίας ὁρμηθεῖσα πρὸς βορέαν διῆξε, λύκος τε ἐς τὴν πόλιν ἐσῆλθε, καὶ σεισμὸς ἐγένετο, τῶν τε πολιτῶν τινες κεραυνοῖς ἐφθάρησαν, καὶ **θόρυβος ἐν τῷ Λατίνῳ ὑπὸ γῆς ἐξηκούσθη**· καὶ αὐτὰ οἱ μάντεις ἀκέσασθαι ἐθελήσαντες **ὀργίζεσθαί σφισι δαιμόνιόν τι ὡς καὶ ἱερῶν τινων ἢ χωρίων οὐχ ὁσίων ἐποικουμένων** ἔφασαν). ἐνταῦθα ὁ Κλώδιος τὸν Κικέρωνα μεταλαβὼν τῷ τε λόγῳ πολὺς ἐνέκειτο, ὅτι τὸ ἔδαφος τῆς οἰκίας ἱερωμένον τῇ Ἐλευθερίᾳ κατῳκοδόμησε, καὶ ἐπῆλθέ ποτε ἐπ᾽ αὐτὸ ὡς καὶ ἐκ θεμελίων αὖθις αὐτὴν ἀναιρήσων (39.20.1–3).

in contione recitavit: This is presumably the same *contio* described at 8. *Recito* is the normal word used to describe a magistrate reading out, or having read out, a proposal to the people (Crawford 1996: 1.11; *ThLL* XI, 2 364.40–55 [P. Pieroni]). In the case of legislation, written copies of the text were displayed publicly on whitened boards for the people to consult over a period of several days (Morstein-Marx 2004: 8; for a depiction of one possible scenario from

Pompeii, see Nappo 1989: 87–88). It seems likely that Clodius would have made similar accommodations for the public display of the haruspical response.

scriptum etiam illud est, id quod audistis: Three possibilities suggest themselves for when the senators could have heard this section of the response. First, Cicero may simply refer to his summary of Clodius's *contio* at 8 (*sacra et religiones neglegi violari pollui questus est*). While this summary could provide an approximate equivalent of *LOCA SACRA ET RELIGIOSA PROFANA HABERI* (for *sacrum* as "shrine" see Plaut. *Curc.* 471; *OLD* s.v. 2), Cicero's lengthy exposition here would seem to require a more direct allusion to "places." A second possibility is that Cicero refers to a public reading of the response at some time before he began his speech. Since we know that witnesses to a prodigy were present before the senate began its deliberations (Liv. 22.1.14, 27.11.3), it is likely that the response of the *haruspices* would have been presented orally at that time (Plut. *Sulla* 7.3–6). This recitation would have either constituted part of the senate's formal considerations (*relatio*), or been given in the period before the *relatio* when texts were read to the senate (O'Brien Moore 1935: 708–709). Third, Cicero refers to the *contio* at which Clodius had read out the response. Several considerations favor this final option: 1. this relative clause—"as you have heard"—is in the immediate context of Clodius's public reading; 2. the sentence following the quotation of the response contains a verb (*dixit*) whose subject, Clodius, is more clear if the context is what the senate had heard from Clodius the previous day; 3. though admittedly this has less force, if *id quod audistis* referred to what *Cicero* had just said, one would have expected some sort of qualifying adverb (e.g., *nuper*); for a fourth consideration, see the next note.

LOCA SACRA ET RELIGIOSA PROFANA HABERI: "Sacred and hallowed places have been desecrated." Cicero reports this and all other clauses of the response in indirect statement. If the argument concerning *id quod audistis* in the previous note is correct, this is the only clause of the response that Cicero explicitly attributes to Clodius having mentioned in his *contio* (for a possible exception see 34: *de Alexandrinis esse video sermonem*). As a result, Cicero gives the impression that Clodius concentrated solely on this portion of the *responsum*, in contrast with Cicero's more holistic and systematic approach. Cicero had good reason both to begin with and to concentrate on this particular clause. It is the most damning for his case, since the entire senate would surely recall that Cicero rebuilt his house on the site of an alleged shrine to Libertas; at the same time, however, the decision of the pontifices the preceding October to restore to him his property provides strong authority for the clause not applying to him. See further the next note.

Dio's summary of this section of the response points to Cicero's situation even more damningly: οἱ μάντεις...ὀργίζεσθαί σφισι δαιμόνιόν τι ὡς καὶ ἱερῶν τινων ἢ χωρίων οὐχ ὁσίων ἐποικουμένων ἔφασαν ("The haruspices declared that a divinity was angry at [the Romans] since some temples or holy places were being inhabited"; 39.20.2; for fuller context see 9n on *de fremitu*). Arnob. *nat.* 7.9.2 seems to have this event in mind in the satirical speech that he puts into the mouth of a sacrificial ox: *"numquid erui* **sacratissimos** *lucos aut* **religiosa** *quaedam* **loca** *substructionibus pollui* **profanavi***que privatis?"*; for Arnobius's familiarity with *har. resp.* see 20n.

The etymology of *profanus* remains in dispute (WH 1: 454). Some scholars posit with Varro *ling.* 6.54 the sense of "in front of" (*pro*) the "sacred space" (*fanum*), while others offer refinements of the notion of Char. *gramm.* p. 305.20–22 B that it means "far removed from the sacred space" (e.g., Wagenvoort 1949, following Wackernagel 1916: 239–240; Lennon 2014: 42–43; and esp. Benveniste 1960: 46–49; full listing of ancient etymologies at Maltby 1991: 499). Ancient authors often preserve the distinction that Cicero does here between this adjective and *religiosus* and/or *sacer*; see, for example, Trebatius's definition: *profanum id proprie dici…quod ex religioso vel sacro in hominum usum proprietatem conversum est* (Macr. *Sat.* 3.3.4; other testimony at *ThLL* X, 2 1661.56–73 [S. Brenner, J. Blundell]). Gaius *inst.* 2.5–6 defines the *sacrum* as what has been consecrated through the Roman people, the *religiosum* through a private person (Rives 2011 surveys the legal evidence); see further 14n.

dixit domum meam a religiosissimo sacerdote, P. Clodio, consecratam: For the many ironic references to Clodius as a *sacerdos*, see Nisbet 1961: 159 ("after the Bona Dea incident he must have made the joke so many times that the name had stuck"). Despite the palpably ironic use of this alleged quotation, Cicero offers here what must have been the key part of Clodius's argument. It seems plausible, even likely, that Clodius did in fact say something akin to this in his *contio* and, as a *XVvir*, he could rightly lay claim to the title *sacerdos* (26n). The adjective *religiosus*, whose superlative form drips with sarcasm in the Ciceronian context, where he has just reminded his listeners of the Bona Dea scandal, commonly occurs elsewhere to insult Clodius (4n). And yet the word also appears with greater regularity in a positive sense, including in superlative form, to describe someone as "practiced in religious matters" or "faithful to the observances of religion" (*OLD* s.v. 3 and 7a; see esp. Fest. p. 289 M: *religiosi dicuntur, qui faciendarum praetermittendarumque rerum divinarum secundum morem civitatis dilectum habent*). Hence, the normally positive connotation of *religiosus* would make it a perfectly reasonable adjective for Clodius to have used in his *contio* to describe himself and his actions. Given the centrality of the consecration of Cicero's house to an interpretation of the response, it is intuitively likely that Clodius's reference had a prominence and wording in his *contio* analogous to what it is given in Cicero's speech.

consecratam: For a clear account of the distinction between *dedicatio* (entailing the surrender of ownership of property or possessions) and *consecratio* (transference from the human to the divine realm), both of which are required for the creation of sacred space, see Nisbet 1939: 209–210. In the context of the consecration of his home, however, Cicero often conflates the two processes, as here (cf. *dom.* 119, 122). For Cicero's tactical use in *dom.* of this confusion see Stroh 2004, esp. 323–330.

10–11 (*parebo*)

Cicero prefaces his defense against Clodius's charge by stressing that the entire response, not just the portion quoted, represents a divine warning about the danger represented by Clodius. This section is clearly set off stylistically. The main verbs receive particular emphasis from the word order—*gaudeo... reperietis* (first position); *sed primum expiabo* (second position)—with these prefatory remarks capped by a cretic + spondee clausula with verb in final position (*religionīquĕ pārēbō*).

de toto hoc ostento: Cf. 10: *ex hoc toto prodigio atque responso*. The various nouns used to refer to the Roman prodigy seem interchangeable, although Cicero and other ancients attempt to make distinctions (*div.* 1.93: *quia... ostendunt portendunt monstrant praedicunt, ostenta portenta monstra prodigia dicuntur*; Maltby 1991: 437). Rosenberger, however, notes a tendency for *ostentum* and *portentum* to describe signs dealing with inanimate nature, *monstrum* and *miraculum* with animate, while *prodigium* is the blanket term (1998: 7–8, with previous bibliography), a distinction that roughly holds for this speech (but cf. 18, where *portenta* seems the generic designation).

haud scio an: A literal interpretation ("I hardly know whether...") and its earliest occurrences (e.g., Plaut. *Epid.* 543; LHS 2: 2.543) indicate that the phrase originally marked uncertainty. By the time of Cicero, however, who favors the formulation in his speeches from the 50s, it has rather come to denote probability (KS 2: 2.520–521; cf. *OLD* s.v. *scio* 4b ["in cautious assertions"]). Von Albrecht 2003: 103 conjectures that *haud*, a negator favored in early Latin poetry, becomes common in Cicero's writings from the fifties on account of his active engagement with poetry at that time.

multis his annis: "In the past several years"; for the use of the demonstrative *hic* in an ablative construction to indicate recent past time, see *ThLL* VI, 3 2720.78–2721.1 (H. Schmid, V. Bulhart, W. Ehlers).

nuntiatum sit: The passive form of the verb *nuntiare* is conventionally used for the official announcement of a prodigy to the senate (cf. 63). The passive construction draws attention to the phenomenon itself rather than to the witnesses reporting it, who nearly always remain anonymous (Luterbacher 1904: 44–45); cf. 23n.

causam ēssĕ dīcēndī: The cretic + spondee ending helps explain the hyperbaton of *causam... dicenti* (all alternatives yield a less desirable double molossus). At the same time, the sequence yields what Powell 2010: 176 classifies as a "short-range" hyperbaton, in which "one, always comparatively unfocused, constituent intervenes between the separated elements," resulting in focus on the enclosing phrase, here *causam dicendi* (cf. 2010: 182 on *esse*). The emphasis would of course make sense, since the speech itself is what Cicero is "speaking."

ex hoc toto prodigio ātquĕ rēspōnsō nos…prope iam voce Iovis Optimi Maximi praemoneri: Cicero here picks up *de toto hoc ostento* (10), and with the addition of *responso* suggests that both the prodigy and the response arise from the will of the gods. This is the first step in a process by which Cicero ultimately identifies as identical the prodigy, the response, and divine intention (Corbeill 2010a: 151–153; cf. 18, 20 [*haruspicum vocem*], 23 [*ille fremitus nuntiet*], 37 [*haruspices haec loquuntur an…dii?*], 44, 55; for *voce* see 20n). The comments of Beard 1991: 50 on written oracles that are delivered to cities aptly apply to the written haruspical response, *mutatis mutandis*: "The oracular text…was more than a document of public information; it was more, even, than a permanent written validation of the spoken word of the god. For, among a community where few people would have the opportunity themselves to travel to distant oracular shrines, the text itself could *become* the word of god" (emphasis original). For the use of *atque* before a consonant, here presumably used to produce a cretic + spondee rhythm, see nn. on 3 and 18.

de istius scelere ac furore: The words *scelus* and *furor* are often paired in Cicero to underscore the religious violations of an enemy of the state (Taldone 1993: 12–13).

de impendentibus periculis maximis: "About the threat of unparalleled dangers." In his discussion of the development, beginning with Cicero, of the so-called *ab urbe condita* construction (13n: *post sacra constituta*), Laughton 1964: 98 identifies this as an early example using the present participle: "The participle can be taken as attributive ('quae impendent'), but I believe that Cicero intended the prepositional phrase to be equivalent to 'impendere pericula maxima'. This interpretation finds strong support in a number of genitive examples, in which Cicero seems to have been exploring new ground."

prope iam voce Iovis Optimi Maximi: The likelihood that Cicero intends to draw a parallel between Jupiter Best and <u>Greatest</u> and "the threat of the <u>greatest</u> (*maximis*) dangers" is supported by the similar position of these adjectives following the word they modify. For the cult of Jupiter Optimus Maximus, or Jupiter Capitolinus, whose temple on the Capitoline was the most important in the city, see Wissowa 1912: 125–129; *RE* 10.1.1135–1139 (C. Thulin). Jupiter did not normally play a significant role in the prodigy process. He seems to be mentioned here in his role as chief Roman deity, a role that also explains why the *haruspices* list him first among the gods to whom reparations are due in expiating the prodigy (20). For an analogous situation in which Jupiter Capitolinus assists Cicero, see *Catil.* 3.22: *quibus ego si me restitisse dicam, nimium mihi sumam et non sim ferendus: ille, ille Iuppiter restitit; ille Capitolium, ille haec templa, ille cunctam urbem, ille vos omnis salvos esse voluit*. Cicero inserts *prope* ("as if through the voice") to avoid claiming to have certain knowledge of Jupiter's will; cf. *Catil.* 3.19: *prope fata ipsa* (Dyck 2008: 195: "added advisedly"). A less likely interpretation is that Cicero alludes to the founder of the *disciplina Etrusca*, Tages, whom some sources record as Jupiter's grandson (20n).

** *praemoneri*: this is the reading of G; *promoneri* P *promoveri* EH. The choice seems easy; *promoneo* would seem to have the required sense (cf. 20: *praemonstrare*), but the only other possible Ciceronian attestation occurs at *Att.* 4.12=SB 81, where it is normally emended; see Watt 1964: 400, Shackleton Bailey 1965-1970: 2.188.

READ *praemoneri*.

11 *expiabo religionem aedium mearum*: "I shall free my home from any religious restrictions." The noun *religio* and its affiliates (8n) occur twelve times within sections 11-12, referring to any potential violation of the relationship between the divine and human that may be evidenced in Cicero's house (cf. *dom.* 69: *ne quis oreretur... qui in meis aedibus aliquam religionem residere diceret*, 104, 127). For this sense, compare Cicero's paraphrase of the decree of the pontifices, most of whom are named in section 12, that had followed Cicero's speech on his house and brought about this freedom from *religio*: "*posse sine religione eam partem areae mihi restitui*" ("that part of my property can be restored to me without any religious scruple"; *Att.* 4.2.3=SB 74). For the collocation *religionem expiare* in Cicero see *Verr.* 2.1.8: *religiones deorum immortalium expiandae*, 2.4.111; *Mil.* 73: *[Clodii] supplicio...sollemnes religiones expiandas*; cf. *Tusc.* 1.27: *inexpiabili religione*, *Phil.* 1.13: *inexpiabiles religiones*. At Liv. 31.13.1 the phrase *expiatis omnibus religionibus* describes the expiation of a series of prodigies that had occurred throughout Italy.

** *scrupulus*: *scripulus* PH, Maslowski; *scrupulus* GE, Peterson. The two forms are often confused in codices (e.g., Varro apud Char. *gramm.* 134.2 B; Caper *gramm.* 7.111.10). Both nouns derive from *scrupus* ("small stone," uncertain etymology), with the "i" form apparently influenced by *scriptum* (Vaan 2008: 547-548). Accordingly, the two spellings have clear, if not absolute, semantic domains, with the neuter *scripulum* describing measurements and the predominantly masculine form *scrupulus* describing sources of anxiety. Semantics here favors *scrupulus*, as does the sense of *residere*; the masculine gender follows the rule for the formation of diminutives (KS 1: 983).

11 (*Sed quae...referretur*)

Cicero begins his remarks on the portion of the response regarding profaned places by asserting that his own home has been determined to be free from religious taint by all three Roman bodies capable of such a determination.

Sed...tandem: "And yet in the end"; in rhetorical questions the particle *tandem* carries a tone of urgency or impatience, with Cicero here addressing the doubts of the hypothetical "someone" of the previous sentence (Risselada 1998: 110-113; 51n). Contrast its use at 50.

in hac urbe tanta: "In such an immense city as this." The combination of a demonstrative adjective with an adjective or adverb of quantity is common in Latin; examples in Nägelsbach 1905: 404-405. The word order, however, is unusual for Cicero, where the noun normally follows the form of *tantus* (*hic/iste/ille* + *tantus* + noun). Of the six examples that I have found in the speeches of *tantus* standing last, five have a clear syntactic explanation (*Quinct.* 82; *S. Rosc.* 97; *Sull.* 68; *Phil.* 6.2, 11.14; semantics seems to explain *Cael.* 52). Here Cicero emphasizes the uniqueness of his house by employing an unexpected word order ("in this city [probably gesturing with *hac*], which is so large"); the displacement of *tanta* also creates anticipation for the subsequent phrase *tam vacua atque pura*.

ab ista suspicione religionis tam vacua atque pura: For *vacua* compare *dom.* 116: *domus illa mea prope tota vacua est* ("nearly that entire house of mine is free [from religious scruple]"). Cicero had to add the qualification *prope* ("almost") for the speech from the previous September since, as he goes on to say, one-tenth had been occupied by the portico of Catulus, which had contained the shrine of Libertas. Since in the interim the *pontifices* have decided that the consecration of the shrine in Cicero's home was conducted improperly, Cicero no longer needs to qualify his claim. *Pura* describes the state of the house as a consequence of this pontifical decision (*atque* adding a more emphatic adjective—here in the sense "and therefore," as often; Ciceronian examples at *ThLL* II 1052, 57–75 [A. Klotz]). For the adjective as a technical term in Roman religion and its relationship with *vacuus/vacare* see Ulp. *dig.* 11.7.2.4: *purus autem locus dicitur, qui neque sacer neque sanctus est neque religiosus, sed ab omnibus huiusmodi nominibus vacare videtur* ("a place is said to be *purus* that is neither *sacer* nor *sanctus* nor filled with *religio*, but is seen to be free from every designation of this type").

una mea domus iudiciis omnibus liberata in hac urbe sola est: Cicero distinguishes here other homes in Rome, that are in a static sense "free of religious sanction" (using the adjective *liberae*), from his own, which has been actively "set free" by every adjudicative body (*liberata...est*). Forms of the verb *libero* occur seven times in sections 11–16, six in reference to Cicero's home, and it is difficult not to see a sly allusion to the shrine of Libertas, whose improper consecration allowed for this "freedom," as well as perhaps a pun on the ancient etymologies that construe *religio* as a "binding" force (8n and *OLD* 4b s.v. *obligo*; for the pun in Cicero, see *Balb.* 34 [*obligari*]; *div.* 1.7 [*obligemur*]; cf. Costa 1964: 1.145–146). Livy's account of the founding of the temple of Jupiter Optimus Maximus on the Capitoline provides a close parallel for Cicero's formulation. Before construction could begin, Tarquin had to deconsecrate (*exaugurare*) the shrines that were already standing on the spot (1.55.2: *et ut <u>libera a ceteris religionibus</u> area esset tota Iovis templique eius quod inaedificaretur, exaugurare fana sacellaque statuit*).

The pleonasm *una...sola* is not uncommon in Cicero's orations; see 14 below (*uno illo solo antistite*) and, e.g., *Verr.* 2.2.13: *unam solam scitote esse civitatem Mamertinam*; 2.2.185: *ex uno oppido solo*; 2.3.202; 2.5.95; *Tull.* 34; *Mur.* 18. The non-standard placement of *omnibus* after its noun underscores the contrast with these two adjectives that bracket it (Marouzeau 1922: 1.172 notes that *omnis* is postponed in Cicero's orations in 384 of 1795 occurrences).

Lentule...Philippe: Since Cicero has at last turned to the business for which the senate is meeting, he fittingly addresses the two consuls of 56, Gnaeus Cornelius Lentulus Marcellinus and Lucius Marcius Philippus (2n), who had made the motion that the senate debate the meaning of the haruspical response. Both men are addressed by their cognomen alone, although it is normal in senatorial speeches to use a double name for address (Adams 1978: 146). Since during this period primarily members of the elite possessed cognomina (Kajanto 1965: 19, 132), the name carried special prestige and direct address by cognomen alone indicated either informality or contempt, neither of which would apply in this case (Adams 1978: 145–146, who notes that the *Philippics* provide an unusual exception). Both here and at the one other time that Lentulus is addressed by cognomen alone (21), it is in direct appeal in requesting the addressee to make a judgment (the verb *appello* is used in both instances), here as consuls and later to Lentulus as *septemvir epulo*. I suggest that Cicero employs the odd usage in order to make his appeal similar to that used in a court of law, where "sustained double naming is not usual" (Adams 1978: 146–147). Clodius is on trial. When Cicero comes to address Lentulus in a different context, he changes to the more usual form of praenomen + cognomen (22n).

ex hoc haruspicum responso: The most natural way of understanding *hoc* in the context is as a reference back to the clause cited at 9 (*LOCA SACRA ET RELIGIOSA PROFANA HABERI*), rather than to the entirety of the text produced by the *haruspices*. If so, this would indicate that Cicero considered the entire "response" to consist of multiple *responsa* (see further Introduction E.1).

decrevit senatus ut de locis sacris, religiosis ad hunc ordinem referretis: This senatorial decree will have marked the penultimate stage in the prodigy process (see Introduction F.1). Once a priestly body delivers its response, the senate can decide either to reject its findings or to decide upon reparations (61n). That discussion would have been initiated by a formal proposal on the part of the current consuls (*relatio*, cf. *referretis* and Mommsen 1887–1888: 1.209–210; Wissowa 1912: 391). Wiseman 1974: 164 points out that this decision to refer the matter of the prodigy to the senate must indicate that some senators agreed with Clodius that the decision made about Cicero's house the previous fall merited reconsideration, a point that Cicero takes care to avoid in the speech (cf. Tatum 1999: 217 and compare 17n: *vidi...quendam murmurantem*).

The absence of a conjunction between the two adjectives *sacra* and *religiosus* (*asyndeton bimembre*) is characteristic of early Latin (LHS 2: 831ε; Timpanaro 1988; but cf. Adams 2021, esp. 683–686), including religious texts (Lehmann 1886: 23, citing *Iuppiter Optimus Maximus*). This particular combination of *sacer* and *religiosus* also occurs at 30 and Marcian. *dig.* 48.13.4 (Preuss 1881: 103), although Cicero elsewhere uses the conjunction (9: *LOCA SACRA ET RELIGIOSA*; *leg.* 3.31; on the variation see Preuss 1881: 10–11). The words in such a construction usually are, as here, semantically related or near synonyms

(*OLS* 2: 614). Considering the rarity of adjectives in asyndeton in literary texts of the classical period (Timpanaro 1988: 11–35), it would be tempting to insert here a conjunction, were it not for the repetition of the same phrase at 30 (cf. Shackleton Bailey on *Att.* 1.16.8=SB 16). Given this evidence, therefore, I assume that Cicero here quotes from the consular motion; for asyndeton in senatorial proposals see Adams 2021: 265–268.

sola in hac urbe / **omni** religione / **omnibus** iudiciis liberata est: Cicero again stresses the uniqueness of his home (cf. 11n above), here by varying word order and placing the adjectives at the beginning of their respective cola. Nisbet 1990: 354 discusses the favorable rhythms at these particular colon boundaries (cretic + spondee, the second one resolved; double trochee).

primum ... deinde ... postea: In a methodical tricolon, Cicero relays specifics about his repeated claim that his house was freed from religious taint "by every possible authority." In so doing, he once again demonstrates that Clodius, whose ineffectiveness he describes in the first colon, is pitted against the combined wishes of those featured in the remainder of the sentence: the Roman people, senate, and *pontifices*.

in illa tempestate ac nocte rei publicae: Cicero's mention of a storm recalls his earlier use of the ship of state metaphor (*tempestate*; 4n). He often associates figuratively the darkness of night with danger to the state; at *S. Rosc.* 91 men during the reign of Sulla "were rushing about in the shadows as if eternal night had spread over the republic" (*qui, tamquam si offusa rei publicae sempiterna nox esset, ita ruebant in tenebris*; see Landgraf 1914: 184).

stilo illo impuro Sex. Cloeli ore tincto: "With a pen made wet by Sextus Cloelius's notoriously (*illo*) disgusting mouth." Grammatically, the form *illo* could modify either *stilo* or *ore*. Word order does not help resolve the ambiguity, since when *ille* means "that [in]famous," it can either precede or follow the noun (KS 2: 1.622; many examples of both occur in this speech, e.g., 4: *illo die* vs. 5: *stipitem illum*, both in a negative sense). Appeal to prior contexts in which Cicero discusses Cloelius's "mouth," however, make it likely that *ore* is the noun modified. In Ciceronian oratory "when accompanied by a modifier *os* receives an added dimension and tends to refer more specifically to vices or reprehensible actions" (Corbeill 1996: 102); if such a principle is applied here, then, one would understand *illo* as emphasizing *impuro ore* ("that notoriously disgusting mouth"), which would carry particular potency given the connotations attached to the *os impurum* throughout Latin literature (Adams 1982: 213; Richlin 1992: 26–29, 99, 149–151). Richlin 1992: 29 notes in particular that it seems "probable ... that *impurus* always carried at least the suggestion of the meaning 'contaminated by oral-genital contact.'" And in fact in *dom.* Cicero devotes a great deal of attention to Cloelius's *os* but not, as here, in its capacity at legislation, but rather in cunnilingus, particularly with Clodia, Clodius's sister, where Cloelius's mouth is characterized as *impurissimum* (*dom.* 26; Corbeill 1996: 112–123). That a reference to oral sex would be understood here need not rely, however, on the memory of the references in *dom.* (as likely as that may be). Cicero's entire phrase also attracts attention by its peculiarity— why would a Roman *stilus*, normally made of hard materials such as bronze, iron, or ivory—be "wet" from a person's mouth? (I have found no comparable example in classical Latin of the combination with *tingo*; in Cicero's speeches, the verb appears only at *Verr.* 2.4.59, to describe dyeing). The most accessible interpretation is that Cloelius's mouth metaphorically "stains" the stylus (for the *stilus*, including images of it near the mouth, see DS 4: 1510–1511 [G. Lafaye]; for the mouth contaminating drinking cups, Kay 1985: 90–91). The impurity of his mouth, in other words, spills over to the writing implement by which he composed Clodius's legislation.

Asconius calls Sextus Cloelius a *scriba* (*Mil.* p. 33.6 Clark), although it is unclear whether he worked for Clodius in a personal capacity or as a civil servant. He is referred to several times in Cicero, as here, for his assistance in drafting legislation during Clodius's tribunate, but he performed several other duties on Clodius's behalf as well, and according to Asconius he spearheaded the cremation of Clodius's body that precipitated the destruction of the senate house in 52 (*Mil.* p. 33.5–8 Clark). Damon 1992 offers a detailed account of his life and career.

**Cloeli: *cloelii* PG; *cloelius* H; *clodii* E. For the certain reading *Cloeli* see Shackleton Bailey 1960.

ne una quidem attigit littera religionis: It appears that in composing the legislation that would result in Cicero's exile Clodius did not mention his plans to consecrate part of Cicero's Palatine property (cf. *dom.* 115: *monumentum iste umquam aut religionem ullam excogitavit?*, with Nisbet 1939: xvii, 206–209). For the objective genitive after *littera*, compare the similar contexts at *dom.* 104: *religionis verbum*, 128: *unum ostende verbum consecrationis*. The short-range hyperbaton of *una...littera* combines with *ne...quidem* to make the modifier *una* especially emphatic: "not one single letter" (Powell 2010: 176–177; for the hyperbole see *ThLL* VII, 2 1520.82–1521.17 [H. v. Kamptz]).

deinde eandem domum populus Romanus, cuius est summa potestas omnium rerum, comitiis centuriatis omnium aetatum ordinumque suffragiis eodem iure esse iussit quo fuisset: Cicero turns from a negative argument about the untainted status of his house to three positive judgments: that of the people, the senate, and the college of pontifices. The first refers to the popular vote in the centuriate assembly on August 4, 57, that recalled Cicero from exile and restored all rights and privileges that he had lost. The occasion resulted in the only known law passed by the centuriate assembly between the years 70 and 49 (Taylor 1966: 103–104). Cicero was justly proud of the event, and refers to it repeatedly in his orations and correspondence (e.g., *Att.* 4.1.4=SB 73: *mirifico studio omnium aetatum atque ordinum*; *p. red. in sen.* 27–28; *p. red. ad Quir.* 17–18; *Pis.* 35–36). Since he was restored with the same rights that he had had previously, the ownership of his property must perforce enjoy the same conditions (this conclusion is supported by the mood of *fuisset*, as a subjunctive in implied indirect discourse following *iussit*).

Cicero frequently asserts that the greatest political power lay in the electoral authority of the people: see, e.g., *leg. agr.* 2.17 (*omnes potestates, imperia, curationes ab universo populo Romano proficisci convenit*), *p. red. in sen.* 27 (*comitiis centuriatis, quae maxime maiores comitia iusta dici haberique voluerunt*) and, for its contrast with the senatorial authority that acts to confirm that power (as at 11), see *leg.* 3.28 (*cum potestas in populo, auctoritas in senatu sit*). Laser 1997: 26–31 analyzes the historicity of Cicero's claim, which also finds voice in his treatises (*rep.* 1.39: *populus... [est] coetus multitudinis iuris consensu et utilitatis communione sociatus*). Debate over the extent to which Rome constituted a democracy, at least in theory, has stimulated much recent debate; see especially Millar 1998 and the challenges from Hölkeskamp 2010.

non quo... sed ut: Cicero prefers the older construction *non quo* to *non quod* (LHS 2: 2.588); the resumption with a purpose clause is extremely common, including at *dom.* 69, which describes the same occasion (*non quo dubitaret... sed ne*).

ut huic furiae, si diutius in hac urbe quam delere cuperet maneret, vox interdiceretur, decrevistis: *Dom.* 69 gives further details about this senatorial edict that gave the *pontifices* the authority to pronounce on the *religio* of Cicero's house and to silence anyone who spoke against their decision. The pronouncement was made on the motion of Marcus Bibulus some time after (*postea*) the August 4 date of the people's vote for Cicero's recall. The sequence of four finite verbs, each in a different construction, is a feature of high literary style; cf. *Catil.* 4.19: *atque haec non ut vos, qui mihi studio paene praecurritis, excitarem, locutus sum* (Courtney 1999: 1). Note how Clodius's *vox* "intervenes" (literally, *interdico*: "is mentioned between") between his own potential actions and those realized by the senate. *ThLL* VII, 1 2173.65–66 (E. Hermans) notes that this verb normally describes actions of the praetor, and gives only this example of the senate. Lebreton 1901: 176 cites only one other occurrence of the passive of *interdico* in Cicero (*Balb.* 26: *interdicto [praemio]*); KS 2: 1.336.

Cicero repeats at 33 the hyperbolic accusation that Clodius wished to destroy Rome (*urbem eam quam delere voluisti*).

ad pontificum collegium: During the Republic, the college of the *pontifices* had three general areas under their jurisdiction (Wissowa 1912: 501–523, esp. 513–519; Beard 1990: esp. 36–39; BNP 1: 24–26): 1. they acted as specialists in the performance of state ritual; 2. they exerted control over the religious behavior of individuals, which could overlap with areas of law; 3. they acted as advisors to the senate, as here, in a conflict between matters of state and of religion (Mommsen 1887–1888: 2.45–47). The majority of *pontifices* simultaneously held high political office and were themselves members of the senate (BNP 1: 27–29; 12n). During the late Republic they were chosen by a complicated combination of nomination by current *pontifices*, election by a special tribal assembly of the people, and cooptation of the electoral victor by the rest of the college (Linderski 1972: 191-192). Their leader, the *pontifex maximus*, was elected by this same popular assembly after the death of the previous holder (details in Taylor 1942b).

12-13

Cicero stresses the authority of those pontifices who had unanimously declared his home free from religious taint, and lists by name most of those involved, contending that their number exceeds those present at any pontifical decision in the history of Rome. Their decision was affirmed the following day at a well-attended meeting of the senate.

in maximis superstitionibus: In public discourse of the late Republic the noun *superstitio* occurs, as here, in a predominately negative sense, as beliefs or behaviors that contrast with recognized state religion; cf., e.g., Cic. *nat. deor.* 1.117: *horum sententiae omnium non modo superstitionem tollunt, in qua inest timor inanis deorum, sed etiam religionem, quae deorum cultu pio continetur*, 2.71: *maiores nostri superstitionem a religione separaverunt*, with Pease 1955-1958: 738; Fest. p. 289 M; Santangelo 2013: 38-47. BNP 1: 216-227 trace the varied meanings of *superstitio* up through Christianity, when it comes to describe chiefly non-orthodox belief. Cicero's use of the plural indicates that he is thinking of a variety of reasons that Romans may feel *superstitio* (cf. BNP 1: 217: "the term *superstitio* was used initially to categorize the improper behaviour of individuals rather than groups").

unius P. Servili aut M. Luculli responso ac verbo: That is, simply one authoritative *pontifex* had the jurisdiction to restore Cicero's home; Cicero makes the same point at 13, where he adds the qualification that the *pontifex* must be "experienced" (*perito*). Lenaghan 1969: 81 conjectures that these particular *pontifices* are named since they acted as *pontifex maximus* while Caesar was in Gaul, for which there is no evidence. It seems more likely that Cicero refers, probably tendentiously, to the single priest who, chosen annually, could make decisions over private affairs, and that Servilius and Lucullus held that post for 57 and 56 (Pompon. *dig.* 1.2.2.6: *actiones apud collegium pontificum erant, ex quibus constituebatur, quis quoquo anno praesset privatis*); this status would accord with the fact that they were among the most senior of the *pontifices*, both having been coopted before 76 (Taylor 1942a: 394, 411; cf. *dom.* 132-133; *pace* Mommsen 1887-1888: 2.46, who notes that occasions when a sacral decision regarding a private individual did not involve the state are doubtful). Note that the use of *responso* implies that the *responsum* of the pontifical college has authority equal to that of the *haruspices*.

de *sacris publicis*, de *ludis maximis*, de *deorum penatium Vestaeque matris caerimoniis*, de *illo ipso sacrificio* quod *fit pro salute populi Romani*, quod *post Romam conditam huius unius casti tutoris religionum scelere violatum est*, quod *tres pontifices statuissent*, id *semper populo Romano, semper senatui, semper ipsis*

dis immortalibus, <u>satis</u> sanctum, <u>satis</u> augustum, <u>satis</u> religiosum esse visum est: The sentence seems designed to impress, beginning with the broad spheres of public cult over which the *pontifices* exercise authority, and ending with the respect widely felt for this authority by the gods and the Romans; except, of course, by Clodius. The construction of the sentence, balancing parallelism with misdirection, can be outlined as follows: two prepositional clauses in isocolon and homoioteleuton, introduced by *de* and describing a general realm of religion; two more clauses introduced by *de* turn to specific religious rites, with the second further described by two relative clauses introduced by *quod*; a third *quod* sets up expectations of a tricolon, which is belied by the subjunctive verb (*statuissent*), whereupon the listener realizes that this clause is a generalizing relative describing the subject of the main clause (*id*). Finally, the sentence regularizes with two consecutive tricola in anaphora (*semper*; *satis*), with the main verbs closing the sentence in a favored ditrochee (*ēssĕ vīsūm ĕst*).

de ludis maximis, de deorum penatium Vestaeque matris caerimoniis: In parallel with the generalizing *de sacris publicis*, I render *ludi maximi* as "the most prestigious games" and not as a specific reference to the *Ludi Romani*, which receives the designation *Ludi Maximi* only occasionally (Wissowa 1912: 453 n. 3).

The *di penates* are the household gods carried by Aeneas from Troy to his new Italian homeland; they have no equivalent in the Greek pantheon (Dubourdieu 1989: 161–217 surveys the literary and iconographic traditions). The precise meaning of their name was disputed even in antiquity (Maltby 1991: 462). After a thorough analysis of ancient and modern views, Dubourdieu 1989: 13–33 concludes that the stem *pen-* conveys the notion both of interiority (cf. *penitus*, *penetro*) and nourishment (*penus*), and that the suffix *-ates* demonstrates that the term *penates* is an adjective, as one would expect from its normal occurrence in the combination *di penates* (Dubourdieu 1989: 29–33). In accordance with this etymology, the term *di penates* designates those gods who protected food stored in the internal spaces of the home. This duty of overseeing the well-being of the home explains the association between the *penates* and the cult of Vesta. Among the most important duties of the Vestal Virgins was the protection of the *Penus Vestae*, the inner sanctum of Vesta's temple in the Roman forum that contained a mysterious collection of sacred objects central to Rome's safety (Dubourdieu 1989: 454–469). Included among these objects, according to Tacitus, were the *penates* of the Roman people (*ann*. 15.41.1, Dubourdieu 1989: 467–469). Numerous other sources attest to the close association of Vesta and the *penates* (Weinstock 1937: 440–449; 37n [*penates…di*]).

Vesta's epithet "mother," which may seem odd applied to a virgin goddess, commonly occurs (e.g., *Font*. 47, *dom*. 144; *CIL* VI 32414=Dessau 4930 [247 CE]). It concerns both her divine power (Wissowa 1912: 26–27, on *mater* and *pater*) and her status as one of the oldest Roman deities (Wissowa 1884–1937b: 241–242; at Verg. *Aen*. 2.296 she appears among the ancestral gods brought from Troy).

de illo ipso sacrificio quod fit pro salute populi Romani: As the next clause makes clear, the reference here is particularly to those annual state rites of the Bona Dea that occur in December (37n). It is improbable that her identification with *Terra/Maia* existed in Cicero's day (Macr. *Sat.* 1.12.21–29, citing Cornelius Labeo) or else he surely would have connected the prodigy of the earth tremors to Clodius's disruption of her rites six years earlier. For the tautology *sacrificio quod fit* see 37n.

huius unius casti tutoris religionum: Clodius of course; the ironic adjective *castus* has special force here given that his violation of the Bona Dea gave rise to the charge of *incestum* (4n).

quod tres pontifices statuissent: Mommsen 1887–1888: 2.46 n. 2 and Wissowa 1912: 514 cite only this passage as evidence for three *pontifices* being able to make a decision on behalf of the entire college. Courtney 1989: 51 adds Marcell. *dig.* 50.16.85: *Neratius Priscus tres facere existimat collegium, et hoc magis sequendum est* ("Neratius Priscus judges that three constitutes a *collegium,* and this should be followed instead"; this occurs under the rubric "Meanings of expressions," and there is no direct reference to the *pontifices*).

at vero: The opening words *at vero* mark a strong contrast between the technicality that three *pontifices* are needed to make a decision on behalf of the college and the decision about Cicero's house, where Cicero implies that all *pontifices* present voted for its restoration. To stress their unanimity and prestige—eight of the *pontifices* attained the consulate, and all but two seem to have been senators in 57 (Lenaghan 1969: 95)—Cicero names thirteen of the fifteen members of the *collegium,* in addition to the *rex sacrorum,* the *flamen Martialis* and *Quirinalis,* and three *pontifices minores* (for another partial list from probably 70, see Macr. *Sat.* 3.13.11; Taylor 1942a: 400–404). The two regular *pontifices* omitted from this catalogue are easily accounted for: Julius Caesar, *pontifex maximus*, was serving as proconsul in Gaul, whereas Lucius Pinarius Natta was presumably omitted since it was his dedication of the shrine of *Libertas* that was being contested (Rüpke 2008: 840; as Tatum 1999: 190, 311 n. 92 points out, the omission does not have to indicate that Pinarius was not in attendance). Publius Lentulus is named first, as consul during the year of the meeting, with the remainder of the members listed by seniority in the order in which they joined the *collegium* (Taylor 1942a). For biographical details about the people listed, see the relevant entries in *RE*, Szemler 1972, Rüpke 2008; further discussion in Lenaghan 1969: 81–91, Bergemann 1992: 25–35. There is little reason to doubt that the deep political involvement of the priests—Pinarius is the only one not known to have held political office (*MRR* 2: 601)—and their membership in elite families informed their decision in Cicero's favor. In the following notes I provide details only for those figures who are known to have had a major role in Cicero's recall and restoration or in the career of Clodius.

P. Lentulus: Publius Cornelius Lentulus Spinther (*RE* 238) first appears in the historical record as curule aedile in 63, when he supported the consul

Cicero against the Catilinarian conspirators (*p. red. ad Quir.* 15; Sall. *Catil.* 47.4). He actively worked with his colleague Q. Metellus Nepos to facilitate Cicero's recall even when still consul designate for 57 (*Sest.* 70; Schol. Bob. p. 122.21–27 Stangl) and receives frequent expressions of gratitude in Cicero's speeches after his return (full list at Kaster 2006: 271).

P. Servilius, M. Lucullus: See nn. on 2 and 12. Perhaps acting as *pontifex maximus* in Caesar's absence, Lucullus spoke on behalf of the entire college when the senate met to discuss their decision about Cicero's house (*Att.* 4.2.4=SB 74).

Q. Metellus, M.' Glabrio, M. Messalla: Quintus Caecilius Metellus Creticus (*RE* 87) and Manius Acilius Glabrio (*RE* 38). Marcus Valerius Messalla Niger (*RE* 266) as consul in 61 urged the senate to adopt harsh measures after the Bona Dea incident (*Att.* 1.13.3=SB 13, 1.14.5–6=SB 14).

L. Lentulus flamen Martialis: Lucius Cornelius Lentulus Niger (*RE* 234) presided over the official state cult of Mars as one of the three *flamines maiores*. Of the other two, the *flamen Quirinalis* occurs later in the list, and there was at this time no *flamen Dialis*, the priest of Jupiter (Rüpke 2008: 734–735). He is probably the L. Lentulus who supported C. Lentulus in the prosecution of Clodius in 51 (Schol. Bob. p. 89.26 Stangl).

P. Galba, Q. Metellus Scipio: Publius Sulpicius Galba (*RE* 55); Quintus Caecilius Metellus Pius Scipio Nasica (*RE* 99) was defended by Cicero in 60, apparently on a charge of electoral bribery (*Att.* 2.1.9=SB 21); he became Pompey's father-in-law in 52.

C. Fannius: Gaius Fannius (*RE* 9) was one of the prosecutors of Clodius following the Bona Dea controversy (*Att.* 2.24.3=SB 44).

L. Claudius rex sacrorum: The ancients identified the *rex sacrorum* as the priest originally tasked with carrying out the sacral duties of the king following the expulsion of the monarchy (for a critical discussion, see BNP 1: 54–61). During the historical period he was barred from taking part in political life and by the republican period performed a variety of duties, such as sacrificing on the Kalends of each month and retaining information about the festal calendar.

Suetonius writes that the Claudii chose not to use the name *Lucius* after two family members with that praenomen had been convicted of crimes (*Tib.* 1.4), an anecdote that has prompted emendation elsewhere (e.g., Syme 1956: 133–134, followed by Briscoe and Shackleton Bailey, who emend to C. at Val. Max. 8.1 absol. 6). Briscoe 2012: 110–111 lists a total of four Lucii Claudii (including this one), three if not all of whom seem to be patrician. There is no valid reason to emend away here our Lucius Claudius (*RE* 21), about whom nothing else is known.

M. Lepidus,...M. Scaurus, M. Crassus, C. Curio: Taylor 1942a: 399–400 argues that these four *pontifices* were elected by popular vote on account of the influence of the First Triumvirate, Scaurus through Pompey, the other three through Caesar and Crassus. Marcus Aemilius Lepidus (*RE* 73), in his early 30s at the time of *har. resp.*, went on to become *pontifex maximus* upon Caesar's assassination, and a member of the Second Triumvirate the following year. Marcus Aemilius Scaurus (*RE* 141) was related by marriage to many prominent figures of the late Republic: stepson of Sulla, brother-in-law of Manius Glabrio and Pompey (whose third wife, Mucia, he married), his most prominent relationship with Cicero occurred a few months before *har. resp.*, as presiding praetor in Sestius's trial. In 54 he was defended by both Clodius and Cicero (and Hortensius; Ascon. *Scaur.* p. 20.16–18 Clark) in an extortion trial that produced the now fragmentary *Pro Scauro*. It is uncertain whether Marcus Licinius Crassus is to be identified with the triumvir and two-time consul (*RE* 68) or, more likely, his eldest son (*RE* 56; see Taylor 1942a: 393–394). Gaius Scribonius Curio (*RE* 10) was approaching the age of seventy at this time. An advocate for Cicero's punishment of the Catilinarians (*Att.* 12.21.1=SB 260), he later supported Clodius in the aftermath of the Bona Dea incident, including defending him at his trial (*Att.* 1.14.5=SB 14; Schol. Bob. p. 85.16–17). Cicero and he wrote invective pamphlets against each other (Crawford 1994: 227–263 for fragments and discussion of Cicero's contribution, which was only made public during Cicero's exile, much to his chagrin; for Curio's, see *Att.* 3.12.2=SB 57). Eventually, he and Clodius fell out of favor (e.g., *Att.* 2.7.3=SB 27, 2.8.1=SB 28) and, by the time of Cicero's return from exile, he appear to have reconciled with Cicero (McDermott 1972: 410–411).

Sex. Caesar *flamen Quirinalis*: This priest of the cult of Quirinus could be one of two men from the period named Sextus Julius Caesar; see Lenaghan 1969: 89–90. Regardless of the precise identification, he would have been a cousin of Julius Caesar.

Q. Cornelius, P. Albinovanus, Q. Terentius, *pontifices minores*: The *pontifices minores* served as assistants to the main *pontifices* in duties ranging from herald to scribe; the matter of Cicero's house is the only one for which their official participation is attested (Wissowa 1912: 518–519). Neither Quintus Cornelius (*RE* 51) nor Publius Albinovanus (*RE* 3) can be positively identified; Lenaghan 1969: 90–91 provides possibilities. As tribune of the plebs in 58, Quintus Terentius Culleo (*RE* 44) attempted unsuccessfully to have the law exiling Cicero made invalid on the grounds that it was directed against an individual (*privilegium*: *Att.* 3.15.5=SB 60).

<u>c</u>ausa <u>c</u>ognita, **duobus locis dicta**, m**A**xim**A** frequenti**A** Amplissimorum Ac s**A**pientissimorum civium Adst**A**nte: This long catalogue concludes with a rising tricolon of ablative absolutes in which internal alliteration and assonance mark each member. Mommsen 1887–1888: 2.47 points out that Cicero's language here equates the pontifical response with a legal *iudicium* and *causa* (cf. 13: *ita est enim interpretatio illa pontificum ut eidem potestatem habeant iudicum*, with Mommsen 1887–1888: 2.49 n. 4).

There are two possibilities regarding what is the second separate hearing to which Cicero refers here, in addition to the case argued before the *pontifices* on the occasion of the delivery of *De domo sua*. One candidate is when the *pontifices* of senatorial rank delivered a report on October 1 in the curia, at the senate meeting described at 13 (Lenaghan 1969: 91–92). Cicero notes that at this session the *pontifices* were asked how they had come to their decision (*Att.* 4.2.4=SB 74: *quid essent in decernendo secuti*), which could reasonably be construed as a kind of second hearing. Alternatively, Stroh 2004: 322 posits on the basis of *dom*. 3–4 a senate meeting that took place before the occasion of *De domo sua* at which Cicero was not present, and suggests that Cicero's absence provided the opportunity for M. Calidius to deliver his *De domo Ciceronis* (Quint. *inst.* 10.1.23). On this reading, only the *pontifices* who were members of the senate could have offered their opinion, whereas at the meeting on October 1 the *pontifex* Marcus Lucullus spoke on behalf of the entire college. For this reason I prefer the first option, but certainty seems impossible.

omni religione / una mente /omnes līběrāvērūnt: The emphatic placement of the adjectives in first position in their cola stresses the unanimity of the decision; compare 11n. The long sentence ends with the favored cretic + spondee clausula.

13 *post sacra constituta*: "Since the establishment of our sacred rites"; see Laughton 1964: 84–99 for the development of the so-called *ab urbe condita* construction, "whereby a predicative participle, usually past, coalesces with its noun in such a way that the two together form a complex of substantival character" (84); he notes that the majority of uses in Cicero occur after *post* (87: "well over fifty instances"). Woodcock 1959: 75–76 comments that the construction's "apparent concreteness recommended it to the Latin mind, and it came to be preferred to an abstract noun with a dependent genitive," adding that it was not widely adopted until classical times, with Cicero, and particularly Livy and Tacitus, favoring it, but Caesar and Sallust offering few examples. Bolkestein 1980 and 1981 offer detailed linguistic analysis. See too 24, 40.

quorum eadem est antiquitas quae ipsius urbis: Although Romulus, Rome's founder, is said to have brought to Rome the religious rites of Alba Longa and to have adopted the local worship of Hercules at the Ara Maxima (Liv. 1.7.3–15), it is traditionally Numa Pompilius, Rome's second king, who receives credit for the establishment of the most important Roman *sacra* that would have been known in Cicero's day; see, e.g., Liv. 1.19–21 with Ogilvie 1965: 93–105. Cicero will elaborate at 18–19 on how Rome's preeminence as a city is founded on the proper relationship between the human and the divine.

ne de capite quidem virginum Vestalium: Cicero's claim here is a bit tendentious. It had only been since Sulla that the number of *pontifices* rose from nine to fifteen (Shackleton Bailey 1991a: 109 n. 18) and there are only two trials of Vestals attested since then, both in 73, for which we have no information concerning how many *pontifices* participated (*TLRR* nos. 167–168). Sources describe the *pontifex maximus* as carrying out the punishment of an unchaste Vestal after investigation by all the *pontifices* (*leg.* 2.22.7; D. H. 2.67.3, 2.68.3;

cf. Plut. *Numa* 10.7 and Plin. *ep.* 4.11.6–7) with the entire college bearing responsibility for its decision (Liv. 4.44.11–12, 8.15.7–8; Ascon. *Mil.* pp. 45.20–46.6 Clark; *RE* 8A: 1747 [C. Koch]; Greenidge 1901a: 377–380). It has been much debated whence the *pontifices* derived this authority (Cornell 1981 reviews the issue, with bibliography).

quamquam...iudicasse: The logic of this difficult sentence seems to be as follows. In investigating a serious religious misdeed (*facinus*)—such as a Vestal's inchastity or neglect of her rites—a large number of priests acting as judges is desirable, whereas the exposition of a principle of *religio* (such as that about Cicero's house) can rest on the decision of simply one learned priest. And yet despite this practice, Cicero asserts that the decision about his house involved a higher number of *pontifices* than had ever participated in the capital trial of a Vestal.

ita est enim interpretatio illa pontificum ut eidem potestatem habeant iudicum: On the *pontifices* as equivalent to judges in legal proceedings, see 12n. At the meeting in which the college addressed the senate on this issue, the consul and *pontifex* Lucullus provided a clearer distinction: "the *pontifices* had been the judges on religious matters; the senate is the judge about human law" (*Att.* 4.2.4=SB 74: *religionis iudices pontifices fuisse, legis ⟨es⟩se senatum*). Similarly, at *dom.* 1 the authority of the *pontifices* resides in "wisely interpreting religious issues" (*religiones sapienter interpretando*). Gildenhard 2011: 308–311 observes that, outside *dom.*, *har. resp.*, and a passage in Justinian (Pompon. *dig.* 1.2.2.6), words related to *interpretari* are never applied to the *pontifices* since the verb implies that they act as mediators between gods and human beings, which is not one of their functions (Beard 1990: 35–39).

The particle *enim* appears third in the sentence, rather than second, since the verb *est* has attached itself to the adverb *ita*, which thereby receives focus because it anticipates the *ut* clause (Adams 1994a: 28).

religionis explanatio vel ab uno pontifice perito recte fieri potest: For the ability of one pontiff to represent the entire college see 12n. For the ablative of agent after *fio* see *ThLL* VI, 1 123.66–75 (O. Hey).

quod idem in iudicio capitis durum atque iniquum est: Halm conjectures *esset* for *est*, the unanimous reading of the codices (Orelli *et al.* 1856: 909). The contrafactual form is attractive, since in Cicero's Rome a single judge could not convict someone of a capital crime. The indicative does, however, yield suitable sense, and it is possible that Cicero means to recall actions of tyrants and dictators, such as the Sullan proscriptions.

postero die: The senate meeting of October 1, which continued until the next day (12n). Before the introduction of the Julian calendar in 45, September had twenty-nine days (Michels 1967: 16–22).

frequentissimus senatus: Cicero uses the positive form of *frequens* in a technical sense to refer to a quorate senate, whereas the superlative always has a non-technical sense ("very crowded"; Ryan 1998: 36–41). The use of the superlative here caps earlier occurrences of the adjective in positive and comparative forms to describe the "crowded" pontifical college (13.4: *frequens*) and "more numerous" *pontifices* (13.9–10: *frequentiores*), all gathered to consider Cicero's case.

sententiae principe: "The first to put forward the motion"; for the expression compare *dom.* 10 (on Cicero's proposal to put Pompey in charge of the grain commission): *quaero in ipsa sententia, quoniam princeps ego sum eius atque auctor, quid reprendatur*; *Balb.* 61. *Princeps* carries here simply the notion of temporal precedence and is not to be confused with the technical term *princeps senatūs*, the senator who was always allowed to present his opinion first in debate; that honor largely fell into abeyance some time after Sulla, although the term remained in use throughout the republican period (Suolahti 1972; Ryan 1998: 137–170, esp. 168–170). Ryan 1998: 247–248 assesses our evidence for consuls designate such as Lentulus having priority in addressing the senate.

P. Lentulo et Q. Metello consulibus: For this Lentulus, see 12n. Quintus Caecilius Metellus Nepos (*RE* 96), Clodius's first cousin or perhaps half-brother (Tatum 1999: 34–36), had a contentious relationship with Cicero early in his career. In December 63, as tribune of the plebs Metellus publicly criticized Cicero's execution of the Catilinarian conspirators, even encouraging his criminal prosecution (Dio 37.42). Consequently, he prevented Cicero from giving his address to the people as outgoing consul (*fam.* 5.2.6–8=SB 2). In early January of 62, after Metellus had attacked Cicero in a *contio*, Cicero responded by publishing the now fragmentary *Contra contionem Q. Metelli* (Crawford 1994: 215–226). Their relationship over the next few years seems to have remained tense, since Cicero writes to Atticus from exile in July 58 that he considered Metellus, now consul-designate, to be his enemy (*Att.* 3.12.1=SB 57: *inimico consule designato*). Cicero's greatest fears seem to have been unfounded, however, as Metellus did not resist his recall claiming, according to Cicero, that the well-being of the state should supersede private enmity (*Sest.* 72, cf. 87; *p. red. in sen.* 5, 9; *p. red. ad Quir.* 9, 15; *dom.* 7, 70; Boll 2019: 31–34 provides a good analysis). Despite occasional conflicts with Cicero's allies during his consular year, such as a violent clash with Sestius in late January (*Sest.* 79), Metellus continued to support Cicero's recall. In spring 56, around the time of *har. resp.*, Cicero receives a letter from him in which he denounces Clodius and reaffirms their previously close ties of friendship (*fam.* 5.3=SB 11, with Shackleton Bailey 1977a: 292).

alii qui honoribus populi Romani antecedebant: The pronoun *alii* refers to those senators who spoke after Lentulus had stated his own view and whom Cicero emphasizes were distinguished by high political office (*honores*). At this period of the Republic, upon taking office the year's consuls determined the order in which senators would be asked their opinion (*rogatus sententiam*), normally beginning with former consuls, and that order apparently prevailed for the entire year (Ryan 1998: 259–276).

multa de conlegi iudicio verba fecissent: The phrase *verba facere* is the technical term to describe senatorial deliberation on a specific proposal (Mommsen 1887–1888: 3.957 n. 3).

omnesque idem scribendo adessent: After the senate passed a *senatus consultum*, the magistrate who had first proposed it asked fellow senators to witness the drafting of the text, consisting normally of those who had favored the measure (*fam.* 15.6.2=SB 112). The formula *scribendo adesse* occurs as early as the 186 BCE *SC de Bacchanalibus* (*CIL* I² 581, 2; cf. 43: *cui feriendo... interfuerat*; for Cicero see Lebreton 1901: 385–386). It was unusual to have as many witnesses as Cicero claims here, with eleven being otherwise the highest number attested (Mommsen 1887–1888: 3.1004–1005; *RE* suppl. 6.801–802).

domum meam iudicio pontificum religione liberatam videri: Julius Victor, without citing *har. resp.* by name, offers this as an example of Cicero using proof that relies upon the judgment of experts (*rhet.* p. 403.3–4: *scientium iudicatu, cum domum suam dicit a religione pontificum sententia liberatam*).

14–15

Cicero proceeds to reiterate how, given the fact that the senate has confirmed the judgment of the *pontifices* about his house, the *haruspices* must be referring in their response to other *LOCA SACRA ET RELIGIOSA*. As a result, he suggests that the consuls make a motion confirming precisely that. Cicero offers as additional proof of his entitlement to his property the many senatorial edicts that have been passed to protect it since the decision of the *pontifices*.

14 *De hoc... loco sacro... sacris... sacer*: The polyptoton of *sacer*, along with the *hoc* emphatically referring back to previous decisions about his property, reinforces that the clear answer to this rhetorical question is "No." The adjective *sacer*, like *religio* and its affiliates, takes its meaning from the relationship between the human and the divine (cf. 9n). Anything declared *sacer*, be it a human being, an object, or a location, is deemed as no longer subject to human jurisdiction (*ius humanum*) but as consecrated to the divine realm; the process of creating the *sacer/sacrum* is, moreover, always conceived of as a public and not a private act (*RE* 4: 896–902; Fest. p. 321 M; Gaius *inst.* 2.5–6). Accordingly, the term occurs in our earliest legal texts, such as the *Lapis Niger* inscription (*ILLRP* 3: 2–3: *sakros esed*; context uncertain), as well as in the Twelve Tables, where a patron who has done harm to a client is declared *sacer* (VIII, 10 Crawford: *si patronus clienti fraudem fecerit, sacer esto*), and it continues to be used throughout the legal tradition with the associated words *sanctus* and *religiosus* (Rives 2011). In the context of his house, Cicero, in claiming that it "was not judged to be *sacer*" (*sacer non esse iudicatus sit*), is using *sacer* synonymously with the two combined adjectives from the response, *SACRA ET RELIGIOSA*. The entire Republican state apparatus—the people, the senate, and the *pontifices*—has judged that the state denies the "sanctity" of Cicero's home. The essays in Lanfranchi 2018 offer a survey of scholarship on the meaning of *sacer* and include consideration of the recent work of René Girard and Giorgio Agamben, with separate chapters on the evidence for the concept of the sacred throughout the ancient Italian peninsula.

verum referte, quod ex senatus consulto facere debetis: The particle *verum* marks an abrupt break, introducing a new topic (Saur 1913: 91; KS 2: 2.79–80). Following Cicero's lengthy preamble on the proper status of his house, it is time for discussion in accordance with the senatorial motion that originally put the matter before the *haruspices*. Cicero therefore turns to speak directly to both consuls in charge of the senatorial proceedings, emphatically requesting that they now offer a *relatio* that specifies the parameters of the discussion (11n). The technical meaning of the verb *referte* makes the turn to direct address less harsh, since it is the job of the consuls to put forth a *relatio*.

The following sentence is structured as a rising tricolon connected by *aut*, with Cicero offering three possible outcomes of a consular *relatio*, each of which he proceeds to demonstrate would be redundant: 1. the consuls, who have acknowledged authority over religious affairs, will be required to conduct a *cognitio* on an issue upon which they have already acted (Pina Polo 2011: 250–261); 2. the senate will judge on a topic upon which they have already decided with near unanimity; 3. the decision will be sent back to the *pontifices*, who had pronounced on the subject the previous October.

uno illo solo antistite sacrorum dissentiente: Clodius, of course, in his capacity as "assistant" at the rites of the Bona Dea; the noun *antistes*, rarely used in connection with Roman cults, has disparaging connotations (Wissowa 1912: 483). For the tautology *uno...solo* see 11n. Cicero specifies elsewhere that the senate vote was 416–1, which is surprising considering that he had other opponents in attendance (*p. red. in sen.* 26, with Boll 2019: 199).

id quod certe fiet,—ad pontifices reicietur: Once the senate determines on this occasion that the response of the *haruspices* represents a situation in which the gods must be appeased, it will of necessity consult the *pontifices* to decide on the nature of the expiation (Mommsen 1887–1888: 3.1061; Wissowa 1912: 391, 514–515). Compare Liv. 41.16.2, where the senate seeks advice from the *pontifices* about how to atone for a ritual that had been conducted improperly (*cum ad senatum relatum esset senatusque ad pontificum collegium reiecisset*). On *reicere* as a technical term for referring an issue to another body (or tabling for a later date) see Mommsen 1887–1888: 3.979 n. 1.

sacra religionesque et privatas et publicas: Wissowa 1912: 398–406 outlines in detail the different spheres of public and private ritual; for rites within individual families in particular, see 32n. Beard 1990: 37–38 gives examples of the diverse areas in which the *pontifices* could affect private worship. See 18n for the authority of the *maiores* in religious matters.

quid ergo? ii possunt aliud iudicare ac iudicaverunt?: Seyffert 1878: 103–117 notes that questions introduced by *quid ergo* expect, as here, a negative response. In light of the examples that Seyffert gives from Cicero, in which *quid ergo* is a separate question immediately followed by a second, I have punctuated as *quid ergo? ii possunt aliud iudicare ac iudicaverunt?* There are numerous parallels in the speeches of *quid ergo?* Followed by a new question introduced by a demonstrative (e.g., *div. in Caec.* 40: *quid ergo? Haec in te sunt omnia?*; *Verr.* 2.4.102: *quid ergo? Hoc solum auditione expetere coepit...?*; *Caec.* 50: *quid ergo? Hoc interdictum putamus...?* Given these parallels, it is worth noting that the codices are divided between *ii* **PG** and *hi* **EH**). For the brachylogy ("Can these men decide anything other than [what] they already have"), frequent in clauses of comparison in both Latin and English, see KS 2: 2.566–567.

haud scio an: The subordinating subjunctive form *sint* is understood from the main verb *sunt* (cf. *De orat.* 2.62: *videtisne quantum munus sit oratoris historia? Haud scio an flumine orationis et varietate maximum*). The phrase *haud scio an* introduces a cautious assertion (10n).

paene cunctae: The adjective *cunctus* normally has a meaning indistinguishable from *omnis*, as is clear when the two words occur in a series (e.g., *dom.* 132: *tum autem ordines omnes, deinde Italia tota, post cunctae gentes*; several examples in *ThLL* IX, 2 611.6–50 [F. Oomes, W. Ehlers]). The adjective apparently originated in sacral language, and so belongs to a higher register throughout Latinity (Hofmann 1948: 285–286), which may explain its occurrence here amid a number of legal technical terms. In addition, it occurs when a single exception is stated or implied, as seems to be the case here (*ThLL* IV 1400.38–50 [K. Wulff], citing however as the earliest prose example Plin. *nat.* 2.25: *uno... praeferendo cunctis bonis*).

iure optimo, sed tamen iure privato, iure hereditario, iure auctoritatis, iure mancipi, iure nexi: "With an unobjectionable title; and yet it is with a title granted through private law—either hereditary, or based on authority, or based on property transfer through sale or debt." This sequence of six consecutive phrases, marked off clearly by anaphora of *iure*, begins with a simple specification: those homes in Rome held by an indisputable title (*iure optimo*) in fact hold their title through private law only (*iure privato*). Cicero then concisely lists in an anaphoric series of descending cola (7, 6, 5, and 4 syllables respectively) the various aspects of private law under which one can possess property. I will discuss these in turn, the final three of which offer apparently insurmountable problems of interpretation, although I hardly think that one needs to resort to the desperate solution of Karsten 1879: 408 of deleting all four terms as the imaginings of a declaimer. First, the *ius hereditarium* refers to the general right to hereditary accession, here to that of a legal heir to inherit the title of property from a previous, legitimate, owner; for use of the term in legal texts see, e.g., Iulian. *dig.* 35.2.87.1. The sense of *auctoritas* as found in the phrase *ius auctoritatis*, clearly contrasting with hereditary possession, is much contested (a thorough summary of the debate at Yaron 1967: 195–208). The most plausible interpretation of the use here is that it refers to rights to property that proceed from either *usus* or direct purchase, as attested by the person from whom those rights were originally acquired (Crawford 1996: 658–660; cf. Shackleton Bailey 1991a: 110 n. 21: "a title resting on an affidavit by a person of credit"). Such a provision is attested as early as the Twelve Tables (Lex. *XII tab.* [Cic. *top.* 23]; more examples at *ThLL* II, 1213.81–1214.23 [K. Münscher]). Given the brevity of Cicero's reference, however, certainty must remain in doubt. Equally uncertain is the difference between the final two means of ownership listed, *iure mancipi* and *iure nexi*. In his correspondence Cicero couples *mancipium* and *nexum* in a metaphorical expression in which he contrasts the paired terms with possession through usufruct (*fam.* 7.30.2=SB 265); as noted by Greenidge 1901a: 71 n. 1, Cicero implies with both terms a type of full ownership. The ancient practice of *mancipatio* occurs in the transfer of ownership of all kinds of property, including slaves, animals, and houses, that originally involved grasping the property with the hand (*manu capere*) and reciting a formula; in the case of land and buildings the mancipation could take place at a distance (Gaius *inst.* 1.119–122; Watson 1968: 16–20). How this form of ownership transfer is to be distinguished from that via *nexum* seems irresolvable. The two terms are paired without clear difference in meaning as early as the Twelve Tables and not fully understood by the time of the Republic (Lex *XII tab.* VI.1 Crawford, with discussion at Crawford 1996: 652–656, who concludes that "Cicero, *de har. resp.* 14, cannot be taken to show that the two were different" [655]). It is possible that Cicero refers to the transfer of ownership as a result of an unpaid debt, as opposed to a purchase through *mancipatio*, but this is only a guess.

nego esse ullam domum aliam privato eodem quo quae optima lege, publico vero omni praecipuo et humano et divino iure munitam: The verb *nego* stands in first position in strong opposition to *haud scio* ("I suppose... [but] I assert that no other home"), thereby contrasting the condition of other houses in Rome with Cicero's own. For the double ellipsis of the verb in the two consecutive relative clauses (*quo [eae domus sunt] quae optima lege [sunt]*) compare *leg. agr.* 2.29 (quoting the tribune Rullus): "*tum ei xviri...eodem iure sint quo qui optima lege*" ("At that time those decemvirs...have the same right as [do those] who [are protected by] the most sound laws"); cf. *leg. agr.* 3.11. As at *leg. agr.* 2.29 (Manuwald 2018: 253), Cicero here adopts legal language, perhaps even quoting the resolution of the senate from the previous fall that he proceeds to allude to; see too *Phil.* 5.45: *sit pro praetore eo iure quo qui optimo* (as this example illustrates, in this formulation *optima lege* and *optimo iure* are synonymous; Botsford 1909: 186–187).

Ius publicum encompasses any proceedings that involve the state and, as Cicero delineates here, was concerned with an individual's participation in either civil or religious proceedings, each administered by two different classes of individuals. As we have seen, it is the *pontifices* who concern themselves with the *ius sacrum*, matters involving lapses in ritual or in behavior relating to divine activity (Greenidge 1901a: 373–380 is especially good at distinguishing the two areas). All other offenses against the state fall under the rubric of the *ius civile* which, as the name indicates, can include the conduct of individuals as Roman citizens (*cives*); cf. Papin. *dig.* 1.1.7: *ius autem civile est quod ex legibus, plebis scitis, senatus consultis, decretis principum, auctoritate prudentium venit.* Cicero will return again in the next section to how he is protected by both limbs of the *ius publicum*.

15 *primum... deinde / primum... deinde*: The collocation *primum... deinde* appears over two hundred times in Cicero but its repetition in consecutive sentences occurs in only four other instances (at *Clu.* 81 the sequence *primum... deinde... postremo* is repeated in order to highlight the differences between opposing arguments; at *fam.* 7.3.2=SB 183 and *top.* 77 the second sequence is a subset of the first). In this example both instances of the *primum* clause treat the rebuilding of Cicero's home, while those marked by *deinde* mention the legal measures taken by the senate to ensure that Clodius and his gangs not interfere with this rebuilding. Aside from the fact that each portion of the second set goes into greater detail, there seems no reason for the repetition.

aedificatur ex auctoritate senatus pecunia publica: In response to a senatorial decree, the consuls the previous September had made an assessment of the amount of damage that had been done to Cicero's property on the Palatine, as well as to his Formian and Tusculan villas, and agreed to finance repairs (*Att.* 4.1.7=SB 73, 4.2.5=SB 74, where Cicero complains that the assessment of his villas was too low). Asconius points out that Cicero can be tendentious in his occasional claims for the unprecedented nature of this decision (Ascon. *Pis.* P. 13.4 Clark: *hoc Cicero oratorio more, non historico, videtur posuisse*), listing several other occasions when the senate authorized public sums for the construction of private property. In the end, however, he rescues Cicero from an outright lie by observing that only here were those funds used for a *rebuilding* (pp. 13.22–14.3 Clark).

contra vim nefariam huius gladiatoris tot senati consultis munita atque saepta est: For Clodius as a gladiator see 1n, and for the possible senatorial decrees alluded to, 8n. These would include the Oct. 1–2 meeting at which the senate placed responsibility for any subsequent violence (*vis*) on the tribunes who supported Clodius (*Att.* 4.2.4=SB 74). The principal codices are here split on what form of the genitive of *senatus* should be read: *senati* PE[1]H, *senatus* GE[2]. At 8n I argue that the similar phrase *ducentis... senati consultis* is a quotation of Clodius and that Clodius affected the archaic form of the genitive. Accordingly, I have chosen to read here as well the form *senati*; Cicero chose the unusual morphology to recall Clodius's complaint of being "transfixed" by countless instances of *SC*.

Note how the earlier metaphorical use of *munio* at 14, describing Cicero's house protected by human and divine laws, becomes literal in light of the mention of a "gladiatorial attack"; the doubling with the verb *saepio* stresses the need for additional defenses.

isdem: The demonstrative adjective is used here in anticipation of the *quibus* two lines below, where the relative clause describes a typical duty of the consuls (in this case, P. Cornelius Lentulus Spinther and Q. Caecilius Metellus Nepos, consuls of 57). For the senatorial meeting alluded to, see *Att.* 4.2.4=SB 74 where, however, the duty of enforcing the decree is given to all magistracies (*senatui placere...auctoritatem ordinis ab omnibus magistratibus defendi*; see too 16 below: *a magistratibus defendendam...magistratus omnes*).

cum ille saxis et ignibus et ferro vastitatem meis aedibus intulisset: For this incident, see 58n.

** *aedibus*: *sedibus* PE¹H, *(a)edibus* GE²: Peterson and Maslowski read *sedibus* with the best codices; Shackleton Bailey 1991a: 230 reads *aedibus*. Cicero uses *aedes* several times of his home in *dom.*—51, 62, 69, 81, 100, 107 (*bis*), 116 (*I*), 128 (*ter*); in no case does Maslowski report a form of *sedes* as a variant. By contrast, *sedes* is used of groups of homes (as is usual "in good prose": LS s.v. IIβ) at *dom.* 61 (of enemies) and 106 (of Romans generally). At 108 Libertas is described as occupying Cicero's house *ut se ipsa tamquam in captivis sedibus conlocaret*, where *sedibus* is needed for pun on *libertas/captivis*, and at 143 as distinct from *domus*: *haec [est] restitutio <u>in domo, in sedibus</u>, in aris, in focis, in dis penatibus reciperandis*. While Cicero does use *sedes* twice in the *peroratio*—145: *ero in meas sedis restitutus* and 147: *manibus...vestris in sedibus meis conlocetis*—he seems to be referring to all his property and not solely his Capitoline residence, as here. Finally, in *har. resp.* the plural noun *aedes* is used exclusively for his home (twice in 11). Paleographical considerations support the hypothesis that this is a copyist's error: *ThLL* I 907.68–70 (K. Prinz) notes that the two words are confused in the codices *saepius* and the mistake here of *meis (a)edibus* for *meis sedibus* is easily accounted for as dittography of the letter [s].

decrevit senatus eos qui id fecissent lege de vi, quae est in eos qui universam rem publicam oppugnassent, teneri: The history of the various laws on public violence (*de vi*) during the Republic is difficult to reconstruct since they were superseded by subsequent legislation and so left little trace in the later record. As this passage makes clear, such acts of violence were construed as being against the state (*contra rem publicam*), with the result that an attack on Cicero becomes by senatorial decree an attack on the state and the culprit, in this case Clodius, an enemy of the state. Riggsby 1999: 79–119 offers a full discussion of the Ciceronian evidence for legislation and trials *de vi*. For *tenere* in the technical sense of being under the jurisdiction of a law see, e.g., *Phil.* 11.11 (*leges eum non tenent*); Gaius *inst.* 1.3 (*olim patricii dicebant plebi scitis se non teneri*); LS s.v. B2g. On the ability of the senate to make decisions on legal matters, see the parallels cited at Mommsen 1887–1888: 3.1067–1068.

post hominum memoriam: In the sense of "in human memory," the phrase occurs frequently in Cicero (twenty times), but only rarely elsewhere: *Lex Gabin. Calp.* [*CIL* I² 2500] 12 of 58 BCE (*post hominum me[moriam]*), *Bell. Hisp.* 15.6, and three times in Nepos (Nepos also has *omnium post memoriam*).

qui meam domum violasset contra rem publicam esse facturum: Nothing else is known of this decree, which presumably occurred in 56 since *vobis referentibus* refers to the current consuls; Lenaghan 1969: 100–102 discusses possibilities. For Cicero identifying himself with the republic in speeches *post reditum* see 3n.

16

Cicero concludes this section by asserting that his own home has received more attention from the Roman senate than any public work or any other private domicile. And yet he is detailing these facts not from arrogance, but out of gratitude for the senate's benefactions toward him.

16 *Nego ullo de opere publico...putarit*: After arguing for the unique legal status of his home as a private possession, Cicero repeats the verb *nego* in first position (cf. 14) to assert how its status is distinct from Rome's public structures as well. The apparently casual sentence has a careful structure. A descending tricolon of prepositional phrases begins the sentence (*de*: 7, 5, 3 syllables), which terminates in a series of four approximate isocola (9, 10, 10, 9 syllables), each of which ends with passive periphrastic infinitives whose homoioteleuton underscores their emphatic meanings (*aedificandam,... liberandam,...defendendam,...poeniendam*); a closing clausula of a favored ditrochee caps the sentence (*-ām pŭtārīt*). The balance within the isocola is further enhanced by the rare use of the preposition *ab* to express agency after a gerundive. Lebreton 1901: 414–415 cites 23 examples of this construction in the orations vs. 457 uses of the dative but cannot discern a consistent reason for the variation. Here the explanation seems stylistic rather than semantic, with the preposition *a* providing a balance with *ex* (cf. *Planc.* 8: *si a populo praeteritus est,...a iudicibus condemnandus est*). Perhaps also the preposition stresses the human agency involved: the *pontifices*, magistrates, and judges all have decided on Cicero's behalf (5n).

post hanc urbem constitutam: For the construction see 13n.

a iudicibus poeniendam: Cicero's reference to a panel of judges would seem to be in anticipation of possible trials that might occur as a result of the two senatorial decrees mentioned in section 15. The verb *poenio* has here the rare sense of "to avenge"; *ThLL* X, 2 2656.50–55 (G. Clementi) cites only three other certain examples, all from Cicero (*de orat.* 1.220, *rep.* 3.15, *Phil.* 8.7). All four passages describe vengeance on behalf of impersonal objects (*domus, dolor, fana, nex*), which perhaps makes the unusual semantics less jarring.

P. Valerio: Liv. 2.7.5–12 narrates how Publius Valerius Publicola (*RE* 302), during his first consulship in 509, was thought to be aiming at kingship because of the construction of a house on the heights of the Velian Hill and how, in response, he razed it and built another at the hill's base. Cicero's version is the earliest for Valerius receiving his site at public expense (*publice*, as emended; see next note), a tradition followed by Ascon. *Pis.* p. 13.13–16 Clark. Plut. *Publ.*

10.3–4 adds, contrary to these sources, that the people also paid for the house (cf. Plin. *nat.* 36.112). For an assessment of the sources, with bibliography, see Beck 2009, esp. 361–365.

** *in Velia publice*: The codices all read *in villa publica* except for a correction in P (the nonsensical *in ulla publica*). The emendation is earliest attested from J. M. Palmerius, as recorded in Graevius 1696: 520–521 (cf. Ascon. *Pis.* p. 13.14–15 Clark).

privato iure...publice: For the distinction, see discussion in section 14.

ne nimis gloriari viderer: Cicero again reveals his awareness that he has a reputation for boasting of his achievements (17n).

** *cum sint*: *cum sint* PH, *quae sint* GE. Shackleton Bailey 1987: 275 proposes reading *quae sunt* to avoid the awkward repetition of *cum* but does not account for the resulting construction of the *quae* clause.

adrogāns vĭdĕātūr: In the first speech to the people during his consulship, Cicero expresses a similar fear while offering thanks for their support in the election: "I am afraid that talking in front of you about myself will be a mark of arrogance, but to be silent a mark of ingratitude" (*leg. agr.* 2.2: *de me autem ipso vereor ne arrogantis sit apud vos dicere, ingrati tacere*; cf. *inv.* 1.22 on avoiding *arrogantia* in the exordium). The final five syllables of this sentence invite comment since they match the typical close to a dactylic hexameter, a meter characteristic of epic poetry in Greek and Latin. Quintilian expresses unequivocal disapproval in ending a sentence with this so-called heroic clausula: "the dactyl is not well placed before a spondee since we condemn using a verse ending at the close of a prose sentence" (*inst.* 9.4.102). Ciceronian practice supports Quintilian's verdict: occurring an estimated 8.3 percent of the time in "normal" Latin prose (De Groot 1921: 106), it appears in fewer than 1.86 percent of the sentences in Cicero's orations (Keeline and Kirby 2019: 176, who do not allow resolutions in this calculation; Fraenkel 1968: 198–200 provides qualifications, and notes that most instances involve words of four or five syllables, as here). As a result of this avoidance, Zielinski 1904: 206 proposed the seemingly attractive emendation ⟨*esse*⟩ *videatur*, a rhythmic ending favored by Cicero to such an extent that the ancients mocked him for it (2n; Kinsey 1971: 164 notes that Cicero uses this same wording c. 80 times). I propose to keep the transmitted text for two reasons: first, prose rhythm presents a preference, not a hard and fast rule. Second, Cicero does on occasion use this epic ending to mock an opponent's way of speaking and, since Cicero is here calling attention to his own reputation for boastfulness, it is possible that he uses the rhythm in humorous self-reproach. In other words, in asserting that his listeners should not find his proclamations here "arrogant," he blatantly uses an unacceptable rhythm. E. Adams 2013 gives several examples of Cicero's rhetorical exploitation of heroic clausulae, normally to humorous effect; see esp. her discussion at 39–41 of *Phil.* 2.63 (*veniamus ad splendidiora*).

17

Cicero turns from the honors bestowed upon him to the subject of his own self-praise, which he justifies by relating an exchange he had had in the senate on the previous day with Clodius.

17 Quamquam si me tantis laboribus pro communi salute perfunctum ecferret aliquando ad gloriam in refutandis maledictis hominum improborum animi quidam dolor, quis non ignosceret?: *Quamquam* is used here not as a conjunction but adverbially, as often, "to introduce a new main sentence which is opposed to, or corrects, what has gone before" (Woodcock 1959: 205), here by qualifying why self-praise is in this instance justified ("and yet"). In the subsequent sentence word order echoes sense: Cicero's alleged boasting (*ecferret aliquando ad gloriam*) separates his signal service to Rome (*me...perfunctum*) from the slanders of the opponents of the republic (*in refutandis maledictis hominum improborum*; for this sense of *improbus* see Manuwald 2021: 113). The *si* clause then ends with what prompts the boasting in this case: *animi quidam dolor* ("a kind of mental anguish"), which recalls Cicero's justification for his attack on Clodius at the beginning of the speech (3: *dolore me elatum et iracundia*, with note). The sentiment that he only resorts to self-praise when compelled to do so closely resembles *dom.* 93 (to Clodius): *et quoniam hoc reprehendis, quod solere me dicas de me ipso gloriosius praedicare, quis umquam audivit cum ego de me nisi coactus ac necessario dicerem?*

vidi enim hesterno die quendam murmurantem: The specification of time as *hesterno die* recalls the opening two words of the speech and provides an initial indication that this exchange took place at the previous day's senate meeting. This possibility is strengthened by the subsequent detail that the verbal altercation between Clodius and Cicero took place before an audience of Roman *equites* and senators (17: *probantibus et vobis et equitibus Romanis*; cf. 1: *et vestra dignitas et frequentia equitum Romanorum praesentium*). Cicero is possibly being vague on the situation since more specificity might show that the anonymous "murmurer" is a senator, and he wishes throughout the speech to give the (*prima facie* unlikely) impression that his colleagues are united with him in their opposition to Clodius (cf. 11n). The pronoun *quidam* can refer to someone known but whom the speaker for whatever reason, sometimes in disparagement, chooses not to name directly; cf. Cic. *off.* 3.58: *Pythius...quidam*; Hor. *serm.* 1.9.3: *quidam notus mihi nomine tantum*; KS 2: 1.642–643.

The verb *murmuro* occurs only here in the orations (*admurmurare/admurmuratio* occurs five times, always in the sense of "murmur *in approval*"; *commurmuror* at *Pis.* 61 introduces sarcasm).

** ferre: C. Halm (in Orelli *et al.* 1856: 911), followed by Peterson, conjectured *ferri* for *ferre* of all the codices. Maslowski retains *ferre* without comment, which receives some support from 17: *qui ferre me non potest*. The reading *ferre* has the difficulty that one would need to understand *se* or sim. as its subject (Wolf 1801: 331: "Cicero haud dubie addidisset *se*"), but ellipsis of the personal pronoun in indirect speech is common in all periods of prose (Landgraf 1914: 129; KS 2: 1.700–701) and this is in particular the tendency if the pronoun would need to be repeated as here, e.g., *Tusc.* 1.60: *nec me pudet...fateri nescire [sc. me] quod nesciam*).

ab hoc eodem impurissimo parricida: Given the sexual connotations of the adjective *impurus*, heightened by being given in the superlative, Cicero probably expects part of his audience to recall the associations that the charge of *parricida* held for Clodius the previous September (*dom.* 26: *patricida, fratricida, sororicida*). See Corbeill 1996: 117–118: "beginning with the common rhetorical slander *patricida*, 'traitor,' Cicero exploits the popular etymology of this word—'father killer'—and the slang meaning of *caedo*—'to cut down (with one's penis)'—to suggest with the following two words (*fratricida, sororicida*) that Clodius engages in incest with both his brother and sister (cf. *Sest.* 16: *fraternis flagitiis, sororiis stupris*). The insinuations may not stop here; *patricida* seems to conceal a similar reference.... When Cicero has occasion later in the speech to impugn Clodius' adoption into the plebs by Fonteius, a man younger than Clodius, he refers to their peculiar father/son relationship as follows:... *nego istam adoptionem pontificio iure esse factam: primum, quod eae vestrae sint aetates, ut is, qui te adoptavit, vel filii tibi loco per aetatem esse potuerit vel eo, quo fuit* (*dom.* 36: '...I say, [Clodius,] that that adoption of yours was not conducted in accordance with pontifical law: first, because the ages of the two of you are such that the man who adopted you could, by dint of his age, either occupy for you the position of a son or that [position] in which he used to be (*eo, quo fuit*).' Cicero implies with the phrase *eo, quo fuit*...that Clodius' adoptive father has already served Clodius as an object of the man's lusts. As the younger man, Fonteius could fill the role either of Clodius' son or, as Cicero asserts has in fact been the case, of his boy lover." For the details of Clodius's adoption, see nn. at 44 and 57.

cuius essem civitatis: Lenaghan 1969: 105 points out that the question is double-edged. On the one hand, Clodius is impugning Cicero's municipal origins and implying that he is not a true citizen of Rome. This was a common invective topos; in the case of Cicero, hostile epithets include "immigrant Roman citizen" and "Rome's third foreign king" (Sall. *Catil.* 31.7; *Sull.* 22 with Berry 1996a: 182; generally, Corbeill 2002: 206–207). On the other hand, for those who believed that Cicero was justly exiled, the question could not be answered since he would be a man without a state. It is principally at this second implication that Cicero's reply is directed.

respondi me, probantibus et vobis et equitibus Romanis, eius esse quae carere me non potuisset: Clodius had taunted Cicero in an analogous way the previous fall, presumably in response to Cicero's boasting about his recall: "Are you the one that the senate could not do without, that the elite mourned, that the republic longed for?" (*dom.* 4: '*tune es ille...quo senatus carere non potuit, quem boni luxerunt, quem res publica desideravit...?*'). Many such boasts survive, e.g., *Pis.* 16: *neque enim me stante et manente in urbis vigilia… umquam se illi rem publicam delere posse duxerunt*; *fam.* 6.6.2=SB 234 (46 BCE): *nam cum me ex re publica expulissent ii qui illam cadere posse stante me non putarunt*; and, most notoriously, *o fortunatam natam me consule Romam!* (Cic. *carm. frg.* 11, with Ewbank 1933: 124; for which compare *Flac.* 102: *o Nonae illae Decembres quae me consule fuistis! quem ego diem vere natalem huius urbis aut certe salutarem appellare possum*). In a thorough account that begins from this anecdote, Allen 1954 places Cicero's alleged conceit in a contemporary political context, noting that there is "no evidence to show that Cicero was more vain than his contemporaries" (1954: 122). It is worth noting that Cicero's remark is prompted by a verbal attack and that the bulk of his self-praise occurs in justifying his actions during the Catilinarian conspiracy, which ultimately resulted in his exile (Quint. *inst.* 11.1.18–19; Nicholson 1992: 23–29).

ut opinor: The first-person singular present indicative form of this verb is used more than 100 times in the speeches, both with and without *ut*. Although Landgraf 1914: 106 gives many examples of Cicero using the verb to escape the impression of pedantry or excessive knowledge, it can also, as here and as commonly in the *philosophica*, mark a logical inference (Laurand 1936–1940: 97; Reid 1885: 256: "to pronounce a confident judgment on insufficient evidence"). The point here is that Cicero can predict Clodius's reaction to his remark even if he were not sure of having heard it.

quid igitur responderem?: The imperfect subjunctive represents the original deliberative subjunctive *quid respondeam?* (KS 2: 1.181; contrast the contrafactual *respondissem* in the next response).

** litterate respondissem: ThLL VII, 2 1533.55–58 (W. Buchwald) lists this passage as the sole example of the adverb meaning "literally" ("fere i.q. ad litteras, ad verbum"), but also considers that it may be used here ironically. Shackleton Bailey 1979: 267–268 believes such a joke not up to Ciceronian standards and suggests *vix litterate* ("'That would not have been a very clever answer'"). Nevertheless *litterate* may be retained since the irony is clear without the addition of *vix*—"What a clever answer [that would have been]!"

an tacuissem? desertum negotium: "Or should I have stayed silent? But then the case is closed"; presumably *a me* is understood. I use the metaphor "case closed" since the only parallels for the expression *negotium deserere* that I have found are from legal texts (Ulp. *dig.* 5.1.10: *plane si quis cognita rei veritate suum negotium deseruerit*; Paul. *dig.* 13.6.17.3; Tryph. *dig.* 27.2.6; cf. ThLL V, 1 676.68–677.37 [E. Vetter]). Cicero's point is that yielding in an *altercatio* by not responding will cause a speaker to lose face (see final note in this section).

potest quisquam vir in rebus magnis cum invidia versatus: Normally a pronoun, *quisquam* may be used as an adjective to modify a word designating a person (LHS 2: 196). The combination with *vir* is not common and is used either when it is necessary to specify sex (e.g., Ter. *Eun.* 578, Quint. *decl. mai.* 3.2) or to stress, as here, the impossibility of what is being said (cf. 38n). The use of *vir* may also be impugning Clodius's masculinity by contrast (e.g., nn. on 6, 42). Cicero uses the construction *versor cum* in particular to describe involvement with abstract concepts, with the preposition expressing a loose sense of accompaniment (e.g., *Rab. perd.* 29; *Phil.* 1.18). Hence my translation "who is engaged in important affairs and who has envy as his companion."

sine sua laude: "Without praising himself"; Cicero not rarely uses a pronominal adjective where an objective genitive would be expected (i.e., *sine sui laude*; see Lebreton 1901: 98–99). For *suus* in particular, see, e.g., *Caec.* 77: *ipse pudore quodam afficeretur ex sua laude* ("A kind of modesty would prevent him from [hearing] praise of himself"); *Verr.* 2.3.68; *Balb.* 32.

at ipse non modo respondet quidquid potest, cum est lacessitus, sed etiam gaudet se ab amicis quid respondeat admoneri: The exchange depicted in this section gives a glimpse of a type of back and forth, characterized by humorous abuse and personal attack, that must have been common in the senate (*Att.* 1.16.10 preserves a classic recounting of one such *altercatio*). For these situations, rhetorical treatises stress that barbs given in reply must be, or seem, spontaneous (of the type *in respondendo*); see *de orat.* 2.230 (*omnino probabiliora sunt, quae lacessiti dicimus quam quae priores, nam et ingeni celeritas maior est, quae apparet in respondendo*) with Leeman et al. 1989: 3.230–231. The point of the second half of this sentence is to mock Clodius's rhetorical ineptitude, which forces him to rely on the wit of his friends; Quintilian warns against being prompted by others during an exchange, "because it sometimes happens that we are embarrassed by our own credulity and by the stupidity of others" (*inst.* 6.4.8: *quo nonnumquam accidit ut nostra credulitate aliena stultitia erubescamus*). It is striking that in sections 16 and 17 forms of the verb *respondere* occur six times, three to describe Cicero's possible responses, one that of a hypothetical person (*quisquam vir*), and the final two that of Clodius's failed understanding of the art of response. Given that the current session of the senate revolves around how best to interpret the document of the *haruspices*, it would seem that Cicero is making an oblique reference to his own ability, and Clodius's inability, to understand the haruspical "responses" (so Beard 2012a: 36: "Enigmas, answers, responses and interpretations are, he suggests, at the centre of *both* political *and* religious discussion" [emphases original]; cf. nn. at 12 and 21). It is, then, not surprising that the next sentence prompts the senate to consider the serious nature of what the *haruspices* have said in response (cf. 18: *gravitate responsi*).

18–19

Cicero defends himself from suspicions that his interest in philosophy indicates a lack of belief in the gods. To counter this claim he praises Rome's unparalleled sacred apparatus, especially emphasizing, unsurprisingly, the role of the *haruspices*. He concludes by asserting that respect for the power of the gods is in fact Rome's defining characteristic and the reason for her greatness. This seeming digression—asserting his own traditional piety and recommending that his fellow senators feel the same—provides an essential prelude to Cicero's subsequent line-by-line reading of the response. Among the numerous discussions of this passage see most recently Guillaumont 1984: 32–36; Gildenhard 2011: 330–338; Santangelo 2013: 102–107; Valvo 2014.

18 *Sed quoniam... commotum*: This section occurs in all manuscripts after the end of section 16 (*adrogans videatur*). There is no obvious reason for the lines being transposed to that earlier section, but they are clearly out of place there, disrupting as they do the discussion of Cicero's allegedly excessive boasting. Here the sense fits well, as well as the manner in which *neque is sum* follows naturally after *ego enim fateor*.

videamus nunc quid haruspices dicant: Having offered at sections 9–17 a thorough argument for the sanctity of his house (*mea causa expedita est*), Cicero signals that he will resume an analysis of the haruspical response. He prefaces that analysis, however, with sections 18–19, where he asserts his own piety in a passage that he marks as a digression only afterward (20: *qua re, ne plura de re minime loquar dubia*; for this common technique, see Canter 1931: 360–361).

ego... ego... ego: The repeated use of the first-person pronoun, combined with five first-person singular verb forms over the course of one sentence, emphatically opposes Cicero to anyone who might argue for his irreligiosity. Such an insinuation likely constituted part of Clodius's arguments during both his *contio* on the response and the previous day's senate meeting (a portion of which he has just recounted in section 17).

et magnitudine ostenti et gravitate responsi et una atque constanti haruspicum ⟨voce⟩ vehementer ēssĕ cōmmōtūm: A rising tricolon (7 + 7 + 11 [?]) and favored clausula of cretic + spondee underscore Cicero's assertion of his belief in the significance of recent events. Note that the prodigy (*ostentum*) is distinguished both from the response (*responsum*) and from the words of the *haruspices*. By the close of the speech, Cicero effectively equates these three separate phenomena (10n; Corbeill 2010a: 151–153).

The collocation of *unus* and *constans* occurs elsewhere only at Cic. *ac.* 1.31 (where it is often emended). *ThLL* IV 538.37–38 (F. Burger) construes the two adjectives in hendiadys (sc. "the single unanimous voice"), which also fits the parallel at *Pis.* 34: *consentiente atque una voce*. Cicero normally avoids the conjunction *atque* before a consonant in his post-Verrine speeches. Exceptions include instances when the juxtaposition produces a desirable clausula (see 10n): "In *pro Sulla*, every case of *atque* before a consonant helps the rhythm, whether at a break within the sentence or at the end" (Berry 1996a: 53). This does not apply here, where the colon presumably continues through the suggested supplement, *voce*. Context may, however, explain the exception. Given the preceding interconnected series of three instances of *et*, the use of that particular conjunction here would be inelegant and potentially confusing, whereas the use of *-que* would yield five consecutive long syllables. The combination *ac c-* was also not an option—*ThLL* II 1048.84–1049.5 (A. Klotz) cites only five possible examples from the post-Verrine orations (no discernible avoidance occurs in *Verr.*: see *ThLL* II 1048.75). Because of the indisputably conscious aversion of *atque* plus consonant, Hutchinson 1995: 487 proposes that occurrences not clearly used for rhythmic purposes should be regarded either as "textually suspect" or as employed to lend "dignity" to a passage. Since the codices here do not offer an alternative reading, the most likely explanation would be that suggested by Hutchinson 1995 (488–490), namely that *atque* + consonant serves "to give weight to particular concepts, and dignity to the style," in particular when the conjunction connects two related words, as in the apparent hendiadys here. Such an interpretation also accords well with the phrase's place in the final portion of a rising tricolon and with the fact that it describes the haruspical response.

** *voce* is a conjecture of Nicolaus Angelius (1515), accepted by all modern editors. The supplement seems nearly certain: the noun occurs fifteen times elsewhere in the speech (along with three forms of *voco* and one instance of *vocabulum*); the juxtaposition with *ostentum* and *responsum* recalls one the speech's motifs (see nn. on 10, 20); the adjectives *unus* and *constans* make an appropriate pair; and, most convincingly, the collocation *constans vox* occurs at *div.* 1.20=*carm. frg.* 3.51 in reference to a haruspical response.

si cui forte videor plus quam ceteri qui aeque atque ego sunt occupati versari in studio litterarum: After asserting how deeply the prodigy under discussion concerns him, Cicero unexpectedly turns to deny accusations of atheism. I translate vaguely *versari in studio litterarum* ("to be involved in the study of the written word"), since I believe that Cicero himself intends to be vague as he begins his assessment of the influence of literary study on religious belief. Only does the subsequent context make clear that the word *litterae* refers here specifically to the study of philosophy (he would have avoided the Greek loan words *philosophus* and *philosophia*, which occur in Cicero's orations always in a pejorative sense and, in relation to a Roman, only in *Pis.*; Hine 2015: 14–19). His coy formulation concerning his studies arises from a sensitivity to anti-intellectualism at Rome during this period, particularly regarding philosophy (Volk 2021: 23–36).

Cicero would have been exposed to the skeptical views of the Academy as early as 88, during Philo of Larissa's stay in Rome, and this philosophical stance came to inform the views of his interlocutors in later philosophical treatises such as *De natura deorum* and *De divinatione*, both produced over a decade after *har. resp.* (*Brut.* 306; Powell 1995: 18–23). Even prior to *har. resp.* Cicero had made no secret during public appearances of his philosophical training. In the *Pro Murena* of 63, for example, he needles Cato for his severe adherence to Stoic principles (see esp. 61–66, which he introduces with *de studiis humanitatis quae et mihi et vobis nota et iucunda sunt disputabo*) and famously advertises his broad education in *Pro Archia* of 62 (e.g., *Arch.* 2). In the poem on his consulship, of uncertain date, Cicero expresses a sentiment similar to that given here, namely that he devotes to literature whatever time he can spare from politics (*div.* 1.22=*carm. frg.* 3.78 [the muse Urania addressing Cicero]: '*quod patriae vacat, id studiisque nobisque sacrasti*'). Cicero was later to claim that his orations are "packed with the opinions of philosophers" (*nat. deor.* 1.6: *orationes…refertae philosophorum sententiis*; for a full discussion see Gildenhard 2011, esp. 1–18). Regarding his contemporaries, Griffin 1989 provides a balanced discussion of the intersection of philosophy and politics in Rome, which continues with Griffin 1995, where she surveys the various types of allusions found in Cic. *fam.* to provide an idea of the extent and range of philosophical knowledge among Cicero's contemporaries (see now Volk 2021: 55–110); for intellectual life more generally, Rawson 1985 provides a full selection of testimony.

his delecter aut utar omnino litteris: Cicero brackets the verb *utar* with *aut…omnino* to stress its contrast with the preceding *delecter* ("I am in fact not the kind of person who enjoys—or makes use of at all—those writings"). For analogous uses of *aut omnino* to qualify an earlier, stronger, verb see *Verr.* 2.2.69: *nihil erat in causa quod metuendum aut omnino quod dubitandum videretur*; *dom.* 14; *Sest.* 140; *Phil.* 2.111: *respondebisne ad haec, aut omnino hiscere audebis?*; LHS 2: 499. For the hyperbaton of *his…litteris* see next note.

** his: Shackleton Bailey 1991a: 230 follows, without argument, Peterson's *Mk* in reading *iis* (Maslowski reads *his* and gives no variants in his apparatus). Changing the reading without strong manuscript support seems unjustified. Furthermore, in the long-range hyperbaton deployed here, emphasis is placed on the first element (*his*), in this case presumably to signal the postponed subsequent relative clause (Powell 2010: 174–175, who notes that determiners such as *hic* are commonly given focus in this construction; see, e.g., *Verr.* 2.1.109: **hoc** *reperies in omnibus statui* **ius quo**…).

quae nostros animos deterrent atque avocant a religione: The indicative mood of the verbs indicates that Cicero has in mind specific texts, presumably the teachings of Epicurus, which he cannot of course name explicitly lest he implicate himself in being too familiar with this school of philosophy. *Deterreo* has its literal force here ("frighten"), perhaps a sarcastic pun on the Epicureans' claim that their belief in the apathy of the gods helps eliminate the fear of death among human beings. Note too the playful word order, which replicates meaning in placing "our minds" as distant as possible from *religio*.

ego vero primum habeo auctores ac magistros religionum colendarum maiores nostros: Despite emphatically asserting this as his own opinion (*ego vero*), Cicero hardly says anything controversial in claiming the Roman ancestors as the authorities for religious ritual (for this general sense of *religionem colere* see *Font.* 31, *leg.* 2.15). Abundant testimony attributes this position to the *maiores*, in particular *Mil.* 83: *maiorum nostrorum sapientia qui sacra, qui* *caerimonias, qui auspicia et ipsi sanctissime coluerunt et nobis suis posteris tradiderunt* (testimony and discussion in Roloff 1938: 109–114; Pease 1955–1958: 983). On the mutual compatibility between the wisdom of philosophers and the practice of the Roman ancestors when it comes to religion, compare the response of Cotta in responding to the Stoic Balbus how it is possible for one man to be both learned in Greek philosophy and a *pontifex* (*nat. deor.* 3.6: *a te enim philosopho rationem accipere debeo religionis, maioribus autem nostris etiam nulla ratione reddita credere*; cf. *div.* 2.148).

Note Cicero's use here of *auctores*, which the context (*litterae* used twice in the previous sentence) might lead his audience to expect to mean "authors (of written texts)" that will lead one toward religion, in opposition to those writings of unnamed Epicureans that impel readers away from it (*a religione*, emphatically closing the previous sentence). Instead, *auctor* has the sense of "instigator" or "teacher," a sense immediately confirmed by the following *magistros*, so that Cicero separates his book-learning, which is suspect to some of the senators and was likely a theme of Clodius's *contio*, from his respect for and familiarity with Roman ritual and convention (for the frequent use by Cicero of *auctorem habere* to assert past authority, including of written texts, see ThLL II 1206.23–40 [T. Bögel]). The notion of a religion passed down through authoritative teachers rather than learned from books corresponds with the speech's emphasis on orality rather than writing in interpreting the prodigy (Beard 2012a).

tanta fuisse sapientia: The placement of *fuisse* tends to emphasize the word that precedes it, here to stress the degree of wisdom of the ancestors as well as to anticipate the result clause (Adams 1994a: 19–24). At the same time, however, the separation of *sapientia* from *quorum* also draws attention to this noun, as the relative clause continues the contrast between communally inherited religious wisdom and the individual works of "philosophers" (a connotation of *sapientis* at 19; cf. *off.* 2.5, where *philosophia* is defined as *studium sapientiae*). See Courtney 1993: 170 for *sapientia* as practical, Roman, prudence.

ut satis superque prudentes sint qui illorum prudentiam non dicam adsequi, sed quanta fuerit perspicere possint: The adverb *super* occurs in Ciceronian prose only in this common alliterative phrase (Wölfflin 1881: 274; also at *Q. Rosc.* 11, *Flacc.* 66). The context here would seem to counter the common claim that the phrase is colloquial (cf. Horsfall 2008: 460). For the use of the interjected phrase *non dicam* to draw attention to a subsequent and more accurate formulation cf., e.g., *Clu.* 133: *nullum ob totius vitae non dicam vitium sed erratum*; 182: *nullo adhibito non dicam viro...sed bono viro*; and, more fully, *Mur.* 23: *non dicam operam perdidisti, sed illud dicam, nullam esse in ista disciplina munitam ad consulatum viam*. Cicero seems to have become especially drawn to this phrase in the speeches delivered after exile (*p. red. in sen.* 1, 8, 16; *Sest.* 46, 108; *Vatin.* 21; *Balb.* 10; *Pis.* 10, 23, 30, 53 [*bis*], 75). The usage contrasts with *ne dicam* which suggests "a stronger epithet by explicitly refusing to insist on it" (Gotoff 1993: 203; KS 2: 1.824–825).

Note the play between *prudentes* and *prudentiam*: the sufficiently "wise" are those who simply recognize, rather than achieve, the "wisdom" of the *maiores*. There may also be a play on *perspicere*, "to see completely," since *prudentia* derives from *pro+video*, "to foresee" (8n; for a full discussion of the adjective and noun in the context of Cicero and Roman religion, see Santangelo 2013: 56–68). Santangelo 2011b: 47–48 argues that Cicero uses these terms to anticipate his subsequent allusions to the role of prophecy in Roman religion (18: *praedictiones…praedixerint*). The general conceit recalls the famous Socratic paradox that knowledge consists chiefly in knowing the limits of one's own knowledge (e.g., *ac.* 1.16: *haec esset una hominis sapientia, non arbitrari sese scire quod nesciat*).

qui statas sollemnisque caeremonias pontificatu, rerum bene gerundarum auctoritates augurio, fatorum veteres praedictiones Apollinis vatum libris, portentorum expiationes Etruscorum disciplina contineri putaverunt: Valerius Maximus lightly adapts this sentence, and regularizes its grammar, to open the main portion of his *Facta et Dicta Memorabilia* (1.1.1: *maiores statas sollemnesque caerimonias pontificum scientia, bene gerendarum rerum auctoritates augurum obseruatione, Apollinis praedictione⟨s⟩ uatum libris, portentorum depulsi⟨one⟩s Etrusca disciplina explicari uoluerunt*; Köves-Zulauf 1972: 43, with bibl.; Wardle 1998: 75–76).

In praising the foresight of Rome's ancestors, Cicero concentrates on the compartmentalization of religious duties that they had developed: the *pontifices* oversee regular religious ceremonies and festivals; the *augures* those religious events that have bearing on the proper conduct of state affairs; the *quindecimviri* the Sibylline books; and the *haruspices* the expiation of prodigies. Cicero opens the *De domo sua* of the previous autumn with a different emphasis on the foresight of the *maiores*: "While many things, pontifices, have been discovered and instituted by our ancestors through divine guidance, nevertheless nothing is more brilliant than their desire to place the same individuals in charge of both the affairs of the immortal gods and of the most important matters of state. As a result, our most prominent citizens preserve religious duties through wise guidance of the state, and the state through proper observance of religious duties" (*dom.* 1: *cum multa divinitus, pontifices, a maioribus nostris inventa atque instituta sunt, tum nihil praeclarius quam quod eosdem et religionibus deorum immortalium et summae rei publicae praeesse voluerunt, ut amplissimi et clarissimi cives rem publicam bene gerendo religiones, religiones sapienter interpretando rem publicam conservarent*). This is of course part of the speech's *captatio benevolentiae*, since Cicero's audience of *pontifices* constitute the supreme example of those who are in charge of both state and religion (however inexact this characterization may be; see Nisbet 1939: 65). For similar reasons, a change in the religious situation forces a change in emphasis in *De haruspicum responsis*. In separating out here the specific capacities of the chief priestly colleges, Cicero must offer a silent corrective: the Etruscan *haruspices* do not, so far as our evidence tells us, belong to the class of those men in charge of "the most important matters of state" (*summae rei publicae*) even though, as the next sentence of *har. resp.* makes clear, they have served an important function in the recent history of the republic. In his later treatises, where the *haruspices* are no longer the focus, Cicero reduces this quadripartite division to a threefold one of pontifices, augurs, and, jointly, the *quindecimviri* and *haruspices* (*nat. deor.* 3.5; cf. *leg.* 2.20.5–6 with 2.21.8, 2.30–31). According to Augustine (*civ.* 6.3 p. 249.17–19), Varro divided the three books of his *Antiquitates rerum divinarum* so that *primus sit de pontificibus, secundus de auguribus, tertius de quindecimviris sacrorum*; there is no mention of *haruspices* (Cardauns 1976: 17=frg. 4).

The sentence is carefully crafted. The balance of four near isocola describing the religious bodies (16/16/17/17) and a concluding [double] cretic + spondee (*cōntĭnērī pŭtāvērūnt*) create a slight dissonance with the syntax, where the mode of designation of each body varies within a consistent ablative construction by: 1. name of college (*pontificatu*); 2. priestly action (*augurio*); 3. physical means (*libris*); 4. specialized training (*disciplina*). If the variation is meant to serve any purpose, it does effectively show that the wisdom of the ancestors escapes easy categorization (as shown by the varied skills of the priests) and yet fits into a neat system (as demonstrated by the overall syntax). It may also be relevant that the sequence of ablatives ascribes action not to individual human agents, but to various non-human aspects of each priesthood. Santangelo 2011b: 48 makes an excellent observation about Cicero's choice of the verb *contineri*: "The foresight of the ancestors is celebrated because they decided to limit the potential options of their divinatory practices. The emphasis is on *contineri*: augury sets a limit on the use of power, the Sibylline books provide a framework for ancient prophetic utterances, and the Etruscan discipline sets rules for the expiation of prodigies." The following notes treat separately each group of religious figures.

statas sollemnisque caeremonias pontificatu: For the *pontifices* see 11n. In the adjectival pairing *statas sollemnisque*, *sollemnis* designates an annual event while *status* indicates that it occurs on a fixed day: Fest. p. 344 M: *stata sacrificia sunt, quae certis diebus fieri debent.... sollemnia sacra dicuntur, quae certis temporibus annisque fieri solent*; Wissowa 1912: 440 n. 3. For the alliterative collocation outside Val. Max. 1.1.1 see Cato *orat.* XV.59, *Tusc.* 1.113, Liv. 3.15.4.

rerum bene gerundarum auctoritates augurio: Full technical discussions of augury may be found in *RE* 2: 2313–2344 (G. Wissowa), Linderski 1986, and Driediger-Murphy 2019. The Ciceronian juxtaposition *auctoritates augurio* occurs several times (e.g., *leg.* 2.31, *nat. deor.* 2.12) and presumably involves an instance of etymological play (Ov. *fast.* 1.611–612; Neumann 1976: 220–223).

fatorum veteres praedictiones Apollinis vatum libris: The origins of the Sibylline books (*Apollinis vatum libris*) are uncertain and their precise makeup varied over time (on the Sibyl throughout antiquity, see Parke 1988; for the

Roman manifestation, Wissowa 1912: 534–543, Orlin 1997: 76–115). Cicero is our earliest source explicitly to connect the books with Apollo. Like the Etruscan writings used by the *haruspices,* this collection of Greek verse oracles originated from a foreign source, according to legend purchased from a mysterious old woman by the Etruscan king Tarquinius Superbus. Stored in the temple of Jupiter Optimus Maximus on the Capitoline until the time of Augustus, the original books were destroyed in a fire in the time of Sulla and a second collection reassembled from various sources throughout the Mediterranean (see esp. D. H. 4.62, relying on Varro). During our period, the books were kept by the *quindecimviri sacris faciundis* who, like the *haruspices,* consulted their sacred books at the request of the senate during the prodigy process and recommended possible means of expiation (see Introduction F.1). In 56, Clodius was a *quindecimvir* (26n). The plural of *vates* here cannot refer to the *quindecimviri,* who simply consulted the sacred books, but presumably to the succession of individual Sibyls whose utterances were collected and came to constitute the Sibylline collection (Guillaumont 1984: 34 n. 56); alternatively, it may refer to prophetic collections added later, such as the *carmina Marciana* (Pease 1920, 1923: 253; Wardle 1998: 77).

** ***praedictiones***: The major codices read *praedicationes*; LA[1] have *praedicatione* (*praedictione* A[2]). Peterson and Maslowski adopt *praedictiones,* an emendation found in the *recentiores* (an analogous confusion exists in the manuscripts at Val. Max. 1.1.1). While *praedicatio* makes possible sense, its principal use during the classical period is of encomiastic speech. It is likely that the major codices are influenced by the later meaning, ubiquitous in Christian texts, of the preaching of divine themes (*ThLL* X, 2 544.9–547.5 [P. Gatti]). Confusion of the two nouns is frequent: *ThLL* X, 2 570.26–28 (J. Ramminger).

** ***expiationes***: This is an emendation of Sigonius; most codices read *explanationes* (*explationes* P[1]). Val. Max. 1.1.1 is of no help here, where modern editors emend to *depulsi⟨one⟩s* the reading of the manuscripts (*depulsis*). While *explanatio* makes good sense, its corruption here can be in part attributed to the presence of the noun at 13 (on the interpretive practice of *pontifices*; otherwise an uncommon noun in Cicero, occurring five times and in the orations only at 13). The conjecture *expiationes* receives support from the following considerations: 1. it accounts for the nonsensical *explationes* of the first hand of P; 2. the parallel use at 21, where there is no textual variant (cf. too 35 and 57, of Clodius); 3. Valerius Maximus's rendering *depulsiones,* which is a suitable synonym of *expiationes* but not *explanationes.*

nostra memoria: Rather than list examples of accurate warnings by the *haruspices* from throughout Rome's history, Cicero invokes events that would have happened within the lifetime of his senatorial audience, thereby appealing even to the most skeptical among them. Similarly, in the *Catilinarians* Cicero professes to pass by early historical precedents for killing a rebellious citizen in order to focus on more recent parallels (*Catil.* 1.3: *nam illa nimis antiqua praetereo* with Dyck 2008: 70). The implied chronology of the sequence *primum... post... tum* is reinforced by accompanying words denoting time (*Italici belli... Sullani Cinnanique temporis... hanc recentem*), with the entire progression expressed in a rising tricolon (15 + 19 + 22, assuming the monosyllabic *tum* does not elide).

Italici belli: For prodigies during the Social War for which the *haruspices* were consulted see, e.g., Cic. *div.* 1.99, 2.59 (cf. Plin. *nat.* 8.221). Other accounts of prodigies during the period do not explicitly mention the *haruspices*: Cic. *div.* 2.54; Plin. *nat.* 2.98, 2.238. MacBain 1982: 100–101 contains a helpful table.

Sullani Cinnanique temporis: In addition to sources cited in the previous note, Plut. *Sull.* 7.2–6 attests to a proliferation of prodigies in 88 BCE that entailed participation of the *haruspices* and presaged the conflict between Sulla and Marius. For Cinna, see too *nat. deor.* 2.14 with Pease 1955–1958: 585; *div.* 1.4: *saepe hariolorum etiam et vatum... praedictiones*; Plin. *nat.* 2.92. Lenaghan 1969: 108–109 has an interesting note on Cicero's tendency to omit mention of his fellow Arpinate Marius when referring to the violence of this period; cf. van der Blom 2010, *passim*. For a brief survey of the activities of Sulla and Cinna at this time see 54n, and 2n for the adjectival forms *Sullanus* and *Cinnanus*.

hanc recentem urbis inflammandae delendique imperii coniurationem: The reference is unmistakably to the Catilinarian conspiracy of 63. The threats of burning down the city and destroying the state are a continually recurring part of Cicero's rhetoric concerning these events: see Dyck 2008: 70 on *caede atque incendiis* (*Catil.* 1.2) as "a paraphrase for Catiline's program." In his *Third Catilinarian* Cicero refers back to prodigies of 65, when images of gods and men, as well as bronze tablets containing laws, were struck by lightning. On that occasion the *haruspices* were summoned, and they included among their predictions *caedes atque incendia* and *totius urbis atque imperi occasum*, a combination of which Cicero alludes to here (*Catil.* 3.19–20, *div.* 1.19–20 [=*carm. frg.* 6.33–59], Dio 37.9.2 and 37.34.3–4, and perhaps 38.7.3; mentioning prodigies but not *haruspices*: Obseq. 61). In the same context he lists prodigies in 63 that included comets in the night sky, lightning bolts, and earth tremors, which again included the participation of the *haruspices* (*Catil.* 3.18, *div.* 1.18–21 [=*carm. frg.* 6.1–65], 2.47; cf. Obseq. 61, Plin. *nat.* 2.137, Dio 37.25.1–2).

praedixerint: The context requires *haruspices* to be understood as the subject, as implied in *Etruscorum disciplina*. This carefully crafted result clause closes with a single and significant verb, emphatically placed at sentence end in a double cretic clausula with both word accents on the first longum: ā́ntĕ prǣ-dī́xĕrīnt ("they warned in advance").

19 deinde: This adverb looks back to *primum* in 18 and moves beyond Roman institutions to introduce the learning about the gods that Cicero has acquired outside this tradition (*etiam cognovi*: "I have also learned about"). The preceding section had offered the first part of Cicero's justification of his piety,

De haruspicum responsis 19

as he praised the wisdom of Rome's ancestors for the division of labor among the various priestly bodies. He now turns to the second portion of his justification with a more general claim: anything that he has heard or read from previous learned men seems merely derivative of the ancestral religion of Rome's founders.

** *siquid habui oti*: Omitted in H; *siquid habui tolli* P; *siquid habuit tolli* GE. Orelli (Orelli *et al.* 1856: 911) proposed *siquid habui otii*, which gives the required sense: "whenever I have had any free time [to learn about philosophy]," i.e., even though I have been so involved with other matters (18: *occupati*; for the orthography *oti* see 4n). The parenthesis again deflects charges that he may have been too preoccupied with the sorts of studies that can make one skeptical about the gods.

etiam cognovi multa homines doctos sapientisque et dixisse et scripta de deorum immortalium numine reliquisse: As the combination of *et...et* makes clear, *multa* is to be understood as the substantized direct object of both *dixisse* and *reliquisse*, to which in the latter case is attached the predicative participle *scripta* ("learned scholars have both said and left behind in writing many things about the power of the immortal gods"). For *relinquo* followed by a predicate, see Merguet 4: 275 [IV], *Verr*. 2.5.112: *id quod scriptum reliquit*, *de orat*. 3.148; Laughton 1964: 62–63 notes that *scribo* commonly occurs in this construction in Cicero. Here Cicero probably did not write *scripsisse* in order to provide with the participle *scripta* a clear construction for the prepositional phrase *de deorum immortalium numine*. The learned men that Cicero has in mind are Greek philosophers (18n); naming them here would potentially undercut his claim that such study occurs only in his rare moments of free time.

The neuter noun *numen* occurs three times in this speech, all in section 19. Much has been written on the original meaning of this noun, which describes the power inherent in divine and sacred things, in particular gods (*RE* 17: 1273–1291 [F. Pfister] assesses the full range of primary material). The possibility that the word provides access to an early pre-animistic stage of Roman religion has been much debated (see, e.g., Rose 1935; Wagenvoort 1947: 73–83; Weinstock 1949; Rose 1951; Fasciano 1971), but this point is irrelevant to an understanding of the word in Cicero, who attributes the power solely to the gods throughout his corpus, except on one occasion each to the *populus Romanus* (*p. red. ad Quir.* 18) and to the senate (*Phil.* 3.32). The two parts of Varro's definition (*ling.* 7.85)—that *numen* means "power," in part based on its etymology from *nuere*, "to nod"—fits Ciceronian usage, where the noun encompasses the particular power that manifests itself in divine will (Fenechiu 2008).

divinitus perscripta: The metaphorical application here of *divinitus* ("brilliantly composed") to describe every detail (*per-*) of the writing of previous philosophers differs from his more cautious use of the adjective *divinus* elsewhere in the speech (2n; for the metaphorical use of *divinitus* see *ThLL* V, 1

1618.10–32 [A. Gudeman]). While the adverb need not always retain its literal sense (cf. Shackleton Bailey 1965–1970: 319: "*divinitus*...the idea hardly required divine inspiration"), the context here, and the lack of apology for the metaphor, suggests that the gods assisted the work even of Greek philosophers, further protecting Cicero from charges of impiety for studying them. For another possible use of *divinitus* in the speech, see 40n.

ea maiores nostri docuisse illos, non ab illis didicisse videantur: Lenaghan 1969: 109 aptly compares *nat. deor.* 3.5 (Cotta speaking): *cum de religione agitur, Ti. Coruncanium, P. Scipionem, P. Scaevolam, pontifices maximos, non Zenonem aut Cleanthem aut Chrysippum sequor, habeoque C. Laelium, augurem eundemque sapientem quem potius audiam dicentem de religione...quam quemquam principem Stoicorum* (immediately afterward Cotta offers the division of Rome's religion into the three parts governed by the *pontifices*, augurs, and *quindecimviri* with *haruspices*; cf. 18n). *Tusc.* 1.1–2 offers a more detailed assessment of the superiority of Rome's traditions to Greek philosophy, while *De oratore* concludes with an analogous assertion about the superiority of Crassus to the Greeks in teaching rhetoric: '*tu vero...conlegisti omnia...ita divinitus ut non a Graecis sumpsisse sed eos ipsos haec docere posse videare*' (3.228). Beard 1986 analyzes how Cicero's final religious treatise, *De divinatione* of 44, represents an attempt to synthesize Greek philosophy with traditional sacred practice at Rome.

etenim quis est tam vaecors: The particle *etenim* ("for in the end") has the function of "toning down a challengeable utterance" by offering an explanation of how Greek thinkers were independently able to come to the same conclusions about the gods as early Romans (Kroon 1995: 196–198). The colorful adjective *vaecors* ("insane") occurs on the early Roman stage (Livius Andronicus, Pacuvius, Accius) and is found five other times in the orations, all in those composed between 57 and 55 BCE, three times to describe Clodius and twice of Piso. Considering its rarity, its use here to describe one who doubts the power of the gods likely is intended to recall its application to Clodius earlier at 2 (note the indicative *est*). The remaining three instances in Cicero outside his oratory occur in an etymology (*Tusc.* 1.18) and in two translations from Greek poetry, one from early and one from late in his life (*Arat.* 424, where the adjective is added in a section that exhibits "a most unusual example of expansion" [Ewbank 1933: 211], and *Tusc.* 2.20, where the Sophoclean original has simply "crafty" [δολῶπις]). It is likely that Cicero here intends this evocative word to allude to literary tragedy, as it will more explicitly later in the speech (for the tragic resonances of *vaecors* in Cicero, see Kubiak 1989).

qui aut, cum suspexit in caelum, deos esse non sentiat, et ea quae tanta mente fiunt ut vix quisquam arte ulla ordinem rerum ac necessitudinem persequi possit casu fieri putet: In the passages discussed in this and the next note, Cicero addresses two alternative views of the gods (*aut...aut*), the first here being atheism. For the Stoic sentiment that the design of the universe supports the existence of the gods see, e.g., *nat. deor.* 2.4 (Balbus): *quid enim potest esse tam apertum tamque perspicuum, cum caelum suspeximus…, quam esse aliquod numen praestantissimae mentis quo haec regantur?* (*Mil.* 83; Pease 1955-1958: 546 lists parallels). The verb *suspexit* has here a frequentative sense ("whenever he looks to the heavens"), a sense common for the perfect and pluperfect indicative in subordinate clauses in Cicero and Caesar, but rare later (Lebreton 1901: 222–223).

aut, cum deos esse intellexerit, non intellegat eorum numine hoc tantum imperium esse natum et auctum et retentum: Cicero offers the alternative view that is the mark of a "madman" (*vaecors*), one that is in accordance with Roman Epicureanism: the gods exist, but do not concern themselves with human affairs (for a Ciceronian summary of Epicurean theology, see the speaker Velleius at *nat. deor.* 1.43–51). The chiastic structure of this clause, with an indirect statement preceding and then following the governing verbs, separated only by *non*, results in the juxtaposition of the two forms of *intellego*, thereby underscoring the limitations of Epicurean theology: they understand that the gods exist, but do not realize the implications of that understanding. In addition, the four instances of elision in the closing indirect statement echo the Stoic view of the interconnectedness between the gods and the Roman state, with the three participles combining in a rising tricolon to create a favored double trochee clausula: *hoc tantum imperium esse natum et auctum ĕt rĕtēntūm*. For a different type of mirroring of sense and syntax, but for similar ends, see the Stoic Balbus's account at *nat. deor.* 2.19: *Quid vero tanta rerum consentiens, conspirans, continuata cognatio quem non coget ea, quae dicuntur a me, conprobare?* (derivatives of *cum*— "together with"—in fact pervade all of Balbus's narrative in Book 2). *Pace* Lebreton 1901: 223, the perfect subjunctive *intellexerit* here is best explained not as frequentative but as concessive— "although he has understood that the gods exist, he [nevertheless] does not understand…."

In the famous sentence beginning *quam volumus licet*, Cicero asserts the superiority of the Romans over all peoples in their devotion to the divine while he simultaneously acknowledges Roman inferiority in other areas. Several authors from Greek and Roman antiquity offer analogous testimony, beginning as early as Polybius in the second century BCE, who sees the unparalleled ubiquity of religious ritual at Rome as a means of controlling the unpredictability of the masses (6.56.6–12). Roman texts tend to be less suspicious, such as the claims found on an early inscribed letter from Telos by M. Valerius Messala (quoted in a note later in this section), or the assertion of the Stoic Balbus in *nat. deor.* 2.8 (*et si conferre volumus cum externis, ceteris rebus ut pares aut etiam inferiores reperiemur, religione, id est cultu deorum, multo superiores*), or the succint sentiment of Horace: "Roman,…you rule because you consider yourself below the gods" (Hor. *carm.* 3.6.5: *[Romane,] dis te minorem quod geris, imperas*; Pease 1955-1958: 566–567 cites a broad range of Greek and Roman parallels; Muth 1962: 247–249).

Commentary

Cicero here adopts the form of the so-called priamel, by which a speaker creates a list that highlights a "climactic term by enumerating or summarizing a number of 'other' examples,... which then yield... to the particular point of interest or importance" (Race 1982: ix, who surveys the form throughout Greek and Roman literature, but omits consideration of Roman prose; for evidence that the figure is Indo-European, see West 2007: 116–117). The structure recalls the most famous priamel in Roman literature, at Verg. *Aen.* 6.847–853: *excudent alii spirantia mollius aera / (credo equidem), vivos ducent de marmore vultus, / orabunt causas melius, caelique meatus / describent radio et surgentia sidera dicent. / tu regere imperio populos, Romane, memento / (hae tibi erunt artes), pacique imponere morem, / parcere subiectis et debellare superbos*. Although it is unlikely that Vergil intends to recall our passage here, it is worth noting the change in emphasis: while Cicero sees piety as the area in which Romans compete with the Greeks and their arts, Vergil's speaker Anchises locates Roman *artes* in military superiority and clemency. Other portions of Anchises's speech are, however, indebted to Cicero, in particular his *De consulatu suo* (Setaioli 1975: 8–12; Gee 2013: 96–98) and *Somnium Scipionis* (Horsfall 2013: 485, 515–516, with bibliography); more generally, see Grilli and Crawford 1984. Cairo 2020: 80–83 observes how Cicero asserts here a Roman collective identity from which the speech's rhetoric necessarily excludes Clodius.

quam volumus licet...ipsi nos amemus: For the conjunction *quam* + *vis* employing other forms of the verb *volo*, see KS 2: 2.443 Anm. 1; LHS 2: 2.603. The concessive compound *quam volumus* and the verb *licet* are not redundant: "Although it is fine...that we hold ourselves in high esteem" (Bailey 1947: 3.1645; *pace* KS 2: 2.444 Anm. 2, who call the combination a "verstärkte Form").

nec numero Hispanos: Önnerfors 1995: 8 cites only this passage of Cicero as testimony to the large population of the Hispani, to which one may add Mela 2.86: *ipsa Hispania... viris equis ferro plumbo aere argento auroque etiam abundans* (*RE* 8: 2028 [A. Schulten] catalogues population data in ancient authors; for modern demographic studies, estimating c. 3.5–4.1 million inhabitants during the Roman era, see Carreras 1995–1996 and Gozalbes Cravioto 2007: 194–195). It is likely that Cicero has in mind here the many and more visible cities that lie on the Mediterranean coast rather than the more sparsely populated regions inland (cf., of Baetica, Mart. Cap. 6.630: *oppida centum septuaginta quinque habitantium multitudine frequentata*). These large urban populations of Hispania are noted in Book 3 of Strabo, one of whose key sources is Cicero's contemporary, Posidonius.

nec robore Gallos: By contrast with the comment on the *Hispani*, Roman acknowledgment of the superior strength and size of the Gauls is a common trope of Greek and Roman panegyric (Men. Rhet. 369). Among Roman authors see, e.g., Caes. *Gall.* 2.30.4: *plerumque omnibus Gallis praemagnitudine corporum suorum brevitas nostra contemptui est* (cf. 1.39.1, 4.1.9); for the Greek background to this conception, see Gruen 2011: 141–147. Vegetius's version of this sentence (see below) stresses the superior numbers of the Gauls (*multitudinem*) rather than their physical superiority, which he cites as a characteristic of the Germani (as typically do later authors: Vell. 2.106.1 with Woodman 1977: 143; Tac. *Germ.* 4, 20.1–2; Isid. *orig.* 9.2.97). While *robur* can indeed refer to manpower (*OLD* s.v. 6b), Cicero's attribution of greater population to the Hispani makes it unlikely that this is the meaning here.

nec calliditate Poenos: The shrewdness of the Carthaginians was proverbial, as reflected in the ironic expression *Punica fides* ("Carthaginian trustworthiness"; see Otto 1890: 291). For the origins and growth of the concept, and the ambivalent view by Romans of the Carthaginians, see Gruen 2011: 115–140, who points out that the mention of Punic *calliditas* occurs here "in a surprisingly positive context: the Romans do not surpass them in cunning, any more than they surpass Gauls in strength, Greeks in art, or Italians in sensibility" (133).

nec artibus Graecos: A traditional contrast (Russell and Wilson 1981: 274 on Men. Rhet. 369), memorably encapsulated in Hor. *epist.* 2.1.156: *Graecia capta ferum victorem cepit* ("Captured Greece captured its fierce conqueror"). The Romans continually referred to their inferiority to the Greeks in fine arts; see Petrocheilos 1974: 55–62. Gruen 1992: 131–141 offers a balanced survey of the domination of Greeks in all areas of the arts during the Republican period.

nec denique hoc ipso huius gentis ac terrae domestico nativoque sensu Italos ipsos ac Latinos: This last clause presents a number of difficulties of interpretation. With the final use of *nec* in anaphora Cicero depicts the *Itali* and *Latini* as being as discrete a community from the Romans as are the Greeks, Hispani, and Gauls; at the same time he marks them as uniquely distinct by the relative length of this clause and the emphasis on these peoples' proximity (*hoc, huius*). And yet, despite the gradual extension of Roman citizenship to Italian communities following the Social War, there did remain throughout the late Republic a lingering prejudice that the *Itali* remained a separate class (Toll 1997: 34–40 surveys this prejudice and how it informs Vergil's portrayal of the *Itali* in the *Aeneid*; cf. 17n. For an historical survey of the origins and aftermath of the Social War see Keaveney 1987). The distinction between Romans and *Latini / Itali* can be traced to the foundation legend of Rome itself, where the development of a narrative of Trojan refugees founding Rome within Italian Latium "would bring mutual esteem to Romans and Latins and establish a pedigree that connected Rome to the Hellenic world"; see Gruen 1992: 6–51 (quotation from 50), who traces the legend from its putative beginnings in the fourth century BCE. It is also possible that Cicero recalls here specifically the historical investigations of Cato, who devoted Books 2–3 of his *Origines* to an account of Italian communities outside Rome (Book 1 covered Rome). While the fragments make clear that he was aware of the diversity of the *Itali* in language and customs, "it would not be altogether surprising if Cato had formed a view of Italy that was united by the toughness and warlike spirit of its various component peoples" (*FRHist* 1: 212 [T. J. Cornell]). Such a conception can be found in non-historical texts of the Republican period that see the extra-urban inhabitants of Italy both as "rustic" barbarians and as morally superior (Dench 1995: 67, 73–80, who also considers negative portrayals).

While the *Latini*, like the urban Romans, technically comprised a subset of the *Itali*, they formed a distinct subgroup not simply because of geography, but because it is "probable that the Latins formed a linguistic, cultural, and religious community long before the emergence of organized city-states in the 6th cent. BC" (*OCD* s.v. "*Latini*"). Various legal benefits that had accrued to the Latins over the years involving intermarriage (*conubium*), trade and contracts (*commercium*), and migration made it so that those who had not attained full Roman citizenship nevertheless had access to most civic privileges (Sherwin White 1973: 96–118). Although the Latins had become full Roman citizens after the Social War, Cicero here appeals to what he perceives as their particular qualities as a distinct ethic group. I know of no parallel instance of this distinction being applied to contemporary Latins in the surviving Ciceronian corpus.

The way in which Cicero characterizes these two groups contains other unique features. The emphatic repetition of deictic and intensive adjectives (*hoc ipso huius... ipsos*) seems intended to emphasize the proximity that these two groups have with the urban Romans, but their precise nuance is difficult to discover (for *huius*, cf. Vell. Pat. 2.15.2, where the Italians are called from the Roman perspective **homines eiusdem et gentis et sanguinis**). Furthermore, none of the combinations *sensus nativus, sensus domesticus,* or *sensus terrae,* occurs elsewhere in extant Latin, with the two adjectives further underscoring that Cicero is moving in his comparison to communities closer to Rome (presumably *nativus* has the sense of "inborn" and *domesticus* indicates that what Cicero describes is particularly characteristic of these peoples). Finally, Cicero employs *Italus* in a rare substantival use, which occurs only here in his corpus and seems to have a poetic resonance (elsewhere in Republican prose only at *Rhet. Her.* 4.43. Sallust, Varro, Livy, and later authors use for the substantive *Italicus*, which is Cicero's only adjectival form; see Sittl 1900: 124).

A final point to consider is the meaning of *huius gentis ac terrae... sensu*. It is best here to take the two genitives as characteristic—"with the sense appropriate to this people and land"—rather than objective, which would make little sense with *gentis*. The Romans attributed to the Latin / Italic *gens* a distinct *sensus* in several areas. Horace, for example, speaks of the sharp Italian sense of humor (*serm.* 1.7.32: *Italum acetum*; Corbeill 1996: 6). In a less complimentary fashion, Cicero's rhetorical works indicate distinctions between Italic and Roman speakers. The interlocutor Brutus calls Italian orators from outside Rome *externi*, to which Cicero replies that "their speech is not characterized by a kind of 'urbanity'" (*Brut.* 170: *non est eorum urbanitate quadam quasi colorata oratio*; cf. 172 *nescio quo sapore vernaculo* describing Granius; see too *de orat.* 3.42–46 on orators affecting a rustic accent to convey antiquity, where he mentions the *Latini* in particular at 3.43). Related to this rusticity is Cicero's mention of the land (*terrae*), which recalls the encomiastic motif in praise of the fertility and abundance of the Italian countryside (*laudes Italiae*), as expressed for example by Cicero's contemporary Varro (*rust.* 1.2.3–7; further, Thomas 1988: 1.179–180 on Verg. *georg.* 2.136–176). From here arises the common Roman equation of the rustic idyll with simple morals and the good life: Cato *agr.* 1.4; *S. Rosc.* 75: *vita... haec rustica quam tu agrestem vocas parsimoniae, diligentiae, iustitiae magistra est* with Landgraf 1914: 158–160; Sen. *ep.* 94.69–70. It is surely significant that these people who are so closely tied to their land occupy the place in which were heard, as will be discussed in the next section, the rumblings that have occasioned the day's senate meeting.

hac una sapientia: The phrase caps a rising tricolon that emphasizes how Roman religious devotion combines the three distinct areas of outward respect (*pietas*), internal sentiment (*religio*), and acquired wisdom (*sapientia*; 18n). *Hac* points forward to the following causal clause, and the unemphatic rhythm (dactyl + cretic; *-ā săpĭentĭā*) further indicates that there is more to follow. Cicero's formulation here resembles a portion of the poem on his consulship where the muse Urania addresses Cicero: "your ancestors, whose piety and faith has distinguished itself and whose wisdom has conquered all, have especially honored the gods and their energetic power" (*div.* 1.21=*carm. frg.* 68–70: *rite etiam vestri, quorum **pietasque** fidesque / praestitit et longe **vicit sapientia cunctos**, / praecipue coluere vigenti numine divos*).

regi gubernarique: The verbs appear to be synonymous when applied to divine guidance (*nat. deor.* 1.52, 1.100, 2.73), with the *abundantia* here underscoring the control that the gods have over creation. As often with paired words in Cicero, one term is literal (*rego*) while the other is metaphorical (*guberno*, literally "to steer a ship"; see 1n).

perspeximus: The emphasis on personal perception, especially through sight, is characteristic of Roman understanding of the divine, and recalls the use earlier of *suspexit* (also used in a frequentative sense).

omnis gentis nationēsquĕ sŭpĕrāvĭmŭs: The climax of the priamel is marked by one of Cicero's favored clausula (resolved cretic + cretic). Although Cicero and other authors do occasionally distinguish between the nouns *gens* and *natio*, with *natio* marking a smaller unit of which *gens* denotes the whole, they are more often synonymous, as here, where the redundancy allows Cicero unambiguously to cover all human beings (*ThLL* VI, 2 1848.55–65, 66–82 [G. Meyer]; *ThLL* VI, 2 1843.56 notes that *gens* is normally favored by Cicero in the proportion 252/160). Note the ambiguity of Cicero's assertion here, meaning both "we have <u>surpassed</u> all nations and tribes <u>in</u> our piety etc." and "we have <u>conquered</u> all nations and tribes <u>because of</u> our piety etc." (cf. *div.* 1.21, quoted in above note on *hac una sapientia*). For the notion that the gods put the Romans at the head of the Mediterranean see *IGR* 4: 1557.12–17=Sherk 1969: no. 34.11–17 (193 BCE): καὶ ὅτι | μὲν διόλου πλεῖστον λόγον ποιούμενοι διατελοῦ|μεν τῆς πρὸς τοὺς θεοὺς εὐσεβείας, μάλιστ' ἄν τις στο|χάζοιτο ἐκ τῆς συναντωμένης ἡμεῖν εὐμενείας | διὰ ταῦτα παρὰ τοῦ δαιμονίου· οὐ μὴν ἀλλὰ καὶ ἐξ ἄλ|λων πλειόνων πεπείσμεθα συμφανῆ πᾶσι γεγονέναι | τὴν ἡμετέραν εἰς τὸ θεῖον προτιμίαν ("Someone would surmise that we continually and entirely place the greatest importance in reverence to the gods from the good will we receive from the divine on this account. For many other reasons as well, we are entirely persuaded that our respect for the gods is apparent to all"; further testimonia on the gods' support of the Roman military in Harris 1979: 118–125).

Perhaps aware of this ambiguity, Vegetius adapts Cicero's remarks for his own purposes, capping his version with an unequivocal acknowledgment of Roman superiority in military training (*mil.* 1.1). Context requires that he omit mention of the Italians and Latins, and he adds the Germani; verbal echoes of Cicero are marked in **bold**: *Nulla enim alia re uidemus populum Romanum orbem subegisse terrarum nisi armorum exercitio, disciplina castrorum usuque militiae. Quid enim aduersus* **Gallorum** *multitudinem paucitas Romana ualuisset? Quid aduersus Germanorum proceritatem breuitas potuisset audere?* **Hispanos** *quidem non tantum* **numero** *sed et uiribus corporum nostris praestitisse manifestum est;* **Afrorum dolis** [cf. Cicero's *calliditate Poenos*] *atque diuitiis semper impares fuimus;* **Graecorum artibus** *prudentiaque nos uinci nemo dubitauit. Sed aduersus omnia profuit tironem sollerter eligere, ius, ut ita dixerim, armorum docere, cotidiano exercitio roborare, quaecumque euenire in acie atque proeliis possunt, omnia in campestri meditatione praenoscere, seuere in desides uindicare.*

20

Cicero returns to the response to treat another three topics: 1. the nature of the prodigy itself; 2. the expiations (*postiliones*) prescribed by the *haruspices*; and, most importantly, 3. what human error could have prompted this divine sign?

20 *ne plura de re minime loquar dubia*: The type of short-range hyperbaton separating *minime* from *dubia* places special emphasis on the adverb and tends to occur "at points of relatively high rhetorical tension" (Powell 2010: 176–177, 179–180 [quotation from 180]; cf. *S. Rosc.* 112 [as emended]: *quod* **maxime** *videtur grave eis qui* **minime** *ipsi leves sunt*). Having established the piety of the Romans and hence having eliminated any potential skepticism on the part of his fellow senators concerning the validity of both the prodigy and his own personal convictions, Cicero can direct their attention to the remainder of the haruspical response.

adhibete animos et mentis vestras, non solum auris, ad haruspicum vocem admovete: *Mens* and *animus* are often paired to describe the faculties of emotion and reason with no discernible distinction in meaning (*ThLL* VIII 714.6–29 [J. B. Hofmann]). For the stress Cicero places throughout the speech on "voice," by which he links the expression of human beings and gods, see Beard 2012a. In particular, the connotations of the voice (*vox*) develop as the speech progresses. Early on (10), the rumblings outside Rome represent "nearly" (*prope*) the voice of Jupiter Optimus Maximus. Here, the voice interpreting that same rumbling derives from the authoritative training of the *haruspices* (*disciplinam*). Finally, at the end of the speech, both the rumblings and the haruspical interpretation conflate to become "the very voice of the immortal gods" that provides warning to the Romans (62: *vox ipsa deorum immortalium*, 63).

IN AGRO LATINIENSI: The word order of the response reflects the language of prodigy reports, by which the location of the event appears first (e.g., Liv. 43.13.3–6: *Anagnia… Menturnis… Reate… Cumis…*, etc., and numerous examples in Obseq.). The precise location of the *ager Latiniensis* is unknown. It is presumably to be identified with the *ager Latinus* which, along with the *ager Fidenas*, is on the east side of the Tiber (Plin. *nat.* 3.53). The most likely inference from Pliny's account is that the *ager Latinus* lies on the left bank of the Tiber, not far from the confluence of the Anio, approximately five miles from Rome. By contrast, Coarelli 2005: 203 without argument locates it on the *mons Albanus* nearly fifteen miles south-east of Rome, near the sanctuary of Jupiter Latiaris. A number of points tell against Coarelli's identification, most significantly the fact that Dio in his listing of prodigies from this year separates out a series that occurred on the Alban Mount from this single earth tremor "in the Latin [territory]" (ἐν τῶι Λατίνωι; 39.20.1–2). Cicero's description of the noise as being heard near Rome (*in agro propinquo et suburbano*) also seems more fitting for the area between the city and Fidenae than the more distant Alban Mount. Finally, it is likely that part of the reason that the *haruspices* were summoned is that the prodigy occurred near what was once Etruria (see Introduction F.2.b). The geology around the *ager Latinus* remains susceptible to earth tremors (Quilici and Quilici Gigli 1978: 152 n. 32).

AVDITVS EST STREPITVS CVM FREMITV: The noun *strepitus*, with its related verbal forms, denotes "a (wild, confused) noise, din of any kind" (LS s.v. I; Schubert 2010 convincingly demonstrates that it cannot refer to harmonic musical sounds [LS s.v. II]). Livy uses similar language to describe a prodigy in a temple (29.14.3: *cum horrendo fragore strepitum*). For the similar *fremitus*, see 9n. Turfa 2012: 31–33 suggests that the combined noise refers to thunder, based on a reference in an extant brontoscopic calendar that apparently dates to archaic Etruria (126: "a loud noise in the heavens over Latium"). The closest parallel I can find for such a meaning is Jupiter's thunder at Plaut. *Amph.* 1062: *strepitus, crepitus, sonitus, tonitrus*. It seems likely, however, that the prodigy here involves some form of seismic activity (parallels in Wülker 1903: 18). Cicero refers to it later in this section with the word *motus* (*hoc tam novo tantoque motus*; cf. 63), and derivations from *movere* commonly describe earth tremors (Luterbacher 1904: 53). Also, it would be odd to describe thunder as occurring "in" the *ager Latiniensis*.

The juxtaposition of the consonant cluster -ST ST- (without sense break) is avoided throughout many genres of classical Latin. It never occurs in Vergil, while Horace, Lucretius, and Catullus use it only once, the latter apparently to convey the sense of dull stupidity (78.5: *Gallus homo est stultus*). Thomas 2011: 70–71 offers a fuller account of the poetic data, where he notes on the sometimes emended Hor. *carm. saec.* 26 that "the awkwardness may be part of the effect" (cf. too Orelli 1886: 1.606). Latin prose exhibits a similar avoidance. In the thirty-four extant books of the historian Livy, relevant instances appear only three times (Thomas 2011: 71). In oratory, Quintilian (*inst.* 9.4.37–38) advises against having a succession of "s" sounds at word break, as in *ars studiorum*, noting that Servius Sulpicius avoided beginning a word with any consonant when the preceding word terminated in "s" (further Lausberg 1998: § 968; cf. Adams 2007: 127–128). In Cicero's fifty-eight extant orations, there are five occurrences of -*st st*-; three occur in *har. resp.* This includes section 20, where Cicero paraphrases the *haruspices*, using an unusual hyperbaton to preserve the consonantal combination—*exauditus in agro propinquo et suburbano e**st** **st**repitus quidam* (2n considers the combination *quam e**st** **st**atim*). The suspicion that the combination was considered cacophonous and awkward is further indicated by the fact that twelve of the forty occurrences throughout Cicero occur as Catullus's did, with a form of the word *stultus*, meaning "stupid." The following table summarizes Ciceronian usage (I include one instance in *Rhet. Her.*). For comparative purposes, note that words beginning with *st*- occur 1,701 times in Cicero, those ending with -*st* (principally *est* and compounds) 2,758 times:

	Speeches	Treatises	Letters
Total occurrences of -*st st*-	14	19	6
Strong break in syntax	9	9	2
No break in syntax	5 (3 in *har. resp.*; *Verr.* 2.3.199; *Phil.* 5.31)	10	4
Percentage occurrences w/no break in syntax	36%	53%	66%

Given the rarity of these consonant combinations and the special context of the prodigy, the most attractive conclusion for its appearance here is that the haruspical text has been designed to imitate the unnatural sound of earth tremors by employing a combination of sounds deemed unnatural in Latin. Note too that the sequence of words causes an unavoidable pause in speaking, a gap between the two occurrences of [st] that mimetically produces an effect of words being separated in a "wordquake": *AVDITVS EST // STREPITVS*. One may compare the interjection frequently used in Roman comedy to impose silence—*st!*—which enacts this type of break to create an analogous pause in external sound, as Jerome notes: "when we want to request silence, we restrict the breath by clamping our teeth in order to force the sound 'st'" (*epist.* 20.5.1: *quando silentium volumus imperare, strictis dentibus spiritum coartamus et cogimus insonandum 'st'*). A second pause between words occurs at the end of the sentence with *cum // fremitu*. A third instance in which "phonological repetition can in fact have a great deal of meaning" may be noted (Katz 2000:

346, in an analysis of the clustering of [st] in Catull. 39): the threefold repetition of *-itu-* (the first time with lengthened [i]). Rhetorical treatises stress that such partial rhymes should be used only sparingly (*Rhet. Her.* 4.22.32; Aquila *rhet.* 42; in detail, Guggenheimer 1972: 13–140). In Cicero, however, when sound effects of this sort do occur they normally underscore an underlying idea (Laurand 1936–1940: 131–135; Gotoff 1979: 230–231).

Just as Marouzeau 1946: 28 hears in the repeated [st] at Verg. *Aen.* 4.443–444 the sharp noises of a wind-wracked forest, so too the repeated syllables here suggest the shaking of the earth, and it requires little imagination to associate the gaps between words with fissures in the ground. This effect agrees with Quintilian's advice to use harsh words in describing forbidding content (*inst.* 8.3.17: *in rebus atrocibus verba etiam ipso auditu aspera magis convenient*). An analogous effect is created at Pacuvius frg. 263 Schierl (*strepitus, fremitus, clamor tonitruum et rudentum sibilus*), where Schierl 2006: 536–537 notes that the repetition of *u* and *s* "bringt das Tosen des Sturms zum Ausdruck" (536) and compares Plaut. *Amph.* 1062 (quoted above) and Enn. *trag.* 4: *unde oritur imber sonitu saevo et spiritu* (Jocelyn 1967: 170–171 is more cautious). Fraenkel 2007 [1922]: 243–244 compares the Plautine passage to Iguvine Table VIB 60, which describes violence to be inflicted on the enemies of Iguvium and contains a striking repetition of [(i)tu] sounds: ***tursitu tremitu hondu holtu ninctu nepitu sonitu savitu preplotatu previlatu*** (cf. Liv. 1.12.10: *sese strepitu sequentium trepidante equo*, of a horse startled by sounds).

One peculiarity, however, must be noted. This marked instance of language mirroring content originates not with Cicero, but with the Latin translation that he has of an Etruscan text. Some evidence survives concerning the care that Romans could take in translating Etruscan writings. Tarquitius Priscus translated the *Ostentaria*, apparently at the end of the republic, and the few extant fragments indicate that he attempted to preserve its original form (Thulin 1905–1909: 3.76–77; Rawson 1985: 28 n. 51). For Cicero's own sensitivity to replicating sound effects of an original while translating, in this case in his own Latin rendering of the Greek of Aratus, see Katz 2009: 79–84. In the case of the haruspical response, although we cannot know what the Etruscan version sounded like, I suggest that the Latin translator has conveyed through sound a philosophical point made in the original: much as the natural world intrudes upon human affairs, so too does it affect human language. Indeed, a prime contender for the Latin translator of this response is the first-century BCE scholar Nigidius Figulus (Piganiol 1951: 85–86; for other candidates such as Tarquitius Priscus and perhaps Aulus Caecina see Rawson 1985: 28–30). Nigidius was a contemporary and colleague of Cicero, who characterizes him in one of his treatises as "a keen and careful explorer of those things that seem hidden by nature" (*Tim.* 1: *acer investigator et diligens earum rerum quae a natura involutae videntur*). He is likely to have been of Etruscan heritage and the fact that he translated an Etruscan brontoscopic calendar into Latin amply attests to his interest in the Etruscan language and divination (*CIL* I² 2640; Turfa 2012: 6). One intriguing example of Nigidius's explorations on grammar survives, in which he posits that divine nature is actively involved in the production of language—our lips protrude when we say "you," for example (*tu* and *vos* in Latin), because the lips are gesturing toward the person to whom we refer (Gell. 10.4). To someone with a mind like that—or to any of the senators sympathetic to this possibility—it would be appropriate to create an earth-shaking sound with the words *AVDITVS EST // STREPITVS CVM // FREMITV.* See too 62n.

   mitto haruspices, mitto illam veterem ab ipsis dis immortalibus, ut hominum fama est, Etruriae traditam disciplinam: For meaning and sense, including the emphatic use of *mitto*, compare the words of Jupiter at the close of Plaut. *Amph.* 1132–1134: *hariolos, haruspices / mitte omnes; quae futura et quae facta eloquar, / multo adeo melius quam illi, quom sum Iuppiter* ("Forget about all the seers and *haruspices*. I will proclaim much better than both what will be and what has been, since I am Jupiter"). The ability for Cicero and the senate to dispense with the *haruspices* derives not, however, from their divine status but from their expertise in being able to interpret independently the meaning of the haruspical response, an expertise that Cicero stresses increasingly as the speech proceeds (cf. 54n; Volk 2021: 310–311).

   Lenaghan 1969: 110 views this claim of divine origin of the Etruscan books as "slightly exaggerated." More likely, Cicero considers divine the supernatural being Tages, who emerged from the earth to teach the *disciplina Etrusca* to mortals (see Introduction E.1). The use of *ipsis* supports this assumption, as the legend depicts "Tages himself" dictating the details of the *disciplina* to the Etruscans or, as Cicero has it elsewhere as well, "to all of Etruria" (*div.* 2.50; Fest. p. 359 M; Ov. *met.* 15.558–559; for the metonymy, see Lebreton 1901: 75–76). While the uncertainty expressed about Tages's true nature at *div.* 2.51 accords with the doctrinal skepticism of the speaker "Marcus" (*estne quisquam ita desipiens qui credat exaratum esse, deum dicam an hominem?*), other sources describe a genealogy that depicts Tages as the son of Genius and grandson of Jupiter (Fest. p. 359 M; Cens. 4.13 [where Lachmann reads *puer...divinus* for *puer...divinitus* of the codices]; Schol. Lucan. B 1.636; Schultz 1916–1924; Pease 1920, 1923: 435–437; De Grummond 2006: 23–27). It is of course essential to Cicero's argument to claim divine origins for the response; at the same time, however, the complete acceptance of Etruscan practice could risk alienating some of his fellow senators. Hence the attribution of the story to unspecified "talk" (*fama*; for another interpretation see Thulin 1906a: 4). Cicero practices this kind of equivocation elsewhere in his oratory to conceal his learning about non-Roman culture, as famously demonstrated by his feigned ignorance of Greek art (*Verr.* 2.4.4–5; Vasaly 1993: 109–110 and 18n above).

   nos nonne haruspices esse possumus?: Cicero favors the particle *nonne* (c. 260 instances as opposed to c. 14 in Plautus) "since most of his texts in some way or other are directed to an audience which he likes to involve" (*OLS* 1: 326). In this case, the uncommon postponement of *nonne* fronts the already emphatic use of the pronoun *nos*, underscoring the assertion at section 19 concerning how Romans excel all other nations in their perception of religious matters. The emphatic contrast also serves to mask a slip in logic, since it is in any case always the senate, and never the *haruspices*, who act as the ultimate "interpreters" in every case involving a prodigy. For a more emphatic statement of this claim see 25: *pro di immortales! qui magis nobiscum loqui possetis, si essetis versareminique nobiscum?*

exauditus in agro propinquo et suburbano e͟s͟t͟ s͟trepitus quidam reconditus et horribilis fremitus armorum: Cicero's use of the discordant juxtaposition of -*st st*- echoes the response. The hyperbaton with *est* that enables the juxtaposition also increases focus on the fronted participle *exauditus* (Adams 1994a: 40–43) and so, along with the preverb *ex*-, word order serves to emphasize the act of hearing (*ThLL* V, 2 1190.38–41 [G. Burckhardt]). *ThLL* XI, 2 405.7–8 (J. Schafer) gives this as the only example of *recondo* to describe sound, but cf. *Brut.* 274: *reconditas exquisitasque sententias* ("unusual and precious thoughts").

Cicero mentions only here that the rumbling resembled, or was accompanied by, the clashing of arms (Dio 39.20.1–2 mentions only a rumbling). Several parallels for the clashing of weapons as a prodigy survive in the compilation of Julius Obsequens: Obseq. 45 (100 BCE, with the same noun: *fremitus armorum ex inferno auditus*), 57 (83 BCE), 65a (48 BCE), and 69 (43 BCE). One may compare the phenomenon of the rustling of sacred weapons (Wülker 1903: 19), where the verb is normally *(pro)movere* (Luterbacher 1904: 53).

quis est ex gigantibus illis: As at *Cato* 5, Cicero depicts the Giants as the paradigm for beings who refuse to abide by the will of the gods (Powell 1988: 109–110, with parallels). Although the Giants belong to the mythical past of his audience of senators, Cicero vividly brings them into contemporary Rome through the present tenses of *est* and *fateatur*, which indicate their potentiality, rather than their unreality (contrast the objections of Wolf 1801: 335–336 to the tense of *est*: "quasi aliquem Gigantem tum superesse aut inter Senatores esse significare velit"). By referring to these mythical figures, Cicero introduces into the speech the third, poetic, element of the tripartite theology that came to be identified with Varro, having already included the civic element of the prodigy process and the natural element of the rumblings in the earth (Cardauns 1976: 18–20 has the relevant fragments; Corbeill 2020). The exemplum of the Giants also suits the context: like the rumblings of the prodigy, they are born of the earth and so suitable judges of any subterranean activity (for evidence that the Romans etymologized *Gigas* as "born from earth," see Maltby 1991: 259). In his prose treatise on the gods, by contrast, Cicero emphatically denies the Giants' existence (*nat. deor.* 2.70: *haec et dicuntur et creduntur stultissime et plena sunt futtilitatis summaeque levitatis*).

quos poetae ferunt: Cicero also refers to poetic versions of myth, in particular from tragedy, at 39 (where see note), 57, 59, and 62. Portents, drama, and

Etruscan intervention will have had a long association with one another in Rome. As early as 364 BCE, according to the well-known account in Livy, a protracted plague prompted the Romans to resort to various means of appeasing the gods, in the course of which were introduced the earliest examples of publicly staged performances at Rome (7.2, with full discussion at Oakley 1997–2005: 37–72; for the continued interconnection of drama and religion, in particular festivals, see Padilla Peralta 2020: esp. 141–150). Livy explicitly tells us that this new form of entertainment was designed as a means of expiation (7.2.3, 7.3.1; Weinreich 1916: 390–392 on drama as expiation) and principally involved entertainment by a group of dancers "summoned from Etruria" (Liv. 7.2.4: *ludiones ex Etruria acciti*). Livius Andronicus, the putative founder of Latin literature, was to develop these early performances into Greek-inspired dramatic performances (Liv. 7.2.8–13). The associations of poetry, prodigy, and Etruria nevertheless continued. A series of prodigies in the year 207 BCE included the birth of a hermaphrodite at Frusino, for which the *haruspices* were summoned; subsequently, the *pontifices* decreed that three groups of nine girls should process through the city singing a hymn that had been composed by Livius Andronicus as "an organic part of the act of worship" (Liv. 27.37.7–10; Fraenkel 1957: 379–380). It is likely that Cicero's consistent appeal to poetic parallels in this speech owes something to these long-standing associations.

praemonstrare et praecinere: In a further move to clarify the role of the *haruspices*, it is now the gods, and not the Etruscan priests or the tremors themselves, who are said to be warning about potential future events (for *monstrare* originating from *monere*, see 26n). The role of the gods will become especially prevalent in the closing sections of the speech (62–63).

POSTILIONES: All codices read *postulationes*, which was corrected by Orelli et al. 1856: 912 (at 31 P¹ reads *postilio*, P²GE *postillo*, H *postulatio*). Like *postulatio*, this noun derives from the verb *postulo*, indicating a divine "demand" for an expiatory ritual (*ThLL* X, 2 229.17–18 [J. C. Korteweg]; cf. Varro *ling*. 5.148, Wissowa 1912: 545–546), an etymology congruent with Cicero's gloss at 21 (*audio quibus dis violatis expiatio debeatur*). Lenaghan 1969: 111 observes that the *haruspices* use the word here to denote the demand for expiation, whereas at 31 Cicero uses the word to refer to the ritual itself. Outside of glossaria and Tironian notes (*Not. Tir.* 100.61, where it is listed among architectural terms[?]), *ThLL* X, 2 229.18–33 (J. Korteweg) records the word only twice outside this speech. Varro *ling*. 5.148 cites his contemporary Procilius (*RE* 2) for an account of the origins of the *Lacus Curtius* in which the *haruspices* include in their response the need for a *postilio* to the Manes. In Arnobius the word occurs in a context containing a clear allusion to this section of *har. resp.* (*nat.* 4.31; for Arnobius's familiarity with this speech see nn. on 8, 9, 21, 23). Champeaux 1995: 66, 80 n. 15, citing Suet. *Aug.* 29.4, suggests that forms of the verb *desidero* had come to designate this notion by Suetonius's day. For another haruspical text that includes suggestions for expiation, compare Cicero's account of the response given in his *De consulatu suo*, where the *haruspices* recommend turning a statue of Jupiter to face east (*div.* 1.20). Although the institution of a festival is particularly common in the case of earthquakes (Mommsen 1887–1888: 2.136 n. 2), it is not recorded what form of expiation, if any, occurred on the occasion marked by *har. resp.*

IŎVĪ, SĀTV̄RNŌ, NĒPTV̄NŌ, TĒLLV̄RĪ, DĪS CÆLĒSTĬBV̄S: In a similar way that the earlier clause had an -*st st*- consonantal sequence avoided by Cicero, this "haruspical" sequence of divinities has an internal rhythm uncharacteristic of the orator, with the second syllable initiating a sequence of thirteen consecutive long syllables (cf. Nisbet 1990: 358–359; I take this list as constituting a single, lengthy colon). The phrase does end, however, with a favored Ciceronian rhythm (molossus + cretic). The prevalence of spondees could have been felt to add dignity (*or.* 216). The epithet *di caelestes* also belongs to elevated style (rather than *di superi*; Dyck 2004a: 133). Similarly, the asyndeton in listing the names of gods represents an archaic feature (Penney 2005: 38–40).

Jupiter ranks first in the list not only as the chief Roman deity but also as possessing the "voice" that warns the senate through the earthquake (10). In a chapter on the manner by which particular gods were chosen as the recipient of expiatory rites following seismic activity, Aulus Gellius notes the uncertainty over whether earth tremors were caused by wind or water or some divine whim (Gell. 2.28.1). This uncertainty may account for the presence in the list of Jupiter (winds), as well as that of Neptune (seas), and their relationship to the earth would account for both Tellus (31) and Saturnus (see Wissowa 1884–1937a: 427–428; less convincing interpretations in Wuilleumier and Tupet 1966: 15 n. 2 [associations with lightning] and Rosenberger 1998: 64 [Latium as *Saturnia tellus*]). It may also be significant that P. Sempronius Sophus's dedication of the temple of Tellus in Rome in 270 BCE occurred in response to an earthquake (Flor. 1.19.2). The final, general, reference to the *di caelestes* is included to ensure that the correct god is not omitted, for which one may compare the common formula of the type *si deo, si deae*. Gellius remarks that this proviso compensates for any uncertainty in the case of earthquakes in particular (2.28.2–3; additional examples and discussion in Appel 1909: 83–84, Guittard 2002).

Alternatively, the *haruspices* may have been following strictly Etruscan guidelines in their choices, as indicated in their practice of extispicy; see Dumézil 1970: 672: "It may be thought that the examination of the liver of a victim, with its precise divine localizations, provided the list of angered gods. Jupiter, Saturnus, and Neptunus are inscribed on the liver of Piacenza—and probably, with names which we cannot understand, Tellus and the Di Caelestes." In fact, van der Meer 1987 does find on the liver equivalents for each of the gods named in the response: Jupiter=*Tin*, Saturn=*Satre*, Neptune=*Nethuns*, and Tellus=*Tlusc* (see his index for a discussion of each god).

21–29

Cicero offers a full account of the claim of the *haruspices* that certain "games have been conducted less carefully and polluted" (*LVDOS MINVS DILIGENTER FACTOS POLLVTOSQVE*). He questions directly Lentulus, *septemvir epulo*, and the *pontifices* to show that all the rites at the games that Lentulus's college had sponsored were performed *summa cum caerimonia* (21). Cicero then turns to his own explanation for this clause of the response: the disruption of the Megalesia by Clodius and his minions in April of this year. The argument includes an account of the origins of these games (26–27).

21 <u>audio</u> **quibus** dis *violatis expiatio debeatur, sed* **hominum** *quae ob delicta* <u>quaero</u>: This example of chiasmus, by which the two main verbs flank the two subordinate constructions that they govern (both indirect questions), is an inverse of the type found at 19, where the subordinate clauses (indirect statements) flank the verbs. Cicero makes much use of chiasmus at the level both of individual words or phrases (40n) and of cola or clauses, as here. While the chiastic ordering of clauses is natural in Latin prose (LHS 2: 2.696–697; Leeman 1963: 22, citing Hermog. *Inv.* 4.3), it is nevertheless clear here how Cicero achieves emphasis by employing variation. The word order allows him to begin with certain information (we have just learned that the gods have been angered) to the as yet unknown (what is the reason for the anger) which, we learn, is the information that Cicero seeks (*quaero*). The *haruspices* have given guidance regarding the divine element (*dis*); it is now incumbent on Cicero and the senate to decide about the human factor (to underscore this point the noun *hominum* is emphatically placed outside its clause).

LVDOS MINVS DILIGENTER FACTOS POLLVTOSQVE: Having argued at length that the clause of the response stating that "sacred and hallowed places have been desecrated" does not apply to his own property, Cicero goes on the offensive against Clodius with the charge that "games have been conducted less carefully and polluted." In his paraphrase of the charge later in this section Cicero adds details not in the response itself that allow him to implicate Clodius all the more easily (*neglegentia* **contemptum** *aut scelere*... *pollutum*).

Arnobius seems to allude to this section of the speech in his treatise against pre-Christian religion at Rome. In this particular passage an anonymous interlocutor responds to Arnobius's critique of the prodigy process at Rome, in particular the belief that the anger of the gods can be expiated (those portions most reminiscent of *har. resp.* are highlighted in bold): "*Quid terrarum fremitus, quid motus, quos esse accepimus factos, quod essent acti per indiligentiam ludi nec ad suam formam condicionemque curati, instauratis his tamen et curiosa observatione repetitis superorum conquievisse terrores et ad hominum curam familiaritatemque revocatos?*" (*nat.* 7.38.2: "'What about the rumbling and tremors of the earth that we have heard occurred because games had been conducted negligently and not administered in accordance with their proper manner and circumstances? [We read in the annals of history] that nonetheless, if these games had been reinstated and repeated with meticulous observance, the frightful behavior of the gods became calm and they were recalled to their friendly concern for human beings'").

Lentule: For Cn. Cornelius Lentulus Marcellinus, consul of 56 and Cicero's long-time ally, see 2n. The reference to his priesthood (*tui sacerdoti*) is the only evidence that Lentulus must have been one of the *septemviri epulones* (Rüpke 2008: 638, no. 1350). This priestly group, originally consisting of three members, was established in 196 BCE as the fourth major college of priests (after the *pontifices, augures*, and *decemviri*). Their chief duty seems to have involved overseeing the rituals taking place at the games, as attested only here, including the feast in honor of Jupiter (Liv. 33.42.1; 21n).

Why does Cicero mention these games? There were two regular occasions for an *epulum Iovis*, at the *Ludi Romani* and *Ludi Plebei* of September 13 and November 13, respectively (Scullard 1981: 186). Cicero refers to the September event, which marked the founding of Jupiter's Capitoline temple and included a *pompa circensis* in imitation of a triumphal parade, such as Cicero describes here (Wissowa 1912: 127, 423, 452–453; full discussion at Bernstein 1998: 51–78; see further next n.). It is likely relevant that these games were in honor of Jupiter Optimus Maximus, who is the first deity for whom a *postilio* is demanded. And yet it makes little sense for Cicero to comment on their success unless he himself had something to do with them. If Clodius had mentioned them in his *contio*, which is the most likely explanation, it would have been due to a rumor that there had been a ritual error in the games that he linked to Cicero's return the previous month. But this is all conjectural. Wiseman 1974: 166 is more sanguine: "Sheer rhetorical trickery enabled [Cicero] to appeal to Marcellinus the consul, whose priesthood involved him only in Jupiter's games..., and his description of the outrageous events [at the Megalesia in April]...owes less to the truth than to his hatred of Clodius, his unparalleled oratorical inventiveness and his audience's imperfect memory of the facts when so much had happened in between."

tensae, curricula, praecentio, ludi, libationes epulaeque ludorum: Dionysius of Halicarnassus's narrative of the opening of the first celebration of the *Ludi Romani* may be compared with the items in Cicero's list (7.72–73, following Fabius Pictor [*FRHist* 1: 15]): 1. young Roman men; 2. charioteers with horses; 3. individual athletes; 4. dancers, accompanied by musicians; 5. dancing satyrs; 6. bands of flute and lyre players; 7. people carrying censers and vessels belonging to the state and the gods; 8. gods on men's shoulders (not on *tensae*). Cicero's order may reflect the actual succession of events at the *ludi*: images or attributes of the gods process on carts, followed by the chariot holding the magistrate in charge; a musical prelude to the games proper, or perhaps to a sacrifice, follows; finally, at the central point in the festival, fifteen days long in Cicero's day, occurred the feast in the presence of the gods. The notes that follow treat each of these points individually; Latham 2016: 19–43 offers a full survey of the features of the late Republican circus procession.

tensae: Sinnius Capito, a late first-century BCE scholar, writes that the *tensa* "is a vehicle on which is carried into the circus the attributes (*exuviae*) of the gods to their couch during the circus games. They were made both of ivory, as in Titinius's play *Barbatus*, and of silver" (Fest. p. 364 M: *tensam ait vocari Sinnius Capito vehiculum, quo exuviae deorum ludicris circensibus in circum ad pulvinar vehuntur. fuit et ex ebore, ut apud Titinium in Barbato, et ex argento*; Hudson 2021: 62–64). With the apparent exception of another passage of Titinius (Non. p. 494), all extant uses of the word *tensa* occur in a sacred context, and a storeroom was designated for these wagons on the Capitoline (*RE* 5: 534–535 [C. Koch]; DS 5: 115–116 [V. Chapot] catalogues visual representations). Sinnius specifies that these *tensae* conveyed not images of the gods, which were carried on stretchers by individuals (D. H. 7.72.13; Macr. *Sat.* 1.23.13), but various attributes of the deities (some scholars think that the *exuviae* are in fact images or statues, for which *ThLL* V, 2 2130.34–61 [H. Kornhardt] offers no parallel: Lenaghan 1969: 112; Weinstock 1971: 284–285; Bernstein 1998: 43–44; for contrasting explanations of these *exuviae* see Versnel 1970: 260–261 and Latham 2016: 56–59).

curricula: The *prima facie* reference here is to the chariot racing that occurred at the festival (Lenaghan 1969: 112, Shackleton Bailey 1991a: 114) and was reserved during this period for the final day (Graillot 1912: 85); for the possibility of a bad omen occurring at the circus see Liv. 39.7.8–9. However, Cicero normally includes chariot-racing as part of the *ludi* and not separately as would be required here (*leg.* 2.22 with Dyck 2004a: 313–314). Moreover, chariot racing sits oddly among the other items in the list closely connected with ritual. A possible alternative is to understand *curricula* as referring to the chariot that carried the aedile at the games, who entered the circus together with the *tensae*. Bernstein 1998: 52–57 provides textual and visual evidence for this chariot; see too the engraving of a now lost sarcophagus in Beard 2009: 283. The distinction preserved in Charisius that the masculine *curriculus* designates the chariot while the neuter form describes the course or act of racing, does not receive support from Latin practice, where either gender is available to describe the chariot (*gramm.* p. 97.22–25 B; *ThLL* IV 1505, 68–71 [K. Wulff]). The plural for singular, however, would be unusual (first at Plin. *nat.* 7.96).

praecentio: As its etymology indicates, this noun refers to a musical performance that takes place before an event (*praecinere* in 20 has a different sense). The games provided multiple opportunities for such preludes: before and during sacrifices (23n); at lectisternia and *epulae* (*Tusc.* 4.4, Sol. 5.19); in the opening procession led by the magistrate in charge (D. H. 7.72.5, 13; Bernstein 1998 54–55 on a late Republican relief). Since the noun appears here in the singular, Cicero probably refers to this latter procession (Wille 1967: 52).

libationes epulaeque ludorum: The Romans regularly offered libations of wine, normally accompanied by incense, before meals dedicated to deities (*RE* 6A: 2.2136–2137 [K. Hanell]). During the *Ludi Romani*, the feast overseen by the *septemviri epulones* occurs on the Ides of September, that is, at the chronologically central point of the festival (Scullard 1982: 183, 186–187; for the only known image of the feast see Crawford 1974: no. 437.2a). The date is significant, in particular as marking the anniversary of the founding of the Republic and the dedication of the temple of Jupiter Optimus Maximus (Versnel 1970: 270–273). At this period, the feast took place in the presence of those images and attributes of the gods that would have been carried in the opening procession of the games (Wissowa 1912: 518).

pontifices: Cicero appositely addresses the *pontifices*, the majority of whom are in attendance and who, he has just noted, are in charge of Rome's regular ceremonial rituals (18: *statas sollemnisque caerimonias*; 11n).

si quid est praetermissum aut commissum: Cicero clarifies the distinction between these verbs two sentences later: *praetermitto* refers to a ritual act being performed improperly, usually by being omitted altogether, *committo* to the performance of an act that is offensive to the gods, either a *scelus* (*div.* 1.55) or a violation of religious custom (*leg.* 2.20–22, in a passage redolent of archaic language). Cicero asserts here that there were no ritual errors in the *ludi* presented in the fall, providing him with a natural segue to the *scelus* that Clodius engineered at the recent celebration of the Megalesia.

illa eadem renovata atque instaurata celebrantur: The neuter plural forms, rather than the expected masculine with *ludi* understood, presumably refer generally to the events that comprise the games; cf. *ThLL* VII, 1 1975.73 (K. Alt); 48n. The neuter continues more naturally with *nihil* and *omnia*. The participles *renovata* and *instaurata* are virtual synonyms (*Verr.* 1.11, *prov. cons.* 19), with the latter being the more technical term, referring to *instauratio*, the ritual repetition of a religious act or event (23n). The verbs *celebrare* and *facere* are those most commonly used for the organization of the games (Bernstein 1998: 76 n. 304).

** *quando*: This reading appears in the *recentiores*, with *quanto* in the major manuscripts. The reading *quando* follows naturally from the previous question—which set of games were violated, <u>when</u> precisely did the violation occur, and what was the cause? The sequence "when and how" is commonly attested in questions in Cicero (e.g., *or.* 117: *quando autem id faciat aut quo modo*; *div.* 2.80: *quando aut a quibus*), whereas something analogous with *quanto et quo?* never occurs.

respondebis et pro te et pro conlegis tuis, etiam pro pontificum conlegio: Lentulus is being addressed, as the following makes clear, even though the previous queries had been addressed to both him and the *pontifices*. For the probability that the verb *respondebis* suggests the haruspical *responsum* under discussion, see nn. on 12 and 17. The likelihood of such a play increases in light of Cicero's assertion at the beginning of section 20 to his fellow senators: "Surely can't we ourselves be *haruspices*?" The sequence *et...et...etiam* groups three items for which the first two have more in common, so that *etiam* has the sense of "as well as" or "and especially" (cf. *p. red. in sen.* 33: *et pro me et mecum etiam post me*; *Att.* 11.5.3=SB 216; Varro *rust.* 1.47; Löfstedt 1911: 136–137).

<u>omnia</u> sollemnia ac iusta ludorum <u>omnibus</u> rebus observatis <u>summa</u> cum caerimonia: Cicero seems to be thinking of three distinct ways in which Lentulus would confirm that the previous year's *ludi* were performed properly: in the performance of all the traditional components (*sollemnia ac iusta*), in the watchfulness for bad omens, and in the due observation of ritual.

22

Cicero credits Lentulus with a leading role in maintaining calm at the recent disruption of the Megalesian games.

22 Quos igitur haruspices "<u>ludos minus diligenter factos pollutosque</u>" esse dicunt: The question of which games are responsible for the prodigy is resumed from 21 (*quos ludos* and *qui...ludi?*) now that the first option—a disruption at the *ludi Romani*—has been firmly rejected. This newest mention triggers a second double ring composition, since the question that introduces this section receives a preliminary answer at 23 (*quos...ludos esse pollutos*) and a final assertion at 27 (*castissimos ludos...pollueres*). The legalistic repetition of key words from the response is typical of religious language (BNP 1: 32–34; cf. 23) as is the joining of near synonyms by the conjunction *-que* (Adams 2016: 77). The insertion of the noun *haruspices* into the hyperbaton *quos... ludos* seems at first odd but has in part been placed there so as not to disrupt the quotation of the response (21: LVDOS MINVS DILIGENTER FACTOS POLLVTOSQVE).

illa mater Idaea: Cybele, or Mater Magna (for this epithet see 24n), was the great mother goddess of Anatolia, where her cult extended back at least to the early first millennium BCE (Roller 1999: 27–115). She was venerated in Greece by the beginning of the sixth century, becoming associated with various gods of the Greek pantheon, with assimilation to Demeter in particular (Roller 1999: 119–234). Of special interest to the Romans was Cybele's connection to Mt. Ida in the Troad, from which derives the epithet *Idaea*, one consistent with her original status as a type of mountain deity (Roller 1999: 2. Her cult on the Cretan Mt. Ida led to occasional confusion and conflation; see Roller 1999: 170–174). The sanctuary at Troy had particular relevance on account of its connections with the legend of Aeneas (Gruen 1990: 18–20; Roller 1999: 206, 270–271).

Besides a brief narrative in Diodorus Siculus (34.33.1–2), our earliest source for the Mater Magna's reception into Rome is *har. resp.* 22–27, an account that can be supplemented by several later references, in particular Liv. 29.10.4–11.8, 29.14.5–14 (27n). At Rome a festival was instituted in her honor, the Megalesia (see note below on *Megalesia illo die*), and she was granted a temple on the southwest corner of the Palatine Hill. This location was perhaps chosen on account of her legendary role as protector of Aeneas since the area contains several other monuments from Rome's earliest history (*LTUR* 3: 206 [P. Pensabene]; for physical remains see 24n). In mythical form she made frequent appearances in Roman literature beginning in the late Republic (e.g., Varro [Rolle 2017: 27–122]; Lucretius [24n]; and Vergil [Wiseman 1984]; E. Simon, "Kybele," in *LIMC* 8: 1.744–766, 8: 2.506–519 catalogues visual representations). Wiseman 1985: 198–206 sketches a religious and social context for worship of Mater Magna in the Republic, concluding with speculations that Catullus 63 represents a hymn commissioned for the Megalesia as a warning to Romans not to engage in excessive devotion to the goddess.

** *Idaea*: *Idaea* is a certain correction of Faernus (in Graevius 1696: 526), easily derived from the nonsensical reading *daea* in P (*dea* is in the rest of the tradition). Although the epithet *Mater Dea* in reference to Cybele does occur once (Hyg. *fab*. 191.1), *Idaea* is far more common, appearing three times elsewhere in Cicero and often in later Latin; cf. 24n.

***te,—te, Cn. Lentule,…spectatorem esse voluit*:** The immediate repetition of the second-person pronoun is common in oratory and drama but avoided for apparently stylistic reasons in other types of poetry (Wills 1996: 82, citing *Mur*. 81; *dom*. 124: *tu, tu*; *Phil*. 2.91, 13.41). When Cicero addressed Lentulus earlier, he used only the cognomen (11n), whereas here and at 22 he uses the formal address normally employed for a man of high status, that of praenomen + cognomen (Adams 1978: 152–154). As Lenaghan 1969: 114 notes, Cicero refers to Lentulus as a *spectator* at the Megalesia, as distinct from how he designated his formal role as *septemvir epulo* at the *ludi Romani*. For an explanation of why Cicero stresses that Lentulus was simply another member of the festival crowd see 22n.

***cuius abavi*:** P. Cornelius Scipio Nasica, who seems to have been Lentulus's great-great-great-grandfather (*atavus*) rather than great-great-grandfather (*abavus*; *RE* 4: 1595–1596 [F. Münzer]). Codices read *abavia* (with [i] seemingly written over an erasure in P). Since the genealogical imprecision is as likely to be Cicero's as the result of scribal error, there is no necessity to emend the text beyond the easy *abavi*. For the story referred to see 27n.

***Megalesia illo die*:** The Megalesia festival in honor of the Mater Magna began annually on April 4, the anniversary of her image's arrival in Rome from Anatolia. The only festival with a Greek name (Μεγαλή being the equivalent of the Latin *Magna*), it was marked by non-Roman elements, the most striking being the Mater Magna's castrated priests, whose ecstatic procession left a vivid impression (see, e.g., Lucr. 2.600–655, Varro apud Aug. *civ*. 7.25–26; Beard 2012b explores the tension between the cult and the Roman state). By Cicero's day the Megalesia continued until April 9 with banquets, circus games, and performances of dance and drama (Wissowa 1912: 574–575; Scullard 1981: 97–100; Bernstein 1998: 186–206, with full bibliography).

The precise date (*illo die*) on which this disruption at the theater occurred has received much discussion (Benner 1987: 113 offers possibilities in addition to those considered here). Stage performances were held only between April 4 and 9, with the 10th devoted to activities in the circus (Graillot 1910: 84–85). Since Cicero delivered his *Pro Caelio* on April 4, in which Clodius's sister Clodia was a major antagonist (it is unlikely that Clodius himself spoke for the prosecution, *pace* Dyck 2013: 7; see *TLRR* no. 275 n. 3), it is reasonable to assume, though not impossible, that Clodius would not have staged a demonstration on a day that involved both such an important legal event for his family and the opening ceremonies of games over which he presided as aedile. Lenaghan 1969: 117 notes that *ad Q. fr.* 2.6=SB 10, containing an account of April 5–7, does not mention this disruption and so he "tentatively" dates it to April 8. Since Cicero himself, however, observes that the event did not require a repetition of any part of the games, it likely attracted little attention at the time until Cicero worked it up for *har. resp.* and so his failure to mention it to his brother is not conclusive (Wiseman 1974: 161 n. 14). Following a suggestion of Benner 1987: 114, Tatum 1999: 211–212 argues that the incident was in fact a riot, perhaps spontaneous, in reaction to the scarce grain supply. Since the senate met on April 5 to grant more funds to Pompey as grain commissioner (*ad Q. fr.* 2.6.1=SB 10), Tatum sees this action as a response to popular unrest and so dates the riot to April 4 or 5. If Clodius's participation in the opening procession was attended by throngs of his adherents, this provides additional support for April 4 (cf. Wiseman 1974: 161). On balance, therefore, April 4 or 5 seems the most likely date for this incident, with April 4 slightly more so. If this dating is accurate, it would support even more the notion that the disruption was not planned by Clodius (see above).

** **haud scio an vivere nobis atque his de rebus iam queri ⟨non⟩ liceret**: Long 1856: 445 first noted that *non* must have dropped out "if Lentulus had not chosen to be a spectator on that day, we should not now be alive" (cf. Mueller 1863: 327). KS 2: 2.522 Anmerk. 4 note that in constructions after *haud scio* and *nescio an* the subordinate clause can omit the negative in post-classical prose, but no secure example occurs before then.

vis enim in*numerabilis* incitata / *ex omnibus vicis* conlecta / *servorum* / *ab hoc aedile religioso* / *repente* ⟨*e*⟩ *fornicibus ostiisque omnibus* / in *scaenam signo dato* inmissa / in*rupit*: This sentence contains syntactic and stylistic oddities. The first is the pronounced separation of the noun *vis* from the partitive genitive that it governs, *servorum*. While *vis* plus the partitive genitive of persons commonly occurs in Cicero—e.g., *S. Rosc.* 9 (*vis adversariorum*), *Verr.* 2.2.160 (*vis hominum*), and esp. *dom.* 96 (*omnium perditorum et coniuratorum incitata vis*)—there is no parallel for such a pronounced separation (cf. Caes. *civ.* 2.6: *magna* **vis *eminus missa* **telorum**, also with intervening participle; cf. Liv. 26.45.1, 30.10.7). Although this is not strictly an instance of hyperbaton according to the criteria established by Powell 2010 since the intervening words and phrases all modify *vis*, the separation is nevertheless marked and the theme that Cicero will emphasize in this account—Clodius's use of slaves (*servorum*)—is further highlighted by not being grammatically associated with the surrounding syntax. A second unusual feature is the series of participles in asyndeton (underlined above). Laughton 1964: 133–134 persuasively argues that *incitata* must be attributive ("a countless excited mob"; see *dom*. 96 above) and that the position of *servorum* acts to separate the two predicative participles (less convincingly, he notes the favored clausula of *-lēctă sērvōrŭm* [cretic + spondee]). Third, we meet again repetition of *in*, as both preverb and preposition, to characterize Clodius's actions (1n). Lastly, military language pervades the sentence (*ex omnibus vicis; signo dato; inmissa; inrupit;* Lenaghan 1969: 116). For the sarcastic use of *religioso*, see 4n.

Cicero on numerous occasions describes Clodius's followers as consisting largely and even, as here, entirely of slaves (see the full catalogue in Favory 1976: 117, Tab. 1; cf. Flambard 1977: 122–125, who presumes that Cicero includes freedmen under this designation). The correspondence with Atticus indicates that his description does not constitute simply rhetorical hyperbole: he describes Clodius in November 57 going from neighborhood to neighborhood (*vicatim*), "openly extending to slaves hope for freedom" and "employing the counsel of slaves" (*Att*. 4.3.2=SB 75: *servis aperte spem libertatis ostendere.... servorum consiliis utitur*); later in the same letter Clodius is said to have levied a contingent of runaway slaves (4.3.4; cf. Plut. *Crass*. 2.7). Kühne 1966 analyzes how Clodius owed much of his success at winning over the slave element to his exploitation of the *collegia*. In the end, whatever one makes of the composition of Clodius's followers on this particular day of the *ludi*, Tatum 1999: 211–212 provides the most judicious assessment of the event: "in view of the expense of the aedilician games and their importance for cutting the *bella figura* for subsequent electoral success, the idea that Clodius intentionally alienated the upper classes and the citizen population of the city must be considered absurd."

The combination of *e fornicibus ostiisque* would seem to be a hendiadys—"from arched doorways"—but Cicero may also imply more. An *ostiarius* ("doorman") is a slave (Schmeling 2011: 94), and so mention of people coming out of *ostia* further suggests that Clodius's men are of that class. Analogously, men coming "out of archways" may contain a double entendre on the meaning of *fornix*, which can mean "brothel" (first securely attested at Hor. *serm*. 1.2.30, where it is associated with "the lowest class of prostitute"; Gowers 2012: 97). Prostitutes in antiquity, both male and female, were often slaves.

tua tum, tua, Cn. Lentule, eadem virtus fuit: Unlike the repetition of the pronoun *te* earlier in this section, the repetition of the second-person pronominal adjective with one word intervening occurs throughout all genres of Latin and is particularly characteristic of hymns (Wills 1996: 83–85). Cicero probably intends such an encomiastic tinge. At the same time, the repeated [*tu*] sounds anticipate both the vocative *Lentule* and his characteristic *virtus*, and recur with reference to Lentulus with unusual frequency as the sentence progresses (*tuo*... *aspectum, impetum tuum*).

in privato quondam tuo proavo: P. Cornelius Scipio Nasica Serapio (*RE* 354) was maternal great-grandfather of Lentulus and the grandson of the Scipio Nasica who received the Mater Magna (27n). Cicero uses Nasica to provide an *exemplum* of a Roman who acted courageously during a public emergency despite not holding elected political office (*privato*; cf. *Catil.* 1.3), much as Cicero emphasizes that Lentulus, although consul, acted at the games of 56 while only a spectator. The brevity of the reference to Nasica attests to its familiarity to Cicero's senatorial audience. In 133 BCE, when Tiberius Gracchus was seeking an unprecedented second consecutive term as tribune of the plebs, the year's consul chose not to intervene. As a result, Nasica encouraged all senators who wished to oppose this move to rise up in protest. During the subsequent conflict Gracchus was killed (Plut. *TG* 19). Cicero will compare Clodius more explicitly to Ti. Gracchus at 41.

te, nomen imperium, vocem aspectum, impetum tuum: This sequence begins with what the other Romans in attendance have chosen to follow—Lentulus as a whole (*te*)—who then breaks down into four of the features that attract them to him. Cicero often lists virtues and merits in asyndetic pairs, and I have punctuated these accordingly (Adams 2021: 480): "authority, power" describe Lentulus's abstract qualities whereas "voice, look" are concrete. Following this description of Lentulus's imposing persona, the other spectators at last follow his "energetic attack" (*impetum tuum*) upon Clodius and his men.

stans: No longer seated as spectators, the senate, *equites*, and all good men (*omnes boni*; see 5n) rise up to join Lentulus against Clodius much as the senate and *publicani* rose up to support Cicero against Clodius at the previous day's senate meeting (2n). The singular form of the participle to modify all three groups, while unobjectionable grammatically, nevertheless helps reflect their unity of purpose.

servorum eludentium: The intransitive sense of *eludere* seems to indicate that the slaves are "making mock" of the Romans in attendance, both literally and figuratively (cf. *Mil.* 32: *[Clodius] speraret posse eludere*). The tense, voice, and meaning contrast with the perfect and passive verbs restricting the spectators (*vinctum, constrictum, impeditum*). Note too the pun on *ludi*; the mass of slaves are "outplaying" others at the games (for the pun *ThLL* V, 2 429.67–79 [F. Krohn]). Benner 1987: 99 makes the interesting suggestion that the slaves are in fact doing something more formal, usurping the theater so as to stage their own mockery of Clodius's political opponents.

senatum populumque Romanum vinctum ipso consessu et constrictum spectaculis atque impeditum turba et angustiis: The phrase *senatus populusque Romanus* (SPQR), while not a formal political designation until the age of Augustus, nevertheless occurs frequently in late Republican texts as shorthand for the essential unity of the Roman state (Mommsen 1887–1888: 3.1257–1259; Moatti 2017: 40–48). As noted above with the participle *stans*, the sense of these two groups as a single entity is reinforced by the singular number of the accompanying participles, which is the regular construction (Mommsen 1887–1888: 3.1257, with n. 2). The participles, organized into a rising tricolon, all have the literal meaning of binding with chains or other methods, as the things binding them progress outward, from the seats they occupy, to the seating area more generally (*OLD* 3, s.v. *spectaculum*; *Sest.* 124), to the crowds blocking their egress. As Cicero makes clear below, a separate section at the *ludi* was set off for the senate (24n, where I also discuss a hypothetical reconstruction of seating at the Megalesia).

23

Cicero describes the various lapses in ritual that can force reperformance of a rite. The relative triviality of these lapses is intended to contrast with the instance under discussion, when Clodius and his gang of slaves invaded the Megalesia.

23 *an*: The particle here introduces a direct question meant to provide a more favorable alternative to another statement or question (*ThLL* II 5.7–8: "*an* pandit sententiam bipartitam cuius altera pars probatur ex opposita priore" [F. Vollmer]). In this instance, the hypothetical lapses and subsequent reparations catalogued and asserted as universally accepted are contrasted with Clodius's disruption of the Megalesia. See further Nisbet 1939: 74 and KS 2: 2.169, who note that this use of *an* is found seldom outside Cicero, from whom they quote several examples. *Dom.* 123 offers a very close parallel both for the use of *an* and for content: *An si postem tenuerit pontifex et verba ad religionem deorum immortalium composita ad perniciem civium transtulerit, valebit in iniuria nomen sanctissimum religionis: si tribunus plebis verbis non minus priscis et aeque sollemnibus bona cuiuspiam consecrarit, non valebit?* In both instances, without this introductory particle, the listener would not know that the entire long sentence was a question until (at the earliest) the main verb several lines later (*dubitabimus* here and *valebit* in *dom.*).

an si ludius…placantur: This passage lists a number of details that might affect a religious event and so require the repetition of an individual ritual or even an entire set of games. Such a repetition, called *instauratio*, is recorded frequently in our sources (*RE* suppl. 14: 197–205 [W. Eisenhut], who offers at 204–205 a full list of instances from Livy). As Cicero notes, proper performance could be marred by a ritual mishap—even something so seemingly trivial as a piper missing a note or a boy dropping the reins of a wagon—or by an event affecting the games from the outside, such as an errant thunderbolt or, as here, slaves invading the theater (for other ritual faults, see *div.* 1.55 [before *ludi*], Liv. 25.16.1–4 [before a sacrifice]). It has been claimed that *instauratio* in the case of festivals applies only to the *ludi Romani* and *Plebeii* (Wissowa 1912: 454; Latte

1960: 250). While it is true that we have evidence for only these games, unless Cicero is guilty of special pleading, it seems that the practice could apply to the Megalesia as well (and to the Apollinares; see Fest. p. 326 M with Taylor 1937: 291–292). Arnobius clearly recalls this passage in his discussion of *instauratio* (*nat.* 4.31; cf. the misplaced frg. at 7.44): *si in caerimoniis vestris rebusque divinis* **postilionibus** *locus est et piaculi dicitur contracta esse commissio, si per imprudentiae lapsum aut in* **verbo** *quispiam aut* **simpuvio deerarit**, *aut si rursus in sollemnibus ludis curriculisque divinis commissum omnes statim in religiones clamatis sacras,* **si ludius constitit aut tibicen repente conticuit** *aut si* **patrimus ille** *qui vocitatur* **puer omiserit** *per ignorantiam* **lorum** *aut* **terram tenere non** *potuit*. See further individual notes below, and North 1976 for a general analysis of the role of conservatism and punctiliousness in Roman religion.

si ludius constitit: The Romans had conflicting etymologies for the term *ludius*, with some authors deriving it from a "playful behavior" exhibited in performance (*lusus*), others from the "Lydian" origins of the Etruscans, who were thought to have played a significant role in the development of Roman public entertainment (20n; etymologies in Maltby 1991: 350). Regardless of the origins of the word, it was primarily applied to dancers who performed with gestures that were normally deemed vulgar by our elite texts (*ThLL* VII, 2 1768.78–80 [H. Beikircher]). Dionysius describes their role in the opening procession of the *ludi* (21n) as well as before the stage performances (D. H. 2.71.3–4). Numerous texts narrate an incident about a "lead dancer" in an opening procession displeasing Jupiter because of inappropriate movements, thereby necessitating an *instauratio* (full sources in Pease 1920, 1923: 191–192 on *div.* 1.55; Corbeill 2010b: 86–92). For possible images of dancers in a procession see Ryberg 1955: 148, with figs. 80b, 82a, and 82c.

aut tibicen repente conticuit: According to Roman sources, music at a ritual event served primarily not to entertain spectators or honor gods, but to shield the officiants from disruptive or inauspicious noises since any break in the music could represent an ill omen (Plin. *nat.* 28.11; Wille 1967: 36–38). Pliny notes an analogous belief that sudden silence at a banquet augured bad luck to all present (provided there is an even number of guests; *nat.* 28.27, with Wolters 1935: 93–95). Ryberg 1955 (e.g., figs. 29, 30, 38a) contains visual depictions of these musicians at ritual activities. Inscriptions document that the flute-players who performed at public rites belonged to a *collegium*, as illustrated by a curious incident from 311 BCE that underscores the essential role of the flute in Roman ritual (Liv. 9.30.5–10). The guild of *tibicines*, denied by the censors their annual banquet in the temple of Jupiter, left in a body to Tibur in protest, whereupon the senate contrived to get them back, panicked at rites being deprived of this crucial element (9.30.6: *eius rei religio tenuit senatum*; cf. Ov. *fast.* 6.667–668). This story provides an *aition* for the *Quinquatrus minusculae*, a raucous festival for the *tibicines* held annually from June 13 to 15 (Scullard 1981: 152–153).

puer ille patrimus et matrimus: The lexicon of Festus records that these adjectives describe a child for whom both parents are living (Paul. Fest. p. 125 M: *matrimes ac patrimes dicuntur, quibus matres et patres adhuc vivunt*; cf. p. 93.24–25 and *pater patrimus* at Fest. p. 298 M). In contrast, a scholiast to Vergil (Serv. Auct. *georg*. 1.31) defines the terms as referring to children whose parents were married through *confarreatio*, a rite required for holders of certain priesthoods, or for their parents (Hersch 2010: 24–27). Since this form of marriage seems rarely to have been practiced in the late Republic it is unlikely, *pace* Lenaghan 1969: 119, that this is the meaning of the terms here. See C. Koch, *RE* 18: 2250–2252, who reviews the numerous occasions when *patrimi et matrimi* were required for successful performance of a ritual.

** *tensam non tenuit* is a conjecture by Ant. Augustinus (in Graevius 1696: 527–528). All codices of Cicero read *terram non tenuit aut* (at P¹E¹, *a* G) *tensam*, while those of Arnobius (23n) have *terram tenere non potuit*. To touch the ground in prayer is firmly attested for the Republican period (Varro *rust*. 1.2.27, Macr. *Sat*. 3.9.12), but there is a marked difference between touching (*tangere*) and holding (*tenere*; cf. Marcell. *med*. 25.13). Furthermore, it is difficult to imagine how this child is expected to "hold" the ground while leading a wagon in procession. The most economical explanation for the oddity is that the incorrect reading *terram* emerged early in the tradition, supplanting the rare word *tensam*, thereby becoming the reading known to Arnobius (Guidetti 2009: 243–246, however, cogently argues for Arnobius also writing *tensam*). An alternative, correct, reading was put in the margin by a scribe (*aut tensam*), which then was incorrectly inserted into the text (Guaglianone 1966; Guidetti 2009: 235–237 convincingly refutes the objections of Le Bonniec 1974).

si tensam non tenuit, si lorum omisit: The best explanation for this juxtaposition is to interpret it as a type of hendiadys. Cicero makes an etymological play in the first half, while specifying in the second the precise type of ritual error involved: "if the boy dis<u>car</u>ded the <u>cart</u> by dropping the reins." For ancients deriving *tensa* from *teneo/tendo*, see in particular Ps. Ascon. *Verr*. p. 255.8–9 Stangl: "[Some say they are called *tensae*] because the reins are <u>stretched</u> in front of them and those leading them enjoy <u>holding</u> the reins in their hands and touching them" (*quod ante ipsas lora* **tenduntur**, *quae gaudent manu* **tenere** *et tangere qui eas deducunt*; cf. Diom. *gramm*. 1: 376.10, Adnot. Lucan. 1.531). Alternatively, Guidetti 2009: 241–243 uses a frieze from the late third century CE depicting a *tensa* in procession to argue that Cicero should be taken literally, and that a single *puer* is expected to process while grasping the wagon and simultaneously retaining a hold on the reins. Aside from the fact that it is difficult to imagine a boy being able to walk steadily in the position illustrated on the relief, Plutarch states that holding the reins in the left hand, as depicted, constitutes a ritual violation (*Cor*. 25.3).

si aedilis verbo aut simpuio aberravit: Plin. *nat*. 28.10–29 provides the most detailed and clear expression of the power of the spoken word in Rome to affect the more-than-human world and the corollary importance of precise wording in reciting prayers; see especially 28.11: *videmusque certis precationibus obsecrasse summos magistratus et, ne quod verborum praetereatur aut praeposterum dicatur, de scripto praeire aliquem rursusque alium custodem dari qui adtendat, alium vero praeponi qui favere linguis iubeat, tibicinem canere, ne quid aliud exaudiatur* ("We see that holders of the highest political offices have prayed using fixed formulas and that someone dictates to them from a written text in order that no word be omitted or spoken at the wrong point, and that further one person is provided as a guard to keep a watch and another to tell people to maintain silence, and that a flute-player perform so that nothing extraneous is heard"). Köves-Zulauf 1972, esp. 19–63, provides an excellent and thorough analysis of this passage as well as the topic more generally.

Paul. Fest. p. 337 M offers the clearest definition of the *simpuium*: "a very small utensil not unlike a *cyathus*, from which wine is poured during sacrifices" (s.v. *simpulum: vas parvulum non dissimile cyatho, quo vinum in sacrificiis libabatur*). Texts trace its origins back to Numa (e.g., Iuv. 6.343), which mention it almost exclusively in the context of ritual action. Zwierlein-Diehl 1980 provides a thorough analysis of its use, with many images.

I have adopted the reading *simpuio*, found in P[1], from Maslowski, who cites the study of Brinkmann 1908 (see Maslowski's apparatus for other readings).

eaque errata expiantur: The elisions mirror the sense of the ritual errors being erased. These phonic tricks continue in the passage cited in the next note.

l<u>u</u>dos ad l<u>u</u>ctum ... pro festis paene funesti: The alliterative play calls attention to how Clodius has transformed what should be festive play into gloomy mourning; as often in Cicero, the soundplay marks a climax, here to the extended protasis of the condition.

quos ille fremitus nuntiet ludos esse pollutos: When referring to the announcement of a prodigy the verb *nuntiare* is either in the passive or the subject is unexpressed (10n; but see 62). Earlier in the speech, Cicero had linked as one unit the prodigy and its interpretation by the *haruspices*. Here, it is the personification of the prodigy itself that offers the response: "The prodigy, in other words, not only announces itself, but it also proffers, as the *haruspices* had done, its own interpretation" (Corbeill 2010a: 152; Plin. *paneg*. 5.3 offers a rough, but weak, parallel). The words of the *haruspices* and the sounds of the earth have become equated.

24

Cicero mentions how the Mater Magna has been making her presence felt on the outskirts of Rome, signaling her unhappiness about the recent disruption at the Megalesian festival.

24 ac si volumus: These three words mark a transition from the human action that disrupted the games to the divine actions that were prompted by it; cf. *inv*. 1.2: *ac si volumus huius rei quae vocatur eloquentia ... considerare principium*.

hanc Matrem Magnam: The deictic *hanc* could simply mean the goddess "here in Rome" as opposed to her manifestations in the eastern Mediterranean but it is not unlikely that Cicero points from the curia in the direction of her temple across the forum upon the Palatine. In either case, he stresses Cybele's proximity in a sentence that details her recent activities in Latium (*hanc* is repeated in the sentence, followed by *haec... haec*).

Mater Magna is the preferred word order for designating the goddess, with the reverse occurring in classical Latinity only at *Cato* 45, perhaps for rhythmic reasons (Ziegler 1969: 850: "*Matris Magnae acceptis* wäre horribel"); when the order *Magna Mater* occasionally occurs in poetry the two words are in hyperbaton (Catull. 35.18: *Magna Caecilio incohata Mater*; Lucr. 2.598, 640; *Prec. Terr.* 15). Neither combination occurs in the thirty-two inscriptions containing the epithet, the preferred form being *Mater Deum Magna Idaea* (seventeen times, often abbreviated as *MDMI*; Ziegler 1969: 848–849, who surveys the varied forms used by Christian writers at 851). The order found here is also reflected in most occurrences of the Greek equivalent Μήτηρ Μεγάλη (Henrichs 1976: 253–254 n. 3).

cuius ludi violati, polluti, paene ad caedem et ad funus civitatis conversi sunt: "The violation and disruption of whose games nearly led to the death and destruction of the state." Cicero's formulation echoes the portion of the response on the games (*LVDOS MINVS DILIGENTER FACTOS POLLVTOSQVE*), thereby implicitly connecting them with Clodius's Megalesia. The replacement of a causal clause such as *quod sunt ludi violati* with a simple noun-participle combination (*ludi violati*) first appears in classical Latin and is not uncommon in Cicero, particularly with the perfect passive participle (KS 2: 1.766–767; Laughton 1964: 7–8). Shackleton Bailey 1991a: 115, less satisfactorily, construes all three participles with *sunt*.

Truncating this part of the response yields the homoioteleuton *lúdi... pólluti*, a variation of which appear at 23 and 25 (*ludos esse pollutos*; cf. 21.11: *POLLVTOSQVE. quos ludos?*).

hanc, inquam, accepimus agros et nemora cum quodam strepitu fremituque peragrare: For *inquam* after a repeated word see 4n. Cicero implies that talk is circulating (*accepimus*; cf. *tradita sunt*) about recent activities of the Mater Magna, wandering through the fields surrounding Rome while making noises that Cicero characterizes with the same words as the *haruspices* had used to describe the prodigy (cf. 20: *STREPITVS CVM FREMITV*). The nouns *strepitus* and *fremitus* would aptly describe the ecstatic music, singing, and dancing of Cybele's attendants, or the roaring of the lions that draw her chariot (Lenaghan 1969: 120; cf. Catull. 63.8–11, 21–26, 82). This is the first step by which Cicero equates Cybele with Tellus, one of the gods to whom the *haruspices* say that reparations are owed and the one to whom the Romans would most likely attribute an earth tremor (20n). Varro, who has numerous references to Cybele across his corpus (Rolle 2017: 25–122), also identifies the Mater Magna with

Tellus and interprets each of her attributes as having significance regarding the care and cultivation of the earth (frg. Aug. *civ.* 7.24=frg. 267 Cardauns; cf. too Serv. Auct. *Aen.* 3.113). If the composition of Varro's work can in fact be dated to the period of 62–55 BCE (Jocelyn 1982a: 164–177), then Cicero could well have relied on this eminent scholar's support for his remarks here (for a dating to 46 BCE, see Horsfall 1972: 120–122, Tarver 1996: 39–48).

Michels 1966 speculates that Cicero's digression on Cybele inspired the composition of Lucr. 2.598–660: "Cicero's speech suddenly made the cult of Magna Mater a topic of popular talk and of learned debate" (679). The verbal and thematic connections she makes are not entirely convincing; for the least tenuous, see 57n. The Lucretian passage occurs in a context in which the poet describes the earth as a nurturing force and Phrygia as the birthplace of agriculture (2.612–613), a link that may further explain why Cicero digresses to such an extent about Cybele, given the speech's allusions elsewhere to the recent establishment of a corn commission with Pompey at the head (nn. at 22 and 31). Also relevant may be Varro's explanation for the goddess's epithet: "she is great because she produces food" (frg. Aug. *civ.* 7.24=frg. 267 Cardauns: *Magnam, quod cibum pariat*).

haec igitur vobis, haec populo Romano et scelerum indicia ostendit et periculorum signa patefecit: Cicero further equates Cybele with both the prodigy and its potential consequences: she has indicated not only that a moral fault has occurred but that repercussions will ensue should reparations not be made. Moreover, she has publicized these warnings both to the senate and to the Roman people at large.

nam quid ego de illis ludis loquar? quos in Palatio nostri maiores ante templum in ipso Matris Magnae conspectu Megalesibus fieri celebrarique voluerunt: The phrase *de illis ludis* resumes discussion of the *ludi* which Clodius's gang of slaves disrupted and at which Lentulus was spectator, in other words the *ludi scaenici*, or dramatic performances. Cicero makes clear with the reference to the Palatine that he does not refer here to the *ludi* more generally, which would include the *ludi circenses*, events in the Circus Maximus that were reserved for the last day of the festival. The staging of plays in the precinct of this temple, which would have occurred from April 4 to 9, is well attested: it was here that Plautus's *Pseudolus* premiered in 191 BCE, and that at least four of Terence's six plays were staged between 166 and 161 (Taylor 1937: 289–291). Goldberg 1998 provides a plausible reconstruction of the conditions of performance in this area, beginning from modern excavations conducted by Pensabene (*LTUR* 3: 206–208 [P. Pensabene], with bibliography). He conjectures that a wooden stage would have been erected on the flat space directly in front of the temple, which lay atop the concrete vaulting that supported the entire precinct, and that the spectators would have sat on the temple steps and in adjoining spaces, with a maximum audience consisting of c. 1,600 (1998: 6–8, 13–14).

The phrase *in ipso Matris Magnae conspectu* contains an important ambiguity. On one level it means "in full view of [the temple of] the Mater Magna," with the genitive of the god's name acting as a colloquial shorthand (cf. English "I'm at Louise's"; for this ellipsis after prepositions see Wölfflin 1885). On another level, a hearer could interpret the phrase as meaning "in full view of the Mater Magna," i.e., that the goddess herself witnessed these events (Jenkyns 2014: 28). Such a scenario would allude to the parade that preceded theatrical performances at the Megalesia and terminated with a *sellisternium*, where an image of the goddess, or only her attributes, sat in as a spectator (Latham 2016: 165–167, with images); for the widespread notion that gods embody their cult statues see Sen. *frg.* 35–36 (Aug. *civ.* 6.10); Gordon 1979: 7–8; *ThesCRA* 2: 463–468 (N. Icard-Gionolio); and esp. Kiernan 2020: 196–221. Through this ambiguity Cicero distances himself from openly asserting before the senatorial audience a belief that the Mater Magna literally resides in her temple while simultaneously allowing this interpretation for those who wish to believe that such embodiment exists (for similar equivocation in this passage, see *accepimus* and *quodam*).

This mention of the temple of Mater Magna contains a conspicuous omission that would have been well known to Cicero's audience, namely that Clodius's house was in close proximity to, and perhaps even overlooked, the temple (Carandini 2017: 1.230 with 2, Tab. 64). It is possible that Cicero does not yet wish to recall the associations between the Claudii and the goddess' reception at Rome in 204 until he can incorporate it into his attack on Clodius (27n).

nam quid ego de illis ludis loquar?: I follow Shackleton Bailey 1987: 275 in putting a question mark after *loquar* rather than *voluerunt*. Aside from the reason that he gives (the games have already been mentioned, so an adjectival relative clause would be out of place) and that then *illis* clearly looks back to the earlier discussion of the games (see previous note), the change also produces a neat tricolon of clauses beginning with connecting relatives in polyptoton (*quos... qui... quibus*; cf. *quo... quo* at lines 28–29).

qui sunt more institutisque maxime casti sollemnes rĕlĭgĭōsī: For the sense of *more institutisque* ("by custom and practice"), see *off.* 1.148: *quae vero more agentur institutisque civilibus, de his nihil est praecipiendum*. The rising tricolon of the three adjectives is solemn, concluding in a resolved double trochee, with the syllable count of the third member equaling the sum of the first two (2 + 3 + 5). Each of these adjectives would fit uneasily in describing the Galli, the eunuch priests of Cybele, who were associated with the Roman cult since its inception (Roller 1999: 274–279). The presence of these priests during the Megalesia would have been conspicuous since they did take an active and visible part in the procession that opened the festival (D. H. 2.19.3–5; Ov. *fast.* 4.181–190; Summers 1996: 342–351). Their self-castration and ecstatic music and dancing were so foreign to Roman sentiments that Cicero is understandably reticent about them in the speech (see 22n). It would seem that Cicero disingenuously employs these stately adjectives to preempt any criticism of the serious nature of the occasion.

quibus ludis primum ante populi consessum senatui locum P. Africanus iterum consul ille maior dedit: In 194 BCE Publius Cornelius Scipio Africanus the Elder (*RE* 336) recommended during his second consulship an innovation in seating arrangements at theatrical performances (for context, see Gruen 1992: 183–222, esp. 202–205). In 65 BCE, nine years before *har. resp.*, Cicero has occasion to mention this same incident in one of his two speeches defending Gaius Cornelius, tribune of the plebs in 67, on a charge of *maiestas*. On that occasion, Cicero records the same information, with the slightly different emphasis that Africanus "allowed" rather than initiated the change, and he adds the detail that he received criticism for it: *P. Africanus ille superior, ⟨ut⟩ dicitur, non solum a sapientissimis hominibus qui tum erant verum etiam a se ipso saepe accusatus est quod, cum consul esset cum Ti. Longo, passus esset tum primum a populari consessu senatoria subsellia separari* (Ascon. *Cornel.* p. 69.14–18 Clark=Cic. *or. frg.* 27 Crawford). In preserving this fragment, Asconius attributes the difference to the fact that Cicero followed in *Pro Cornelio* a version of the events also found in Valerius Antias, whereas in *har. resp.* he adopts a different tradition (the author's name supplied by Asconius is lost in a lacuna). Asconius reasonably explains the discrepancy as an instance of Cicero's "oratorical shrewdness" in using the same historical *exemplum* for two opposing purposes (p. 70.13–15 Clark: *non praeterire autem vos volo esse oratoriae calliditatis ius ut, cum opus est, eisdem rebus ab utraque parte vel a contrariis utantur*). He argues that since the *Pro Cornelio* involved defending a *popularis* tribune it suited Cicero to say at the time that Scipio regretted a decision that probably gave rise to popular resentment, whereas in *har. resp.* the senatorial audience would have appreciated the notion that the great Scipio not only expressed no regrets about separating out the senators but that he was the main instigator (p. 70.25 Clark: *ipsum etiam dedisse dicit*; cf. Liv. 34.54.4–7, who records contemporary rumors that made a similar distinction).

Another discrepancy that Asconius mentions has a more complicated history. He tells us that Antias dates this seating innovation not to the Megalesia but to the *ludi Romani*, and that the aediles had acted on that occasion at the instigation of the censors (p. 69.21–24 Clark). One reason that Antias will have chosen the *ludi Romani* is his belief that the first stage performances at the Megalesia did not occur until 191; see Liv. 36.36.5. Asconius then cites his second source, who preserves a third option, namely that the change occurred at votive games that had been given by Scipio and his colleague Ti. Sempronius Longus. Other ancient authorities are also split on whether the innovation occurred at the *ludi Romani* (Liv. 34.44.5, 34.54.4) or Megalesia (Val. Max. 2.4.3, 4.5.1). The historical record, therefore, shows clear uncertainty over which games first saw this innovation. There is, however, no reason to follow

Asconius here in accusing Cicero of duplicity since this passage from *har. resp.* and the fragment of *Pro Cornelio* can both be construed as referring to the Megalesia; whether this attribution is historically correct or not cannot be determined. As a result, Cicero may be guilty of historical imprecision and of reorienting emphasis, but there is no evidence that he has deliberately falsified history (Damon 1997: 262–263 offers an argument for Cicero's accuracy). For clear accounts of this issue from various perspectives, and for recent bibliography, see Damon 1997 (Livy), Bernstein 1998: 193–195, and *FRHist* 3: 348–349 (T. J. Cornell, on Antias).

It is worth mentioning that the immediate context of *har. resp.* is filled with praise of various members of the Cornelian *gens* for their importance to the state's well-being: Lentulus, the current consul and an *epulo Iovis* (21–22); the Nasica who killed Tib. Gracchus (22); and the Nasica who in 204 welcomed the Magna Mater (22). Here yet another Cornelius, Africanus, recognized the importance of maintaining class distinctions in public, distinctions that the actions of Clodius at the recent games had blurred.

ut eos ludos haec lues impura pollueret?: Cicero once again employs a feminine noun, *lues* ("plague"), as a metaphorical equivalent for Clodius (6n; for *impurus* see 11n). The word occurs only here in Cicero. *ThLL* VII, 2 1797.21–44 (R. Maltby) records this as the first time the word is applied scornfully to a person; all subsequent occurrences appear in poetry until the Christian writers. A clear attraction of using the word here is its resonance with LVDOS...POLLVTOS of the response, which is echoed in this clause with ludos...pollueret. Lenaghan 1969: 123 cites as a parallel for the sentiment *Cael.* 33–35, where App. Claudius Caecus upbraids Clodia for sullying his major achievements—the peace of Pyrrhus and the *Aqua* and *Via Appia*—though in that passage, unlike here, much of the point is that Clodia was acting in ways embarrassing to her own ancestor.

manus adferebantur: The metaphor of "bringing hands" to or upon someone in violence is common (*OLD* s.v. *affero* 9b). The impropriety of the violence is underscored by the fact that it is being perpetrated by slaves on freeborn men (*liber*) and threatened against freeborn women (*matrona*).

ex ultimis terris arcessita: See 27n.

qui uni ludi ne verbo quidem appellantur Latino: For the plural form of *unus* with the meaning "only, alone," see KS 2: 1.657. Other Roman sources attest that the name *Megalesia* derived from the Greek form of Cybele's epithet Μήτηρ Μεγάλη (Varro *ling.* 6.15; *Fast. Praen. Apr.* [*CIL* I^2 p. 235]), and Cicero seems to be correct in his claim that it is the only Roman festival with a non-Latin name (Varro *ling.* 6.12 and Ov. *fast.* 1.329–330 offer both Greek and Latin etymologies for the *Agonalia*; cf. Paul. Fest. p. 10 M). Roller 1999: 283–285 discusses other features of the Roman cult that adopted Greek features, such as the singing of her hymns only in Greek (Serv. *georg.* 2.394). Despite these Hellenic elements, however, there is no evidence that festivals analogous to the Megalesia took place in the Greek East (Roller 1999: 279). Cicero makes a similar claim about the adoption of the cult of Demeter in Rome, saying that her Roman counterpart Ceres always had Greek priests and that the elements of her rites had Greek names (*Balb.* 55).

hos ludos servi fecerunt, servi spectaverunt, tota denique hoc aedile servorum Megalesia fuerunt: The verb *facio* is regularly used to describe the action of the person in charge of organizing the games (e.g., *Verr.* 1.31, 2.5.36; *Sest.* 117; 26 below) and so adds special point to the claim of the *haruspices* that "games have been conducted less carefully" (*LVDOS MINVS DILIGENTER FACTOS*). Cicero's subsequent (and confusing) narrative of how these slaves intruded on the Megalesia does not at all clarify the hyperbolic claims in this tricolon of how Clodius's aedileship facilitated the holding of the games by the slaves, their attendance as spectators after taking control of the original audience, and ultimately their presence as the only persons in attendance. As noted above (22), it is difficult to imagine that such an uprising, were it to have happened as described, escaped mention in other sources, in particular Cicero's correspondence from this period (cf. Wiseman 1974: 160–161). Nevertheless, this uncertainty must be balanced against the fact that Cicero is speaking in the presence of Lentulus, who is credited with quelling the disturbance, and other senators who would have been in attendance, which indicates that some truth content must lie behind this vague narrative.

For the predicate genitive *servorum* used in a similar context, see 25: *alter [consessus] servorum totus esset*.

25–26

Cicero turns at last to describe the nature of the disruption at the Megalesia. The incursion of slaves does not simply foreshadow a danger to the state; it is the danger itself.

25 pro di immortales! qui…: Variants of this interjection—for instance, preceded by *o* rather than *pro*, or simply appearing as the bare vocative *di immortales*—occur as early as Plautus (twenty-six times) and frequently in Cicero (including fifteen times in his correspondence). Here Cicero adds emphasis by following the interjection with a direct address to the gods. Although this trope in turning from exclamation to address is formulaic in Plautus (e.g., *Amph.* 455: *di immortales, obsecro vostram fidem*), it is first attested in Cicero only in the speeches after exile, where he uses it several times (*p. red. in sen.* 9: *di immortales, quantum mihi beneficium dedisse videmini…quanto maius dedissetis*; *dom.* 104: *o di immortales!—vos enim haec audire cupio—P. Clodius vestra sacra curat*, etc.; *Cael.* 59; *Sest.* 93: *o di immortales! quemnam ostenditis exitum nobis?* etc.). The remaining example in the Ciceronian corpus occurs at *Phil.* 4.9: *o di immortales! avertite et detestamini, quaeso, hoc omen!* (cf. Ps. Cic. *exil.* 9: *vos, vos optestor, di immortales, qui meae* *menti lumina praetulistis*). As these examples demonstrate, the interjection is often followed by a question. See also 42n.

magis nobiscum loqui possetis si essetis versareminīquĕ nōbīscūm: The collocation of the roughly synonymous verbs *essetis versareminique* is not a redundancy, since *essetis* alone could be taken to mean that Cicero is doubting the existence of the gods (which of course is precluded by the context); as a result, the more active *versaremini* is added. Translate: "Could you speak with us more [clearly] if you were present here among us?" *Versor* has *deus* as its subject also at 62: *nolite enim id putare accidere posse... ut deus aliqui delapsus de caelo coetus hominum adeat,* **versetur** *in terris, cum hominibus conloquatur*, where a divine epiphany is again rejected, but the existence of the gods is not denied (see 62n); cf. too the similar *div*. 1.79: *quid igitur expectamus? an dum in foro nobiscum di immortales, dum in viis* **versentur***, dum domi?*

Although both instances of the prepositional phrase *nobiscum* are necessary in their respective contexts, their emphatic sense is reinforced by repetition, chiastic order, and position of the second phrase at sentence end (with favored clausula of cretic + spondee). The repeated use in each case with a "middle" deponent stresses reciprocity—the gods speak with us (not *to* us) and interact with us; Adams 2016: 46 notes a similar nuance of *loquor* in Plautus. It is worth noting that Cicero addresses all the gods, and not only the Mater Magna, in a typical gesture not to risk omitting any relevant deity (20n).

significastis ac plane dicitis: As in the previous note, the two verbs do not constitute a hendiadys. The gods have "signaled" through the "sign" of the earth tremors with the result that (*ac*, "and therefore"; 11n), through the irruption of the slaves into the Megalesia, they now "plainly speak" to human beings about the meaning of the response, as indicated by the fact that the indirect statement that depends upon these verbs contains part of that response (*ludos esse pollutos*). For *signum* used to indicate a prodigy, see *div*. 1.77 with Pease 1920: 226; for *significo* in the sense indicated, see 26 (*significatum*), 32; *div*. 1.2; Tib. 2.1.25–26: *viden ut.../ significet placidos nuntia fibra deos*; Ov. *met*. 15.576: *quid sibi significent, trepidantia consulit exta*.

inquinatum deformatum, perversum conturbatum: As noted at 22 (*te, nomen imperium, vocem aspectum, impetum tuum*), the quadripartite asyndeton is divided into two pairs containing approximate synonyms, the first being more concrete, the second abstract ("stained and misshapen, perverted and completely disturbed"; cf. *Phil*. 11.2: *inuisitatum inauditum, ferum barbarum*. Marouzeau 1946: 247–249, in a key discussion of Cicero's use of synonyms, does not recognize this tendency).

omne servitium: "The entire slave population"; for abstracts used to indicate a concrete group of several individuals, see KS 2: 1.81–82, who compare *Verr*. 2.5.9: *coeptum esse in Sicilia moveri aliquot locis servitium suspicor*. Cicero uses the plural *servitia* in the same sense (*Flacc*. 97).

permissu magistratus liberatum: "Set free by a magistrate's authority." Cicero uses *liberatum* with deliberate ambiguity: is he simply "letting the slaves loose" on the unsuspecting spectators or, more ominously, literally granting them freedom? The manner of expression suggests a formal act: the ablative *permissu* with names of various magistracies in the genitive is common, and its presence in inscriptions indicates that it is likely a technical phrase (*ThLL* X, 1 1550.19–41 [N. Delhey]). Furthermore, Cicero's mention of Clodius's position as a magistrate has clear ironic overtones: even though he is an elected public official, he is "freeing" slaves; compare his sarcastic reference to Clodius as a *sacerdos* (9, 26). Outside his rhetorical invective Cicero mentions Clodius's promises of freedom to slaves in his capacity as a private citizen (*Att.* 4.3.2=SB 75; 22n); as aedile, on the other hand, he would also have had access to slaves owned by the state (Becker 2017: 221–222 and n. 399; Nippel 1988: 19–20), although Cicero would presumably have mentioned if *servi publici* were part of Clodius's group, in particular since it is unlikely that public slaves could be used to coerce citizens (Nippel 1988: 183–184 n. 9; 1984: 22) or that they could be manumitted at the whim of a single magistrate (judging from municipal legislation; see Gonzalez and Crawford 1986: 171, 192–193, 222). As is often the case with Cicero, the ambiguity of expression allows the listeners to use their imaginations.

omne servitium, permissu magistratus liberatum, in alteram caveam [scaenam codd.] inmissum, alteri praepositum, ut alter consessus potestati servorum obiceretur, alter servorum totus esset: The opening portion is constructed as a tricolon diminuens (11 + 9 + 7), with the participles at clause end in epistrophe (*permissu magistratus liberatum, in alteram caveam inmissum, alteri praepositum*). The three decreasing phrases describe increasing degrees of the pollution involved: apparent manumission by a magistrate, invasion of one section of the audience, and control over the other. The sequence *alteram ... alteri/alter ... alter* allows the most alarming element of Clodius's alleged actions—that slaves took over an entire section of the theater—to be in emphatic position at the end of the sequence.

This passage presents as vexing an interpretive challenge as any in *har. resp.* The main crux involves how to construe *scaenam*, the unanimous reading of the codices. How can there be two *scaenae* at a single theatrical performance? When not conceding despair (Long 1856: 447: "I do not understand"; Wuilleumier and Tupet 1966: 50 n. 1: "Mention imprécise"; Courtney 1960: 99: "I have not been able to get any clear picture of what is happening"), scholars have offered several interpretations, none completely satisfactory. The commonest explanation is that Cicero is being imprecise in his use of *scaena* (properly, "stage"), or that the word refers not to the stage but to the space occupied by the audience (a meaning otherwise unattested). A second option allows *scaena* its normal meaning, with Cicero referring to two different performances on the same day, played out on two separate stages. Hanson 1959: 14 n. 29 and 24–25 presents this option, tentatively proposing that one stage stood in front of Cybele's temple, with a hypothetical second erected somewhere on the cliff face that went down to the Circus (followed by Wiseman 1974: 168–169). However, the fact that Cicero situates the games explicitly *in ipso Matris Magnae conspectu* makes a second, more distant venue less probable (24; cf. Arnob. *nat.* 7.33: *[Mater Magna] conspexerit*; Aug. *civ.* 2.4: *matre spectante atque audiente*); see too the reasonable objections of Goldberg 1998: 8–9. A third option, "recommended by its simplicity" by Lenaghan 1969: 125, is that Cicero indeed refers to two separate performances, but in the same space before the temple and on different days. Goldberg 1998: 8–9 opts for this explanation as "easier to square with Republican practice" and points to *leg.* 1.47 for *scaena* meaning "performance" (cf. English "the stage"). This proposal has attractions, but the natural way of construing the passage rests uncomfortably with this interpretation: the sequence *alteram...alteri / alter...alter* implies simultaneous action, not two events separated by a day or more, and the phrase *in alteram scaenam inmissum* seems to describe intrusion into a real physical space ("sent onto the stage"), as in the closely parallel uses of the same verb at 22, 25, and 26 (cf. 47).

A fourth and final option, also proposed by Lenaghan 1969: 125, points toward a solution: the two *scaenae* refer to two different seating areas in one theater, at one performance. Such a scenario certainly jibes well with Cicero's description, but encounters the objection with which we began, namely, that *scaena* is nowhere clearly attested as referring to the seating area of the audience, an area normally referred to as the *cavea*. I propose therefore to emend the reading of the codices to *caveam*. A number of points in the immediate context supports this reading. First, Cicero has just referred to the measure from 194 BCE by which Africanus created special seating at the Megalesia, partitioned into two parts to separate the senate from the people, and he imagined that this innovation gave Clodius special opportunity to commit sacrilege at his own version of the festival (24: *quibus ludis primum ante populi consessum senatui locum P. Africanus iterum consul ille maior dedit, ut eos ludos haec lues impura pollueret*). The reading *cavea* continues this characterization, and it gives the historical digression on Scipio more relevance. Second, within the sentence itself, the two contrasting nouns modified by forms of *alter* would then refer by synecdoche to the same feature, as one would expect, with *consessus* referring to the seated people occupying each *cavea* (cf. Serv. *Aen.* 5.340: *cavea consessus est populi*; for the collocation *consessus caveae*, see Lucr. 4.78, Verg. *Aen.* 8.636, Tac. *ann.* 13.54.3). Third and most persuasively, section 26, which describes this disruption in similar language, strongly supports *cavea* as the original reading: *servos de cavea exire iubebant; tu in alteram servos immisisti, ex altera liberos eiecisti*. Fourth, corroborating evidence in Cicero for the *cavea* having two parts occurs at *Cato* 48: *qui in prima cavea spectat...qui in ultima*, where Powell 1988: 200 offers the gloss *in prima parte caveae*; for other passages in which the plural of *cavea* refers to portions of the seating area in a single theater, see *ThLL* III 629.39–41 (H. Hoppe), citing Stat. *silv.* 1.6.28 (Vollmer 1898: 307: "einzelne Sitzreihe"), Claud. 20.404, Drac. *laud. dei* 3.198.

Finally, the alteration of *caveam* to *scaenam* can be reasonably explained paleographically. The spelling *cavia* occurs frequently in codices of other texts (*ThLL* III 628.29–33 [H. Hoppe]), leaving open the possibility of confusion between *caviam* and *scenam*, with -*vi*- being misconstrued as -*n*- at some stage; either the resultant *canam*, or indeed the original *caveam*, would then be easily emended by a scribe to *sc[a]enam* as a result of the earlier description of this same event (22: *in scaenam... inmissa*). Furthermore, indisputable evidence for confusion between the two words lies a few sentences later (*scaenam caveam⟨ve⟩*; see note); regardless of what one reads there, the codices show clearly not only that *scaena* and *cavea* could be confused, but that such a confusion occurred elsewhere during the transmission of the text. Emend *scaenam* to *caveam*.

examen apium: A swarm of bees can be an omen of future wealth or power, as Cicero himself attests for Dionysius of Syracuse (*div.* 1.73, with Robert-Tornow 1893: 35–39 and comparative evidence at Pease 1920–1923: 220). Far more often, however, and particularly in Roman culture, a swarm's sudden appearance presages danger both as a private omen and on public prodigy lists (Robert-Tornow 1893: 43–60). Significantly, this type of prodigy seems to have been of particular concern to the *haruspices*, who always consider swarming of bees a "forbidding portent" (Plin. *nat.* 11.55: *dirum... ostentum*; full references in Wülker 1903: 16, with Thulin 1905–1909: 3.98–101 on the involvement of the *haruspices*). Indeed, Dio included swarms of bees gathered in Rome's shrine to Asclepius as among the portents preceding the proscriptions of 43 that resulted in the death of Cicero (47.2.3). It is presumably just an odd coincidence that the priestesses of Mater Magna were called "Honeybees" (*Melissae*; Lact. *inst.* 1.22.20) and the wine jug at the rites for the Bona Dea a "honeypot" (*mellarium*; Macrob. *Sat.* 1.12.25).

**scaenam caveam⟨ve⟩: This is a conjecture of Mommsen (in Orelli *et al.* 1856: 914). P¹ reads *caenam caveam*; examination of a digital copy of P indicates that P² added dots beneath each letter of *caveam* and an 's' before *caenam*. The remaining codices read *sc(a)enam*. Klotz 1915: 136 conjectured simply *caveam*, presumably understanding *scaenam* as a gloss that had been inserted into the text. I have chosen to read *scaenam caveam⟨ve⟩* with Mommsen, with the -*ve* having dropped out by haplography before <u>ve</u>nisset. My emendation of *scaenam* to *caveam* in the previous sentence can be used in support of this reading, since Cicero will then have already mentioned Clodius disrupting events both on the *scaena* (=initial disruption; 22) and *cavea* (=second instance). Combining both areas here in the hypothetical case of a bee swarm would then recall both of Clodius's acts. But the decision is difficult.

putaremus; videmus universi repente: Each of these four words serves to emphasize the immediacy and enormity of Clodius's offense. The contrafactual verb form *putaremus* for the hypothetical prodigy of the swarm of bees sits juxtaposed with the indicative *videmus*, in the emphatic present tense to mark the real prodigy of the "swarm" of slaves. The adjective *universi* is not otiose but emphatic (Gesner 1753: 275, *contra* Markland and Wolf), either imagining as earlier that all the senators present had also attended the Megalesia (e.g., *nobis* at 22) or, if not, that Cicero's description allows them to "see" it in their mind's eye. Finally, the adverb *repente* receives focus, as it often does (see Merguet 1877–1884: 4.284–285), by its distance from the verb it modifies (*inmissa*). The sentence then concludes with another emphatic use of the present tense (*non commovemur*), to underscore that the effects of this recent festival are still being felt.

examina tanta servorum: ThLL V, 2 1162.78–1163.35 (F.-L. Junod) notes that the noun *examen* applies strictly to bees. Given that swarming normally constitutes a bad omen in the Roman world (note above on *examen apium*), the rare metaphorical application of the word to groups of human beings often has negative or hostile associations (of slaves also at Plaut. *Truc.* 534 [by conjecture], Hor. *epod.* 2.65; of refugees and suppliants at Stat. *Theb.* 3.196, 11.39, 12.472; of the dead at Stat. *Theb.* 1.95, 11.82, *silv.* 5.3.284; of soldiers at Hor. *carm.* 1.35.31, Sil. 4.159).

atque in apium fortasse examine nos ex Etruscorum scriptis haruspices ut a servitio caveremus monerent: For this sense of *atque* ("and as a matter of fact") see 8n. The adverb *fortasse* qualifies the prepositional phrase rather than the finite verb: "in the *hypothetical case of* a swarm of bees" (Shackleton Bailey 1991a: 116: "if there *had* been a swarm of bees, it may be that..." [emphases original]; for the construction see, e.g., *Mil.* 69: *fortasse in motu aliquo* and further examples in ThLL VI, 1 1142.31–62 [O. Hey]). Thulin 1905–1909: 3.100 offers support for Cicero's claim that Etruscan haruspicy saw in bee prodigies a potential loss of freedom, apparently by analogy with the fact that a swarm cannot survive without its sole leader (Plin. *nat.* 11.56).

26 quod igitur ex aliquo diiuncto diversoque monstro significatum caveremus, id cum ipsum sibi monstrum est et cum in eo ipso periculum est ex quo periculum portenditur: "When that very thing which we would have watched out for when signified by some unconnected and separate warning is in fact [note indicative *est*] a warning of itself and when danger resides in the very thing from which danger is predicted." The word *monstrum* denotes a prodigy and seems synonymous with other Latin designations, despite Varro's attempt to make distinctions based on etymology: ostentum *quod aliquid hominibus ostendit;* portentum *quod aliquid futurum portendit;* prodigium *quod porro dirigit;* miraculum *quod mirum est;* monstrum *quod monet* (frg. Serv. Auct. *Aen.* 3.366; 10n). Nevertheless, since the etymological sense of "warning" (*moneo*) does seem particularly suitable here I have used that word in my translation. The participle *significatum* resumes the use of the finite form of the verb from earlier in this section (where see note), here to describe the warning giving a warning about itself. The collocation of the two participles *diiunctus* and *diversus* also occurs at *Manil.* 9, to describe the distant and opposing regions from which the Romans could expect war; the point here is that, since the senate would normally devote its attention to a potentially hostile sign whose interpretation was so foreign as to be up for debate, they should be particularly cautious about one that signifies itself as a portent of its own danger.

Cicero is here elaborating on his sophistic attempt to equate the "swarms" of slaves with a non-existent portent of swarming bees by expressing in alarming language and tortuous syntax an alleged paradox: there is no need to search for the meaning of mysterious portents since this attack of slaves on the theater is a prodigy that "predicts" its own existence. Gildenhard 2007: 151 expresses well Cicero's aim: "[Cicero] interprets the recent upheaval at the Games as an unmistakable sign that the system of 'advance warning' is, in crucial respects, currently out of order. In his view, the vital gap in time between 'alarm' and 'disaster', which afforded the Roman community a decisive window of opportunity to re-establish proper relations with the divine, has disappeared. Clodius is both portent and portended evil, a divine warning of impending danger and the danger itself."

pater tuus: Clodius's father, Appius Claudius Pulcher (*RE* 296) held the aedileship in or before 91 BCE, having been unsuccessful in his first attempt at election (*MRR* 2: 21; *Planc.* 51); nothing else is known about his presentation of the Megalesia in that year. Following the praetorship in 89, the censors removed him from the senatorial rolls in 86 for disregarding the summons of a tribune. During the reign of Sulla his stature was restored, and his election to the consulship of 79 followed (2n). He died in 76 during his proconsulship in Macedonia and Thrace; the testimony of Varro *rust.* 3.16.2 that he left his family in poverty has been doubted. Tatum 1999: 32–36 provides an up-to-date assessment of Appius and other members of Clodius's immediate family, concluding that "the Claudian poverty...is—and was intended to be recognized as—a humorous fiction" (36; details in Tatum 1992).

patruus: Gaius Claudius Pulcher (*RE* 302), elder brother of Appius, was curule aedile in 99 and renowned for the splendor of his games, decorating the stage with *trompe l'oeil* paintings and introducing elephants into the arena (e.g., *Verr.* 2.4.6: *aedilitatem magnificentissimam*, and 133; Plin. *nat.* 8.19, 35.23; Lazzeretti 2006: 100–101). He reached the consulship in 92 and appears to have died soon thereafter.

is mihi etiam generis sui mentionem facit: Cicero's comparison of past Claudii to Clodius's own recent activity prompts him to recall a recent boast that Clodius had made about his family roots. The trope that an opponent has failed to live up to the standards of an ancient and hallowed family is a familiar one (Corbeill 1996: 79–83) and Clodius's reference to his own venerable ancestors presumably originated in the context of demeaning Cicero's less distinguished lineage (17n). The pronoun *mihi* appears to be an ethical dative, signaling Cicero's presence as a silent observer of Clodius's boast (Roby 1892: 2.§§1150–1151). For the possibility that Clodius made this allusion in his recent *contio* see Corbeill 2018: 184–185.

Athenionis aut Spartaci exemplo: The Romans had a fear of slaves felt even in proverbial expressions (Fest. p. 261 M: *quot servi, tot hostes*; Otto 1890: 319–320). Cicero continues to exploit that anxiety by equating Clodius's actions at the Megalesia with two recent slave revolts with which his senatorial audience would have been fully familiar. In 104–103 BCE Athenion (*RE* 6), a Cilician slave transplanted to Sicily, assisted Salvius Tryphon in a rebellion against Rome, becoming sole leader upon Tryphon's death in 102. He was killed the following year, or perhaps in 100, in hand-to-hand combat with the consul M.' Aquillius (Diod. 36.7.1–2, 36.8–10.1). Cicero uses Athenion's name as a sobriquet for a henchman of Clodius, probably Sex. Cloelius (*Att.* 2.12.2=SB 30; see Shackleton Bailey 1965–1970: 1.376).

Spartacus was a Thracian slave, sold to perform as a gladiator in Campania (the following relies on F. Münzer, *RE* 3A: 1528–1536). He led a major slave uprising on the Italian peninsula between 73 and 71 that is recorded in many ancient sources. Following several victories over Roman troops, these sources estimate his troops to have numbered at their peak between 60,000 and 120,000 men. Marcus Licinius Crassus, at the head of eight Roman legions, ultimately quelled the rebellion after battles that had extended over several months (*MRR* 2: 123). Spartacus died fighting. Lenaghan 1969: 128 makes the intriguing suggestion that the *ludi* of Spartacus to which Cicero alludes are "the funeral games which [Spartacus] gave in honor of Crixos, at which games he made Roman captives fight in gladiatorial contests" (Flor. 2.8.9, Oros. *hist.* 5.24.1; cf. App. *BC* 1.117).

illi ... servos de cavea exire iubebant: tu in alteram servos inmisisti, ex altera liberos eiecisti: The exclusion of slaves from public festivals, as inferred here, is attested for the Secular Games by Zosimus 2.5.1. See Scheid 2015: 80, who also assesses the evidence for the Megalesia (81–85) and concludes that the exclusion of slaves continued until the time that Cicero delivered this speech. Paul. Fest. p. 82 M preserves a general formula that excludes, among other groups, foreigners (*hostis*) and captives from certain unspecified sacred rites, an exclusion that doubtless included slaves (*lictor in quibusdam sacris clamitabat: hostis, vinctus, mulier, virgo exesto*, "The lictor used to proclaim at certain sacred events 'May foreigners, captives, women, and virgins remain outside'"). Richlin 2014 provides a powerful case for slaves attending stage performances of Plautus, although not necessarily at *ludi*. For the two parts of the *cavea*, see 25n.

antea voce praeconis: The adverb *antea*, clearly contrasting with *tuis ludis*, must point to Clodius's actions as marking an exception and not mean that the separation of free and slave populations is no longer in force when Cicero is speaking (*pace* Krauter 2004: 121, whom Scheid 2015: 84–85 sensibly counters). Cicero introduces the *praeco* here to contrast the ability of earlier Claudii to manage a crowd of slaves through voice alone rather than using slaves to resort to the physical violence (*manu*) wielded by Clodius. On the wide range of duties of the *praecones* who accompanied the various Roman magistrates, see Mommsen 1887–1888: 1.363–366; Bond 2016: 21–58. *RE* 22: 1196 (K. Schneider) lists evidence for their duties at the *ludi* in particular, of which Plautus's *Poenulus* offers an intriguing parallel. The speaker of the prologue commands the *praeco* to grab the attention of those attending the play (11: *exsurge, praeco, fac populo audientiam*; cf. *Asin.* 4). The speaker then reminds the various audience members of the etiquette appropriate to their station—male prostitutes, for example, may not sit in front of the stage and wetnurses should not take their nurslings to the play. Included among these commands is the injunction that "slaves should not prevent the freeborn from having a place" (23: *servi ne opsideant, liberis ut sit locus*). It is unclear whether this passage indicates that the presence of slaves at dramatic performances presented a problem, perhaps because of limited seating, or whether the humor arises from the absurdity of the situation that Plautus imagines.

ne hoc quidem tibi in mentem veniebat, Sibyllino sacerdoti, haec sacra maiores nostros ex vestris libris expetisse?: One might expect *Sibyllino sacerdoti* to appear in the vocative rather than in agreement with the dative *tibi* (as at, e.g., *Q. Rosc.* 45: *tibi vero, Piso, diu deliberandum . . . est*; *div. in Caec.* 20: *si tibi, Q. Caecili*). The dative is unlikely to involve attraction, for which LHS 2: 179 *Zusatz* a) gives only one example (Pap. Tjäder 8 II 1 from 564 CE). By placing the phrase in the dative, however, its appositional quality is emphasized: "Did it not even occur to you, as a priest of the Sibyl, that . . . ?" *Har. resp.* provides the only evidence that Clodius was a member of the *quindecimviri sacris faciundis* in 56 (*MRR* 3: 58, to which add 27, *sacerdotium ipsum*; Rüpke 2008: 625 no. 1265 n. 4 notes that *dom.* 105—*quem umquam audisti maiorum tuorum, qui et sacra privata coluerunt et* publicis sacerdotiis praefuerunt, *cum sacrificium Bonae Deae fieret interfuisse*—"is more pointed if Clodius himself was a priest"; Tatum 1999: 200–201 discusses a consultation of the Sibylline Books in January in which he assumes that Clodius participated). For this priesthood and the Sibylline books, see Parke 1988: 136–151, 190–215.

conquiris: Markland 1745: 347 rightly notes that this verb cannot refer to the simple consultation of written records, for which one normally uses *adire* or *inspicere*, but to some system of "gathering together," a system that he finds irrelevant for the *quindecimviri*. Gesner 1753: 275–276 counters, however, by arguing that the consultation proper is denoted by Cicero here with *attrectas* and that hence *conquiris* refers to the gathering and assessment of the various sources of the Sibylline prophecy, a process that Tacitus notes happened at least on occasion (*ann.* 6.12). More likely, however, *conquiris* simply refers to the sifting and selection of whatever portions of the preserved oracles are deemed relevant to a given situation, whether this involved reading through the entire set or relying on an index (Orlin 1997: 82–83). Such an interpretation would provide special nuance to *impia mente*, which implies that Clodius selects the oracles "with impious <u>intention</u>" (*OLD* s.v. 7); it also explains Cicero's emphatic distinction in the sentence between those books that belong to the entire college (*vestri*) and those that Clodius himself (*tu*) chooses to consult—tendentiously, as Cicero implies. In this reading, the tricolon of the sentence follows a logical sequence, as Clodius "gathers" (*conquirere*) the appropriate oracles of the Sibyl, before "reading" them (*legere*) while "handling" their texts (*adtrectare*).

violatis oculis: Markland 1745: 347–348 rightly sees a problem, in that the context would seem to demand not "with eyes that have been violated" but "with eyes that have violated [sc. the rites of the Bona Dea]." Cicero seems here, as elsewhere, to be conflating the notions of physical and moral "blindness." For a close parallel see *In Clod. et Cur.* frg. 20 (Crawford): *quo loco ita fuit caecus, ut facile appareret, vidisse eum quod fas non fuisset,* which was construed correctly by the ancient scholiast (Schol. Cic. Bob. pp. 88.33–89.2) as alluding, in the words of Crawford 1994: 254, "to the blindness which is visited on those who have seen what it is not right for mortals to see in a religious context." In this case of course Clodius's invasion of the Bona Dea festival constituted the impropriety. The passages she cites for comparison demonstrate the inconsistency with which Cicero employs the trope: *dom.* 105 (referring only to Clodius's *caecitas mentis*), 129 (unspecified *caecitas*); *har. resp.* 38 (*caecitas* as possible punishment), 48 (*caecus amentiā*); *Sest.* 17 (*caecus atque amens*). A comparison with Clodius's great ancestor Appius Claudius Caecus is either implicit or explicit in these passages; see nn. on 8, 38.

contaminatis manibus adtrectas: Lennon 2014: 31: "*contaminare* represents one of the clearest examples of a word referring to a physical action resulting in [religious] pollution." He appositely cites *Catil.* 1.29, where those men who murdered Saturninus, the Gracchi, and Fulvius Flaccus are explicitly noted as not marked by *contaminatio* since the murders of these men were justified (see further Dyck 2008: 117).

27–29

Cicero emphasizes the reverence felt toward the Mater Magna in the history of Rome and of other peoples in order to contrast the behavior of Clodius who, during his tribunate, violated her most prominent shrine in Phrygia by taking it from Deiotarus, the rightful king, and ceding it to his son-in-law Brogitarus.

27 Cicero begins with a condensed version of a story told or alluded to in numerous ancient accounts, most fully at Liv. 29.10.4–11.8, 29.14.5–14; out of the vast modern bibliography, Gruen 1990: 5–33 and Roller 1999: 263–285 analyze the event from different perspectives, while offering readable narratives that critically assess the sources. My précis here follows Livy. In 205 BCE, when Hannibal had been fighting the Romans throughout the Italian peninsula for over a decade, a series of stone showers prompted consultation of the Sibylline books. Here was found the prophecy stating that a foreign-born enemy would be driven from Italy if the Idaean mother were brought to Rome from Phrygia. Accordingly, a Roman legation went east, consulting the oracle at Delphi en route, who advised that the goddess be welcomed upon their return by the best man in Rome. The embassy continued to Attalus, king of Pergamum, who conducted them to the goddess's shrine at Pessinus. In 204, the Romans returned with a small dark stone that the locals had identified as an aniconic representation of the Mater Magna. Most prominent among those welcoming the goddess was Publius Scipio among the men, joined by Claudia Quinta among the women. As noted earlier, the Mater Magna was ultimately given a temple at a prominent location on the Palatine, and the Megalesia was instituted in her honor.

Cicero selectively chooses to recall those points most relevant to the issue under debate in the senate: Publius Scipio as ancestor of the current consul and Claudia as ancestor of Clodius; most significantly, he begins his account by stressing the perilous state of Rome at the time these events took place.

hac igitur vate suadente quondam, defessa Italia Punico bello atque ⟨ab⟩ Hannibale vexata: The three ablative absolutes at sentence opening, combined with the expressions of time and agent, reflect a style of historical narrative that efficiently provides the setting necessary for the subsequent narration of a past event (Krebs 2018: 115–116 catalogues Caesar's more prevalent use of this technique). The adverb *quondam* ("once [upon a time]") is included to reinforce the temporal function of the clauses, which is less common in Cicero than one might expect (Laughton 1964: 105–106). The use of three ablative absolutes in succession, in particular in different tenses (present and perfect), is a Latin formula inherited by Cicero (Laughton 1964: 115–117).

In 205, when the Sibyl was consulted, Hannibal's overwhelming victories on the peninsula were already in the past, with the result that the claim that Italy was being "harassed by Hannibal" overstates the case (Gruen 1990: 6–7, who cites other similar ancient testimony). The inaccuracy suits Cicero's rhetorical purpose; by associating the summoning of the Mater Magna with the resolution of a past crisis, he suggests that Clodius's violation of that same goddess's festival and ancient shrine is what has precipitated the current crisis. Perhaps not coincidentally, *vexo* is a verb that Cicero in particular associates with the actions of Clodius (e.g., 40, 48; *dom.* 3; *Mil.* 26).

sacra ista: Although the adjective *ista* need not always have a derogatory sense (see Nisbet 1939: 169–170 on *dom.* 120, where *ista auctoritate* refers to the authority of the *pontifices* before whom he speaks), its use here indicates that Clodius is still uppermost in Cicero's mind (cf. 27: <u>tua</u> *soror*) and its irony is made clear by juxtaposition with *nostri* ("those rites over which *you* have authority *our* ancestors once brought from Phrygia"; cf. the contrast of *vestri* and *tu* at 26). The reference eases the transition to the story of Rome's acquisition of the Mater Magna, in which a role was played by Clodius's ancestor, from whose probity Clodius's sister, Clodia, has diverged.

ex Phrygia: Livy 29.10.5 and 34.3.8 records that the Romans received the goddess from Pessinus in Phrygia, as opposed to the testimony of Varro and Ovid that she arrived from the Troad (Varro *ling.* 6.15; Ov. *fast.* 4.247–272). Gruen 1990: 15–19 concludes that the Livian version is in error, arising from the fact that Cybele's cult at Pessinus was the major one known to the Romans in the late second and early first centuries BCE. In the third century, by contrast, her summoning from the Troad would have constituted part of a series of moves to emphasize Rome's ancestral ties with Troy (Rolle 2017: 112–116 supports with additional arguments; *contra* Fantham 1998: 145). Although Cicero's reference to Phrygia might at first seem to concur with Livy's account, Lenaghan 1969: 130 points out that "Cicero's 'ex Phrygia' is non-committal; it could mean either Pergamum or Pessinus" (see too Rolle 2017: 115), noting that *ex Phrygia*, like *ex ultimis terris* (24), could indicate simply that the icon originated in Pessinus, not that the Romans in 204 traveled there to retrieve it. If Cicero's geographical imprecision here is in fact intentional, and he did know that the embassy went to the Troad, it serves a rhetorical purpose. By alluding to Pessinus as the original home of the Roman manifestation of Mater Magna, he increases Clodius's sacrilege against her when he turns to narrate his complicity in violating her shrine at Pessinus (28–29 below).

quae vir is accepit qui est optimus populi Romani iudicatus, P. Scipio: Publius Cornelius Scipio Nasica (*RE* 350; 22n), the ancestor of the consul Lentulus, was the first of the Cornelian *gens* to hold the cognomen *Nasica* (Kajanto 1965: 237). When the Delphic oracle, or in some versions the Sibylline books, instructed that the Mater Magna should be welcomed to Rome by its *vir optimus*, the senate chose Nasica (Liv. 29.14.6–8; full sources at *RE* 4: 1495 [F. Münzer]), a young man who was not yet quaestor, becoming consul only in 191 (*MRR* 2: 556). Although Livy was unable to discover the criteria governing the senate's selection (Liv. 29.14.9), the choice of the cousin of the future Scipio Africanus, whatever his inherent virtues, must have acted as an endorsement of Scipio's plan to invade northern Africa, while his youth helped shield him from envy (Gruen 1990: 25–26, Roller 1999: 281–282, with bibliography).

The noun *vir*, seemingly redundant with *is*, serves two purposes: 1. to contrast with *femina*, also occupying first position in its clause; 2. to allude to Scipio's selection as Rome's *vir optimus*.

femina autem quae matronarum castissima putabatur, Quinta Claudia: The particle *autem* acts here as a light adversative, similar to Greek δέ, contrasting the man chosen (*vir*) with the woman (KS 2: 2.91–92; cf. 5, where it introduces the second of two opposing *si* clauses). Given its usefulness in rational argumentation, it is unsurprising that Cicero prefers the particle in his prose treatises, where it occurs c. 2,650 times in comparison with about 650 times in the speeches (*ThLL* II 1576.54–59 [K. Münscher]). Claudia Quinta (*RE* 435) was a descendant, perhaps granddaughter, of Appius Claudius Caecus (38n). She first receives mention here and in *Pro Caelio*, where her exemplary virtue serves as a reproach to Clodia, Clodius's sister (*Cael.* 33–34; 27n). In contrast with Nasica, her story expanded with retellings and allusions in a wide variety of ancient sources, including a drama performed at the Megalesia and a statue erected in the vestibule of Mater Magna's temple (textual sources in Roller 1999: 265 n. 10; for drama, Ov. *fast.* 4.326; for visual renderings, Bömer 1964: 146–151. Köves 1963: 335–347 reconstructs the historical context to determine why a woman of the Claudian *gens* was selected). Presumably because of this legendary connection, houses containing members of the Claudii, including Clodius, lay in the area behind the sanctuary of Mater Magna (Bruno 2017: 230).

The most well-known supplement to Claudia's myth involves her miraculous rescue of the goddess's ship when it became stranded in the shallows of the Tiber en route to Rome, most famously related at Ov. *fast.* 4.255–349 (also, e.g., Sil. 17.23–47; Stat. *silv.* 1.2.245–246). The most significant alteration to the account in *har. resp.*, however, is the detail first found in Seneca (frg. 80 [Hier. *adv. Iovin.* 1.26]), and often later, that Claudia was not a *matrona*, but a Vestal, whose chastity was redeemed by this feat. Bömer 1964: 146–147 has convincingly demonstrated that this confusion rests on a misreading of *Cael.* 34.

If we consider Cicero's formulation here to be parallel to that describing Nasica, it is possible to read *castissima femina* as a designation analogous with *optimus vir*, and that perhaps Claudia received this honor as a result of a process of selection conducted by the Roman *matronae* (Plin. *nat.* 7.120, with Val. Max. 8.15.12; I owe this suggestion to Lewis Webb). As with Nasica, it is probable that political considerations contributed to this choice: of the censors of 204, C. Claudius Nero belonged to the same *gens*, while the other, M. Livius Salinator, was probably connected to the Claudii by marriage (Liv. 23.2.6). Choosing as representative of the best men and women a member of two of the most prominent *gentes* at the time, the Cornelii and Claudii, "exemplified closing of the ranks, a show of unity in leadership" (Gruen 1990: 26).

cuius priscam illam severitatem [sacrifici] mirifice tua soror existimatur imitata: Cicero makes a similarly sarcastic rebuke to Clodia when addressing her in the person of Appius Claudius Caecus at *Cael.* 34: "*nonne te, si nostrae imagines viriles non commovebant, ne progenies quidem mea, Quinta illa Claudia, aemulam domesticae laudis in gloria muliebri esse admonebat?*" ("'Surely, if the portraits of your male ancestors weren't troubling you, wasn't at least my descendant, the famous Quinta Claudia, reminding you in the case of female renown to be a rival for our family's praise?'"). The sarcasm is increased with the use of *existimatur*, which echoes the analogous verbs of judging applied to the cases of Nasica and Claudia (*est . . . iudicatus*; *putabatur*). For Clodius's hatred of *severitas*, see 5n.

**The lemma is the reading of the major codices. *Sacrifici* was deleted by Ernesti 1810: 909–910 and is followed by all recent editors. The reading *mirifica* of the major codices is normally changed, following the *recentiores*, to *mirifice*, an adverb favored by Cicero (forty times in the full corpus), the use of which in the correspondence befits the tone here. Alternatively, Sydow 1941: 168 suggests that a noun in the ablative has dropped out that would account for both readings, e.g., *sacrificii mirifica ⟨cura⟩*, with the reference being Clodia's poisoning of her husband. There is a parallel for this sense of *cura* at Hist. Aug. *Aurelian.* 21.4: *post…sacrificiorum curas*. Sydow's suggestion certainly makes the irony more clear than does the simple change to *mirifice* and has the advantage of keeping the reading of the codices. The resultant jingle of the repeated *-rific-* sound may seem harsh, but Cicero recommends such wordplay in contexts of humorous abuse (*de orat.* 3.206: *habet interdum vim, leporem alias…paulum immutatum verbum atque deflexum*, with examples at *de orat.* 2.249 ["*quid hoc Naevio ignavius?*" severe Scipio], 2.256; Leeman *et al.* 1989: 276; 59n; for such soundplay concerning Clodius, see 4n). Nevertheless, Sydow's emendation does not give the sense required here of *severitas*, which is surely meant to refer to Claudia's chastity (and Clodia's lack thereof). The most economical solution is to delete *sacrificii* and emend *mirifica* to *mirifice*.

nihil te igitur neque maiores tui coniuncti cum his religionibus, neque sacerdotium ipsum, quo est haec tota religio constituta, neque curulis aedilitas, quae maxime hanc tueri religionem solet, permovit: The sentence wraps up the section begun at 26 (*illi cum ludos facerent*) by referring both to Claudia and the two Claudii who had put on the Megalesia previously (*maiores tui*), to Clodius's position as a *quindecimvir* overseeing the Sibylline books (*sacerdotium*), and to the curule aedileship that gave him the authority to sponsor the Megalesia (for the close association of this magistracy and the Megalesia see Bernstein 1998: 199–200, esp. n. 475). The adverbial sense of *nihil* to begin the sentence anticipates the subsequent series of negators (*neque…neque…neque*), comprising a rising tricolon of 16 + 18/19 + 21 syllables. For the redundant series following *nihil* ("epexegetic negation"), which is especially common with *neque…neque*, see *OLS* 1: 726–727. Note that each colon has an adjectival clause attached that contains a form of the word *religio*, which in each instance Clodius has failed to observe.

quo minus: The clause of negative prevention following *permoveo* seems to occur only here (*ThLL* X, 1 1568.66–68 [W. J. Claassen], which notes a few Christian examples of the verb governing an *ut* clause; KS 2: 2.257–258).

castissimos ludos / omni flagitio pollueres, / dedecore maculares, / scelere obligares: An asyndetic descending tricolon (10 + 8 + 6) balances in chiastic fashion the polysyndetic rising tricolon of the main clause. Thematically, ascribing to Clodius the pollution of the games (*ludos…pollueres*) recalls *LVDOS…POLLVTOS* of the response. Lennon 2014: 33 notes the religious connotations of *maculare*; for *obligare* compare *dom.* 20, also to Clodius: *cum…populum…Romanum scelere obligasses*. There is likely a play here between *obligares* and the triply-repeated *religio* in the main part of the sentence (11n): by ignoring the three aspects of his life that expect adherence to *religio*—his ancestry, quindecimvirate, and curule aedileship—Clodius succeeds in "binding down" the games.

28–29: Deiotarus I (*RE* 2), tetrarch of the Tolistobogii of Galatia, had a long history of alliance with the Romans that dated back to their conflict with Mithradates VI of Pontus, when he offered 30,000 troops to Lucullus in 72 (Sullivan 1990: 164). In 59, as part of Pompey's settlement in the aftermath of the Third Mithradatic War, the senate awarded Deiotarus additional lands in Asia Minor and the title of "king" (Adcock 1937); there is no evidence, however, that Pessinus was among them. He went on to have dealings with numerous generals and statesmen with claims in Asia Minor, including Caesar, Cato, and Marcus Antonius. Deiotarus's relationship with Rome continued beyond the end of the Republic (Sullivan 1990: 165–169), and he came to develop an especially close relationship with Cicero, whom he had helped during the latter's proconsulship in Cilicia. In 45 Cicero defended Deiotarus before Caesar on a charge of plotting his assassination (the extant *Pro rege Deiotaro*, of which Cicero himself had a low opinion: *fam.* 9.12.2=SB 263).

Cicero preserves our only evidence for Deiotarus's conflict with his son-in-law Brogitarus and for Clodius's legislation from his tribunate of 58, with this passage offering the fullest version (*LPPR* 397; for Clodius's possible motives, see Tatum 1999: 168–170). According to Cicero, Clodius's law made Brogitarus joint king, thereby giving him authority over Pessinus, who subsequently installed there a new priest to oversee Mater Magna's cult. Other references appear at *dom.* 129 and *Sest.* 56 (cf. *ad Q. fr.* 2.8.2=SB 13), both of which also mention that Clodius restored exiles to Byzantium, a separate piece of legislation that has no relevance to this section, which concentrates on profanation of the Mater Magna and her priesthood. Cicero alludes elliptically to these exiles only later, in a general catalogue of Clodius's misdeeds (59n). Despite Cicero's implications here, it is unclear what claims either Deiotarus or Brogitarus had to Pessinus before Clodius's legislation (Coşkun 2018: 125–128).

Cicero begins by answering his own rhetorical question of why he should be surprised at Clodius's behavior at the Megalesia (*quid ego id admiror?*). A causal relative clause ("Since you [*qui*]...") contains perfect subjunctive verbs in a tricolon detailing Clodius's crimes against the temple of Mater Magna at Pessinus (*vastaris... vendideris... detraxeris*). The syntactic tricolon develops semantically with three events of increasing gravity (sacking of Pessinus > "sale" of temple > abuse of head priest) and is then capped by a colon of summation (*omnia... perverteris*). For this construction, of a tricolon describing specifics followed by what seems a fourth element, but which in fact provides an expansion of the previous three cola see, e.g., nn. on 29, 32.

28 *Pessinuntem ipsum, sedem domiciliumque Matris deorum*: For Pessinus see 27n. Cicero uses the collocation of *sedes* and *domicilium* over a dozen times in his corpus. The noun *domicilium* is a technical term employed in law as a synonym for *domus*, and the combination with *sedes* reflects the redundant specificity typical of legal language (Costa 1964: 1.49 n. 1; further Grillo 2015: 239). The phrase occurs not infrequently with a pathetic tone of loss or potential loss (cf. Caes. *Gall.* 1.31.14; Liv. 45.38.7), such as in the analogous context of the plundering of a temple of Diana and Apollo at *Verr.* 2.5.185.

Brogitaro Gallograeco: Little is known about Brogitarus beyond what can be reconstructed from Cicero. The son-in-law of Deiotarus, his sister was a concubine of Mithradates VI; he is referred to in inscriptions as tetrarch and in one coin of c. 58–53 BCE as "king, friend to the Romans" (*ΒΑΣΙΛΕΩΣ ΒΡΟΓΙΤΑΡΟΥ ΦΙΛΟΡΩΜΑΙΟΥ*; *RE* suppl. 7: 82–83; Adcock 1937: 16; Magie 1950: 2.1235–1236). Since Cicero never mentions him in his correspondence while proconsul in Cilicia, he is probably dead by spring of 51.

This is the earliest Latin occurrence of the ethnic *Gallograecus* (the geographical designation Γαλλογραικία occurs at Strabo 12.5.1). The Romans called the Galatians of Asia Minor *Gallograeci* in recognition of their Celtic origins before they migrated eastward in the early third century BCE. Liv. 38.16 offers the earliest ancient account; see Briscoe 2008: 71–76 and, for details, Strobel 1996: 124 (naming), 236–257 (migration).

impuro homini ac nefario: For the "brave men and true" word order by which *homo* creates a hyperbaton see Adams 2021: 220 and 46n. Cicero uses a similar formulation to describe Brogitarus at *Sest.* 56: *Brogitaro, impuro homini atque indigno illa religione* (referring to Magna Mater).

cuius legati te tribuno dividere in aede Castoris tuis operis nummos solebant: The verb *divido* describes the divvying out of money; the suggestion of bribery is often present, as more commonly with the noun form *divisor* (cf. 42). The term *divisor* originally designated private agents who distributed by tribe among the Roman populace private gifts from patrons, or the profits from war spoils. This practice came to be exploited by candidates for public office as a mechanism for distributing bribes in order to sway elections (Liebenam 1905, with full citations). After much resistance, legislation was eventually enacted in the 60s BCE in an attempt to curb the practice, including a *lex Tullia* from Cicero's consulship in 63 (Gruen 1974: 216–224). The activity described here is probably the same alluded to more succinctly in the list of the various illegal activities of Clodius's tribunate at *dom.* 129 (*cautiones fiebant pecuniarum*). In 55 BCE, Cicero reports that Clodius requested an official legation to the East, in part to collect some of the money owed him from Brogitarus and the Byzantines; for unknown reasons, he never went (*ad Q. fr.* 2.8.2=SB 13: *illud autem quod cupit Clodius est legatio aliqua (si minus per senatum, per populum) libera aut Byzantium aut ⟨ad⟩ Brogitarum aut utrumque, plena res nummorum*).

The temple of Castor stood in the south-east portion of the Roman forum, officially designated as the *aedes* or *templum Castoris* but dedicated in the early fifth century to both Castor and Pollux (Suet. *Iul.* 10.1; further references in *LTUR* 1: 242 [I. Nielsen]). At some point during the first half of the second century, a tribunal was inserted into its steps, and expanded during a restoration in 117; from this spot orators, in particular tribunes of the people, could address the populace assembled in tribes (Morstein-Marx 2004: 57–59). Elsewhere as well Cicero identifies the temple as a site for Clodius's illegal activities while tribune (*dom.* 110; *Pis.* 11). No doubt in part as a result of these developments, the area became a locus for much of the political struggles of the late Republic (*LTUR* 1: 242–243 [I. Nielsen]). The chambers beneath the temple podium served to store moneys both public and private, a circumstance that provides a further indication of why Clodius chose the site to receive payments from the legates of Brogitarus (*Quinct.* 17; Iuv. 14.260 with Schol. Iuv. 14.260 and Courtney 1980: 583).

The feminine singular noun *opera* originally indicates the effort exerted to complete a specific task (*opus*) and then comes metonymically to refer to the people who expend that effort (*ThLL* IX, 2 665.27-67 [P. Flury]). Cicero frequently uses the term in the plural to describe groups hired, particularly by Clodius, to support violent activities of dubious legality (e.g., *Att.* 1.14.5=SB 14, of 61 BCE). The *operae* are characterized by Cicero either as slaves or as motivated by money, as here (e.g., *dom.* 79: *conductis operis non solum egentium sed etiam servorum*, where Nisbet 1939: 142 construes *operae* as meaning "services"; *Vatin.* 40. For Clodius's use of slaves, 22n).

totum illum locum fanumque vendideris: Cf. *Sest.* 56: *fanum… sanctissimarum atque antiquissimarum religionum venditum pecunia grandi Brogitaro*. The collocation of *locus* and *fanum* occurs again at 28 (*in illo loco fanoque*) and apparently nowhere else in Latin (cf. *Verr.* 2.4.110: *fani, loci, religionis illius*). The second term, *fanum*, constitutes a subset of the first, as often in Latin (cf. 22: *di immortales atque illa mater Idaea*; KS 2: 2.24-25, who notes that *et* is the commoner conjunction in this construction). The resulting emphasis on the word *fanum* contrasts with the fact that this alleged sale takes place in the Roman temple of Castor, thereby adding a further layer to Clodius's impiety.

sacerdotem ab ipsis aris pulvinaribusque detraxeris: The language not accidentally recalls the description of Clodius's violation of the rites of Bona Dea (8: *qui pulvinaribus Bonae deae stuprum intulerit*; 33: *quo pulvinari? quod stupraras*; cf. too 9: *ab altaribus religiosissimis fugatus*). It is unclear precisely what action Cicero describes here. Strabo notes that the priest at Pessinus was originally a person of political importance (12.5.3: οἱ δ' ἱερεῖς τὸ παλαιὸν … δυνάσται τινὲς ἦσαν) and Polybius 21.37.4-7 records the names of the high priests as Attis and Battakos, not as that of a king (Diod. 36.13 mentions a priest named Battakes coming to Rome in 102 in the trappings of a king; cf. Plut. *Mar.* 17.5-6). Up until the mid-second century at least, these priests were treated by the local kings as independent rulers (Walbank 1979: 3.150; Roller 1999: 193–194). From the reference here, however, and its résumé at 29 it is commonly assumed that the situation changed with Clodius's legislation, so that part of Cicero's indignation is that the new law allowed Brogitarus to succeed as the chief priest in Pessinus (Lenaghan 1969: 132–133, with hesitation; Kaster 2006: 246; Tatum

1999: 169 thinks that Deiotarus is the *sacerdos* being replaced, which surely Cicero would have emphasized if this were the case). Adcock 1937: 16 instead assumes that Brogitarus was simply given the right to appoint a new priest (also Magie 1950: 1236, Coşkun 2018: 122 n. 15). I favor this latter interpretation if only because, had Brogitarus indeed become high priest, one would have expected Cicero to refer unambiguously to such a radical change.

omnia illa quae vetustas, quae Persae, quae Syri, quae reges omnes qui Europam Asiamque tenuerunt semper summa religione coluerunt perverteris: For the extreme antiquity of the worship of the Anatolian antecedents of Mater Magna see 22n. The use of an abstraction for a collective noun as an alternative to a concrete expression (*vetustas=vetusti*: "men of old") is a construction found already in Plautus and one that becomes increasingly productive throughout Latinity (LHS 2: 747–748). For *vetustas*, as well as for the combination of this abstraction with concrete nouns describing people, see *Mil.* 98: "de me... semper populus Romanus, semper omnes gentes loquentur, nulla umquam obmutescet vetustas" (*OLD* s.v. 5). This vivid use of the noun, repeated again at 29, may also be intended to anticipate a clause of the response discussed later in the speech, SACRIFICIA VETVSTA OCCVLTAQVE MINVS DILIGENTER FACTA POLLVTAQVE (37, where Cicero argues that *vetusta* refers to worship of the Bona Dea).

There is no clear evidence that the Persians and Syrians worshipped the cult of Mater Magna, but Roller 1999: 185 notes that beginning in late fifth-century Greece the eastern aspects of her cult came to receive more emphasis, with the result that she became "increasingly identified with the Trojans and Persians." Cicero could be tapping into a similar Roman belief about the more exotic aspects of the Roman version of her cult. For evidence of her worship throughout Asia Minor and Europe, in some cases indisputably favored by kings, see Roller 1999: e.g., 111, 188, 193–194, 198, 206. The single word, and singular verb, *perverteris*, isolated at the end of the tetracolon, contrasts Clodius's actions with the antiquity, ubiquity, and intensity (*semper summa religione*) of Mater Magna's worship.

nostri maiores: *ThLL* VIII 144.30–33 (V. Bulhart) lists only sixteen examples from Latinity of this word order, of which three occur in *har. resp.* (24, 27). The inversion of the expected order (*maiores nostri*) normally signals a contrast between Rome's ancestors and those of other peoples (Landgraf 1914: 147). Here, in sandwiching and isolating Clodius through the syntax (as subject of *perverteris*), Cicero implies that Clodius's ancestry does not include nostri maiores but is as foreign as that of the other non-Roman peoples mentioned in the preceding clause (cf. 28: *nostri imperatores*, 29: *nostri nominis*).

refertam urbem atque Italiam fanorum: Of the approximately fifty examples in Cicero in which the adjective *refertus* governs a noun, it is normally construed with the genitive of persons; this is the only example in Cicero of the genitive of things (KS 2: 1.441–442 cite outside this passage only Gell. 1.8.1:

librum multae variaeque historiae refertum; cf. Sall. *hist. frg.* [Pap. Corp. 28] 4: *r[ef]ertus ir⟨a⟩e et doloris*). It is unclear why Cicero uses the genitive here; personification seems unlikely and rhythm is not a consideration, and he does not seem to be avoiding the ablative form *fanis*, which frequently occurs elsewhere in his corpus.

nostri imperatores maximis et periculosissimis bellis huic deae vota facerent, eaque in ipso Pessinunte ad illam ipsam principem aram et in illo loco fanoque persolverent: Val. Max. 1.1.1 is clearly adapted from this passage: *Matri deum saepe numero imperatores nostri compotes victoriarum suscepta vota Pessinuntem profecti solverunt*, with the notable addition of "very often" *saepe numero* (for another example of Valerius's use of *har. resp.* in 1.1.1 see 18n). Lenaghan 1969: 135 notes that "there is no other evidence whatsoever that the Roman commanders actually went to Pessinus and paid their vows there after victory." He cites an incident in 189 when priests came to Cn. Manlius Vulso, who was near Pessinus, assuring him of victory over the Galatians (Polyb. 21.37.4–7; Liv. 38.18.9) and, more aptly, in 102 when the priest Battakes came to Rome to request purificatory rites for unspecified defilement of Cybele's temple, promising military victories to the Romans (Diod. 36.13), in exchange for which the senate vowed to the goddess a temple (Plut. *Mar.* 17.5–6; on both incidents see Roller 1999: 290–291). Even if Roman generals had made vows to the Mater Magna in the latter case, they would presumably have done so at Rome. It seems improbable that they would have traveled all the way to "Pessinus itself" to fulfill a vow. Cicero likely manufactures this possibility to contrast Clodius's behavior (cf. his emphasis on the sacredness of Pessinus: *ad <u>illam ipsam principem</u> aram et in <u>illo</u> loco fanoque*). Wardle 1998: 86 offers other possibilities.

The phrase *in ipso Pessinunte* is unusual. Normally when pronominal adjectives modify names of cities the locative form is used without a preposition (KS 2: 1.479, adding only *Att.* 11.16.1=SB 227: *in ipsa Alexandrea*, where the preposition is clearly used for symmetry). *Fam.* 2.12.2=SB 95, though emended, confirms that Cicero considered Pessinus the name of a city (*Diogenes tuus... a me cum Philone Pessinunte⟨m⟩ discessit*).

29 quod cum Deiotarus religione sua castissime tueretur: The antecedent to *quod* is *loco fanoque*; as an expression in hendiadys it is construed as one singular concept (28n). The phrase *sua religione* is apparently an ablative of means—"through his own sense of religious obligation"—where *sua* puts Deiotarus on a par with the other kings who preserve her cult *summa religione* (28) as well as with Rome's own generals. Parallels include *Font.* 45: *ulterior Hispania... <u>religione sua</u> resistere istorum* [sc. *Gallorum*] *cupiditati potest*; Val. Max. 8.2.2: *C. Aquilius,...iudex addictus,...prudentia et <u>religione sua</u> mulierem reppulit*.

quem unum habemus in orbe terrarum fidelissimum huic imperio atque amantissimum nostri nominis: The hyperbolic use of *unus* with a superlative adjective is a common colloquialism found already in Plautus, and occurs in *har. resp.* also at 34, 45, 49, and 57 (Hofmann 1980: 243, §97; LHS 2: 193–194).

On the issue of whether such instances represent a weakening of *unus* in its development into an indefinite article see 49n.

Brogitaro... addictum pecunia tradidisti: Lenaghan 1969: 137 cites several parallels to show that the use of *addico* to mean "give over for sale" is "a favorite expression of Cicero." *ThLL* I 576.39–60 (A. Klotz) lists examples with ablative of price.

atque hunc tamen Deiotarum saepe a senatu regali nomine dignum existimatum, clarissimorum imperatorum testimoniis ornatum: The participles have a concessive sense, as anticipated by the particle *tamen* ("although Deiotarus was deemed worthy... nevertheless you..."). The granting of the title "king" occurred as a result of Pompey's settlement in 59 (texts specifying that the assignment was done by the senate include *Att.* 5.17.3=SB 110; *Deiot.* 10; *Bell. Alex.* 67.1; for controversy over this interpretation see Lenaghan 1969: 137). The position of the adverb *saepe* indicates that it is to be construed with both participles, with *existimatum* meaning "deemed worthy of" rather than "granted" (cf. *Deiot.* 10 with Lenaghan 1969: 137–138: "'Saepe' refers to the honorific use of the new title, not to any repetition of the grant").

tu etiam regem appellari cum Brogitaro iubes: Clodius passed this legislation as tribune through the plebeian assembly, an unprecedented but legal maneuver (Tatum 1999: 169). The only other references to this portion of the *leges Clodiae* are at *dom.* 129 (*regum appellationes venales erant*) and *Sest.* 56 (*appellati reges a populo qui id numquam ne a senatu quidem postulassent*). In both passages, *pace* Kaster 2006: 246, the plural need not be "meaningless" but could refer to the fact that the legislation reaffirmed Deiotarus as king while also making him co-regent with Brogitarus (see next sentence). In highlighting that Clodius ignored the normal procedure by which the senate concerns itself with international affairs—which of course his audience of senators would be well aware of—Cicero sets the power of the single *tu* of Clodius against the entire senate (*a senatu*). Further evidence that Cicero intends to identify Clodius with his plebiscite lies in the use of the verb *iubeo*, the technical term for describing the authority of a decision made by the people as a whole (see, e.g., *Verr.* 2.2.161: *senatus decrevit populusque iussit*, with Schwameis 2019: 492).

sed alter est rex iudicio senatus per nos, pecunia Brogitarus per te <u>appellatus</u> *** <u>alterum</u> putabo regem...: The unanimous reading of the codices is *appellatus alterum*, where the rest of the sentence makes clear that *alterum* must refer to Brogitarus. As a result, Kayser 1862: xli posited a lacuna in which there would have occurred a second reference to Deiotarus. Maslowski follows in printing a lacuna while recording a number of conjectures, the most paleographically attractive of which, *appellatus alter. eum* of Jeep 1863: 5–6 (deleting *Brogitarus* as a gloss) goes contrary to Cicero's normal oratorical practice, whereby each instance of *alter* stands in similar positions in its clause (as, e.g., at 25); the nearest parallel to the order proposed, which is in fact not very close, is *Pro Cornelio I* frg. 4 Crawford: *duos laqueos in causa esse propositos, ut, si me altero expedissem, tenerer altero* (cf. *inv.* 2.69). Lenaghan 1969: 138–139 assesses other conjectures, none completely convincing.

Despite uncertainty about the original reading, the sense is clear since it repeats attacks contained in the previous two sentences, with another pointed contrast between the rationality of the senate and the greed of Clodius (*iudicio senatus per nos, pecunia…per te*). In fact, to remedy this redundancy, it is worth considering what Lenaghan 1969: 139 calls "the simplest, but not the most convincing, solution," namely the suggestion of Schütz 1816: 159 to delete *pecunia Brogitarus per te*, although it then becomes a challenge to explain how this clause would have entered the text as a gloss.

alterum putabo regem, si habuerit unde tibi solvat quod ei per syngrapham credidisti: "This other one I'll consider a king if he has had the means to pay you what you loaned him through a bond." The joke rests on the proverbial wealth of kings; Brogitarus can prove himself a king by making good on the loans he received from Clodius. The pun on royal wealth recalls another that Cicero had made in the senate five years earlier, when Clodius was disappointed in not receiving an expected inheritance from Q. Marcius Rex, whose cognomen means "king" (*Att.* 1.16.10=SB 16: "*regem appellas*" *inquam* "*cum Rex tui mentionem nullam fecerit?*"; *ille autem Regis hereditatem spe devorarat*). The joke here may also be intended to recall the proverb *rex erit qui recte faciet; qui non faciet non erit* (Porph. *Hor. epist.* 1.1.62: "Whoever behaves correctly will be king; whoever doesn't, won't"; cf. Otto 1890: 300). Then the joke would be that if Brogitarus does *recte* by repaying his debt to Clodius, he can properly be called "king."

A *syngrapha* refers to a type of promissory note (cf. 34). The word appears at *dom.* 129 in the same context: *si tuus scriptor… non syngraphas cum Byzantiis exsulibus et cum legatis Brogitari faceret*. The feminine form is to be distinguished from the masculine *syngraphus*, referring to either a passport (e.g., Plaut. *Capt.* 450, with Lindsay 1900: 229) or another sort of written contract (e.g., Plaut. *Asin.* 238), a distinction that seems not to be observed in Greek (*LSJ* s. vv.). The noun *syngrapha* occurs thirty-four times in Cicero, particularly in his correspondence, but rarely outside Cicero in classical Latin, only once each in a fragment of Julius Caesar's oratory, Seneca, Suetonius, and Gaius.

quod tibi nummum nullum dedit: This clause introduces a summary of the most important of the "many regal characteristics" of Deiotarus. The entire sentence is arranged in a rising tetracolon with anaphora of *quod* (governing in each case emphatic indicative verbs). As at 28, a rising tricolon (9 + 34 + 43) is capped by a fourth member (56 syllables) that provides a summation of the previous three points. As often in Cicero, "*cum* introduces the general statement and *tum* the particular application, on which the main stress is laid" (Nisbet 1939: 65).

The surface meaning of the first regal characteristic is clear—Deiotarus never tried to buy favors from Clodius. As Lenaghan 1969: 138 observes, however, Clodius may have expected payment for reappointing Deiotarus as king in 59. *Nummus* often occurs to denote a very small sum, particularly in a negative context, i.e., "not a penny" (*OLD* s.v. 3c).

quod Pessinuntem: Shackleton Bailey 1987: 275 proposes deleting *quod* because "It was not specially 'regal' of Deiotarus not to repudiate that part of Clodius' law which confirmed his title." This interpretation seems too literal and was already anticipated by Wolf 1801: 348, who notes that the point, which recurs in this section, is that Deiotarus accepted that portion of Clodius's law which reaffirmed a decision of the senate. A second if lesser argument against deleting *quod* is that it would destroy the careful structure of the tetracolon mentioned above.

caeremonias ab omni vetustate acceptas: "Rites that have been welcomed by all the ancients." For the sense of *vetustate* see 28n, where it again describes persons from antiquity involved in the worship of Cybele. Two factors favor this interpretation over the alternative sense of "time-honoured cult" (Watts 1923: 353; cf. Shackleton Bailey 1991: 118, "immemorial rituals"): first, *omnis* is difficult to construe as modifying *vetustas* in this context (*fam.* 6.10b.2=SB 222 is not parallel), whereas the combination *omnis vetustas* occurs elsewhere as a personification (Sen. *nat.* 4A.17: *in eadem opinione omnis vetustas fuit*; Gell. 10.24.4: *pleraque omnis vetustas sic locuta est*); second, understanding the *ab* as expressing agency provides a direct contrast with the immediately following *a Brogitaro*.

sed ut haec haruspicum responsa redeam, ex quibus est primum de ludis, quis est qui id non totum in istius ludos praedicatum et responsum esse fateatur?: Cicero signals clearly the end of his lengthy excursus on the portion of the response that treats the games. With the phrase *est primum de ludis* ("the first [response] is about the games"), he indicates that this clause constituted the first portion of the response.

When the negator *non* is positioned at the beginning of a clause it indicates an emphatic denial, which is appropriate for this question, capping as it does an extensive discussion of the games (*OLS* 1: 731). Not uncommonly a pronoun, here *id*, precedes the negating word (e.g., *Lael.* 24: *quis est, qui id non maximis efferat laudibus?*; KS 2: 1.818–819).

** praedictum: This is the reading of all the codices. Markland 1745: 349, in full-blown sarcasm, detects a problem here with the tense, as a prediction "of a thing past": "*Tiresias*... was not a greater *Conjurer* in his way than our Author's *Haruspices* are, who *foretel*, not in the Vulgar method, concerning things *future*, but concerning things which are *already done* and *over*." Gesner 1753: 277 counters reasonably (though not for Wolf 1801: 350: "Plus quam humana est haec divinatio") that it was not the games being "predicted" by the *haruspices* but their consequences for the state and he convincingly points to 26 for this conception (*id... ipsum sibi monstrum est et cum in eo ipso periculum est ex quo periculum portenditur*). Courtney 1960: 97 suggests emending to *praedicatum* and notes the reading of the *recentiores* (and several codices of Val. Max. 1.1.1) at 18 *fatorum veteres praedicationes*; but see note *ad loc.*

30

Returning to the violation of sacred and religious sites, Cicero mentions a house bought by Clodius containing a chapel that had been destroyed.

Sequitur de locis sacris, religiosis: Cicero resumes with the portion of the response that incriminates him most, on the violation of sacred places, which he has already spent sections 9–17 attempting to refute. On account of his use of the verb *sequitur*, scholars assume that this section followed in the response directly after that about neglected and polluted games. For the asyndeton bimembre *de locis sacris, religiosis* see 11n.

It is rare in Latin for a bare prepositional phrase to act as a noun, in this instance as the subject of a verb; cf. *leg.* 2.34: *sequitur... de iure belli* (LHS 2: 411 notes that the construction, in imitation of the ability of the Greek article to substantize, begins with Cicero and is generally rare). Lebreton 1901: 88–90 provides known parallels in Cicero, adding that these constructions are more commonly accompanied by a pronoun acting as a definite article, e.g., *Sest.* 136: *concludam illud de optimatibus* (LHS 2: 191–194).

de mea domo dicere audes? committe vel consulibus vel senatui vel conlegio pontificum tuam: To underscore the differences between his and Clodius's homes, Cicero places them at opposite ends of their respective sentence, putting each possessive adjective in an unexpected and therefore emphatic position (Marouzeau 1922: 133 remarks on how the position of *mea* anticipates a contrast). For the rising tricolon specifying the consuls, senate, and pontifices as those who have rendered verdicts (4 + 4 + 8), see 14n, where the three options are separated by *aut... aut... aut* (cf. *ut dixi antea* in the next sentence). The etymological origins of the conjunction *vel* fit the second-person address here—"whether you want the consuls or senate or pontifices": "*vel* still performs a function in second-person contexts, which betrays its origin (from *velle* 'to want')" (Torrego 2009: 461; LHS 2: 500–502). Moreover, by using *vel* rather than *aut* in this instance Cicero stresses that whatever option Clodius chooses will yield the same result: that Clodius's home is as tainted as Cicero's is not. For an analogous use where all three options are explicitly applicable, see Planc. Cic. *fam.* 10.4.1=SB 358: *habeo causas plurimas, vel... vel... vel...*, also in a second-person address.

quidem... at: This correlation is very rare (Solodow 1978: 32–33); KS 2: 2.82–83 notes that the combination gives the introductory *quidem* a strong concessive sense.

Q. Seio, equite Romano, viro optimo, per te apertissime interfecto: Quintus Seius Postumus (*RE* 12) is known only from this passage and *dom.* 115 (cf. *dom.* 129), where his murder is detailed. At the time that Cicero left for exile, Seius refused to sell his home to his neighbor Clodius. After Clodius threatened to block his access to daylight, Seius asserted, according to Cicero, that Clodius would never own the house as long as he was alive. Clodius accordingly poisoned him openly (*apertissime*) and purchased his home at auction at a price nearly half its valuation.

The precise position of Seius's house cannot be ascertained but a reasonable guess can be made. Recent excavations on the northwest corner of the Palatine, combined with mentions in Cicero, have given a good indication of the makeup and residents of the city block on which Cicero and Clodius both had homes. There had been abundant discussion of the area previously; some of the key analyses include Allen 1939, who offers full literary documentation and previous bibliography, but whose conclusions are not always acceptable; the reconstruction of Nisbet 1939: 206 is convincingly refuted by Allen 1940; see too Cerutti 1997. Most recently, the investigations of a team of researchers led by Andrea Carandini, employing the analyses of Krause 2001 and Coarelli 2012, have placed the discussions on a new level. A member of that team, Bruno 2017: 2.230–232 provides a clear analysis to show that before Cicero's exile a series of structures stood facing the Capitoline Hill and overlooking the forum, with Clodius's house being most westward, followed by the Porticus Catuli and then Cicero's house; see her illustrations in Carandini 2017: 1, Tab. 64, 281a (with M. Ippoliti) and for bibliography on the recent archaeology, see Bruno 2017: 271 n. 214. References in Cicero allow us to situate the residence of Seius in relation to these three points. First, Cicero tells us that Clodius planned after his exile to join together two prominent houses, which are most easily taken as referring to those of Cicero and Seius (*dom.* 115: *duas… et magnas et nobilis domos coniungere*; Coarelli 2012: 317 interpets as that of Cicero and Clodius). Later in this same passage is related the threat from Clodius that he would disrupt Seius's access to daylight, which presumes that they occupy adjacent houses and that Seius's does not stand on one of the Palatine's edges, since this would have given him access to unimpeded light. The most economical conclusion, therefore, is that Seius's home lies between that of Cicero and Clodius, to the south of the Porticus Catuli on an internal street, the so-called Clivus Palatinus. For a reasonable plan of the location of Seius's house, see Carandini 2017: Tab. 281a, no. 6 (the more detailed discussion of Coarelli 2012, esp. 314–319, differs in several particulars).

Unless expressed otherwise, the agent connected with the actions of an ablative absolute is assumed to be the subject of the main sentence (KS 2: 1.772). As a result, the addition of *per te* here is unnecessary, and allows Cicero to underscore Clodius's involvement in Seius's murder (and create a sarcastic phonic repetition: <u>per te</u> a<u>p</u>er<u>t</u>issime in<u>t</u>er<u>f</u>ecto).

sacellum: Wissowa 1912: 469 distinguishes between two types of *sacella*. First, those for public cults, to which most textual sources refer and which could minimally consist of an altar in an uncovered space, presumably with an image of the god nearby (see Trebatius, quoted in next note; Fest. p. 318 M: ⟨*loc*⟩*a dis sacrata sine tecto*; Rosenberg 1920: 1625); the term is particularly well attested to describe shrines for the Lares Compitales (Wissowa 1912: 470 n. 4). The second category of *sacellum* encompasses domestic shrines on private property, which must be the type to which Cicero refers here, dedicated to some deity important to Seius. The *sacellum* as a place of worship was significant enough for Varro to have devoted to them the entire fifth book of his *Antiquitates rerum divinarum* (Aug. *civ.* 6.3; Cardauns 1976: 47–48). Fridh 1990 provides a thorough discussion of the range of meanings of the word throughout classical antiquity.

Contrary to what Cicero implies in this section, the destruction of a private shrine by a new owner did not seem to constitute a religious violation, which is perhaps why he does not dwell on this point. Cicero himself, in fact, provides clear evidence: in his quest for a shrine in which to memorialize his deceased daughter Tullia after her death in 45, he expresses concern that, wherever it should be erected, future owners could demolish it since it would be only "somewhat consecrated" (*quasi consecratum*: *Att.* 12.19.1=SB 257; cf. 12.36.1=SB 275; Wissowa 1912: 469 n. 7).

** ***sacellum dico fuisse ⟨et⟩ aras***: All codices read *sacellum dico fuisse aras*; P² has the perplexing addition of the letters *st* written above the text, between the second "a" and the "s" of *aras*. The emendation adopted by Peterson is to read *et aras*, apparently understanding the addition of P² as the misplaced and incorrectly written transmission of an original *et* (for the value of this hand in correctly supplying omissions in P see Maslowski 1981: xviii). Two objections, however, can be raised against this reading, aside from the fact that the reading of *et* is uncertain to begin with. The first objection concerns word order. The emphatic position of *aras* comes as an unexpected afterthought following the infinitive *fuisse* (of course, if we knew anything about Seius's *sacellum*, this position could be explained). Two pieces of evidence, however, seem to support this emphasis. First, Fest. p. 154 M shows that a *sacellum* could contain more than one altar and that their removal seems to constitute the final step in the site's desecration—*Mutini Titini sacellum fuit in Veliis, adversum murum Mustellinum in angi⟨portu⟩, de quo aris sublatis balnearia sunt ⟨f⟩acta domus Cn. D⟨omitii⟩ Calvini* ("The shrine to Mutinus Titinus was on the Velian Hill, opposite the Mustelline wall in an alley. The altars were removed from it and baths were built for the home of Gnaeus Domitius Calvinus"). Second, the jurist Trebatius in fact defines a *sacellum* as *locus parvus deo sacratus cum ara* (Gell. 7.12.5) where *ara* is also in an emphatic position; if *et aras* is to be read we would see Cicero putting the word in an analogously emphatic position. The second objection involves rhythm. Maslowski 1981: 103 reads only *sacellum dico fuisse*, following objections to the rhythm of *-ō fŭīssĕ ĕt ārās* raised by Zielinski 1904: 206. This concern seems unwarranted, however, since if one allows elision of *fuisse et* the final four syllables yield a double trochee, a favored rhythm that occurs in almost 29 percent of this speech's clausulae (Keeline and

Kirby 2019: 175 and cf. *orat.* 212–215). Both objections to *et aras* at sentence end, therefore, disappear on closer examination. Given the unanimity of the codices, the odd note in P², and the reasons cited for the emphasis on altars, I have chosen to read *fuisse ⟨et⟩ aras*. But the decision is difficult.

tabulis...censoriis: For the use of *tabulae* in Roman public and private life to contain in written form items ranging from financial records to pontifical documents to curses see Meyer 2004: 24–43; note in particular her comment, with full citations of ancient references, that "on *tabulae* were recorded the ritual utterances of the censors as well as the results of their quinquennial census— land, buildings, and census-class of all the citizens, along with any public contracts and public expenses and income down to the number, size, and even posture of plundered statues" (25–26; see too Kübler 1932; full discussion of censorial duties at Mommsen 1887–1888: 311–469). The most recent census at the time of *har. resp.* occurred in 61/60 (*MRR* 2: 179), when Seius would have still been in residence. Lenaghan 1969: 141 doubts Cicero's testimony here— "For the censors to keep records of all such shrines and chapels in Rome would be a staggering task"—although this evidence is accepted without comment by Mommsen 1887–1888: 2.1.434 n. 4 and Kübler 1932: 1900. Indeed, the censors at this period were expected to include in their assessments all of an individual's valuable personal property (Suolahti 1963: 39–40). Since we are unaware of the nature of Seius's *sacellum*, and we know that the previous holders of the censorship came close to completing their duties (Suolahti 1963: 476), it seems more likely that Cicero is presenting here a plausible situation than that he is manufacturing an improbable circumstance that would have been obvious to his senatorial audience.

With the combination *firmabo ac docebo* ("I will confirm and elaborate"), Cicero distinguishes between proving Clodius's destruction of the shrine and discussing the consequences (cf. Amm. 21.12.18: *multa...locutus et vera, quibus...firmatum...Iuliani docebat imperium*; for *atque/ac* preceding the more emphatic member of a pair see 11n).

agatur modo haec res: On *modo* as an adverbial equivalent to the conjunction *dummodo* see LHS 2: 616.

** *res quod*: Shackleton Bailey 1991a: 230 reads *res quam* (with Ernesti 1810: 911) rather than *res quod* of the archetype. This emendation certainly makes clearer sense, but it is possible to construe *quod* as referring to the entire previous clause ("let this affair be attended to, [an action] which needs to be referred..."). Analogously, Mueller 1896: cxxxiii understands the clause in a pregnant sense, as equivalent to *quod fieri necesse est, ut referatur*.

ex eo senatus consulto quod nuper est factum: That is, the senatorial motion that put the matter of the prodigy to the *haruspices* (14n).

** *ad nos necesse est*: This is the reading of all major manuscripts, with *vos* occurring in some *recentiores*. Shackleton Bailey 1991a: 119 n. 46 reads *nos*: "Cicero speaks as a senator to senators," as often in this speech in the context of the prodigy (e.g., 19, 24, 25; cf. 11: *ad hunc ordinem referretis*). *Nos* also has the advantage of not disrupting the continual address to Clodius (30–31: *tenes... de domo tua*).

31

Cicero defends himself from a point that Clodius had presumably raised in his *contio*: that the goddess Tellus is upset with Cicero for not fulfilling his duty as her *curator*. Cicero counters that the violation of Tellus's rites can be traced instead to Clodius's brother, Appius Claudius.

Interpretation of this section relies on uncertain conjecture, causing Watts 1923: 354 n. b to write: "Long says here, 'There is no difficulty in translating the rest of the chapter, but it is unintelligible.' I fear I can do no more than endorse Long's statement." I offer below what I hope is an intelligible interpretation, but with little confidence that it accurately represents Cicero's meaning in all its details.

in qua tamen ita est inaedificatum sacellum ut alius fecerit, tibi tantum modo sit demoliendum: "Where a shrine has been built over in such a way that someone else has been doing the overbuilding, and you only have to destroy it." For the use of *tamen* to signal a parenthetical aside in a relative clause, see OLD s.v. 6. The discussion of the verb *inaedificare* in Fridh 1990: 179–182 provides a useful context within which to understand this aside. He shows convincingly that the verb here has the sense of "build over, build upon," and that Seius (the presumed referent of *alius*) had built over a shrine in his home, thereby beginning the process of desecration (cf. Shackleton Bailey 1991a: 119: "a chapel has been walled up"). Fridh 1990: 181 maintains that the desecrated shrine was originally public, rather than a private one built within the house at an earlier stage, but I do not see how we can be sure. Clodius then completed the process of alleged desecration through demolition.

de aliis: Sc. *domibus*. The logical progression of what follows (*enim*) indicates that Cicero is going to turn from Clodius's home to another one which could involve the profanation of sacred spaces, namely, the home of Appius Claudius, Clodius's brother.

putant enim ad me non nulli pertinere magmentarium Telluris aperire: The substantive *magmentarium* is the emendation of Mommsen (Orelli *et al.* 1856: 916) for the otherwise unattested noun *acmentarium* of the major manuscripts (*actamentarium* is the reading of E at 31.5; Latte 1960: 389 n. 2 suggests the also unattested *augmentarium*). The word is explained in a late glossary as: *magmentarium ἐφ' οὗ τὰ σπλάγχνα τιθέμενα τοῖς βωμοῖς προσφέρονται* (*Gloss.*[L] II Philox. MA 24, a set of glosses extant in one ninth-century manuscript). The precise sense of the gloss is disputed, but the best interpretation seems to be "*magmentarium*: where entrails are stored, and then brought to the altars"; that is, the *magmentarium* is a storehouse for the animal parts before they are offered to Tellus (so Weinstock 1934: 805; Latte 1960: 389 n. 2; Marcattili 2020:

105–108). Regardless of its precise function, Cicero clearly indicates that the *magmentarium* is a place that should be protected from desecration.

As the preeminent goddess of the earth, Tellus is of major importance to the traditional agrarian economy of the Roman state (Wissowa 1912: 192–195; 191–208 surveys all the numerous major and minor gods associated with agriculture). Varro describes her as the goddess who receives and nourishes seeds, adding that she is the first agricultural deity addressed in the prayers of the *pontifices* (Aug. *civ.* 7.23=Varro frgs. 265–266 Cardauns; see further Weinstock 1934). Since Tellus is one of the gods to whom the *haruspices* recommend reparations, it is natural that Cicero's opponents would exploit any possibly negative associations that he may have with this deity (Clodius is surely among the unnamed *non nulli*). This passage indicates that Cicero was procurator of the cult of Tellus, and the accusation recorded is that he was expected to render accessible her *magmentarium*, presumably to her priest, or perhaps even to the general populace, a circumstance that would have been particularly crucial during the grain scarcity prevailing in Rome at this time. For this sense of *aperire*, see *ThLL* II 212.71–213.4 (O. Prinz); of particular relevance to this context are Liv. 30.17.6, where the caretakers of all the shrines in Rome lay them open so that the people are able to visit and give thanks, and Fest. p. 250 M, who describes the *penus*, the inner part of the temple of Vesta, being opened to the Vestals and *pontifex maximus* only on specific dates (Wissowa 1912: 159–160). In response to this accusation Cicero, who has already implicated Clodius in violating Tellus by identifying her with the Mater Magna whose recent festival he disrupted (24n), defends himself by associating the violation of the *magmentarium* with another member of Clodius's family. It is odd that he does not stress again in this rebuttal the connection of Tellus with Mater Magna.

nunc sanctissimam partem ac sedem maximae religionis privato dicunt vestibulo contineri: That is, in contrast with talk that it had been accessible recently (*nuper id patuisse dicunt*), the passage to the *magmentarium* has now become obstructed through its incorporation into the forecourt of a private home. Festus cites a parallel for this sort of domestic usurpation of divine space under the principate of Augustus (p. 154 M, quoted at 30n). Cicero underscores the sacrilege of private property imposing on the religious realm both by the juxtaposition of *maximae religionis* and *privato*, as well as by the short-range hyperbaton that places special emphasis on the introductory adjective *privato* (Powell 2010: 176–177). Marcattilli 2020: 109–110 has suggested that Appius, contrary to Cicero's claim that he removed the *magmentarium* (*sustulit*), in fact incorporated it into his home in order to facilitate private worship of Tellus on behalf of the Claudian *gens*.

The home adjacent to the temple of Tellus to which Cicero refers would presumably have been known to most of his senatorial audience. Weinstock 1934: 805 argues that the reference is to the ancestral home of the Tullii in the Carinae district of Rome, now owned by Quintus Cicero (*LTUR* 2: 204 [E. Papi]), which seems to have been near the temple of Tellus (*ad Q. fr.* 3.1.14=SB 21; see *LTUR* 5: 24–25 [F. Coarelli] for the temple's location). The chief obstacle to this conjecture is that it leaves unexplained the reference to Clodius's brother in the subsequent section, a reference that Weinstock acknowledges as "unverständlich." To account for this allusion, Fridh 1990: 182 n. 24 offers the unlikely hypothesis that Cicero refers to L. Pinarius Natta, Clodius's brother-in-law. Courtney 1960: 98–99 offers what must be the correct interpretation. He points out that all mentions of repairs to Quintus's house during this period refer to his house on the Palatine, not in the Carinae, and that "it is Appius Claudius who has incorporated the shrine into his house, and Cicero is connected with the business solely because the temple is under his *curatio*; the house of Quintus has nothing to do with it" (1960: 99). He cites as supporting evidence a letter from 50 BCE in which Marcus Caelius mentions that he has begun proceedings against Appius for a shrine in his home (Cael. Cic. *fam.* 8.12.3=SB 98: *coepi sacellum, in domo quod est, ab eo petere*). This solution is accepted by most recent scholars (Lenaghan 1969: 142–143; Shackleton Bailey 1991a: 119; *LTUR* 5: 246 [J.-P. Guilhembet: "peut être"]; Carandini 2017: 2, Tab. 89 inset C provides a speculative map orienting the houses of Quintus and Appius with the temple of Tellus) and makes sense of the otherwise confusing sentence that follows.

multa me movent: With this short alliterative sentence Cicero specifies three aspects of the desecration of the *magmentarium* that particularly concern him. The subsequent list is organized as a rising tricolon (14 + 44 + 58), with the first two cola introduced by *quod*, and the third by a reprise of this introductory phrase (*movet me etiam*).

quod aedes Telluris est curationis meae: The duties of *curatio* did not constitute a formal office during the Republic. Although aediles seem to have provided general oversight of temples (Becker 2017: 184), other magistrates could be delegated tasks by the *populus Romanus* that technically stood outside the normal duties of their respective magistracy. The numerous duties could include serving on a grain commission, overseeing the minting of coins, or being caretaker of public buildings, including temples (Leonhard 1901: 1761–1770; for sacred buildings, Mommsen 1887: 2.667–671). The only independent evidence for Cicero as *curator* for the temple of Tellus comes from a letter of 54 where he writes to his brother that he is caring for the building and has placed a statue of Quintus beside it (*ad Q. fr.* 3.1.14=SB 21: *de aede Telluris et de porticu Catuli me admones. fit utrumque diligenter. ad Telluris quidem etiam tuam statuam locavi*). This particular duty may have been assigned because of the proximity of the temple to the family home of the Tullii (Richardson 1992: 378; *LTUR* 5: 24 [F. Coarelli]), or perhaps even as a product of Pompey's recent appointment as head of the grain commission, an appointment that Cicero wholeheartedly supported (*Att.* 4.1.7=SB 73, where he notes that Pompey named him the chief of his fifteen legates; 4.2.6=SB 74; Balsdon 1957: 16–18).

quod is qui illud magmentarium sustulit mea domo pontificum iudicio liberata secundum fratrem suum iudicatum esse dicebat: As argued above, the unnamed speaker is Appius Claudius Pulcher (*RE* 297), Clodius's eldest brother. Appius appears to have been a fine representative of the famed arrogance of the Claudii (Shackleton Bailey 1965-1970: 1.396). His relationship with Cicero was checkered: as praetor in 57 he did not vote for Cicero's recall, offering steadfast support to his brother (*MRR* 2: 200). By 54, however, Cicero writes to a colleague that the two of them have a good relationship (*fam.* 1.9.4=SB 20: *cum Appio... in gratia*), although the tone of their own correspondence over the next few years, as well as Cicero's mentions of him elsewhere, varies drastically (*fam.* 3.1-13=SB 64-76; Gruen 1974: 353-354). Subsequent to *har. resp.*, Appius went on to obtain high office, the consulship in 54 and censorship in 50. Cicero succeeded him after his proconsulship in Cilicia (53-51) and writes to Atticus of the damage inflicted on the locals by Appius's greed (e.g., *Att.* 5.16.2=SB 109, 5.17.6=SB 110).

The preposition *secundum* in legal parlance has the sense of making a decision "in favor of" someone, and the reference is to the pontifical decision rendered in the episode that prompted Cicero's *De domo sua*. In a letter to Atticus Cicero records Clodius making the same claim soon after the verdict at a *contio* called by Appius in his capacity as praetor (*Att.* 4.2.3=SB 74: *nuntiat populo pontifices secundum se decrevisse;... hortatur ut se et Appium sequantur et suam libertatem ut defendant*). Cicero remarks that even the lowest of the Romans (*infimi*) either marveled at or mocked Clodius's insanity on this occasion. It is natural for Cicero to attribute here the same sentiment to Appius.

in hac caritate annonae, sterilitate agrorum, inopia frugum: All three nouns refer to the same phenomenon, namely the grain shortage in Rome of 57 BCE as a result of which Pompey was granted a command over the grain supply.

eodem ostento Telluri postilio deberi dicitur: For *postilio* see 20n. Cicero's reference to *eodem ostento* ("by the same portent") is to be noted. The adjective *eodem* allows him to equate the grain shortage of the previous sentence with the rumblings in the earth that have prompted the senate meeting. The rumblings provide a warning to the Romans, and the previous year's famine provides an example of the real threat portended.

32

Cicero alludes to two more recent instances of shrines being desecrated, by L. Piso and Sex. Serranus, respectively.

vetera fortasse loquimur: "Maybe I'm talking about things that are out of date." As the adverb *fortasse* hints, Cicero here speaks sarcastically, as he does in the next sentence when he says "But still, we are currently neglecting events of the past." As he points out in the intervening portion, it is a universal law of humanity that the gods have inalienable rights to property that has been dedicated to them, rights that have been violated by the actions of Appius Claudius in building part of his home over the shrine of Tellus. To underscore the antiquity of this observation, Cicero uses the noun *mortales*, a word with generally more solemn associations than *homines* (Fronto in Gell. 13.29; Cramer 1889: 342–343; 32n).

quamquam hoc si minus civili iure perscriptum est, lege tamen naturae, communi iure gentium sanctum est ut...: The adverb *quamquam* often introduces a main clause in Cicero; here it acts as a corrective particle to show that the notion of divine property in fact remains relevant ("of course," "in fact"; cf., e.g., *Planc.* 4: *quamquam, iudices, si quid est...*; KS 2: 2.444 Anm. 3). The pronoun *hoc* stands in emphatic position in anticipation of the subordinate *ut* clause.

For the *ius civile* see 14n. The *ius gentium* ("law of peoples") often corresponds to the modern idea of international law but, as indicated by its apposition with *lex naturae*, Cicero intends it here to be understood in a more strictly theoretical sense as synonymous with the law of nature (cf. *off.* 3.23: *natura, id est iure gentium*; Jolowicz and Nicholas 1972: 102–107). See Gaius *inst.* 1.1: *quod vero naturalis ratio inter omnes homines constituit, id apud omnes populos peraeque custoditur vocaturque ius gentium quasi quo iure omnes gentes utuntur* ("That which has been established among all human beings by natural reason is preserved equally among all peoples and is called *ius gentium*, as all peoples make use of this law"). Cicero equates the two concepts to underscore that, as a belief shared by all human beings, the inviolability of divine property must be respected, even if such a provision is not explicitly covered under Roman statute law.

ut nihil mortales a dis immortalibus usu capere possint: In Cicero, the noun *mortales* is normally accompanied by an indefinite adjective of quantity such as *multi, omnes,* or *cuncti* (Lebek 1970: 255), which allows Cicero to stress the universal destiny of mortals. That function is served here by the emphatic juxtaposition with *nihil* (where *ut nihil* is itself an emphatic alternative to the expected *ne quid*: KS 2: 2.209–210). For the two other exceptions in oratory—*Marcell.* 22 and *Phil.* 2.114—a form of *immortalis*, as here, underscores the transient nature of mortality (cf. *Verr.* 2.4.80, *Catil.* 4.7; Meillet 1982: 328–329 notes that Indo-European conceptions of the divine already include this emphasis on human mortality). Wills 1996: 458–459 observes that, contrary to what one might expect, the contrasting pair of *mortales / di immortales* is rare among poets.

The principle of usucaption (*usucapio*) entailed "the acquisition of ownership of property by continued possession for a certain time;...in particular it was necessary that the possession should have begun in good faith and that there should have been a *iusta causa* for its inception" (Jolowicz and Nicholas 1972: 151–152). The tenet may date as early as the XII Tables, and had reached its basic form by the end of the Republic; this passage of Cicero is our only evidence that usucaption of sacred property was not allowed under the Roman *ius civile* (for the case of wine used in libations, see Arnob. *nat.* 7.31; Watson 1968: 4, 21–22).

** ***neglegimus***: The present tense is the reading of H and *recentiores*; other manuscripts read *neglegemus* (**PG**) and *negligemus* (**E**). Shackleton Bailey 1991a: 230 follows Mueller 1896: cxxxiii and other *recentiores* in reading *neglegamus*. The present indicative, however, appositely picks up the same form of *loquimur* (see note), whereas the hortatory subjunctive would imply that Cicero is willing to ignore past violations of natural law, which does not serve his purpose. The translation of Watts 1923: 357 captures the tone well: "But, neglecting antiquity as we do."

cum maxime: This non-subordinating phrase occurs commonly in Cicero as an intensified form of the adverb *maxime*—"most of all, especially" (*ThLL* VIII 74.32–48 [V. Bulhart]). Its origins are uncertain. Hand 1836: 3.599–603 has a full discussion, and presumes that originally a verb from the context is understood in subordination to *cum*; so here, "Shall we also neglect those things that are happening [now], especially when [those things are happening]." Baiter suggested emending to *nunc cum maxime* (Orelli 1856: 916). Although Cicero uses the phrase elsewhere (Landgraf 1914: 242–243), the addition seems unnecessary (Hand 1836: 3.600).

L. Pisonem quis nescit his temporibus ipsis maximum et sanctissimum Dianae sacellum in Caeliculo sustulisse?: This passage provides our only evidence for a shrine of Diana on the Caelian. D. Palombi (*LTUR* 2: 13–14) connects its destruction with the crackdown on foreign cults by Piso and Gabinius during their consulship in 58, as attested by Varro (Tert. *apol.* 6.8, *nat.* 1.10.17–18=Varro frg. 46a–b Cardauns; cf. Arnob. *nat.* 2.73). Since these sources refer only to Egyptian cults, however, the connection with Diana must remain uncertain; activity in 58 may also stretch the limits of Cicero's assertion that this happened *his temporibus ipsis*. In part because there is scanty evidence for the syncretism of Diana with Isis at this period, Malaise connects the destruction of Diana's *sacellum* instead to the general neglect of Roman religion lamented by Varro *apud* Aug. *civ.* 6.2=frg. 2a Cardauns (Malaise 1972: 381).

** ***in Caeliculo***: *Caeliculus* is attested here only but is presumed, along with the similarly named *Caeliolus* (Varro *ling.* 5.46), to be part of the Caelian Hill. Rodríguez Almeida (*LTUR* 1: 208) identifies it with the area later occupied by the temple of Claudius and called the *minor Caelius* at Mart. 12.18.16. Courtney 1989: 51, noting that second-declension diminutives in *-culus* are rare, follows Graevius 1696: 535 in emending the Ciceronian text to *Caeliolo*. However, the existence of examples of such forms in the classical period (Catull. 57.7 and Cels. 2.12.2: *lecticulus*; Cels. 2.17.9 *panniculus*; KS 1: 986 offers a full list), and particularly the semantic parallel in the diminutive of "mountain" in Char. *gramm.* p. 196.25 B (*mons monticulus*) and in the early second-century CE inscription Sent. *leg. Aug. pr. pr.* (*CIL* III 567) 17 and 19, provide sufficient grounds for retaining the unanimous reading of the manuscripts.

qui sacrificia gentilicia illo ipso in sacello stato loco anniversaria factitarint: Regular sacrifices that take place on behalf of a familial group (*gens*) are a subclass of the *sacra privata* (nn. on 8, 14): "private rites take place on behalf of individual people, their families, or their clans" (Fest. p. 245 M: *[sacra] privata, quae pro singulis hominibus, familiis, gentibus fiunt*). There are scattered references to individual Roman *gentes* during the late Republic holding annual sacrifices, such as that of the Fabii on the Quirinal (Liv. 5.46.2) or of the Julii for the god Vediovis (*ILLRP* 270). Cicero notes in *dom.* that one potentially disgraceful consequence of Clodius's being adopted by Fonteius (57n) is that it forced him to abandon the ancestral rites of the Claudian *gens* (*dom.* 35: *sacra Clodiae gentis*, with Nisbet 1939: 98). Smith 2006: 44–50 collects and assesses these references, noting how the preservation of gentilician rites was a special concern of the *pontifices*.

The phrase *stato loco* refers to the particular designation of this chapel as the appropriate, and presumably sole, location for performing these particular rites (for the importance of place, see the story of the Fabii cited above). While this phrase would appear otiose after the emphatic designation that precedes it—*illo ipso in sacello*—Wolf 1801: 352 notes that it allows Cicero to anticipate the reference to *loca* in the next sentence.

** ***anniversaria***: This is a conjecture of Naugerius 1519 for the masculine forms in the codices (*anniversari* P¹GH, *anniversarii* P²E). Parallels do exist for the adjective modifying people in an adverbial sense, e.g., Flor. *epit.* 1.12.1: *adsidui vero et anniversarii hostes ab Etruria fuere Veientes*. However, the adjective more often appears in factitive constructions in the accusative, as conjectured here; cf. the analogous word order and bracketing construction at *rep.* 2.12: *quos [ludos] tum primum anniversarios in circo facere instituisset*; Varro *rust.* 1.16.4: *coloni potius anniversarios habent vicinos, quibus imperent*.

quaerimus di immortales quae loca desiderent, quid significent, de quo loquantur?: The proleptic placement of the subject *di immortales* before the indirect question gives it emphasis (*OLS* 2: 983), underscoring Cicero's conception, as stressed elsewhere, that the prodigy represents the gods speaking directly to mortals. The first member of the tricolon contains a double reference: first, to the *locus* of the previous sentence regarding gentilicial sacrifices that have had to be abandoned; and second, to the wording of that portion of the response that this section treats (30: *de locis sacris, religiosis*).

a Sexto Serrano sanctissima sacella suffossa, inaedificata, oppressa, summa denique turpitudine foedata esse nescimus?: Cicero gives a third example of the violation of sacred shrines by a member of the elite which, like the previous two, is attested only here. As with Appius Claudius and Lucius Piso, Cicero had clear personal reasons for accusing Serranus of sacrilegious activities. Sextus Atilius Serranus (*RE* 70) was quaestor in 63, the year of Cicero's consulate, and tribune of the plebs in 57. Cicero alleges that he did Serranus great favors during his quaestorship (*p. red. ad Quir.* 12; cf. *Sest.* 72) which, contrary to Cicero's expectations, Serranus failed to reciprocate in his tribunate (*ad Q. fr.* 1.4.3=SB 4). At its outset, he withdrew support for Cicero's recall (*Sest.* 72, where Cicero alleges that he was bribed; cf. *Pis.* 35); in January he freed those gladiators of Clodius who had been imprisoned by Milo (*Sest.* 85; 34n); and in October he threatened to veto a senatorial edict concerning the restoration of Cicero's house (*Att.* 4.2.4=SB 74). Note the repetition of nine [s] sounds at the beginning of the sentence (with four more concluding it) and the use of the plural form *nescimus*. Since normal Ciceronian practice would have Serranus here being addressed for the first time as *Sex. Atilius* (7n), the alliteration (and consonance) seems intentional. For recommendations to avoid alliteration see *Rhet. Her.* 4.18; the catalogue of Ciceronian examples in Straub 1883: 131–134 does not include as extreme an example as this. Wilkinson 1963: 13 remarks that "there was one point on which all ancient critics were agreed—that an excess of sibilants was peculiarly cacophonous." Here the combination seems to convey exasperation and disdain (cf. 38n).

The indirect statement follows a familiar structure for this speech, with a tricolon describing the physical violation of the shrines capped by a fourth colon providing an overall generalization (28n). The first three participles follow the chronology of the desecration: first, the *sacella* are literally undermined (*OLD* s.v. *suffodio* 1), then built over (*inaedificata*; 31n), and finally access to them is blocked (for this sense of *opprimere* see *Mil.* 85: *obrutae arae... quas ille... substructionum insanis molibus oppresserat*; *OLD* s.v. 3a). The final verb, *foedo*, describes the metaphorical disgrace caused by the physical destruction and appears principally in poetry and post-Augustan prose (*ThLL* VI, 1 997.32–33 [F. Vollmer]). Lennon 2014: 31–32 notes that the verb denotes "an act of polluting, or of making something 'foul' or otherwise unclean" and that derivatives of *foedus*, which occur five more times in the speech, "appear to evoke physical repulsion or fear." The association with religious pollution causes it to sit logically as the climax (*denique*) of a series of negatively charged participles.

33

Cicero abruptly turns from the senate to address Clodius and to contrast once more the relative degrees of religious taint in each of their homes.

tu meam domum religiosam facere potuisti?: Cued by the juxtaposition of *nescimus / tu*, this sudden change of grammatical subject resumes the theme, brought up especially at 11–12, that Cicero's home is not one of the *loca religiosa* warned of in the response. The follow-up questions regarding Clodius's insanity and sacrilegious behavior indicate that Clodius's sheer presence can make a place *religiosus*—i.e., filled with religious taint (cf. 33: *quid habet mea domus religiosi nisi quod impuri et sacrilegi parietem tangit?*). The answer to the question posed here then is yes, he could, but not in a way sanctioned by Roman ritual.

The Roman rhetoricians call the technique used here *subiectio*, "a mock dialogue (and so a monologue) with question and answer (mostly with several questions and answers), included in the speech to enliven the line of thought" (Lausberg 1998: §§771–775, with examples). In this instance the answers increase the invective tone by highlighting various religious crimes of which Clodius is guilty.

Beginning with this question, interrogative pronouns and adjectives appear in first position in six consecutive clauses, moving from four feminine forms to two neuters. Six forms of the relative pronoun, also in varying cases and genders, constitute the replies. Such extensive repetition, with the introductory words often in polyptoton, occurs frequently in Cicero's orations at points of climax, although such a close accumulation of analogous forms and sounds is unparalleled. If one includes the capping question and the words *quidem* and *nisi quod* the letter "q" is repeated fifteen times in close succession. Compare (and contrast) *Clu.* 167: *quod autem tempus veneni dandi illo die, illa frequentia? per quem porro datum? unde sumptum? quae deinde interceptio poculi? cur non de integro autem datum?*; *Deiot.* 12: ***quantum*** *nomen illius fuerit,* ***quantae*** *opes,* ***quanta*** *in omni genere bellorum gloria,* ***quanti*** *honores populi Romani,* ***quanti*** *senatus,* ***quanti*** *tui quis ignorat?* The sound patterns are further enhanced by the homoioteleuton of the series of six pluperfect verbs in final position of each "answer": *amiseras…disturbaras…iusseras…scripseras…stupraras…conlocaras*. The relentless sequence hammers home the frequency of Clodius's crimes and is capped by a final rhetorical question of summation: "What religious pollution does my house have other than that it shares a party wall with someone impure and sacrilegious?" (*quid habet mea domus religiosi nisi quod impuri et sacrilegi parietem tangit?*).

** **quam amiseras**: *qua miseras* is the reading of P[1], *et qua amiseras* of the remaining major codices. As emended, this initial relative clause disturbs the parallelism of three consecutive relatives in the ablative, as well as the syntax, since one must skip over this clause to understand *domum* as the object of the next two verbs (*disturbaras, incendi iusseras*). If we read *[et] qua* with all major witnesses, then syntax is restored and sense is fine: "With what mind? [With that one] with which you had lost [my home]." However, although *amitto* can describe the loss of one's own home (Val. Fl. 4.448), the verb does not make good sense in describing the loss of a home at the hands of another. Furthermore, the speech's motif of Clodius's madness (e.g., 1n) fits well the idea here of Clodius "losing his mind" (for *mentem amittere* see Sen. *Herc. f.* 1259–1260, Filastr. 151.2). This would appear to be an instance where the text printed yields proper sense rather than a more elegant syntax.

qua disturbaras: The verb *disturbo* commonly takes as its object a word describing man-made structures, which makes it easy to understand *meam domum* here despite the disruption of the syntax (cf. 58, *dom.* 113; *ThLL* V,

1 1552.76–1553.8 [K. Nelz]). For the combination with *manus* see *dom*. 103, again describing the actions of Clodius and his men: *porticum… manibus vestris disturbare cuperetis.*

qua incendi iusseras: Cicero's mentions Clodius setting his home on fire also at *dom*. 62: *domus ardebat in Palatio non fortuito, sed oblato incendio* (see too 15, *dom*. 113, *Pis*. 26; Cicero refers to its general destruction at *dom*. 60, 103, 146, and see 58n). Tatum 1999: 158 details Clodius's historical justification for this destruction.

qua lege? quam ne in illa quidem impunitate tua scripseras: "During that time when you would have been unpunished" (*in illa quidem impunitate tua*) refers of course to Clodius's tribunate of 58; for his legislation see 11n. *ThLL* VII, 1 347.40–48 (V. Bulhart) gives several parallels for this sense of *illa* ("i. q. ὁ πρίν").

quo pulvinari? quod stupraras: By imagining a sacred couch that could have been used to mar the scrupulousness of the former site of his home, Cicero bends reality so as to connect Clodius once again with the disruption of the rites of the Bona Dea. Cicero uses *stupro* in his oratory only twice, both in allusion to this incident (the other is at *dom*. 125, in a literal sense). Gesner 1753: 278 cites for the metaphorical use *Att*. 1.18.3=SB 18: *constuprato… iudicio*, where it again refers to the Bona Dea scandal ("debauched trial," Shackleton Bailey 1965–1970: 1.175). Through these rare figurative applications of the verb Cicero characterizes Clodius as a practitioner of sexual violence that reaches beyond the human to violate religion and legal procedure. For the connotations of the violent sexual activity of *stuprum* and its associations with the sacred couch, see 8n.

quo simulacro? quod ereptum ex meretricis sepulcro ⟨in⟩ imperatoris monumento conlocaras: Cicero alleged that the statue to the goddess Libertas erected on the site of his home originally depicted a prostitute from Tanagra and had been stolen by Clodius's brother Appius Claudius Pulcher and brought to Rome (*dom*. 111–112; cf. *dom*. 51, 116, 131, *leg*. 2.42: *templum Licentiae*). The irony of the statue's origins is underscored by the use of *simulacrum*, which implies that the statue depicts a divinity (Dyck 2008: 193). For the widespread popularity during the Republic of repurposing Greek statues for a new Roman context, see Cicero's exchange with Atticus concerning the decoration of his Academy, e.g., *Att*. 1.3.2=SB 8, 1.4.3=SB 9, 1.6.2=SB 2, 1.8.2=SB 4, with Neudecker 1988: 8–18 and, more generally, Zanker 1979. The reuse of Greek funerary sculpture in particular would not have been surprising at this period, and apparent parallels from the early principate are extant (Bell 1998). E. Papi (*LTUR* 3: 188–189) surveys the theories concerning what form the entire shrine to Libertas may have taken; see too Berg 1997: 131–132, Begemann 2015.

The "monument of a general" is the Porticus Catuli, erected by Quintus Lutatius Catulus, consul in 102 (*RE* 7). As proconsul in 101, jointly with Marius he defeated the Germanic tribe of the Cimbri, who had invaded northern Italy. He was awarded a triumph and built as monuments a vowed temple to Fortuna Huiusce Diei in the Campus Martius and the Porticus Catuli on the Palatine, the latter adorned with spoils from his victory (*dom.* 102; Val. Max. 6.3.1; cf. 58). This portico occupied the site formerly containing the home of M. Fulvius Flaccus, who was executed in 121 for his support of Gaius Gracchus, after which his home was demolished (Roller 2010: 161–162 assesses Catulus's reason for choosing this site). Clodius acquired this property in 58, which appears to have been between his own house and that of Cicero (30n). He proceeded to alter the monument by incorporating into it one-tenth of Cicero's former home, erasing Catulus's name from the dedicatory inscription and, as this passage clearly implies, constructing the shrine to *Libertas* within it (on this last point see Nisbet 1939: 207–209). Following the decision of the *pontifices* in October 57, the senate decreed that the portico be restored at state expense according to its original dimensions (*Att.* 4.2.5=SB 74), a restoration that Clodius hindered through violent means (*Att.* 4.3.2=SB 75). Tatum 1999: 159–166 contains a comprehensive discussion, with citation of ancient sources and recent bibliography.

**The preposition *in* is supplied only by the *recentiores*, but *in* + ablative (or the locative) is the principal construction in Cicero's oratory for the more than one hundred occurrences of the verb *collocare* (exceptions include *Vatin.* 39: *aliis iam se locis conlocarunt*; *Cael.* 65: *quo loco collocati fuerant*). Its omission from the tradition is easily explained as haplography before *imperatoris*.

impuri et sacrilegi parietem tangit: The party wall (*paries*) referred to here is presumably one that Cicero formerly shared with Seius, but which now belongs to Clodius (Allen 1939: 140–141; on the proximity of Clodius's house to Cicero's, see 30n). Lennon 2014: 30–31 notes concerning the verb *tango* that "Contact with any impure person or substance can potentially lead to [religious] contamination, depending on context," a connotation that underscores the ideas behind *impuri et sacrilegi*. The combination of these two substantives also occurs at Apul. *met.* 9.9, interestingly of men who have stolen from the shrine of the Mater Magna.

itaque ne quis meorum imprudens introspicere tuam domum possit ac te sacra illa tua facientem videre, tollam altius tectum, non ut ego te despiciam, sed tu ne aspicias urbem eam quam delere voluisti: The sentence at first seems illogical. How will raising the roof of Cicero's home prevent members of his *familia* from looking into Clodius's house? Shackleton Bailey 1979: 268 explains well that they would have been looking into Clodius's windows from Cicero's roof, and so originally Clodius's house was higher. I do not see, however, the necessity of also following him in emending to ⟨*etiam*⟩ *altius* (Maslowski includes it in his apparatus but not his text).

The ironic use of *illa tua* instead of the more normal *ista* (KS 2: 1.620 with 622 Anm. 6) mocks Clodius's ritual behavior (see, e.g., nn. on 4 [*religiosus*] and 9 [*sacerdos*]) and perhaps even prompts his senatorial audience to wonder what precise rites these could be (57n). In particular, by saying that he does not wish members of his household to be witnesses—and that he is even willing to remodel his home to ensure it—Cicero intends his listeners to imagine them to entail, as in the Bona Dea incident, illicit sexual behavior. The allusion is especially pertinent since this sentence brings to a close the discussion resumed at 30 on the portion of the response DE LOCIS SACRIS RELIGIOSIS. Although adding a second reason for raising his roof is slightly illogical (Wolf 1801: 353: "Inepte additur alia causa, postquam dictum est, *ne quis meorum* etc."), it allows Cicero to end this section with a joke by playing on both the literal meaning of *despicere* ("to look down") and the figurative ("to look down upon, despise"); note too the paronomasia of *despiciam / aspicias*. For the rhetorical effect of humor here, compare the introductory n. to 9 (*responsum haruspicum*)–19.

The syntax of the sentence seems to end with *urbem* ("so that you may not look out on the city") and a non-favored clausula of choriamb + trochee (Keeline and Kirby 2019: 164 n. 21), but there follows unexpectedly the punchy conclusion *eam quam dēlērĕ vŏlŭīstī*, containing the favored clausula of (resolved) cretic plus trochee (2n).

34–35

Cicero turns to the section of the response mentioning *oratores* who have been killed. After quickly acknowledging the recent deaths of the Alexandrian ambassadors, he concentrates on two different instances of murder that implicate Clodius and Piso.

34 *sed iam haruspicum reliqua responsa videamus*: Following a series of seemingly random references to the portion of the response mentioning the violation of sacred and hallowed places Cicero returns to a discussion of the text proper (for this resumptive force of *sed* see LHS 2: 487a). The reference to the "remaining responses" implies that Cicero will discuss every portion of the response in this speech.

ORATORES: As his subsequent discussion makes clear (e.g., *ius legatorum*), Cicero here interprets *orator* in its original sense of "legate" (Varro *ling.* 7.41, Fest. p. 198 M; additional testimonia in Neuhauser 1958: 119–151; Linderski 1995b: 457–464 treats the word's eventual displacement by *legatus*). It is highly probable that Clodius interpreted the word in the same way in his *contio* (see below). The hypothesis of van den Bruwaene 1948: 90–92 that the response is a remnant of one produced in the early 80s to discredit the followers of Marius leads him to understand this clause as referring to the deaths in 87 of the orators M. Antonius, Julius Caesar Strabo, and Q. Lutatius Catulus. Setting aside other objections, his entire reconstruction rests on a view of the response as a partisan political document, a view to which I do not subscribe.

CONTRA IVS FASQVE: The Romans recognized as a component of international law (*ius gentium*; cf. 32n) the guarantee of foreign ambassadors to conduct their business without fear of harm. Coudry 2004: 555–560 maintains that this principle was stronger under the Republic than in the Greek world and was reinforced both by historical *exempla* and by the opinions of Roman jurists (see, e.g., Pompon. *dig.* 50.7.18, citing Q. Mucius Scaevola, an older contemporary of Cicero). Although the terms *ius* and *fas* are sometimes used synonymously, when juxtaposed *ius* denotes human law, and *fas* divine (Serv. *georg.* 1.269: '*fas et iura sinunt*': *id est divina humanaque iura permittunt: nam ad religionem fas, ad homines iura pertinent*; Isid. *orig.* 5.2.2; Oakley 1997–2005: 2.421; for the use of these terms in Roman law see Kaser 1971–1975: 1.23–26). Cicero's gloss on the pair in his own discussion would seem to follow this convention (34: *hominum praesidio... divino iure*), where the term *ius divinum*, as always, acts as a synonym for *fas* (Orestano 1939: 195–196, with n. 2; cf. 14: *et humano et divino iure*). Orestano 1939 traces the historical development of the terms *fas* and *ius* (both *divinum* and *humanum*); for the point under consideration here see especially 271, with n. 220.

de Alexandrinis esse video sermonem: Even from our limited historical perspective, the notorious incident of the Alexandrian ambassadors from the previous year would be the obvious inference for any contemporary to make regarding the response's assertion that "*oratores* have been killed contrary to divine and human law." In 57 an embassy of one hundred citizens of Alexandria, led by the Academic philosopher Dio, was on its way to the senate to request that it not restore to the throne Ptolemy Auletes, who was in Rome at the time. Several legates were murdered or beaten en route to Rome from the Bay of Naples, as well as in Rome, while others were bribed or intimidated not to complete their mission. The senate in late 57 did subsequently vote for Ptolemy's restoration, allegedly on account of bribes, but then revoked that decision when the Sibylline books advised against it. Only a few months before *har. resp.*, the issue resurfaced when Dio was murdered (Dio 39.12–16 offers the fullest ancient account; Wiseman 1985: 54–62 provides a clear narrative of the complex background, Coudry 2004: 558–559 of the legal complications). Cicero had reasons not to dwell on the obvious inference to be made from this portion of the response. As recently as the previous month, in his celebrated defense of Marcus Caelius Rufus, Cicero spoke on behalf of Romans who had been involved in the murders (Cic. *Cael.* 23–24, with Austin 1960: 152–153). Earlier, in late 57 or early 56, he successfully defended Publius Asicius against charges of murdering the Egyptian ambassadors (Crawford 1984: 138–140). As a result, it seems inevitable that Clodius would have made this link in his *contio* (Lenaghan 1969: 150 has reservations). While the vagueness of *sermo* discourages precise identification, Cicero's subsequent reference to Clodius (*quaero ab illo*) indicates that he was at least a prominent participant in this "talk"; see further Corbeill 2018: 174, 185–186.

quem ego non refuto: These four words represent an unusual but unavoidable admission on Cicero's part, an admission underscored by the emphatic use of *ego*. Given his role in defending men successfully on related charges (see previous n.), he could hardly deny before an audience of senators that the haruspical response might refer to the case of the Alexandrian ambassadors.

sic enim sentio, ius legatorum, cum hominum praesidio munitum sit, tum etiam divino iure esse vallatum: "I understand that the rights of embassies have been not only fortified by the safeguards of human beings but also protected by the ramparts of divine law." The verb *vallo*, when used metaphorically as here, refers to a stronger type of protection than does the more general *munio*, signifying that someone or something has been entirely surrounded, as by a Roman palisade (*vallum*; Liv. 33.5.5–12 provides a clear description). This contrast is supported by other cases in which the verbs are paired in a metaphorical sense, with word order again implying that *vallo* describes superior protection: *Tull.* 49: *[maiores nostri] non iniuria, quo magistratu [sc. tribunatu plebis] munitae leges sunt, eius magistratus corpus legibus vallatum esse voluerunt*; Val. Max. 2.2.1: *silent...salubritate munitum et vallatum undique*.

On the subjunctive form of all codices (*munitum sit*) rather than the infinitive, compare the close syntactic parallel at *leg. agr.* 3.13: *iam totam legem intellegetis cum ad paucorum dominationem scripta sit tum ad Sullanae adsignationis rationes esse accommodatissimam* (Manuwald 2018: 102 emends *scripta sit* to *scriptam*), with LHS 2: 625 ("Der Unterschied zwischen dem partitiven und dem koordinierenden *cum-tum* zeigt sich in der or[atio] obliqua darin, daß im ersten Fall der *cum*-Satz stets im Konj. steht... während bei rein koordinierendem *cum-tum* beiden Glieder wie Aussagesätze behandelt werden"; cf. Lebreton 1901: 345–346; Orlandini and Poccetti 2017: 77–78). LHS also notes that the second clause is often, though not always, accompanied by a strengthening particle such as *vero*, *maxime*, or, as here, *etiam*.

** *vallatum*: The major codices read *velatum* here, which has no appropriate sense. Since, as mentioned in the previous note, one expects a verb with a meaning analogous to *munire*, but more emphatic, the best alternative is to read *vallatum* with some *recentiores*.

quaero ab illo: A person hearing Cicero's claims would assume this anonymous tribune to be Clodius. Lenaghan 1969: 151 notes that the actions here described of releasing prisoners into the forum is attested only for his satellite Sextus Serranus, tribune of 57 (*Sest.* 85: *gladiatores ex praetoris comitatu comprensi, in senatum introducti, confessi, in vincla coniecti a Milone, emissi a Serrano: mentio nulla. forum corporibus civium Romanorum constratum caede nocturna*...; 32n), but elsewhere in *Pro Sestio* Cicero attributes what is apparently the same event to Clodius's tribunate (*Sest.* 95: *in tribunatu carcerem totum in forum effudit*; cf. 78). Furthermore, the address to Clodius after this sentence—*nec confero nunc in te unum omnia*—strongly implies that the activity that Cicero has just described is to be attributed to Clodius. If these references are to the same event in January 57 (Kaster 2006: 315), when Clodius was no longer tribune, this would appear to be another instance of intentional vagueness, conflating Clodius with his henchman so that he shares blame for their actions. The technique is ubiquitous in Ciceronian oratory; for some specific instances, see Corbeill 1996: 112, 119–124; 35n.

indices: The reading of P; the remaining major codices have *iudices*, which makes no sense in the context. Maslowski includes in his apparatus the conjecture *audaces* of Lambinus 1566: 704=1830: 265–266, which supplies good sense and is not so difficult paleographically (Lambinus in fact prefers *iudicatos* ["quod magis probo"] but in the Republic the substantive is attested only for condemned debtors; *de orat.* 2.255; *ThLL* VII, 2 621.8–21 [F. Oomes]). Cicero frequently employs the adjective *audax* as a substantive (Merguet 1877–1884: 346–347; cf. *ThLL* II, 1245.18–1246.13 [O. Hey]). For the sense of *indices* see next note.

qui omnis indices tribunus e carcere in forum effudit: Other descriptions of this or similar events in *Pro Sestio* do not mention informers (*indices*). Cicero does, however, use *index* to describe the followers of both Catiline and Clodius, where the word has the sense of "spy" (*Sest.* 95; *Mur.* 49 with Adamietz 1989: 188).

cuius arbitrio sicae nunc omnes atque omnia venena tractantur: Cicero underscores the current threat of Clodius and his henchmen through the use of the present tense (supplemented by *nunc*), the frequentative suffix *-to* (*tractantur*), and the unnecessary repetition of *omnes / omnia*. The word *sica* has particularly ominous overtones since in Ciceronian oratory these daggers are always employed against the state and its representatives (e.g., *Catil.* 1.16, *Mil.* 37; Dyck 2008: 96). Cicero's formulation also recalls the title of the *lex Cornelia de sicariis et veneficiis*, passed by Sulla in 82 BCE, which covered arson, murder, and theft, or the intent to commit any of these crimes (6n). This was the law under which occurred the prosecutions defended by Cicero in his extant speeches *S. Rosc.* and *Clu.* Although the precise phrase *sicas tractare* appears only here, the verb frequently occurs to indicate the "wielding" of various other weapons (e.g., Liv. 7.32.11, Hor. *ep.* 1.18.52–53, Ov. *fast.* 5.397). Conversely, *venena tractare* has a parallel only at Hor. *carm.* 2.13.8–10 to describe the witch Medea (*venena Colcha...tractavit*). Compare Hor. *carm.* 1.37.26–28, of Cleopatra, which neatly combines the act of piercing the flesh and poisoning: *fortis et asperas / tractare serpentes, ut atrum / corpore conbiberet venenum.*

qui cum Hermarcho Chio syngraphas fecit, ecquid sciat unum acerrimum adversarium Hermarchi, Theodosium, legatum ad senatum a civitate libera missum sica percussum: For *syngrapha* see 29n. Hermarchos (*RE* 2), Theodosius, and the incidents described are mentioned only here, although the context suggests that Theodosius was a legate from Chios (*RE*² 5: 1929 [F. Münzer]). Designation as a free state (*civitas libera*) allowed a city to be governed by its own laws and exempted it from a number of impositions, such as Roman garrisons and tribute; precise privileges and duties varied from state to state (Lintott 1993: 36–40; for Chios in particular see Sherk 1969: 351–353). For the construction *unum acerrimum* see 49n.

35 nec confero nunc in te unum omnia: "And yet I am not now attributing everything to you alone" (for this adversative sense of initial *nec* see KS 2:

2.42d). Even if his listeners were meant to understand some of the preceding crimes to have been perpetrated by Serranus, Cicero here addresses Clodius and implies that in fact all the preceding allegations had been directed at him.

hoc et tu tibi confidis magis et nos prope iure diffidimus: *Hoc* is ablative, "for this reason," that is, because there are so many criminal types around. The adverb *prope* helps strike a defiant tone as an answer to *magis*: despair would "almost" be justified, but not quite. As one would expect, the contrasting pair *confido / diffido* appears frequently throughout Latinity, and is especially favored by Cicero (e.g., *Q. Rosc.* 11, *Clu.* 63, *Sest.* 135). Contrary to *ThLL* V, 1 1101.57–58 (S. Tafel) *diffidimus* appears here in an absolute sense ("we lack confidence").

Platorem ex Orestide, quae pars Macedoniae libera est: Cicero gives additional details about this incident in his account at *Pis.* 83–84, written in the following year. While proconsul of Macedonia, Piso received lavish hospitality at Plator's home and in exchange invited him to visit in Thessalonica. There, as a result of a bribe from the people of Dyrrachium, Piso ordered a doctor to kill Plator by opening his veins even though Plator had requested the traditional punishment of a beheading. He also flogged to death Plator's aged companion, Pleuratus. Nisbet 1961: 151–152 provides more details.

Plator is a well-attested Illyrian name (Schulze 1933: 30 n. 3), as suits his homeland Orestis, a region of western Macedonia inhabited by the Orestae people (*RE* 18: 960–965 [J. Schmidt]; Talbert *et al.* 2000: Map 49). In 196 the Orestae were given free status by the Romans for their cooperation in the war against Philip V (Polyb. 18.47.6 with Walbank 1957–1979: 2.616; Liv. 33.34.6). It is not attested to what extent they may have been affected by Aemilius Paulus's reorganization of Macedonia in 167 (Liv. 45.29.4–6) but this passage makes clear that they retained their free status. Cicero stresses this status in order to indicate that Piso, as proconsul of Macedonia, should have had only limited authority over the citizens of Orestis (Lintott 1993: 39–40).

legatum: Plator should be an ambassador for this example to suit the context of *har. resp.*, although Cicero does not mention this fact in *In Pisonem*. As Nisbet 1961: 152 notes, however, in that account the phrases "*fide tua* and *Pleuratus eius comes*... suit the story of a deputation."

ad nostrum, ut se ipse appellavit, 'imperatorem': If the senate had not already realized that Cicero refers to Piso, this allusion would have banished any lingering doubt. Cicero enjoys claiming that Piso had unjustly been hailed as *imperator* by his troops, referring to him by this term multiple times, always in a sarcastic context (*prov.* 4, 7, 15; *Pis.* 38, 44, 53–55, 61, 70, 91–93, 97; *ad Q. fr.* 3.1.24=SB 21). An inscription from Samothrace, however, attests that Piso had in fact received some sort of formal recognition of this title (*IG* XII, 8: 242 a,b): [ἡ βουλὴ καὶ ὁ δῆμος Λεύκιον Καλπόρνιον] Λευκίου υ[ἱὸν Πείσ]ωνα τὸν αὐτοκράτορ[α καὶ πάτ]ρωνα τῆς πόλεως : "The people and council [honor] Lucius Calpurnius Piso, son of Lucius, *imperator* and patron of the city"; see

Bloch 1940: 485–490 and Nisbet 1961: 160. Cicero mentions a trip by Piso to Samothrace at *Pis.* 89, which he may have made in order to participate in the mysteries there (Bloch 1940: 488–489). For independent assessments of Piso's proconsulship, see Nisbet 1961: 172–180, Goldmann 2012: 154–162.

propter pecuniam, quam ab eo extorquere non poterat: This differs from Cicero's account in *Pis.*, where he says that Piso was paid by the people of Dyrrachium to dispose of Plator (83: *accepta pecunia a Dyrrachinis ob necem hospitis tui Platoris*) and that Plator was thrown into prison so that he would die a less honorable death.

legato, socio, amico, libero foedissime et crudelissime venas incideret: The sequence *legato, socio, amico, libero* is notable for its homoioteleuton and the identical number of syllables in each word. In terms of content, the violation of any of these alliances would have been disgraceful enough; the fact that Piso violated all four makes the murder all the more heinous. The combination of superlative adverbs that follows further enhances the suspense about what this doctor did, pointing as they do to how he violates principles of both religion (*foedissime*; 32n) and humanity.

The phrase *venas incidere* also describes Plator's death at *Pis.* 83. In later Latin it appears in texts describing the action of doctors and practitioners of folk medicine (e.g., Cels. 2.10.1, 7.15.1, and often; Scrib. Larg. 16; Plin. *nat.* 29.126) or to describe suicide (e.g., Vell. 2.22.2, Tac. *ann.* 16.19.1, Suet. *Cal.* 38.4).

secures suas cruentari scelere noluit: That is, by severing Plator's head as he had requested (*Pis.* 83). Although the execution of the sons of Brutus, the first consul, is the only instance of capital punishment recorded within the city of Rome during the Republican period (Liv. 2.5.8, D. H. 5.8.5, Plut. *Publ.* 6.3), Mommsen 1899: 916–918 notes that public decapitations were regularly staged outside the city by promagistrates. Cicero pretends sarcastically that Piso did not use this traditional form of execution in order not to sully the axes that were bundled in the fasces and so represented his proconsular authority, implying instead that Piso intentionally chose a punishment that would be more drawn out (cf. Cicero's depiction of Verres's cruelty at *Verr.* 2.5.118–120). Nisbet 1961: 152 offers a more generous interpretation: "Even if Cicero's account is not fictitious, this method of execution avoided the pain and publicity of the *mos maiorum*, and must be considered a concession to Plator."

nomen quidem populi Romani tanto scelere contaminavit: With the particle *quidem* Cicero ironically contrasts Piso's concern for bloodying his fasces with his lack of concern for staining Rome's religious purity (for "adversative" *quidem* see Solodow 1978: 75–82). The words *scelus* and *contaminare* convey notions of religious pollution (nn. on 5, 26).

ipsius supplicio: This must refer to expiation through punishment of Piso. Watts 1923: 361 takes it to be Clodius's punishment because he interprets the *ille* of the previous sentence to refer to him, surely wrongly given the account at

Pis. 83–84. Still, Watts does isolate a problem. What does Piso's punishment for murdering an ambassador have to do with anything? See next note.

quales hunc carnifices putamus habere, qui etiam medicis suis non ad salutem sed ad necem utatur?: The pronoun *hunc* would seem to refer, as it has previously, to Clodius, present in the senate (contrast *ille* at 35, appropriate since one would assume that Piso is in Macedonia at this time). The sentence's close, however, makes this identification impossible, since it is of course the doctor of Piso, not Clodius, who brings about the death of Plator. This seems to be yet another case of rhetorical slippage, by which the close association of Clodius and Piso causes their actions to be confused and even conflated (34n; cf. 5n, on Ligus). Suetonius points up a similar irony in his account of how Nero used doctors to "care for" hesitant suicides (Suet. *Nero* 37.2: *medicos admovebat qui cunctantes continuo curarent: ita enim vocabatur venas mortis gratia incidere*).

36

The next clause of the response treats the breaking of oaths. Cicero argues that this must apply to the judges who had been bribed to acquit Clodius during the Bona Dea trial in 61.

FIDEM IVSQVE IVRANDVM NEGLECTVM: In his interpretation of this clause, which he implies follows immediately upon the previous charge (36: *recitemus quid sequatur*), Cicero construes the subject as a hendiadys, with the first part representing the abstract concept behind an oath, the second its concrete administration (1n): "the honesty of oath-taking has been neglected." Compare *off.* 3.104: *qui ius... iurandum violat, is fidem violat* ("Whoever violates an oath violates trust"; Ogilvie 1965: 103: "*fides* is the guarantee of *iusiurandum*"). For the same pairing see *off.* 3.43 (*contra ius iurandum ac fidem*), citing Enn. *scaen.* 403.

quid sit per se ipsum: For *esse* in the sense of "signify" see *OLD* s.v. 18b. The prepositional phrase *per se ipsum* ("by itself") indicates that to explain this portion of the response Cicero needs additional information, which he proceeds to supply.

ex eo quod sequitur suspicor: Shackleton Bailey deletes as a gloss the entire phrase *ex eo quod sequitur*, although it is attested in the best manuscripts (1985: 146; cf. his reevaluation at 1987: 276). This clause is, however, anticipated by the preceding *hoc quid sit per se ipsum*: "It isn't easy for me to explain what this means by itself, but <u>from what follows</u> I imagine...." The reference is to 37, the clause of the response that succeeds this one on breaking oaths: *SACRIFICIA VETVSTA OCCVLTAQVE MINVS DILIGENTER FACTA POLLVTAQVE*. The verb *suspicor* ("I imagine") is repeated in the next sentence (*suspicer*) and in the noun form *suspicio* in 37. Cicero affects coy uncertainty in an interpretive context where he is far from dubious (cf., e.g., 37: *quis praeter hunc unum? obscure dicitur quae sacra polluta sint?*). In Roman as in modern practice, this feigned

214   *Commentary*

ignorance sets up the punchline for the joke that follows. Compare the ironic use of *credo* (2n).

de tuorum iudicum manifesto periurio: With *tuorum* Cicero returns attention to Clodius, last addressed at 35. Clodius is ever at the forefront of the mind of Cicero, and therefore of his senatorial audience. Cicero alludes here to Clodius's acquittal after the Bona Dea scandal by a jury vote of thirty-one to twenty-five; Cicero of course was convinced that bribery was involved, with Crassus the primary supplier of funds. This charge gives the possessive adjective *tuorum* a sarcastic edge—the judges "belonged" to Clodius (*Att.* 1.16.5, 10=SB 16; *In Clod. et Cur.* frg. 30 [Crawford]; Plut. *Cic.* 29.8; Schol. Cic. Bob. p. 85.32–34, p. 90.20–30; for a balanced assessment of Cicero's charge see Tatum 1999: 82–84). Members of a Roman jury swore oaths in advance of a case (*off.* 3.43–44, Ps. Ascon. *Verr.* 1.17 p. 210.13–14: *iurabant in leges iudices, ut obstricti religione iudicarent*; Greenidge 1901a: 474). The use of *peri̱urium* initiates an etymological play on the *IVS IVRANDVM* of the response—*peri̱urium*, *coni̱urasti*—thereby linking Clodius to the transgression not only logically but etymologically.

quibus olim erepti essent nummi nisi a senatu praesidium postulassent: In response to threats of violence from Clodius's supporters, the jurors had asked that a bodyguard accompany them on the day that the verdict was to be delivered. The senate duly granted this request (*Att.* 1.16.5; Plut. *Cic.* 29.6; for the nature of this *praesidium*, see Lintott 1968: 89–92). Cicero recalls here a witticism made by Q. Lutatius Catulus soon after the trial, which he related to his friend Atticus in July 61 more directly than here but using much the same words: "When Catulus had seen one of the jurors he said 'Why did you all request a bodyguard from us? Were you afraid that your money would be stolen from you?'" (*Att.* 1.16.5=SB 16: *quorum [iudicum] Catulus cum vidisset quendam, "quid vos" inquit "praesidium a nobis postulabatis? an ne nummi vobis eriperentur timebatis?"*). The allusiveness of the reference indicates that the joke, now nearly five years old, had become a favored chestnut, the authorship of which was well known (cf. Sen. *epist.* 97.6, Plut. *Cic.* 29.8, Schol. Cic. Bob. p. 90.29–30). Such an interpretation is preferable to that of Lenaghan 1969: 152: "It is quite natural that Cicero should transmit this quip as if it were his own."

quod sic statuo: This causal clause, anticipated by *haec*, is added to govern the indirect statement that follows since it is rare for *causa est* to govern acc. + inf. (KS 2: 1.695 and LHS 2: 359 cite only Vitruv. 9.1.16).

** **insigne periurium et te ipsum tamen in crimen ab iis** *quibuscum coniurasti non vocari*: This is a difficult textual problem; **PGE** read for the underlined portion *insigne periurium et te ipsum tamen in periurium et te ipsum inprime (im- G) ab his*; **H** reads *insigne periurium et te ipsum tamen in periurium inprime ab his*.

Madvig 1871–1884: 3.225–226 removes the second *et te ipsum* in **PGE** as dittography and concludes that from the resulting *in periurium prime* "is easily made" ("facile fit") *in periuri crimen*, since once *crimen* had been corrupted, *periuri* became *periurium*. This does make sense, in which case H perhaps had what we have in **PGE** and removed only *et te ipsum* because of dittography. Merguet cites ten other examples of *in crimen vocare* in Cicero's oratory (for the genitive of the charge, see *Balb*. 5 and *Scaur*. frg. 3). Maslowski, following Klotz 1915: 142, prints *in [periurium] crimen*, and Courtney 1989: 51 convincingly justifies the deletion of *periurium* on the basis of the size of a column of the archetype ("21–22 letters or slightly longer," following Clark 1918: 272–280). He conjectures that the two consecutive lines read *periurium et te ipsum tamen in / periurium et te ipsum inprime* (the scribe realized his mistake with *te ipsum*, at which point he copied the corruption of *in crimen*). This reconstruction also explains the absence of the second *tamen*.

quibuscum coniurasti: Elsewhere in his orations Cicero uses the verb *coniuro* only to describe the actions of slaves or of those involved in the Catilinarian conspiracy. Its use here to refer to the collusion of judges supports the notion that the verb occurs here for the sake of a pun with *ius iurandum*. As Ferratius 1729: 395 observes, although Clodius perjured himself at the trial, he nonetheless kept his promise to pay bribes out to the jurors.

37–39

To confirm that the breaking of oaths refers to the Bona Dea incident, Cicero turns to the accompanying clause of the response on the violation of "ancient and secret rites." Additional evidence that Clodius violated the will of the gods during that affair lies in the madness that they have inflicted on him once a human jury was found incapable of reaching a guilty verdict. The section closes with the madness of Clodius being compared to famous instances of madness in literature.

37 haec esse subiuncta: When used in reference to written texts, the verb *subiungo* suggests subordination or some sort of desirable textual addition: Plin. *nat. praef.* 33: *quid singulis contineretur libris huic epistulae subiunxi* (describing a table of contents); Quint. *inst*. 3.9.5: *prooemio non narrationem subiungit sed propositionem*; Serv. Auct. *Aen*. 4.384: *debuit "absens" "quamquam" subiungere, ut esset "quamquam absens"* ("Vergil should have added *quamquam* to *absens*, so as to yield *quamquam absens*"; this use occurs often in the Servian tradition). Such a meaning fits the context here, since Cicero has just referred to this particular clause of the response as providing supplemental information for his own interpretation (36n).

** **in haruspicum responso haec esse subiuncta**: The phrase *in haruspicum responsum* is the reading of all codices (E reads *subiecta* for the verb). Shackleton Bailey 1987: 276, following Baiter in Orelli 1856: 917, notes that *subiungo* followed by *in* + acc. seems unattested elsewhere and so emends to the dative *responso*, deleting *in*. The other two uses of *subiungo* in the speeches are followed by *sub* + acc. (*Verr*. 2.1.55, *leg. agr*. 2.98). A full search of PHI confirms that the dative is the rule (e.g., *de orat.* 1.218: *placet omnis artis oratori subiungere*; *orat.* 94), even in parallel contexts of talking about a text (see citations in previous note). For the simplex form *iungo*, ThLL VII, 2 657.60–64 (H. v. Kamptz) records the earliest example of *in* + acc. in Grattius, then Gaius. A more plausible suggestion is to read *in haruspicum responso*, with the phrase dependent upon *video* rather than *esse subiuncta* ("I see in the haruspical response"; I owe this suggestion to Thomas Keeline). The parallels justify emending the construction of *in* + acc.; changing *responsum* to the ablative is simplest paleographically.

SACRIFICIA VETVSTA OCCVLTAQVE <u>MINVS DILIGENTER FACTA POLLVTAQVE</u>: The formulation echoes the earlier part of the response regarding the disruption of games (21: LVDOS <u>MINVS DILIGENTER FACTOS POLLVTOSQVE</u>). The underlined portion does not seem intended to recall any sacral formulations (all extant instances of *minus diligenter* elsewhere occur in non-religious contexts). The tautology of *sacrificium facere* is common throughout Latin and is found elsewhere in this speech (12: *quod fit*; 32: *sacrificia…factitarint*), particularly in the litany at 37, where *[sacrificium] fit* is repeated five times in short succession. The verb *polluo*, although surprisingly rare, usually describes in prose authors the defilement of religious rites (ThLL X, 1 2567.48–67 [P. Pieroni]; Fantham 2012: 60), with a particular concentration in *har. resp.*, where it governs *sacra et religiones* (8), *ludi* (21, 22, 23, 24, 25, 27), *caerimoniae* (29), *sacra* (37), and, as here, *sacrificia* (cf. Serv. Auct. Aen. 4.234). Van den Bruwaene 1948: 89–90 implausibly believes that this clause refers to events in 88 BCE (cf. 34n).

haruspices haec loquuntur an patrii penatesque dii?: When a disjunctive question conveys a concise contrast, as here between priests and gods, the conjunction *an* does not typically have a question word such as *-ne* or *utrum* attached to the first part (KS 2: 2.525c). As with single questions introduced by *an*, the second part in this instance "serves as a supplement, correction, or specification of the preceding words of the speaker/writer" (OLS 1: 331). It is not simply the Etruscan priests who recognize the polluted rites of the Bona Dea; Cicero offers the correction that it is the Roman gods who are in fact speaking. For the identification of the response with the gods, who speak through the prodigy to the *haruspices*, see 10n.

Nisbet 1939: 193–194 argues that this and the other pairings of *patrii* and *penates* in Cicero (*Verr.* 2.4.17; *Sul.* 86; *dom.* 144; *Sest.* 45) represent two distinct groups: the public, ancestral gods and the collection of *penates* found in individual homes; for both aspects see Weinstock 1937 (esp. 421–422) and 12n. By contrast, Berry 1996a: 306 considers the expression tautologous and "that by *penates* Cicero means the *publici penates*" (cf. Dubourdieu 1989: 98). Considering that the city *penates* were held in the temple of Vesta (Tac. *ann.* 15.41.1), and that the ritual of the Bona Dea violated by Clodius involved rites in honor of the *penates* (12), Berry's interpretation has attractions. Since, however, the combination is used here in a context where Cicero at other points in the speech refers to the gods as a collective (*di immortales*: 11, 32, 53), I prefer to see not redundancy, but a reference to two sets of deities, those of the state and those of the household, which in total represent all deities that speak through the prodigy. There is also a certain piquancy in giving voice to domestic *penates* in a speech involving the fate of Cicero's home.

multi enim sunt, credo, in quos huius malefici suspicio cadat: The meaning of this part of the response, Cicero contends, is in fact blatantly obvious in its application not to many, but to one individual (for the ironic use of parenthetical *credo*, see 2n). The noun *suspicio* adds to the irony (36n). As he does frequently in his oratory, Cicero uses the noun *maleficium* to describe the misdeed of the improper sacrifice as a synonym for the rhetorically colorless synonym *delictum* (*ThLL* VIII 174.62–63 [K. Brink] lists 72 occurrences in the orations, 16 in *inv.*, and 32 in *Rhet. Her.*, as opposed to only 3 in the *philosophica*; Mommsen 1899: 11 n. 4). There may also be wordplay in describing the improper *sacrificium* as a *maleficium*. For the idiom *in aliquem cadere* see 53n.

quid planius, quid religiosius, quid gravius dici potest?: Cicero "answers" this rhetorical question by quoting the response: VETVSTA OCCVLTAQVE. Forms of the adverb *plane* often signal irony (*ThLL* X, 1 2346.71–73 [I. Reineke]), and there may be further irony in the fact that these "secret" rites could not be revealed "with more clarity."

Fraenkel 1968: 190–191 notes that the rhythm spondee + iamb (including resolution into anapest + iamb), although normally undesirable as a clausula, occurs in Cicero with exceptional frequency in short cola, particularly lists, and especially in short questions, as here (*quĭd plānĭŭs*; note the analogous rhythm in the rest of the sentence: *quid rĕlĭgĭōsĭŭs /quid gravius dīcī pŏtēst*). A non-interrogative example occurs at 60: *iām nōn pŏtēst*.

Lentulum, gravem oratorem et disertum: Lucius Cornelius Lentulus Crus (*RE* 218) was the principal speaker for the prosecution in the Bona Dea trial of 61, in which role he was joined by Cn. Cornelius Lentulus Marcellinus and L. Cornelius Lentulus Niger (Schol. Cic. Bob. p. 85.16, 89.25–26; Val. Max. 4.2.5). As praetor in 58 he was an expected ally of Cicero in the days preceding his exile (*ad Q. fr.* 1.2.16=SB 2; *Pis.* 77). Elected to the consulship for the fateful year of 49, he passed with his fellow consul the senatorial decree that precipitated civil war. Fleeing to Egypt after the Battle of Pharsalus, he was executed in prison by Ptolemy XIII in September 48 (Caes. *civ.* 3.104.3; Plut. *Pomp.* 80.4; Oros. *hist.* 6.15.28).

This is the only fragment we have of Lentulus's oratory; the one parallel in Latin outside this speech for either *occultus* or *vetustus* used to describe the Bona Dea rites is in the third-century antiquarian Cornelius Labeo's reference to a *ritus occultior* of the goddess (Macrob. *Sat.* 1.12.21). At *Brut.* 268 Cicero offers a mixed assessment of Lentulus as an orator that is not inconsistent with his description here: *satis erat fortis orator, si modo orator, sed cogitandi non ferebat laborem; vox canora, verba non horrida sane, ut plena esset animi et terroris oratio; quaereres in iudiciis fortasse melius, in re publica quod erat esse iudicares satis* ("he had sufficient energy as an orator—if he was in fact an orator—but he didn't tolerate the labor of thinking. His voice was melodious, his words not at all unpolished, so that his speech was both energetic and frightful. Maybe you would look for something better for the courtroom, but you would consider what he did have as sufficient for politics"). For the "brave men and true" (*gravem oratorem ac disertum*) construction see 46n.

ex Etruscis libris in te conversa atque interpretata: For the collocation of the two verbs see Quint. *decl.* 313.7: *perniciosum sit interpretari legem et ad ingenia utriusque [sc.* defendant and prosecutor*] converti*. Similarly, Cicero is saying that the words of the response have been interpreted and, as a result of that interpretation, redirected from their Etruscan source to apply to Clodius (for this use of *converto* see 47). Although *interpretor* can mean "translate" (Liv. 23.11.4, 45.29.3; it is emended out of *leg.* 2.29), it is unlikely to have such a meaning here, since Cicero nowhere else wishes to acknowledge that the response has been rendered into Latin from Etruscan, presumably so that the text can appear as objective as possible (cf. 53n; for the *libri Etrusci* see Introduction E.1). Similarly, no agency is ascribed to who is doing the interpreting since, as he has just implied, the response represents an objective text whose interpretation is apparent to all.

etenim quod sacrificium tam vetustum est quam hoc quod a regibus aequale huius urbis accepimus?: Although evidence for the cult of Bona Dea can be traced back no further than the first century BCE, written sources do claim an earlier, mythical existence. Plutarch equates her rites with the Greek Gynaeceia, claiming her as one of Dionysus's mothers, while in Phrygia she was the mother of King Midas (*Caes.* 9.3; cf. *Quaest. Rom.* 20.268e; for the Greek syncretism see De Sanctis 1953: 278–280). In Rome she became a Dryad identified as either the wife or daughter of Faunus (Brouwer 1989: 324–327 has a full listing of sources). Propertius, perhaps following Varro, imagines her cult as preexisting Hercules's establishment of the *Ara Maxima*, which would make it older than the city of Rome (4.9 with Hutchinson 2006: 205). While it is of course clearly to Cicero's advantage to stress the antiquity of the cult, the researches of the first-century BCE antiquarians Butas (*RE* 2), and Sextus Clodius (*RE* 13), in addition to Varro, make clear that her origins were also the subject of contemporary speculation (Macrob. *Sat.* 1.12.27=Varro frg. 218 Cardauns; Arnob. *nat.* 5.18). Staples 1998: 32–36 analyzes Bona Dea's antiquity through the lens of gender.

non solum curiosos oculos excludit sed etiam errantis: For the notion that not only willful but also accidental viewing of secret rites constitutes a violation, see 8n. A passage in Lactantius's third-century CE treatise *Institutiones Divinae*, in which he discusses those who strive to discover the secrets of divine providence, contains several resemblances to this portion of *har. resp.*

(3.20.2–4; for his familiarity with Cicero's depiction of Clodius more generally, see *inst.* 1.10.14). The parallel contexts, combined with verbal echoes, make it almost certain that Lactantius knows at least this portion of the speech (Bryce 1990: 33–34, noting only the parallel with *curiosos oculos*, is more skeptical); there is no disputing that Lactantius's teacher Arnobius frequently referred to it (20n). I have printed in bold the imitations in Lactantius, with those portions of the speech corresponding most closely indicated afterward in parentheses: *in quo illos non excordes tantum fuisse arbitror, sed etiam inpios, quod in secreta caelestis illius providentiae* **curiosos oculos** (37: <u>curiosos oculos</u>) *voluerint inmittere. Romae et in plerisque urbibus scimus esse quaedam* **sacra quae aspici a viris nefas habeatur** (8: <u>sacra quae viri oculis ne imprudentis quidem aspici fas est</u>). *abstinent igitur* **aspectu** (8: <u>non solum aspectu virili... violarit</u>) *quibus contaminare illa non licet, et si forte* **vel errore vel casu quopiam vir aspexit**, *primo poena eius, deinde* **instauratione sacrificii** (cf. imitation of Arnobius in 21n) *scelus expiatur. quid his facias qui inconcessa scrutari volunt? nimirum multo sceleratiores qui arcana mundi et hoc caeleste templum profanare inpiis disputationibus quaerunt quam qui aedem Vestae aut* **Bonae Deae** *aut Cereris* **intraverit** (37: <u>intrare</u>). **quae penetralia quamvis adire viris non liceat** (37: <u>quod... sacrificium... nemo umquam adiit... vir</u>; 44: <u>quo eum adire fas non fuerat</u>), *tamen a viris fabricata sunt.* Cf. also 3.20.7: **non enim descendit aliquis e caelo** (62: <u>nolite... id putare accidere posse... ut</u> *deus aliqui delapsus de caelo coetus hominum adeat*).

non modo improbitas sed ne imprudentia quidem: Cicero frequently uses an abstract noun in place of a pronoun or noun describing a person (Lebreton 1901: 42–49 for numerous instances); cf. 42: *in domesticis... germanitatis stupris*. The abstractions echo in syntax and sense the concrete reference to the eyes that has preceded and make clear, if not so already, the association with Clodius; for the use of feminine grammatical genders, see 6n.

quod quidem sacrificium nemo ante P. Clodium omni memoria violavit: According to Prop. 4.9.61–62 Hercules had, before the founding of Rome, broken into a sanctuary of the Bona Dea to drink from a stream inside. Strictly speaking, however, he did not disrupt a *sacrificium*.

Cicero presents the main verbs in this passage in descending order of sacrilegiousness, from violation (*violavit*) to illicit entry (*adiit*) to neglect (*neglexit*) to witnessing from afar (*aspicere*), in order to end with one of the main points of this section, namely, that even a minor infringement constitutes a major offense.

nemo vir: The point, of course, is that women are welcome at the ceremonies but since *nemo*, as a noun of epicene gender, does not specify sex, Cicero adds *vir* (cf. 8n). Note that in Cicero *nemo*, not *nullus*, is always the adjective when the noun modified designates a person (LHS 2: 204–205; cf. the frequent, though tautological, *nemo homo*).

quod [sacrificium] fit per virgines Vestalis, fit pro populo Romano, fit in ea domo quae est in imperio, fit incredibili caerimonia: The Vestals supervised the ritual of the Bona Dea, and this seems to be the one rite in which they were in charge of the actual sacrifice (Wildfang 2001: 250–253). The common formula *pro populo [Romano]* indicates that the festival was celebrated for the welfare of the Roman state (cf. 12: *pro salute populi Romani*; ThLL X 2720.33–39 [M. Ottink]; Wissowa 1912: 217 n. 3, 398–399) and it appears frequently to characterize her rites (e.g., *Att.* 1.13.3=SB 13; *leg.* 2.21; *Iuv.* 9.117; Ascon. *Mil.* p. 49.16–17 Clark). For the requirement that the ritual take place at the home of a man holding *imperium*, see 4n. The final part of this tetracolon on the "unbelievable ceremony" may seem a misstatement, considering that Cicero refers to mystery rites that men could not have witnessed; nevertheless, ancient sources preserve several details concerning the rituals involved (for *caerimoniae* see 8n). Brouwer 1989: 369 provides a concise summary.

cuius ne nomen quidem viros scire fas est: As with the goddess Roma, whose real name cannot be revealed lest the disclosure compromise Rome's safety (e.g., Plin. *nat.* 3.65, 28.18; Macrob. *Sat.* 3.9.3), so too the actual name of Bona Dea is shrouded in secrecy and was the subject of learned speculation as early as Varro (frg. 218 Cardauns; Serv. Auct. *Aen.* 8.314).

quam iste idcirco Bonam dicit quod in tanto sibi scelere ignoverit. non ignovit, mihi crede, non: Cicero makes sarcastic remarks about Clodius's special relationship with Bona Dea elsewhere (*Att.* 2.4.2=SB 24: *iste sacerdos Bonae Deae*; *dom.* 110: *bonam esse oportet, quoniam quidem est abs te dedicata*; *in Clod. et Cur.* frg. 13 Crawford). In light of these precedents, I consider it likely that Clodius made a remark such as this in his *contio*—"the goddess is 'good' because she forgave me" (Corbeill 2018: 186). Since he would have expected Cicero to mention the Bona Dea incident in his own speech, Clodius would have been wise to pre-empt any such accusations in advance. Given Cicero's vehemence when mentioning the Bona Dea, it is easy to forget that Clodius was, in the end, acquitted of all wrongdoing. It would serve as a clever reminder of that acquittal to stress the goddess's "beneficence" (for this as the original sense of the epithet *Bona* see Marouzeau 1956: 230–231).

The subjunctive of alleged cause (*ignoverit*), immediately followed by the emphatic and negated indicative (*non ignovit*), is an example of *correctio* (*Rhet. Her.* 4.36: *correctio est quae tollit id quod dictum est, et pro eo id quod magis idoneum videtur reponit*; Lausberg 1998: §786). Straub 1883: 104–105 lists additional Ciceronian examples; for this speech see 51, 60. Here the correction is followed by an imagined exception, introduced by the sarcastic *nisi forte* (39n). Cicero's speeches and *philosophica* and, with one exception, *fam.*, have only the word order *mihi crede*; by contrast, *crede mihi* is the preferred order in *Att.* On the basis of this and other evidence Landgraf 1914: 187 argues that *mihi crede* is the more elevated expression. Adams 2016: 204, however, pointing to the tendency for personal pronouns to follow the focus of a phrase, in this case the imperative (Adams 1994b), concludes that the difference is not so much one of stylistic register as of persona: "it would only have been a person of marked self-esteem who would regularly have written *mihi crede*." This description certainly fits Cicero as authoritative orator. Wills 1996: 120 cites the repetition of *non* here as a rare example of "negative reinforced in conclusion," comparing Ov. met. 11.684: *"nulla est Alcyone, nulla est" ait*; Pers. 4.23: *ut nemo in sese temptat descendere, nemo*.

   te iudices ēmiserunt ēxcussum et ēxhaustum: A similar repetition of *e(x)* occurs at 4. *ThLL* V, 2 1313.37–46 (B. Rehm) suggests that the use of the verb *excutio* here represents a technical legal term attested otherwise only much later, designating that a defendant or other claimant is deprived of all his funds (e.g., Ulp. *dig.* 29.4.2.1; cf. Shackleton Bailey 1991a: 122: "relieved of every penny"). If so, this would be another joke about Clodius's bribery of the judges (36n), and *exhaustum* would have a similar double sense of "exhausted" and "drained of resources" (for the latter sense see *ThLL* V, 2 1410.59–76 [H. G. Wackernagel]). The verb *emitto* may also have witty connotations suggesting, among other things, Clodius being "sent away" upon detection in Caesar's house (cf. 44n).

   opinio illius religionis: "The general belief of that cult." As the *enim* at the beginning of the next sentence indicates, the following two sections will illustrate that Clodius did indeed lose his "sight" but not in the literal sense.

   38 quis enim: It is not unusual to find *quis*, rather than *qui*, as the masculine interrogative adjective; the chosen form often seems to be determined, as here, by whether the following word begins with a vowel (Adams 2016: 48–51, more cautiously Keeline 2021: 131; cf. 59n). This claim is supported by the fact that in classical Latin *(ali)quid* rarely appears as an adjective and *(ali)quod* rarely as a substantive, neither of which words would elide with a vowel in the following word (Löfstedt 1956: 2.81 n. 2). Löfstedt 1956: 2.82–96 analyzes the usage throughout Latinity.

   quis... vir sciens viderat: "What man knowingly had witnessed." In contrast with seeing the event with "wandering eyes" (37: *errantis [oculos]*; cf. 57n), Clodius was very conscious of his actions. At *dom.* 105 the phrase *nihil viderat sciens* is used to contrast Clodius with his ancestor Appius Claudius Caecus, who lost his sight through no fault of his own (38n). Note the ironic repetition of *scire* in the subordinate clause: one who "knowingly" intrudes upon the rights will come to "know" the punishment.

   quisquam poenam quae sequeretur id scelus scire posset?: The pronoun *quisquam*, normally occurring in negative or implicitly negative contexts, makes clear that the answer is "no one" (or else a pronoun such as *aliquis* would be used). No one can know how violation of the Bona Dea is penalized since no one has previously committed such an act. The sequence of sibilants and voiceless velar plosives in regular alternation contributes to the contemptuous tone (32n).

222   *Commentary*

An tibi luminis obesset caecitas plus quam libidinis?: "Would blindness in your eyes hinder you more than blindness in your passions?" In other words, even if Clodius were struck blind his lust and reckless ambition would remain active. For the moral blindness visited upon the sacrilegious in particular see 26n. Sen. *dial.* 1.6.1, in a remark that echoes Cicero's subsequent argument here, notes that the gods protect good men from "blind passion" (*libidinem caecam*), whereas presumably bad men remain subject to its power. Cicero's replacement of adjective by abstract noun, followed by a noun in the genitive (i.e., *caecitas libidinis* rather than Seneca's *libido caeca*), acts to emphasize the sense of the expected adjective, a construction that becomes particularly pronounced in imperial Latin (LHS 2: 152, who cites *Att.* 8.12.5=SB 162: *tristitiam illorum temporum* rather than *tristia illa tempora*). The noun *lumen* in both singular and plural forms can refer to "eyesight" (*ThLL* VII, 2 1818.35–62 [W. Ehlers]); doubtless the singular was used here for the alliteration with *libidinis*.

ne id quidem sentis, coniventes illos oculos abavi tui magis optandos fuisse quam hos flagrantis sororis?: The reference to Clodius's famous blind ancestor resumes the trope of not living up to the past achievements of one's family (2n), with Cicero sardonically saying that even blindness would be preferable to the allure of his sister. Appius Claudius Caecus (c. 340–after 280 BC; *RE* 91), is often noted as the first Roman whose career can be reconstructed with reasonable certainty. Originally bearing the cognomen *Crassus* (Frontin. *aq.* 1.5), he acquired the name *Caecus* after becoming blind some time late in life—Cicero, unsurprisingly, remains silent about the story that his blindness was divine punishment for tampering with the cult of Hercules (Oakley 1997–2005: 3.383). According to an extant *elogium* (*CIL* XI.1827), he held all major political offices, including that of consul (twice), dictator, *interrex* (three times) and, famously, censor from 312–308. During his censorship he sponsored the building of Rome's first major road (*Via Appia*) and aqueduct (*Aqua Appia*) and conducted the first revision of the list of senators. His speech from 280 persuading the senate not to surrender to Pyrrhus still survived in Cicero's day (*Brut.* 61). Cicero enjoys bringing up Caecus as a counterexample to the behavior of Clodius (e.g., 8, 26; *in Clod. et Cur.* frg. 20 Crawford; *Mil.* 17) as well as that of his sister Clodia (*Cael.* 33–35).

The verb *coniveo* means "to close" and is particularly used of the eyes. Cicero seems to favor the word, using it fifteen times in his corpus. The objection of Markland 1745: 351 that the verb nowhere else refers to eyes shut from blindness appears to be correct; *ThLL* IV 321.10–21 (E. Lommatzsch) cites only this example in its entry *de oculis*. But the metaphorical sense, common in Cicero, of "turning a blind eye," or conniving (e.g., 52), and the context of Caecus, makes the sense of literal blindness comprehensible. Moreover, the present participle contrasts well with the open, "burning," eyes of his female descendant. Although Cicero elsewhere alleges that Clodius had committed incest with more than one sister (9n), his delivery of the *Pro Caelio* just a few months earlier this year makes the probable referent here Clodia, the wife of the consular Quintus Metellus Celer and most likely the model of Catullus's "Lesbia," against whom was directed harsh invective in that speech, including charges of incest (*Cael.* 32, 36, 78). This probable identification seems confirmed by the reference to the "blazing" nature of Clodia's eyes at *Cael.* 49 (*flagrantia oculorum*), one of many traits that characterize her as a "forward and shameless prostitute" (*proterva meretrix procaxque*; Griffith 1996 suggests that burning eyes conveyed inchastity). Clodia's eyes attract elsewhere the attention of Cicero, who frequently applies to her the nickname "cow-eyed" ($\beta o \hat{\omega} \pi \iota s$), a Homeric epithet used of Hera, herself a famous perpetrator of sibling incest (*Att.* 2.9.1=SB 29, 2.12.2=SB 30, 2.14.1=SB 34, 2.22.5=SB 42, 2.23.3=SB 43). Skinner 2011 offers a sympathetic biography of this Clodia Metelli.

deorum. homines te in re foedissima defenderunt: Note that this instance of *homines*, picking up on *hominum* in the previous sentence, is juxtaposed with its antithesis, *deorum*. There then follows five more instances of *homines* in anaphora and polyptoton to explain that Clodius's acquittal by fellow Romans can be attributed to their moral failings, not to his innocence. These six instances of human fallibility are met with one simple rhetorical question about punishment that comes from the gods (39: *a dis quidem immortalibus*).

For the connotations of religious pollution for the adjective *foedus*, see 32n. There was only one speaker for the defense in the Bona Dea trial, C. Scribonius Curio (12n). The plural verb may be rhetorical or, as Lenaghan 1969: 155 suggests, could refer less technically to Clodius's prominent supporters at the time, such as M. Pupius Piso and Q. Fufius Calenus, respectively consul and tribune in 61 (*Att.* 1.16.1-2=SB 16, 1.14.5-6=SB 14).

hominibus iniuria tui stupri inlata in ipsos dolori non fuit: The act of *stuprum* makes the reference to the Bona Dea ritual unmistakable (nn. on 4, 8). Here, however, the detail that particular individuals took no offense from the act clearly points as well to Clodius's alleged sexual encounter with Julius Caesar's wife, Pompeia. When Caesar was asked at the trial about why he had divorced her, rather than incriminate Clodius, he made the famous remark that Caesar's wife should be not only free of vice, but beyond suspicion (Suet. *Iul.* 74.2; Plut. *Cic.* 29.9, *Caes.* 10.9; Dio 37.45.2). For Cicero's cool attitude toward Caesar in this speech, see nn. on 45, 47.

homines tibi arma alii in me, alii post in illum invictum civem dederunt: Unnnamed like Caesar, Pompey is unmistakably the "unconquered citizen." The phrase *invictus civis* also occurs to describe Pompey at *Pis.* 34 (*clarissimi atque invictissimi civis*; cf. *Verr.* 2.5.153: *illa dextera invicta*, *leg. agr.* 2.52: *invicta... manu*) and is used in only one other place in Cicero, to describe Milo (*Mil.* 101). For Clodius taking up arms against Cicero and Pompey, see 58n.

prorsus concedo: "I fully admit." The adverb *prorsus* here introduces the general summation of a preceding list, and so signals that Cicero has concluded his account of the manifold ways that Clodius has benefited from the violent and irresponsible actions of human beings (*ThLL* X, 2 2160.40–2161.36 [C. Wick], who notes that *prorsus* normally occurs in first position in this sense. Cicero deviates from this normal practice in order to retain the various forms of *homines* in first position).

39 ***A dis quidem immortalibus quae potest homini maior esse poena furore atque dementia?***: The non-standard word order, with *poena* in a long-range hyperbaton with *quae* and the ablative pair closing the sentence, emphasizes the contrast between the human benefits to Clodius just listed and his divine punishment. Cicero has attributed *furor* to Clodius since the speech's opening (2n) and, beginning with this passage, *dementia* becomes an analogous identifying characteristic (41n; Berno 2007: 80 provides a catalogue of terms describing Clodius's insanity).

nisi forte in tragoediis quos vulnere ac dolore corporis cruciari ac consumi vides, graviores deorum immortalium iras subire quam illos qui furentes inducuntur putas: The phrase *nisi forte* nearly always has a sarcastic edge, as here in introducing an alternative view of divine punishment that is subsequently discarded (37, 55; *ThLL* VI, 1 1134.67–1135.10 [O. Hey]). With the mention of tragedy, Cicero returns more explicitly to the poetic element of the tripartite conception of theology, an element that he will ultimately reject at the speech's close (nn. on 20, 62). The notion that mental madness is more serious than physical travails has already been anticipated at 38, where Cicero contrasts the specific case of physical versus moral blindness. As he details in *Pis.* 42–50, again calling on tragedy for evidence, even good men can be subjected to physical punishment, whereas madness is directed by the gods solely against the guilty (see the excellent analysis of Gildenhard 2011: 181–190). As a result, "in contrast to 'criminal insanity' in modern law, which diminishes liability, the insanity of his adversaries that Cicero alleges in his orations is a symptom of guilt" (Gildenhard 2011: 114). Notably, Clodius's madness does not arise from physical causes such as one encounters in the drunken *furor* of Marcus Antonius (*Phil.* 2.101, cf. 6). Thurn 2018: 171 notes that Clodius's bibulousness in fact receives only oblique references (she cites *Mil.* 56, to which add 55: *plenus vini*). Indeed, given that the aim of *har. resp.* is to determine divine intention, it is unsurprising that Clodius's *furor* is depicted as arising solely from the judgment of the gods.

It is worth noting the emphasis on the staged performance of tragedy: Cicero refers to "seeing" characters "led onstage" (*inducuntur*; 57n), and to hearing "shrieks and groans." While such a description clearly increases vividness, it nevertheless differs from Cicero's normal references to tragedy, which regularly derive from written texts (Goldberg 2000: 51–53).

non sunt illi eiulatus et gemitus Philoctetae tam miseri, quamquam sunt acerbi: While enroute to the Trojan War, the Greek archer Philoctetes was left behind on the island of Lemnos after his companions had become repulsed by the odor emanating from his infected snakebite. Years later he was rescued and brought to Troy when it was discovered that the city could not be captured without him. He is the subject of an extant Sophoclean tragedy, a prominent scene of which portrays him racked with pain from his wound. Cicero seems to have in mind the *Philocteta* of his older contemporary Accius, several fragments of which are extant (Acc. *trag.* 520–568 *TRF*); see in particular 549–551 (*iaceo in tecto umido, / quod eiulatu questu gemitu fremitibus / resonando mutum flebilis voces refert*), quoted at *Tusc.* 2.33 in order for Cicero to contrast with groans (*ingemiscere*) the onomatopoetic noun *eiulatus*, formed from the exclamations of grief or pain (*[h]ei/heu*; cf. *Tusc.* 2.55). The application of the nouns there in a negative characterization of the inability to endure pain may give an added dimension to *miseri* here (*ingemescere non numquam viro concessum est, idque raro, eiulatus ne mulieri quidem*; the notions are also contrasted in an analogous context at 2.19; *fin.* 2.94; Cicero alludes to Philoctetes as a paradigm of suffering at *fam.* 7.33.1=SB 192, *ad Q. fr.* 2.9.4=SB 12, *fin.* 5.32, *fat.* 36–37). When applied to the human voice, the adjective *acerbus* describes a harshness that verges on the unnatural (e.g., Quint. *inst.* 11.3.169, with Wille 1967: 483 n. 780).

quam illa exsultatio Athamantis et quam senium matricidarum: Cicero again alludes to mythical subjects that are known to have been depicted on the Roman stage, in this case as maddened by the gods, and that would have been familiar to his senatorial audience (Brook 2016: 48–52, with bibliography). Athamas (*RE* 2), mythical king of Boeotia, had twin children, Phrixus and Helle, through his wife Nephele. When Athamas's second wife Ino was plotting to dispose of these stepchildren, they were rescued by a flying golden sheep and Phrixus was transported to Colchis, while Helle fell into what later became known as the Hellespont ("sea of Helle"). Ino went on to raise her nephew Dionysus, whereupon a jealous Juno sent Furies to drive Athamas insane who then, in the commonest version, proceeded to murder one of his and Ino's sons, believing him an animal. Athamas was the subject of an eponymous play by Accius, the details of which are obscure (Acc. *trag.* 189–195 *TRF*); Lenaghan 1969: 157 points out the (presumably coincidental) aptness of frg. 189 to Clodius: *prius quam infans facinus oculi vescuntur tui* ("Before your eyes feast on an unspeakable crime"). He also appears in an *Athamas* of Ennius, which seems not to have featured his madness (*TrRF* 2: 107–110) and perhaps in an *Ino* attributed to Livius Andronicus (*TrRF* 1: 50–52). Although the noun *exsultatio* normally contains the connotations of "jumping about" in joy, its meaning here can be most conveniently glossed from the pairing of the participial form *exsultantem* with *furentem* at the beginning of the speech to describe Clodius (1; cf. *rep.* 2.68, of animals). As with Clodius, Athamas's madness had manifested itself in lack of control over the body.

The most well-known matricides from the tragic stage are Orestes and Alcmaeon. As immortalized in Aeschylus's *Oresteia* trilogy, Orestes avenged the death of his father Agamemnon by murdering his mother Clytemnestra; he was pursued by avenging Furies until absolved of guilt by a jury of Athenian citizens (and ultimately Athena). Whether Orestes had committed justifiable murder had already become a stock subject of the rhetorical schools in Cicero's youth (*inv.* 1.18; cf. Quint. *inst.* 3.11.4–6). Roman theatrical audiences too would have been familiar with the mythical cycle involving Orestes (Brook 2016: 66–68). The *Aegisthus* of Livius Andronicus included an account of the death of Agamemnon, but the fragments do not indicate whether Orestes appeared as a character (*TrRF* 1: 33–41), while the main theme of Ennius's *Eumenides* would certainly have been the matricide and its moral and legal implications (*TrRF* 2: 124–129). Pacuvius wrote *Dulorestes*, centered on Orestes's plot to murder his mother (Pacuv. *trag.* 113–160 *TRF*), and *Hermonia*, named after Orestes's wife, which included a scene in which he is harassed by the Furies (Serv. *Aen.* 4.473; Pacuv. *trag.* 161–190 *TRF*; his *Chryses* also had Orestes as a major character). Accius had one play, an *Aegisthus* (Acc. *trag.* 22–29 *TRF*), that treated the aftermath of the matricide, and two others in the cycle whose contents cannot be reconstructed, *Agamemnonidae* and *Clytemnestra* (*trag.* 43–48, *trag.* 30–42 *TRF*). *Clytemnestra* was restaged at the dedicatory ceremonies for the Theater of Pompey, the year after the delivery of *har. resp.* (*fam.* 7.1.2=SB 24). Alcmaeon and his brother Amphilochus, while still boys, were commanded by Amphiaraus the seer to kill their mother Eriphyle, an injunction later repeated by Apollo at Delphi. Alcmaeon, like Orestes, was driven mad by Furies upon completing the act until after much wandering the river god Achelous purified him of his crime. Ennius's *Alcmeo* treated the matricide (*TrRF* 2: 49–60), as did Accius's *Epigoni* (Acc. *trag.* 285–306 *TRF*). Accius also wrote an *Alcmeo* (Acc. *trag.* 58–70 *TRF*), and another play treating aspects of Alcmeon's story, *Alphesiboea* (Acc. *trag.* 71–81 *TRF*); neither plot can be reconstructed with certainty. Each of the characters alluded to here receive frequent mention across the range of Cicero's works; all three are grouped together also at *Tusc.* 3.11, Orestes and Athamas at *Pis.* 47. In her analysis of Cicero's use of the *exemplum* of Orestes in defending Milo for murdering Clodius, Brook 2016: 60 notes that Orestes in particular "seems to have been a favourite example of Cicero's, used to illustrate many different concepts: madness, especially guilt-inspired madness (*Pis.* 46–47, *Tusc.* 3.11), justifiable homicide (*Inv.* 1.18–19, [Cic.] *Rh. Her.* 1.17, 25–26), the wickedness of parricide (*S. Rosc.* 66–67) and friendship, focusing on Orestes' relationship with Pylades (*Fin.* 1.65, 2.79, 5.63; *Amic.* 24)."

Since the advanced age of the most well-known tragic matricides never arises as an issue, it is highly unlikely that *senium* here is a genitive plural, *pace* Watts 1923: 367 ("long-lived matricides"), Lenaghan 1969: 157. Although reasonable emendations have been suggested, such as *insania* (Jeep 1862: 10–11) and *somnium* (Wolf 1801: 361, after some *recentiores*), Garatoni 1786: 321–322 observed long ago that *senium*, the reading of the best codices, makes good sense and provides a neat contrast with *exsultatio*. It is an abstract noun in the neuter nominative singular, derived from *senex*, and occurs in early drama in the sense of "wretchedness" or "gloom," with no direct reference to age (e.g., Plaut. *Truc.* 466, Pacuv. *trag.* 301 *TRF*, Acc. *trag.* 316 *TRF*) as well as in Cicero (*Mil.* 20). Thurneysen 1906: 179–180 derives the origins of the word not from human old age, but from the waning of the moon (*senescere*; cf. Slușanski 1974: 566–567).

tu cum furiales in contionibus voces mittis, cum domos civium evertis, cum lapidibus optimos viros foro pellis, cum ardentis faces in vicinorum tecta iactas, cum aedes sacras inflammas, cum servos concitas, cum sacra ludosque conturbas, cum uxorem sororemque non discernis, cum quod ineas cubile non sentis, tum baccharis, tum furis, tum das eas poenas quae solae sunt hominum sceleri a dis immortālibūs cōnstitūtā: Cicero moves from the fictions of the tragic stage to an emphatic expression of facts about Clodius in the present. Each verb in this sentence's nine instances of *cum* occurs in the indicative, stressing the frequency of Clodius's illicit activities ("whenever") and referring to actions that either have already been mentioned in the speech or that will be related later (or both). The main clause that follows consists of a tricolon of *tum* in anaphora, also with verbs in the present indicative (ending with a favored double cretic + anceps), which offer a succinct statement of what these actions signify: Clodius is crazed. The combined twelve verbs take the emphatic first word, *tu*, as their subject and are active in sense, so that it is no exaggeration to say that Clodius dominates the sentence. This domination terminates with the closing relative clause, which contains a passive statement of fact about the penalties that have been firmly ordained for Clodius by the gods (cf. *Pis.* 46). Gildenhard 2007: 165 notes well Cicero's logic here: "the workings of the human mind are not accessible to empirical inspection. By inverting the presentation of cause and effect, the orator enhances the *evidentia* ('vividness') of his discourse."

I offer here comments and cross-references on the actions ascribed to Clodius. The first adjective in the sentence, *furiales*, recalls not only Cicero's depiction from the beginning of Clodius and his followers as Furies (nn. on 2, 4) but anticipates the subsequent depiction of Clodius in this sentence, wielding burning torches in Fury-like fashion, and ultimately characterized as embodying *furor* itself. The second and fourth accusations, of overturning the homes of citizens and setting them aflame, unmistakably includes the destruction during Cicero's exile of both his own home and his brother's (58n, with additional possibilities), while the third recalls earlier descriptions of violence in the forum (6n). The burning of temples refers to the temple of the Nymphs (57n) and perhaps that of Castor (Manuwald 2021: 104–105) or other unidentified temples (Keeline 2021: 285), while the next two *cum* clauses, mentioning the stirring up of slaves and disruption of games, clearly recalls the disturbance at the Megalesia (e.g., 22, 25–26). The list concludes by turning from the political to the personal, with more jokes about Clodius's incest with his sister (9n); the remark about his not being able to distinguish his wife from his sister recalls the famous joke directed at Clodia a few months earlier, where it is Cicero himself who has trouble with this distinction: "with that woman's husband—I mean brother. I always make this mistake" (*Cael*. 32: *cum istius mulieris viro—fratrem volui dicere; semper hic erro*). In the main clause, the verb *baccharis* becomes very much a living metaphor in the context of Furies and tragic scenarios. Fantham 1972: 49 notes that Plautus uses *bacchari* "only of actual Bacchic orgies (*Am*. 703) or alcoholic revelry (*Mil*. 856, applied to a drinking vessel)." Gildenhard 2007: 153 captures the tone well: with the verbs *baccharis* and *furis* "Clodius has, as it were, stepped out of the tragic imagination into Roman reality."

corporis quidem nostri infirmitas multo subit casus per se, denique ipsum corpus tenuissima de causa saepe conficitur: "deorum tela in impiorum mentibus figuntur." qua re miserior es cum in omnem fraudem raperis oculis quam si omnino oculos non haberes: This series of gnomic statements is one of two selections from *har. resp.* contained in the twelfth-century collection known as *Florilegium Gallicum*, compiled probably at Orléans and including selections from thirty-six verse texts and thirty-four prose texts. As excerpted for this anthology, the text contains only minor variations for the sake of simplification (omission of *qua re*; word order changed to the more standard *oculis raperis*; *haberes* changed to indicative *habueris*). These readings ultimately derive from a sister text to **P** whose archetype is designated **R** (Maslowski and Rouse 1984: 79–88, who include a stemma on 104 superseding that in Maslowski 1981: xxxiii). For the other excerpt see **54n.

Of particular note in this passage is the sentence *deorum tela in impiorum mentibus figuntur* ("The spears of the gods are fixed in the minds of the impious"). This gnomic sentiment almost certainly derives from a Roman play, presumably a tragedy. Aside from its dramatic subject matter, the rhythm is inappropriate for prose: Cicero in his oratory avoids the clausula used here (cretic + molossus); instead the entire phrase yields a typical dramatic meter, the iambic senarius: *dĕōrŭm tēlă ĭn īmpĭōrŭm mēntĭbŭs / fĭgŭntūr*. Havet 1897 first noted this possibility, although he overstates his case that a word formed of three longs (*figuntur*) is always preceded in Ciceronian prose by a tribrach or trochee. *TrRF* 1: 196 includes this as *frg. adesp.* 17 with the line break reproduced here (following Klotz 1953: *frg. adesp.* 265–266). It is also significant that Cicero provides no syntactic transition into the quotation, such as a particle or conjunction, and does not put *mentibus* earlier in the sentence to provide contrast with the preceding *corpus*. His neglect at identifying text and author is insignificant; Jocelyn 1973: 62–63 notes that Cicero has an unusual number of such quotations in his speeches from 56 and 55, often quoted anonymously (for hidden quotations elsewhere see *leg. agr.* 2.93 with Manuwald 2018: 391; *Sest*. 45, 126; list at Radin 1911: 211–213). Finally, the notion of the gods deliberately inflicting upon someone a madness that hastens that person's downfall, which appears as early as Homer and Hesiod (Dodds 1951: 38–41), is a prevalent motif of tragedy; Gildenhard 2007: 176 aptly compares Soph. *Ant*. 622–624: τὸ κακὸν δοκεῖν ποτ' ἐσθλὸν / τῷδ' ἔμμεν ὅτῳ φρένας / θεὸς ἄγει πρὸς ἄταν. The presence of a quotation here further enhances the effect already mentioned, that the mythical and the civic theologies—the theology of the poet and that of the orator—occupy the same level of discourse, thereby uniting Clodius with antagonistic figures from myth and literature (39n).

40

Cicero turns from the faults listed by the *haruspices* to the third and apparently final portion of the response, in which they warn what those faults may portend. Dissension among the elite will lead to death and destruction in its ranks, ultimately resulting in some form of tyranny. Unsurprisingly, Cicero proceeds to identify Clodius as the source of this dissension.

40 *de his omnibus*: This phrasing is another indication that Cicero has now quoted the entirety of that portion of the response that treats the faults requiring expiation. Reading *his* instead of *iis* makes this possibility even more likely; see next note and Introduction E.1.

** *de his omnibus*: All codices and Maslowski read *his*. Peterson conjectures *iis,* presumably as a more natural antecedent to the following *quae*. Although the two forms are consistently confused in manuscripts, a case can be made for *his*. The deictic is used throughout *har. resp.* to refer to the words of the response, perhaps because a copy was posted or otherwise available to the audience of senators (e.g., 9: *responsum haruspicum hoc recens de fremitu*, 11, 29).

***commissa esse*:** As the context of the response indicates, when the verb *committo* refers to human actions, it normally refers to those that are morally reprehensible; cf. 7, 21n, and *ThLL* III 1910.45–1912.33 (H. Mertel).

***iam a dis immortalibus*: The reading of P[1] is the nonsensical *iam immortalibus*, which is corrected by P[2] to *a dis iam immortalibus* (adopted by Peterson and Maslowski). The remaining major codices GEH read *a diis immortalibus*. Halm (Orelli *et al.* 1856: 919) conjectures *iam a dis immortalibus* ("fort[asse] recte" notes Maslowski in his apparatus). Of the more than 500 occurrences of the phrase *di immortales* (in all grammatical cases) found in a search of the entire PHI corpus, in only approximately twenty is the noun separated from the adjective. Most of these instances are unremarkable, with the intervening word being a clitic (*-que*; *-ne*; enclitic *'st*) or a word that is normally postpositive (forms of *inquam*; *ne…quidem*; *denique*; *quidem*; *non…tantum…sed…quoque*; cf. Sen. *contr.* 9.2.7 "*di tibi*" inquit "*immortales*"). In three cases in Cicero, the word in the hyperbaton creates a rhetorical emphasis (*ego* 1x; *di ipsi immortales* twice). The only case at all unusual is Plin. *nat.* 36.118: *deorum quaedam immortalium…portio*, a highly rhetorical passage in which *quaedam* introduces a metaphor (the Roman people represent "a part of the gods, as it were"). There is no clear rhetorical or stylistic reason for the unusual position of *iam* in P[2], which is readily explained by the corrector incorrectly inserting the missing *a dis*, perhaps even confusing *iam* with the first syllable of the word before which the two words should be placed, *imm-* (or some abbreviation such as *īm-*).

READ *iam a dis immortalibus*. This fits normal usage, and the readings of P are easily accounted for. A possible sequence could be as follows: the archetype read simply *iam immortalibus*; this was faithfully reproduced by P¹, whereas GEH made the easy correction of *iam* to *a dis*, which was inserted by P² in the wrong place.

moneri. monent: While the repetition is hardly necessary, there is no sufficient reason to follow Lambinus 1566: 704 in deleting *monent* as "supervacaneum et inane" (for more egregious examples of apparently unnecessary repetition of verbs see, e.g., *Verr*. 2.1.80 [*dico*], *S. Rosc*. 99 [*video*]). The apparent redundancy in fact adds a desired emphasis, as is reflected in the slightly incongruous semantics that results from the repetition. The introductory conjunction *ne* would seem to introduce a fearing clause—this is what the Romans are to fear if reparations are not made (cf. 54: *ad quem metum*). The normal construction after *moneo*, however, is a negative indirect command; in particular this instance seems to be of the type that follows oracles or written texts (*ThLL* VIII 1412.27–47 [W. Buchwald]): "The gods warn/advise [us] that there not be carnage…." Forms of *moneo*, first used here in this sense, come to proliferate as the oration progresses (44, 45, 53, 54 [twice], 55, 56, 57, 61). By stressing the notion of an indirect command, responsible agency is transferred from the gods to the Romans themselves, a move that anticipates the emphatic plea with which the entire speech closes.

NE PER OPTIMATIVM DISCORDIAM DISSENSIONEMQVE PATRIBVS PRINCIPIBVSQVE CAEDES PERICVLAQVE CREENTVR AVXILIOQVE DIVINITVS DEFICIANTVR, † QVA RE AD VNVM IMPERIVM PECVNIAE REDEANT EXERCITVSQVE PVLSVS DOMINATIOQVE ACCEDAT †: I offer here the text of this passage, incorporating the emendations discussed in the following notes. I translate: "[The gods warn] that through discord and disagreement of the best men there not arise death and danger for the fathers and leading men, and that they not be without help from a divine source, † because of which circumstance wealth would revert to a single ruler and there would occur the driving away of the army and despotism †." Despite serious textual problems, the general tenor of the warning is clear—unless reparations are made to the gods, civil dissension will result in autocracy. This portion of the response seems to reflect the Etruscan conception that prodigies can signal a "new age" that follows in the wake of political turmoil (Plut. *Sull*. 7.2–5, with Santangelo 2013: 89–91; Cens. 17.6). The Etruscan brontoscopic calendar preserved in John of Lydus also predicts several instances of civil unrest (Piganiol 1951: 80–81; I quote the Greek text from Turfa 2012: 73–85). The closest parallel to this clause occurs under September 25: "if it should thunder, a tyrant will rise up from the dissension in the state; he will himself be destroyed but the powerful will be overthrown with unbearable punishments" (ἐὰν βροντήσῃι, ἐκ διχονοίας τοῦ πολιτεύματος τύραννος ἀναστήσεται, καὶ αὐτὸς μὲν ἀπολεῖται, ζημίαις δὲ ἀφορήτοις οἱ δυνατοὶ ὑποστήσονται). Compare too the entries for June 20 (διχονοίαν ἀπειλεῖ τῶι δήμωι), July 15 (διχονοία ἔσται τοῦ δήμου), and July 23 (ἡ διχονοία τοῦ δήμου παυθήσεται). Similarly, the prophecy of Vegoia predicts as a consequence of moving boundary markers on land "many disagreements among the people" (Grom. p. 351.9: *multae dissensiones in populo*; cf. 53n). Even if this Latin prophecy does not derive from an Etruscan original (see Adams 2003: 179-182 for evidence, with earlier bibliography), the author nevertheless would intentionally have chosen language that suggested Etruscan influence. Finally, the haruspical response in 63 warned, in Cicero's paraphrase, "that slaughter, conflagrations, and destruction were being readied for the state, and at the hands of citizens" (*Catil.* 3.21: *cum esset ita responsum, caedes, incendia, interitum rei publicae comparari, et ea per cives*).

PER OPTIMATIVM DISCORDIAM DISSENSIONEMQVE: The pair *discordia / dissensio* occurs in the same order three additional times later in *har. resp.*, each discussing this clause in the context of the activity of, unsurprisingly, Clodius (46, 50, 53). Some minor support for the unCiceronian origins of the Latin translation of the response can be found in the fact that the remaining two instances of the pair in Cicero outside the speech reverse the order (*Phil.* 8.8; *Lael.* 23), as do the next two occurrences in Tacitus (*Agr.* 32.1, *dial.* 40.4); the remaining occurrences I have found occur in the *har. resp.* order (Gell. 2.12.1; Serv. *Aen.* 7.542; Lact. *ira* 24.12). The term *discordia* recurs twelve times in the remainder of the speech and usually in the plural. When Cicero uses abstract substantives in the plural, especially with possessive or genitive forms, it most often denotes repeated action (Lebreton 1901: 32-38, esp. 33-36). For instances of the plural of *discordia* subsequent to this section, most with plural possessives, see 43, 44, 45, 46 (twice), 50, 53, 54, and 63 (the penultimate word of the entire speech). The many plurals support rhetorically the claim that Clodius has been fomenting discord repeatedly. Pallottino 1948-1949: 170 suggests that the Etruscan word *natinusnal*, part of the Etruscan religious calendar that appears on the Capua tile, derives from the name of a Fury and corresponds with the Latin *discordia*; if so, this provides an intriguing parallel for the response's concern with "dissent and discord."

It is important to note here that the term *optimates* represents the translation of an Etruscan term whose connotations are lost to us. In Republican Rome, the term *optimates*—the "best" men in Rome—was malleable; it did not represent a political party in the modern sense and was used in accordance with the rhetorical aims of a speaker (Brunt 1988: 35-36, 54-66). This is amply demonstrated by Cicero's recent appropriation of the word to describe in effect all those citizens of Rome beyond the criminal and bankrupt (*Sest.* 96-135; Kaster 2006: 31-37). Although Cicero aims both in *Sest.* and *har. resp.* to isolate Clodius as an enemy to good reason and statesmanship, he does not define *optimates* so expansively here, glossing the term for his own purposes as "the most renowned and deserving citizens" (53: *cum di immortales monent de optimatium discordia, de clarissimorum et optime meritorum civium dissensione praedicunt*).

PATRIBVS PRINCIPIBVSQVE: The combination occurs elsewhere only in the singular to describe an individual, in particular the emperor Augustus (Hor. *carm.* 1.2.50: *ames dici pater atque princeps*; Manil. 1.7; at *Phil.* 8.22 the context makes clear that *principes* refers to the leaders of the senate). Mommsen 1887–1888: 3.836–838 notes that Cicero normally distinguishes between *patres* (senate of the kings) and *patres conscripti* (Republican senate) but that he also occasionally uses *patres* to designate leaders of the elite more generally (1887–1888: 3.837 n. 5: "die Spitzen der Aristokratie ohne bestimmte Beziehung auf die Patricier und den Senat"), for which he cites only this passage and *rep.* 1.48–49 and 3.37. Sallust and Livy, by contrast, use the term *patres* to designate the senate as a whole, as does Cicero in his verse in the context of divination (*div.* 1.20–21).

Given the general Ciceronian usage, the translation of the response offered by the *haruspices* seems intentionally ambiguous, thereby allowing the interpreter to consider the two words either as virtual synonyms referring to Rome's leading statesmen and generals or as making a distinction between the senate and leaders of the non-senatorial elite.

CREENTVR: Both at *S. Rosc.* 85 and here Landgraf 1914: 175 considers the use of *creare* as a synonym of *inferre* to be an archaism. It is worth noting that *periculum* is also the subject at *S. Rosc.* 85 (in the sense of "trial"), which indicates that the response here is to be taken as ambiguous, pointing either to politically-motivated trials or to vague "dangers." For other archaic elements in the response see Introduction G.2.

** AVXILIOQVE DIVINITVS DEFICIANTVR: The adverb *divinitus*, the reading of some of the lesser witnesses, is adopted by Maslowski and Shackleton Bailey 1991a: 230. The major codices contain nonsense: *diminuitis* P¹, *diminutis* P²GE, *diminuti* H. Koch 1868: 14, comparing *Catil.* 2.29, conjectured *divini numinis*, which is adopted by Peterson in the OCT; Lambinus 1566: 704=1830: 266 emended to AVXILIISQVE DIMINVTIS EFFICIANTVR, which makes excellent sense of the confusion in the manuscripts and eliminates the abrupt change in subject, but it is unclear what kind of *auxilium* one is to imagine if the gods are no longer specified.

READ *divinitus*. The readings of the better manuscripts are likely influenced by *deminutio* / *diminutio* on the next line, so it is not essential that a conjecture be paleographically plausible (a virtue of Koch's suggestion). Furthermore, *divinitus* seems unlikely to be a medieval conjecture, which may mean that the reading of the *recentiores* that contain *divinitus* arises from a now lost codex that contained independent readings. Finally, the unusual syntax of *divinitus*, whether construed with *auxilio* or (less probably) *deficiantur*, may be explained by the fact that it sounds "haruspical" (cf. Cens. 17.5, discussing Etruscan *saecula*: *portenta mitti **divinitus**, quibus admonerentur unumquodque saeculum* *esse finitum*; "portents are sent from a divine source, through which they are warned that each age has come to a conclusion"). For the adverb *divinitus* modifying a noun, see Verg. *georg.* 1.415–416: *quia sit divinitus illis / ingenium aut rerum fato prudentia maior.*

** **AD VNVM IMPERIVM PECVNIAE REDEANT**: This is the reading of most manuscripts, with some *recentiores* having *provinciae* instead of *pecuniae* (Maslowski sees a small erasure in P after *pecuniae* that seems to indicate an original reading of *pecunia*). Peterson obelizes this entire phrase. Lambinus 1830: 266 cites Cicero's later reference back to this passage at 54 (*ne in unius imperium res reccidat*) to support the emendation *AD VNIVS IMPERIVM RES REDEAT*, and is followed by Wuilleumier and Tupet 1966: 60, Maslowski, Shackleton Bailey 1991a: 230. Although I have not seen it stated explicitly, the emendators must presume that *pecuniae* was inserted at 40 from a marginal gloss on an original reading of *res*.

These emendations seem attractive, but the evidence of *har. resp.* 54 becomes less persuasive when one notes that other portions of this section of the speech contain loose paraphrases of the response, so that verbal precision is not to be expected (as the change from *redeat* to *reccidat* indicates; cf. too the plural forms of *discordia* and *dissensio* cited above). Furthermore, a case can be made for *ad unum imperium* of the manuscripts. In a practice that becomes prevalent in the empire, Cicero uses the abstract *imperium* to designate an individual person (*rep.* 1.60, *leg.* 1.23; *ThLL* VII, 1 581.31–42 [O. Prinz]; Adams 2003: 181–182); the phrase would then mean here "to one man of power," and the unusual nature of such a construction would be in keeping with other aspects of the haruspical response that have already been noted.

Courtney 1989: 52, following Busche 1917: 1359–1360 (who presents no argument), suggests reading *RES CVNCTAE* for *PECVNIAE* and cites in possible support the brontoscopic calendar for July 14: ἐὰν βροντήσηι, εἰς ἕνα τὴν πάντων δύναμιν ἐλθεῖν φράζει (Turfa 2012: 75). This has the benefit of retaining the *redeant* of the codices and is also easier to explain paleographically. I cannot, however, find a parallel for *res cunctae* being used to refer to the state, whereas both Sallust and Lucretius use the phrase to refer broadly to "everything" or "all creation" (Lucr. 2.290, 874; Sall. *Catil.* 8.1, *Iug.* 2.1). Rather than seeing *pecuniae* as a gloss, a case can be made for retaining this reading. The plural of *pecunia* is hardly uncommon even in prose writers such as Cicero and Livy (*ThLL* X, 1 942.62–63 [H. Ramminger]) to indicate the property of separate individuals (*ThLL* X, 1 942.64–69) or, in later Latin, and as early as Nepos, simply to indicate a very large amount of cash or goods (*ThLL* X, 1 942.70–943.9). For Ciceronian examples of the distributive use (appropriate with *ad unum imperium*), see, e.g., Cic. *Verr.* 2.2.30: *omnes omnium pecuniae positae sint in eorum potestate*, 2.4.71; *leg. agr.* 2.61; *Phil.* 2.41: *in multas...pecunias alienissimorum hominum...invasit.* The plural also fits the context of the haruspical prophecy since each of these Ciceronian examples describes the inappropriate acquisition of money from others, in a usage that dates to Gaius Gracchus: *legationes... a regibus... sumptus atque pecunias maximas praebent* (apud Gell. 11.10.6). Finally, the unusual (but acceptable) use of the plural would explain why **P** originally seems to have read, or been emended to, the singular *pecunia*. (For an additional argument, see next note) The sense of *REDEANT* would remain the same: wealth reverts back into the hands of one individual (as it had in the days of the kings).

READ (cautiously) with the major manuscripts QVA RE AD VNVM IMPERIVM PECVNIAE REDEANT.

** *EXERCITVSQVE PVLSVS DOMINATIOQVE ACCEDAT*: Most manuscripts read *EXERCITVSQVE APVLSVS DIMINVTIOQVE ACCEDAT*; the only variation occurs with the noun *apulsus*, which is the reading of **GE**; *pulsus* is in **P²H** and the word is omitted in **P¹**. No obvious conjectures arise for *apulsus*, which does not elsewhere exist (*appulsus* is used chiefly of ships; *aspello* occurs in Plautus, and once in Cicero in a translation of Aeschylus at *Tusc.* 2.25). Of many conjectures the suggestion of Lambinus 1566: 704=1830: 266—*EXERCITVSQVE PVLSVS AD DIMINVTIONEM ACCEDAT*—yields good sense, although *diminutio* comes as an anticlimax after the preceding list of dangers that threaten.

As Lambinus recognized, reading *pulsus* of **P²H** as a participle fits the context semantically; *pello* occurs frequently in the sense of driving away a military foe (*ThLL* X, 1 1010.61–1011.18 [I. Reineke]; 1010.73–75 for *exercitus* acting as direct object). For the so-called *ab urbe condita* construction—"and the driving away/defeat of the army"—see 13n. But what of *diminutio*? Some help can be found in a later paraphrase of this section of the response: *neque enim ullus alius discordiarum solet esse exitus inter claros et potentis viros nisi aut universus interitus aut victoris dominatus ac regnum* (54). A comparison yields the following equivalences: *OPTIMATIVM* ~ *inter claros et potentis viros*; *DISCORDIAM DISSENSIONEMQVE* ~ *discordiarum*; *PATRIBVS PRINCIPIBVSQVE CAEDES PERICVLAQVE CREENTVR* ~ *universus interitus*; *QVA RE AD VNVM IMPERIVM PECVNIAE REDEANT* ~ *regnum*; *EXERCITVS PVLSVS* ~ *victoris*. If these correspondences are recognized, then one would expect *dominatus* to match the word hidden by the *DIMINVTIO* of the codices. A conjecture that will fill this gap, fit the overall sense, and require only minor alteration paleographically is *DOMINATIO*. Aside from the meaning being suitable for the sense, *dominatio* is also rhetorically appropriate as the dramatic final part of the response (Sall. *Catil.* 17.5 uses it to describe what the *nobiles* expected from participation in the Catilinarian conspiracy). The occurrence of the notion of *dominatio* in other prophecies further supports this reading: when told of the birth of Octavius, Nigidius Figulus predicted that "a lord (*dominus*) has been born on earth" (Suet. *Aug.* 94.5: *dominum terrarum orbi natum*)—we may also recall that Nigidius is a strong contender for the translator of the response. Cf. too the parallels in the words attributed to L. Cotta at *dom.* 68: *qui* *me... vi armis **dissensione** hominum et **caede** instituta novoque **dominatu pulsum** esse dixit*. Finally, if one reads *dominatio*, then keeping PECVNIAE would seem all the more justified, since with *ad unum imperium res reddat* the later occurrence of *dominatio* would be redundant.

haruspicum verba sunt haec omnia, nihil addo de meo: Cicero takes particular care to show that the response is entirely the product of the *haruspices* since this section would be particularly damning to the recently renewed triumviral alliance between Caesar, Pompey, and Crassus. The strict chiastic structure provides emphasis for this point, with the contrasting *omnia / nihil* offering the transition, and with *haruspicum / de meo* at the opening and close literally distancing the words of the *haruspices* from those of Cicero, a separation further stressed by the hyperbaton of *nihil* and *de meo*. The phrase *de meo* offers an example of the common idiomatic use of the neuter substantive where one might expect *de me* or, here, *de meis [verbis]* (Don. Ter. *Ad.* 940: *acutius 'de te' dictum est quam 'de tuo'*; ThLL VIII 920.55–62 [V. Bulhart]). Compare the English idiom "a friend of mine," which is usually explained as deriving from "a friend of my [friends]" (Hatcher 1950).

quod obscurus non erat: Sc. *error noster*.

hōc enim etiam turpius adflictatur res publica quod ne ab eo quidem vexatur, ut tamquam fortis in pugna vir acceptis a forti adversario vulneribus adversis honeste cadere videatur: That is, the loss to the republic is all the more shameful since the opponent is such a thoroughly wretched person, in contrast with opponents from the past. For this application of the verb *afflicto* and its non-frequentative form *affligo*, see *Sest.* 1 (*rem publicam afflictam*), on which Kaster 2006: 110 notes: "The image of the battered commonwealth..., whether used alone or with a complementary metaphor,... is almost unique to C[icero] and occurs with striking frequency in [*Sest.*], where it supports his strategy of identifying his own calamity with the commonwealth's"; for a full demonstration of such metaphors of the body politic see Walters 2020. In the phrase *ne ab eo quidem* the demonstrative pronoun *is* has the sense of *talis*, as often, here introducing a clause of result: "not even by the sort of person...." The pronoun refers, of course, to Clodius; cf. *Catil.* 1.22: *neque enim is es, Catilina, ut...*; KS 2: 2.248. The notion that the republic is being attacked by an unworthy opponent is underscored by the fact that it is being felled not by wounds inflicted in face-to-face combat (*vulneribus adversis*) but, it is implied, by being stabbed in the back when either not looking or, more sinisterly, while running away.

** ***honeste***: This is a conjecture of Gryphius; the codices are divided between *et honestis* P²GE and the nonsensical *homines* P¹H. While *et honestis* is acceptable in meaning (see Tac. *ann.* 1.49.3: *pectoribus inpiis honesta vulnera accepissent*), it seems redundant after the common expression *vulneribus adversis* and both the rhythm and sense of the sentence expect *cadere* to have an adverb (for the notion cf. *Rab. perd.* 37: *honeste moriendi facultatem*; *Phil.* 3.35: *honeste decumbant*).

41

Cicero compares Clodius with notoriously fiery tribunes from Rome's past (the Gracchi, Saturninus, Sulpicius). He devotes unexpected attention to their speaking abilities, presumably in silent contrast with that of Clodius, which has been characterized as crazed and irrational since the speech's beginning (1–2: *stultissimis interrogationibus; furentem exsultantemque; cum quibusdam fractis iam atque inanibus minis; sine voce*). Despite the clear disagreements that these past figures had had with the elite, fighting against them at least provided the consolation of conferring *dignitas* on their senatorial opponents.

41 *Ti. Gracchus*: Before a senatorial audience Cicero expresses ambivalence about the Gracchi, as here, recognizing their talents while simultaneously critical of how they used them. Van der Blom 2010: 103–107 offers a helpful survey, with bibliography, that illustrates how Cicero's attitudes toward the brothers varied depending upon audience and genre; see too the attempt of Tracy 2012 to find consistency in Cicero's occasional embrace of *popularis* stances (in particular 85–87 on the Gracchi). In his *De oratore* of the following year Cicero puts in the mouth of Crassus a similar sentiment of ambivalence regarding the brothers (3.226): "*doleo quidem illos viros in eam fraudem in re publica esse delapsos; quamquam ea tela texitur et ea in civitate ratio vivendi posteritati ostenditur, ut eorum civium, quos nostri patres non tulerunt, iam similis habere cupiamus*" ("I grieve that those men fell into the trap that they did in the case of the republic; although the cloth that is currently being woven and the type of life suitable for citizens that is being displayed for posterity are such that we now want to have citizens like those men whom our ancestors could not tolerate"; cf. Scaevola at *De orat.* 1.38). For other passages in which the Gracchi compare favorably with contemporary popular politicians see, e.g., *leg. agr.* 2.81, *Catil.* 1.3 and 4.4, *dom.* 24, *Vatin.* 23, *Sest.* 105, and in particular the dialogue between Marcus and Quintus about the tribunate of the people being a necessary evil (*leg.* 3.19–26). Grillius, a rhetorician from probably the fifth century CE, is particularly perceptive on Cicero's ambivalence regarding the two men: *sed quaeritur, cur hic ⟨inter⟩ optimos rhetores Gracchos enumeret, cum eos constet conturbasse rem publicam. hoc igitur respondemus in hoc loco Ciceronem verum loqui; nam si consideremus, iustum erat, quod moliebantur senatus consultis, ut populo agrum suum redderent, quem nobilitas occupaverat. ob hoc ergo perturbasse rem publicam iudicati, quia commutatus civitatis status vel in melius nocet. Cicero ergo quod in quibusdam orationibus illos reprehendit non verum iudicat, sed blanditur nobilitati* (*in Cic. inv.* 1.5.17–22 Jakobi=598.24–31 Halm).

Cicero begins his chronological account of past tribunes with the elder brother, Tiberius Gracchus. As a nominative in first position, Tiberius appears in parallel syntax with the mention of Clodius two sentences earlier (40: *idem iste*); that Cicero intends a contrast is indicated by the lack of a conjunction to unite this sentence with the previous. Tiberius Sempronius Gracchus (c. 163–133 BCE; *RE* 54) was born to a distinguished father of the same name; his mother Cornelia, a woman renowned for her erudition, was daughter of Scipio Africanus the Elder. Elected to the tribunate in 133, Tiberius dedicated most of his year in office to the redistribution of land to the disenfranchised poor, including veterans of Rome's wars. After a series of disruptions, the senate and people eventually voted his agrarian proposal into law. He made the unprecedented move of standing for re-election as tribune of 132 and during a demonstration he and over three hundred of his followers were killed by members of the senate. *MRR* 1: 493–494 lists the principal ancient sources on Tiberius. Plutarch provides a readable ancient, Stockton 1979 an accessible modern, biography of both him and his brother Gaius.

convellit statum civitatis: Cicero often employs the metaphor of "uprooting" the state and its institutions (*Caecin*. 51, *Pis*. 4, *Brut*. 115). Val. Max. 6.3.1 applies Cicero's formulation to describe the actions of both Gracchi: *statum civitatis conati erant convellere*. *Status civitatis* is, "with *status rei publicae*, one of the two phrases C[icero] uses when he wants to denote what we would call a constitution or what a Greek would call a *politeia*" (Kaster 2006: 109; 60 n. 1). Among Tiberius's actions as tribune, Cicero would be thinking of his unprecedented steps to bypass the senate with his agrarian bill, to remove a fellow tribune from office, to wrest control of financial affairs traditionally maintained by the senate, and to run for a second consecutive year as tribune (Stockton 1979: 82–84; see too 43n). Cicero accuses Clodius of attacking the *civitatis status* at 45.

qua gravitate vir, qua eloquentia, qua dignitate: The noun *vir* is included to make clear the syntax of this sequence of ablatives, which denote characteristics of Tiberius (KS 2: 1.226–227) rather than express manner with the verb *convellit*. Discounting *vir*, the emphatic anaphora underscores the pathos of the entire section: Tiberius Gracchus disrupted the state, but he did so with elegance (and, incidentally, while maintaining his masculinity). For assessments of Tiberius's oratory see, e.g., *Brut*. 103–104 (along with C. Carbo): *ingenium ad bene dicendum fuit.... nam et Carbonis et Gracchi habemus orationes nondum satis splendidas verbis sed acutas prudentiaeque plenissimas*. Manuwald 2019: 1.184–199 offers additional ancient testimony and oratorical fragments.

nihil: The fronting of *nihil* to precede the result clause further emphasizes this already emphatic negative adverb; the placement of *non* to introduce the indirect statement in the passage describing Gaius achieves the same effect (KS 2: 1.819).

ut: Cicero's presentation of the four tribunes offers a fine example of his skillful way of including variation within a series of parallel clauses. Each section begins with different ways of foregrounding the person described: Tiberius Gracchus occurs in the nominative in first position; his brother also occurs in the nominative, but is preceded by the main verb (*secutus est C. Gracchus*); Cicero then returns to nominative in first position to introduce Saturninus, who is here accompanied by an intensifying adjective (*ipse Saturninus*); he then closes this catalogue with a rhetorical question to introduce his account of Sulpicius (*nam quid ego de Sulpicio loquar?*). After these brief introductory remarks, a consecutive clause introduced by *ut* follows in each instance, detailing the results of their combined eloquence and demagoguery; the two devoted to the Gracchi do not contain a semantic signal in the main clause, whereas the remaining two are preceded by *ita* and *tanta* respectively.

a patris avique Africani praestabili insignique virtute: Tiberius's maternal grandfather was the great general Publius Cornelius Scipio Africanus (*RE* 336; 24n), who defeated Hannibal at Zama in 202, effectively ending the Second Punic War. Tiberius bore the same name as his father, Tiberius Sempronius Gracchus (*RE* 53), who had a promising military and political career that would not have presaged the radical politics of his two sons. He served as tribune of the plebs in the 180s (supporting his future father-in-law Africanus when accused of taking bribes; *MRR* 1: 376), held the consulship twice (177 and 163 BCE), celebrated two triumphs, and was elected censor in 169. He died in 154. Cicero contrasts the behavior of the Gracchi with their eminent ancestry at *Catil.* 1.4 (*interfectus est propter quasdam seditionum suspiciones C. Gracchus, clarissimo patre, avo, maioribus*); *de orat.* 1.38; *off.* 2.43, 2.80; *Brut.* 126. For application of the topos to Clodius see 26n.

praeterquam quod a senatu desciverat deflexisset: In the subordinate clause, *praeterquam* introduces the comparison ("other than"), with *quod* in this construction originally referring back to a single noun or demonstrative (e.g., *div.* 2.28: *at id, praeterquam quod fieri non potuit, ne fingi quidem potest*). Later the *quod* extended its range of reference to an idea, as here the area in which Tiberius differed in virtue from his ancestors (KS 2: 2.270–272). The juxtaposition of the indicative of what Tiberius did do (*desciverat*) with the subjunctive of what he did not adds to the pathos of unfulfilled promise, as does the repetition of the preverb *de-*, stressing the deviation from his ancestors' stability (*praestabili*). *Desciscere* characterizes Tiberius's actions also at 43, where Cicero describes a particular instance of his conflict with the senate.

*C. Gracchus, qu*o *ingENi*o, *quA eloquENtiA, quanTA* **VI**, *quanTA gra***VI***TAte* d*icen*d*i*: Gaius Sempronius Gracchus (c. 154–121 BCE; *RE* 47) began his political career serving on the land commission that was instituted by Tiberius's agrarian law. He was elected tribune of the plebs for 123 and, in a move attempted unsuccessfully by his brother before being murdered, for the year 122. He initiated numerous important and controversial pieces of legislation that aimed to alleviate the burdens of the poor and disenfranchised. These included provisions for the founding of several colonies, the administration of grain to Roman citizens at low prices, and the regulation of service in the military (*MRR* 1: 513–514, 517–518 for ancient sources). After standing unsuccessfully for a third term as tribune, he died during a riot at which several of his supporters were slain by senatorial opponents. As Cicero's tribute here makes clear, Gaius had a reputation as a forceful and dramatic orator, and he also elsewhere praises his *ingenium, eloquentia,* and *gravitas* (*Brut.* 125; cf. Liv. *perioch.* 60, Vell. 2.6.1). Plutarch maintains that he was the first speaker to address the people not when they were assembled in the crowded space between the speaker's platform and the senate house but in the more wide open forum, a move that Plutarch hailed as a step toward "democracy" (*Vit. C. Gracch.* 5.3). Cicero remarks that had he lived longer he doubts that anyone could have equaled him in eloquence and he recommends Gaius, before any others, as the speaker that an aspiring orator should read (*Brut.* 126; extensive fragments and testimony at Manuwald 2019: 1.256–317).

This concise synopsis of Gaius's speaking ability finds Cicero engaging in his own self-conscious, even competitive, display of eloquence. As noted above in the parallel description of Tiberius, the ablatives of characteristic employed here are usually accompanied by a noun in apposition such as *homo* or *vir*; here *vir* is understood from the earlier description of Tiberius (KS 2: 1.227 for Ciceronian parallels), an ellipsis which, in addition to the repetition of the nouns *gravitas* and *eloquentia*, serves to unite the like-minded brothers. Gaius's reputation as a more forceful speaker (Liv. *perioch.* 60; Vell. 2.6.1), however, is reflected in the more emphatic description. The tricolon of Tiberius increases to two bicola for Gaius, and the repeated noun *gravitas* is specified for him not as a general trait, but as a characterizing his speaking ability (*dicendi*). Finally, the repetition of sounds as marked above unites each set of bicola, which, together with the prominent assonance, suggests the famous musicality of Gaius's delivery.

ipse L. Saturninus: Lucius Appuleius Saturninus (*RE* 29) was tribune of the plebs in 103 and 100, during which time he passed popular measures in the tradition of the Gracchi such as a law setting lower prices for grain and the distribution of land in Italy and Africa to military veterans. Before he could enter a third term as tribune of 99, he was arrested for organizing a violent mob in support of Glaucia's illegal bid for the consulship (51n) and subsequently murdered before a trial could take place (*MRR* 1: 563, 575–576). Although not in agreement with Saturninus's politics, Cicero also displays admiration for his character and determination elsewhere (*Sest.* 37, 101, 105).

The abbreviation for the praenomen *Lucius* (*L.*) is omitted in **P**. For Cicero's regular inclusion of the praenomen in lists of historical actors from the past whom he has not mentioned earlier in a speech, even those well known, see, e.g., *Verr.* 2.3.209, *Catil.* 1.3–4, and cf. 7n.

ita fuit effrenatus et paene demens ut actor esset egregius et ad animos imperitorum excitandos inflammandosque perfectus: In his *Brutus*, Cicero classifies Saturninus among the *seditiosi*, noting that his exaggerated physical presence only gave the illusion of possessing the highest degree of eloquence (*Brut.* 224: *L. Appuleius Saturninus eloquentissimus visus est: magis specie tamen et motu atque ipso amictu capiebat homines quam aut dicendi copia aut mediocritate prudentiae*). The physical aspects of delivery—appearance, gesture, clothing—constitute *actio*, which is picked up here by the agent noun *actor*; for the significance of dramatic and exaggerated movements to tribunician oratory see Corbeill 2004: 107–139. Cicero describes Saturninus in terms similar to those used to characterize Clodius. Both were capable of oratory designed to rouse the masses, here characterized as *imperiti* ("naive"), an adjective that Cicero uses "virtually as a formula" to describe the Roman people assembled at *contiones* (Morstein-Marx 2004: 68 and n. 3). And just as Saturninus is "unbridled" (*effrenatus*), so too is Clodius's *furor* (2, 52). The next descriptor, however, adds an important qualification that distinguishes the two tribunes: whereas Saturninus's behavior verged on madness (*paene demens*), Clodius's was truly insane (33: *qua mente? quam amiseras*; 39; 48; forms of *demens* occur at 51 and 55). As Cicero goes on to argue, it is precisely this type of madness about which the prodigy warns (44).

** *actor*: This is a conjecture of Madvig 1871–1884: 3.226 for *auctor* of the codices. He reasons that an *auctor* should have some *auctoritas* ascribed to him and not simply *industria et vis* as here. In addition, Saturninus being an *egregius actor* accords well with Cicero's allusions to his *actio* in *Brut.* 224 (quoted in previous note).

nam quid ego de P. Sulpicio loquar?: In his prose treatises Cicero often uses the particle *nam* in doxographical lists to introduce a new proper name, perhaps with an ellipsis understood: "⟨I need hardly mention X⟩, for…" (Pease 1955–1958: 1.216–217). The suitability of including Sulpicius in this catalogue of famous tribunes is further demonstrated by the interrogative *quid*, which introduces the rhetorical figure of *praeteritio*, indicating that this concluding information is so well known as not to need mentioning (but that Cicero nevertheless proceeds to mention); cf. *Lael.* 104: *nam quid ego de studiis dicam…?*

Publius Sulpicius Rufus (*RE* 92) appears in *De oratore* as a young interlocutor eager to hear the discussion of the great orators M. Antonius and L. Crassus (dramatic date Sept. 91). As tribune in 88 he worked to ensure that Italians who had recently received citizenship were fairly assigned to urban tribes and he opposed Julius Caesar Strabo's illegal bid for the consulship (43n). Overturning the appointment of Sulla, he arranged for Marius to obtain the command in the Mithridatic Wars (54n). When Sulla marched on Rome in retaliation, Sulpicius was put to death and his legislation revoked. Although none of his speeches survived into the late Republic (*Brut.* 205), Cicero deemed Sulpicius, together with C. Cotta, the best speaker of his generation (Manuwald 2019: 2.56–73), a judgment reflected in his concise assessment at *Brut.* 203: *fuit enim Sulpicius vel maxime omnium, quos quidem ego audiverim, grandis et, ut ita dicam, tragicus orator. vox cum magna tum suavis et splendida; gestus et motus corporis ita venustus ut tamen ad forum, non ad scaenam institutus videretur; incitata et volubilis nec ea redundans tamen nec circumfluens oratio.*

The abbreviation for the praenomen *Publius* (*P.*) is omitted in **P**. See 7n and compare 41.

** *ubertas*: The unanimous reading of the codices is *brevitas*. It is difficult to see how *brevitas* contributes to the type of persuasion Cicero here attributes to him (Long 1856: 457; Lenaghan 1969: 162). The quality of *brevitas*, moreover, does not match how he characterizes Sulpicius's oratorical exuberance elsewhere (*de orat.* 2.88–89, 2.96, 3.31 [*verborum... copia*]; *Brut.* 203 [see previous n.]). Four solutions suggest themselves: Cicero intends to convey with *brevitas* a quality beyond its normal meaning, but no such quality suggests itself; Cicero mischaracterizes an orator that he saw in action (*Brut.* 203); Sulpicius's style changed over time (Lenaghan 1969: 162), which seems to be true (*de orat.* 2.88–89) but presumably Cicero describes Sulpicius in all these passages when he was at the height of his powers; the transmitted text is corrupt. The only emendation of which I am aware is *ubertas*, suggested by Shackleton Bailey 1985: 146–147 (cf. 1987: 276), who notes that "*ubertas* is a quality attributed to Sulpicius's model Crassus in *Balb.* 3." More to the point, at *de orat* 2.96 Sulpicius's oratory is described as insufficiently "compact" (*pressa*), and compared to the *ubertas* of crops. The change from *ubertas* is easily explicable, the noun having the same four initial letters as *breuitas*.

ut posset vel ut prudentes errarent vel ut boni minus bene sentirent perficere dicendo: The rhetorical figure of using an adjective and adverb of the same stem in close proximity, here *boni / bene*, is characteristic of colloquial Latin and particularly favored by Plautus (e.g., *Amph.* 278: *optumo optume optumam*; *Curc.* 521: *bella belle*; Hofmann 1980: 231, §88). Cicero employs the figure less frequently (e.g., *Att.* 3.23.5=SB 68: *miserum misere perdidi*) but the particular combination found here occurs in early formal prose; see, e.g., the prayer preserved in Cato *agr.* 134.3: "*bonas* preces *bene* precatus sum" or the formular phrase at Cic. *off.* 3.61: "*ut inter bonos bene agier oportet*" (Dyck 1996: 571; see too *off.* 3.70, *fam.* 7.12.2=SB 35). In this instance, however, Cicero negates the common figure through the addition of *minus*, thereby further characterizing Sulpicius's persuasive capabilities as perverse.

It is difficult to see the difference between the two alternatives presented: "He could cause the wise to err or the honorable to think dishonorably." The reference to *boni* adds a political dimension (5n), but presumably the *prudentes* must also be involved in politics to be misled by a tribune. Watts 1923: 371 attempts to make a distinction by translating the second half as "undermine the loyalty even of the loyal" (cf. Shackleton Bailey 1991a: 124, "shake the loyalty of the loyal"). When one notes the other redundancies and repetition in this short sentence—the awkward repetition of *dicendo*, the triple homoioteleuton of *-tas*, the three instances of *ut* in two different constructions, the non-committal use of *vel... vel* (30n), the collocation *boni minus bene*, and perhaps even the picking up of *perfectus* with *perficere*—it is tempting to suggest that Cicero here, as he had with Gaius Gracchus, is alluding to the young Sulpicius's verbal excesses, his *ubertas* (*de orat.* 2.88: *et verbis effervescentibus et paulo nimium* *redundantibus*). Without any excerpts of his oratory, however, this suggestion must remain conjectural.

molestum... molestia: In keeping with its etymology, the adjective and noun refer to the difficulty of ridding oneself of a troublesome obstruction (*moles*).

quandām tămēn dīgnītātēm: As the favored clausula of double-cretic + anceps underscores, Cicero signals the end of his account of the four historical tribunes through ring-composition of the "worthiness" at stake in these struggles. The *dignitas* attributed to Tiberius Gracchus at the opening is here retained at the end by the opponents of all four tribunes.

42–44 (*careret*)

To set up a contrast with the four tribunes just mentioned, Cicero presents a moralizing account of Clodius's public and private life that begins from the death of his father. He then returns in section 43 to the four tribunes to claim that, unlike Clodius, they were not driven by selfish motivations even though their cause was unjust. A vivid description of Clodius at the Bona Dea festival closes the section. These biographical facts have equipped Cicero with additional evidence for associating Clodius with the dangers portended in the haruspical response.

42 hic vero de quo ego ipse: The deictic *hic*, referring to Clodius as he listens in the senate house, juxtaposed with the emphatic *ego ipse* denoting his enemy Cicero, returns the subject from tribunician struggles in the historical past to the here and now. Grammatically, *hic* is the subject of the three verbs following the interjection *pro di immortales*. The disjunctive particle *vero* contrasts the *dignitas* of the Gracchi, Saturninus, and Sulpicius with the unmanliness that has characterized Clodius throughout his personal and political life.

pro di immortales: See 25n. It is uncommon for interjections introduced by *pro* to occur other than at the beginning of a sentence (*ThLL* X, 2 1438.48–53 [J. Ramminger]), and this placement of the exclamation is uniquely emphatic in Cicero. In particular, of the remaining seventeen instances of *pro di immortales* in his corpus, this is the only time that the exclamation divides a grammatical subject from its predicate (all twenty-seven Plautine instances begin a sentence or phrase). Following this emotional break Cicero segues into a studied rising tricolon in anaphora.

[hic] quid est: "What sort of thing is this man?," in contrast with *hic quis est*, "Who is this man?" The neuter pronoun *quid* is often used with masculine and feminine nouns to ask about essence, rather than identity (e.g., *nat. deor.* 1.60: *roges me, quid aut quale sit deus*; KS 2: 1.33). At the same time, the use of the neuter gender here has particular point in introducing doubts over Clodius's masculinity, which will be questioned over the next several sections (beginning with *a viro*).

quid valet: "What power does he have?" For the internal accusative with the intransitive verb *valeo* see, e.g., *fam.* 6.5.1=SB 239: *polliceor ei studium quidem* *meum... quantum valeam quantumque possim*; *Lig.* 23: *haec querela... quid valet?*

quid adfert: The verb *afferre* can have the sense of "to bring with hostile intent" (*OLD* s.v. 9; cf. 24n). The tricolon has moved from questioning Clodius's essence, to his potentiality, to his current activity.

quod di omen obruant!: "May the gods avert this omen!" A second interjection invoking the gods immediately after *pro di immortales!* continues the high emotional register. In this instance, a belief in the potential for uttered language to affect the external world necessitates the exclamation. Once Cicero has raised the possibility of the fall of the Roman state (*si cadet*), he must speak out to prevent his words from being realized. For other passages attesting to the Roman sensitivity to averting verbal omens, see *ThLL* IX, 2 575.47–56 (F. Oomes) and the collection at *RE* 18, esp. 356 (E. Riess); Pease 1921: 286; and more generally Lateiner 2005: 45–50.

Markland 1745: 351–352 notes correctly that Cicero "always writes" *avertant* in this formulation and includes the use of *obruere* as evidence for non-Ciceronian authorship (for *omen avertere* see *ThLL* II 1323.2–6 [E. Bickel]). Nevertheless, *obruere* can apply to the erasure of speech and language: 57.30–31: *iste parentum nomen... obruit*; *rep.* 6.25.3: *sermo autem omnis ille... obruitur hominum interitu*; Varro *ling.* 6.2: *quae [nomina] obruta vetustate... eruere conabor*.

a viro tamen confecta: This clause obliquely responds to the tricolon of rhetorical questions that introduce the *ut* clause—"What sort of thing is Clodius, what power does he have, what force is he using?" The answer, "nothing/none," becomes clear with the addition of the particle *tamen*—even if the state falls, "at least" let it seem to have been destroyed by a real man. The biographical sketch that follows details why Clodius cannot be considered a fully Roman *vir*. In the earlier invective that centered on Clodius's actions regarding the Bona Dea, it was essential that he be a *vir* to expose the enormity of the male violation of those female rites; see nn. on 8, 37. At this point in the speech, however, as he turns to the larger and more significant issue of how the response indicates Clodius's threat to concord among the elite, Cicero employs the common invective trope of impugning an opponent's masculinity. For the ideological connection between this trope and the stability of the state see Corbeill 1996: 128–173.

qui post patris mortem: The review of an opponent's early life in order to find evidence for current behavior constitutes a common motif in oratorical invective; for a classic example see *Phil.* 2.44–50 (where Cicero does not so mechanically signpost the steps in Antonius's development, and where he employs a wider variety of rhetorical tropes). The principle behind the practice is that past conduct provides a legitimate predictor for current and future behavior (Riggsby 2004). The sequence of topics is clearly set out by Cicero when he anticipates needing to defend the past actions of his client Flaccus from a similar attack. The correspondence with Cicero's invective at *har. resp.* is striking: *cum adulescentiam notaris, cum reliquum tempus aetatis turpitudinis maculis consperseris, cum privatarum rerum ruinas, cum domesticas labes, cum urbanam infamiam, cum...[in provinciis] vitia et flagitia protuleris,...*(Flacc. frg. Mediol.). The technique is recommended in the rhetorical tradition: *Rhet. Her.* 2.5: *in eo debebit esse occupatus ut ad eam causam peccati quam paulo ante exposuerit vita hominis possit accommodari; inv.* 2.32–33; Quint. *inst.* 7.2.28–34. For a full list of recommendations for, and examples of, *argumenta ex vita* for both the defense and the prosecution see Berry 1996a: 273–275.

Cicero uses direct and damning language here, only occasionally obfuscating with innuendo to lend his account a false sense of decorum. He also structures Clodius's biography in a precise chronology (for a slight deviation see n. on *deinde iam robustus* etc.): first (*primam*) his earliest youth in and around the home; then (*deinde*) his adventures as a young adult; afterwards (*post*) the period 68–67 and his experiences with the army and judicial bribery; further crimes (*inde*) committed in the provinces in the year 64, followed by (*unde*) his subsequent political career in Rome.

primam illam aetatulam suam ad scurrarum locupletium libidines detulit: A similar formulation describes the youth of Gabinius (*p. red. in sen.* 11: *cuius primum tempus aetatis palam fuisset ad omnium libidines divulgatum*). Cicero begins his account at the beginning, employing the adjective *primam* rather than the adverb *primum* in order to emphasize the early age at which Clodius's decadence began ("the notorious [*illam*] beginnings of his tender youth"). The uncommon diminutive *aetatula* underscores the context. Before Cicero it is applied solely to the youth of women, often prostitutes, or of young boys who are the object of pederastic attention (Plaut. *Persa* 229; the sole exception is *fin.* 5.55), and Cicero had used the same noun a month or so earlier to describe the homoerotic life of the young Gabinius (*Sest.* 18). The avoidance of the more expected *aetatem* (and perhaps *primum*) also allows Cicero to imply Clodius's effeminacy less directly through the unusual rhyming string of four grammatically feminine terminations (*primam illam aetatulam suam*; 6n).

The noun *scurra* can designate in Latin a kind of professional jester and musician, known particularly for his biting wit, but in Cicero the term more commonly refers by extension to "the amateur man about town, city wit and scandal-monger whose chief characteristic also is malicious intent" (Corbett 1986: 4; 59–61 on Cicero). In referring to their wealth Cicero implies that Clodius, whose family was allegedly impoverished with the death of his father (26n), required payment for his services, as he makes explicit at *Sest.* 39, where Clodius is described as acting as a "whore for wealthy *scurrae*" (*scurrarum locupletium scorto*). At the same time since Clodius's *scurrae* act as perverse proxy fathers, Cicero seems to be playing on the proverb that it is easier for a *scurra* to become a wealthy man than a respectable father of the household

(*Quinct.* 55: *vetus est "de scurra multo facilius divitem quam patrem familias fieri posse"*; Otto 1890: 314, no. 1614).

quorum intemperantia expleta in domesticis est germanitatis stupris volutatus: For the sexual euphemism *intemperantia* see Adams 1982: 222 n. 2. Continuing with the order followed at *Sest.* 39, Cicero introduces incest as the second charge after male prostitution. However, rather than specifying the singular object of Clodius's attentions as in the later speech (*cum sororis adultero*), Cicero's vagueness in vocabulary and syntax allows room for innuendo. Cicero often employs an abstract noun in place of a pronoun or a noun that directly describes a person or persons (37n), and here the required sense of *germanitas* to mean "of his sibling[s]" is in fact attested for later Latin (e.g., Apul. *met.* 5.27: *fallacie germanitatis inductă*; Courtney 1989: 52). Despite parallels, however, the usage remains odd, and one wonders why Cicero does not simply use a plural noun, as elsewhere, if he simply wished to refer to more than one sister (e.g., *cum sororibus*; 59). The ambiguity, it would appear, is precisely the point—the preceding sentence hinted at Clodius prostituting himself to men in his youth, while the one following continues to stress his passivity in sexual relations. Sandwiched in between these accusations Cicero adds the vague but steamy claim that Clodius "played around at home having sex with his siblings," which could refer to a sibling of either sex (although I doubt this would have concerned Cicero, it is unclear whether Clodius and all his siblings had the same parents and therefore technically shared ties of *germanitas*; see Tatum 1999: 33–36 and the detailed refutation in Tansey 2016: 127–129). Cicero offers the accusation of sex with a brother with equal vagueness (and deniability) at *dom.* 26 (*fratricida, sororicida*, with Corbeill 1996: 117–118) and *Sest.* 16 (*fraternis flagitiis, sororiis stupris*). Schol. Cic. Bob. p. 127.26–27 specifies that *Sest.* 16 refers to his brother Appius (on this identification see Kaster 2006: 410), which would also fit the context of *har. resp.*: as older brother and guardian to Clodius following their father's death (Varro *rust.* 3.16.2), the charge would continue the theme of Clodius's sexual passivity. The final oddity is the construction of the genitive *germanitatis*. Lambinus 1566: 704 remarks that the formulation is impossible in Latin and suggests emending to *in domesticis germanisque stupris*. But once again, the odd syntax appears to be precisely the point, as the construction could be equally an objective ("the sexual violation of his sibling[s]") or a subjective genitive ("his sibling's/siblings' sexual violation [of him]") or, of course, both, depending on the sex of his partner. The charges of incest against Clodius had become so common by this point (Kaster 2006: 409–411) that the use of the vague *germanitatis* afforded Cicero the opportunity for colorful variation while at the same time allowing each of his hearers in the senate to imagine for himself the range of the word's implications. The verb *voluto* also occurs in the context of incest at 59; see further Adams 1982: 193–194, who suggests that "*volutor cum sorore / fratre* had originally been a non-sexual set phrase. If so its transfer to the sexual sphere would have constituted a metaphor akin to that of 'playing'."

deinde iam robustus provinciae se ac rei militari dedit, atque ibi piratarum contumelias perpessus etiam Cilicum libidines barbarorumque satiavit: The introductory phrase *iam robustus* continues the attack on Clodius's sexual passivity (for the passive sexual connotations of *perpessus* see *ThLL* X, 1 1629.5–9 [U. Dubielzig]). Although now mature (*robustus*), Clodius still services older men sexually, a particularly taboo offense to the Romans. Clodius served in the military under Lucullus (42n), at some time before his capture by Cilician pirates in 67 (Strabo 14.6.6; App. *BC* 2.23; Dio 36.17.2–3, 38.30.5; Tatum 1999: 49–50; for date *MRR* 2: 148). Cicero presumably inverts the order of events to maintain a coherent narrative of Clodius's sexual history. Since the hendiadys of *Cilicum . . . barbarorumque* constitutes simply an expansion of *piratarum*, the sense of *etiam* must be "in addition to" the lusts of the *scurrae* at Rome and his siblings at home. By contrast with Clodius's fate, another well-known story that circulated about the capture of young Julius Caesar by Cilician pirates stresses his success at retaining his dignity, including his sexual purity (Vell. 2.41.3–42; Suet. *Iul.* 4; Plut. *Vit. Caes.* 1.8–2). Piracy greatly threatened Rome's trade in the eastern Mediterranean beginning from the second century until it was widely suppressed by Pompey in 67–66, with the Cilicians being such a prominent component that their ethnonym became synonymous with "pirate" (App. *Mith.* 92–93; Magie 1950: 1.281–301 has a general survey).

In a section of the fragmentary speech *De aere alieno Milonis*, Cicero also recalls Clodius's childhood to his audience (*or. frg.* A 15.19: *quis non meminerit pueritiam tuam?*), and compares the story of being ransomed from pirates with that of bribing the jurors at the Bona Dea trial, where he was "a second time bought from pirates" (*or. frg.* A 15.20: *iterum a piratis redemptum*, with Schol. Cic. Bob. p. 173.19 and Crawford 1994: 285; for the bribed jurors see 36n).

exercitu L. Luculli sollicitato per nefandum scelus: Clodius served on the staff of his brother-in-law Lucius Licinius Lucullus when Lucullus acted as proconsul in Bithynia, Pontus, and Cilicia (*MRR* 2: 111; 2: 139–140). According to Plutarch and Dio, Lucullus's strict discipline and unwillingness to court the common soldiers had made him unpopular and there were rumors that he would be recalled to Rome (Plut. *Lucull.* 33.1–2; Dio 36.16; Tatum 1991a: 572). The mutiny instigated by Clodius occurred at Nisibis during late winter 68 or early spring 67 and Plutarch marks it as the beginning of the decline of Lucullus's military career; subsequently, Clodius deserted both Lucullus and his troops (Plut. *Lucull.* 33–34; Dio 36.14.3–4, with Moreau 1982: 175–182, Tatum 1991a). Lucius, who died c. 57, was the brother of M. Lucullus, possibly the proxy *pontifex maximus* at this time (12n).

recenti adventu suo cum propinquis suis decidit ne reos faceret: "Freshly arrived in Rome, he came to an agreement with his relatives not to prosecute them" (literally, "not to make them defendants"). For this use of *recens* to refer to events in the past ("when his arrival was fresh," not "at his recent arrival"), compare *fam.* 5.17.2=SB 23: *proxime recenti adventu meo.* Upon returning to the capital from the East, Clodius would have been expected to make his mark as an orator, and the normal way of doing so quickly and effectively would have been through high-profile prosecutions (David 1979; David 1992: 497–589). Cicero pretends here that Clodius stooped so low as to contemplate even the prosecution of his closest relatives. As Lenaghan 1969: 163 neatly observes, "it was an easy charge to make, since it concerned something that did not happen" (cf. Tatum 1999: 53–54). The construction of *decīdo* with *cum* and a final clause appears elsewhere only in legal texts; see Paul. *dig.* 35.2.3.1: *si...heres cum creditoribus deciderit, ne solidum solveret...*; Ulp. *dig.* 44.4.4.6: *si is...cum debitore decidit...ut nomen emeret*; Scaev. *dig.* 2.14.44, 26.7.59. If, as it appears, the phrase is a technical term, Cicero's use of legal language to describe Clodius's alleged collusion makes the insult all the more ironic.

a Catilina pecuniam accepit ut turpissime praevaricaretur: For Catiline, see 5n. The asyndeton between the two main clauses, made easier by their parallel syntax and word order (prepositional phrase + main verb + *ut/ne*), reinforces the expectation raised by *recenti adventu suo* that Clodius made these arrangements with all speed while at the same time implying that both moves entailed bribes. The verb *praevaricor* refers to collusion with an opponent to achieve a specific outcome in a trial, in this case in Catiline's trial in 65 for extortion while governor of Africa; for other references to collusion with Catiline see *Pis.* 23, *TLRR* no. 212. In writing to Atticus Cicero, who had at one point been planning to defend Catiline, does refer to the cooperation of Clodius as prosecutor, although he does not indicate any possibile illegality: *iudices habemus quos volumus, summa accusatoris voluntate* (*Att.* 1.2.1=SB 11; see too Ascon. *tog. cand.* p. 87.13–15 Clark, with Marshall 1985: 98–99). Gruen 1971: 59–62 dismisses Cicero's claim here, arguing that the charge of collusion arose principally from the fact that Catiline was acquitted (see too Tatum 1999: 53–55).

cum Murena se in Galliam contulit: Lucius Licinius Murena (*RE* 123) attended his father as governor of Asia between 83 and 81. After holding the quaestorship in 75, like Clodius he served under Lucullus in the campaigns against Mithradates and upon his return to Rome was elected praetor (65), which led to the propraetorship in Gaul in 64–63 to which Cicero alludes. He became consul in the election for 62, which saw Catiline defeated, and subsequently came under prosecution for illegal canvassing. Defended by Crassus, Hortensius, and Cicero (whose speech survives as *Pro Murena*), he was acquitted; nothing is known of his life following his consulship. This is the only evidence for Clodius being on Murena's staff in Gaul; Broughton conjectures that he served as military tribune (*MRR* 2: 164).

in qua provincia mortuorum testamenta conscripsit, pupillos necavit, nefarias cum multis scelerum pactiones societatesque conflavit: Tatum 1999: 56 doubts the credibility of all Cicero's claims here. A telegraphic version of the first charge occurs in the same sequence of accusations against Clodius from

Sest. 39 to which reference has already been made (*cum testamentario*). The context here in *har. resp.* clarifies that the term *testamentarius* involves the forging or improper alteration of wills by Clodius, for which there are no other references. Evidence for the frequency of the charge can be found in the only other use of the substantive *testamentarius* in Cicero, where it occurs in a litany of crimes (*off.* 3.73: *de sicariis, veneficis, testamentariis, furibus, peculatoribus*) and must refer without further qualification to the false creation of wills. Champlin 1991: 82–102 surveys the range of testamentary forgery in the Roman world—from single words to entire documents—and attests to the ubiquity of the practice. In addition to forgery, Cicero accuses Clodius of killing legitimate heirs. *Pupilli* are a special class of beneficiary (Pompon. *dig.* 50.16.239 pr.); as young men no longer under the protection of their fathers, their murder evokes particular pathos. The final accusation, of forging criminal alliances, is more vague and therefore more widely applicable to whatever activity the senatorial audience wishes to imagine.

quaestum illum maxime fecundum uberemque campestrem totum ad se ita redegit: Cicero provides a striking series of accusatives to reflect the idea of Clodius accruing profit (*quaestum*) from electoral bribery bit by bit. Each adjective has point. Cicero suggests with *illum* that the activity was well known. The pair *fecundum uberemque*, in addition to underscoring the amount of Clodius's profit, offers an agricultural pun on *campestrem*, which refers to the urban location of the bribery, the *Campus Martius*, but which literally describes open fields and plains (for this usage see, e.g., *leg. agr.* 2.96, Liv. 30.33.9 [*uber*], Tac. *ann.* 1.79.2 [*fecundus*]). The final and emphatic *totum* ("all of it") anticipates the next sentence: Clodius did not share the profits since he systematically proceeded to murder his associates.

The verb *redigo* describes the payment of funds from one source to another; here Clodius is envisioned as diverting to his own pocket funds from electoral candidates that are intended for bribing voters. For the construction compare *Att.* 7.1.9=SB 124: *scripsi…me quicquid posset nummorum ad apparatum sperati triumphi ad te redacturum*.

ut homo popularis fraudaret improbissime populum: Cicero again plays with etymology to stress the inapplicability of a political term (cf. 41n). He particularly enjoys this *figura etymologica*, which he employs to discredit the claim of "popular" politicians that they work for the people: *Rab. perd.* 13; *dom.* 77: *ubi tu te popularem, nisi cum pro populo fecisti, potes dicere?* (for the joke see Nisbet 1939: 140); *Sest.* 110 (on the name *Publicola*, literally seeming to mean "the people's supporter"): *id [nomen] erit populare?* "*est enim homo iste populo Romano deditus*" (cf. *rep.* 2.53 with Corbeill 1996: 83); *Sest.* 114; *Vatin.* 39; *or. frg.* A 9.9. Near the end of his life, Cicero applies the same paronomasia to himself: *me commovet propterea quod popularem me esse in populi salute praeclarum est* (*ad Brut.* 9.2=SB 7). Robb 2010 offers a comprehensive overview of the connotations of the much discussed term *popularis*.

*** *idemque vir clemens divisores omnium tribuum domi ipse suae crudelissima morte mactaret*: Codex G reads *demens* (Peterson records it for P also, which I would support from autopsy; Maslowski does not note this possibility). It is easy to understand the reading in G considering that madness is associated with Clodius throughout the speech (for forms of *demens* alone see 39, 51, 55). By contrast, the murderous context makes the better attested reading, *clemens*, clearly ironical, and is thereby the preferred *lectio difficilior*. Courtney 1989: 53, citing *p. red. in sen.* 17, suggests that the reference to *clementia* "means that Clodius objected to Cicero's execution of the Catilinarians." Although the alleged actions described in this sentence belong to 63, it is difficult to read a reference to the Catilinarian conspiracy in this one adjective.

For *divisores omnium tribuum* see 28n. For the unusual and hence emphatic position of *ipse* beside a form of *suus*, compare Quint. *inst.* 2.15.8: *Galli…Sulpici filium suis ipse manibus circumtulerat*; LHS 2: 190; *ThLL* VII, 2 350.64–72 (F. Tietze).

43 *exorta est*: The verb *exorior* often has the sense of appearing suddenly out of an unexpected source (*ThLL* V, 2 1571.3–6 [G. Meyer]). By putting the verb in first position, Cicero reflects this sense, and forces the listener to wait through an unusually long sequence of nouns in the dative before ending with the grammatical subject (*funesta quaestura*); cf. 4n (*erupturum*).

rei publicae, sacris, religionibus, auctoritati vestrae, iudiciis publiciis: In addition to being relevant to the events of Clodius's quaestorship, each item in this asyndetic series has direct relevance to the response and Cicero's reading of it: the state of the republic (40, 55, 60), the violation of religious rites (9, 21, 37), the authority of the senate (40), and the public trial concerning the Bona Dea incident (36). For the sequence *sacris, religionibus* see 8n.

quaestura: Clodius held the quaestorship in 61. Even though the Bona Dea incident occurred in December 62 while he was still quaestor designate, Lenaghan 1969: 165 observes that since the trial took place in 61 Clodius's quaestorship can justifiably stand for the scandal and its aftermath.

deos hominesque, / pudorem, pudicitiam, / <u>senatus auctoritatem</u>, / ius, fas, / leges, iudicia / violavit: This long catalogue in asyndeton repeats in different words, but in much the same order, many of the concepts listed in the previous clause: here the first four words allude to elements involved in the religious violation of the Bona Dea, the last four to those related to the subsequent legal and judicial process. Emphatically placed in the middle of both lists is the authority of the senate, which will now meet to judge Clodius's relationship to ritual and legal matters. Except for *senatus auctoritatem*, the enumeration consists entirely of binary phrases, a complementary set of words that give the impression of a totality (Krostenko 2004: 245–247; see 22n). The components of each of these pairs have varying relationships with each other: gods and men constitute a merism expressing the two groups to which ritual applies, *pudor* and *pudicitia* the abstract and concrete forms of sexual purity (see nn. on 1, 9), *ius* and *fas* human vs. divine law (34n), *leges* and *iudicia* legislation and the processes that this legislation governs. Krostenko 2004: 259 characterizes these structures as representing "the words of a *vir* who knows how things work and knows how to talk about them in such a way as to show that he knows." Cicero produces a similarly paired list of the qualities in Rome that Milo has preserved by murdering Clodius. Cicero imagines Milo freely admitting to the murder (*Mil.* 77, with Keeline 2021: 294): "*adeste, quaeso, atque audite cives! P. Clodium interfeci, eius furores, quos nullis iam legibus, nullis iudiciis frenare poteramus, hoc ferro et hac dextera a cervicibus vestris reppuli, per me ut unum ius aequitas, leges libertas, pudor pudicitia maneret in civitate.*" Langlands 2006: 302–305 notes how the pairing *pudor* / *pudicitia* appears "alongside major institutions of Roman society, as if these qualities too are part of the institutional structures that regulate that society" (303). Their violation constitutes an attack on the Roman state.

atque HIC *ei* GRADUS—*o misera tempora stultasque nostras discordias!*—*P. Clodio* GRADUS *ad rem publicam* HIC: The noun *gradus* commonly denoted a step on Rome's *cursus honorum* (*ThLL* VI, 2 2152.64–2153.21 [U. Knoche]), the succession of elected offices that an aspiring politician sought to hold, beginning for patricians with the quaestorship as here and ending with the consulship or censorship. The altered order of nouns after the interjection is pointed: as has been noted, Cicero takes care to use vocabulary that connects the actions of Clodius with the language of the response (*discordia*, for example, recalls 40). By specifying the referent of *ei* immediately after the mention of *discordia*, Cicero indicates that Clodius's acquiring the quaestorship marked the beginning of the conflict observed by the *haruspices*. For the sarcastic specification of Clodius's praenomen *P[ublio]* cf. 8n.

In Cicero exclamatory *o* normally introduces the accusative of exclamation for nouns (79 examples :: 22 without), whereas the tendency is slightly reversed with pronouns (e.g., *me miserum!* 10 examples without *o* :: 7 with; LHS 2: 48).

** *primus* ⟨*fuit*⟩ *et aditus ad popularem iactationem atque ascensus*: While the sense of this passage is clear, it is difficult to determine precisely what Cicero wrote. The principal codices have the following variations: *primus est* H; *primis est* P; *primum est* GE. The adjective *primus* is undoubtedly correct, and Madvig 1871–1884: 3.226 emends *est* of all the codices to *fuit et*. While the present tense of *est* can be made to make grammatical sense—"this first entrée into the republic (i.e., the quaestorship) is [an] approach and ascent to popular sway"—Madvig is surely correct that Cicero would hardly characterize in this way the quaestorship in general.

Cicero signals the end of his early biography of Clodius—from first youth to his entry into elected office—by returning briefly to the *exempla* of the four historical tribunes that had introduced it. Rather than concentrating on their individual oratorical skills as earlier, Cicero instead explains the motivations that each had had in abandoning the senatorial for the popular cause. The actions of all are explicitly attributed to *dolor* ("grievous indignation") at 44 (cf. *dolori* [Tiberius], *dolor* [Gaius], *dolore* [Saturninus]), the same emotion to which Cicero appeals in justifying his disdain for Clodius; see nn. on 3, 4, and 17. Although Cicero's apology for these tribunes has an obvious rhetorical purpose, Tatum 1999: 13 well points out that "the strategy...is inconceivable unless it was actually the case that Romans, particularly senators and equestrians, expect patterns of behavior like the ones Cicero outlines" (cf. Tatum 1999: 88).

invidia Numantini foederis: During his quaestorship of 137, Tiberius acted as envoy for the consul Gaius Hostilius Mancinus (*RE* 18) to negotiate a treaty with the Numantines after the Romans had suffered a series of defeats. Since he had struck the agreement without consultation of the senate, it was proposed that he and Mancinus be surrendered to the Numantines as prisoners; in the end, only Mancinus was handed over, but the Numantines refused to accept him and he returned to Rome (sources at *MRR* 1: 485). Cicero attributes Tiberius's political shift, and the state's subsequent loss of his oratorical talents, to the same senatorial "envy" at *Brut.* 103: *propter turbulentissimum tribunatum, ad quem ex invidia foederis Numantini bonis iratus accesserat, ab ipsa re publica est interfectus* (cf. Vell. 2.2.1; Quint. *inst.* 7.4.13; Dio 24.83.1–3).

cui feriendo...interfuerat: The phrase *foedus ferire* is the customary way to describe the "striking" of a treaty (*ThLL* VI, 1 516.58–61 [W. Bannier] lists thirty-nine occurrences). The vivid expression invited etymological speculation even in antiquity (those deriving from the adverb *foede* are catalogued in Maltby 1991: 237–238). Servius provides the most likely derivation, that it derives from the "striking" of a sacrificial hog to finalize the agreement (Serv. *Aen.* 10.154: *propter porcum qui de lapide feritur*). This interpretation accords with the curse that Livy records as spoken at the moment of sacrifice against anyone who violates a treaty: "*tum illo die, Iuppiter, populum Romanum sic ferito ut ego hunc porcum hic hodie feriam; tantoque magis ferito quanto magis potes pollesque*" (Liv. 1.24.8; cf. 9.5.3, Varro *rust.* 2.4.9). For the construction of *interesse* with the dative gerundive, see *ThLL* VII, 1 2283.12–15 (A. Szantyr) and cf. 13: *scribendo adessent*.

C. Mancini consulis: Upon his return to Rome after the Numantines had refused to accept him as prisoner, Mancinus endeavored to resume his career as a senator. He was initially refused on the grounds that his surrender to the enemy deprived him of Roman citizenship, but a law was passed restoring these privileges and he was even elected to the praetorship for a second time (*RE* 8: 2.2511 [F. Münzer]; for the praetorship see Pompon. *dig.* 50.7.18). The interlocutor Crassus in *De oratore* characterizes the incident of the Numantine treaty and its consequences for the consul Mancinus as the most important case involving civil law for an aspiring orator to know (*de orat.* 1.181–182). For discussion and bibliography of the numerous allusions see Reinhardt 2003: 278.

252   *Commentary*

dolori et timori: Quint. *inst.* 7.4.13 notes that Tiberius's fear was that the charge of making the Numantine treaty would be transferred from Mancinus to himself. For *dolor*, see 43n.

a gravitate patrum desciscere: At *prov. cons.* 18, Cicero regrets how the Gracchi disappointed the expectations raised by the successful career of their father: *patrem dico, cuius utinam filii ne degenerassent a gravitate patria*. The parallel prompted Shackleton Bailey to read here *patria* for *patrum* (1985: 147; 1991a: 125). Despite the striking similarity, the emendation is unnecessary. The same verb has just been used, also of Tiberius's alienation from the senate, at 41 (*a senatu desciverat*). The repetition here, together with the fact that the context assumes that Cicero would continue talking about the *senatus severitas*, ensures that the reference is to to senators and not a biological father.

C. autem Gracchum mors fraterna, pietas, dolor, magnitudo animi ad expetendas domestici sanguinis poenas excitavit: The concrete act—the murder of his brother Tiberius—is accompanied in the same grammatical case by the abstract qualities of Gaius that manifested themselves as a result of this murder and motivated him to take vengeance (for his exemplary devotion to his brother see Bannon 1997: 127–135). Along with *dolor*, this list includes another quality that Cicero chooses to redefine to suit his rhetorical purposes. In his *De partitione oratoria* he includes as a chief characteristic of *magnitudo animi* the ability to endure wrongs, and in particular those that are unjust (77: *magnitudo animi... est... altitudo animi in capiendis incommodis et maxime iniuriis*; cf. *parad.* 16, of M. Atilius Regulus). Here it is the same quality that prompts Gaius to take vengeance.

Although the adjective *domesticus* is not uncommon in the speeches, Cicero clearly intends Gaius's desire to avenge "bloodshed within his family" (*domestici sanguinis*) to echo the similar description of Clodius's "sex with his siblings," including his own brother[s] (42n: *domesticis... germanitatis stupris*).

Saturninum, quod in annonae caritate quaestorem a sua frumentaria procuratione senatus amovit eique rei M. Scaurum praefecit, scimus dolore factum esse popularem: As with Tiberius, the act driving Saturninus's move to popular politics occurred while serving his country as quaestor. Little is known about this incident from 104 beyond what Cicero relates here. Saturninus's duties included transporting grain from Ostia to Rome when for unclear reasons the senate took away this commission; additional sources include Sest. 39 (where he is also a negative foil to Clodius), Diod. 36.12. The sequence *dolore factum esse popularem* will be echoed in describing Clodius's less admirable transformation to the popular cause (44: *a stupro est factus repente popularis*). Cicero rarely uses the perfect indicative (*amovit, praefecit*) in a *quod* causal clause where logic requires the pluperfect (Lebreton 1901: 218); he may be suggesting here the close interval between the cause of Saturninus's removal from office and its actual occurrence (cf. the emphatic *scimus*).

Sulpicium ab optima causa profectum, Gaioque Iulio consulatum contra leges petenti resistentem: As Powell 1990: 457–458 notes, *ab optima causa profectum* cannot be Latin for "after abandoning the optimate cause" as had been the prevailing view (influenced by passages such as *de orat.* 3.11, *Lael.* 2, both quoted in next n.). Rather, the phrase *ab optima causa profectum* indicates that in opposing Strabo's candidature Sulpicius had right on his side ("starting with the best intentions"). For this regular sense of *proficiscor ab* to indicate not deviation from a prior course but progress from a point of origin see *ThLL* X, 2 1710.27–56 (I. Hajdú): "qui initium quoddam capiunt eoque nituntur fundamento."

Gaius Julius Caesar Strabo Vopiscus (*RE* 135) appears in *De oratore* as the interlocutor best qualified to speak on the role of humor in oratory (*de orat.* 2.216–290; Manuwald 2019: 2.32–47). He became aedile in 90 and afterwards, in violation of the customary sequence of the *cursus honorum* that he then hold the praetorship, sought the office of consul, apparently for 87 (*Phil.* 11.11; Lintott 1971: 446–449). Sulpicius and his tribunician colleague of 88, Publius Antistius, put up legal resistance to this attempt, which eventually escalated to violence (*Brut.* 226; Ascon. *Scaur.* p. 25.8–11 Clark). The year following this ultimately unsuccessful attempt at the consulship Strabo was killed in the purge following Marius's return to Rome in 87 (*de orat.* 3.10; Liv. *perioch.* 80). Marshall 1985: 144–145 surveys scholarly discussion of these events.

longius quam voluit: "Further than he had intended." The capricious nature of the "popular breeze" makes it hard to control; for this meaning of *velle* see *OLD* s.v. 16. Powell 1990: 458 argues that Cicero refers in particular to the fact that Sulpicius's turn toward popular causes caused him to alienate many of his former friends and allies, for which see especially *de orat.* 3.11: *quibuscum privatus coniunctissime vixerat, hos in tribunatu spoliare instituit omni dignitate*; *Lael.* 2.

popularis aura: Attested first and only here in Cicero, the phrase occurs frequently in later Latin prose and poetry, always with a contemptuous tone; Quintilian contrasts the "popular breeze" with the fixedness of *gravitas senatoria* (*inst.* 11.1.45). *ThLL* II 1479.49–76 (O. Hey) provides a full list, including variations such as *aura vulgi / populi*; see too Kaster 2006: 326–327. Vergil's application of the term in *Aeneid* Book 6 invites particular speculation. In his description of the residents of Hades, immediately after the mention of the early Roman king Tullus, Vergil notes that the king "Ancus [Marcius] follows boastfully, even now delighting too much in the popular breezes" (*Aen.* 6.815–816: *sequitur iactantior Ancus / nunc quoque iam nimium gaudens popularibus auris*)—perhaps Tullus / Marcius is a sly nod to Marcus Tullius, the apparent coiner of the phrase?

44 *nulla enim potest cuiquam male de re publica merendi iusta esse causa*: Although none of these four tribunes (*in his omnibus*) had a just cause for their actions since they acted against the state, they were nonetheless serious and

254 Commentary

driven by a sense of masculine pride. The mention of "manly spirit" (*animi virilis*) invites the contrast with the Clodian persona that follows, just as the previous two references to *popularis* politics set up the punch line.

**The major codices have a variety of readings: *merendae* P, *merenti* GH, *meriti* E, while the *recentiores* contain *merendi*. The reading *merenti* is easily explicable by a scribe creating an adjective in agreement with the common idiom ("for anyone behaving badly in regards to the state"), modifying *cuiquam* and dependent upon *iusta*. However, the construction of the noun *causa* with a gerund in the genitive and dative of reference is ubiquitous throughout Cicero: *Font.* 22: *causa nobis tacendi* ("the reason for our being silent") and above at *har. resp.* 10: *mihi... datam non modo iustam sed etiam necessariam causam... dicendi* ("not only a just but even a necessary reason for speaking has been given to me"). It is best, then, to print *merendi* in light of these parallels and the reading of P, which is difficult to account for otherwise, and its status as the *lectio difficilior* after *cuiquam*. It is also worth noting that *merendi* makes the clause periodic since *causa* is necessary to complete the construction, whereas with *merenti* the required syntax ends with *esse*.

P. Clodius a crocota, a mitra, a muliebribus soleis purpureisque fasceolis, a strophio: The use of the preposition *a* + ablative recalls Cicero's characterization of Sulpicius immediately above (43: *Sulpicium ab optima causa profectum*: "starting with the best intentions") and the parallel underscores how, rather than beginning from a situation of well-intended politics, Clodius's transformation into a *popularis* began with transvestism and sacrilegious sexual behavior (for *ab* meaning "[immediately] after," see *ThLL* I 37.71–38.61 [E. Lommatzsch]). Through word order, Cicero describes Clodius enacting a textual striptease, followed by a seduction (Leach 2001: 337–338). The garments mentioned at the beginning of this catalogue are not only associated with women, as one would expect given that Clodius is described as disguising his sex in order to penetrate the Bona Dea, but when worn by men they have strong connotations of effeminacy and luxury (Heskel 2001: 139–140). First removed is the *crocota*, a saffron-colored outer robe that when worn by men in Aristophanes signifies "doubtful masculinity or an undeniably feminine demeanor" (Cleland *et al.* 2007: 107); for the effeminizing connotations in Latin, see Naev. *trag.* 43 *TRF*: *crocotis malacis* ("in delicate gowns"; cf. Plaut. *Aul.* frg. 1). Clodius then doffs a second piece of clothing designated by a Greek, and hence suspect, word: the *mitra* (worn by Clodius also at *or. frg.* A 14.22; for the sarcastic resonance of Greek words in Cicero's speeches, see Laurand 1936–1940: 72–74). This headdress had inescapable associations with effeminacy (Cleland *et al.* 2007: 127; Serv. Auct. *Aen.* 4.216: *sane quibus effeminatio crimini dabatur, etiam mitra eis adscribebatur*; *ThLL* VIII 1160.79–1161.2 [H. Rubenbauer]). Since the next item removed, the slippers (*soleae*), suits either sex (Cleland *et al.* 2007: 173–174), Cicero specifically designates Clodius's as appropriate for women (*muliebribus*). Next to drop from Clodius's body, like Salome's veils, are *fasceolae*, bands wrapped about various parts of the limbs and torso (Schol. Hor. *sat.* 2.3.255). Their effeminate associations when worn by men are further enhanced by the diminutive termination of the noun (*-ola*) and their luxurious purple color (Cleland *et al.* 2007: 67; used of Clodius without the suffix at *or. frg.* A 14.22, where they wrap around his feet). At last, Clodius removes the breastband, a final comic touch since it is unclear how this undergarment would enhance his disguise (Clodius's breastband appears also at *or. frg.* A 14.24; Astrid Khoo points out to me *per litteras* that breastbands could be visible, citing Aristoph. *Thesm.* 637–642, in which Mnesilochus, who is also infiltrating a religious ceremony restricted to women, wears a breastband evident to other characters [τὸ στρόφιον]; for the possibility that Clodius is trying to create the impression that he has breasts, see Gibson 2003: 208 on the problematic passage Ov. *ars* 3.274).

a psalterio: The Greek-derived noun *psalterium* ("lute") has associations with effeminacy and unRoman behavior in a well-known oratorical fragment from the previous century in which Scipio Aemilianus laments the state of Roman education (Scip. min. *or. frg.* Macrob. *Sat.* 3.14.7: *docentur praestigias inhonestas:* **cum cinaedulis et sambuca psalterioque** *eunt in ludum histrionum, discunt cantare, quae maiores nostri ingenuis probro ducier voluerunt: eunt, inquam, in ludum saltatorium inter cinaedos virgines puerique ingenui*). In Cicero's catalogue the noun marks a transition from the preceding items of clothing to the following two neuter words describing Clodius's behavior (*a flagitio, a stupro*), creating the image of Clodius tossing aside the final element of his female disguise in order to engage in the active sexual activity that Romans identified with the male.

a flagitio, a stupro est factus repente popularis: Cicero's litany of shame ends with a pair of nouns that form a virtual hendiadys ("disgraceful sexual behavior"), combining as they do characteristics of an abstract fault of the mind (*flagitium*) with a vividly concrete fault of the body (*stuprum*; see 8n, and 1n for this type of combination). He pairs these nouns with Clodius's external appearance also in his description of the Bona Dea rites at *dom.* 105: *non solum aspectu, sed etiam incesto flagitio et stupro caerimonias polluit* ("he has defiled rituals not only with his gaze, but with his vile sexual behavior"). As Cicero effects for Clodius a symbolic sex change from feigned woman to active male, the removal of Clodius's feminine disguise enables him to be involved in *stuprum* as a man. It is notable how the series of terminal *-a* sounds, suggesting femininity, ends with the revealing of Clodius as male (*est factus*). The *haruspices* appear to have specialized in diagnosing not only androgyne prodigies, but also cases when people undergo sex changes from female to male—they are attested as being summoned for two such cases, the *(quin)decimviri* and pontifices for none (Liv. 24.10.10, 13; Plin. *nat.* 7.36; MacBain 1982: 119). The contention that Cicero suggests here that Clodius is a prodigy suitable for treatment by the *haruspices* is supported by the fact that, following Cicero's one other extensive description of Clodius's tranvestism, the orator interjects dramatically *o singulare prodigium, o monstrum!* ("A unique prodigy, a sign!"; *or. frg.* A 14.22 with Crawford 1994: 255). For a general discussion of the function of prodigies in Ciceronian invective, see Corbeill 2008.

ancillarum beneficio emissus esset: The slave-girl accomplices, with their diminutive suffix (anc<u>illa</u>), contrast with the vengeful *mulieres*. This detail is recounted also at *Att.* 1.12.3=SB 12; Plut. *Caes.* 10.4, *Cic.* 28.4; Schol. Bob. p. 91.3–5 Stangl. As Leach 2001: 338 notes: "Although he may have shed his feminine costume, there remains the humiliating obligation to the women who rescued him from some undefined *terminus*. How can a man who owes his salvation to the *beneficium* of an *ancilla* be a sturdy supporter of the people?" The verb *emitto* is used in the same context at 4, and later of Clodius's dismissal from the subsequent trial for *incestum* (37; cf. *Sest.* 134, *Pis.* 95, where in each case the release is considered inappropriate). Nisbet 1961: 168 notes that the verb can describe the release of a caged animal in the arena (more examples at *ThLL* V, 2 501.42–76 [B. Rehm]); especially relevant here is *Rhet. Her.* 4.51 (*sicut e cavea leo emissus*) where the comparison is with someone acquitted by a jury unwisely. In each occurrence in *har. resp.* suspicious members of the Roman community—bribed jurors and slave-girls—are represented as Clodius's accomplices, allowing him to escape from just punishment.

res publica cive tali careret: All other instances of the combination *talis civis* in Cicero describe an outstanding citizen (e.g., *Flacc.* 104–105, *p. red. in sen.* 19, *Mil.* 66; cf. Milo at 7) and in each case *talis* always precedes the noun (except when in correlation with a following *qualis*). The ironic use here is signaled both by the preceding paronomasia *populari...populus* and by the postponement of *tali* to follow *cive*.

44 (*Hanc ob amentiam*)–52

Having capped Clodius's biography with the incident of his crossdressing in 62 BCE, Cicero briefly narrates the political turmoil that has characterized Clodius's activities from his unprecedented bid for the tribunate to the present day. Throughout this section Cicero ties Clodius's behavior to the portion of the haruspical response quoted at 40. He concentrates on how Clodius's tribunate in particular is the cause of the DISCORDIAM DISSENSIONEMQVE among the Roman elite, and he calls for the senate to unite against him and his allies.

44 <u>Hanc</u> ob amentiam in discordiis <u>nostris</u>: For the use of *discordia* in this speech, see 40n. The chiastic order of adjective-noun / noun-adjective serves to separate Clodius (*hanc=eius*) from the senate (*nostris*), while at the same time tellingly juxtaposing "madness" and "discord," visually illustrating how the latter proceeds from the former. Cicero also plays with etymology by juxtaposing Clodius's lack of mind (*a+mens*) with the senate's riven feelings (*dis+cor*; for this sense of *cor*, see *ThLL* IV 935.79–936.83 [F. Reisch]).

de quibus ipsis his prodigiis recentibus: The adjective *ipse* follows its noun frequently in Cicero (345x vs. 544x when it precedes; Marouzeau 1922: 186). Here, as at 45 (*de quo ipso*) with its similar antecedent (*discidium*), *ipsis* is best understood with the preceding *quibus [discordiis]*. A further indication that the adjective does not belong with the following *his prodigiis recentibus* is that in Cicero *ipse* never immediately precedes *hic* when the latter is accompanied by a substantive (Fischer 1908: 130–131; cf. LHS 2: 408).

a dis immortalibus: While the gods are indeed responsible for conveying the prodigies, it is the *haruspices* who supplied the warning about elite discord. As noted at 20, as the speech proceeds, Cicero elides the warnings from the *haruspices* to become those of the gods themselves and, eventually, the view of any clear-thinking member of his audience.

arreptus est unus ex patriciis: This and the following sentence refer to Clodius's irregular election to the office of tribune of the plebs for which, born a patrician, he should have been ineligible. According to Dio 37.57.1, Clodius first tried to have some of the tribunes of 60 BCE propose opening the office to patricians. Failing in this, he attempted to have his own individual status changed to plebeian through a vote of the *comitia centuriata*; it is this move that Metellus, Clodius's brother-in-law and consul of 60, after offering initial support, ultimately blocked with the cooperation of the senate (*Att.* 1.18.4=SB 18, 1.19.5=SB 19, 2.1.4–5=SB 21; *Cael.* 60; Dio 37.51.2). Tatum 1999: 90–102 provides a reliable discussion and bibliography concerning our evidence for the transition of patricians to plebeian status along with the legal and religious controversies that surrounded Clodius's failures at gaining such status. Ultimately, Clodius realized his goal through his adoption into a plebeian *gens* by a man that Cicero claims was no more than twenty years old (*dom.* 34), a ceremony over which Pompey presided as augur (45n). Since his father was deceased, Clodius was no longer under paternal authority. As a result, the adoption could take place only through a *lex curiata*, which was passed through the efforts of Julius Caesar in his capacity as consul and *pontifex maximus* (45n). Immediately afterwards, Clodius's newly adoptive father manumitted him (ancient sources at Tatum 1999: 284 n. 85). Cicero offers a detailed, albeit tendentious, account of the technicalities involved at *De domo sua* 34–42 (on which see Tatum 1999: 104–108; 57n). In reading Cicero's invective on this topic it is worth noting that although patricians could not become tribune, the tribunate was hardly restricted to members of the non-elite. Between the period 78 and 49, almost 30 percent of known tribunes were from plebeian families that had previously held the consulship, while at least thirteen more had reached praetorian rank (Gruen 1974: 181–189).

tribuno: For the grammatical attraction of this word from the expected accusative into the dative case, see LHS 2: 99 (cf. Liv. *perioch.* 50: *consuli fieri non licebat*, where the subject is not expressed; several parallels, most with subject understood, in *ThLL* VII, 2 1360.63–83 [W. Buchwald]). Contrast, e.g., *Balb.* 29: *si civi Romano licet esse Gaditanum*.

** non liceret: This is the reading of all codices. Ernesti 1810: 917 deleted *non*, understanding the emphasis of the sentence to be on the uniqueness (*unus*) of this event ("Etenim an eum noluerunt tribunum fieri?"; he is followed by Shackleton Bailey 1991a: 126, who translates "Clodius was snatched up to be the only patrician eligible for the tribunate"). Wolf 1801: 369, however, compares *leg.* 3.21, also referring to Clodius: *neminem in nos mercede ulla tribunum potuisse reperiri, nisi cui ne esse quidem licuisset tribuno* ("No one could be found at any price [to work] against us, except the one for whom it had not even been allowed to become tribune"). In light of this parallel, *non* makes good sense: "This single patrician was snatched up, for whom it was not permitted that he become a tribune." The sarcasm underlying the remark fits well with the sentence that follows, which notes that the possibility of Clodius acquiring the tribunate was originally resisted by the year's consul and the senate. Tatum 1999: 281–282 n. 21 points that Cicero's description here is imprecise, since Clodius was not in fact made tribune while a patrician, but only after being adopted into a plebeian *gens*, a transition that made his election technically legal.

45 This section opens with one of the longer sentences in the speech as well as one of the hardest to follow, in part because Cicero coyly avoids naming names (*adfinis et sodalis, is consul, eo...auctore*). Two of the triumvirs are deliberately alluded to in dense syntax in order to obfuscate as much as possible their contribution to Clodius's actions as tribune. In addition, the vague referents of *is* (Caesar), *illi* (Clodius), and *eo* (Pompey) convey the impression of confusing and shifting alliances. Steel 2007 analyzes Cicero's tactic of avoiding names in passages of both praise and blame; particularly applicable here is her remark that "to attack people without naming them, even if their identity can be deduced, would seem to lessen the offence to them" (110). See too nn. on 47, 48.

anno ante frater Metellus: The reference is to 60 BCE, the "year before" the consulship of Julius Caesar, when Clodius was elected tribune. The consul that year was Q. Caecilius Metellus Celer (*RE* 86), who was married to Clodius's sister. He served as Pompey's legate in Asia in 66 together with his brother Metellus Nepos and became urban praetor of 63, in which year he led an army against the Catilinarian conspirators but came into conflict with Cicero on account of the latter's disagreements with Nepos, who had become the newly elected tribune of 62 (*fam.* 5.1–2=SB 1; for more on Nepos see 13n). In his consulship of 60 Metellus opposed Pompey on both political and personal grounds (Pompey had divorced his sister Mucia for alleged infidelities; Plut. *Pomp.* 42.6–7; Shackleton Bailey 1965–1970: 1.299). Cicero suggests that he was murdered by Clodia soon thereafter (*Cael.* 59–60; Schol. Cic. Bob. *Sest.* p. 139.8–10 includes Clodius as a second suspect). After Celer's death, Cicero praises him as *socio laborum, periculorum, consiliorum meorum* (*Sest.* 131).

De haruspicum responsis 45

The sense of *frater* is contested (cf. note below on *frater consul*). There is no instance of the word meaning "brother-in-law." Shackleton Bailey 1977b maintains that he and Clodius shared the same mother, making them half-brothers, which would necessitate that he and his wife Clodia had different mothers for their marriage to be legal. Tatum 1999: 35–36 and Tansey 2016: 124–126 summarize an unpublished study by T. W. Hillard, M. Taverne, and C. Zawawi which argues that they were in fact cousins on their fathers' side (*frater patruelis*, often abbreviated to *frater*, for which see Shackleton Bailey 1977b: 148, *ThLL* VI, 1 1254.83–1255.18 [F. Vollmer]). This would allow Clodia Metelli to remain a full sister to Clodius, as is implied at 42. Most recently, Tansey 2016: 120–140 provides a full discussion that includes valid objections to both reconstructions and offers several new possibilities (stemmas on 134–138).

concors etiam tum senatus, principe Cn. Pompeio sententiam dicente: The combination *concors senatus* seems not to occur anywhere else in Latin, but cf. *prov.* 47: *concordia senatus*, Tac. *dial.* 40.4: *nulla in senatu concordia*, and the fact that between 63 and 43 the senate occasionally held meetings in the temple of Concordia (*LTUR* 1: 317 [A. M. Ferroni]; cf. 61n). Cicero clearly uses the uncommon adjective, occurring only one other time in the speeches, to mark a contrast with the *discordia* predicted in the response.

**The text in the lemma is that of the manuscripts, except that all codices read the easily emended *principi* (*princi* P¹)... *dicenti* and P alone reads *senatu senatus*. In light of the latter Lambinus 1832: 267 tentatively suggested *concors etiam tum senatus, senatus principe*, an emendation followed by Peterson and Lenaghan 1969: 168. However, despite the fact that Cicero regularly refers to Pompey broadly as a *princeps* (e.g., *p. red. in sen.* 4: *princeps... civitatis*; *prov. cons.* 41: *principem civium*; *fam.* 3.11.3=SB 74: *omnium saeculorum et gentium principis*), there is no record of his holding the official title of *princeps senatus*, a position that in any case had lost much of its relevance by the late Republic. Ryan 1998: 168–224 demonstrates clearly, contrary to what is commonly assumed, that while the privileges of the *princeps senatus* were reduced under Sulla, the title did not fall into abeyance (his suggestions for emending this passage at 204–205 are unacceptable). The meaning here is simply that Pompey was the first person to render his opinion in the senate on this particular occasion. This is our only evidence that Pompey objected to Clodius's bid to become plebeian.

excluserat acerrimeque una voce ac mente restiterat: The sense of unanimity underscored by the phrase *una voce ac mente* is reinforced by the use of singular verbs with the compound subject *Metellus et... senatus* (for the expectation of a plural verb see *OLS* 1: 1248–1251, who acknowledges that a full semantic analysis has not been made on this issue).

id: As commonly, the pronoun is the post-positive antecedent of the introductory *quod*, and provides a subject to *perturbatum itaque permutatum est*. The same construction occurs in the result clause that follows.

post discidium optimatium: Cf. 40: PER OPTIMATIVM DISCORDIAM DISSENSIONEMQVE. This sentence is the closest that Cicero comes to saying that the division of the *optimates* resulted from the creation of the First Triumvirate in 60 (Lapyrionok 2008: 29–30). The only action of the unnamed Caesar and Pompey that he emphasizes, however, is the adoption of Clodius as a plebeian. Cicero does not dwell on any of their other activities but instead quickly turns his attention to the tribunate that resulted from this adoption.

ita perturbatum itaque permutatum est: The anaphora of *ita* combined with the partially rhyming dispondees *perturbatum / permutatum est* gives the phrase a serious and solemn quality (*perturbo* is a particular favorite of Cicero, used 135x in contrast with 16x for the simplex *turbo*: ThLL X 1829.48 [M. Erwin]).

adfinis et sodalis, clarissimus vir: The noun *adfinis* refers to relationship by marriage; it is disputed what was the precise familial relationship between Pompey and Clodius. Pompey had divorced Clodius's half-sister Mucia in late 62, so it is difficult to agree with Shackleton Bailey 1983 that this is the connection to which Cicero refers for Pompey's actions in 60 (as dated by *frater consul*), especially since that divorce seems to have been an unhappy one (note above on *anno ante frater Metellus*). Cicero also alludes in correspondence from 51 to a marriage between Pompey's son Gnaeus and Clodius's niece (*fam.* 3.4.2=SB 67, 3.10.10=SB 73; cf. Dio 39.60.3, on 54 BCE). On the basis of this passage from *har. resp.*, Hillard proposes that this later union began in 60, and perhaps was planned as early as 62. He argues that Cicero is able, by alluding to the ties between Pompey and Clodius at that time, to claim that Pompey's eventual choice to support Clodius arose from these marriage connections and not from any antipathy toward the orator (1982: 35–36). Tatum, however, rejects this hypothesis on the basis of Dio 38.15.6, which alludes to the marriage of Mucia as a tie between the two men as late as 59, and therefore dates the marriage of Gnaeus and Clodius's niece rather to 56 (endorsed by Seager 2002: 181–182). He particularizes further that the marriage would have occurred prior to *har. resp.*; the resulting chronological inaccuracy of Cicero seeming to call the two men *adfines* in 60 on the basis of this match is, he goes on to claim, "not foreign to the technique of Ciceronian oratory" (1991b: 128–129). It is difficult to reconcile between these two reconstructions but, on balance, it seems preferable to imagine with Hillard that it is in fact the union of Gnaeus with Clodius's niece in 60 that is being referred to here.

Cicero's use of the term *sodalis* is fraught with equal uncertainty. The designation can describe members of a group organized for religious functions; the bonds among such *sodales* made their relationship analogous to blood or marriage relations in the sense that they were not expected to pursue each other in court (Hellegouarc'h 1963: 109–110). There is no evidence that Clodius and Pompey had such a connection. *Sodalis* could also describe the member of a *sodalicium*, a term always used in a pejorative sense to describe a group that distributed bribes in order to secure votes in an election; in the year following the delivery of *har. resp.* the *lex Licinia de sodaliciis* was passed to curb such activity (*Planc.* 36–48; Hellegouarc'h 1963: 109–110). Hillard, reviewing the evidence for Clodius engaging in electoral bribery since 62, including the allusion at 42, suggests that *sodalis* refers here to questionable canvassing by Pompey and Clodius in L. Afranius's bid for the consulship of 60 (1982: 36, 42–43). One wonders, however, what advantage Cicero would gain in *har. resp.* from implicating Pompey in such activity. Finally, the term can be used generally to describe men with various types of special links, such as comrades in war or simply close friends. Dio 38.15.6 notes that Clodius had had extensive military service under Pompey (Tatum 1991b: 126–127 discusses a possible occasion). It is either this or the more generic use of *sodalis* to which Cicero refers here. His point is that, despite their familial connection (*adfinis*) and close ties outside the family (*sodalis*), Pompey nevertheless initially opposed Clodius's plan to become part of a plebeian *gens*.

qui illum reum non laudarat: "Who had not praised him when on trial." Pompey seems to have retained his neutrality when Clodius was defendant (*reus*) during the Bona Dea proceedings, stating publicly no more than that he supported the trial preparations that were being organized by the senate (*Att.* 1.14.1–2, 6=SB 14; cf. 1.16.11=SB 16). It is unlikely that *laudarat* is used here technically to refer to his refusal to deliver a *laudatio* of Clodius (Moreau 1982: 205–207), particularly since Pompey was awaiting a triumph and hence could not have attended the trial (Hillard 1982: 41 n. 42). That Pompey adopted a guise of neutrality suits both the Latin and the context (Hillard 1982: 41, followed by Tatum 1999: 85).

is consul: This is the first clear allusion in the speech to Julius Caesar, consul of 59, who would have been campaigning in Gaul when it was delivered. As elsewhere, however, Caesar is not named (cf. the omission of his name at 4, 38, and from the list of *pontifices* at 12, where see note). Although no one in his audience would be unaware of the reference to his consulship, not including the name appears to soften the criticism (cf. Kaster 2006: 150).

The adoption of a man no longer under the authority of his father, as Clodius was, was called *adrogatio*, and could proceed only when the college of *pontifices* had determined that there were no technical objections; after this a special session of the *comitia curiata* voted on the adoption (Watson 1967: 82–88). Accordingly, Cicero adds *consul* here to indicate Caesar's actions in calling together the curiate assembly by dint of that office (Bleicken 1957: 355; cf. *Sest.* 16: *hanc...beluam...solvit subito lege curiata consul*; cf. *Att.* 2.12.2=SB 30). Caesar would then have presided over the vote of the *lex curiata* in his capacity as *pontifex maximus*. Cicero complained that this particular *lex* was passed with irregular speed, three hours after promulgation, rather than after the normally prescribed twenty-four days (*Att.* 2.7.2=SB 27; *dom.* 39, 41; cf. Suet. *Iul.* 20.4); for the dubious legitimacy of Cicero's objection see Tatum 1999: 106.

qui illi unus inimicissimus esse debuerat: "Who ought to have been Clodius's single greatest enemy." When Curio related to Cicero in April 59 the news of Clodius's intention to stand for election as tribune, he characterized in similar language Clodius's intentions: he is seeking the office "both as the greatest enemy of Caesar, and to rescind all his laws" (*Att.* 2.12.2=SB 30: '*et inimicissimus quidem Caesaris, et ut omnia*' inquit '*ista rescindat*'; cf. *Att.* 2.9.1=SB 29). Since this remark in *har. resp.* presumably also includes reference to Clodius's alleged affair with Caesar's wife (38n), its coyness is notable.

eo fecisse auctore se diceret cuius auctoritatis neminem posset paenitere: The reference is to Pompey, who became augur at a young age, no later than 71 BCE (Rüpke 2008: 846, no. 2756), and in that capacity provided divine authorization for the *comitia curiata* that approved Clodius's adoption (*Att.* 2.9.1=SB 29, 2.12.1=SB 30, 8.3.3=SB 153; cf. Dio 38.12.2). He may also have assisted Caesar in taking the auspices on that occasion (Linderski 1986: 2193 n. 172). The repetition of the antecedent within the relative clause (of the type *locus, quo in loco*) ensures accuracy and so is typical of legal and religious language (LHS 2: 563); the variant here, incorporating the repetition of a related form (*auctore... auctoritatis*) occurs not infrequently in literary texts (Landgraf 1914: 92). Since Cicero purports to be quoting Caesar, it is perhaps not coincidental that this construction commonly occurs in the first book of his *Bellum Gallicum* (Paslay 1918: 348), which is likely to have been in circulation by this time (Wiseman 1998).

iniecta fax est foeda ac luctuosa rei publicae: In abrupt asyndeton after the tortuous sentence that recounted the maneuvering for Clodius's adoption comes this concisely expressed and vivid metaphor describing the result of that adoption: Clodius as a torch cast upon the state (cf. 45: *flamma*). For the associations of the epithet *fax*, especially with the Furies, see 4n, where it describes Piso and Gabinius. As he does throughout the speech, Cicero employs grammatically feminine words to describe Clodius (6n).

** Manuscripts vary on word order: *fax est* **PG**, *est fax* (*fas* **H**[1]) **EII**[2]. It is best here to follow **P** and **G**; in this way, *est* brings focus to *fax* (Adams 1994a), the most significant component of the metaphor.

petita est: The verb continues the metaphor of the torch; Cicero uses the verb *peto* to describe a lightning strike in his poetry (*carm. frg.* 3.37), and it is used often in later poetic texts to describe attacks with fire (*ThLL* X, 1 1951.69–75 [U. Dubielzig]; Sen. *Tro.* 445; *Octavia* 688, 851). Cf. *petebantur* at 45.

totus denique civitatis status: For *civitatis status* as the Latin equivalent for "constitution," see 41n.

haec enim certe petebantur, cum in me cognitorem harum omnium rerum illa flamma illorum temporum coniciebatur. excepi et pro patria solus exarsi, sic tamen ut vos isdem ignibus circumsaepti me primum ictum pro vobis et fumantem videretis: Cicero, together with the other most important features of the republic, bursts into flame as a result of Clodius's attacks. While Cicero several times employs the metaphor of "burning" as a result of unpopularity (*invidia*; e.g., *Catil.* 1.29: '*tum te non existimas invidiae incendio conflagraturum?*' [*patria* speaking], with Dyck 2008: 116), the sustained imagery here, culminating in the orator "going up in smoke" (*fumantem*), is particularly striking.

The vivid indicative form *coniciebatur* is used in the *cum inversum* clause and is made even more vivid by the rare use of the imperfect (KS 2: 2.338–342; OLS 2: 245–248). The perfect tense of *excepi*, juxtaposed in asyndeton with the imperfect, describes in turn the instantaneous moment when Cicero received the flame on behalf of the state, with the senate already engulfed in these same figurative fires. To understand that Cicero here stands metaphorically for his home, subsequently damaged by Clodius and his mob, ruins the effect (so H. Rubenbauer, *ThLL* VI, 1 1539.40–42).

46 ** *sed etiam crescebat inter eos odium a quibus nos defendi putabamur*: All codices read *in eos* except E, which has *in consules* (presumably at some point *eos* was construed as the abbreviation *cos*). Shackleton Bailey 1991a: 127 judges the reading "nonsense," perhaps overharshly, and emends to *inter eos*, which Berry 1993: 175 deems "a certain correction." Madvig 1871–1884: 2.141 takes a different approach to the problem by retaining *in* and reading *nos non defensi* (or simply *non defensi*) in light of the division in the manuscripts (*defensi* PG, *defendi* EH); in this interpretation the hatred is directed against those who did not support Cicero. I have chosen to print with Shackleton Bailey *inter eos*, which fits better the context of discord among the elite that Cicero stresses throughout this section. The decision between *defendi* and *defensi* is more difficult, but the progressive sense of the present infinitive rather than the perfect participle suits the context, describing those working continuously for Cicero's recall from exile ("by whom we were thought to be defended," rather than "to have been defended").

***isdem auctoribus, Pompeio principe*:** The consecutive ablative absolutes more vividly present the various conditions and actors at work to engineer Cicero's recall than would have the ablative of agent with *ab*. In the first months of his exile, Cicero's correspondence with his brother makes clear that he viewed Pompey as a traitor for not standing up to Clodius (*ad Q. fr.* 1.3.9=SB 3, 1.4.4=SB 4; *Att* 10.4.3=SB 195, from 49 BCE, shows that nearly a decade later his disappointment had still not disappeared). Pompey's increasing discontentment with the actions of Clodius, however, eventually led him to work for Cicero's return, prompting a tribune to propose his recall in the senate as early as July 1, 58, a proposal that was vetoed by Aelius Ligus (*Sest.* 67–68; for Ligus see 5n). Pompey nevertheless continued in his attempts, communicating about the issue in September with Caesar in Gaul (*Att.* 3.18.1=SB 63; cf. *fam.* 1.9.9=SB 20) and, spurred by Clodius's violent protests of the following year (see, e.g., *Sest.* 84–88) and following a motion from the consuls, he proposed before the senate in July 57 that Cicero be recalled as the savior of the state, with the added suggestion that the vote be made by the people (e.g., *p. red. in sen.* 29; *dom.* 38–39; *Sest.* 73–74, 129; Dio 39.8.3). For a full overview of Pompey's actions during these years see Seager 2002: 101–109.

qui cupientem Italiam, flagitantis vos, populum Romanum desiderantem non auctoritate sua solum, sed etiam precibus ad meam salutem excitavit: Even before the senate meeting of July 57 that brought the issue of Cicero's restoration before the Roman populace, Pompey traveled throughout Italy to stir up support; much of the language here is echoed at *p. red. in sen.* 29 (see too *p. red. in sen.* 31; *dom.* 25, 30; *Pis.* 80; *Mil.* 39; cf. Vell. 2.45.3). The order of nouns in the tricolon roughly mirrors Pompey's campaign, from traveling around Italy, to meeting with the senate in July, to addressing the populace in advance of their vote in August (cf. *dom.* 30). Kaster 2006: 333 comments well on the situation of Pompey as Cicero describes him here, who both persuaded through his authority and lowered himself to supplication: "In a request based on *auctoritas* the petitioner occupies the superior position and expects to gain his aim just because the other party is disposed to grant it; in supplication, the hierarchical positions are reversed, as the petitioner presents himself as the dependent party."

rēstĭtūtī sŭmŭs: Cicero concludes the sentence describing his restoration with a favored double cretic. The attractive rhythm provides a segue into the next phase of the argument, that with Cicero's return concord among the orders is at last possible, provided that Clodius can be eliminated.

sit discordiarum finis aliquando, a diuturnis dissensionibus conquiescamus: Although both halves of this chiastically structured sentence assert the same objective, the repetition of *discordiarum* and *dissensionibus* echoes the language of the response (40n.).

eadem ista labes: *Eadem* here contrasts with Cicero's supporters, described as *isdem auctoribus* directly above. The opposing sides are the "same" as before, the difference now being that Cicero is back to offer his assistance. Once again, a feminine noun describes Clodius (6n). Cicero uses the epithet *labes* to describe Verres (*Verr.* 1.2), Gabinius (*Sest.* 20, 26; *Vatin.* 25), and Piso (*Pis.* 3, 56), as well as Clodius (*dom.* 2, 107, 133), and the epithet is later applied to bad emperors and their rivals (Opelt 1965: 139, 169–170). The noun *lābes* (>*labor*, "to slip, fall down") can refer to destruction or ruin and, when applied to a person, to the instrument of that ruin (cf. passages such as *Verr.* 1.1.2: *labem et perniciem provinciae*; *dom.* 2: *labes ac flamma rei publicae*). The metaphorical "ruin" that is Clodius remains the subject of the verbs as it goes on to hold *contiones* and stir up trouble, with Clodius the human being reemerging at 46 (*ab isto*). The relationship is unclear between this noun and *labes* ("stain"), which seems to be the sense of the epithet at, e.g., *Sest.* 20: *labi illi et caeno* (see *ThLL* VII, 2 768.57–60 [P. Flury]).

** ⟨***modo his se***⟩**,** ***modo vendat illis***: For Clodius "selling" himself, see 1n. Lambinus first filled this suspected lacuna with *se modo his* (1830: 267). Baiter

1862 placed the adverb first (*modo se his*) to better account for the three words being omitted by haplography (Willis 1972: 112–113), and is followed by Peterson. Klotz 1915: 149 altered to *modo his se* and is followed by Maslowski. With this order the unemphatic personal pronoun *se* gives focus to *his*, which is fitting given its contrast with *illis* (Adams 1994b).

nec tamen ita ut se quisquam, si ab isto laudatus sit, laudatiorem putet, sed ut eos quos non amant ab eodem gaudeant vituperari: Cicero's formulation is a clear allusion to the rhetorical categories of praise (*laus*) and blame (*vituperatio*) that young orators were taught and that Cicero came to master (Corbeill 2002: 199–201; Thurm 2018: 64–75). Through this allusion Cicero criticizes Clodius as an orator who sells his services not to praise, but only to increase dissent among his hearers.

After asserting that Clodius makes improper use of his rhetorical training, Cicero proceeds to express what he finds remarkable about the reactions that his fellow Romans, serious and wise as they are, have to that rhetoric. The main construction consists of a tricolon, on the one hand clearly marked by the sequence *primum…deinde…postremo* while on the other simultaneously varied in the constructions governed by *miror* (first the accusative *homines*, then clauses introduced by *quod, si,* and *quod* again). The first two parts of the tricolon treat what these Romans do, namely allow respectable fellow citizens to be abused by the impure Clodius while believing that the abuse can have effect. The third, climactic, portion expresses what they do not realize: that Clodius could at any moment turn on them.

The repetition of the noun *homo* is worth noting. The first occurrence (*homines*) refers to the elite who have been encouraged to discord by Clodius, while the second *hominem* apparently refers to Pompey (Lenaghan 1969: 170). Then the final two instances (both in the genitive *hominis*) describe Clodius in a derogatory context, a frequent connotation of the singular form (1n).

quemquam clarum hominem atque optime de re publica saepe meritum…perditi hominis profligatique maledictis: Cicero has previously employed this type of conjunct hyperbaton, in which a noun intervenes between two associated adjectives (the "brave men and true" construction), at 2n (Piso and Gabinius), 28 (Brogitarus, where the noun is also *homo*), and 37 (Lentulus Crus). The pattern is found in Latin prose and poetry of all periods, and the unexpected word order provides focus for both adjectives, placed as they are at the beginning and end of a sense unit (Devine and Stephens 2006: 586–591; Chahoud 2018: 146–147). The two negative adjectives describing Clodius receive further emphasis here through alliteration and homoioteleuton (*perditi…profligati*). In both instances, the intervening noun is *homo*, whose empty semantics has the force of a pronoun and thereby gives the flanking adjectives even greater prominence (Chahoud 2018: 147–148, citing *ThLL* VI, 3 2882.13–58 [C. O. Brink]; cf. 28n).

The use of the pronoun *quisquam* after a verb of wondering (*miror*) indicates that the object of wonder is about something that the speaker would not have expected to happen (KS 2: 1.638–639). Cicero marvels at the possibility, which he would have deemed unlikely, that his colleagues prefer the slanders of Clodius over the well-established patriotism of someone like Pompey, the principal person to be identified with *hominem*.

deinde si: The verb *miror* takes a *si* clause as its object rather than the expected *quod* (as in the previous and following clauses) if the statement about which wonder is expressed is only possible or if, as here, it is still in question (KS 2: 2.424–425). The wonderment is further reinforced by the emphatic position of *posse* ("is it possible?"), the aside *id quod minime conducit ipsis* ("something that hardly befits them"), and the repetition of *cuiusquam* (see previous note). By using *si* as the conjunction Cicero expresses his skepticism that a man such as Clodius could damage anyone's reputation through his speech.

illius furentis ac volaticos impetus: All codices agree on this reading, although it is tempting to emend to *volatici* so that the word describes Clodius (taking *furentis* as genitive). The adjective has the sense of "flighty" or "fickle," and Clodius's fickleness is precisely the point in this context. While there is no problem with understanding hypallage here, with the "fickleness" transferred from Clodius to his violent actions, this is the only example from the classical period in both LS and *OLD* in which the adjective is applied to something inanimate (*Att.* 13.25.3=SB 333: *Academiam volaticam* is a personification), with the *ThLL* archive containing examples only from Ambrose (*sermo*), Augustine (*affectus?, spiritus*), Cassiodorus (*imaginatio*) and a late panegyric (*arma*). While it is general practice for pronominal adjectives in oblique cases to be accompanied by a noun, there are several instances in Cicero of *ille* occurring in the genitive with an unaccompanied adjective: *Verr.* 2.5.162: *nulla vox alia illius miseri*; *leg. agr.* 2.49: *illius absentis dignitatem* (predicative); *dom.* 41: *ad illius miseri causam*; *Tusc.* 5.62; *fam.* 14.4.3=SB 6; cf. *Rhet. Her.* 4.65.

47

Cicero implicates the First Triumvirate in his exile, while simultaneously claiming that their complicity was a product of Clodius's delusions.

ex hac nimia non nullorum alienatione a quibusdam: "As a result of this wholesale alienation of not a few people from certain individuals." The anonymity of the pronouns *nonnulli* and *quidam* accords with Cicero's previous efforts at obfuscating which members of the elite were actively involved in supporting Clodius during his tribunate (45n). As with the thinly veiled reference earlier at 46 (*quemquam*), it would seem that *quibusdam* refers to Pompey, with the direct identification being further confused by the plural number. For numerous examples of Cicero's use of the plural to refer to one person, see Nisbet 1939: 106–107 (on *dom.* 41, where *quosdam viros fortis* refers only to Julius Caesar); KS 2: 1.86–87 discusses the rhetorical plural more generally.

Gelzer 1937: 6, on the contrary, sees the pronoun as being truly plural and referring to the three members of the triumvirate, presumably in light of Cicero's subsequent naming of all three members. It seems more natural, however, to see *quibusdam* as picking up the references to Pompey that had preceded rather than as looking forward to the triumvirs.

levius: Sc. "than now," when the entire republic is suffering rather than Cicero alone. Since Clodius has broadened his attack, Cicero feels compelled to act. The following sentence contains a six-fold repetition of *nisi* (governing five clauses), concluding with a short and punchy apodosis. The repetition of *nisi* in a series of contrary-to-fact conditions conveys the idea of how easily it could have been to avert Clodius's emergence as the tormentor of Cicero and the republic.

an iste nisi primo se dedisset iis quorum animos a vestra auctoritate seiunctos esse arbitrabatur, nisi eos in caelum suis laudibus praeclarus auctor extolleret: For the use of *an* see 23n. The adverbial *primo* governs the contrafactual clauses concerning all the things Clodius did to make it seem that he was allied with the triumvirs, and anticipates *postea quam* at 48, which introduces the steps he took to oppose the triumvirs, in particular Caesar, when their alliance proved illusory.

If the identification of Pompey alone with *quibusdam* in the previous sentence is correct, Cicero now for the first time turns to the ways in which Clodius used—falsely, Cicero claims—the threat presented by all three triumvirs (*iis, eos*) to advance his political agenda. He makes the same claim, with similar examples, at *Sest.* 39–40, the only other place in the post-exile speeches where the triumvirs are singled out by name (on the passage see Kaster 2006: 211–216). Cicero describes the relationship between the senate and the triumvirate also at 50 (*qui a vobis seiuncti videbantur*), where again their dispute with the senate is depicted as illusory. Cicero may be rewriting recent history here: the extent to which Clodius had initially "surrendered himself" to this alliance is a matter of debate among modern scholars. Gruen 1966 offers a reassessment of Clodius's relationship with the triumvirs during his tribunate to argue that in the majority of his actions he can be seen acting as an independent agent; he considers Cicero probably accurate here in finding Clodius's public assertions of triumviral support to be without substance (1966: 126–127). For a more recent assessment of Clodius's complicated maneuverings with the alliance, see Tatum 1999: *passim*, esp. ix–x, 102–103 (Pompey), 108–111 (esp. Caesar), 151–154, 172–175.

Woodman 2018: 228 notes that the expression *aliquem laudibus/laude extollere* "seems something of a set phrase" (Sall. *Iug.* 15.2; cf. *Iug.* 4.2 [*laudando*]) and suggests that at Tac. *ann.* 4.41.3 it implies a reference to the rhetorical teachings on speeches of praise or blame (cf. *inv.* 1.22: *nostram causam laudando extollemus, adversariorum causam per contemptionem deprimemus*). The addition of *in caelum* ("to high heaven") is frequent in Cicero, particularly in his correspondence (*ThLL* III 91.10–14 [W. Bannier]). Woodman's suggestion that the phraseology recalls rhetorical terminology would fit the ironic description of Clodius as a "renowned authority" (*praeclarus auctor*), a tone underscored by the inclusion of the adjective *praeclarus*, which Cicero employs in an ironic sense numerous times throughout his corpus (e.g., *Cluent.* 14: *[Sassia], illa egregia ac praeclara mater*, *Flacc.* 36: *[Asclepiades] praeclarus iste auctor suae civitatis*; *ThLL* X, 2 488.25–63 [P. Gatti]); Landgraf 1914: 200 points out that in such cases the adjective nearly always precedes the noun.

nisi exercitum C. Caesaris—in quo fallebat, sed eum nemo redarguebat—nisi eum, inquam, exercitum signis infestis in curiam se inmissurum minitaretur: Clodius's threat to call down upon the senate the armed troops of Caesar was an empty one, as made emphatically clear in the parenthesis by Cicero, who certainly would not want it to get back to Caesar in Gaul that he thought there was any truth lying behind Clodius's words (cf. *Sest.* 42: *intenta signa legionum existimari cervicibus ac bonis vestris falso, sed putari tamen*). Nevertheless, Clodius's alleged threat does have some basis in fact. Later historians note that, while Clodius was beginning his quest to have Cicero exiled, he held a *contio* outside the city that included Caesar, who was preparing to leave for Gaul with his army (Plut. *Cic.* 30.3–5; Dio 38.17.1–2). Cicero alludes to this episode elsewhere in the speeches after his exile where, as here, he questions claims that Caesar was then his enemy (*p. red. in sen.* 32: *erat alius ad portas cum imperio in multos annos magnoque exercitu, quem ego inimicum mihi fuisse non dico, tacuisse, cum diceretur esse inimicus, scio*; cf. *dom.* 5: *exercitus terrore*, 131; *Sest.* 52; *leg.* 3.25). Boll 2019: 221–222 suggests that the phrase *ad portas* at *p. red. in sen.* 32 (also at *Sest.* 41) alludes to the threat of "Hannibal at the gates" during the Second Punic War (for the proverb, Otto 1890: 158–159); if so, the threat as reproduced by Cicero at *har. resp.* would not be so different as it may first appear from his other accounts. The fact that Clodius's brother, Gaius Claudius Pulcher, had control of Caesar's troops in Italy during this period would lend further credence to this threat (*Sest.* 41; *MRR* 2: 198). Modern historians dispute whether Caesar's troops would have been near Rome at this time (Lenaghan 1969: 171–172).

nisi se Cn. Pompeio adiutore, M. Crasso auctore, quae faciebat facere clamaret: The two nouns *adiutor* and *auctor* are also paired or listed together at *p. red. ad Quir.* 9; *dom.* 30, 66 (both of Pompey); *Sull.* 34 with Berry 1996a: 207. For Pompey's shifting alliances between Cicero and Clodius, see nn. on 45, 46; Lenaghan 1969: 172–173; Seager 2002: 101–109. The noun *auctor* most likely alludes principally to Crassus's financial support for Clodius's activities (according to Cicero, it was his bribes that led to Clodius's acquittal in 61 on the charge of sacrilege; see 36n). The wealth of Crassus, obtained through the mining of silver (Plut. *Crass.* 2.5) and through real estate, often acquired as a result of the previous owners' misfortunes (Ward 1977: 70–73), had become a well-worn conceit by the time of his death (e.g., *Att.* 1.4.3=SB 9, *Tusc.* 1.12; Sall. *Catil.* 48.5;

Plin. *nat.* 33.134); nevertheless, contrary to what is commonly believed, this Crassus did not carry the cognomen *Dives*, "the rich" (Ward 1977: 46–47). At *Sest.* 39–41 Cicero also mentions Clodius's claim of Crassus's support, only to reject it; during Cicero's exile, Crassus assisted in securing his return, but often through intermediaries and not to Cicero's full satisfaction (*fam.* 14.2.2=SB 7; see further Ward 1977: 243–245).

For the vagueness of the phrase *se... quae faciebat facere* compare *Verr.* 2.5.176: *ea quae faciebat tua se fiducia facere dicebat*, where again Cicero uses the emphatic indicative in the relative clause in *oratio obliqua*.

in quo uno non mentiebatur: An important proviso, since it allows Cicero to ascribe blame only to Piso and Gabinius and exculpate the First Triumvirate. For Piso and Gabinius see 2n.

48

Cicero marvels at Clodius's mad attempts to vitiate the legislation that Caesar had passed during his consulship.

48 *idem postea quam / respirare vos a metu caedis, / emergere auctoritatem vestram e fluctibus illis servitutis, / reviviscere memoriam ac desiderium mei / vidit*: Once again, Cicero disrupts a regular and symmetrical construction to create a particular emphasis. Here a tricolon, each limb of which is introduced by a present infinitive in anaphora and asyndeton, metaphorically describes the senate rescued from drowning. The metaphor is immediately suggested by the idea of one being able to breathe once more (*respirare*), then made explicit by the image of emerging from waves, until finally the memory of Cicero is restored to life. A grammatical subject in the accusative follows each introductory infinitive. After this, in the first two cola there occurs a prepositional phrase plus a noun in the genitive; in the final colon, however, the phrase is omitted, thereby stressing the isolated genitive: Cicero. Although there are no explicit indicators, it is possible that Cicero intends his hearers to imagine the senate as the helmsman of a metaphorical ship-of-state, an image to which Cicero frequently appeals in this period, e.g., *dom.* 137, *Sest.* 25, *prov.* 38; see further 4n.

vobis se coepit... venditare: See 1n (*totus venierat... venditaret*).

tum leges Iulias contra auspicia latas et hic et in contionibus dicere: The historic infinitive occurs only three other times in Cicero's orations from the 50s (*Sest.* 74, *Pis.* 69, *Mil.* 29); elsewhere it is almost entirely restricted to his correspondence and to early speeches, in particular the *Verrines* (Perrochat 1932: 39–41, who cites but does not discuss the *har. resp.* passage; generally, *OLS* 1: 526–531). Perrochat notes two registers in Cicero, the colloquial (not relevant here) and the artistic. Of the latter, context usually indicates confusion or excitement and more than one infinitive form occurs. I suggest that the preceding *coepit* here influences the choice; once Clodius began selling himself to attack Caesar, the historic infinitive underscores the abruptness of Clodius proclaiming his opposition at *contiones* and in the senate house. For parallel constructions after *coepit*, see *Rhet. Her.* 4.14 (on the plain style): *clarius eadem et alia dicere coepit.... tum vero iste clamare...* (a single infinitive); *Verr.* 1.25: *comitia nostra... haberi coepta sunt. cursare iste homo potens* (several more infinitives follow).

The *leges Iuliae* referred to here are those laws passed by Caesar during his consulship in 59 (sources in *MRR* 2: 187–188; for an evaluation, see Gruen 2009: 31–35). Caesar, with the support of Crassus and Pompey, succeeded in passing agrarian legislation early in the year despite opposition from his consular colleague Marcus Calpurnius Bibulus (*RE* 28) and three tribunes. Afraid for his life, Bibulus secluded himself in his home and, for the majority of what remained of his year in office resorted to *obnuntiatio*, that is, regularly declaring on days scheduled for voting on legislation that the auspices were unfavorable, thereby ceasing public business until the next lawful opportunity (*Att.* 2.16.2=SB 36; *dom.* 39–40; Suet. *Iul.* 20.1–2; Plut. *Caes.* 14.1–9, *Pomp.* 47.3–48.4; Dio 38.1–6). Bibulus only observed the sky for omens, however (48n); he did not take the important subsequent step of delivering these notices personally to Caesar, the magistrate in charge. As a result, Caesar's legislation seems to have been legal from the point of view of the augural process (Linderski 1989: 222–225; Tatum 1999: 129–30 is more circumspect). Accordingly, Caesar ignored these alleged signs and continued to pass significant legislation for the remainder of his consulship (full summary of ancient references in Driediger-Murphy 2019: 158–160).

in quibus legibus curiata illa lex quae totum eius tribunatum continebat: The law allowing Clodius's adoption into a plebeian family, thereby enabling his election to the tribunate, passed during Caesar's consulship (nn. on 44, 45). As Clodius surely must have known, Bibulus had also on the day of this vote announced that he was watching the sky for omens (*Att.* 2.9.1=SB 29, with 2.12.1=SB 30; *dom.* 39, *prov.* 45; 48n). The precision by which *legibus* is repeated within the relative clause (and further repeated in the singular form *lex*) is typical of legal language (45n).

** **quod caecus amentia non videbat**: Ernesti 1810: 919 suggested emending the relative pronoun *quam*, the universal manuscript reading, to *quod* on the basis that Cicero is alleging that Clodius failed to recognize not a single law, but the principle that repealing Caesar's legislation would necessarily vitiate his adoption. He is followed by Madvig 1877–1884: 2.142 and Shackleton Bailey 1991a: 230 (who at 1987: 276 unnecessarily suggests *id quod* or *quam rem*).

For other references to Clodius's moral blindness see 26n. Cicero seems here to be playing on the idea of not "seeing" as a result of mental "blindness" (cf. the pun at 8n).

producebat fortissimum virum, M. Bibulum: The word *produco* is the appropriate verb for bringing someone forward in a *contio*, as Clodius does here in his capacity as tribune (Mommsen 1887–1888: 1.201; *ThLL* X, 2

1634.21–36 [J. Ramminger]); the imperfect tense used throughout this section underscores the fact that Clodius interrogated Bibulus and the augurs on more than one occasion (cf. 48: *et hic et in contionibus*). The absurdity that Cicero emphasizes is that, if all Julian laws are declared void on the basis of being passed against the auspices, this would include Clodius's adoption, thereby nullifying the subsequent acts of his tribunate, including the law bringing about Cicero's exile. Lenaghan 1969: 174–175 surveys the various ways in which modern scholars have interpreted Clodius's motives here, from assuming that Clodius really was mentally unstable to imagining, as Lenaghan does, that this was an empty threat meant to intimidate Caesar (see too Linderski 1989: 223–224).

Cicero expressed skepticism about the reputation that Bibulus had earned for his opposition to Caesar in 59 (*Att.* 2.19.2=SB 39: *Bibulus in caelo est, nec qua re scio, sed ita laudatur quasi ⟨qui⟩ 'unus homo nobis cunctando restituit rem'*). After his return from exile, however, Cicero publicly describes Bibulus with fulsome language (*dom.* 39: *praesens vir singulari virtute, constantia, gravitate praeditus, M. Bibulus*), presumably in no small part because it was he who had proposed putting the question of Cicero's house before the *pontifices* (*dom.* 69). The homoioteleuton of *fortissim<u>um</u> vir<u>um</u> Marc<u>um</u> Bibul<u>um</u>* recalls Cicero's description of Milo in its emphasis on masculinity (6n).

quaerebat ex eo, C. Caesare leges ferente de caelo semperne servasset: "He asked him whether he had continuously observed the auspices when Caesar was passing his legislation." The enclitic question particle *-ne* attaches to the most important word in the sentence; in order to nullify all Caesar's legislation it is essential that Bibulus observed the auspices "always" throughout the year (Driediger-Murphy 2019: 151 argues that the adverb indicates that the watching extended into the actual time that legislation was passed; this is possible, but is not the natural way of interpreting the Latin). It is rare to find *-ne* displaced beyond first position in the indirect question, and there are few parallels for displacement to seventh place (KS 2: 2.504–505; cf. next n., where *-ne* is in fifth position). The expression *de caelo servare* is a technical term from augury, referring only to the seeking out of bird signs; it does not include *obnuntiatio* (note above on *tum leges Iulias contra auspicia latas*). For the elliptical sense of the phrase—"to watch for [something] from the sky," see Nisbet 1939: 202–203; the ellipsis likely has the function of preventing the observer from prejudging precisely what will be observed. For attestations of the phrase, and a discussion of what such observation of the sky entailed, see Driediger-Murphy 2019: 127–157, esp. 133–137.

augures interrogabat, quae ita lata essent rectene lata essent. illi vitio lata esse dicebant: For the delayed position of *-ne* see previous note, and for the regular construction of using a generalizing neuter form *quae lata* instead of the expected feminine *quae latae* (sc. *leges*) see KS 2: 1.61–62; 21n. Note once again the precise repetition characteristic of religious/legal language (28n).

Linderski 1986: 2165–2167 observes that this is the only text in which *vitio* ("faulty") is used in an augural context for the otherwise regular *contra auspicia* ("contrary to the auspices"). He argues that the phraseology with *vitium* had neutral connotations since it could refer to any ritual mistake, intended or accidental, whereas the phrase *contra auspicia* "was politically charged for it stressed an active disregard and contempt for the auspices" (1986: 2166). As a result, the augurs are being careful here in their public response not to make a decision about intentionality, by contrast with Clodius's bald statement earlier in the *contio* and senate that "the Julian laws were passed *contra auspicia*." Linderski 1986: 2208–2212 also makes the important point that the augurs are expressing personal opinions after being summoned to a *contio* by a tribune, not rendering an official response on behalf of their college, which would have taken place only before the senate (for which there is no evidence in this instance). He argues that Cicero intentionally obfuscates this distinction in order to use augural authority as evidence that Clodius's tribunate was indeed illegitimate (see Linderski 1989: 224 on Cicero's "self-interest hiding under the mask of ignorance").

ferebant in oculis hominem quidam boni viri et de me optime meriti: "Some good men who were my benefactors used to hold this man very dear." Otto 1890: 249–250 lists other examples of the idiom *aliquem in oculis ferre*, and compares the Greek expression ἐπὶ τῶν ὀφθαλμῶν περιφέρειν. Note once again Cicero's care not to name those members of Rome's elite who had once offered support to Clodius. Lenaghan 1969: 175 aptly compares section 50 and the similarly phrased *fam.* 1.9.19=SB 20, also of Clodius: *quoniam quidam nobiles homines et de me optime meriti nimis amarent inimicum meum meque inspectante saepe eum in senatu modo severe seducerent, modo familiariter atque hilare amplexarentur.*

auctorem, ut praedicare est solitus, consiliorum suorum: Pompey, whom Clodius described earlier as playing the "assistant" (*adiutor*), is here promoted by him to a more active role (47n).

inibat gratiam a non nullis: This idiom meaning "to gain the favor of" or "to win approval from" (*ab aliquo gratiam inire*) occurs in the comic playwrights and thenceforward throughout Latin prose (*ThLL* VI, 2 2218.69–81 [O. Hey]).

49

One Roman who particularly suffered at the hands of Clodius was Pompey.

49 tum … tum … tum: The tricolon of temporal adverbs does not give precise dates, but they do follow a chronological sequence, starting from the height of Clodius's tribunate of 58. The three episodes describe: his first attacks on Pompey following Cicero's departure from Rome (Seager 2002: 103–105 assesses Clodius's motives); an attempt to assassinate Pompey; forcing Pompey to seek refuge in his house.

** *est elatus spe posse se*: The readings of the major codices are: *elatus spe posse se* P² (*se* is ommitted in P¹) GE; *est ratus se posse* H. Most modern editors, including Maslowski, print the majority reading *elatus spe posse se* (presumably understanding *est ratus* of H to be a misconstrual of *elatus* of the apodosis). Ellipsis of forms of *esse* with the perfect passive participle is occasionally attested in Cicero but is more common in historians such as Livy, Curtius, and Tacitus, occurring with increasing frequency in later Latinity (KS 2: 1.13; LHS 2: 422; for Varro, see Laughton 1960: 10). Such omissions, however, usually occur in a colloquial context or in a passage of speedy narration, neither of which applies here. As a consequence, I have added *est* according to the suggestion of Wolf 1801: 373–374, who places it after *elatus*, as does Peterson in the OCT. The supplement also creates concinnity within the tricolon (*est elatus, est… deprensa, obsessus… est*). Although Reid 1886: 162 does point out that *est* "readily" drops out in manuscripts after words ending with "s," I have chosen to put *est* before the participle, where it gives focus to *vero* and preserves the order of H (the combination *vero est* occupies second position at five other places in the speeches). The temporal adverb *tum* would also influence the position of *est*; see 49n. I should note, however, that there does not seem to be sufficient research on the omission of *est* with the perfect participle, and KS 2: 2.632 seems correct in suggesting that "die Sache verdient nähere Untersuchung" (cf. the cogent discussion of Keeline 2021: 151–152).

quoniam togatum domestici belli exstinctorem nefario scelere foedasset: Cicero alludes here to his actions during the Catilinarian conspiracy, which he consistently characterizes as civil war (Dyck 2008: 127. The phrase *bellum civile*, first attested at *Man.* 28, was not yet the standard formulation; see Arena 2020). He extinguished the conflict while "wearing a toga" in his capacity as consul, when he did not hold a regular military command (cf., e.g., *Catil.* 2.28=3.23: *me uno togato duce et imperatore*; *dom*. 99: *consul togatus armatos vicerim*, 101: *exstinctor coniurationis et sceleris… videar*; Gildenhard 2011: 196–200). Both Cicero's contemporaries and later declaimers recognized this boast as a trope susceptible to mockery, particular his ancillary claim that weapons of war should yield to the toga of diplomacy (Quint. *inst.* 11.1.24; Ps. Cic. *in Sall*. 7: *an ego tunc falso scripsi 'cedant arma togae', qui togatus armatos et pace bellum oppressi?*; for this often-quoted tag from Cicero's epic poem *De consulatu suo* see Courtney 1993: 172). The explicit juxtaposition of *externorum bellorum hostiumque victorem* allows Cicero to equate Pompey's actions as warrior with his own as consul, as he does frequently in his career beginning with his consulship; see, e.g., *Catil*. 2.11, 4.21, and particularly the now lost letter in which Cicero annoyed Pompey by "placing himself with a haughty boastfulness above all the illustrious generals" (Schol. Cic. Bob. p. 167.26–27 Stangl: *quod quadam superbiore iactantia omnibus se gloriosis ducibus anteponeret*; Nicolet 1960: 240–252). Steel 2001: 166–173 offers other examples of

Cicero's claims that oratorical ability placed him on a par with Rome's military leaders.

The *scelus* that Clodius committed against Cicero is principally his exile and all the difficulties attendant upon it such as the illegitimate consecration of the site of his home. The final three words, all associated with religious pollution, point to this act in particular: for *scelus* see 5n; for *foedare*, 32n. The adjective *nefarius* derives from the noun *nefas* (>*for, fari* "to speak") and refers literally to any "unspeakable" act. Cognate forms commonly occur in Ciceronian invective in a variety of contexts (in this speech also at 3, 15, 28, 42 [twice], 55), but in every case "the possibility of divine anger/retribution appears present" (Lennon 2014: 39, with literature).

illum etiam, illum externorum bellorum hostiumque victorem: Wills 1996: 76 notes that the gemination of demonstrative pronouns (*illum*) is rare in comedy and is atypical of poetry more generally until after the Augustan age. The repetition here, together with *etiam*, stresses that Cicero is comparing his own actions with that of Pompey. Courtney 1989: 53 notes that the paired genitives after *victorem* "represents first a cognate accusative (*bellum vincere*), then a direct object." For the phenomenon of two different genitives dependent upon one noun see KS 2: 416–417.

tum est illa in templo Castoris scelerata et paene deletrix huius imperi sica deprensa: Asconius supplies our fullest account of this event, which he dates to August 11, 58: "When Pompey entered the senate, a slave of Clodius is said to have dropped a dagger. After the dagger was brought to the consul Gabinius, it was reported that the slave had been ordered by Clodius to kill Pompey. Pompey straightaway returned home and from that moment on kept himself in his house. He was also besieged by Clodius's freedman Damio, as I have learned from the *Acta* of that year" (pp. 46.22–47.1 Clark: *cum...Pompeius in senatum venit, dicitur servo P. Clodi sica excidisse, eaque ad Gabinium consulem delata dictum est servo imperatum a P. Clodio ut Pompeius occideretur. Pompeius statim domum rediit ⟨et⟩ ex eo domi ⟨se⟩ tenuit. obsessus est etiam a liberto Clodi Damione, ut ex Actis eius ⟨anni⟩ cognovi*). The numerous other descriptions of, or allusions to, this incident by Cicero and later authors adds nothing substantial to Asconius's account (see 6n, 58n, *dom.* 67, *Sest.* 69, *Pis.* 28, *Mil.* 18; full listing at Keeline 2021: 136). Marshall 1987: 125 argues that Pompey deliberately staged this and other reported attempts to assassinate him in order to buttress popular support and to create suspicion concerning his opponents among the political elite; his retreat to his house did not originate from fear but "was another tactic devised by Pompeius to reinforce the concept of his indispensability." Seager 2002: 106, by contrast, thinks that it was indeed a plot of Clodius, but that he purposefully staged an unsuccessful attempt simply to frighten Pompey; if so, it seems to have worked (cf. Seager 2002: 179 on Marshall). Clodius's involvement is further indicated by the fact that this particular meeting of the senate was held in the temple of Castor, a notorious locus for his tribunician activities (28n).

Adams 1994a: 38–39 lists examples in which temporal adverbs (here *tum*) act as "influential hosts" of *esse* in periphrastic constructions, in this case drawing it away far from the participle (*deprensa*); compare the less extreme example below: *umquam fuit clausa*. *Deprensa* completes the periodicity of the sentence by supplying the word governing *in templo Castoris*.

** ***omnis angustias, omnis altitudines <u>moenium obiectas</u>…perfregit***: This is the reading of Maslowski, Wuilleumier and Tupet, and Peterson. All codices but one agree in reading for the underlined portion *omnium obiecta tela* (P omits *tela*). It is possible to explain this reading only if one accepts a harsh zeugma with *perfregit*, which would also apply to *altitudines* in isolation (so Gesner 1753: 281–282, citing *S. Rosc.* 22, which is normally emended). Lambinus 1830: 268 originally suggested *montium obiectas*, which Baiter 1856: 923 improved with the change of *montium* to *moenium*. The zeugma also becomes less harsh with Baiter's reading, since *altitudines moenium* can be taken as a periphrasis for *alta moenia* and, if one understands *angustiae* to refer to mountain passes (*ThLL* II 59.73–83 [O. Hey]), Sil. 5.160 (*perfractas Alpes*) provides a suitable parallel for *perfregit*. One order of corruption could be: *moenium obiectas > moenium obiecta* (haplography before *semper*) > *omnium* (supplying a third adjective in anaphora) *obiecta > omnium obiecta tela* (supplying a needed noun; not adopted by P). Parallels for *altitudo moenium* occur at Sall. *hist. frg.* 4.14; Liv. 26.46.1, 26.48.4; Curt. 4.6.21; Tac. *hist.* 3.20.2, 3.30.2.

vi ac virtute: The several parallels in Wölfflin 1881: 280 (to which add Quadrigarius *FRHist* 24: 3) suggest that this alliterative pair echoes the language of military reports. See Adams 2005: 73, who speculates that the military narrative containing this phrase at Plaut. *Amph.* 191 "must have had its stylistic origins in such spoken genres as military reports to the senate and generals' prayers of thanksgiving after battle, as well as in battle descriptions in early tragedy and epic" (cf. Christenson 2000: 175–176). If this is correct, then it is tempting to see irony in the phrase when one considers that the context is Pompey, under siege, being unable to leave his house at Rome.

obsessus ipse est domi: For the many references in Cicero to Pompey being shut up in his home see 6n. Asconius claims that he learned from the *Acta* that Clodius's freedman Damio, otherwise unknown, coordinated this siege of Pompey's house (quoted in 49n). He presumably refers to the *Acta Diurna Populi*, established by Caesar during his consulship to record senatorial proceedings along with other, less official news (Suet. *Iul.* 20.1; details in Marshall 1985: 55–57).

The fronting of the participle and its separation from *est* serves to emphasize it (Adams 1994a: 40–42). At the same time the phrase visually finds Pompey (*ipse*) trapped in his home. There again seems to be irony in the fact that

Pompey's being "besieged" in his home is what ultimately "freed" Cicero from the abuse of others (*liberavit*).

non nulla imperitorum vituperatione timiditatis meae: When two genitives depend upon a single substantive as here, the governing noun regularly occurs between a preceding possessive form (*imperitorum*) and a following objective (*timiditatis*; KS 2: 1.416 A3). Cicero also calls "naive" (*imperiti*) those citizens who were swayed by the reckless rhetoric of the tribune Saturninus (41). He makes clear in the next sentence that the alleged "timidity" of which he is accused is the abandonment of his own house in order to go into exile, an act which he claims here and elsewhere to be not the result of cowardice but a planned move to spare the republic more violence.

The sentence following again depicts the situation of Pompey (*nam si Cn. Pompeio*) as paralleling that of Cicero (*certe mihi*): just as Pompey was correct in not choosing to leave his house forcefully during Clodius's tribunate (it was *miserum* for him to stay at home, but not *turpe*, since his potential assassination would inevitably have led to widespread violence), so too it was mournful (*luctuosum*) for Cicero to leave his own home to go into exile (*exire domo mea*) but his departure was ultimately beneficial to the state. Compare Cicero's characterization of his day of exile at *Sest*. 27: *rei publicae* **luctuosum***, mihi* **ad domesticum maerorem gravem***, ad posteritatis memoriam* **gloriosum**.

viro uni omnium fortissimo quicumque nati sunt: LHS 2: 193 considers the combination of *unus* + superlative, occurring as early as Plautus, to mark an early stage in the development of *unus* into the indefinite article. Pinkster 2015: 1115 argues rather that this sense develops only much later and interprets the meaning in contexts such as this as "the single bravest of all men." The type *unus omnium* + superlative also occurs in our earliest Latin (LHS 2: 165), and over a dozen times in Cicero (cf. 56: *unus omnium mortalium . . . deterrimus*). It seems best to interpret the combination as an emphatic tautology, in particular given the tendency for the adjectives *unus* and *omnium* to be juxtaposed (cf. Dougan 1905: 1.23). The fulsomeness of the praise of Pompey is increased by the addition of the unnecessary relative clause *quicumque nati sunt*. Since the aim of the sentence is to justify Cicero's own inaction at the time of his exile, the praise indirectly but clearly transfers to him as well; compare *p. red. ad Quir.* 16 (*Cn. Pompeius vir omnium qui sunt fuerunt erunt virtute sapientia gloria princeps*), where the hyperbolic praise of Pompey also reflects on Cicero.

quam diu ille tribunus plebis fuit: *Sest.* 69 and Plut. *Pomp.* 49.2 confirm that Pompey secluded himself at home for the remainder of Clodius's tribunate.

lucem non aspicere, carere publico: "To gaze at the light [of day]" is an expression that occurs mostly in Cicero; beyond its literal meaning (e.g., *Sest.* 20) it can have the metaphorical connotations of being alive, or of coming back to life (Crass. *or. frg.* Cic. *de orat.* 2.226; *nat. deor.* 2.96, *Brut.* 12; Liv. 9.6.3). The phrase *carere publico* ("to keep out of the public eye") also describes Pompey's activities during this period at *Mil.* 18: *caruit foro... Pompeius, caruit senatu, caruit publico; ianua se ac parietibus... texit.* For this sense of the neuter substantive *publicum* see *ThLL* X, 2 2460.25–2461.58 (K.-H. Kruse). Liv. 22.61.9 combines the two ideas in describing disgraced legates: *non foro solum... sed prope luce ac publico caruerint.*

velle se in Carinis aedificare alteram porticum: Pompey's home in the Carinae district of Rome originally belonged to his father Cn. Pompeius Strabo. Plutarch describes it as "modest and simple" (*Pomp.* 40.5: μετρίως καὶ ἀφελῶς ᾤκησεν). Clodius did not realize his veiled threat to replace it with a portico as he had tried to do with Cicero's home (hence "a second portico," with the first being the altered Porticus Catuli; see 33n). After Pompey's death, however, it is likely that another enemy of Cicero, Marcus Antonius, confiscated it; for further details see *LTUR* 2: 159–160 (V. Jolivet).

** **Palatio**: This is the reading of all codices and is in itself unexceptional; the brachylogy of "Palatine" for "portico on the Palatine" is as natural in Latin as in English (Lebreton 1901: 95–96 list several examples from Cicero). Nevertheless, Shackleton Bailey 1985: 147 tentatively suggests emending to *Palatinae*, with *porticui* understood (see Plin. *nat.* 36.38.1: *Palatinas domos Caesarum*; Gell. 4.1.1). Although he does not elaborate further, the change is tempting for several reasons: first, it makes Clodius's threat more pointed, since it explicitly alludes to his usurpation of Cicero's portico (33n); second, it provides a clear referent for the mention of a "second portico" (*alteram porticum*); finally, it corresponds well with the required sense of *respondere*. On the other hand, it is possible that Clodius in his *contiones* did indeed say *Palatinae*, but Cicero refuses to write this since it would recall unnecessarily Clodius's temporary victory over him regarding his own house. Cicero does use the adjective *Palatinus* four times, once to describe a palaestra (*Att.* 2.4.7=SB 24), twice Clodius's tribe (*dom.* 49, *Sest.* 114), and once Clodia as *Medea Palatina* (*Cael.* 18); three of these instances occur in speeches after his return from exile.

mihi exire domo mea ad privatum dolorem fuit luctuosum: In all his works, including the correspondence, Cicero avoids referring to his own banishment with the standard terms designating exile (*exsulo, exsul, exsilium*), preferring instead colorful metaphors such as *calamitas* or euphemisms, as here "to leave my home" (the commonest is *discessus*, "departure"). The three main exceptions occur when countering an opponent's use of exile vocabulary (*ad Q. fr.* 3.2.2=SB 22 [Gabinius]; *dom.* 72–76 and *parad.* 27–32 [Clodius]); similarly Dio 39.60.1 notes that Cicero was called a φυγάς in the senate, apparently by Crassus (cf. *fam.* 1.9.20=SB 20). Lastly, Cicero refers to his pondering the possibility of *exilium* at *Sest.* 42. See Robinson 1994 and especially Riggsby 2002: 167–172. At least one declaimer seems unaware of this distinction. In addition to the title, the author of *Pridie quam in exilium iret oratio* puts the noun *exilium* into the mouth of "Cicero" on three occasions (22, 29, 30).

278   *Commentary*

The insertion of the copulative form *esse* after the prepositional phrase prompts the listener to anticipate a contrast, in this case *ad rationem rei publicae gloriosum* (Adams 1994a: 15–19).

50–52

Cicero returns to the theme of how certain members of the elite tolerate Clodius simply because he hates their own enemies. He devotes particular attention to how Clodius's negative treatment of Pompey causes, counterintuitively, Pompey to gain support. This section goes on much longer than necessary to make this basic point, in particular since it is one that has already been made in section 46, and Cicero expends little effort to make this repetitive digression entertaining (there are few jokes or instances of harsh invective, and only one brief exemplum). The best explanation for the excursus is that, by stressing Clodius's unpredictability on a political level, Cicero underscores how the response's reference to OPTIMATIVM DISCORDIAM DISSENSIONEMQVE must be attributed to him, thereby providing a transition to his discussion of the next section of the response.

50 *Videtis igitur hominem per se ipsum iam pridem adflictum ac iacentem perniciosis optimatium discordiis excitari*: With *videtis* Cicero returns to the present time and to the current situation of Clodius, who is referred to with the disparaging noun *homo* (1n) and accompanied by two adjectives that describe his self-inflicted decline since Cicero's recall (Lenaghan 1969: 178). Cicero had just used the same verb *adfligere* to describe Clodius's treatment of Pompey (49); the repetition is presumably accidental, although *per se ipsum* (i.e., "and even to himself") may indicate an intentional reminiscence, underscoring how Clodius's strategy has backfired. The phrase *optimatium discordiis* of course recalls the most recent clause of the response under discussion, but Cicero is likely using word order to play with his audience's expectations. As the sentence proceeds, the listener/ reader would first take this causal ablative phrase with the preceding participles *adflictum ac iacentem* ("lying dashed to the ground because of the destructive discord among the elite"), but then this interpretation must be reassessed upon reaching the next and final word of the clause—*excitari*. Rather than being harmed by this discord, Clodius, perversely, is "roused" back into action as a result of it.

cuius initia furoris dissensionibus eorum qui tum a vobis seiuncti videbantur sustentata sunt: The mention of Clodius's madness recalls the beginning of the speech, where Cicero vividly illustrates that Clodius's rage persists (*furor*, 2n). For the sequence of two genitives (*cuius, furoris*) dependent on a single substantive see 49n. The verb *sustento* means literally "to hold up from underneath," i.e., "to support" or "maintain," with the result that there is a slight paradox in the notion of receiving support from political dissension. The referent of *eorum* is the triumvirs (47n). Courtney 1989: 53 notes that the objective genitive *eorum* can represent a prepositional phrase (here, *cum eis*: "disagreement with those people"); see KS 2: 1.415b, who cite, e.g., *Tusc.* 1.27: *excessu vitae*; *de orat.* 1.98: *earum ipsarum rerum aditum*; OLS 1: 1000–1001.

reliqua iam praecipitantis tribunatus etiam post tribunatum obtrectatores eorum atque adversarii defenderunt: "Their detractors and enemies defended what was left of his tribunate when it was already in decline—and even afterward." The neuter plural *reliqua* here refers to the "residue" of Clodius's actions that had remained even after his term as tribune had officially ended, in particular his legislation carried out soon before leaving office. For the phrase *praecipitantis tribunatus*, see *dom.* 40: *praecipitante iam et debilitato tribunatu* ("when your tribunate was sinking to its impotent close": Nisbet 1939: 105). The pair of virtual synonyms *obtrectatores* and *adversarii* is best taken as a hendiadys: "those who openly spoke in opposition [to the triumvirs]." For the combination, see Q. Cic. *pet.* 40: *[tuorum] obtrectatorum atque adversariorum rationes et genera cognoscito*; Gell. 17.1.11.

ne a re publica rei publicae pestis removeretur restiterunt: KS 2: 2.256–261 lists a full range of verbs of hindering that govern *ne* (for *resisto*, see Nep. *Att.* 3.2, Liv. 23.7.4). The repetition of the preverb *re-* in the two adjacent verbs reinforces the strength of the resistance of Clodius's supporters. Since Cicero generally avoids sequences of the letter [r] (Kraffert 1887: 718), the four further instances of the sequence *re / er*, even though semantically unrelated, provide additional emphasis; compare Verg. *Aen.* 9.261–262: *revocate parentem, / reddite conspectum; nihil illo triste recepto*, with Hardie 1994: 121 and, generally, Wills 1996: 437–438.

etiam ne causam diceret: Clodius's supporters prevented him from pleading a case in court by twice over the course of 57 blocking Milo's attempts to prosecute him *de vi* (7n). Cicero is recapitulating in more concise form edicts produced in early 57 by the consul Metellus Nepos, the praetor Appius Claudius Pulcher, and a tribune of the plebs to prevent the first prosecution (*Sest.* 89: "*ne reus adsit, ne citetur, ne quaeratur, ne mentionem omnino cuiquam iudicum aut iudiciorum facere liceat*," with Kaster 2006: 305–306).

etiam ne privatus esset: This clause seems to allude in a more cryptic way to the second of these foiled occasions to bring Clodius to court. The consul Nepos succeeded in preventing Milo's attempt at prosecution in November 57 by creating obstructions until Clodius could be elected aedile and therefore no longer be a private citizen (*privatus*); for details and bibliography see Kaster 2006: 316. On the extent to which the aedileship ensured immunity from prosecution, see 1n.

** **etiamne in sinu**: The codices universally read *etiam ne in senatu* (**P** has a clear space after *etiam*); Angelius's emendation *in sinu* has been the accepted reading ever since his 1515 edition. It is very difficult in reading the text silently—delivery is of course another matter—not to take *etiam + ne* as introducing the third element of a tricolon in anaphora of *etiamne* (or fourth, if we include the *ne* clause preceding *restiterunt*) detailing what these opponents to the triumvirs sought to prevent. Even granting that Cicero is generally less sensitive about such repetitions, the ambiguity created here is unusual. If we do have the introductory words to a fourth clause of prevention, then one most posit a more drastic issue with the manuscripts than would be solved by emending *senatu* > *sinu*. First, one would need a subjunctive verb: "they prevented him even from ----- in the senate" (*resisterunt… etiam ne in senatu…*); it is difficult to think of an appropriate verb (parallels could suggest *de eo detraheretur* [*Phil.* 2.2], *accusaretur* [*or.* 129], *oppugnaretur* [*fam.* 1.9.19=SB 20]; and perhaps best *esse prohiberetur* [Caes. *Gall.* 7.33.3]). Note too the awkward zeugma of *in sinu atque in deliciis* ("in their embrace and among their favorites"), which also complicates the simple emendation to *in sinu*. As it is, I strongly suspect a lacuna after *in senatu*. Despite these objections I have chosen to retain the conjecture *in sinu* (for support for this phrase, see next note). I have found no other discussion of this issue.

in sinu atque in deliciis quidam optimi viri viperam illam venenatam ac pestiferam habere potuerunt: For the sentiment that many members of the elite valued Clodius see 48n. The noun *deliciae* covers a range of meanings, from innocent object of diversion to source of sexual pleasure (Adams 1982: 171, 196–197, 220). The epithet chosen to describe Clodius, *vipera*, also hints at a sexual connotation by recalling the sexual invective from his moral biography (cf. 42n). First, immediately after using an emphatically masculine noun that is unnecessary for the syntax, the "men" (*viri*) who hold Clodius to their breast, Cicero places special emphasis on the feminine gender of the word describing Clodius (*-am -am -am ac -am*); second, outside of this instance of invective and one later in the speech, where Cicero calls Clodius a *serpens* (55, also a feminine noun), comparisons with a snake are reserved for women (Opelt 1965: 144). The abusive epithet *pestifer* first occurs in Cicero's speeches after exile, particularly to describe Clodius or things and people associated with him (*p. red. in sen.* 3 [*annus*]; *dom.* 2 [*tribunatum*], 85; *Sest.* 78; *prov.* 3 [Piso and Gabinius]); the word then typifies Antonius and his associates. Clodius is also spoken of more directly as himself a *pestis* (4n). Given these associations, it is likely that Cicero alludes to the fable of the man who revived a frozen snake by holding it in its breast (if we retain the conjecture *in sinu*), only to be killed by its bite when it revived (Phaedr. 4.20; cf. Otto 1890: 372–373, to which add Theognis 602).

tandem: Questions that contain the particle *tandem* request additional, specific information after a clear situation has been presented (Risselada 1998: 105–106). Here, Cicero has acknowledged more than once that Clodius received unexpected support from respectable members of the elite. He now asks how it is that they expect to benefit from this support. The answer of his imagined interlocutors follows immediately.

"volo," inquiunt, "esse qui in contione detrahat de Pompeio": When *detrahere* has the metaphorical sense of "taking down" an individual through defamation the object of that defamation is expressed by *de* + ablative: see *de illius amplissima dignitate detrahere* later in this section and *ThLL* V, 1 831.16–39 (P. Graeber). In its literal sense the verb takes the accusative, as at 28 (*sacerdotem ab ipsis aris pulvinaribusque detraxeris*). Clodius's defamation of Pompey before an assembled audience of citizens well illustrates the theatrical element of Roman politics. Plutarch preserves a memorable example from the year 56, at a time when he tells us that Pompey had chosen to neglect public affairs to spend time with his new, young wife. Clodius addresses the crowd with an orchestrated call-and-response: " 'Who is the licentious general? What man is looking for a man? Who scratches his head with one finger?' As Clodius pulled up his toga and shook it, the mob, just like a chorus well-trained in responsion, answered each time with a loud shout: 'Pompey!' " (Plut. *Pomp*. 48.7: 'τίς ἐστιν αὐτοκράτωρ ἀκόλαστος; τίς ἀνὴρ ἄνδρα ζητεῖ; τίς ἑνὶ δακτύλῳ κνᾶται τὴν κεφαλήν;' οἱ δέ, ὥσπερ χορὸς εἰς ἀμοιβαῖα συγκεκροτημένος, ἐκείνου τὴν τήβεννον ἀνασείοντος ἐφ' ἑκάστῳ μέγα βοῶντες ἀπεκρίναντο: 'Πομπήϊος'; Corbeill 1996: 164–165). Cicero describes from the same year an even more vivid scene which includes Clodius's followers attacking Pompey spontaneously (*Q. fr.* 2.3.2=SB 7; Dio 39.19.1–3; Morstein-Marx 2004: 134–135).

accipiat ut a me dicitur; dicam quidem certe quod sentio: Lenaghan 1969: 179 gives parallels for what he calls "ingenuous protestations of sincerity." In this case, Cicero attempts to hide any such accusations of ingenuousness by stressing that he welcomes his hearers to report to Pompey what he is about to say; cf. *dom*. 25, also about Pompey: *dicam ipso audiente quod sensi et sentio, quoquo animo auditurus est* (see too *Sest*. 85, *Vat*. 15, *prov*. 18). Rhetorically, the aside indicates to the senators, some of whom may by now be losing interest, that Cicero is about to say something important.

me dius fidius: This exclamation, appearing already in Plautus, occurs several times in Cicero as shorthand for *ita me Dius Fidius iuvet*. In this context Dius Fidius is the god to whom one swore an oath before making an assertion (compare English "So help me God!"). For the development of this god from a manifestation of Jupiter to an independent deity, see Wissowa 1912: 129–131.

tum de illius amplissima dignitate detrahere cum illum maximis laudibus ecferebat videbatur: The conceit that Clodius's praise in fact acts to degrade Pompey's stature will dominate the following two sections. Particular emphasis in the current formulation is derived from the *tum…cum* construction, in which both finite verbs are in the indicative: at the very moment when Clodius offered the greatest praise, at that moment Pompey was seen to decline in dignity. The conceit that flattery from an evil person is in fact the worst criticism while abuse is the highest praise occurs elsewhere in Cicero (*Vatin*. 29, 41; *Pis*. 72; Kaster 2006: 330). Nisbet 1961: 140 notes the converse sentiment at Naev. *trag*. 14 TRF: *laetus sum laudari me abs te, pater, a laudato viro* ("I am happy to be praised by you, father, a man worthy of praise"), quoted by Cicero at *fam*. 5.12.7=SB 22, 15.6.1=SB 112; *Tusc*. 4.67.

51 C. Glaucia: Cicero records that C. Servilius Glaucia (*RE* 65) was of lowly birth but had a reputation for his sharp wit, rising to prominence on account of his popular appeal (*Brut.* 224; for jokes attributed to him see *de orat.* 2.249, 263). Cicero's references show a mix of disdain and admiration (*Rab. Post.* 14: *homo impurus sed tamen acutus*; *Brut.* 224), and he records L. Crassus using the epithet "excrement of the senate house" to describe him, an expression that Cicero asserts should be avoided despite a certain claim to truth (*de orat.* 3.164: "*stercus curiae*"). In 102 the censor Metellus Numidicus tried unsuccessfully to have Glaucia expelled from the senate (App. *BC* 1.28), after which he held important political offices in rapid succession: tribunate of the plebs in probably 101 (*MRR* 2: 645, 3: 59) and praetorship in 100, during the early tenure of which he was an ally of Marius (App. *BC* 1.29). In December of that year, Glaucia made the unusual move to stand for election as consul for 99 and was killed during the same disturbance that saw Saturninus murdered (41n). His death occurred after the senate authorized the consuls, one of whom was Marius, to acquire weapons and arm citizens in order to restore order (*Rab. perd.* 20; App. *BC* 1.33; full list of sources at *MRR* 1: 574–575). Outside of this passage from *har. resp.* there is no other evidence of Glaucia shifting from praising Marius to criticizing him, although the latter part of 100 would have provided opportunities.

The historical exemplum offered here is unusual in its brevity and in standing alone. In terms of content, moreover, it offers no particulars, simply equating Clodius's actions with that of Glaucia. Cicero's choice of *exemplum* seems dictated by two points: by being a great general, Marius offers a good parallel for Pompey; by being a fellow Arpinate, *homo novus,* and exile, Marius offers a close parallel for Cicero (he refers to all these elements in the recent *p. red. in pop.* 19–21). As a result, the *exemplum* once again places Pompey and Cicero in analogous positions (see nn. on 49, 58). Marius provides an *exemplum* for Cicero on a variety of occasions; see van der Blom 2010 *passim*, esp. 181–182, 188–189, 277–278 (as *homo novus*); 203–208, 259–263 (as exile).

demens et iam pridem ad poenam exitiumque praeceps: Cicero emphasizes at the beginning of the oration how Clodius's combination of insanity and recklessness had resulted in his collapse in the senate on the previous day (2: *cuius ego de ecfrenato et **praecipiti furore** quid dicam?*).

quod quidem miror: "This is the very thing that I marvel at, namely that while they are pleased with the former action [abusing Pompey] when they are angry, the latter [attacking the senate] is not unpleasant to such good citizens." The neuter accusative pronoun *quod* simultaneously refers backward as a loose connecting relative to the assumption underlying the previous sentence—that Clodius's abuse of Pompey and of the senate are somehow qualitatively distinct—and points forward to the indirect statement that is governed by *miror*. Other Ciceronian examples of this type of transitional phrase include: *dom.* 140: *quod quidem minime mirum est, in tanto scelere tantaque dementia ne* *audaciae quidem locum ad timorem comprimendum fuisse*; top. 3: *quod quidem minime sum admiratus eum philosophum rhetori non esse cognitum*. See further KS 2: 2.320–321, LHS 2: 572γ, who characterize the anticipatory use of *quod* as a colloquial way of providing clarification.

alterum... alterum: In an AB-AB order, the first alternative refers to attacking Pompey, the second to attacking the senate. In the *cum* clause, Cicero characterizes those opponents of Pompey who are pleased with Clodius's attacks as "angry" (*iratis*), presumably in part by his alliance with Caesar and Crassus, of which Cicero avoids explicit mention (see nn. at 45, 47). By contrast, in the main clause he wonders why the same group is not upset by Clodius's attacks on the senate; presumably this group of *tam boni cives* includes mostly senators themselves and is identical with the *optimi viri* of the next sentence.

id: This pronoun must refer only to Clodius's abuse of Pompey, and not to that of the senate as well, as only becomes clear from the remainder of the sentence (the lack of clarity provides Wolf 1801: 376 with further evidence for non-Ciceronian authorship: "Scil. *Pompeium a Clodio vituperari*, ut recte subaudit Manutius, sed divinitus, non ex bene vincto sermone"). His abuse of Pompey will no longer please Rome's elite since as of his recent *contio* the two men have, according to Clodius, reconciled.

legant hanc eius contionem de qua loquor: Dio 39.29.1 refers to this *contio*, delivered in the wake of Clodius's reconciliation with Pompey, but without specifying a date. In a letter to Lentulus Spinther from December 54, however, Cicero describes in detail his own estrangement from Pompey in spring 56 and how after Luca Clodius became reconciled with him and the other triumvirs (*fam*. 1.9.9–10=SB 20). So this *contio* must have been recent, some time between April and the delivery of *har. resp.* It is likely that it is identical with the *contio* that Clodius had delivered regarding the haruspical response (see next note). For more on this *contio*, and for the evidence that *contiones* were written out and available for distribution and private reading, see 8n.

in qua Pompeium ornat—an potius deformat? certe laudat, et unum esse in hac ciuitate dignum huius imperi gloria dicit et significat se illi esse amicissimum et reconciliationem esse gratiae factam: If this is indeed from Clodius's recent speech on the response, it contains the longest nearly verbatim quotation. Clodius will have offered these words of reassurance in reference to the portion of the response that warned of imminent disaster and death among Rome's elite as a result of internal discord. By insisting that his feud with Pompey is over, Clodius can argue that, contrary to what some may believe from his past politics, he no longer wishes to foment dissension in the higher ranks. For Cicero's use here of *correctio* (*ornat—an potius deformat?*), see 37n. The two verbs *dicit* and *significat* have distinct meanings. *Dico*, as usual, introduces in indirect discourse an actual or approximate quotation, whereas *significo* is followed by a statement for which the person reporting it makes no claims to accuracy (cf. 25n): "he *says* that there is one man in this state worthy of the glory of this empire and *indicates*...that he has been reconciled to his favor." Other than at 25, Cicero uses the two verbs in parallel only at *de orat.* 3.203 (where irony is defined as *alia dicentis et significantis dissimulatio*) and *fam.* 5.13.2=SB 201. It is clear from what follows in the speech that Cicero does not accept that Clodius and Pompey have reached a reconciliation.

The genitive *gratiae* is objective; the same phrase occurs at *Rab. Post.* 32, *p. red. ad Quir.* 13 (*gratiarum*); Balb. Cic. *Att.* 9.7a.1=SB 174A; cf. *Catil.* 3.25: *reconciliatione concordiae*, *ThLL* XI, 2 396.25–40 (J. Ramminger).

52 quod ego quamquam quid sit nescio, tamen hoc statuo: As above (51n), the connecting relative *quod* refers loosely back to an idea described in the previous sentence rather than to a specific word. Here Cicero indicates that he does not understand what Clodius means in saying that he and Pompey have reconciled. For the verb *esse* having the word "mean" or "signify," see *OLD* s.v. *sum* 18. The main clause, *hoc statuo*, employs an authoritative verb to counter Clodius's claims for reconciliation in mock syllogistic fashion: 1. Clodius praises Pompey; 2. he says he has become Pompey's friend; 3. "although I don't understand this, I nevertheless am of this opinion," that if he were indeed his friend, how could he have praised him? For this sense of *statuo*, see *OLD* s.v. 13.

videant...quam se cito inverterit: The long space intervening between verb and predicate contains a tricolon of relative clauses that characterize in detail the subject of *videant*: those men who turned a blind eye to Clodius's disruptive activities when they thought he was hostile to Pompey. The extended description of their support contrasts with the concise presentation of Clodius's change of alliance ("how swiftly he has changed").

conivebant: This is the reading of the *recentiores*. All major codices have *contuebant*. *ThLL* IV 794.18–19 (A. Gudeman) cites the active voice of *contueor* only, and with hesitation, in a fragment of Pacuvius (*trag.* 6 *TRF*), and then again not until the sixth century CE (Greg. Tur. *glor. conf.* 84). For the sense of *coniveo* see 38n where, as here, the verb occurs in a play on seeing vs. blindness. Here the contrast is with the notion of "seeing" expressed in the governing verb *videant* (cf., e.g., *leg. agr.* 2.77, *Catil.* 2.27, *Cael.* 59).

nunc enim iam: Cicero frequently uses *nunc* and *iam* pleonastically, with the current state of affairs often contrasted explicitly with a time in the past, as here with *antea*; cf. *Verr.* 2.3.5: *non moleste fero...eam vitam quae mihi sua sponte antea iucunda fuerit nunc iam mea lege et condicione necessariam quoque futuram*. Additional examples at *ThLL* VII, 1 114.52–63 (J.-B. Hofmann).

se...venditabat: Cicero continues to recall accusations from the speech's opening. This phrase describes Clodius at 1 and 48; the former refers to a different group of "buyers," but the latter may refer to the same incident.

si reditus ei gratiae patuerit: Markland 1745: 354 cites parallels where the prepositional phrase *in gratiam* is the only construction following the noun *reditus* in Cicero (*in gratiam* had already been suggested by Lambinus. The phrase *in gratiam redire* occurs five times in *prov.* alone; see Grillo 2015: 179).

It is better, however, to understand *gratiae* as a genitive paralleling the sense of *reconciliationem...gratiae* (51n) and the grammar of *dissensionibus eorum* (50n). The construction is probably also affected by the contrasting *opinionem gratiae* in the relative clause (Wolf 1801: 378).

inrepat: It is possible that Cicero continues with his recent characterization of Clodius as a snake (50: *vipera*), a characterization soon to be repeated (55: *serpens*, a noun cognate with *inrepo*, as recognized by Ambr. *hex.* 5.14.46). More likely, however, Cicero simply employs a dead metaphor found elsewhere in his oratory to describe sneaky activity, e.g., *Arch.* 10: *ceteri... aliquo modo in eorum municipiorum tabulas inrepserunt; Pis.* 1: *obrepsisti ad honores errore hominum*; Fantham 1972: 116 n. 1.

53–55 (*morietur*)

Having exposed Clodius's reconciliation with Pompey as a fiction, Cicero isolates two words from the response—*DETERIORES* and *REPVLSOS*—to claim that the *haruspices* chose these adjectives specifically to designate Clodius and his followers. The words do not describe those members of the *optimates* for whom danger is portended. Instead, if the elite can resolve those differences that in recent history have led to autocratic rule, the prodigy can be readily expiated, leaving Clodius powerless and without purpose.

53 definiri: ThLL V, 1 344.2-3 (T. Bögel) categorizes this passage as an instance of the meaning "*finire, facere finem*," surely incorrectly. A prodigy urges human action, and on this occasion Clodius and Cicero argue, respectively, for what they think is the correct course to follow. Only after such a decision is made do the gods allow an end to be made. As a result, the sense here accords better with the notion of restricting understanding within prescribed bounds (344.72–345.7). Cicero will then proceed to himself define to whom this suggestion does and, more significantly, does not apply.

hoc quidem verbo: That is, by the word *optimates*. There is surely a play here on Clodius and his followers not being the "best"; see puns on *boni / optimates* at *Att.* 2.5.1=SB 25, 8.1.3=SB 151, 13.40.1=SB 343, 14.10.1=SB 364, with Corbeill 1996: 209 n. 58.

de gregalibus eius aut de consiliariis: A motif of this speech's invective involves comparing Clodius and his followers to animals: a beast to be hunted (7n), a wild horse (2n), a domesticated animal not possessing reason (5n). A far more colloquial animal comparison, which may be a dead metaphor by Cicero's day, is to refer to a group gathered for a specific purpose as a "herd" (*grex*) and its members as *gregales*. The latter can have a neutral tone, such as in describing a soldier of the rank and file (*ThLL* VI 2316.45–65 [G. Burckhardt]) but its three uses in Cicero's oratory all refer to the nameless followers of Clodius and his allies, with the two other instances equating them with Catiline's adherents (*dom.* 75: *Catilinae gregales; Sest.* 111. The noun *grex* also normally, but not always, has negative connotations in the speeches). The word appears here in hendiadys with the more descriptive *consiliarii*, creating the oxymoronic notion of a "mob of advisors."

habent Etrusci libri certa nomina: Cicero here refers back to the mention of *hoc verbo* and underscores how the response does in fact spell out Clodius's involvement, but as the producer, not victim, of dissension among the elite. Despite the literal meanings of *hoc verbo* and *certa nomina*, they are unlikely to imply that the *libri Etrusci* were written in Latin or consulted in translation. See further the Introduction E.1.

in id genus civium cadere: Cicero particularly favors the idiom *in aliquem cadere* ("to pertain to someone or something"); see *ThLL* III 30.64–31.12 (K. Hoppe; *in aliquid*, 31.18–66). It occurs at two other points in *har. resp.* (37, 56), in each case as part of Cicero's philological analysis of how to interpret the response.

DETERIORES, REPVLSOS: For these two adjectives see 56n.

quod iam audietis: Cicero will discuss these two words from the response after he quotes their context at 56 (*NE DETERIORIBVS REPVLSISQVE HONOS AVGEATVR*). It is no accident that he begins his discussion by treating these adjectives in isolation since, taken as a whole, the passage seems to reflect Cicero's current situation more accurately than Clodius's: Cicero reached the consulship (*honos*) as a *novus homo* (*deterior*; for negative epithets used of Cicero as *novus homo* see Vretska 1961: 2.18–19); he was then subsequently restored (*honos*) from his status as an exile (*repulsus*; see further 56n). On this reading the response judges Cicero's return to Rome to be a mistake.

hos appellant quorum et mentes et res sunt perditae longeque a communi salute diiunctae: With the terms *deteriores* and *repulsi*, the *haruspices* refer to "men whose thoughts and affairs have become corrupted and far removed from the common welfare." The word choices deliberately echo previous descriptions of Clodius as crazed (cf. 26: *impia mente*; 33) and "lost" (46: *perditi hominis*), linking this type of character with the danger of separation underscored in the response (diiunctae >< DISCORDIAM DISSENSIONEMQVE). Word order underscores the point, with these people's thoughts and affairs at one end of the sentence "far removed from the common welfare" at its end.

cum di immortales monent: With the verb *monent* begins a long series of virtual synonyms describing the warnings of the gods, nearly all of which have been used already, or will be repeated in the *peroratio*: *praedicunt* (53), *portendunt* (53), *consulendum et prospiciendum* (54), *ostenditur* (54), *admonemur* (54). One is left with the impression that the gods express themselves in as many ways as possible in order to avoid any chance of ambiguity. Further emphasizing the nature of their warnings is the double occurrence of the conjunction *cum* with the vivid indicative mood (*cum...portendunt*).

in tuto conlocant Clodium: The unexpected position of *Clodium* underscores the irony; amid all the threats to the elite there remains safe the outcast Clodius, who is alleged to have been the source of them all. The expression *in tuto* is a common one in both prose and poetry, dating from as early as Plautus (*OLD* s.v. 4a); the noun *loco* is to be understood, which is particularly unnecessary with the verb con*lo*cant.

tantum abest a principibus quantum a puris, ab religiosis: Cicero has called Clodius *impurus* several times already, normally with connotations of religious impurity (e.g., 24, 33). These many references guarantee that the audience will understand that the *religiosi* from whom Clodius is so distant are those whom the adjective describes in its positive sense (for the ambiguity of *religiosus* see 4n). Adams 2021: 428–429, moreover, notes the tendency in Ciceronian oratory for an asyndeton consisting of prepositions in anaphora to contain near-synonyms.

54 o clarissimi atque optimi cives: This is the reading of E, adopted by Maslowski and Shackleton Bailey 1991a: 230; all other codices read *carissimi* for *clarissimi*. The surrounding context makes the reading *clarissimi* all but certain, in particular 53, which warns of "dissension among the most brilliant and meritorious citizens" (*de **clarissimorum** et **optime** meritorum civium dissensione*; cf. 54.9: *claros... viros*). When Cicero addresses the Roman populace in assembly, he invariably uses the vocative form *Quirites* (169 times); *cives* is an alternative when the people are addressed in other contexts, as here in addressing a gathering of senators (Dickey 2002: 286, 315–316). Cicero uses this form rather than the expected vocative *patres conscripti* in order to connect their potential fate with the end of the state.

Following the convoluted syntax that had described the convoluted machinations of Clodius, in turning his attention to the senators Cicero's style radically changes. Between this direct address of his audience and the next portion of the response (55: *NE OCCVLTIS CONSILIIS RES PVBLICA LAEDATVR*), the intervening sentences contain few instances of complex subordination, with sets of contrasts making clear that the issue is a straightforward one of us vs. them (or him). The simplicity of the syntax reflects the clarity of the senate's decision: to eliminate dissension they must eliminate the influence of Clodius.

id quod interitum optimatium sequi necesse est adiungitur: That is, the predictions of the *haruspices* as a whole can be averted by an appropriate senatorial response, but if the potential dangers of which they warn, such as the murder of the *optimates*, are not avoided, then the attendant consequences become inevitable (*necesse est*). Note that Cicero equates the *principes* of the state (54: *caedes principum*) with the *optimates*. It is unlikely, *pace* Lenaghan 1969: 181, that Cicero intends to be referring explicitly to the triumvirs with either of these categories. The vagueness of whose destruction is imminent works to Cicero's advantage in pleading for peace among the elite and suits the general tone of the response.

ne in unius imperium res reccidat admonemur: For the use of this paraphrase to emend the text of the response see 40n. The formulation of a "return" to the rule of one person recalls the ancient theory of anacyclosis, which posits that forms of government are in a constant state of evolution. In this case the response hypothesizes a potential change from an aristocracy (*optimates*) to a monarchy. The theory is formulated most explicitly by Polybius (6.4–9; for its origins see Walbank 1957–1979: 643–647), who posits a fixed and natural order of monarchy, kingship, tyranny, aristocracy, oligarchy, democracy, and ochlocracy, which does not correspond to the order imagined here. In his *De re publica*, begun two years after *har. resp.*, Cicero presents a version of this theory which describes a less fixed sequence, one that would allow the transition from aristocracy/oligarchy to monarchy/tyranny that is anticipated in the response (*rep.* 1.44–45). The Etruscan brontoscopic calendar for July 14 is in agreement with the Polybian model by describing a change from democracy/ochlocracy to the rule of one, but this must surely be a coincidence (cited at 40n).

** The orthography *reccidat* (for *recidat* of all codices) receives support from consideration of prose rhythm (Zielinski 1904: 179), the prosody of poetry (Keeline 2013), and ancient testimony (*ThLL* XI, 2 317.61–73 [R. Rey]). Lambinus 1830: 268 suggests deleting *monemur* (which he prints for *admonemur*) since the final clause introduced by *ne* follows naturally after *adiungitur*, as signaled by *id*. Three points argue for retaining *admonemur*, the reading of all the codices: first, Cicero is intent on stressing the warnings of the gods in this section (53n); second, deletion would destroy the emphatic sequence of three passive verbs in final position; third, 40n provides a parallel for the otiose use of verbs of warning (although there too Lambinus suggested deletion).

nostro sensu coniecturaque raperemur: "We would still be caught up in it due to our own feelings and reason." Cicero contrasts elsewhere the activities denoted by these two nouns (e.g., *ac.* 2.42, *div.* 2.13). The noun *coniectura* is often connected by him and other authors with forms of artificial divination and may even be a technical term (Pease 1920, 1923: 168, 548; LS s.v. II A). At *div.* 1.24, he notes that the responses of *haruspices* rest upon a type of *coniectura* that employs induction from empirical evidence and that therefore they can be fallible (cf. *ac.* 2.107). Cicero has already claimed for the senators an ability to use their reason in such a way that it allows them to act as *haruspices* themselves (20n). With this sentence, he begins equating the products of human reason with the knowledge derived from the warnings of the gods (*deorum monitis*). This stance resembles that taken in a letter written in October of 46 to his friend Aulus Caecina, a member of an established family from the Etruscan city of Volaterrae whose writings on Etruscan religion were a key source for Seneca and the elder Pliny (Rawson 1985: 304–305). In this letter Cicero compares the *ratio* of Etruscan divination with his own *ratio* in predicting the outcome of political maneuvering in Rome (*fam.* 6.6=SB 234, with Corbeill 2012: 254–255). In a similar way, Cicero will demonstrate here that a rational mind can infer from the historical *exempla* of Sulla, Marius, and Cinna how disagreement among the elite normally leads to autocracy and that the senators can understand as well as the gods Clodius's culpability in the current political situation.

For *rapio* used metaphorically to describe someone suddenly being thrust into some surprise situation or way of feeling see *ThLL* XI, 2 106.28–68 (I. Reineke).

** *neque enim ullus alius discordiarum solet esse exitus inter claros ⟨et⟩ potentis viros nisi aut universus interitus aut victoris dominatus et* [*aut* codices] *regnum*: This sentence is excerpted in the twelfth-century *Florilegium Gallicum* with minor variations underlined (see 39n for the *Florilegium*): nullus alius discordiarum solet esse exitus inter claros potentesque viros nisi aut universorum interitus aut victoris dominatus et regnum (Maslowski and Rouse 1984: 83). Of the two conjunctions underlined here, the first (-*que*) provides a necessary supplement for a word omitted by all extant codices of the main tradition. Alternatively, Peterson and Maslowski supply *et* (*et potentis*), following an edition published at Rome in 1471. Since the compiler of the *Florilegium* displays in excerpting "a fair amount of expertise in dealing with the text" (Maslowski and Rouse 1984: 88), the addition of -*que* can as easily represent an independent conjecture for a gap in the manuscripts as an authentic reading. The decision between the two is therefore difficult, but since the rhythm of ēt pŏtēntīs vĭrōs (double cretic) is more favored than that of īntēr pŏtēntīsquĕ vĭrōs, I follow Peterson and Maslowski in printing the former.

The second difference also presents uncertainty. The consensus of the main codices reads *aut regnum*. Madvig 1871–1884: 2.142 points out that only two options are being considered here ("*aut universus interitus aut…dominatus & regnum*"), not three, and so emended to *ac regnum*, and he is followed by Peterson and Maslowski. Lehmann 1880: 568 made the same observation, apparently independently, and proposed *et regnum*. In this instance, since the closing clausulae are identical regardless of the conjunction (cretic + spondee) and since the change from either is easy to account for paleographically, I have chosen to print *et* in light of the possibility that *Florilegium* preserves the reading of an independent witness.

victoris dominatus et regnum: The addition of *regnum* disrupts unexpectedly the periodicity of the sentence and so receives emphasis. There are two possible reasons for this postponement: first, the charge of aiming at *regnum* is a particularly powerful one in oratorical invective (Rawson 1975 offers a nuanced reading of the evidence); second, and more significantly for the context, *regnum* makes clear that the "victor's conquest" will result in the rule of only one, thereby allowing Cicero to make clear that the response does not apply to the triumvirs. To underscore the notion that an autocracy is what the gods portend, the emphasis on the ascension of a "king" continues in each of the three historical exempla that follow (54: *regnaverit*; 54: *regnum*; 54: *regalem*).

** *C. Mario*: Shackleton Bailey 1985: 147 suggests without argument reading *C. Mario* for the simple *Mario* of all manuscripts and editions. A *praenomen* may be dropped in a Ciceronian oration if a large gap does not intervene since that person was last named (7n). At 51 Cicero writes *C. Marius*. Despite the proximity of this earlier reference, I have adopted Shackleton Bailey's supplement for three reasons: first, the context about Marius here differs from the earlier one, making the repeated *praenomen* desirable; second, haplography could account for the dropping of *C.* after an abbreviated form of *cum*; third, the contrasting *L. Sulla* would be better balanced if Marius's name included his *praenomen*.

dissensit cum C. Mario, clarissimo cive, consul nobilissimus et fortissimus, L. Sulla: The mention of Sulla's consulship indicates that Cicero refers to the end of his term in that office in 88. At this time the tribune Sulpicius Rufus attempted to deprive Sulla of his command in the Mithradatic Wars, which had already been awarded to him by the senate, and transfer it to Marius (41n). Driven from Rome by open violence, Sulla returned with an army, where he killed many of his political enemies, including Sulpicius, and forced Marius to seek refuge in Africa; he then left for the war against Mithradates (sources at *MRR* 2: 40). The following year Marius, leading troops newly formed from his veterans, joined with Cinna after his expulsion from the consulship (54n) and helped recapture Rome while Sulla was in the East. Together with Cinna, Marius became consul for 86 and began exacting revenge on his political opponents before dying early in that year; this is presumably the "reign" to which Cicero refers. During Cinna's second consulship of 84, Sulla rebelled, eventually invading Italy and capturing Rome a second time. He was elected *dictator* in 82, and over the next two years proscribed several hundred, perhaps even thousands, of his opponents and passed numerous pieces of legislation designed to strengthen the power of the senate (*MRR* 2: 66–67, 74–76). In 80 he served as consul and died two years later.

Even though Cicero intends this *exemplum* of Marius and Sulla to show how dissension among the elite can lead to kingship, he nevertheless applies to them adjectives in the superlative that describe positive characteristics (*clarissimus, nobilissimus, fortissimus*). As with his depiction of the rebellious second-century tribunes (cf. 41, with notes), the complimentary descriptions are meant to contrast with the current behavior of Clodius, who has no redeeming motivations for his actions.

horum uterque ita cecidit victus ut victor idem regnaverit: "Each was defeated and fell; each then conquered and ruled like a king"; literally "Each of them, when conquered, fell in such a way that (*and yet*) the same man, as conqueror, ruled as a king." The tense of the perfect subjunctive *regnaverit*, in secondary sequence in a consecutive clause after *cecidit*, expresses a particular historical fact whose effects are no longer felt in the time that Cicero is speaking. Lebreton 1901: 227–230 cites numerous examples in Cicero of this sense of the perfect subjunctive, which resembles the Greek aorist. The paronomasia of *victus / victor*, describing the progression from conquered to conqueror, reflects the discussion of cycles in forms of government of which this is an example. For similar reasons, Cicero repeats *uterque* in the *exemplum* that follows (*utrique*; cf. *idem*).

cum Octavio collega Cinna dissedit: Lucius Cornelius Cinna (*RE* 106) and Gnaeus Octavius (*RE* 20) shared the consulship of 87. Despite having sworn to preserve Sulla's consular legislation from the previous year, Cinna soon after taking office proposed a series of measures opposed to that legislation, including a bill to recall Marius. Octavius violently prevented these moves, driving Cinna and his men from the city. Cinna subsequently raised an army and gained the support of leading Romans, including Marius. In late 87, he captured Rome, beheaded Octavius, and succeeded in being elected consul for the next three years until killed by mutinous troops in 84. The testimonia of Cicero, as well as the bulk of ancient sources, consistently describe these years as characterized by violence and despotism (*MRR* 2: 46, 60; for a reassessment of Cinna see Badian 1962, esp. 52–59; Bulst 1964).

The position of *collega* in the sentence is pointed. Although presumably a nominative in apposition to *Cinna*, it could also be understood with *Octavio*: the word order literally joins the two men with this noun while the meaning of the sentence places them in conflict. The dissonant effect is further echoed by the preposition *cum* ("[together] with") being placed at the opposite end of the sentence from *dissedit* (literally, "sat apart").

utrique horum secunda Fortuna regnum est largita, adversa mortem: I have chosen to capitalize *Fortuna* to indicate that the noun is a personification, since the gnomic form of the sentence supports the probability that Cicero alludes here to the notion of "Fortune's Wheel" (*rota Fortunae*, a phrase first attested at *Pis.* 22; see Otto 1890: 142). In his desire to present another instance of two persons (*uterque*) experiencing both positive and negative twists of fate, Cicero plays loose with the historical record since he presumably characterizes as a *regnum* that brief period of Octavius's consulship when he drove out his fellow consul Cinna during a memorably bloody conflict (*Catil.* 3.24, *Sest.* 77), even though Cinna was quickly replaced as consul by L. Cornelius Merula (App. *BC* 1.63–64).

tum sine dubio habuit regalem potestatem, quamquam rem publicam reciperarat: The sentence refers to Sulla's election as *dictator* by the *comitia centuriata* and to his subsequent legislation. The claim that he had "restored the republic" does not seem to be used sarcastically, but reflects a recognized slogan that Cicero uses elsewhere to describe Sulla's activity during his dictatorship (see, e.g., *dom.* 79: *Sulla victor, re publica reciperata*, *Brut.* 311, Liv. *perioch.* 88.1, Aug. *civ.* 2.24; cf. *S. Rosc.* 141, Sall. *Catil.* 11.4). The same phrase was to be adopted as a rallying cry following Caesar's assassination (*Phil.* 3.7: *ad rem publicam recuperandam*, 5.11).

55 *inest* **hoc tempore haud obscurum odium, atque id** *insitum penitus* **et** *inustum* **animis hominum amplissimorum**: The adverb *penitus* often occurs in Cicero, with or without *animus*, to describe feelings and thoughts implanted in the soul (e.g., *Verr.* 2.5.139, *S. Rosc.* 53, *leg. agr.* 2.14 [*odio penitus insito*], *dom.* 25, *nat. deor.* 1.49), and he commonly uses the metaphor of branding (*inustum*) to describe the presence of negative qualities, particularly in regard to the state (Kaster 2006: 154). Cicero here recalls the speech's beginning, where he had argued that his own *odium* toward Clodius was in fact the product of justified anger. Here it is *odium* among the elite that threatens, an *odium* that, Cicero goes on to argue, will be eliminated with the elimination of Clodius. The short sentence abounds in sonic play that echoes this idea. First, Cicero seems to be punning on the name *Clodius* in order to associate him with this rampant political enmity—the elision of the two words *obscurum odium*, combined with the common confusion in pronunciation between [l] and [r] (Quint. *inst.* 1.11.4–5; for Cicero's mockery of this confusion see *fam.* 2.10.1=SB 86 with Shackleton Bailey 1977: 409), would have given him the opportunity to exploit the phonic similarities between "Clodius" and "hatred," just as he had done earlier (*obsCuR/LODIVM*; cf. 4n). Second, the sentence contains an unusual number of elisions, as many as six depending upon Cicero's choice of delivery, which if exploited would underscore the sense of a deeply planted hatred. Finally, we have a variation of what Woodman has termed in his work on Tacitean sound effects "anagrammatical assonance" (2014: 69; cf. 1998: 223–225). Here, in the sequence *insitum penitus et inustum* (cf. *inest*), each word intertwines so as to reflect the deep-seatedness of this hatred, an effect further emphasized by the repetition of the prefix *in-*.

captatur occasio: The phrase occurs first here (but cf. Plaut. *Pseud.* 1022: *occasionem capsit*; ThLL IX, 2 335.45–48 [R. Teßmer]). The referent for what opportunity is being seized is spelled out in the next sentence: those less wealthy wait for an appropriate occasion to act, while the more powerful fear the plans of their enemies.

non tantum: The phrase here is adverbial ("those who are not so strong in resources"). Cicero's audience would not have expected an answering correlative phrase (e.g., *sed etiam*, "not only...but also"). Merguet 1877–1884: 4.700 cites *non tantum* followed by a form of "but also" only three times for the speeches. All attestations occur in the latter part of Cicero's career, around the time of or after *har. resp.*, and two are placed in the unambiguous context of a rhetorical climax: *Vatin.* 36 (immediately after *non solum...sed etiam*), *Mil.* 61 (immediately after *neque...solum...sed etiam* and *neque...modo...sed etiam*); cf. *Scaur.* frg. 5. Landgraf 1914: 134 lists an additional five occurrences from the remaining Ciceronian corpus (*fin.* 1.44; *Tusc.* 2.45, 3.75; *fam.* 5.12.7; *de orat.* 3.52), and notes that the construction never occurs in Caesar and Sallust but is favored in the colloquial writings of Hirtius. One may contrast the many uses in Cicero's corpus of *non modo* and *non solum* (1059 and 861 times respectively; Steele 1896: 156).

qui sine controversia plus possunt, ei fortasse non numquam consilia ac sententias inimicorum suorum extimescunt: Included in the category of the unquestionably powerful who fear their enemies is undoubtedly Pompey, as earlier portions of the speech make clear. There may perhaps also be an allusion to Caesar's concern that he will be prosecuted once he no longer has *imperium* (e.g., Suet. *Iul.* 23), or even generally to all three triumvirs (so Lenaghan 1969: 183). But the referent is very much deliberately left vague, since it accords with Cicero's purpose that any senator listening see the threat as applicable to his own circumstances. The equivocal "perhaps sometimes" (*fortasse non numquam*), which shows Cicero's care not to accuse anyone of cowardice, would apply to all these possibilities.

iam ista serpens, quae tum hic delitiscit, tum se emergit et fertur illuc, compressa atque inlisa morietur: The otherwise abrupt mention of a figurative snake has been prepared by the recent reference to Clodius as a *vipera* (50n). Clodius is described here as a serpent destined to die, but the language used—that he is often "hidden" (*delitiscit*) and will eventually be "crushed" (*inlisa* > *in* + *laedo*) anticipates the portion of the response that is immediately quoted, and thereby implicates Clodius once again with the prodigy that had prompted these warnings: *NEC OCCVLTIS CONSILIIS RES PVBLICA LAEDATVR*. The device used here represents a rare instance in the orations of what Quintilian calls "complete allegory," where there is no clear indication given in the text that the reference to the snake represents a figure of speech. For an ancient discussion of *allegoria / inversio* and its limited application to oratory, see *inst.* 8.6.44–53, in particular section 47: "Oratory frequently has recourse to allegory, but rarely complete allegory; normally it is mixed in with words used literally. Here is an example of complete allegory from Cicero: 'I marvel and lament the fact that everyone is so interested in sinking another that he even scuttles the ship in which he is himself sailing'" (*habet usum talis allegoriae frequenter oratio, sed raro totius, plerumque apertis permixta est. tota apud Ciceronem talis est: 'hoc miror, hoc queror, quemquam hominem ita pessumdare alterum velle ut etiam navem perforet in qua ipse naviget'* [*inc. or.* frg. B 13 Schoell=frg. 3 Crawford]; further Mankin 2011: 253, Lausberg 1998: §§895–901).

55 (*Monent*)–55 (*esse munitam*)

Cicero treats briefly the response's admonition "that the republic not be harmed by secret plans." He tendentiously tries to apply this clause to Clodius's actions, ignoring the seemingly more appropriate option that it refers to the recent renewal of the pact among Caesar, Pompey, and Crassus.

55 Monent enim eidem: The particle *enim* signals an inference made from the solution to Rome's problems just proposed—that is, crushing the "snake" Clodius: "the snake, formerly hidden, will die **crushed**, for (*enim*) the gods warn that through hidden plans the state may be **crushed**." There is consequently no reason to emend to *etiam* (Garatonius 1786: 343) or *autem* (Shackleton Bailey 1987: 276). The pronoun *eidem* presumably refers to the gods, who are last mentioned as responsible for these warnings (54: *deorum monitis*), and yet the ambiguity leaves open the possibility of a reference to the *haruspices*, as throughout the speech (e.g., below at 56: *nullo haruspicum cum* *admonitu*) or even to the *libri Etrusci* (53), all of which have been the subject of verbs introducing parts of the response. Cicero of course intends the ambiguity, since as the speech draws to a close he works to conflate these various sources (10n), ultimately equating them all with his own reliance upon reason (54n).

NE OCCVLTIS CONSILIIS RES PVBLICA LAEDATVR: Cicero has a challenge in trying to convince his audience of senators that the response points to anything other than the recent conference at Luca in early April, when Caesar, Pompey, and Crassus renewed their agreement of mutual cooperation. Although ancient sources record that as many as two hundred members of the senate went north to Luca during this period (App. *BC* 2.17; Plut. *Caes.* 21.5, *Pomp.* 51.4), it is probable that they did not necessarily visit at the same time and that they did not all attend the private meetings of the three (Pelling 2011: 246). Subsequent events at Rome also indicate that any planning made in the north could still be reasonably interpreted as "secret" by the time of the delivery of *har. resp.* (cf. Plut. *Crass.* 15.1–2, *Pomp.* 51.6–8; details in Gruen 1969: 92–99). An indication that neither this nor any other portion of the response was engineered to contain specific references to contemporary events (as modern scholars often assume), but that rather their ambiguity suited them to senatorial debate, is the parallel language present in the haruspical response of 63 (*Catil.* 3.20: *consilia quae clam essent inita contra salutem urbis*; cf. the corresponding part of *De consulatu suo* [*carm. frg.* 3.57–58]: *tum fore ut occultos populus sanctusque senatus / cernere conatus posset*).

Quae sunt occultiora quam eius qui in contione ausus est dicere iustitium edici oportere, iuris dictionem intermitti, claudi aerarium, iudicia tolli?: Cicero appears to quote from Clodius's recent *contio* on the response (the following derives from Corbeill 2018: 187–188). This citation provides a good test case of the extent to which we can trust a passage that Cicero explicitly marks as a quotation from an opponent. As Lenaghan 1969: 184 notes, the final three elements in Cicero's list constitute simply an enumeration of what it entails to declare a *iustitium* (*RE* 10: 1339–1340 [G. Kleinfeller]). He presumably adds these redundant defining clauses in order to make Clodius's alleged suggestion sound more dramatic than it need be. Despite the rhetorical *abundantia*, however, I see no reason to follow Lenaghan further in thinking that, if Clodius did indeed make this proposal for a cessation of public business, he could not have been serious, much less that Cicero simply fabricated the event. A close parallel occurs in Cicero's remarks to the *pontifices* from the previous year, when he rebuked Clodius for declaring during his tribunate similar edicts that ordered shops to be closed (*dom.* 54: *edictis tuis tabernas claudi iubebas*, and 89–90; on the legality of proposing a *iustitium* and Clodius's possible motivations see Russell 2016). Rather than dismiss this evidence, I propose that Clodius made the suggestion to advertise his interest in ensuring a speedy resolution to the current prodigy process. That this particular *iustitium* seems never to have been enacted by the senate need not detract from the seriousness of Clodius's proposal. In fact, in the following decade Cicero uses precisely the same language as he attributes here to Clodius when making the same recommendation, again not followed, in response to the threat of Marcus Antonius (*Phil.* 5.31: *iustitium edici...dico oportere*). Clodius's proposal would have had immediate relevance: freeing the senators from their judicial duties and economic obligations would enable them to devote sufficient time to considering the response. Although the tendency during the Republic was for the higher magistrates to restrict the *iustitium* to moments of dire military emergency, Greenidge 1901b: 175 notes that one also "might be declared for the purpose of directing exclusive attention to some special sphere of administration" (cf. Mommsen 1887–1888: 1.263–264). And in fact, not only do there exist parallels for short periods of *iustitium* called for ad hoc business during the Republican period, but Cicero himself supplies a close analogy from a year and a half later for the type of cessation of business that I hypothesize here, when a *iustitium* seems to have been proposed in November 54 to calm political events in the capital (*Att.* 4.19.1=SB 93, with Shackleton Bailey 1965–1970: 2.225). I hypothesize that Clodius, as aedile of 56, suggested an analogous measure at his *contio* on the haruspical response. The proposed *iustitium* demonstrates the seriousness with which Clodius treated—or pretended to treat—the recent prodigies.

nisi forte existimatis hanc tantam conluvionem illi tantamque eversionem civitatis in mentem subito in rostris cogitanti venire potuisse: The phrase *nisi forte* signals irony, as normally (39n). The noun *conluvio* (and the related form *colluvies*) etymologically indicates the jumble of dregs left after washing (*colluo*) and is used by Cicero only in a metaphorical sense. In *Pro Sestio*, for example, he describes Clodius as "born from the mishmash of every crime" (*Sest.* 15: *ex omnium scelerum conluvione natus*). In other instances, such as here, the notion of movement, as in the swirling of water, predominates, for instance in describing the tumultuous activities of the tribunate of Drusus (*Vatin.* 23: *in Gracchorum ferocitate et in audacia Saturnini et in conluvione Drusi et in contentione Sulpici et in cruore Cinnano*). In the remaining Ciceronian instances the associations are also negative (*Att.* 9.10.7=SB 177; *Cato* 84). The phrase *in mentem venire* normally takes a neuter pronoun as its subject in Cicero since it is the idea that occurs to one, not the thing itself (in this case a "turmoil and overturning"; KS 2: 1.472 lists only four other examples of a nominal subject). Note that if Cicero refers here to the *contio* of the previous day, it would have most likely been delivered from the *rostra*, immediately in front of the senate house.

est quidem ille plenus vini, stupri, somni plenusque inconsideratissimae ac dementissimae temeritatis: The adjective *plenus* governs variously each genitive—"filled with wine and sleep" can be construed as literally surfeit with these items and their associated activity, whereas being "filled with sexual wantonness (*stupri*) and rashness" represents a personality trait; the effect of the

296   *Commentary*

zeugma is to show Clodius displaying a full range of despicable qualities. Each element of the characterization is a stock feature of invective; the catalogue in Craig 2004: 189–192 contains all of these but sleepiness (for this as an indication of moral deviance see, e.g., Sall. *Catil.* 2.8, 13.3: *dormire plus quam somni cupido esset*, where it is associated with *stuprum* and gluttony). Indeed, the first three traits are applied in the same words to Verres and Gabinius (*vini, somni, stupri plenus*: *Verr.* 2.5.94, *p. red. in sen.* 13). Thurm 2018: 166–203 catalogues at length the charge of drunkenness in Cicero's oratory and correspondence and its interrelationship with charges of luxury and lust (cf. 39n). Accusations of *stuprum* occur numerous times in this speech to defame Clodius, with reference to the violation of the Bona Dea, incest, and general notions of sexual misconduct, as here (nn. on 4, 8, 33, 38, 42, 44). The charges of sleepfulness and crazed rashness would seem to be at odds with one another, and both with the point at hand, namely, that Clodius has been actively engaged in secret plans to overthrow the republic. Cicero recognizes this inconsistency and goes on to assert that nevertheless (*verum tamen*) Clodius managed to do so.

nocturnis vigiliis: The plural of *vigilia* often occurs in Ciceronian oratory to indicate a wakefulness devoted to illicit activities, in opposition to the sleepless vigilance undertaken on behalf of the state or other beneficial goals (e.g., *Verr.* 2.4.144: *cuius omnis vigilias in stupris constat adulteriisque esse consumptas*; *Catil.* 2.9: *vigiliis perferendis fortis*). The plural form also contains the more sinister suggestion of a group of armed guards (*OLD* s.v. 1), a suggestion picked up by the reference to "conspiratorial meetings" (*coitione hominum*; for this negative sense of *coitio*, frequent in Cicero, see, e.g., *Clu.* 148, *Planc.* 53).

verbo illo nefario: Wolf 1801: 382 interprets this as referring to what Clodius said more generally in his recent *contio*, as does Long 1856: 466 and, apparently, Watts 1923: 391 ("his outrageous words"). I have not found a precise parallel for *verbum* used in this sense, but for the singular form referring to speaking in general see *de orat.* 1.47: *verbi... controversia*; Liv. 9.19.15: *absit invidia verbo*; Gell. 10.27.3; cf. *Verr.* 2.3.133: *verbo ac simulatione*. Wuilleumier and Tupet 1966: 72 n. 1, however, take this as referring to the single word *iustitium*, as does, seemingly, Shackleton Bailey 1991a: 132 ("this wicked word"). This seems to be the better option, although the rest of the sentence requires us to understand that the threat of the cessation of public business had been bandied about repeatedly since Clodius's *contio*, which hardly sounds like "hidden plans."

perniciosam viam audiendi consuetudine esse munitam: The metaphorical use of road-building occurs commonly, both as applied to negative ends, as here, and positive (*Verr.* 2.3.157; Varro *Men.* 402: *dextimam viam muniit Epicurus*; cf. *ThLL* VIII 1658.42–60 [J. Gruber]). The notion that a lie will become accepted as truth if repeated often enough—the so-called "illusory truth effect"—has been the subject of several recent scientific studies, one of which cites Cato the Elder's famous repetition of "Carthage must be destroyed"

De haruspicum responsis 56

as evidence for its rhetorical use among the Romans (Schnuerch *et al.* 2021). Cicero explicitly appeals to this notion here.

56-59

Cicero turns to the warning from the response about honors being increased for the less respectable members of society (*NE DETERIORIBVS REPVLSISQVE HONOS AVGEATVR*). Having already briefly treated those whom the Etruscan books label as *deteriores* and *repulsi* (53), he now turns to details regarding these two designations, showing in particular that Clodius belongs to the *deteriores* since he has violated natural law by renouncing his family, gods, and country. A rapid-fire listing of Clodius's crimes follows, most of which have already been narrated.

56 *sequitur illud*: As noted at 30, Cicero gives the impression that he is treating the response clause by clause.

NE DETERIORIBVS REPVLSISQVE HONOS AVGEATVR: For the interpretation of this clause as an indictment of Cicero's return from exile see 53n. The substantival use of *deterior* in the masculine gender, signifying a person who is "worse" in character and action, is first met in Plautus where the context is also political (*Poen.* 39; *ThLL* V 798.53-56 [K. Pflugbeil]). Claudius Quadrigarius employs the word in a context similar to Cicero's, noting it as a sign of the injustice of the gods that *deteriores* go unpunished while the *optimi* are not allowed to live long lives (*FRHist* 24: 26: *nam haec maxime versatur deorum iniquitas, quod deteriores sunt incolumiores neque optimum quemquam inter nos sinunt diurnare*); it is just such a fate that Cicero argues that his interpretation of the response will avoid (cf. below, *optimis civibus*). In her discussion of the seventh-century BCE Etruscan brontoscopic calendar Turfa 2012: 33 notes that the words in this clause of the response "invite consideration of the lower orders of a stratified society, a situation just as possible by the late seventh century as it was in the mid-first," comparing Cicero's language to the many places in which the brontoscopic calendar "notes dissension among or troubles for the lower classes and commons." Cicero interprets these words, however, not as referring to class distinctions but to characteristics strictly within the elite that invite moral repugnance in the sphere of both politics and religion (Cairo 2020: 79-80; it is of course a different, and unknowable, matter what was the original significance of the Etruscan text from which the clause is translated). Interpreting this clause as meaning that the morally objectionable should be denied election to additional political office allows Cicero once again to argue that Clodius is being referred to in his position as aedile for the year. For this common sense of *honos* see *OLD* s.v. 5 and, further, the next note, on *repulsi*.

qui sunt igitur repulsi? non, ut opinor, ii qui aliquando honorem vitio civitatis, non suo, non sunt adsecuti: As Lenaghan 1969: 185 notes, rather than treating DETERIORIBVS REPVLSISQVE as a hendiadys, Cicero separates out the

terms to stress the applicability of both negative adjectives to Clodius. In order to do so he stretches the ordinary semantics of the verb *repello*. Although the commonest reference of the noun form *repulsa* is to electoral defeat (*OLD* s.v. 1), Cicero here applies to the verb *repello* the same meaning, one that is otherwise unattested in the lexica. That is, in his considered opinion (17n on *ut opinor*), the participle *repulsi* does not refer to those who have lost an election (*honorem... non sunt adsecuti*), since this applies even to the best citizens. There are two reasons that Cicero is loose with semantics here. First, he intends to contrast his elite allies who have failed in elections with those opponents of his who have failed despite using illegal means (see next note). Second, Cicero wishes to distract the senate from thinking that *repulsi* could refer to exiles such as himself (53n). For Cicero's frequent use of *[ex]pello* (although not *repello*) to refer to his exile, see Robinson 1994: 478–479.

multis saepe optimis civibus atque honestissimis viris: When the adjective *multus* modifies a noun together with a descriptive adjective a conjunction is employed (e.g., *Verr.* 2.5.119: *multi et graves dolores*). When, however, *multus* accompanies a noun phrase that contains a descriptive adjective the conjunction is commonly omitted (e.g., Plaut. *Bacch.* 1020: *plurumis verbis malis*, where the noun phrase *verbis malis* represents the single concept of "slander" or "abuse"; LHS 161, 444; *OLS* 1: 982–984). So here "many of the best citizens and most honorable men." Note the play on *HONOS* from the response: even the *honestissimi* are often deprived of civic *honores*. For the sentiment that electoral success does not necessarily indicate the merit of the candidates, see the extended passage at *Planc.* 7–9, which begins *quid? tu in magistratibus dignitatis iudicem putas esse populum? fortasse nonnumquam est*.

repulsi sunt ii quos ad omnia progredientis, quos munera contra leges gladiatoria parantes, quos apertissime largientis non solum alieni sed etiam sui, vicini, tribules, urbani, rustici reppulerunt: *Ad omnia progredientis* ("those who stoop to anything"); for this negative connotation of *omnia*, compare Catull. 75.3–4: *ut iam nec bene velle queat tibi, si optima fias, / nec desistere amare, omnia si facias*. Lenaghan 1969: 186 understands Cicero here as "clearly referring to P. Vatinius." It is indeed true that Vatinius had suffered defeat in the aedilician elections for 56 despite sponsoring gladiatorial games to drum up votes in contravention of Cicero's *lex Tullia de ambitu* of 63, a point that Cicero had raised in other speeches of spring 56 (*Vat.* 37, *Sest.* 133–135; Schol. Cic. Bob. p. 140.1–10 Stangl). Furthermore, the list of the citizens who have chosen to reject these *repulsi*, moving systematically from closest relatives to the distant rural population, mirrors the development at the close of Cicero's speech against Vatinius (*Vatin.* 39: *quod si ipse, qui te suae dignitatis augendae causa...ferri praecipitem est facile passus,...si te **vicini**, si adfines, si **tribules** ita oderunt ut **repulsam** tuam triumphum suum duxerint,...si cognati respuunt, **tribules** exsecrantur, **vicini** metuunt, adfines erubescunt,...si es odium publicum populi, senatus, universorum hominum **rusticanorum**...*). Lenaghan 1969: 186 also notes

that Vatinius did not carry the members of his own tribe in his attempt to be elected aedile for 56, nor the urban tribe to which Clodius belonged (*Vat.* 36; *Sest.* 114). At the same time, the lack of specificity and the plural number of the participles allows the senatorial audience to apply the references to Clodius as well; cf. the instances of wholesale bribery that Cicero has already mentioned on several occasions (nn. on 28, 36, 42). After all, Cicero begins this definition of *repulsus* by explicitly noting that it does not describe those who have been unsuccessful in obtaining political office, and therefore it can include the aedile Clodius.

** **hi ne honore augeantur monemur. debet esse gratum quod praedicunt**: This sentence offers a difficult textual crux. Maslowski records in his apparatus *monent* GE, *nomen* P, *monemur* H, *recentiores*. Peterson and Maslowski follow G and E in reading *monent*, presumably understanding *hi* as referring to the *repulsi* just mentioned (it is unlikely to refer to the *haruspices*, who are not present in the senate). It is tempting, however, to adopt the reading *monemur* with H, and understand *monent* as the misunderstanding of a scribe who construed the fronted *hi* as the subject of both the subordinate and main clauses, as is often the case in Cicero. A verb in the first-person plural has the further advantages of uniting Cicero with the senate, as at 10, 45, 54, 63, and an original reading of <u>monemur</u> better accounts for the variant *nomen* of P. The fact that the next sentence continues with *haruspices* as the understood subject of *praedicunt* may have further contributed to the corruption to *monent*.

sed tamen huic malo populus Romanus ipse nullo haruspicum admonitu sua sponte prospexit: The Roman people have already averted the potential for the *deteriores repulsique* to accrue further honors by voting to recall Cicero from exile. On the potential for the Roman senate to use reason in order to have prescience compatible with the *haruspices*, see nn. on 20, 54. This potential now extends to any right-thinking Roman citizen.

57 quorum quidem est magna natio, sed tamen: The combination *quidem...sed [tamen]* first appears with regularity in Cicero to mark contrasts in a manner analogous to the Greek construction μέν...δέ. While this contrastive function of *quidem* rarely appears in Varro and Caesar, it eventually becomes ubiquitous in prose and poetry (Solodow 1979: 30–32).

In classical Latin the noun *natio* can designate a person's ethnic or geographic origin, as literally their "place of birth" (from *nascor*); e.g., *inv.* 1.35: *hominum genus...consideratur...in natione, patria, cognatione, aetate. natione, Graius an barbarus*. When the word describes a group of Romans united by a common cause, rather than by situation of birth, Cicero tends to use the word disparagingly in his speeches, in a manner comparable to the pejorative use in English of "tribe"; examples in *ThLL* IX, 1 135.46–53 (F. Spoth). Both Vatinius and Albinovanus, the prosecutor of Sestius, applied the derogatory phrase *natio optimatium* to their political opponents; see *Sest.* 96, 132, and Schol. Cic. Bob. p. 139.18–20 Stangl, which notes that use of the word *natio* aimed to "destroy the dignity of elite men" (*destruens amplissimorum hominum dignitatem*).

eorum omnium hic dux est atque princeps: Cicero refers disparagingly to Clodius on several occasions as leader (*dux*) of the wicked of Rome (*dom.* 96; *Mil.* 56, 95; *parad.* 4.31: *omnes scelerati atque impii, quorum tu te ducem esse profiteris*). The sarcastic use of *princeps* is applied to Clodius only here, although Cicero uses it of other opponents, e.g., Verres (*Verr.* 2.2.34), Catiline (*Catil.* 1.27 [*Patria* speaking]), and Gabinius (*Sest.* 110). It seems to occur here as providing a more suitable transition to the explanation introduced by *etenim*; cf. *Verr.* 2.4.15: *legationis...princeps est Heius—etenim est primus civitatis*. Nevertheless, it is odd that Cicero would reserve the designation for this point in his argument, considering the effort that he has put into denying that Clodius is one of the *optimates* whose dissension will bring about, in the words of the response, the death *patribus principibus*que.

unum hominem deterrimum: For *unus* + superlative, see 49n. Here *unum* clearly carries more force than an indefinite article; fronted to first position in the protasis of the condition, it provides a clear contrast with the first word of the apodosis, *nullum* ("if a poet should wish to bring on stage the single worst human being, he would be able to discover not a single disgrace..."). The contrast continues with the first word of the second clause of the apodosis, *multa*: *multa...praeteriret*; "and *many* he would skip over."

***poeta* praestanti *aliquis* ingenio**: Cicero reserves for special effects this type of interlocking word order (synchysis), consisting of two examples of short-range hyperbaton. Synchysis of the type adj1/ adj2/ noun1/ noun2 seems an inheritance from Proto-Indo-European and occurs not infrequently in both Plautus and Cicero (Hofmann 1980: 272–273, §110; e.g., *Phil.* 2.66: *permagnum optimi pondus argenti*; *Tusc.* 4.7). However, the chiastic order found here (noun1/ adj2/ adj1/ noun2) rarely occurs and seems not inherited from PIE but is rather a feature of the oratorical grand style (Calcante 1986 discusses its appearance in Latin poetry and prose of the first century BCE). An analogous feature in non-dramatic poetry appears to be a separate inheritance, from Greek literary models; see bibliography cited in Harrison 1991: 96.

A passage from *Pro Archia* provides an intriguing parallel to Cicero's usage here. In that speech Cicero comments sarcastically on the fact that citizenship is bestowed on stage-actors while being denied to the poet Archias: *quod scaenicis artificibus largiri solebant, id huic* **summa** *ingeni praedito* **gloria** *noluisse* (*Arch.* 10; "[That grant of citizenship] which [various peoples of southern Italy] were accustomed to bestow on stage actors, they did not wish for this man, endowed with the highest reputation for his talent"). To underscore the difference between the block grant given to people in the theater and the single recognition of Archias, Cicero has employed a singular type of word order (Gotoff 1979: 143–144). Furthermore, since synchysis is a feature found predominantly in poetry, it seems hardly coincidental that the unprosaic word order in both *har. resp.* and *Arch.* describe a poet. In similar fashion, the mention of a hypothetical *poeta* sparks a series of examples of quasi-poetic language that will continue throughout the next few sections, reaching a climax when Cicero returns to the notion of poets attempting in vain to fashion a creature as monstrous as Clodius (59).

inducere: As earlier in the speech (39n), Cicero imagines his poet as a writer of tragedies, "leading onto" the stage his fictive villain; for the metaphor, used as here without explicit reference to a dramatic setting, see *Cael.* 35; Schol. Cic. Bob. p. 138.8–9: *lugubri habitu, ut solent qui pro mortuis inducuntur*; *ThLL* VII, 1 1239.67–1240.37 (J. B. Hofmann). La Bua 2019: 312–313 discusses how Cicero's references to the Roman stage in his oratory "conveyed a message freighted with moral significance" (312).

profecto: The particle expresses a strong opinion but one that the speaker wishes to specify is subjective (i.e., "surely" rather than "truly"; Landgraf 1914: 77). It is most commonly employed by Cicero in apodoses of unreal conditions, as here, to underscore what conclusions the speaker should draw from the necessarily hypothetical situation (Steinitz 1885: 31–36).

multa...in eo penitus defixa atque haerentia: The metaphor continues the imagery of Clodius as a hunted animal; cf. nn. on 4 (*volnerati*), 8 (*confixum*), 39 (*figuntur*, a probable tragic quotation).

Parentibus et dis immortalibus et patriae nos primum natura conciliat: "From the first, the condition of our being born (*natura*) commends us to our parents and the immortal gods and our fatherland." This literal interpretation of the noun *natura* (*OLD* s.v. 1), rather than understanding it as referring to a quasi-divine nature (as does *ThLL* IX, 1 160.44 [I. Hajdú] and Shackleton Bailey 1991a: 132; cf. Watt 1923: 393: "nature...at the hour of our birth"), accords better with the following sentence, where "at the same time" (*eodem tempore*) refers back to the time of birth.

The entire sentence has a deliberate, systematic structure. The trinity of parents (*parentibus*), gods (*dis*), and fatherland (*patriae*), presented in polysyndeton in the first half, corresponds precisely to the areas in which a Roman's life is affected by each of these elements, also presented in polysyndeton (*et suscipimur in lucem et hoc caelesti spiritu augemur et certam in sedem civitatis ac libertatis adscribimur*), as "we Romans" move from being the direct object of the first verb to being the subject of the three verbs of the second half, each of which is in the passive voice. The careful parallelism disappears when each of these categories is applied to the case of Clodius (*parentum*; *deorum*; *quid de patria loquar?*). In that section of the speech long lists prevail, largely in asyndeton, leaving the impression of the jumbled mess that Clodius has left in his wake. It is worth comparing this passage to *p. red. in sen.* 2, where the same trio of parents, gods, and country are praised (cf., less systematically, *p. red. ad Quir.* 5). Rather than showing how Clodius acts contrary to each, however, the different context finds Cicero adding the senate as a fourth essential item, which acts as protector and preserver of the first three, in particular through its role in recalling Cicero from exile.

suscipimur in lucem: This phrase refers to a child's relationship with its parents (*parentibus*), as it emerges from birth into the light of the world, the area watched over by the goddess of childbirth Lucina. Köves-Zulauf 1990: 1–92 provides, with discussion, a full list of parallels for this concept from antiquity to the middle ages (for *suscipere*, see 28–29). He demonstrates that there is no clear evidence to support the widely held notion that the act Cicero describes here involves the father lifting a newborn child from the ground toward the light of the sun as a way of signaling acceptance of it into his household.

Cicero's wording recalls the notion of birthing children "into the shores of light" (*in luminis oras*), a phrase used both literally and metaphorically by Ennius (*ann*. 109; cf. *ann*. 135), including in a passage quoted by Cicero at *rep*. 1.64. The phrase is picked up numerous times by later poets (Skutsch 1985: 259), in particular by Cicero's contemporary Lucretius (e.g., 1.22–23: *nec sine te quicquam dias in luminis oras / exoritur*; 5.781–782, with Köves-Zulauf 1990: 88–99). Cicero's reminiscence of poetic language fits the context here, as he heightens the rhetoric following his mention of a hypothetical poet.

hoc caelesti spiritu augemur: The second simultaneous gift to the newborn arises from the gods (*dis immortalibus*). As often (*ThLL* III 71.4–12 [W. Bannier]), the adjective *caelestis* acts as a synonym for "divine" as Cicero imagines here each human being instilled with a divine element at the moment of birth. Compare Seneca, who describes the human mind (*mens*) not as arising from matter, but as descending from a "distant (*illo*) heavenly spirit" (*dial*. 12.6.7: *non est [mens] ex terreno et gravi concreta corpore, ex illo caelesti spiritu descendit*). Rather than marking the source of that spirit with *ille*, as Seneca does, Cicero uses the deictic adjective *hoc* to designate that the spirit is present among all his listeners—all, that is, but *iste* Clodius.

certam in sedem civitatis ac libertatis adscribimur: The third benefit, unlike the first two, is described in prosaic terms. Each Roman child receives as a gift of the fatherland (*patriae*) citizenship in a secure and free state. The verb *adscribere* is the technical term, here used metaphorically, to describe the entering of names onto a community's rolls as a first step toward full citizenship (*ThLL* II, 773.81–774.5 [A. v. Mess]).

** ***parentum***: Shackleton Bailey 1987: 276 maintains that *parentum*, the reading of all the manuscripts, can never mean *maiorum* in Cicero and suggests emending to *paternum* (note *dom*. 35: *sacris paternis*, in the same context). While *paternum* may be more accurate a designation, the genitive *parentum* nevertheless fits with each subsequent noun that governs it and, stylistically, accords with the precise expansion of the tricolon as discussed above, where *parentum* corresponds with *parentibus* and the phrase *suscipimur in lucem* refers to the role of parents after birth. Furthermore, the use by Cicero's younger contemporary, the poet Catullus, of the phrase *more parentum* (101.7) as a poetic variant for the common *more maiorum* may suggest that Cicero is continuing here with his adoption of a less prosaic tone.

iste parentum nomen, sacra, memoriam, gentem Fonteiano nomine obruit: Cicero asserts that Clodius has obliterated important elements of his ancestral inheritance "through the name Fonteius" (*Fonteiano nomine*). The ablative phrase alludes to Clodius's adoption by a certain Publius Fonteius, a man considerably younger than his adopted son, thereby allowing the patrician Clodius to become a plebeian and qualify for election to the tribunate of the plebs (44n). The adjectival form *Fonteianus* appears only here in classical Latin (Solin and Salomies 1994: 333 give one example of *Fonteianus* as a cognomen at *CIL* VI 18528) and seems to signal that Cicero is treating the change of name ironically (2n; at *dom.* 116 Cicero uses the adjective *Fonteius*), an irony probably underscored by the repetition *Fonteianō nōmine* (Marouzeau 1946: 42–45 provides numerous examples of such repetition used for comic effect). Despite the clarity of the historical reference, it is nevertheless difficult to determine precisely the applicability of the adoption to each of the elements that Cicero lists. This difficulty is exacerbated by the fact that Cicero's claims in this sentence make little sense to us (see below on *nomen*) and conflict in at least one particular from his fuller account at *dom.* 35–41 (see below on *sacra*).

To begin with the claim that the name *Fonteius* has helped Clodius obliterate the "name...that belonged to his parents" (*parentum nomen*). If the noun *nomen* here refers strictly to the *nomen gentilicium*, as often (*OLD* s.v. 1c), Cicero would allude to Clodius's use of the untraditional form of his family *nomen* Claudius (on which see Riggsby 2002b). Two factors tell against this possibility. The first is that Cicero nowhere else criticizes Clodius (or Clodia for that matter) for a deviant spelling or pronunciation of their name and so it is unclear how he would conceive of Clodius as "ruining" it (contrast his jokes on *Pulcher*, Clodius's cognomen; Corbeill 1996: 79–80). A second objection is that it is also unclear how Fonteius's name would have had this effect. Clodius was immediately emancipated by Fonteius upon adoption (*dom.* 37) and there is no evidence that Clodius used the *nomen* of his adoptive father, always retaining instead the well-known Publius Clodius Pulcher (on the varied nomenclature an adopted son could have during this period, see Shackleton Bailey 1991b: 54–59). It is possible that Cicero conveniently ignores Clodius's immediate emancipation, imagining that Clodius lost his birth *nomen* upon adoption (which was then converted to *Claudianus* or *Clodianus*, an alteration that would fit with the verb *obruere*) but there is no evidence of Clodius ever being referred to as *Claudianus* or *Clodianus*.

Next among the items that Cicero alleges Clodius to have ignored are the religious rituals (*sacra*) practiced by his ancestors (for these rites, see 32n). This assertion repeats claims that Cicero had made in a convoluted discussion of the repercussions of Clodius's adoption at *dom.* 34–37. At *dom.* 35, he begins by asserting that adoption normally entails loss of the *sacra* practiced by one's biological family: *sacra Clodiae gentis cur intereunt, quod in te est?* ("Why are the rites of the Clodian family dying out, as far as it concerns you [Clodius]?";

cf. 37). This assertion seems inaccurate: through his emancipation from his father immediately upon adoption, Clodius was able "to retain the gentile name of his birth, his *imagines* and *sacra*, and consequently his inheritance" (Nisbet 1939: 97, quoting Botsford 1909: 163). Cicero does acknowledge at *dom.* 35 that it was indeed Clodius's intention not to lose his *sacra*, but that this act of retention violated pontifical law: *neque amissis sacris paternis in haec adoptiva venisti.... factus es eius filius contra fas* ("And you neither lost your ancestral rites nor entered into those belonging to your adoption.... You became his son contrary to religious law"; for *neque* negating both the ablative absolute and main verb, see Nisbet 1939: 99). If this interpretation of *dom.* 34–37 is correct, then by claiming here in *har. resp.* that Clodius's adoption has negated the familial rites of his ancestral Claudii, Cicero refers not to what the adoption had in fact effected in the eyes of human law (as many in his audience of senators, in particular the *pontifices* in attendance, would have known) but to what has happened in contravention of divine law (*fas*; cf. Weinrib 1968b: 256–257). Such a stance is of course in keeping with the tenor of Cicero's argument throughout the speech, which aims through an analysis of the haruspical response to expose Clodius's actions as an affront to divine will.

Cicero also accuses Clodius of obliterating the "memory (*memoriam*) of his ancestors." As my translation indicates, the noun *memoria* must govern *parentum* as an objective genitive, whereas with the remaining nouns in the series the genitive is subjective, but it is doubtful that Cicero's audience would have noticed the distinction (LHS 2: 65: "Wenn wir von Gen. subiectivus und obiectivus reden, verselbständigen wir logische Kategorien, die lediglich durch die Bedeutung der beiden Subst. näher bestimmt werden, aber keiner irgendwie klar abgegrenzten begrifflichen Kategorie im Bewußtsein des Redenden entsprechen"). The reference here is to the inability of Clodius to live up to the standards of the noble Claudii, a stock element of Cicero's invective against him and, particularly in *Cael.*, against his sister (nn. on 26, 27, 38).

The final item in the list, *gentem*, is the summation of the previous three items: in obliterating his ancestral name, rites, and memory, Clodius destroys his *gens* (*dom.* 116: *non suae genti Fonteiae, sed Clodiae, quam reliquit*; 127: *ille gentem istam reliquit*). Michels 1966: 678 connects this sentence with Lucr. 2.614–615: *qui.../ ingrati genitoribus inventi sint* (in an explanation for why male followers of the Mater Magna practice self-castration).

Cicero caps the sentence with a punning verb: as a result of the name *Fonteius*, derived from *fons* ("fountain, spring"), all these features of the Claudian *gens* are "washed away" (for this sense of *obruo* see *ThLL* IX, 2 153.3–27 [M. Lossau]). The possibility of such a pun is further indicated by the beginning of the next sentence (*deorum ignis*) and the accusation that Clodius set afire the temple of the Nymphs in the Campus Martius (57), who were "devoted to the beneficial effects and uses of springs and water" (Lenaghan 1969: 188). For the centrality of name puns in Republican rhetoric see Corbeill 1996: 57–98.

deorum: After treating Clodius's abandonment of his ancestors, Cicero turns to the second item in his earlier list, his relationship with the gods. Although the noun *deorum* is plural, the list of items that follows makes clear that Cicero is thinking chiefly of objects associated with the rites of the Bona Dea. His greater elaboration in comparison with his account of the ancestors suits the religious subject matter of the speech and, predictably, he uses the list to further connect Clodius's transgressions with the language of the haruspical response.

ignis, solia, mensas, abditos ac penetrales focos...pervertit: For the fires (*ignis*) associated with the Bona Dea rites, see 4n. The use of the plural number for each of the items upset by Clodius underscores the enormity of his sacrilege. In an analogous way, the verb *perverto* is chosen since it carries both literal and metaphorical overtones ("overturned / perverted"). The *solium* is defined by Festus as a seat suitable for an individual and covered with a spread (*soliar*) when used for goddesses at the *sellisternium* (p. 298 M). References to Jupiter's having a *solium* occur especially frequently (e.g., Hor. *ep*. 1.17.34, Verg. *Aen*. 10.116, Stat. *silv*. 3.1.25; *RE* 3A: 929–930 [A. Hug]) and, although there are no extant mentions in texts, Brouwer 1989 offers several images of Bona Dea seated on what appears to be the high-backed *solium* (esp. plates 16–17, 42–44). Cicero also mentions the goddess Voluptas seated on a *solium* (*fin*. 2.69). The noun *mensa* refers to the table used to hold offerings and assorted sacred objects for a god; it could also occasionally serve as an altar (Schaewen 1940: 43–44). The sacred hearths (*focos*) in this passage carry multiple associations. Like the first three items in the list, they have ritual connotations, designating portable burners, such as would presumably have been used for the moveable ceremony at the house of Caesar (*ThLL* VI, 1 989.83–990.69 [F. Vollmer]). At the same time, the accompanying adjectives—"the hidden inner hearths"—shift attention to the synecdochal use of *focus* to designate the stability of home life, as in English "hearth and home" (Landgraf 1914: 61–62). Clodius, in other words, disrupted not only this one specific festival but also overturned the household of the pontifex maximus where the festival took place by instigating the divorce of Caesar from his wife Pompeia (38n).

occulta et maribus non invisa solum, sed etiam inaudita sacra: The previous components of the list included concrete items necessary for the ritual of the Bona Dea—fire, throne, altar, and hearth—while the final, elaborated, element, *sacra*, encompasses the ritual itself. Cicero repeats earlier points about these female rites being forbidden to men's eyes (e.g., 8, 26, 38), and with *occulta sacra* once again ties Clodius's intervention at the Bona Dea with the wording of the response (37: **SACRIFICIA VETVSTA OCCVLTAQVE**, with Cicero's exposition). In classical Latin the adjective *invisus* ("unseen"), in order to avoid confusion with *invisus* ("hateful"), is used only in combination with additional words that clarify the meaning, such as *inaudita*; cf. Cato *agr*. 141: *visos invisosque*; *ThLL* VII, 2 224.65–225.2 (K. Stiewe).

inexpiabili scelere: While the adjective *inexpiabilis* is frequently used metaphorically ("unforgivable"), when employed in a sacral context the adjective retains its etymological meaning to describe something for which one cannot receive atonement from the gods (*Phil.* 1.13 and 11.29, *Tusc.* 1.27; *ThLL* VII, 1 1325.16–17 [A. Szantyr]). For the first time in this speech, Cicero depicts Clodius as a type of prodigy, one for which it is not possible, in contrast with other prodigies that are treated in a timely fashion, to receive expiation (cf. 4n). After Clodius's death Cicero remarks that the senate required frequent expiation for his violation of the Bona Dea, an historically tendentious claim which contradicts the assertion here that the crime is inexpiable: *eum [Clodium], cuius supplicio senatus sollemnis religiones expiandas saepe censuit* (*Mil.* 73, with Keeline 2021: 283).

idemque earum templum inflammavit dearum: Cicero explicitly refers at *Mil.* 73 to Clodius and his gang setting afire the temple of the Nymphs in order to destroy censorial records: *aedem Nympharum incendit ut memoriam publicam recensionis tabulis publicis impressam exstingueret* (cf. *parad.* 31; *Cael.* 78 [of Cloelius]: *qui aedes sacras, qui censum populi Romani, qui memoriam publicam suis manibus incendit*; *Sest.* 95; Suolahti 1963: 33 n. 5). If this allegation is true, it is unclear what Clodius's motivation will have been in destroying public records. Lenaghan 1969: 188 conjectures that it represented an attack on the authority of the censors, but adds that "it may also simply have been an accidental by-product of some other violence." Nicolet aims for more precision, dating the burning to February or March 56 and interpreting it as an attack intended to complicate Pompey's work as grain commissioner by destroying the registration lists found in the temple that contained the names of those entitled to grain distribution (Nicolet 1976: 38–46, followed by Benner 1987: 119–121; Tatum 1999: 211; Kaster 2006: 315 and App. 1; cf. Keeline 2021: 285–286). The site of the temple has been identified with a building on the Marble Plan situated inside the Porticus Minucia Vetus, the probable site of food distribution during the Republic; this association provides further support that Clodius's actions were a direct attack on Pompey's commission (*LTUR* 3: 350–351 [D. Manacorda], following Nicolet 1976: 38–46).

As Clark 1895: 63–64 notes, Cicero was not himself innocent of this sort of activity. Plutarch records that, taking advantage of Clodius being away from Rome, he ventured to the Capitol with a large gang in order to destroy the records of his enemy's activities as tribune (*Cic.* 34.1).

quarum ope etiam aliis incendiis subvenitur: The Nymphae (originally Lymphae), as personifications of water sources, were worshipped by the Romans for their associations with health and well-being; Bloch 1899: 3.540–552 offers a full account of their divine role in the Roman world. Outside this reference, the only other association of Nymphs with fire depends on a conjecture in the inscription of the Arval Calendar that has them sharing with Vulcan and Juturna the festal day of August 23 (*CIL* VI 32482; Bloch 1899: 3.544; Wissowa 1912:

223). I consider it more likely, however, that Cicero does not in fact refer here to an otherwise unknown sacral function of the Nymphs but rather is appending to the bare description of Clodius's incendiary behavior a learned pun on the mythical Nymphs. Playing on their association with springs, an association so marked that they become synonymous with the water that they inhabited (*OLD* s.v. 1b), Cicero is simply remarking that "water" helps put out fires.

58 *quid de patria loquar?*: The regularity of the original listing of the trio of parents, gods, and country in the dative at first receives a regular response in their elaboration, where the first two elements occur in the genitive (57: *parentum... deorum*). For the third and most significant element in his list, however,—the manner in which Clodius has violated his homeland—Cicero disturbs the expected syntax by instead posing an emphatic rhetorical question. This disruption seems to infect the following sentence, which is not only one of the longest in *har. resp.* but is characterized by an avoidance of conjunctions (*salutis mentisque... caede incendiisque... Aeliam et Fufiam* are the exceptions). The marked use of asyndeton reflects the violence and rapidity of what is described: a swift catalogue of the numerous ways in which Clodius has violated nearly every institution of the Roman state, beginning with Cicero's exile (*primum*) and following up with (*deinde*) the numerous acts of violence against the state and its most prominent citizens that he perpetrated in Cicero's absence.

eum civem vi, ferro, periculis urbe, omnibus patriae praesidiis depulit: Cicero refers here to himself in the third person (continued below with *comite, duce*). This unexpected form of reference (rather than the more natural *me*) corresponds with the preceding third-person pronoun *qui* to describe Clodius (rather than *tu*). This simple grammatical maneuver removes Clodius's actions from the area of personal attack, lending the subsequent description an objective and unbiased air. The abrupt change in the construction of the ablatives from means (*vi, ferro, periculis*) to separation (*urbe, praesidiis*) is unusual, and the confused syntax contributes to the confused state of Rome at the time of Cicero's exile. The transition may be eased by the fact that *depello* anticipates a construction specifying "from where," although of the many examples in Merguet 1877–1884: 2.70–71, most are governed by *ab*, less frequently *de* or *ex*; of the four other bare ablative constructions in Cicero cited by KS 2: 1.366 there is no possible ambiguity (e.g., *de orat.* 3.11: *depulsus per invidiam tribunatu*). The safeguards (*praesidia*) which Cicero had lost include the protection afforded by a fair jury trial (for this sense of *praesidium* see *Verr.* 2.2.8, *Sull.* 92).

omnibus patriae praesidiis... quem vos patriae conservatorem esse saepissime iudicaritis: The repetition of *patria* in such close proximity keeps up the theme of this sentence, namely how Clodius's actions are contrary to the well-being of the state (*quid de patria loquar?*).

In December 63 the senate bestowed on Cicero, in recognition of his role in suppressing the Catilinarian conspiracy, the unprecedented title of "father of his country" (*parens* / *pater patriae*), together with other extraordinary distinctions such as a *supplicatio* and *corona civica,* the latter normally reserved for military achievement (*Sest.* 121, *Pis.* 6, *fam.* 15.4.11=SB 110; Plin. *nat.* 7.117; Plut. *Cic.* 23.6; App. *BC* 2.7; Gell. 5.6.15; Kaster 2006: 364–365 doubts whether the title was formally awarded). While there is no evidence that the designation *patriae conservator* was among these honors, Cicero mentions on numerous occasions, particularly following his exile, that the senate had recognized his role as Rome's "savior" (of many examples, compare especially the similar formulation at *dom.* 101: *cuius* urbis servatorem *me esse senatus omnium adsensu* totiens iudicarit; cf., e.g., 122; *p. red. in sen.* 26, *p. red. ad Quir.* 17, *Mil.* 73, *Phil.* 2.2; more examples in Lenaghan 1969: 189). The reference to the epithet being used "repeatedly" supports the idea that it never received formal recognition.

The perfect subjunctive *iudicaritis,* here violating the expected sequence of tenses, has a concessive force in this relative clause of characteristic ("he drove away that man, *even though* you repeatedly deemed him 'savior of the fatherland'"; many parallels at Lebreton 1901: 234–236; *OLS* 2: 537–538).

everso senatūs, ut ego semper dixi, comite, duce, ut ille dicebat: Cicero's positive characterization of Scipio Aemilianus in *De amicitia* reverses the contrast here between a cooperative companion (*comes*) and a self-centered leader (*dux*): *ut facile ducem populi Romani, non comitem diceres* (*Lael.* 96: "so that you might easily call [Scipio] not a member of the Roman people, but its leader"; note similar contrasts at *Marcell.* 11, *Lael.* 37; cf. too *Sull.* 9, *Flacc.* 5). Cicero defends himself elsewhere from claims by Clodius that he exhibits tyrannical behavior, most famously when in response to an attack by Cicero in the aftermath of the Bona Dea trial Clodius complained in the senate "How long shall we endure this king?" (*Att.* 1.16.10=SB 16: '*quousque...hunc regem feremus?*'; see too Cicero's long response to the charge at *Sull.* 21–22, with Berry 1996a: 174–178). Allen 1944 discusses how the accusation underlay Clodius's choice to erect on Cicero's property the shrine to *Libertas*—marking freedom from the tyrant. An additional aspect of Clodius's accusation is that, while it is appropriate for a member of the elite to show leadership (*dux*) over the general Roman populace, among his fellow senators he needs to remain an equal (*comes*); there may also be an allusion to Cicero placing himself on a par with military leaders, for which *dux* is a common designation (49n). Nowhere else in his extant works does Cicero refer to himself as a *senatus comes.* It is possible, however, that Clodius quotes an occasion when Cicero did in fact claim to be *senatus dux* since he does describe himself with this phrase in the 40s while looking back on the events of 63 (*Phil.* 2.17: *praesertim cum senatus populusque Romanus [me] haberet ducem; ad Brut.* 8.3=SB 6; Cicero also occasionally speaks of the senate as having plural *duces:* e.g., *p. red. in sen.* 33, *Sest.* 35).

principem salutis mentisque publicae: Cicero at *Mil.* 90 describes the senate building as *templum...mentis [publicae].* In specifying that the senate, much like the controlling force of the universe in Stoicism, has a mind that controls the rational and intellectual aspect of the state, Cicero contrasts the irrationality with which he has characterized Clodius throughout the speech.

sustulit duas leges, Aeliam et Fufiam: The *leges Aelia et Fufia* broadened the range of those officials who could employ the auspices in order to prevent legislation in the popular assemblies and perhaps even to block elections (*obnuntiatio*; 48n). The two laws seem to have formalized the *mos maiorum* by extending this authority, once restricted to augurs, to curule magistrates and tribunes of the people, or by specifying which political measures could be blocked by the auspices (discussion in Tatum 1999: 127–129). Passage is dated to c. 150 BCE on account of Cicero's reference to its having been in existence for nearly one hundred years in 58 (*Pis*. 10: *centum prope annos*). While the precise intentions behind these laws can only be guessed at, one certain result was reduction in the power of augurs. On January 4, 58, Clodius passed the law referred to here, the precise scope of which is uncertain beyond that it limited the application of the earlier legislation (see, e.g., *p. red. in sen*. 11; *Sest*. 33, 56; *Vatin*. 23; *Pis*. 9; *prov. cons*. 46; Ascon. *Pis*. p. 8.17–22 Clark). The bibliography on the issue is immense (for which see Kaster 2006: 194–196, Manuwald 2021: 125–126), but there seems to be general consensus on two points: 1. Clodius wished to restrict the use of *obnuntiatio* in order to facilitate the passing of his own legislative program; 2. despite Cicero's vociferous objections to it, this *lex Clodia* did not entirely repeal or override the *leges Aelia et Fufia*, as indicated by the fact that C. Cato was prosecuted under the *lex Fufia* in 54 (*Att*. 4.16.5=SB 89). Lenaghan 1969: 190–191 notes that Cicero may have himself benefited from Clodius's law when the senate prohibited *obnuntiatio* from obstructing legislation for his recall. Despite Cicero's frequent mentions of how Clodius's measures limit the power of the auspices, however, it is interesting that he does not raise objections on religious grounds, especially here in *har. resp*. where such an argument would have particular significance (Riggsby 2002a: 187–188).

censuram exstinxit: The same vague and hyperbolic accusation that Clodius's legislation destroyed the functions of the Roman censor occurs at *dom*. 131, *Sest*. 55, *prov. cons*. 46, *Pis*. 9. Asconius offers a more objective perspective, stating that the legislation provided "that the censors, while making the senate rolls, should neither pass over nor disqualify anyone without formal accusation and the judgment of both" (*Pis*. p. 8.24–26 Clark: *ne quem censores in senatu legendo praeterirent, neve qua ignominia afficerent, nisi qui apud eos accusatus et utriusque censoris sententia damnatus esset*; see too Dio 38.13.2; Schol. Bob. p. 132.21–23). Gruen 1974: 257 recognizes one positive side of the measure, as a control on abuses of previous individual censors who had wished to remove people from the senate or equestrian rolls without due cause and the consent of both censors. Tatum 1990: 36–41 reviews the history of the censorial role in revising senatorial membership and stresses that one innovative feature of Clodius's law was its ability to allow senators to defend themselves before formal expulsion. This Clodian law was repealed in 52 by the consul Metellus

Scipio (Dio 40.57.1–3); for an analysis of Scipio's possible motivations see Tatum 1990: 42–43.

intercessionem removit, auspicia delevit: Cicero elsewhere attributes to a single law from Clodius's tribunate the removal of both the ability for tribunes to veto legislation and the right to take auspices: *lata lex est, ne auspicia valerent,... ne quis legi intercederet* (*Sest.* 33; cf. *p. red. in sen.* 11, *prov.* 46; *LPPR* 398). In each passage, as here, Cicero remarks in the same list that Clodius overturned the *leges Aelia et Fufia*. It seems likely therefore, as Mommsen 1887–1888: 2.1.308 n. 3 suggested, that the abolition of the veto and of the auspices refers hyperbolically to a limitation that Clodius's law had put on these two practices in order to control excessive use of *obnuntiatio* (Tatum 1999: 130–133 offers a concise overview). Cicero, in other words, for dramatic effect mentions as separate incidents three results of one *lex Clodia*, interposing among them the independent legislation concerning the censorship in order to increase the illusion that each provision was a distinct law. For a similar rhetorical trick, compare Cicero's treatment of Clodius's alleged threat to declare a *iustitium* (55n).

consules sceleris sui socios aerario, provinciis, exercitu armavit: Cicero colors regular political procedures with loaded vocabulary (*sceleris sui socios, armavit*). For the complicity of Piso and Gabinius, the consuls of 58, in Clodius's tribunician activity see 2n. For Clodius's role in using special legislation to secure them provinces (and hence armies) after their consulship see 3n. As part of these appointments, both men would have been expected to receive funds from the public treasury, which in this instance Cicero construes on several occasions to have "drained the treasury" (cf. *p. red. in sen.* 18; *dom.* 23–24, 55; *Sest.* 54; *Pis.* 28, 37, 57). At *Pis.* 86 he claims that Piso was granted 18,000,000 sesterces to provide his troops with equipment (*vasarii nomine*), which would seem an unusually high sum (Nisbet 1961: 155), and that, rather than spending the funds for their allotted purpose, he accrued interest on them by making loans in Rome.

reges qui erant vendidit, qui non erant appellavit: This refers directly to the Clodian legislation concerning the Galatian kings Brogitarus and Deiotarus (28–29n). The obliquity of Cicero's formulation also allows a reference to Clodius's legislation about the island of Cyprus (*LPPR* 397), which is mentioned alongside the Brogitarus incident at *Sest.* 56–58. Clodius's law led, in Cicero's formulation, to the auctioning of the kingdom and possessions of King Ptolemy of Cyprus (*dom.* 52, *Sest.* 57–58; cf. *dom.* 20, reading *praeconium* with Shackleton Bailey 1979: 264). The affair ultimately drove Ptolemy to suicide (Tatum 1999: 150–151).

Cn. Pompeium ferro domum compulit: For the incident, see 49n. It is worth noting that an analogous formulation occurs earlier in the sentence to describe Clodius driving Cicero into exile (*civem vi ferro periculis urbe...depulit*), another instance of Cicero comparing himself to Pompey (49n).

imperatorum monumenta evertit: Cicero presumably has in mind only the Porticus Catuli, despite the plural number (for which see Nisbet 1939: 155; KS 2: 1.86–87). Clodius did, however, damage this single monument on two occasions: first, during Cicero's exile (33n), and then on November 3, 57 as Cicero's builders were restoring it (*Att.* 4.3.2=SB 75; *Cael.* 78).

inimicorum domus disturbavit: Of the many accusations in this sentence, this one has greatest claim to being comparatively free of hyperbole. Both Cicero and other ancient sources refer on several occasions to Clodius and his gangs attacking the homes of opponents, particularly in the period 58–57 BCE. In addition to general references (*p. red. in sen.* 7: *magistratuum tecta impugnata*, 19; *p. red. ad Quir.* 14; *Sest.* 90), the sources also provide specifics. Asconius cites the *Acta* for evidence that Pompey, following an attempt on his life in summer 58, was driven to take refuge in his home, where he was continually under siege from Clodius's followers (49n). In January 57, the house of Milo too was besieged during the violent unrest that accompanied calls for Cicero's restoration (*Sest.* 85: *domus est oppugnata ferro, facibus, exercitu Clodiano*, 88; for context Tatum 1999: 176–180). Eleven months later, on the morning of November 12, Clodius and his allies staged another attack on this tribune's home (*Att.* 4.3.3=SB 75; cf. *Mil.* 38; Maslowski 1976 discusses dates). In July of the same year, when L. Caecilius Rufus was conducting the *ludi Apollinares* in his capacity as urban praetor, his house was attacked during a riot over the price of grain (*Mil.* 38 with Ascon. *Mil.* p. 48.18–27 Clark). Cicero tells us that during the destruction of the Porticus Catuli on his property in November 57, the same gang threw stones upon the house of his brother Quintus before setting it alight (*Att.* 4.3.2=SB 75: *Quinti fratris domus primo fracta coniectu lapidum ex area nostra, deinde inflammata iussu Clodi inspectante urbe coniectis ignibus*; *Cael.* 78). A week later, the home of Tettius Damio was besieged when Cicero took refuge there to escape another riot (*Att.* 4.3.3=SB 75). Around the time of the delivery of *har. resp.*, Cicero was again taking precautions to protect his property (*Att.* 4.7.3=SB 77, c. April 56) and it seems to have been attacked yet again soon thereafter (Dio 39.20.3 with Kumaniecki 1959: 138).

vestris monumentis suum nomen inscripsit: Despite textual uncertainties, *dom.* 137 seems to indicate that Clodius removed Catulus's name from the portico and added his own. Such an interpretation of Cicero's assertion here, however, would create an inelegant redundancy following the accusation that Clodius had "overturned the monuments of generals" (*imperatorum monumenta evertit*). Furthermore, the portico was presumably built from Catulus's war booty and so did not involve contributions from the senate, as *vestris* implies. An attractive alternative explanation for this accusation has recently become available. In a letter to Lentulus from December 54, Cicero describes a different occasion when certain individuals had "allowed a monument of the senate to be inscribed in bloody letters with the name of an enemy (sc. Clodius)" (*fam.* 1.9.15=SB 20: *monumentum... senatus hostili nomine et cruentis inustum litteris esse passi sunt*). Cicero adds that he had himself contracted the erection of this monument (*operis locatio mea fuerat*), presumably during his consulship, with the result that it cannot refer to the Porticus Catuli. The identification of the monument was the subject of speculation until relatively recently, when Zevi published a series of articles that provide a concrete reference for Cicero's allusion (see esp. Zevi and Fedeli 2013). Two identical inscriptions from the turn of the second century CE had been known since the early twentieth century, commemorating the erection of the circuit walls around Rome's port city of Ostia. This dedication was displayed on both the exterior and interior attic of the so-called Porta Romana, the most prominent gate of Ostia, which greeted those entering the city by land from the direction of the capital. Following a careful reconsideration of the extant fragments of these two texts, Zevi has determined that not only the senate but Cicero when consul and Clodius when tribune played central roles in initiating and completing the construction of the Ostian walls. I cite here a composite reconstruction (I do not indicate the various lacunae in the two exemplars. For details see Zevi 1996–1997: 84–99; minor refinements in Caruso and Papi 2005, Zevi and Manzini 2008): *Senatus Populusque Romanus | coloniae Ostiensium muros et portas dedit. | M. Tullius Cicero co(n)s(ul) fecit locavitque. | P. Clodius Pulcher tr(ibunus) pl(ebis) consummavit et probavit. | Portam vetustate corruptam…* ("The Roman senate and people have gifted to the colony of the people of Ostia city walls and gates. Marcus Tullius Cicero arranged and contracted for this when consul. Publius Clodius Pulcher when tribune of the plebs completed it and gave final approval. The gate, damaged by the passage of time [*the rest of the inscription is fragmentary*]"). Zevi concludes that these inscriptions commemorate the original decision by the senate in 63 to construct defensive walls for Ostia and their subsequent completion under Clodius's tribunate five years later. The unusual association of a tribune with a building project, and with one outside the city, can probably be attributed to provisions included in Clodius's grain legislation. This information was included in the extant inscriptions when the gate underwent restoration in the late first century CE (Zevi 1996–1997 has a detailed account of the inscriptions' discovery and dating, along with a reconstruction of the historical circumstances; Bruun 2023 considers the context of their first- or second-century CE erection).

Although Cicero has chosen for unclear reasons not to be more specific about the allusion here, the vagueness of the accusation does complement well other references in this section to aspects of Clodius's legislation that had not explicitly been mentioned earlier, such as his succinct remarks on Clodius eliminating the censorship, the veto, and the auspices.

inscripsit. *infinita sunt scelera quae ab illo in patriam sunt edita*: The asyndetic and seemingly unending nature of the catalogue of Clodius's crimes is underscored by the meaning of the first word of the following sentence, *infinita*—"endless"—also following in asyndeton. Besides repeating the beginnings

De haruspicum responsis 59

of these two juxtaposed words, the preverb *in-* also anticipates the prepositional phrase *in patriam,* which clues the hearer that this short sentence provides, in a type of ring composition, the closing bracket to the short rhetorical question that had preceded the catalogue—*quid de patria loquar?*

quid?: For the colloquial use of *quid* to attract and hold on to the attention of an audience, see Hofmann 1980: 189–192, §66. Cicero frequently employs the lone pronoun *quid* to preface a question or series of questions, as here; the more emphatic *quid vero?* two sentences later signals change of topic after an intervening question. For the employment of a series of rhetorical questions (*interrogatio*) see Lausberg 1998: §§767–768, who notes that the self-evident answer to the questions "is intended to humiliate the opposing party."

quae [scelera] in singulos civis quos necavit, socios quos diripuit, imperatores quos prodidit, exercitus quos temptavit: Cicero leaves the triad of family, gods, and country to list briefly those crimes that do not fall so neatly into these categories, eventually culminating in the next section with those that Clodius had committed against his own self (*in ipsum se scelera...edidit*). Cicero recapitulates in brief some of the events upon which he had touched earlier. The citizens murdered would include Seius (30n) and perhaps also the anonymous *pupilli* (42n) and *divisores* (42). For his unjust treatment of allies, see the notes on Deiotarus (28–29n) and perhaps the less specific accusations at 42. The final two allegations—of betraying a general and fomenting a military revolt—refer most clearly to the betrayal of Lucullus and subsequent rebellion of his troops at Nisibis (42n), but the noun *imperator* is certain to call to mind Clodius's conflicts with Pompey (e.g., 49n), as well as perhaps the long-dead Catulus (e.g., nn. on 33, 58). The tetradic structure of the sentence adheres to a regular sequence—masculine accusative noun dependent upon the expressed or understood preposition *in*, relative pronoun in masculine accusative plural (*quos*), verb in perfect active with Clodius as understood subject. This regularity, however, receives variation through the use of three different clausulae to terminate each relative clause (double trochee / spondee + anapest / long syllable + cretic / double spondee).

59 ea quanta sunt quae in ipsum se scelera, quae in suos edidit!: The noun *scelera* would have been readily understood by listeners with the phrase *ea quanta sunt*, just as it was understood with the interrogative adjective *quae* in the previous sentence. As a result, its occurrence in the relative clause is unexpected and, further enhanced through hyperbaton, it becomes particularly emphatic. For *scelera*, see 5n; the subsequent question make clear that the word here refers specifically to sexual transgressions (cf. Adams 1982: 202).

quis...quae navis...quis umquam nepos...quam denique tam immanem Charybdim...aut...Scyllam: This tetracolon of rhetorical questions adheres to the pattern of Cicero's introductory exclamation, with the first two sentences describing "crimes" that Clodius committed against himself, the next two against his family and associates. The sequence of questions is carefully structured, introduced by interrogative words in first position, but with morphological forms interchanging. After three questions that claim some relationship with Roman realities regarding Clodius's unprecedented behavior (*umquam...umquam...umquam*), the fourth climaxes (*denique*) by remarking again how even the imagination of poets cannot express the enormities of Clodius's behavior (57n).

omnibus corporis sui partibus: The phrase is deliberately vague. The all-encompassing adjective here ("all") allows Cicero's audience to imagine for themselves the involvement of Clodius's body in an entire range of deviant activities, in particular their sexual use as both an active and passive male. For a more elaborate development of the same conceit see *Catil.* 1.13: *quae libido ab oculis, quod facinus a manibus umquam tuis, quod flagitium a toto corpore afuit?*; *p. red. in sen.* 11 (of Gabinius): *qui ne a sanctissima quidem parte corporis potuisset hominum impuram intemperantiam propulsare* (i.e., the mouth; see Boll 2019: 134). An analogous charge was brought against Cicero in the declamatory schools, such as at Ps. Sall. *inv. Cic.* 5: *cuius nulla pars corporis a turpitudine vacat, lingua vana, manus rapacissimae, gula immensa, pedes fugaces: quae honeste nominari non possunt, inhonestissima* ("No part of his body is free of vice—his idle tongue, thieving hands, boundless gullet, cowardly feet; those [parts] that cannot be honestly named are the most dishonorable"); see further Vretska 1961: 2.43–46. The metaphor of "not sparing the body" is a violent one that occurs elsewhere in the context of rape, e.g., Curt. 3.11.22 (*ne corporibus quidem vis ac libido parcebat*) or lax sexual behavior (Ps. Cypr. *pudic.* 3: *nec corporibus parcens [impudicitiā] nec animis*).

quae navis umquam in flumine publico tam vulgata omnibus quam istius aetas fuit?: The comparison of a ship to a sexualized woman's body is common. The most notorious example occurs in a joke attributed to Augustus's daughter Julia. When asked how, despite her well-known profligacy, all of her children managed to resemble their father Agrippa she quipped: '*numquam enim nisi navi plena tollo vectorem*' ("I never take on a passenger unless the ship's hold is full": Macr. *Sat.* 2.5.9). Analogous examples equating boats with undesirable prostitutes can be found in epigram and Roman comedy (Woodman 1980: 62–63; Jocelyn 1982b: 333–335) and "the imagery was even more derogatory when applied to a male" (Jocelyn 1982b: 333). Furthermore, *flumen publicum* denotes a space that by law any person has the right to use (Marcian. *dig.* 1.8.4; all of *dig.* 43.12–13 treats the subject). This implication, that Clodius is being portrayed as an effeminized male prostitute freely open to partners of either sex, is underscored by the feminine gender of the ship (*quae...vulgata*; 6n). Clodius is accused of prostitution in close proximity with incest also at *Sest.* 39: *cum scurrarum locupletium scorto, cum sororis adultero*.

As often, *aetas* refers specifically, without further descriptors, to adolescence; *ThLL* I 1128.38–1128.47 (J. G. Kempf). For a Ciceronian parallel, compare the account of Verres's youth: *damna, dedecora, quae...aetas ipsius pertulit, praetereantur* (*Verr.* 2.1.33); compare too Cicero's reference to Clodius's *prima aetatula* (42n).

quis umquam nepos tam libere est cum scortis quam hic cum sororibus volutatus?: For *quis* as in interrogative adjective see 38n, and for Cicero's jokes on Clodius's incest with multiple sisters see 9n. It is possible that the noun *nepos* contains a double-entendre for the listener, who would initially construe the word with its base meaning "descendant" (an instinct supported by *libere*) but would reevaluate the word as the sentence continues as having the derived meaning of "playboy" (a frequent sense in Cicero, e.g., in the string of invective terms at *Catil.* 2.7; for the secondary derivation, and a similar pun at Catull. 58.5, see Muse 2009: 303–305). The jingle *scortis...sororibus* seems not to occur elsewhere, perhaps unsurprisingly. Despite its etymology ("leather hide"), the word *scortum* is "not a vulgarism" (Adams 1983: 326), although it is more pejorative than the other common term *meretrix*. *Scortum* may apply to prostitutes of either sex. The verb *est...volutatus* occurs earlier in the context of incest (42n), where the participle is also in final position in hyperbaton with *est*.

quam denique tam immanem Charybdim poetae fingendo exprimere potuerunt, quae tantos exhaurire gurgites possit quantas iste Byzantiorum Brogitarorumque praedas exsorbuit: "And lastly, what kind of enormous Charybdis could poets describe in their fictions that could suck up whirlpools of the same size as the loot that Clodius has drained from the Byzantines and King Brogitarus?" Charybdis first appears in Homer's *Odyssey* as a mythical whirlpool that posed dangers to passing sailors; the Romans commonly situated it in the Straits of Messina alongside the monstrous Scylla (H. W. Stoll in Roscher 1: 888). As a metaphor for a person's all-consuming greed, Cicero's interlocutor Crassus explicitly recommends against using the imagery of Charybdis in *De oratore*, published the year following delivery of *har. resp.* (3.163): *deinde videndum est ne longe simile sit ductum:... 'Charybdim' bonorum, voraginem potius; facilius enim ad ea, quae visa, quam ad illa, quae audita sunt, mentis oculi feruntur* ("Comparisons must not be made with things too remote;... rather than 'a Charybdis of goods' say 'whirlpool'; for the mind's eye is applied more easily to those things that have been seen than to those that have been heard about"). Despite this unambiguous recommendation, the comparison occurs in two more places in Ciceronian oratory. At *Verr.* 2.5.146 (with Scylla and the Cyclops), the comparison may be more suitable since the crimes being compared are situated in Sicily. The same explanation, however, does not apply to Cicero's comparison of Antonius to Charybdis, also in the context of voracious greed (*Phil.* 2.67: *quae Charybdis tam vorax? Charybdin dico? quae si fuit, animal unum fuit; Oceanus me dius fidius vix videtur tot res tam dissipatas, tam distantibus in locis positas tam cito absorbere potuisse. nihil erat clausum, nihil obsignatum, nihil scriptum*). Regarding *har. resp.*, Fantham 1972: 131 conjectures that "the comparison would be justified in Cicero's eyes

316 Commentary

by the monstrous and unique wickedness of his personal enemy," further noting that his criticism elsewhere of the lesser opponent Gellius as a non-mythic whirlpool fits with the prescription offered in *de orat.* (*dom.* 124: *ille gurges*; *Sest.* 111: *gurges ac vorago patrimoni*). Innes 1988: 319 suggests further that the coupling here with Scylla—a more visual image—renders the use of Charybdis more acceptable. At the same time the pair enables Cicero to compare Clodius to two "archetypes of the devouring female" and so continue the effeminizing of Clodius that has dominated the speech (cf. Leach 2001: 345). Oddly, Scylla appears alone as an example of greed and voraciousness at *Sest.* 18, where Gabinius's friends advise him to avoid prosecution as a result of being "in a kind of Scyllan strait of debt" (*in Scyllaeo illo aeris alieni tamquam fretu*). Tastes in metaphor have changed by the time of the empire. Quintilian approves of the comparisons in *Verrines* and *Philippics* as instances of hyperbole (*inst.* 8.6.70–72), with that in the *Philippics* described as a "highlight" (12.10.62: *lumen*). The *Philippics* passage also receives particular attention both in later declamation (Sen. *suas.* 6.5, cf. 6.3) and in historical texts (Dio 45.28.4, 46.14.4; Keeline 2018: 114–115, 179).

For Clodius's bribery of Brogitarus see 28n, which quotes an excerpt of a letter from Cicero to Quintus alluding to Clodius also acquiring money illicitly from "Byzantium." The latter opportunity resulted from Clodius's legislation about King Ptolemy of Cyprus (58n). According to Cicero, along with the seizure and sale of Ptolemy's possessions the same law mentioned the return to Byzantium of men who had been exiled on capital charges (*dom.* 52: *tu lege una tulisti, ut Cyprius rex... cum bonis omnibus sub praeconem subiceretur et exsules Byzantium reducerentur*; cf. *Sest.* 56, 84; Plut. *Cat. min.* 34.4; Schol. Bob. *Sest.* p. 132.33–35 Stangl). Cicero presumes that Clodius approved of their return, together or individually, in exchange for money.

** **exhaurire gurgites possit**: Halm (Orelli *et al.* 1856: 926) deleted *possit* and conjectured *exhauriret* for *exhaurire*, the unanimous reading of the codices. Maslowski retains *exhaurire* and reads *exhaurire gurgites possit* (*possit* **GEH**, omitted **P**, *posset* is read by some more recent manuscripts). It is a difficult decision. In favor of Halm's emendation is the resultant imagery of the verb "in the middle of" the whirlpool of the syntax (*tantos exhauriret gurgites*) and the responsion of the finite forms *exhauriret* with the following *exsorbuit* (although an opposite, and perhaps better, argument could be made about the sequence *exprimere... exhaurire*); finally, *possit* is not essential to the sense, and is in fact somewhat of an anticlimax after *potuerunt* ("What sort of Charybdis have poets been able to describe... which is able to suck down...?" as opposed to "which [was characterized by] sucking down"). In favor of the text printed is the near unanimity of the codices, and the fact that the progressive sense of *potuerunt* expects a present subjunctive (*possit*) rather than an imperfect (*exhauriret*).

aut tam eminentibus canibus Scyllam tamque ieiunis quam quibus istum videtis, Gelliis, Cloeliis, Titiis, rostra ipsa mandentem?: "Or what kind of a

Scylla, with dogs projecting out as famished as [Clodius's] henchmen—Gellius, Cloelius, Titius, and their ilk—as you watch him chomping away at the very *rostra*?" Scylla also appears in a comparison at *Verr.* 2.5.146 with Charybdis, and alone at *Sest.* 18 (59n). Homer describes Scylla as a monster occupying a cave across from Charybdis, with twelve legs and six heads (*Odyss.* 12.73–100). In later visual and literary descriptions she normally has the upper torso of a beautiful woman (*LIMC* 8.1: 1137, 8.2: 784–792 [M.-O. Jentel]). Cicero clearly has in mind a version of the Homeric monster, with its grotesque maw(s), and the legs topped by the members of Clodius's gang rather than dogs (cf. Lucr. 5.892–893). The comparison of one's opponents to dogs is common; for the "dogs" of Clodius see *Pis.* 23 (Cloelius) and *Att.* 6.3.6=SB 117 (Gavius). In a particularly interesting parallel to Clodius "chewing on the rostra," Cicero quotes Verres's description of his associates as "dogs licking my tribunal" (*Verr.* 2.3.28: *horum canum quos tribunal meum vides lambere*). Although the imagery fits in neatly with the metaphor of the ship of state, I can find no parallel for the pun on *rostra*, meaning both a ship's beak and the tribunal from which speakers, and commonly Clodius, addressed the people. As Ernesti 1810: 924 astutely observes, the Clodian Scylla is even worse than the Homeric since it devours not simply people but the very tribunal upon which legislation and other features of Roman politics were debated and made public.

In Latin, the plural of a proper name is frequently used to indicate that the person named exemplifies the traits for which he or she is known (sc. "Gellius, Cloelius, Titius, and their ilk"; see LHS 2: 2.19; Wackernagel 1926–1928: 1.91–92). Gellius (*RE* 1), for whom only the *nomen* is known, is mentioned by Cicero primarily, as here, in combination with other of Clodius's associates (*Att.* 4.3.2=SB 75; *Sest.* 112; cf. *Vat.* 4), except for the extended account at *Sest.* 110–111, where we learn that he was an *eques* whose stepfather was L. Marcius Philippus, consul of 91, and stepbrother of the current consul, L. Marcius Philippus (2n; further details in Kaster 2006: 336–338). That hate-filled invective recounts how, after a scandalous youth, Gellius squandered his patrimony and attempted to devote himself to literature. He is traditionally identified with the elder Gellius of Catullus (74, 88.3, 89.3). For Sex. Cloelius see 11n. Titius (*RE* 2) is known only from Cicero, who specifies that he is a "Sabine from Reate" (*Sest.* 80: *Sabino homini Reatino*) and identifies him as an adherent of Clodius also at *dom.* 21 and *Sest.* 80.

60–61 (*ceciderunt*)

Cicero turns to the last and most dramatic warning of the response, to take care that the current status of the republic not be overturned (*NE REI PVBLICAE STATVS COMMVTETVR*). The only way that the Romans can face all their challenges is through *concordia*, which the gods have indicated can only be realized through the punishment of Clodius.

60 Qua re: Cicero follows his moral biography of Clodius with its logical conclusion (*qua re* = "therefore"): the state will collapse if harmony is not effected through the elimination of Clodius. Here, as often at the close of his orations, Cicero employs an imperative (*providete*) following an inferential adverb in order to exhort the audience to act in accordance with what he has logically argued (Winterbottom 2004: 229).

id quod extremum est in haruspicum responso: The most straightforward interpretation of this statement is that the phase with which it is in apposition as the direct object of *providete*, NE REI PVBLICAE STATVS COMMVTETVR, constitutes the final clause of the haruspical response; see further Introduction E.1.

** ***responso***: The reading *responso* is found in some lesser manuscripts, and was first adopted by Baiter in Orelli 1856: 926. The major codices read *responsu* P; *responsum* GE; *responsis* H, *recentiores*. An ablative is required for the syntax, and *responso* is closest to the reading of the normally reliable P.

NE REI PVBLICAE STATVS COMMVTETVR: The phrase *rei publicae status* refers to the prevailing condition of the state, for which "constitution" provides a rough synonym (41n). Lenaghan 1969: 194 observes that such a warning would seem apt after the meeting of the triumvirs at Luca but here, as elsewhere, I assume that the *haruspices* composed their response independent of political considerations (55n). Coincidentally, Julius Caesar is reputed to have used similar language following Cato's suicide when he remarked that the preservation of the constitution is the role of a good citizen and a *bonus vir* (Macr. *Sat.* 2.4.18: "*quisquis praesentem statum civitatis commutari non volet et civis et vir bonus est*"). For similarities of the haruspical language with the Roman SCU and other ancient texts see Santangelo 2013: 105 n. 88.

Vix haec, si undique fulciamus iam labefacta, vix, inquam, nixa in omnium nostrum umeris cohaerebunt: For the use of *inquam* after a repeated word see 4n. The deictic pronoun *haec*, perhaps accompanied by a sweeping gesture of Cicero to his surroundings and that of his fellow senators, refers emphatically to the current state of Rome. Compare *p. red. in sen.* 4, where the Catilinarian conspirators are described as "those who almost destroyed *these things*" (*qui haec paene delerunt*, with Boll 2019: 109). *ThLL* VI, 3 2706.57–69 provides a full list of parallels (H. Haffter). The verb *fulcire* commonly occurs in prose in metaphors of propping up something fallen or about to fall (*ThLL* VI, 1 1506.23–28 [H. Rubenbauer]). In reference to the state, see *p. red. in sen.* 18, *Phil.* 2.51 (***labentem et prope cadentem rem publicam fulcire***); the combination with *cohaerere* occurs also at *Tusc.* 3.61 (***fulciendi sunt qui ruunt nec cohaerere possunt***).

Given the proliferation of mythical references in this speech, particularly in the final paragraphs, and the emphasis on the interrelationship between human action and the natural world, the formulation *nixa in omnium nostrum umeris* would suggest to some senators that they are being compared to Atlas, who prevented the collapse of the heavens by propping them on his shoulders. Atlas is described by Vergil as the one "who props the heavens on his head" (*Aen.* 4.247: *caelum qui vertice fulcit*; cf. 4.481–482: *maximus Atlas / axem umero torquet stellis ardentibus aptum*).

cohaerebunt. fuit quondam ita firma haec civitas et valens: The perfect tense of *fuit* describing Rome's former stability is emphatically juxtaposed with the uncertain future tense of *cohaerebunt* and further reinforced by the placement of *fuit* (Adams 1994a: 38–39). Cicero uses similar language in looking back at an idyllic time of Rome at *Catil.* 1.3: *fuit, fuit ista quondam in hac re publica virtus ut...* (cf. *Verr.* 2.5.45, *Man.* 32).

posset. iam non potest: For this rhetorical figure (*correctio*) see 37n. While *iam non* and *non iam* normally seem indistinguishable (*ThLL* VII, 1 93.72–96.70 [J. B. Hofmann]), here the fronting of *iam* stresses again the change from a past situation to the present predicament; cf. *expeditus iam non erit*. For the iambic rhythm *iăm nōn pŏtēst* in short cola, see 37n.

aerarium nullum est: Cicero lists in summary fashion the weakness of separate elements of the Roman state that has led to the current situation of imminent collapse: an exhausted treasury, defrauded tax-collectors, leading Romans possessing no authority, discord among the elite, powerless law courts, electoral corruption, loss of senatorial power, and the unlikelihood that an individual will come forward to take a stand. A month or two earlier, Cicero had introduced his ideal of *cum dignitate otium* at *Sest.* 98, which Kaster 2006: 32 succinctly describes as "a personal and communal state in which the best men serve the public interest and enjoy the appropriate reward of personal prestige" (Kaster 2006: 31–37, with bibliography). In that passage Cicero had offered a more comprehensive list of the Republic's ills, many items of which correspond to those here (*religiones, auspicia, potestates magistratuum, senatus auctoritas, leges, mos maiorum, iudicia, iuris dictio, fides, provinciae, socii, imperi laus, res militaris, aerarium*). The most significant items excluded on the present occasion—*religiones, auspicia*—of course constitute the main theme of the speech and so are treated more fully in the next three sections (*har. resp.* also does not treat issues of military expansion). For the one item added in *har. resp.*—defrauded tax-collectors—see 60n.

Until the end of the Republic, Rome's treasury was located in the temple of Saturn, perhaps in its podium (Richardson 1980: 55–56). Shortly before the delivery of *har. resp.*, Cicero wrote to Quintus that discussion in the senate over distribution of public lands in Campania became particularly intense in part due to a scarcity of available funds (*ad Q. fr.* 2.6.1=SB 10, from April 56: *inopia pecuniae*). Cicero would have expected most of his senatorial audience to agree with him in attributing this scarcity to the actions of popular politicians who "drained" the treasury, such as C. Gracchus (*Sest.* 103, *off.* 2.72), P. Vatinius (*Vat.* 5, 10, 29, 36), and of course Clodius, in league with Piso and Gabinius (58n).

vectigalibus non fruuntur qui redemerunt: "Those who have collected the taxes do not profit from them." For this sense of *redimo* see *ThLL* XI, 2 551.5–12 (P. Pieroni). This clause refers most immediately to the *publicani* who are described in the first sentence of the speech as being blocked in the senate by Clodius on the previous day (*publicanorum causam*: 1n). This instance of ring composition helps signal that the speech is coming to a close.

auctoritas principum cecidit, consensus ordinum est divulsus: This consequence of Clodius's actions was also broached at the speech's beginning (5n).

iudicia perierunt: The reference is clear: Cicero elsewhere attributes the demise of the courts to Clodius, in particular during his tribunate (*p. red. in sen.* 19; *p. red. ad Quir.* 14; *Sest.* 73, 85–86, 89, 92), and he has mentioned in *har. resp.* several occasions when Clodius succeeded by various means in subverting the courts: through collusion in the period 68–67 (42n); through a bribed jury in 61 during the Bona Dea affair (36n); and most recently through the intervention of Metellus Nepos, consul of 57, in the two attempts of Milo to bring Clodius to trial (nn. on 7, 50). Clodius also assisted as tribune in preventing the judicial prosecution of Vatinius (*Vat.* 33–34).

suffragia descripta tenentur a paucis: The reference is to a small number of people distributing in advance of voting ballots that have already been filled out, thereby allowing only one option for voting, either *uti rogas* ("yes") or *antiquo* ("no") in the passage of laws, or a candidate's name in the case of elections. *Att.* 1.14.5=SB 14 vividly describes one such occasion involving Clodius's gangs (*p. red. in sen.* 18: *isdem operis suffragium ferentibus* may allude to a similar type of intimidation). At *dom.* 112 Cicero alludes to the possibility that the magistrate in charge of tabulating election results could willfully misinterpret what is written on the ballots (Nisbet 1939: 164). Lintott 1990 provides a survey of electoral corruption during this period and the various attempts to curb it.

bonorum animus ad nutum nostri ordinis expeditus iam non erit: *Expeditus* is adjectival here with the sense "accessible, ready to hand." The phrase *ad nutum* refers to the willingness to heed someone in response to the slightest request, such as the nodding of the head, a gesture commonly attributed to deities as early as Homer (Sittl 1890: 341–344). Horace describes an obedient slave as ready to serve "at the nod" of his master (*ep.* 2.2.6: *verna ministeriis ad nutus aptus erilis*). These connotations show that Cicero laments to his fellow senators not only the possibility that they will lack allies, but that their authority will be diminished as well. For the sense of *iam non erit* ("will no longer be"), see 60n above.

civem qui se pro patriae salute opponat invidiae frustra posthac requiretis: The listing of what the republic currently lacks concludes with its longest clause, which combines praise of Cicero's self-sacrifice in the past with an implied threat that neither he nor others will act in this way in the future. The word order works to dramatic effect, with the public indignation (*invidia*) directed toward the patriot strikingly postponed to the last word of the relative clause in order to place it as far as possible from its target (*civem qui se*). The displacement of *invidiae* also allows it to be set alongside the emphatic and largely unexpected *frustra*, whose sense bleeds over into the relative clause. "As for the citizen who, for the sake of the country's well-being, will stand in opposition to public indignation *in vain* will you all long for him in the future." For a parallel sense of *requiro*, in this case describing the longing of the senate for the exiled Cicero, see *Sest.* 128: *quem curia magis requisivit, quem forum luxit?*; cf. *Pis.* 27. Kaster 2005: 84–103 offers a detailed discussion of the workings of Roman *invidia*.

61 qua re hunc statum qui nunc est, qualiscumque est, nulla alia re nisi concordia retinere possumus: For *qua re* see the first note in 60; here, rather than offering a command to his audience in the second-person plural as earlier (*providete*), Cicero now includes himself in the first-person plural verb *possumus*, a transition that befits his argument regarding the need for concord among the elite. He will stress this unity with particular emphasis in his concluding sentence (63n).

Cicero reserves for the speech's closing argument his only use of the important word *concordia*, the agreement of thought and feeling needed to ensure the harmonious maintenance of the state (Varro *ling.* 5.73: *concordia a corde congruente*; for *cor* as the seat of cognition, see *ThLL* IV 935.79–936.80 [F. Reisch]). The concept *Concordia* had become a deified abstraction in Rome by the fourth century BCE, with her earliest attested cult statue dating to 164 (*dom.* 130), and her appearance on coins beginning in the mid-first century (discussion and images at *LIMC* 5: 1.479–498, 2.333–340 [T. Hölscher]). The literary tradition records the dedication of a temple in her honor at the base of the Capitol to celebrate the reconciliation of the orders following the *leges Liciniae Sextiae* in 367 (*LTUR* 1: 317 [A. M. Ferroni]). In 121, after the murder of Gaius Gracchus, the consul Lucius Opimius vowed another temple, and it was here that the senate met to discuss the Catilinarian conspiracy in 63 (45n). Concord in the state will be produced by concord in the relationship between humans and gods (of which *Concordia* is one). This correspondence facilitates the logical connection with the next sentence (*nam*), which asserts that Clodius must be punished.

illo impunito: The verb *impunio* points back to the speech's opening, where Cicero tells the senate that he had foreseen how the aftermath of the Bona Dea scandal would eventually result in the destruction of the state if the evil resulting from it went unpunished, as it had done in 61 as a result of judicial bribery (4: *erupturum illud malum aliquando, si impunitum fuisset, ad perniciem civitatis*). With the prodigy and the haruspical response that resulted from it, the forum for assessing the need for punishment moves from the human to the divine realm.

This oblique reference is the last direct mention of Clodius in the speech; the obliqueness, however, serves a point. By referring to Clodius with the bare adjective *ille* (rather than by name, or with the more direct deictic *hic* as he had earlier), Cicero excludes him from his current discussion with the other members of the senate. The word *ille* efficiently expels this prodigy from the political community to which he had belonged. Corbeill 2002: 212–215 identifies this form of verbal expulsion as a key function of Roman oratorical invective.

deteriore autem statu ut simus, unus est inferior gradus aut interitus aut servitutis: The fronted adjective *deteriore* recalls that the increase in stature among the *deteriores* is among the warnings of the *haruspices* (56). After the indirect command *ut meliore simus loco*, which acts as grammatical subject to the verb *optandum est*, a second *ut* clause appears here in what one anticipates will be a parallel construction. In addition to the similarities in syntax and vocabulary, *autem* also anticipates a contrasting clause in a way analogous to the Greek δέ (27n). This second *ut* clause, however, does not introduce an indirect command and, further, has no clear grammatical relationship with its main clause. As a result, in addition to breaking the parallelism, it seemingly constitutes a dramatic anacoluthon. The type does not fit the typical categories for anacoluthon, which in any case rarely occurs in Ciceronian oratory (3n): it neither introduces a colloquial tone, nor is it prompted by the complexity of the sentence (for these causes see Mayer 2005: 199–203). Nevertheless, the anacoluthon does serve to emphasize the fronted adjective *unus*: the constitution is just one step away from either destruction or enslavement. The metaphor alludes to a ladder or staircase with the best fortune at top and the worst at bottom; cf. *Balb.* 18: *ex infimo…fortunae gradu*; Hor. *Carm.* 1.35.2: *imo tollere de gradu* (in a hymn to Fortuna); *ThLL* VI, 2 2154.48–61 (U. Knoche). Contrast the related imagery of Fortune's "wheel" (54n).

quo ne trudamur di immortales nos admonent, quoniam iam pridem humana consilia ceciderunt: The adverb *quo* is adverbial "to which [place]," referring to the condition of annihilation or slavery. The contrast between the warnings of the *di immortales* and failed human counsel will become the theme of the speech's closing *peroratio*.

61 (*Atque ego hanc orationem*)–63

Cicero concludes by asserting that he has delivered this speech not simply on account of his political standing—he could just as easily have kept silent, as others have—but because the *haruspices* and the immortal gods have provided him with the authority to do so. The senators must listen to him since he reveals the will of the gods as it is made manifest in the recent prodigies that have occurred in the natural world, and they must make reparations by reconciling their differences among each other.

The ancient rhetorical handbooks stress that the concluding section of a speech, normally called in Latin *peroratio*, have two principal functions: recapitulation and arousal of emotions (listing of ancient sources at Lausberg 1998: §§431–442; on Cicero in particular Winterbottom 2004). Recapitulation is most commonly employed by the prosecution in judicial cases, although seldom in deliberative oratory, which is the category to which *har. resp.* largely belongs (see Introduction B.3). Accordingly, Cicero here offers in his recapitulation simply an oblique reference to the prodigy under discussion, expanding upon its significance by referring to other recent portents. In this way he is able to concentrate upon the arousal of emotions, emphasizing the seriousness of the occasion (*hanc orationem... tam tristem, tam gravem*), its religious significance (*vox ipsa deorum immortalium*), and the imminent threat of future upheaval if matters are not quickly resolved (e.g., *haec eadem profecto quae prospicimus impendentia pertimescetis*).

Atque ego hanc orationem: For *atque* as a transitional particle, in this case to the peroration, see 8n.

non quin hanc personam et has partis, honoribus populi Romani, vestris plurimis ornamentis mihi tributis, deberem et possem sustinere: The combination *non quin* occurs when a proposed reason is immediately denied; since the reason is hypothetical, the subjunctive is used. In this construction *quin* retains its negative sense—"**not** that I did **not** possess the duty and ability" (cf. *Phil.* 7.6: *[Pansam] esse dico... praestantissimum atque optimum consulem, non quin pari virtute et voluntate alii fuerint*; KS 2: 2.385; OLS 2: 295).

In a speech containing several allusions to drama, the closing portion finds Cicero fittingly adopting a theatrical metaphor to describe himself, as a character addressing the senate in words that are both melancholic and stern (*orationem... tam tristem, tam gravem*), and one that is in keeping with the many honors bestowed upon him by the state and citizens of Rome. Wright 1931: 99–100 discusses the use of *partes* in the sense of "dramatic role" and notes on *persona* (originally "mask" and, by extension "character") that "Cicero never used the word without some feeling for its original significance." Cicero attributes his sense that he is obligated to play this role to the series of elected offices he had held without suffering a defeat (*honores*) and to other *ornamenta* given him by the senate (cf. 58n).

tacentibus ceteris: This remark sheds revealing light on how charged the political atmosphere must have been during this period. Cicero claims he could easily have chosen not to speak since "everyone else" had opted to remain silent. He does not provide a reason for this reticence, but it presumably involved a desire not to offend either Clodius or Cicero, the two Romans to whom the haruspical response must have been deemed most applicable. As we have seen Clodius and Cicero, in their turn, wished not to offend members of the triumvirate.

haec oratio omnis fuit non auctoritatis meae, sed publicae religionis: In the spirit of discreet reticence that he has just attributed to his political colleagues, Cicero asserts that the speech that he has just delivered did not arise from him, but from a kind of revelation concerning Rome's civic religion (for *publica religio* see 14n). Contrast the opposite assertion at *S. Rosc.* 143 (*verum haec omnis* *oratio... mea est*), where Cicero goes on to say that he was compelled to speak because of concern for the republic, personal indignation, and the injustice of Roscius's accusers. Landgraf 1914: 265 notes that in that earlier case Cicero claims to be speaking on his own behalf to protect his clients from any repercussions.

mea fuerunt verba fortasse plura, sententiae quidem omnes harupicum: The use of the particle *quidem* is a mark of Cicero's mature style, as "a signal qualifying the importance of what follows immediately in favour of arguments to be mentioned later" (von Albrecht 2003: 108; cf. 57.21n). In other words, the *haruspices* were consulted in order to give the senate the means to resolve the issue, rather than having the senators rely on their own interpretations of the potentially capricious gods. To further stress the importance of their *sententiae*, the word occupies first position, disrupting the balance of the sentence (i.e., the order is A B C / B C A).

ad quos aut referri nuntiata ostenta non convenit aut eorum responsis commoveri necesse est: This relative clause contains a mild anacoluthon, since *eorum* should strictly be *quorum* (3n). Cicero describes here the normal procedure for assessing prodigies (Rosenberger 1998: 17–90). It is the responsibility of the senate to decide whether to refer a matter to a priestly body for consultation. Since the haruspical response was produced as a result of this decision, the senate must needs be "deeply moved" by it. The dilemma Cicero presents ignores other options available to the senators, namely, that they reject the validity of the prodigy altogether, or refer it to another body such as the *XVviri* (for Cicero's use of the dilemma see Craig 1993). Corbeill 2012: 252–259 places this assertion in the context of Rome's relationship with Etruscan religious authority.

62 quod si cetera [sc. ostenta] magis pervulgata nos saepe et leviora moverunt: The use of the simplex form *moverunt* contrasts with *commoveri* in the previous sentence and *permovebit* in this; other portents have not affected the senators as deeply as those being debated. Compare too the odd position of *nos saepe*, which makes *et leviora* appear as an emphatic afterthought—"even though these omens are less serious, they still moved us."

vox ipsa deorum immortalium: See 20n, 63n.

nolite enim id putare accidere posse quod in fabulis saepe videtis fieri, ut deus aliqui delapsus de caelo coetus hominum adeat, versetur in terris, cum hominibus conloquatur: "Do not think that what you often see happening in plays will possibly occur—no god will slip down from the sky to approach a human gathering, spend time on earth, and converse with people." The stage device of the *deus ex machina*, by which a divine figure unexpectedly appears from the sky to resolve dramatic tensions, has had detractors since as early as Aristotle (Arist. *Pol.* 454 b 1–6). Cicero adopts an Aristotelian line here, maintaining that real-life conflicts, even though foreseen and announced by divine figures as in this case, must be resolved only through the actions of the human agents involved. Accordingly, the injunction puts an abrupt end to the numerous references concerning the applicability of tragic drama to Rome's current situation (Gildenhard 2007: 150–155; Corbeill 2020: 187–191). Cicero uses similar language elsewhere to warn his oratorical audience that life is not like the stage, asserting in these instances that guilt arises from an individual's own conscience, not from external divine Furies (*S. Rosc.* 67: nolite enim putare, quem ad modum in fabulis saepenumero videtis, eos qui aliquid impie scelerateque commiserint agitari et perterreri Furiarum taedis ardentibus; Pis. 46: nolite enim ita putare, patres conscripti, ut in scaena videtis, homines consceleratos impulsu deorum terreri furialibus taedis ardentibus; cf. *leg.* 1.40). Landgraf 1914: 140–141 discusses how the topos adopted in these two oratorical examples derives from Aeschin. *Timarch.* 190 and seems to have been taught in Roman schools of rhetoric. Levene 2012: 66–69 argues that Cicero's appeal accords with a common belief among the Romans that the gods typically dwell separately from human contact (cf. 25n). Cicero does not, however, always adhere to this principle, asserting that in times of particular crisis the gods will aid the Romans; see in particular *Catil.* 2.29: [di immortales] iam non procul, ut quondam solebant, ab externo hoste atque longinquo, sed hic praesentes suo numine atque auxilio sua templa atque urbis tecta defendunt.

The construction of *noli* / *nolite* plus infinitive to express a negative command appears to be more formal than its other equivalents, such as *ne* plus perfect subjunctive (*OLS* 1: 352) and the presence of the verb *nolo* represents not simply a direct prohibition, but an "attempt by the speaker to convince the addressee of the non-desirability [sc. *nolite*, "don't wish"] of the realization of the state of affairs involved" (Risselada 1993: 296–300; quotation from 296).

** **delapsus de caelo**: Only P has the preposition *de*; the remaining codices read *e*. When describing something descending from the heavens, Cicero uses the preposition *de* exclusively in his prose works: Cic. *Manil.* 41; *Phil.* 11.24; *fin.* 1.63 (metaphorically); an apparent exception in Cicero's poetry does not describe a descent to earth (*carm. frg.* 1.1: [Lucifer] claris delapsus ab astris / praevius Aurorae). For additional examples of *de caelo* signifying "from heaven" in the context of prodigies, see Nisbet 1939: 202; lightning, by contrast, strikes objects both *e caelo* (*div.* 1.16, 98) and *de caelo* (*div.* 1.92–93).

cogitate genus sonitus eius quem Latinienses nuntiarunt: When the verb *cogito* means "recall" rather than "think," it regularly takes the accusative (*ThLL* III 1463.55–1465.28 [W. Elsperger]; cf. *recordamini* in the next clause). Mention of the earthquake prodigy prompts the repetition -*us* / -*itus* / -*us*, a series of sounds reminiscent of the effects found in the haruspical response (20n). For the identification of the *Latinienses* see 20n.

recordamini illud etiam quod nondum est relatum, quod eodem fere tempore factus in agro Piceno Potentiae nuntiatur terrae motus horribilis: For *referre* as the technical term for referring a matter to the senate, see 11n; for *nuntiare* see 10n. The pronoun *illud* serves as antecedent to the relative clause introduced by the first *quod*, which clause in turn is preparatory for the second *quod* clause; so *OLS* 2: 35 ("what was not discussed before, that"). An alternative explanation is that *quod* introduces indirect statement after *recordor*; so *ThLL* XI, 2 412.63 (M. L. De Seta), citing Suet. *Tit.* 8.1 as the only other non-Christian usage. LHS 2: 2.576 offers a full discussion. Confusion over the double *quod* presumably explains the universal error of *factum* (for *factus*) in the codices, with scribes construing the second *quod* as another neuter pronoun with *illud* as its antecedent.

The *ager Picenus* seems to correspond at least in part with the territory *Picenum*, which lay between the Apennines and the Adriatic Sea, stretching in the time of Augustus from the mouth of the Aesis river in the north to the Matrinus in the south (Plin. *nat.* 3.110; Strabo 5.4.2; Talbert *et al.* 2000: 42). On the coast of this region the Romans founded the colony Potentia in 184 (Liv. 39.44.10, with Briscoe 2008: 368). The earthquake is unmentioned in any other source—if the seismic activity included in Dio's list of portents referred to this event he would probably have noted the location, since it so distant from Rome (quoted in 9n; Beard 2012a: 23 n. 9 leaves the question open). Presumably the senate did not move to recognize this particular quake formally since consideration of the rumblings in Latium had already reached the stage of senatorial debate.

** **multis quibusdam metuendisque rebus**: The unanimous reading of the codices is *quibusdam multis metuendisque rebus*, with the exception that P¹ omits *rebus*. The difficulty with this formulation is the combination *quibusdam multis*: "Indefinite determiners cannot function as determiners of noun phrases containing an adjective of amount, probably because indefinite determiners are by implication understood as denoting (a low) number" (*OLS* 1: 985, citing this passage in n. 74 as "one textually uncertain combination of *quibusdam multis*"). Scholars have suggested numerous emendations for *multis* (see the apparatuses of Peterson and Maslowski). Koch 1868: 14 counters these emendations by citing Ov. *Met.* 15.24: *multa ac metuenda minatur* as evidence that Cicero is here using an alliterative religious formulation otherwise unattested. If Koch is correct, then the most attractive solution, first proposed by Busche 1917: 1360, involves not changing *multis* but simply transposing it with *quibusdam*, a suggestion commended by Maslowski in his apparatus ("fort. recte") and adopted by Shackleton Bailey 1991a: 230. When the order is reversed in this way, with an adjective of amount preceding an indefinite article, the pronoun acts as an intensifier; see *de orat.* 1.91: *innumerabilis quosdam* and *Pis.* 9: *innumerabilia quaedam nova*, the latter rendered by Nisbet 1961: 68 as "quite impossible to count." Willis 1972: 147–148 notes the frequency of transpositions of single words in manuscripts.

pērtĭmēscētīs: The same verb is used at 26, also of the prodigy, but there the first-person plural shows Cicero sharing in the fear; here Cicero separates himself from the senate as sole prophet of the forthcoming calamities, while at the same time couching this assertion of singularity in the first-person plural verb (*prospicimus*). ThLL X, 1 1786.45–48 (K.-H. Kruse) notes that *pertimesco* is rare throughout Latinity outside Cicero (106 times in the orations, twenty-seven in the correspondence; he prefers *extimesco* in the *philosophica*), Ovid (eighteen times), and Gregory the Great (more than 170 times). Cicero especially employs the verb to create a favorable clausula, as here a cretic + trochee (Laurand 1936–1940: 272 n. 3).

63 *haec deorum immortalium vox*: The hypothesis presented early in the speech that the earth tremors seem *almost* to represent the voice of Jupiter (10: *prope iam voce Iovis*) has now developed into an undisputed fact, and is expanded to include all the gods; see further 20n. This expansion resembles the Roman tendency to tack on to a series of prayers to specific deities a more general plea to all divinities with a formula such as *dique deaeque omnes* (see 20n).

** *cum agri atque terrae motu quodam novo contremescunt*: Other than the orthographical variant *contremescunt* / *contremiscunt* recorded by Maslowski, this is the reading of all major codices but E, which has *agris* (Maslowski's note that in **P** *agri* is written in erasure is not detectable on my scan). Because of the possible redundancy of *agri* with *terrae* Jeep 1862: 11 conjectured *maria* for *agri*, by which he saw completed a reference to the trio of *caelum* (=*mundus*), *mare*, and *terra*, citing the close parallel at Catull. 64.205–206: *quo motu tellus atque horrida* **contremuerunt** / *aequora concussitque micantia sidera* **mundus**. Jeep also offered a reconstruction of how the error could have arisen: *cûmariaatque* > *cûagriatque*. The reading of the codices can, however, yield adequate sense: "when fields and the earth tremble" (for the plural *terrae* see *OLD* s.v. 9). Nevertheless, the pair of *ager* with *terrae* is unusual, with the only close parallel known to me being Ov. *fast*. 4.126: *vere nitent terrae, vere remissus ager*.

Another issue not previously noted, however, is that in the previous sentence the collocation *terrae* (gen.) *motus* means "earth tremor" and it is odd that the same combination here yields a different construction. For this reason I would suggest that the error lies with *atque*, the deletion of which offers excellent sense: "the fields [sc. the *Latiniensis* of the response and the *ager Picenus* of 62.33–62.1] shake all over with a strange tremor of the earth." For the notion cf. Ulp. *dig*. 19.2.15.2: *si ager terrae motu ita corruerit ut nusquam sit*. Additional support for deletion of *atque* is discussed at 18n. I have therefore printed *cum agri atque* with the majority of codices, although the simple deletion of *atque* remains tempting.

***inusitato aliquid sono incredibilique*:** For the "brave men and true" word order, see 46n. As discussed there, the order places particular emphasis on the postponed adjective, here *incredibili*, and the repeated negating element of each adjective (*in-*) is a not uncommon feature. For the intrusion of a weak separating term (*aliquid*) see Adams 2021: 221.

procurationes et obsecratio: The verb *procurare* is synonymous with *expiare* as a technical term for the expiation of prodigies (Luterbacher 1904: 55). Here Cicero makes explicit (*quem ad modum monemur*) that he refers to the expiations demanded by the gods in the response (*postiliones*; see 20n). Such a *procuratio* could take many forms, from lustration of the city to a special sacrifice to a *lectisternium* to a *supplicatio* (Lenaghan 1969: 197; *ThLL* X, 2 1572.28–42 [I. Reineke]). Cicero's reference to an *obsecratio*, a public prayer of entreaty that aims to ward off divine anger (Fest. p. 190 M) and that was typically incorporated as part of the ritual of the *supplicatio* (Wissowa 1912: 423–426), indicates that a *supplicatio* comprised at least part of the expiatory ritual imagined here. Livy records an instance from 436 BCE when a series of earthquakes were the driving force behind instituting an *obsecratio* to the people (4.21.5), and two certain occasions when the *haruspices* recommend a *supplicatio* as an appropriate form of expiation (32.1.14, 41.13.3; MacBain 1982: 120).

sed faciles sunt preces apud eos qui ultro nobis viam salūtĭs ōstēndŭnt; nostrae nobis sunt inter nos irae discordiǣquĕ plăcāndǣ: "But prayers are easy in the presence of those gods who willingly show us the way to safety; **our own** anger and disagreements, felt **among ourselves**, must be reconciled **by us**" (for the construction of *apud* see KS 2: 1.525, citing Tac. *ann.* 11.27.1: *sacrificasse apud deos*). Wuilleumier and Tupet 1966: 77 note that each of these two closing clauses ends with the favored cretic + spondee rhythm (2n). The plural forms of the abstract nouns *irae discordiaeque* denote, as often, repeated action (40n). Here they are fittingly followed by the emphatic *placandae* ("they must be reconciled"), a verb commonly used of placating the displeasure of the gods and things associated with them (*ThLL* X, 1 2286.55–2287.26 [L. Pieroni]), an allusion that Cicero surely intends his audience to recognize. After stressing how important it is for the senate to take expiation into its own hands (*nobis quidem*, i.e., "it is *we* who must prepare for expiation and public prayer"), Cicero concludes the speech by asserting that, now that the gods have indicated their displeasure via prodigies, it is up to the senate to remedy the differences that had caused them. The notion that the gods expect humans to act on their own initiative in times of difficulty accords with Cato the Younger's argument, as presented by Sallust, that it is the responsibility of the senate, not the gods, to take strong actions against the Catilinarian conspirators: Sall. *Catil.* 52.29: *non votis neque suppliciis muliebribus auxilia deorum parantur: vigilando, agundo, bene consulendo prospere omnia cedunt. ubi socordiae tete atque ignaviae tradideris, nequiquam deos implores: irati infestique sunt.*

Note that Cicero had begun *har. resp.* by distinguishing himself from the senate (e.g., 1n) and continued to do so throughout the speech (most recently and emphatically at 60). In this final sentence, however, the *ego* and *vos* coalesce into a single, united, *nos* (with Clodius—the *illo* of 61—excluded). Cicero underscores the need for action through a polyptoton of the words referring to the members of the senate (*nostrae nobis... inter nos*). He in effect redirects the familiar repetition of the second- and third-person pronouns and adjectives in beseeching divinities (dubbed by Norden 1913: 143–166 as the "*Du*"- and "*Er*"-*Stil*) by turning the prayers away from the gods and inwardly toward himself and his fellow senators. On this occasion simple prayers are not available; a solution to the crisis requires the concerted effort of all.

Bibliography

Achard, G. 1981. *Pratique rhétorique et idéologie politique dans les discours "optimates" de Cicéron*. Leiden. Mnemosyne suppl. 68.
Adamietz, J. 1989. *Marcus Tullius Cicero, Pro Murena*. Darmstadt. Texte zur Forschung 55.
Adams, E. 2013. *"Esse videtur": Occurrences of Heroic Clausulae in Cicero's Orations*. M.A. Thesis, University of Kansas.
Adams, J. N. 1971. "A Type of Hyperbaton in Latin Prose." *Proceedings of the Cambridge Philological Society* 17: 1–16.
Adams, J. N. 1976. "A Typological Approach to Latin Word Order." *Indogermanische Forschungen* 81: 70–99.
Adams, J. N. 1978. "Conventions of Naming in Cicero." *Classical Quarterly* 28: 145–166.
Adams, J. N. 1982. *The Latin Sexual Vocabulary*. Baltimore.
Adams, J. N. 1983. "Words for 'Prostitute' in Latin." *Rheinisches Museum* 126: 321–358.
Adams, J. N. 1994a. *Wackernagel's Law and the Placement of the Copula "esse" in Classical Latin*. Cambridge. Cambridge Philological Society suppl. 18.
Adams, J. N. 1994b. "Wackernagel's Law and the Position of Unstressed Personal Pronouns in Classical Latin." *Transactions of the Philological Society* 92: 103–178.
Adams, J. N. 2003. *Bilingualism and the Latin Language*. Cambridge.
Adams, J. N. 2005. "*Bellum Africum*." In Reinhardt et al. eds. 73–96.
Adams, J. N. 2007. *The Regional Diversification of Latin, 200 BC–AD 600*. Cambridge.
Adams, J. N. 2016. *An Anthology of Informal Latin, 200 BC–AD 900*. Cambridge.
Adams, J. N. 2021. *Asyndeton and Its Interpretation in Latin Literature: History, Patterns, Textual Criticism*. Cambridge.
Adcock, F. E. 1937. "Lesser Armenia and Galatia after Pompey's Settlement of the East." *Journal of Roman Studies* 27: 12–17.
Albrecht, M. von. 1989. *Masters of Roman Prose from Cato to Apuleius. Interpretative Studies*. Trans. N. Adkin. Trowbridge.
Albrecht, M. von. 2003. *Cicero's Style: A Synopsis*. Leiden. Mnemosyne suppl. 245.
Allen, W. 1939. "The Location of Cicero's House on the Palatine Hill." *Classical Journal* 35: 134–143.
Allen, W. 1940. "Nisbet on the Question of the Location of Cicero's House." *Classical Journal* 35: 291–295.
Allen, W. 1944. "Cicero's House and *Libertas*." *Transactions of the American Philological Association* 85: 121–144.
Allen, W. 1954. "Cicero's Conceit." *Transactions of the American Philological Association* 75: 1–9.
Angelius, N. 1515. *Marci Tulli Ciceronis orationes a Nicolao Angelio Bucinensi nuper maxima diligentia recognitae et excusae*. Florence.
Appel, G. 1909. *De Romanorum precationibus*. Giessen.
Arena, V. 2020. "The Notion of *Bellum Civile* in the Last Century of the Republic." In F. Pina Polo, ed. *The Triumviral Period: Civil War, Political Crisis and Socioeconomic Transformations*. Saragossa. 101–126.

Astin, A. E. 1967. *Scipio Aemilianus*. Oxford.
Austin, R. G. 1960. *M. Tulli Ciceronis pro M. Caelio Oratio*. 3rd ed. Oxford.
Badian, E. 1962. "Waiting for Sulla." *Journal of Roman Studies* 52: 47–61.
Bailey, C. ed. 1947. *Titi Lucreti Cari De rerum natura libri sex*. Oxford. 3 vols.
Balsdon, J. P. V. D. 1957. "Roman History, 58–56 B.C.: Three Ciceronian Problems." *Journal of Roman Studies* 47: 15–20.
Bannon, C. 1997. *The Brothers of Romulus: Fraternal "Pietas" in Roman Law, Literature, and Society*. Princeton.
Beard, M. 1986. "Cicero and Divination: The Formation of a Latin Discourse." *Journal of Roman Studies* 76: 33–46.
Beard, M. 1990. "Priesthood in the Roman Republic." In Beard and North eds. 19–48.
Beard, M. 1991. "*Ancient Literacy* and the Function of the Written Word in Roman Religion." In J. Humphrey *et al.*, eds. *Literacy in the Roman World*. Ann Arbor. 35–58.
Beard, M. 2009. *The Roman Triumph*. Cambridge, Mass.
Beard, M. 2012a. "Cicero's 'Response of the haruspices' and the Voice of the Gods." *Journal of Roman Studies* 102: 20–39.
Beard, M. 2012b. "The Cult of the 'Great Mother' in Imperial Rome: The Roman and the 'Foreign.'" In J. R. Brandt and J. Iddeng eds. *Greek and Roman Festivals: Content, Meaning, and Practice*. Oxford. 323–362.
Beard, M., and J. North, eds. 1990. *Pagan Priests: Religion and Power in the Ancient World*. Ithaca.
Beck, H. 2009. "From Poplicola to Augustus: Senatorial Houses in Roman Political Culture." *Phoenix* 63: 361–384.
Becker, M. 2017. *"Suntoque aediles curatores urbis…": Die Entwicklung der stadtrömischen Aedilität in republikanischer Zeit*. Stuttgart. Frankfurter Historische Abhandlungen 50.
Begemann, E. 2012. *Schicksal als Argument. Ciceros Rede vom "fatum" in der späten Republik*. Stuttgart.
Begemann, E. 2015. "*Ista tua pulchra libertas*: The Construction of a Private Cult of Liberty on the Palatine." In C. Ando and J. Rüpke eds. *Public and Private in Ancient Mediterranean Law and Religion*. Berlin. 75–98.
Behrends, O. 1974. *Der Zwölftafelprozess: zur Geschichte des römischen Obligationenrecht*. Göttingen.
Bell, M. 1998. "Le stele greche dell'Esquilino e il cimitero di Mecenate." In M. Cima and E. La Rocca eds. *Horti Romani. Atti del Convegno Internazionale, Roma, 4–6 maggio 1995*. Rome. Bullettino della Commissione Archeologica Comunale di Roma, suppl. 6. 295–314.
Bendlin, A. 2000. "Looking beyond the Civic Compromise: Religious Pluralism in Late Republican Rome." In E. Bispham and C. Smith eds. *Religion in Archaic and Republican Rome and Italy. Evidence and Experience*. Edinburgh. 115–135.
Benner, H. 1987. *Die Politik des P. Clodius Pulcher*. Stuttgart. Historia Einzelschriften 50.
Benveniste, E. 1960. "*Profanus* et *Profanare*." *Hommages à Georges Dumézil*. Brussels. Collection Latomus 45. 46–53.
Berg, B. 1997. "Cicero's Palatine Home and Clodius' Shrine to Liberty: Alternative Emblems of the Republic in Cicero's *De domo sua*." *Studies in Latin Literature and Roman History* 8: 122–143. Collection Latomus 239.

Bergemann, C. 1992. *Politik und Religion im spätrepublikanischen Rom.* Stuttgart. Palingenesia 38.
Berno, F. R. 2007. "La 'Furia' di Clodio in Cicerone." *Bollettino di studi latini* 37: 69–91.
Bernstein, F. 1998. *"Ludi publici": Untersuchungen zur Entstehung und Entwicklung der öffentlichen Spiele im republikanischen Rom.* Stuttgart. Historia Einzelschriften 119.
Berry, D. H. 1993. Rev. of Shackleton Bailey 1991a. *Classical Review* 43: 174–175.
Berry, D. H. 1996a. *Cicero: Pro P. Sulla Oratio.* Cambridge.
Berry, D. H. 1996b. "The Value of Prose Rhythm in Questions of Authenticity: The Case of *De optimo genere oratorum* Attributed to Cicero." In F. Cairns ed. *Papers of the Leeds International Latin Seminar* 9: 47–74.
Bleicken, J. 1957. "Oberpontifex und Pontifikalkollegium: Eine Studie zur römischen Sakralverfassung." *Hermes* 85: 345–366.
Bloch, H. 1940. "Lucius Calpurnius Piso Caesoninus in Samothrace and Herculaneum." *American Journal of Archaeology* 44: 485–493.
Bloch, L. 1899. "Nymphen." In Roscher, 3: 500–567.
Bolkestein, A. 1980. "The 'ab urbe condita'-Construction in Latin: A Strange Type of Raising?" In S. Daalder and M. Gerritsen eds. *Linguistics in the Netherlands 1980.* Amsterdam. 80–92.
Bolkestein, A. 1981. "Factivity as a Condition for an Optional Expression Rule in Latin: The 'ab urbe condita' Construction and Its Underlying Representation." In A. Bolkestein *et al.* eds. *Predication and Expression in Functional Grammar.* London. 205–233.
Boll, T. 2019. *Ciceros Rede "cum senatui gratias egit." Ein Kommentar.* Berlin. Göttinger Forum für Altertumswissenschaft, Beihefte N.F., 10.
Bömer, F. 1964. "Kybele in Rom. Die Geschichte ihres Kults als politisches Phänomen." *Mitteilungen des Deutschen Archäologischen Instituts. Römische Abteilung* 71: 130–151.
Bond, S. E. 2016. *Trade and Taboo: Disreputable Professions in the Roman Mediterranean.* Ann Arbor.
Booth, J., ed. 2007. *Cicero on the Attack: Invective and Subversion in the Orations and Beyond.* Swansea.
Botsford, G. 1909. *The Roman Assemblies from Their Origin to the End of the Republic.* New York.
Boyce, A. A. 1938. "The Development of the *Decemviri Sacris Faciundis*." *Transactions of the American Philological Association* 69: 161–187.
Brinkmann, A. 1908. "*Simpuvium—simpulum*." *Archiv für lateinische Lexikographie und Epigraphik* 15: 139–143.
Briscoe, J. 2008. *A Commentary on Livy, Books 38–40.* Oxford.
Briscoe, J. 2012. *A Commentary on Livy, Books 41–45.* Oxford.
Brook, A. 2016. "Cicero's Use of Aeschylus' *Oresteia* in the *Pro Milone*." *Ramus* 45: 45–73.
Brouwer, H. H. J. 1989. *Bona Dea. The Sources and a Description of the Cult.* Leiden. Études Préliminaires aux Religions Orientales dans L'Empire Romain 110.
Bruno, D. 2017. "Regio X. *Palatium*." In Carandini ed. 2: 215–280.
Brunt, P. A. 1988. *The Fall of the Roman Republic and Related Essays.* Oxford.
Bruun, C. 2023. "Cicero and Clodius Together: The Porta Romana Inscriptions of Roman Ostia as Cultural Memory." In M. Dinter and C. Guérin eds. *Cultural Memory in Republican and Augustan Rome.* Cambridge. 355–374.

Bryce, J. 1990. *The Library of Lactantius*. New York and London.
Bulst, C. 1964. "*Cinnanum Tempus*: A Reassessment of the *Dominatio Cinnae*." *Historia* 13: 307–337.
Busche, K. 1917. Rev. of *M. Tulli Ciceronis Scripta quae manserunt omnia. Orationum fasc. 21–27, 29*, rec. A. Klotz et F. Schöll (part 1). *Berliner Philologische Wochenschrift* 37: 1353–1361.
Caerols Pérez, J. 1995. "*Arceri oti finibus* (Cic. *Har.* 4): ¿'paz' civil u 'ocio' de los jóvenes aristócratas?" *Estudios Clásicos* 37: 57–92.
Cairo, M. 2020. "A Reading of Cicero's *De Haruspicum Responso*. Some Reflections on Roman Identity." In C. Beltrao da Rosa and F. Santangelo eds. *Cicero and Roman Religion: Eight Studies*. Wiesbaden. 73–86.
Calcante, C. M. 1986. "L'opposizione *synchysis* vs. *concinna transgressio* nel sistema letterario latino del I. sec. a. C." *Materiali e discussioni per l'analisi dei testi classici* 16: 55–76.
Canter, H. V. 1931. "*Digressio* in the Orations of Cicero." *American Journal of Philology* 52: 351–361.
Capdeville, G. 1997. "Les livres sacrés des Étrusques." In J.-G. Heintz ed. *Oracles et prophéties dans l'antiquité*. Paris. 457–508.
Carandini, A., ed., with P. Carafa. 2017. *The Atlas of Ancient Rome. Biography and Portraits of the City*. Trans. A. C. Halavais. Princeton. 2 vols.
Cardauns, B. 1976. *M. Terentius Varro: Antiquitates Rerum Divinarum*. Mainz and Wiesbaden.
Carreras Monfort, C. 1995–1996. "A New Perspective for the Demographic Study of Roman Spain." *Revista de Historia da Arte e Arqueologia* n.s. 2: 59–82.
Caruso, C., and C. Papi. 2005. "L'iscrizione di Porta Romana a Ostia: verifiche e proposte." *Archeologia Classica* 56: 461–469.
Cèbe, J.-P. 1972–1999. *Varron, Satires ménippées*. Rome. 13 vols.
Cerutti, S. 1997. "The Location of the Houses of Cicero and Clodius and the *Porticus Catuli* on the Palatine Hill in Rome." *American Journal of Philology* 118: 417–426.
Chahoud, A. 2018. "Verbal Mosaics: Speech Patterns and Generic Stylization in Lucilius." In B. Breed *et al.* eds. *Lucilius and Satire in Second-Century BC Rome*. Cambridge. 132–161.
Champeaux, J. 1995. "L'*Etrusca disciplina* dans Suétone, *Vie des douze Césars*." In D. Briquel and C. Guittard eds. *Les écrivains et l'"Etrusca disciplina" de Claude à Trajan*. Tours. Caesarodunum suppl. 64. 63–87.
Champlin, E. 1991. *Final Judgments: Duty and Emotion in Roman Wills, 200 B.C.–A.D. 250*. Berkeley.
Christenson, D. 2000. *Plautus: Amphitruo*. Cambridge.
Clackson, J., and G. Horrocks. 2007. *The Blackwell History of the Latin Language*. Malden, Mass.
Clark, A. C. 1895. *M. Tulli Ciceronis pro T. Annio Milone ad iudices oratio*. Oxford.
Clark, A. C. 1918. *The Descent of Manuscripts*. Oxford.
Cleland, L., G. Davies, and L. Llewellyn-Jones. 2007. *Greek and Roman Dress from A to Z*. London and New York.
Coarelli, F. 2005. "*Latiniensis ager*." In A. La Regina ed. *Lexicon Topographicum Urbis Romae: Suburbium*. Rome. 3: 202–203.

Coarelli, F. 2012. *Palatium. Il Palatino dalle origini all'impero*. Rome.
Cole, S. 2013. *Cicero and the Rise of Deification at Rome*. Cambridge.
Corbeill, A. 1996. *Controlling Laughter. Political Humor in the Late Roman Republic*. Princeton.
Corbeill, A. 2002. "Ciceronian Invective." In May 2002: 197–217.
Corbeill, A. 2004. *Nature Embodied. Gesture in Ancient Rome*. Princeton.
Corbeill, A. 2008. "*O singulare prodigium!* Ciceronian Invective as Religious Expiation." In T. Stevenson and M. Wilson eds. *Cicero's "Philippics:" History, Rhetoric and Ideology*. Auckland. 240–254.
Corbeill, A. 2010a. "The Function of a Divinely Inspired Text in Cicero's *De Haruspicum Responsis*." In D. H. Berry and A. Erskine eds. *Form and Function in Roman Oratory*. Cambridge. 139–154.
Corbeill, A. 2010b. "Dreams and the Prodigy Process in Republican Rome." In E. Scioli and C. Walde eds. *"Sub Imagine Somni": Nighttime Phenomena in Greco-Roman Culture*. Pisa. 81–101.
Corbeill, A. 2012. "Cicero and the Etruscan *Haruspices*." *Papers of the Langford Latin Seminar* 15: 243–266.
Corbeill, A. 2014. *Sexing the World. Grammatical Gender and Biological Sex in Ancient Rome*. Princeton.
Corbeill, A. 2018. "Clodius's *Contio de haruspicum responsis*." In C. Gray and C. Steel ed. *Reading Republican Oratory: Reconstructions, Contexts, Receptions*. Oxford. 171–190.
Corbeill, A. 2020. "Varro's Tripartite Theology and Ciceronian Invective in 56 BC." *Aevum Antiquum* 20: 177–193.
Corbett, P. 1986. *The Scurra*. Edinburgh.
Cornell, T. 1981. "Some Observations on the *crimen incesti*." In M. Torelli ed. *Le délit religieux dans la cité antique*. Rome. 27–37.
Coşkun, A. 2018. "Brogitaros and the Pessinus-Affair. Some Considerations on the Galatian Background of Cicero's Lampoon against Clodius in 56 BC (*Harusp. Resp.* 27–29)." *Gephyra* 15: 119–133.
Costa, E. 1964. *Cicerone giureconsulto*. Rome. 2nd ed. 2 vols. Studia juridica 28.
Coudry, M. 2004. "Contrôle et traitement des ambassadeurs étrangers sous la République romaine." In C. Moatti ed. *La mobilité des personnes en Méditerranée de l'antiquité à l'époque moderne*. Rome. Collection de l'École Française de Rome 341. 529–565.
Courtney, E. 1960. "Notes on Cicero." *Classical Review* 10: 95–99.
Courtney, E. 1963. "The Date of the *De Haruspicum Responso*." *Philologus* 107: 155–156.
Courtney, E. 1980. *A Commentary on the Satires of Juvenal*. London.
Courtney, E. 1989. "Notes on Cicero's *Post Reditum* Speeches." *Rheinisches Museum* 132: 47–53.
Courtney, E. 1993. *The Fragmentary Latin Poets*. Oxford.
Courtney, E. 1999. *Archaic Latin Prose*. Atlanta. American Classical Studies 42.
Craig, C. 1993. *Form as Argument in Cicero's Speeches: A Study of Dilemma*. Atlanta.
Craig, C. 2002. "A Survey of Selected Recent Work on Cicero's Rhetorica and Speeches." In May 2002: 503–599.

Craig, C. 2004. "Audience Expectations, Invective, and Proof." In J. Powell and J. Paterson eds. *Cicero the Advocate*. Oxford. 187–213.

Cramer, F. 1889. "Was heißt 'Leute'?" *Archiv für lateinische Lexikographie und Epigraphik* 6: 341–376.

Crawford, J. 1984. *M. Tullius Cicero: The Lost and Unpublished Orations*. Göttingen. Hypomnemata 80.

Crawford, J. 1994. *M. Tullius Cicero: The Fragmentary Speeches*. Atlanta. 2nd ed.

Crawford, M., ed. 1974. *Roman Republican Coinage*. Cambridge. 2 vols.

Crawford, M., ed. 1996. *Roman Statutes*. London. 2 vols. Bulletin of the Institute of Classical Studies, suppl. 64.

Damon, C. 1992. "Sex. Cloelius, *scriba*." *Harvard Studies in Classical Philology* 94: 227–250.

Damon, C. 1997. "From Source to *sermo*: Narrative Technique in Livy 34.54.4–8." *American Journal of Philology* 118: 251–266.

David, J.-M. 1979. "Promotion civique et droit à la parole. L. Licinius Crassus, les accusateurs et les rhéteurs latins." *Mélanges d'archéologie et d'histoire de l'École Française de Rome, Antiquité* 91: 135–181.

David, J.-M. 1992. *Le patronat judiciaire au dernier siècle de la République romaine*. Rome. Bibliothèque des Écoles Françaises d'Athènes et de Rome 277.

De Groot, A. W. 1921. *Der antike Prosarhythmus*. Groningen.

De Grummond, N. 2006. *Etruscan Myth, Sacred History, and Legend*. Philadelphia.

De Sanctis, G. 1953. *Storia dei Romani*. Florence. Vol. 4.2.1.

Dench, E. 1995. *From Barbarians to New Men: Greek, Roman, and Modern Perceptions of Peoples from the Central Apennines*. Oxford.

Devine, A. M., and L. D. Stephens. 2006. *Latin Word Order. Structured Meaning and Information*. Oxford.

Devoto, G. 1933. "I problemi del più antico vocabolario giuridico romano." *Annali della Scuola Normale Superiore di Pisa. Lettere, Storia e Filosofia*. Ser. 2. 2: 225–240.

Dickey, E. 2002. *Latin Forms of Address from Plautus to Apuleius*. Oxford.

Dodds, E. R. 1951. *The Greeks and the Irrational*. Berkeley.

Dougan, T. W., and R. Henry. 1905, 1934. *M. Tulli Ciceronis Tusculanarum Disputationum Libri Quinque*. Cambridge. 2 vols.

Driediger-Murphy, L. 2019. *Roman Republican Augury: Freedom and Control*. Oxford.

Dubourdieu, A. 1989. *Les origines et le développement du culte des Pénates à Rome*. Rome. Collection de l'École Française de Rome 118.

Dufallo, B. 2007. *The Ghosts of the Past. Latin Literature, the Dead, and Rome's Transition to a Principate*. Columbus.

Dumézil, G. 1970. *Archaic Roman Religion*. Trans. P. Krapp. Chicago.

Dyck, A. 1996. *A Commentary on Cicero, "De Officiis."* Ann Arbor.

Dyck, A. 2001. "Dressing to Kill: Attire as a Proof and Means of Characterization in Cicero's Speeches." *Arethusa* 34: 119–130.

Dyck, A. 2004a. *A Commentary on Cicero, "De Legibus."* Ann Arbor.

Dyck, A. 2004b. "Cicero's *devotio*: The Roles of *dux* and Scape-goat in his *Post Reditum* Rhetoric." *Harvard Studies in Classical Philology* 102: 299–314.

Dyck, A. 2008. *Cicero: Catilinarians*. Cambridge.

Dyck, A. 2013. *Cicero: Pro Marco Caelio*. Cambridge.

Epstein, D. F. 1987. *Personal Enmity in Roman Politics, 218-43 B.C.* London.
Ernesti, J. 1810. *M. Tullii Ciceronis opera omnia. Voluminis secundi pars secunda: Orationes.* Oxford.
Ewbank, W. W. 1933. *The Poems of Cicero.* London.
Fantham, E. 1972. *Comparative Studies in Republican Latin Imagery.* Toronto.
Fantham, E. 1998. *Ovid, Fasti Book IV.* Cambridge.
Fantham, E. 2012. "Purification in Ancient Rome." In M. Bradley ed. *Rome, Pollution, and Propriety: Dirt, Disease, and Hygiene in the Eternal City from Antiquity to Modernity.* Cambridge. 59-66.
Fasciano, D. 1971. "*Numen*, réflexions sur sa nature et son rôle." *Rivista di cultura classica e medioevale* 12: 3-20.
Favory, F. 1976. "Classes dangereuses et crise de l'État dans le discours cicéronien (d'après les écrits de Cicéron de 57 à 52)." In *Texte, politique, idéologie: Cicéron. Pour une analyse du système esclavagiste: le fonctionnement du text cicéronien.* Paris. Annales Littéraires de l'Université de Besançon 187. 109-233.
Fenechiu, C. 2008. "The Term *numen* in Cicero's Works." *Les Études Classiques* 76: 95-106.
Ferrary, J.-L. 1991. "*Lex Cornelia de Sicariis et Veneficis*." *Athenaeum* 79: 417-434.
Ferratius, M. A. 1729. *M. Tullii Ciceronis Orationum, Pars III.* Padua.
Fischer, A. 1908. *Die Stellung der Demonstrativpronomina bei lateinischen Prosaikern.* Tübingen.
Flambard, J. M. 1977. "Clodius, les collèges, la plèbe et les esclaves." *Mélanges de l'École Française de Rome, Antiquité* 89: 115-156.
Fraenkel, E. 1957. *Horace.* Oxford.
Fraenkel, E. 1965. *Noch Einmal Kolon und Satz.* Munich.
Fraenkel, E. 1968. *Leseproben aus Reden Ciceros und Catos.* Rome. Sussidi Eruditi 22.
Fraenkel, E. 2007 [1922]. *Plautine Elements in Plautus.* Trans. T. Drevikovsky and F. Muecke. Oxford.
Fridh, A. 1990. "*Sacellum, Sacrarium, Fanum* and Related Terms." In S.-T. Teodorsson ed. *Greek and Latin Studies in Memory of Cajus Fabricius.* Göteborg. Studia Graeca et Latina Gothoburgensia 54. 173-187.
Gallo, I. 1969. *M. Tullio Cicerone, Orazioni Clodiane: De domo sua, de haruspicum responso, pro Milone.* Rome.
Garatoni, G. 1786. *M. T. Ciceronis Orationes* etc. Naples. Vol. 7.
Gee, E. 2013. "Cicero's Poetry." In Steel 2013: 88-106.
Gelzer, M. 1937. "Die Datierung von Ciceros Rede *de haruspicum responso*." *Klio* 3: 1-9.
Gelzer, M. 1939. "M. Tullius Cicero (als Politiker)." *RE* 7A: 827-1091.
Gesner, J. 1753. "Cicero restitutus." *Commentarii Societatis Regiae Scientiarum Gottingensis* 3: 223-284.
Gibson, R. 2003. *Ovid: Ars Amatoria Book 3.* Cambridge.
Gildenhard, I. 2007. "Greek Auxiliaries: Tragedy and Philosophy in Ciceronian Invective." In Booth ed. 149-182.
Gildenhard, I. 2011. *Creative Eloquence: The Construction of Reality in Cicero's Speeches.* Oxford.
Goldberg, S. 1998. "Plautus on the Palatine." *Journal of Roman Studies* 88: 1-20.
Goldberg, S. 2000. "Cicero and the Work of Tragedy." In G. Manuwald ed. *Identität und Alterität in der frühromischen Tragödie.* Tübingen. 49-59.

Goldmann, F. 2012. *Die Statthalter der römischen Provinzen von 60 bis 50 vor Christus: Politisches Handeln in einem Jahrzehnt der Krise*. Diss. Göttingen.
González, J., and M. Crawford. 1986. "The *Lex Irnitana*: A New Copy of the Flavian Municipal Law." *Journal of Roman Studies* 76: 147–243.
Gordon, R. L. 1979. "The Real and the Imaginary: Production and Religion in the Graeco-Roman World." *Art History* 2: 5–34.
Gotoff, H. 1979. *Cicero's Elegant Style: An Analysis of the "Pro Archia."* Urbana.
Gotoff, H. 1993. *Cicero's Caesarian Speeches: A Stylistic Commentary*. Chapel Hill.
Gowers, E. 2012. *Horace: Satires, Book I*. Cambridge.
Gozalbes Cravioto, E. 2007. "La demografía de la Hispania romana tres décadas después." *Hispania Antigua* 31: 181–208.
Graevius, J. G. 1696. *M. Tulli Ciceronis Orationum Tomi Secundi Pars II*. Amsterdam.
Graillot, H. 1912. *Le culte de Cybèle, mère des dieux, à Rome et dans l'Empire romain*. Paris. Bibliothèque des Écoles Françaises d'Athènes et de Rome 107.
Greenidge, A. H. J. 1901a. *The Legal Procedure of Cicero's Time*. Oxford.
Greenidge, A. H. J. 1901b. *Roman Public Life*. London.
Griffin, M. 1989. "Philosophy, Politics, and Politicians at Rome." In Powell 1989 ed. 1–37.
Griffin, M. 1995. "Philosophical Badinage in Cicero's Letters to his Friends." In Powell 1995 ed. 325–346.
Griffith, R. D. 1996. "The Eyes of Clodia Metelli." *Latomus* 55: 381–383.
Grilli, A., and J. Crawford. 1984. "Cicerone." In U. Cozzoli *et al.* eds. *Enciclopedia Virgiliana*. Rome. 1: 774–777.
Grillo, L. 2015. *Cicero's "De Provinciis Consularibus Oratio."* Oxford.
Gruen, E. 1966. "P. Clodius: Instrument or Independent Agent?" *Phoenix* 20: 120–130.
Gruen, E. 1969. "Pompey, the Roman Aristocracy, and the Conference of Luca." *Historia* 18: 71–108.
Gruen, E. 1971. "Some Criminal Trials of the Late Republic: Political and Prosopographical Problems." *Athenaeum* 49: 54–69.
Gruen, E. 1974. *The Last Generation of the Roman Republic*. Berkeley.
Gruen, E. 1990. *Studies in Greek Culture and Roman Policy*. Leiden.
Gruen, E. 1992. *Culture and National Identity in Republican Rome*. Ithaca.
Gruen, E. 2009. "Caesar as a Politician." In M. Griffin ed. *A Companion to Julius Caesar*. Oxford. 24–36.
Gruen, E. 2011. *Rethinking the Other in Antiquity*. Princeton.
Guaglianone, A. 1966. "Cic. *De harusp. resp.* XI 23, 3; Arnob. *Adver. nat.* IV 31, 19 (*terram e tensam*)." *Rivista di Studi Classici* 14: 109–110.
Guggenheimer, E. 1972. *Rhyme Effects and Rhyming Figures: A Comparative Study of Sound Repetitions in the Classics with Emphasis on Latin Poetry*. The Hague.
Guidetti, F. 2009. "*Tensam non tenuit*: Cicerone, Arnobio e il modo di condurre i carri sacri." *Studi Classici e Orientali* 55: 233–248.
Guillaumont, F. 1984. *Philosophe et augure. Recherches sur la théorie cicéronienne de la divination*. Brussels. Collection Latomus 184.
Guittard, C. 2002. "*Sive deus sive dea*: les Romains pouvaient-ils ignorer la nature de leurs divinités?" *Revue des Études Latines* 80: 25–54.

Gummere, J. G. 1934. *The Neuter Plural in Vergil*. Diss. Univ. of Pennsylvania. Language Dissertations 17.

Gunderson, E. 1996. "The Ideology of the Arena." *Classical Antiquity* 15: 113–151.

Haack, M.-L. 2003. *Les haruspices dans le monde romain*. Bordeaux. Scripta Antiqua 6.

Haack, M.-L. 2006. *Prosopographie des haruspices romains*. Pisa and Rome. Biblioteca di Studi Etruschi 42.

Habinek, T. 1985. *The Colometry of Latin Prose*. Berkeley. University of California Publications: Classical Studies 25.

Habinek, T. 1998. *The Politics of Latin Literature: Writing, Identity, and Empire in Ancient Rome*. Princeton.

Hand, F. 1836. *Tursellinus Seu De Particulis Latinis Commentarii*. Leipzig. 4 vols.

Hanson, J. A. 1959. *Roman Theater-Temples*. Princeton. Princeton Monographs in Art and Archaeology 33.

Harders, A.-C. 2008. *"Suavissima soror": Untersuchungen zu den Bruder-Schwester-Beziehungen in der römischen Republik*. Munich.

Hardie, P. 1994: *Virgil: Aeneid Book IX*. Cambridge.

Harris, W. V. 1979. *War and Imperialism in Republican Rome, 327–70 B.C.* Oxford.

Harrison, S. 1991. *Vergil, Aeneid 10*. Oxford.

Hatcher, A. 1950. "The English Construction *A Friend of Mine*." *Word* 6: 1–25.

Haury, A. 1955. *L'ironie et l'humour chez Cicéron*. Leiden.

Havet, L. 1897. "Un nouveau fragment tragique." *Revue de Philologie* 21: 159.

Hellegouarc'h, J. 1963. *Le vocabulaire latin des relations et des partis politiques sous la republique*. Paris.

Henrichs, A. 1976. "*Despoina Kybele*: Ein Beitrag zur religiösen Namenkunde." *Harvard Studies in Classical Philology* 80: 253–286.

Hersch, K. 2010. *The Roman Wedding: Ritual and Meaning in Antiquity*. Cambridge.

Heskel, J. 2001. "Cicero as Evidence for Attitudes to Dress in the Late Republic." In J. L. Sebesta and L. Bonfante eds. *The World of Roman Costume*. Madison, Wisc. 133–145.

Hickson-Hahn, F. 1998. "What's so Funny? Laughter and Incest in Invective Humor." *Syllecta Classica* 9: 1–36.

Hillard, T. W. 1982. "P. Clodius Pulcher 62–58 B.C.: *Pompeii adfinis et sodalis*." *Papers of the British School at Rome* 50: 34–44.

Hine, H. 2015. "Philosophy and *philosophi*: From Cicero to Apuleius." In G. D. Williams and K. Volk eds. *Roman Reflections: Studies in Latin Philosophy*. Oxford. 13–29.

Hofmann, J. B. 1948. "Die lateinischen Totalitätsausdrücke." In *Mélanges de philologie, de littérature et d'histoire anciennes offerts á J. Marouzeau*. Paris. 283–290.

Hofmann, J. B. 1980 [1951]. *La lingua d'uso latina*. Trans. L. Ricottilli of *Lateinische Umgangssprache*. 3rd ed. Bologna.

Hölkeskamp, K.-J. 2010. *Reconstructing the Roman Republic. An Ancient Political Culture and Modern Research*. Trans. H. Heitmann-Gordon. Princeton.

Horsfall, N. 1972. "Varro and Caesar: Three Chronological Problems." *Bulletin of the Institute of Classical Studies* 19: 120–128.

Horsfall, N. 2000. *Virgil, "Aeneid" 7: A Commentary*. Leiden.

Horsfall, N. 2008. *Virgil, "Aeneid" 2: A Commentary*. Leiden.

Horsfall, N. 2013. *Virgil, "Aeneid" 6: A Commentary*. Berlin and Boston.

Housman, A. E. 1909. "*Vester = tuus.*" *Classical Quarterly* 3: 244–248.
Hudson, J. 2021. *The Rhetoric of Roman Transportation*. Cambridge.
Hutchinson, G. O. 1995. "Rhythm, Style, and Meaning in Cicero's Prose." *Classical Quarterly* 45: 485–499.
Hutchinson, G. O. 2006. *Propertius: Elegies, Book IV.* Cambridge.
Innes, D. 1988. "Cicero on Tropes." *Rhetorica* 6: 307–325.
Jeep, J. 1862. *Kritische Bemerkungen zu Ciceros Reden*. Wolfenbüttel.
Jeep, J. 1863. *Kritische Bemerkungen zu Ciceros Reden*. Wolfenbüttel.
Jenkyns, R. 2014. *God, Space, and City in the Roman Imagination*. Oxford.
Jocelyn, H. D. 1967. *The Tragedies of Ennius*. Cambridge.
Jocelyn, H. D. 1973. "Greek Poetry in Cicero's Prose Writings." *Yale Classical Studies* 23: 61–111.
Jocelyn, H. D. 1982a. "Varro's *Antiquitates Rerum Divinarum* and Religious Affairs in the Late Roman Republic." *Bulletin of the John Rylands Library* 65: 148–205.
Jocelyn, H. D. 1982b. "Boats, Women, and Horace *Odes* 1.14." *Classical Philology* 77: 330–335.
Jolowicz, H. F., and B. Nicholas. 1972. *Historical Introduction to the Study of Roman Law*. 3rd ed. Cambridge.
Kajanto, I. 1965. *The Latin Cognomina*. Helsinki. Societas Scientiarum Fennica: Commentationes Humanarum Litterarum 36.2.
Karsten, H. T. 1879. "Cicero: *Orationes post reditum tres; Oratio de domo.*" *Mnemosyne* n.s. 7: 399–410.
Kaser, M. 1971–1975. *Das römische Privatrecht*. 2nd ed. Munich. 2 vols.
Kaster, R. A. 2005. *Emotion, Restraint, and Community in Ancient Rome*. Oxford.
Kaster, R. A. 2006. *Cicero: Speech on Behalf of Publius Sestius*. Oxford.
Katz, J. 2000. "Egnatius' Dental Fricatives (Catullus 39.20)." *Classical Philology* 95: 338–348.
Katz, J. 2009. "Wordplay." In S. Jamison *et al.* eds. *Proceedings of the 20th Annual UCLA Indo-European Conference*. Bremen. 79–114.
Kay, N. M. 1985. *Martial Book XI. A Commentary*. London.
Kayser, C. L. 1862. *M. Tullii Ciceronis Opera Quae Supersunt Omnia*. Leipzig. Vol. 4.
Keaveney, A. 1987. *Rome and the Unification of Italy*. London and Sydney.
Keeline, T. 2013. "*Orthographicum quoddam*: reccido." *Glotta* 89: 126–129.
Keeline, T. 2018. *The Reception of Cicero in the Early Roman Empire: The Rhetorical Schoolroom and the Creation of a Cultural Legend*. Cambridge.
Keeline, T. 2021. *Cicero: Pro Milone*. Cambridge.
Keeline, T., and T. Kirby. 2019. "*Auceps syllabarum*: A Digital Analysis of Latin Prose Rhythm." *Journal of Roman Studies* 109: 161–204.
Kelly, G. P. 2006. *A History of Exile in the Roman Republic*. Cambridge.
Kiernan, P. 2020. *Roman Cult Images: The Lives and Worship of Idols, from the Iron Age to Late Antiquity*. Cambridge.
Kinsey, T. E. 1971. *M. Tulli Ciceronis Pro P. Quinctio Oratio. Edited with Text, Introduction and Commentary*. Sydney.
Klotz, A. 1915. *M. Tulli Ciceronis scripta quae manserunt omnia*, fasc. 21. Leipzig.
Koch, H. A. 1868. "Conjectanea Tulliana." Naumburg.
Köves, T. 1963. "Zum Empfang der Magna Mater in Rom." *Historia* 12: 321–347.
Köves-Zulauf, T. 1972. *Reden und Schweigen: Römische Religion bei Plinius Maior*. Munich. Studia et Testimonia Antiqua 12.

Köves-Zulauf, T. 1990. *Römische Geburtsriten*. Munich. Zetemata 87.
Kraffert, H. 1887. "Kakophonieen im Lateinischen." *Zeitschrift für das Gymnasialwesen* 41: 713–733.
Krause, C. 2001. "*In conspectu prope totius urbis* (Cic. *dom*. 100). Il tempio della Libertà e il quartiere alto del Palatino." *Eutopia* 1: 169–201.
Krauter, S. 2004. *Bürgerrecht und Kultteilnahme. Politische und kultische Rechte und Pflichten in griechischen Poleis, Rom und antiken Judentum*. Berlin and New York.
Krebs, C. 2018. "A Style of Choice." In L. Grillo and C. Krebs eds. *The Cambridge Companion to the Writings of Julius Caesar*. Cambridge. 110–130.
Kroon, C. 1995. *Discourse Particles in Latin: A Study of "nam," "enim," "autem," "vero" and "at."* Amsterdam.
Krostenko, B. 2004. "Binary Phrases and the Middle Style as Social Code: *Rhetorica ad Herennium* 4.13 and 4.16." *Harvard Studies in Classical Philology* 102: 236–274.
Kubiak, D. 1989. "Piso's Madness (Cic. *In Pis.* 21 and 47)." *American Journal of Philology* 110: 237–245.
Kübler, B. 1932. "*Tabulae censoriae*." RE^2 4: 1899–1900.
Kühne, H.-J. 1966. "Die stadtrömischen Sklaven in den *collegia* des Clodius." *Helikon* 6: 95–113.
Kumaniecki, K. 1959. "Ciceros Rede *De haruspicum responso*." *Klio* 37: 135–152.
La Bua, G. 2019. *Cicero and Roman Education: The Reception of the Speeches and Ancient Scholarship*. Cambridge.
Lambinus, D. 1566. *M. Tullii Ciceronis opera omnia, quae exstant*. Paris. 4 vols.
Lambinus, D. 1830. *Tullianae emendationes ex editione Ciceronis operum Lambiniana principe repetitas*. Ed. F. N. Klein. Koblenz.
Landgraf, G. 1914. *Kommentar zu Ciceros Rede "pro Sex. Roscio Amerino."* 2nd ed. Leipzig and Berlin.
Lanfranchi, T., ed. 2018. *Autour de la notion de "sacer."* Rome. Collection de l'École Française de Rome.
Langlands, R. 2006. *Sexual Morality in Ancient Rome*. Cambridge.
Lapyrionok, R. 2008. *"Consensus bonorum omnium": Untersuchungen zur politischen Terminologie der späten Römischen Republik*. Frankfurt.
Laser, G. 1997. *"Populo et scaenae serviendum est": Die Bedeutung der städtischen Masse in der späten Römischen Republik*. Trier. Bochumer Altertumswissenschaftliches Colloquium 29.
Lateiner, D. 2005. "Signifying Names and Other Ominous Accidental Utterances in Classical Historiography." *Greek, Roman and Byzantine Studies* 45: 35–57.
Latham, J. 2016. *Performance, Memory, and Processions in Ancient Rome: The "pompa circensis" from the Republic to Late Antiquity*. Cambridge.
Latte, K. 1960. *Römische Religionsgeschichte*. Munich. Handbuch der Altertumswissenschaft 5: 4.
Laughton, E. 1960. "Observations on the Style of Varro." *Classical Quarterly* 10: 1–28.
Laughton, E. 1964. *The Participle in Cicero*. Oxford.
Laurand, L. 1936–1940. *Études sur le style des discours de Cicéron*. 4th ed. Paris.
Lausberg, H. 1998. *Handbook of Literary Rhetoric. A Foundation for Literary Study*. Trans. M. Bliss, A. Jansen, and D. Orton. Leiden.
Lazzeretti, A. 2006. *M. Tulli Ciceronis, In C. Verrem Actionis Secundae Liber Quartus (De Signis). Commento storico e archeologico*. Pisa.

Leach, E. 2001. "Gendering Clodius." *Classical World* 94: 335–359.

Lebek, W. 1970. *"Verba Prisca": Die Anfänge des Archaisierens in der lateinischen Beredsamkeit und Geschichtsschreibung.* Göttingen.

Le Bonniec, H. 1974. "Une faute rituelle dans la *pompa* des jeux." In *Mélanges de philosophie, de littérature et d'histoire ancienne offerts à Pierre Boyancé.* Rome. Collection de l'École Française de Rome 22. 505–511.

Lebreton, J. 1901. *Études sur la langue et la grammaire de Cicéron.* Paris.

Leeman, A. 1963. *"Orationis ratio": The Stylistic Theories and Practice of the Roman Orators, Historians and Philosophers.* Amsterdam. 2 vols.

Leeman, A., H. Pinkster, and E. Rabbie. 1989. *M. Tullius Cicero: De Oratore Libri III. 3. Band: Buch II, 99–290.* Heidelberg.

Lehmann, C. A. 1880. "Quaestiones Tullianae. Pars V." *Hermes* 15: 354–355, 566–573.

Lehmann, C. A. 1886. *Quaestiones Tullianae. Pars prima: De Ciceronis epistulis.* Prague and Leipzig.

Lenaghan, J. O. 1969. *A Commentary on Cicero's Oration "De Haruspicum Responso."* The Hague.

Lennon, J. 2014. *Pollution and Religion in Ancient Rome.* Cambridge.

Leonhard, R. 1901. "*Cura (curatio)*." *RE* 4: 1761–1773.

Levene, D. 2012. "Defining the Divine in Rome." *Transactions of the American Philological Association* 142: 41–81.

Lévy, C. 1998. "Rhétorique et philosophie: la monstruosité politique chez Cicéron." *Revue des Études Latines* 76: 139–157.

Liebenam, W. 1905. "*Divisor*." *RE* 5: 1237–1238.

Linderski, J. 1972. "The Aedileship of Favonius, Curio the Younger and Cicero's Election to the Augurate." *Harvard Studies in Classical Philology* 76: 181–200.

Linderski, J. 1986. "The Augural Law." *Aufstieg und Niedergang der römischen Welt* 2.16.3: 2146–2312.

Linderski, J. 1989. "The Libri Reconditi." *Harvard Studies in Classical Philology* 89: 207–234 = Linderski 1995a: 496–523.

Linderski, J. 1991. Rev. Brouwer 1989. *Ploutarchos* 7.2: 27–30 = Linderski 2007: 533–536 (with addenda).

Linderski, J. 1995a. *Roman Questions. Selected Papers.* Stuttgart. Heidelberger althistorische Beiträge und epigraphische Studien 20.

Linderski, J. 1995b. "Ambassadors go to Rome." In E. Frézouls and A. Jacquemin eds. *Les relations internationales.* Paris. 453–478 = Linderski 2007: 40–60 (with addenda).

Linderski, J. 2007. *Roman Questions II. Selected Papers.* Stuttgart. Heidelberger althistorische Beiträge und epigraphische Studien 44.

Lindholm, E. 1931. *Stilistische Studien zur Erweiterung der Satzglieder im Lateinischen.* Lund.

Lindsay, W. M. 1900. *The "Captivi" of Plautus.* Oxford.

Lindsay, W. M. 1907. *Syntax of Plautus.* Oxford.

Lintott, A. 1968. *Violence in Republican Rome.* 2nd ed. Oxford.

Lintott, A. 1971. "The Tribunate of P. Sulpicius Rufus." *Classical Quarterly* 21: 442–453.

Lintott, A. 1990. "Electoral Bribery in the Roman Republic." *Journal of Roman Studies* 80: 1–16.

Lintott, A. 1993. *"Imperium Romanum": Politics and Administration*. London and New York.
Lintott, A. 2013. *Plutarch: Demosthenes and Cicero*. Oxford.
Löfstedt, E. 1911. *Philologischer Kommentar zur "Peregrinatio Aetheriae." Untersuchungen zur Geschichte der lateinischen Sprache*. Uppsala.
Löfstedt, E. 1956. *Syntactica: Studien und Beiträge zur historischen Syntax des Lateins*. 2nd ed. Lund. 2 vols.
Long, G., with A. J. Macleane. 1856. *M. Tullii Ciceronis Orationes*. London. Vol. 3.
Luterbacher, F. 1904. *Der Prodigienglaube und Prodigienstil der Römer*. Darmstadt.
MacBain, B. 1982. *Prodigy and Expiation: A Study in Religion and Politics in Republican Rome*. Brussels. Collection Latomus 177.
Madvig, J. N. 1871–1884. *Adversaria critica ad scriptores graecos et latinos*. Copenhagen. 3 vols.
Magie, D. 1950. *Roman Rule in Asia Minor to the End of the Third Century after Christ*. Princeton.
Malaise, M. 1972. *Les conditions de pénétration et de diffusion des cultes Égyptiens en Italie*. Leiden. Études Préliminaires aux Religions Orientales dans l'Empire Romain 22.
Maltby, R. 1991. *A Lexicon of Ancient Latin Etymologies*. Leeds.
Mankin, D. 2011. *Cicero: De oratore, Book III*. Cambridge.
Manuwald, G. 2018. *Cicero: Agrarian Speeches. Introduction, Text, Translation, and Commentary*. Oxford.
Manuwald, G. 2019. *Fragmentary Republican Latin: Oratory*. London. 3 vols.
Manuwald, G. 2021. *Cicero: "Post Reditum" Speeches. Introduction, Text, Translation, and Commentary*. Oxford.
Marcattili, F. 2020. "Il *magmentarium* di Tellus e il *lectisternium* di Cerere." *Revue archéologique* 69: 103–115.
Markland, J. 1745. *Remarks on the Epistles of Cicero to Brutus and of Brutus to Cicero: in a Letter to a Friend. With a Discussion upon Four Orations Ascribed to Marcus Tullius Cicero*. London.
Marouzeau, J. 1922. *L'ordre des mots dans la phrase latine: I: Les groupes nominaux*. Paris.
Marouzeau, J. 1946. *Traité de stylistique latine*. 2nd ed. Paris.
Marouzeau, J. 1956. "*Iuppiter Optimus* et *Bona Dea*." *Eranos* 54: 227–231.
Marshall, B. 1985. *A Historical Commentary on Asconius*. Columbia, Missouri.
Marshall, B. 1987. "Pompeius' Fear of Assassination." *Chiron* 17: 119–133.
Maslowski, T. 1976. "Domus Milonis oppugnata." *Eos* 64: 20–30.
Maslowski, T. 1981. *M. Tulli Ciceronis orationes "Cum senatui gratias egit," "Cum populo gratias egit," "De domo sua," "De haruspicum responsis."* Leipzig.
Maslowski, T., and R. H. Rouse. 1984. "The Manuscript Tradition of Cicero's Post-Exile Orations. Part I: The Medieval History." *Philologus* 128: 60–104.
May, J. M. 1980. "The Image of the Ship of State in Cicero's *Pro Sestio*." *Maia* 32: 259–264.
May, J. M. 1988. *Trials of Character: The Eloquence of Ciceronian Ethos*. Chapel Hill.
May, J. M. 1996. "Cicero and the Beast." *Syllecta Classica* 7: 143–153.
May, J. M., ed. 2002. *Brill's Companion to Cicero: Oratory and Rhetoric*. Leiden.
Mayer, R. 2005. "The Impracticability of Latin *Kunstprosa*." In Reinhardt *et al.* eds. 195–210.

McDermott, W. 1972. "Curio *Pater* and Cicero." *American Journal of Philology* 93: 381–411.

Mebane, J. 2022. "Cicero's Ideal Statesman as the Helmsman of the Ship of State." *Classical Philology* 117: 120–138.

Meillet, A. 1982. *Linguistique historique et linguistique générale*. Paris.

Merguet, H. 1877–1884. *Lexikon zu den Reden des Cicero*. Jena. 4 vols.

Metzger, E. 1997. *New Outline of the Roman Civil Trial*. Oxford.

Meyer, E. 2004. *Legitimacy and Law in the Roman World: "Tabulae" in Roman Belief and Practice*. Cambridge.

Meyer, I. 2003. "Zur Datierung von Ciceros Rede *de haruspicum responso*." *Göttinger Forum für Altertumswissenschaft* 6: 97–109.

Michels, A. 1966. "Lucretius, Clodius and Magna Mater." *Mélanges d'archéologie, d'épigraphie et d'histoire offerts à Jérôme Carcopino*. Paris. 675–679.

Michels, A. 1967. *The Calendar of the Roman Republic*. Princeton.

Millar, F. 1998. *The Crowd in Rome in the Late Republic*. Ann Arbor.

Moatti, C. 2017. "*Res publica, forma rei publicae*, and *SPQR*." *Bulletin of the Institute of Classical Studies* 60: 34–48.

Mommsen, T. 1887–1888. *Römisches Staatsrecht*. 2nd ed. Leipzig. 3 vols.

Mommsen, T. 1899. *Römisches Strafrecht*. Leipzig.

Moreau, P. 1982. *"Clodiana Religio." Un procès politique en 61 av. J.-C.* Paris.

Morstein-Marx, R. 2004. *Mass Oratory and Political Power in the Late Roman Republic*. Cambridge.

Mouritsen, H. 2013. "From Meeting to Text: the *Contio* in the Late Roman Republic." In H. van der Blom and C. Steel eds. *Community and Communication: Oratory and Politics in Republican Rome*. Oxford. 63–82.

Muse, K. 2009. "Fleecing Remus' Magnanimous Playboys: Wordplay in Catullus 58.5." *Hermes* 137: 302–313.

Muth, R. 1962. "Römische *religio*." In R. Muth *et al*. eds. *Serta Philologica Aenipontana*. Innsbruck. Innsbrucker Beiträge zur Kulturwissenschaft 7–8. 247–272.

Nägelsbach, K. 1905. *Lateinische Stilistik*. 9th ed. by I. Müller. Nuremberg.

Nappo, S. C. 1989. "Fregio dipinto dal 'praedium' di Giulia Felice con rappresentazione del foro di Pompei." *Rivista di Studi Pompeiani* 3: 79–96.

Narducci, E. 1997. "Perceptions of Exile in Cicero: The Philosophical Interpretation of a Real Experience." *American Journal of Philology* 118: 55–73.

Neudecker, R. 1988. *Die Skulpturenausstattung römischer Villen in Italien*. Mainz am Rhein. Beiträge zur Erschließung Hellenistischer und Kaiserzeitlicher Skulptur und Architektur 9.

Neuhauser, W. 1958. *"Patronus" und "Orator": eine Geschichte der Begriffe von ihren Anfängen bis in die augusteische Zeit*. Innsbruck. Commentationes Aenipontanae 14.

Neumann, G. 1976. "Zur Etymologie von lateinisch *augur*." *Würzburger Jahrbücher für die Altertumswissenschaft* 2: 219–229.

Nicholson, J. 1992. *Cicero's Return from Exile. The Orations "Post reditum."* New York. Lang Classical Studies 4.

Nicolet, C. 1960. "*Consul togatus*: Remarques sur le vocabulaire politique de Cicéron et de Tite-Live." *Revue des Études Latines* 38: 236–263.

Nicolet, C. 1976. "Le Temple des Nymphes et les distributions frumentaires à Rome." *Comptes rendus des séances de l'Académie des Inscriptions et Belles-Lettres* 120: 29–51.

Nippel, W. 1984. "Policing Rome." *Journal of Roman Studies* 74: 20–29.
Nippel, W. 1988. *Aufruhr und "Polizei" in der römischen Republik.* Stuttgart.
Nisbet, R. G. 1939. *M. Tulli Ciceronis De domo sua ad pontifices oratio.* Oxford.
Nisbet, R. G. M. 1961. *M. Tulli Ciceronis In L. Calpurnium Pisonem oratio.* Oxford.
Nisbet, R. G. M. 1990. "Cola and Clausulae in Cicero's Speeches." In E. M. Craik ed. *"Owls to Athens": Essays on Classical Subjects Presented to Sir Kenneth Dover.* Oxford. 349–359.
Nisbet, R. G. M., and M. Hubbard. 1970. *A Commentary on Horace: "Odes" Book I.* Oxford.
Nisbet, R. G. M., and N. Rudd. 2004. *A Commentary on Horace: "Odes" Book III.* Oxford.
Norden, E. 1913. *"Agnostos Theos": Untersuchungen zur Formengeschichte religiöser Rede.* Leipzig.
North, J. A. 1976. "Conservatism and Change in Roman Religion." *Papers of the British School at Rome* 44: 1–12.
Oakley, S. P. 1997–2005. *A Commentary on Livy, Books VI–X.* Oxford. 4 vols.
O'Brien Moore, A. 1935. "Senatus." Trans. into German by R. Keimer and W. Kroll. *RE* Suppl. 6: 660–800.
Oberhelman, S. 2003. *Prose Rhythm in Latin Literature of the Roman Empire: First Century B.C. to Fourth Century A.D.* Lewiston, NY. Studies in Classics 27.
Ogilvie, R. M. 1965. *A Commentary on Livy, Books 1–5.* Oxford.
Önnerfors, A. 1995. *P. Flavii Vegeti Renati Epitoma Rei Militaris.* Stuttgart and Leipzig.
Opelt, I. 1965. *Die lateinischen Schimpfwörter und verwandte sprachliche Erscheinungen.* Heidelberg.
Orelli, J. C., J. G. Baiter, and C. Halm. 1856. *M. Tullii Ciceronis Opera Quae Supersunt Omnia.* Vol. 2: 2. Zürich.
Orelli, J. C. 1886. *Q. Horatius Flaccus.* 4th ed. rev. J. G. Baiter and W. Hirschfelder. Berlin. 2 vols.
Orestano, R. 1939. "Dal *ius* al *fas*. Rapporto fra diritto divino e umano in Roma dall'età primitiva all'età classica." *Bullettino dell'Istituto di Diritto Romano* 46: 194–273.
Orlandini, A., and P. Poccetti. 2017. "Structures pseudo-subordonnées en *oratio obliqua*." In P. Poccetti ed. *"Oratio Obliqua": Strategies of Reported Speech in Ancient Languages.* Pisa. 77–85. Ricerche sulle lingue di frammentaria attestazione 9.
Orlin, E. 1997. *Temples, Religion and Politics in the Roman Republic.* Leiden.
Otto, A. 1890. *Die Sprichwörter und sprichwörtlichen Redensarten der Römer, gesammelt und erklärt.* Leipzig.
Padilla Peralta, D. 2020. *Divine Institutions. Religions and Community in the Middle Roman Republic.* Princeton.
Pallottino, M. 1948–1949. "Sulla lettura e sul contenuto della grande iscrizione di Capua." *Studi Etruschi* 20: 159–196.
Parke, H. W. 1988. *Sibyls and Sibylline Prophecy in Classical Antiquity.* London.
Paslay, M. G. 1918. "Does the Style of the *Civil War* Justify the Doubt as to Its Authenticity?" *Classical Journal* 13: 343–353.
Pease, A. S. 1920, 1923. *M. Tulli Ciceronis De divinatione liber primus.* Urbana.
Pease, A. S. 1955–1958. *M. Tulli Ciceronis De natura deorum libri tres.* Cambridge, Mass.
Pelling, C. 1988. *Plutarch: Life of Antony.* Cambridge.
Pelling, C. 2011. *Plutarch: Caesar.* Oxford.

Penney, J. H. W. 2005. "Connections in Archaic Latin Prose." In Reinhardt *et al.* eds. 37–51.
Perrochat, P. 1932. *L'infinitif de narration en latin*. Paris. Collection d'Études Latines 10.
Petersmann, H. 1996. "From Concrete to Abstract Thinking: The Development of Moral Concepts in Archaic Latin." In H. Rosén ed. *Aspects of Latin: Papers from the Seventh International Colloquium on Latin Linguistics, Jerusalem, April 1993*. Innsbruck. 665–674.
Petrocheilos, N. 1974. *Roman Attitudes to the Greeks*. Athens.
Piganiol, A. 1951. "Sur le calendrier brontoscopique de Nigidius Figulus." *Studies in Roman Economic and Social History in Honor of Allan Chester Johnson*. Princeton. 79–87.
Pina Polo, F. 1989. *Las "contiones" civiles y militares en Roma*. Zaragoza.
Pina Polo, F. 1995. "Procedures and Functions of Civil and Military *contiones* in Rome." *Klio* 77: 203–216.
Pina Polo, F. 2011. *The Consul at Rome. The Civil Functions of the Consuls in the Roman Republic*. Cambridge.
Pokorny, J. 1959, 1969. *Indogermanisches etymologisches Wörterbuch*. Bern and Munich. 2 vols.
Pompei, A. 2011. "Relative Clauses." In Ph. Baldi and P. Cuzzolin eds. *New Perspectives on Latin Historical Syntax, Volume 4: Complex Sentences, Grammaticalization, Typology*. Berlin. 427–547.
Powell, J. G. F., ed. 1989. *"Philosophia Togata": Essays on Philosophy and Roman Society*. Oxford.
Powell, J. G. F., ed. 1995. *Cicero the Philosopher: Twelve Papers*. Oxford.
Powell, J. G. F. 1988. *Cicero: Cato Maior De Senectute*. Cambridge.
Powell, J. G. F. 1990. "The Tribune Sulpicius." *Historia* 39: 446–460.
Powell, J. G. F. 1995. "Introduction." In Powell, ed. 1–35.
Powell, J. G. F. 2005. "Cicero's Adaptation of Legal Latin in the *De legibus*." In Reinhardt *et al.* eds. 117–150.
Powell, J. G. F. 2010. "Hyperbaton and Register in Cicero." In E. Dickey and A. Chahoud eds. *Colloquial and Literary Latin*. Cambridge. 163–185.
Powell, J. G. F. 2013. "Cicero's Style." In Steel ed. 41–72.
Preuss, S. 1881. *De bimembris dissoluti apud scriptores Romanos usu sollemni*. Edenkoben.
Probert, P. 2015. *Early Greek Relative Clauses*. Oxford.
Quilici, L., and S. Quilici Gigli. 1978. *Antemnae*. Rome. Latium Vetus 1.
Race, W. H. 1982. *The Classical Priamel from Homer to Boethius*. Leiden. Mnemosyne suppl. 74.
Radford, R. 1902. "Use of the Suffixes *-anus* and *-inus* in Forming Possessive Adjectives from Names of Persons." In *Studies in Honor of Basil L. Gildersleeve*. Baltimore. 95–111.
Radin, M. 1911. "Literary References in Cicero's Orations." *Classical Journal* 6: 209–217.
Ramsey, J. 2003. *Cicero: Philippics I–II*. Cambridge.
Ramsey, J. 2006. *A Descriptive Catalogue of Greco-Roman Comets from 500 B.C. to A.D. 400*. Iowa City. Syllecta Classica 17.

Rasmussen, S. 2003. *Public Portents in Republican Rome*. Rome. Analecta Romana Instituti Danici 34.
Rawson, E. 1975. "Caesar's Heritage: Hellenistic Kings and their Roman Equals." *Journal of Roman Studies* 64: 148–159 = Rawson 1991: 169–188.
Rawson, E. 1978. "Caesar, Etruria and the *disciplina Etrusca*." *Journal of Roman Studies* 68: 132–152 = Rawson 1991: 289–323.
Rawson, E. 1985. *Intellectual Life in the Late Roman Republic*. London.
Rawson, E. 1991. *Roman Culture and Society: Collected Papers*. Oxford.
Reid, J. S. 1885. *M. Tulli Ciceronis Academica*. London.
Reid, J. S. 1886. *M. Tulli Ciceronis Pro P. Cornelio Sulla Oratio ad Iudices*. Cambridge.
Reinhardt, T. 2003. *M. Tullius Cicero: Topica*. Oxford.
Reinhardt, T., M. Lapidge, and J. N. Adams, eds. 2005. *Aspects of the Language of Latin Prose*. Oxford. Proceedings of the British Academy 129.
Richardson, L. jr. 1980. "The Approach to the Temple of Saturn in Rome." *American Journal of Archaeology* 84: 51–62.
Richardson, L. jr. 1992. *A New Topographical Dictionary of Ancient Rome*. Baltimore.
Richlin, A. 1992. *The Garden of Priapus: Sexuality and Aggression in Roman Humor*. Rev. ed. Oxford.
Richlin, A. 2014. "Talking to Slaves in the Plautine Audience." *Classical Antiquity* 33: 174–226.
Riggsby, A. 1999. *Crime and Community in Ciceronian Rome*. Austin.
Riggsby, A. 2002a. "The *Post Reditum* Speeches." In May ed. 159–195.
Riggsby, A. 2002b. "Clodius / Claudius." *Historia* 51: 117–123.
Riggsby, A. 2004. "The Rhetoric of Character in the Roman Courts." In J. Powell and J. Paterson eds. *Cicero the Advocate*. Oxford. 165–185.
Risselada, R. 1993. *Imperatives and Other Directive Expressions in Latin*. Amsterdam. Amsterdam Studies in Classical Philology 2.
Risselada, R. 1998. "*Tandem* and *postremo*: Two of a Kind?" In R. Risselada ed. *Latin in Use: Amsterdam Studies in the Pragmatics of Latin*. Amsterdam. 85–116.
Rives, J. 2011. "Control of the Sacred in Roman Law." In O. Tellegen-Couperus ed. *Law and Religion in the Roman Republic*. Mnemosyne suppl. 336. 165–180.
Robb, M. A. 2010. *Beyond "Populares" and "Optimates": Political Language in the Late Republic*. Stuttgart. Historia Einzelschriften 213.
Robert-Tornow, W. 1893. *De apium mellisque apud veteres significatione et symbolica et mythologica*. Berlin.
Robinson, A. 1994. "Cicero's References to His Banishment." *Classical World* 87: 475–480.
Roby, H. J. 1892. *A Grammar of the Latin Language from Plautus to Suetonius*. London and New York. 2 vols.
Rocca, G. 1994. "La *porta scelerata* e la semantica di *scelus*." *Studi Etruschi* 60: 179–182.
Rolle, A. 2017. *Dall'Oriente a Roma. Cibele, Iside e Serapide nell'opera di Varrone*. Pisa.
Roller, L. 1999. *In Search of God the Mother: The Cult of Anatolian Cybele*. Berkeley.
Roller, M. 2010. "Demolished Houses, Monumentality, and Memory in Roman Culture." *Classical Antiquity* 29: 117–180.
Roloff, H. 1938. *"Maiores" bei Cicero*. Göttingen. Diss. Leipzig.

Rose, H. J. 1935. "*Numen inest*: 'Animism' in Greek and Roman Religion." *Harvard Theological Review* 28: 237–257.
Rose, H. J. 1951. "*Numen* and Mana." *Harvard Theological Review* 44: 109–120.
Rosenberg, A. 1920. "*Sacellum*." *RE* 1A: 1625–1626.
Rosenberger, V. 1998. *Gezähmte Götter. Das Prodigienwesen der römischen Republik*. Stuttgart.
Rouse, R. H. 1979. "Florilegia and Latin Classical Authors in Twelfth- and Thirteenth-Century Orléans." *Viator* 10: 131–160.
Rouse, R. H., and M. D. Reeve. 1983. "Cicero: Speeches." In L. D. Reynolds ed. *Texts and Transmission: A Survey of the Latin Classics*. Oxford. 54–99.
Rüpke, J. 2008. *"Fasti Sacerdotum": A Prosopography of Pagan, Jewish, and Christian Religious Officials in the City of Rome, 300 BC to AD 499*. Oxford.
Russell, A. 2016. "Why Did Clodius Shut the Shops? The Rhetoric of Mobilizing a Crowd in the Late Republic." *Historia* 65: 186–210.
Russell, D. A., and N. G. Wilson. 1981. *Menander Rhetor*. Oxford.
Ryan, F. X. 1998. *Rank and Participation in the Republican Senate*. Stuttgart.
Ryberg, I. S. 1955. *Rites of the State Religion in Roman Art*. Rome. Memoirs of the American Academy in Rome 22.
Sanford, E. M. 1939. "The Career of Aulus Gabinius." *Transactions of the American Philological Association* 70: 64–92.
Santangelo, F. 2011a. "*Pax Deorum* and Pontiffs." In J. H. Richardson and F. Santangelo eds. *Priests and State in the Roman World*. Stuttgart. 161–186.
Santangelo, F. 2011b. "Law and Divination in the Late Roman Republic." In O. Tellegen-Couperus ed. *Law and Religion in the Roman Republic*. Leiden and Boston. Mnemosyne suppl. 336. 31–54.
Santangelo, F. 2013. *Divination, Prediction and the End of the Republic*. Cambridge.
Santoro L'Hoir, F. 1992. *The Rhetoric of Gender Terms: "Man," "Woman," and the Portrayal of Character in Latin Prose*. Leiden. Mnemosyne suppl. 120.
Saur, H. 1913. *Die Adversativpartikeln bei lateinischen Prosaikern*. Diss. Tubingen.
Schaewen, R. von. 1940. *Römische Opfergeräte, ihre Verwendung im Kultus und in der Kunst*. Berlin. Archäologische Studien 1.
Scheid, J. 2015. *The Gods, the State, and the Individual: Reflections on Civic Religion in Rome*. Trans. C. Ando. Philadelphia.
Schierl, P. 2006. *Die Tragödien des Pacuvius. Ein Kommentar zu den Fragmenten mit Einleitung, Text und Übersetzung*. Berlin and New York. Texte und Kommentare 28.
Schmeling, G. 2011. *A Commentary on the "Satyrica" of Petronius*. Oxford.
Schnuerch, M., L. Nadarevic, and J. Rouder. 2021. "The Truth Revisited: Bayesian Analysis of Individual Differences in the Truth Effect." *Psychonomic Bulletin and Review* 28: 750–765.
Schubert, C. 2010. "Was bedeutet *strepitus*?" *Glotta* 86: 145–158.
Schultz, W. 1916–1924. "Tages." In Roscher 5: 3–5.
Schulze, W. 1933. *Zur Geschichte lateinischer Eigennamen*. Berlin.
Schütz, C. G. 1816. *M. Tullii Ciceronis Opera Quae Supersunt Omnia ac Deperditorum Fragmenta*. Leipzig. Vol. 8: 3.
Schwameis, C. 2019. *Cicero, "De praetura Siciliensi" (Verr. 2.2). Einleitung und Kommentar*. Berlin.

Scullard, H. H. 1981. *Festivals and Ceremonies of the Roman Republic*. London.
Seager, R. 1964. "The First Catilinarian Conspiracy." *Historia* 13: 338–347.
Seager, R. 2002. *Pompey the Great: A Political Biography*. 2nd ed. Oxford.
Setaioli, A. 1975. "Un influsso Ciceroniano in Virgilio." *Studi Italiani di Filologia Classica* 47: 7–26.
Seyffert, M. 1878. *Scholae Latinae: Beiträge zu einer methodischen Praxis der lateinischen Stil- und Compositionsübungen. Erster Theil: Die Formen der "tractatio."* 4th ed. Leipzig.
Shackleton Bailey, D. R. 1960. "Sex. Clodius—Sex. Cloelius." *Classical Quarterly* 10: 41–42.
Shackleton Bailey, D. R. 1965–1970. *Cicero's Letters to Atticus*. Cambridge. 7 vols.
Shackleton Bailey, D. R. 1977a. *Cicero: Epistulae ad Familiares*. Cambridge. 2 vols.
Shackleton Bailey, D. R. 1977b. "Brothers or Cousins?" *American Journal of Ancient History* 2: 148–150.
Shackleton Bailey, D. R. 1979. "On Cicero's Speeches." *Harvard Studies in Classical Philology* 83: 237–285.
Shackleton Bailey, D. R. 1983. "Brothers or Cousins?" *American Journal of Ancient History* 8: 191.
Shackleton Bailey, D. R. 1985. "More on Cicero's Speeches (*post reditum*)." *Harvard Studies in Classical Philology* 89: 141–151.
Shackleton Bailey, D. R. 1987. "On Cicero's Speeches (*post reditum*)." *Transactions of the American Philological Association* 117: 271–280.
Shackleton Bailey, D. R. 1991a. *Cicero Back from Exile: Six Speeches upon His Return*. Atlanta.
Shackleton Bailey, D. R. 1991b. *Two Studies in Roman Nomenclature*. 2nd ed. Atlanta.
Sherk, R. 1969. *Roman Documents from the Greek East. "Senatus consulta" and "epistulae" to the Age of Augustus*. Baltimore.
Sherwin White, A. N. 1973. *The Roman Citizenship*. Oxford.
Shewring, W. H. 1931. "Prose-Rhythm and the Comparative Method." *Classical Quarterly* 25: 12–22.
Siani-Davies, M. 2001. *Cicero's Speech "Pro Rabirio Postumo."* Oxford.
Sihler, A. 2014. *New Comparative Grammar of Greek and Latin*. Oxford.
Sittl, K. 1890. *Die Gebärden der Griechen und Römer*. Leipzig.
Sittl, K. 1900. "Der Name Italiens." *Archiv für lateinische Lexikographie und Grammatik* 10: 121–124.
Skinner, M. 2011. *Clodia Metelli. The Tribune's Sister*. Oxford.
Skutsch, F. 1910. "*Odium* und Verwandtes." *Glotta* 2: 230–246.
Skutsch, O. 1985. *The "Annals" of Q. Ennius*. Oxford.
Slușanski, D. 1974. "Le vocabulaire latin des *gradus aetatum*." *Revue roumaine de linguistique* 19: 104–121, 267–296, 345–369, 437–451, 563–578.
Smith, C. J. 2006. *The Roman Clan. The "gens" from Ancient Ideology to Modern Anthropology*. Cambridge.
Solin, H. 1987. "Three Ciceroniana." *Classical Quarterly* 37: 521–523.
Solin, H., and O. Salomies. 1994. *Repertorium nominum gentilium et cognominum Latinorum*. 2nd ed. Hildesheim.
Solodow, J. 1978. *The Latin Particle "quidem."* Boulder. American Classical Studies 4.

Stangl, T. 1912. *Ciceronis orationum scholiastae. Volumen II: Commentarios continens*. Leipzig.
Staples, A. 1998. *From Good Goddess to Vestal Virgins: Sex and Category in Roman Religion*. London and New York.
Steel, C. E. W. 2001. *Cicero, Rhetoric, and Empire*. Oxford.
Steel, C. E. W. 2007. "Name and Shame? Invective against Clodius and Others in the Post-Exile Speeches." In Booth ed. 105–127.
Steel, C. E. W. ed. 2013. *The Cambridge Companion to Cicero*. Cambridge.
Steele, R. B. 1896. "The Formula *non modo... sed etiam* and Its Equivalents." *Illinois Wesleyan Magazine* 1: 143–169.
Steinitz, S. 1885. *De affirmandi particulis Latinis: I. Profecto*. Wrocław.
Stockton, D. 1979. *The Gracchi*. Oxford.
Straub, J. 1883. *De tropis et figuris quae inveniuntur in orationibus Demosthenis et Ciceronis*. Würzburg.
Strobel, K. 1996. *Die Galater: Geschichte und Eigenart der keltischen Staatenbildung auf dem Boden des hellenistischen Kleinasien*. Vol. 1. Berlin.
Stroh, W. 2004. "*De domo sua*: Legal Problem and Structure." In J. G. F. Powell and J. Paterson eds. *Cicero the Advocate*. Oxford. 313–370.
Sullivan, R. D. 1990. *Near Eastern Royalty and Rome, 100–30 BC*. Toronto.
Summers, K. 1996. "Lucretius' Roman Cybele." In E. Lane ed. *Cybele, Attis and Related Cults. Essays in Memory of M. J. Vermaseren*. Leiden. 337–365.
Suolahti, J. 1963. *The Roman Censors. A Study on Social Structure*. Helsinki. Annales Academiae Scientiarum Fennicae, ser. B, 113.
Suolahti, J. 1972. "*Princeps senatus*." *Arctos* 7: 207–218.
Sutphen, M. 1901. "A Further Collection of Latin Proverbs." *American Journal of Philology* 22: 1–28, 121–148, 241–260, 361–391.
Sydow, R. 1941. "Kritische Beiträge zu Ciceros vier Reden nach seiner Rückkehr (Fortsetzung)." *Rheinisches Museum für Philologie* 90: 168–174.
Syme, R. 1956. "Piso and Veranius in Catullus." *Classica et Mediaevalia* 17: 129–134.
Szemler, G. 1972. *The Priests of the Roman Republic: A Study of Interactions between Priesthoods and Magistracies*. Brussels. Collection Latomus 127.
Talbert, R. J. A. 1984. *The Senate of Imperial Rome*. Princeton.
Talbert, R. J. A. et al. 2000. *Barrington Atlas of the Greek and Roman World*. Princeton.
Taldone, A. 1993. "Su *insania* e *furor* in Cicerone." *Bollettino di studi Latini* 23: 3–19.
Tan, J. 2008. "*Contiones* in the Age of Cicero." *Classical Antiquity* 27: 163–201.
Tan, J. 2013. "Publius Clodius and the Boundaries of the *contio*." In C. Steel and H. van der Blom eds. *Community and Communication: Oratory and Politics in Republican Rome*. Oxford. 117–132.
Tansey, P. 2016. *A Selective Prosopographical Study of Marriage in the Roman Elite in the Second and First Centuries B.C.: Revisiting the Evidence*. Diss. Macquarie University.
Tarver, T. 1996. "Varro, Caesar and the Roman Calendar." In A. Sommerstein ed. *Religion and Superstition in Latin Literature*. Bari. 39–57.
Tatum, W. J. 1990. "The *Lex Clodia de Censoria Notione*." *Classical Philology* 85: 34–43.
Tatum, W. J. 1991a. "Lucullus and Clodius at Nisibis (Plutarch, *Lucullus* 33–34)." *Athenaeum* 79: 569–579.

Tatum, W. J. 1991b. "The Marriage of Pompey's Son to the Daughter of Ap. Claudius Pulcher." *Klio* 73: 122–129.
Tatum, W. J. 1992. "The Poverty of the Claudii Pulchri: Varro, *De Re Rustica* 3.16.1–2." *Classical Quarterly* 42: 190–200.
Tatum, W. J. 1999. *The Patrician Tribune: Publius Clodius Pulcher*. Chapel Hill.
Taylor, L. R. 1937. "The Opportunities for Dramatic Performances in the Time of Plautus and Terence." *Transactions of the American Philological Association* 68: 284–304.
Taylor, L. R. 1942a. "Caesar's Colleagues in the Pontifical College." *American Journal of Philology* 63: 385–412.
Taylor, L. R. 1942b. "The Election of the Pontifex Maximus in the Late Republic." *Classical Philology* 37: 421–424.
Taylor, L. R. 1949. *Party Politics in the Age of Caesar*. Berkeley. Sather Classical Lectures 22.
Taylor, L. R. 1966. *Roman Voting Assemblies from the Hannibalic War to the Dictatorship of Caesar*. Ann Arbor.
Thomas, R. 1988. *Virgil, Georgics*. Cambridge. 2 vols.
Thomas, R. 2011. *Odes Book IV and Carmen Saeculare*. Cambridge.
Thulin, C. 1905–1909. *Die Etruskische Disciplin*. Göteburg. Göteborgs Högskola Årsskrift 11, 12, and 15. 3 vols.
Thulin, C. 1906a. *Italische sakrale Poesie und Prosa: eine metrische Untersuchung*. Berlin.
Thulin, C. 1906b. *Scriptorum Disciplinae Etruscae Fragmenta*. Berlin.
Thulin, C. 1912. "Haruspices." *RE* VII 2.2431–2468.
Thurn, A. 2018. *Rufmord in der späten römischen Republik: Charakterbezogene Diffamierungsstrategien in Ciceros Reden und Briefen*. Berlin. Philologus suppl. 11.
Thurneysen, R. 1906. "*Senium* und *desiderium*." *Archiv für lateinische Lexikographie und Epigraphik* 14: 179–184.
Timpanaro, S. 1988 [1994]. "Alcuni tipi di sinonimi in asindeto in latino arcaico e in età classica repubblicana." *Rivista di filologia e di istruzione classica* 116: 257–297, 385–428 = *Nuovi contributi di filologia e storia della lingua latina*. Bologna. 1–74.
Toll, K. 1997. "Making Roman-ness and the *Aeneid*." *Classical Antiquity* 16: 34–56.
Torrego, M. 2009. " Coordination." In P. Baldi and P. Cuzzolin eds. *New Perspectives on Historical Latin Syntax. Volume 1: Syntax of the Sentence*. Berlin. 443–487.
Tracy, C. 2012. "Cicero's *Constantia* in Theory and Practice." In W. Nicgorski ed. *Cicero's Practical Philosophy*. South Bend, Ind. 79–112.
Traina, A. 1984. "*Belua* e *bestia* come metafora di 'uomo'." *Rivista di filologia e dell' istruzione classica* 112: 115–119.
Turfa, J. M. 2012. *Divining the Etruscan World. The Brontoscopic Calendar and Religious Practice*. Cambridge.
Ullman, B. L. 1932. "Classical Authors in Certain Mediaeval Florilegia." *Classical Philology* 27: 1–42.
Vaan, M. de. 2008. *Etymological Dictionary of Latin and Other Italic Languages*. Leiden.
Valvo, A. 2014. "Il declino della Repubblica nel *De haruspicum responsis*." In M. Chiabà ed. "*Hoc quoque laboris praemium*." *Scritti in onore di Gino Bandelli*. Trieste. 509–518.
Van den Berg, C. 2008. "The *Pulvinar* in Roman Culture." *Transactions of the American Philological Association* 138: 239–273.

Van den Bruwaene, M. 1948. "Quelques éclaircissements sur le *De haruspicum responsis*." *L'Antiquité Classique* 17: 81–92.
Van der Blom, H. 2010. *Cicero's Role Models: The Political Strategy of a Newcomer*. Oxford.
Van der Meer, L. Bouke. 1987. *The Bronze Liver of Piacenza: Analysis of a Polytheistic Structure*. Amsterdam.
Van Meerdervort, J. P. Pompe. 1850. *Annotationes ad orationem, quae Ciceronis fertur, De haruspicum responsis*. Leiden.
Vasaly, A. 1993. *Representations: Images of the World in Ciceronian Oratory*. Berkeley.
Versnel, H. S. 1970. *"Triumphus": An Inquiry into the Origin, Development and Meaning of the Roman Triumph*. Leiden.
Versnel, H. S. 1976. "Two types of Roman *devotio*." *Mnemosyne* 29: 365–410.
Volk, K. 2021. *The Roman Republic of Letters. Scholarship, Philosophy, and Politics in the Age of Cicero and Caesar*. Princeton.
Vollmer, F. 1898. *P. Papinii Statii Silvarum Libri*. Leipzig.
Vretska, K. 1961. *C. Sallustius Crispus: Invektive und Episteln*. Heidelberg. 2 vols.
Wackernagel, J. 1916. *Sprachliche Untersuchungen zu Homer*. Göttingen. Forschungen zur griechischen und lateinischen Grammatik 4.
Wackernagel, J. 1926–1928. *Vorlesungen über Syntax: mit besonderer Berücksichtigung von Griechisch, Lateinisch und Deutsch*. Basel. 2 vols. Trans. D. Langslow, 2009, as *Lectures on Syntax: With Special Reference to Greek, Latin, and Germanic* (Oxford).
Wagenvoort, H. 1937 [1956]. "*Caerimonia*." *Glotta* 26 (1937) 115–131 = *Studies in Roman Literature, Culture, and Religion*. Leiden. 84–101.
Wagenvoort, H. 1947. *Roman Dynamism. Studies in Ancient Roman Thought, Language and Custom*. Oxford.
Wagenvoort, H. 1949. "*Profanus, Profanare*." *Mnemosyne* 2: 319–332.
Walbank, F. W. 1957–1979. *A Historical Commentary on Polybius*. Oxford. 3 vols.
Walters, B. 2020. *The Deaths of the Republic: Imagery of the Body Politic in Ciceronian Rome*. Oxford.
Ward, A. M. 1977. *Marcus Crassus and the Late Roman Republic*. Columbia, Missouri.
Wardle, D. 1998. *Valerius Maximus: Memorable Deeds and Sayings, Book 1*. Oxford.
Watson, A. 1967. *The Law of Persons in the Later Roman Republic*. Oxford.
Watson, A. 1968. *The Law of Property in the Later Roman Republic*. Oxford.
Watt, W. S. 1964. "Notes on Cicero, *Ad Atticum*, Book 4." *Hermes* 92: 395–407.
Watts, N. H., trans. 1923. *Cicero, Orations: Pro Archia. Post Reditum in Senatu. Post Reditum ad Quirites. De Domo Sua. De Haruspicum Responsis. Pro Plancio*. Cambridge, Mass. Loeb Classical Library 158.
Weinreich, O. 1916. "Zur römischen Satire." *Hermes* 51: 386–414.
Weinrib, E. J. 1968a. "The Prosecution of Roman Magistrates." *Phoenix* 22: 32–56.
Weinrib, E. J. 1968b. "The Family Connections of M. Livius Drusus Libo." *Harvard Studies in Classical Philology* 72: 247–278.
Weinstock, S. 1934. "*Terra Mater* und *Tellus*." *RE* 5B: 791–806.
Weinstock, S. 1937. "*Penates (Di)*." *RE* 19: 417–457.
Weinstock, S. 1949. Rev. of H. J. Rose, *Ancient Roman Religion*. *Journal of Roman Studies* 39: 166–167.
Weinstock, S. 1971. *Divus Julius*. Oxford.

Weiss, M. 2009. *Outline of the Historical and Comparative Grammar of Latin.* Ann Arbor and New York.
West, M. L. 2007. *Indo-European Poetry and Myth.* Oxford.
Wildfang, R. 2001. "The Vestals and Annual Public Rites." *Classica et Mediaevalia* 52: 223–255.
Wilkinson, L. P. 1963. *Golden Latin Artistry.* Cambridge.
Wille, G. 1951. *"Musica romana": Die Bedeutung der Musik im Leben der Römer.* Amsterdam.
Willems, P. 1885. *Le sénat de la république romaine.* Paris. 2 vols.
Williams, C. 2010. *Roman Homosexuality.* 2nd ed. Oxford.
Willis, J. 1972. *Latin Textual Criticism.* Urbana. Illinois Studies in Language and Literature 61.
Wills, J. 1996. *Repetition in Latin Poetry: Figures of Allusion.* Oxford.
Wingo, E. 1972. *Latin Punctuation in the Classical Age.* The Hague and Paris.
Winterbottom, M. 2004. "Perorations." In J. Powell and J. Patterson eds. *Cicero the Advocate.* Oxford. 215–230.
Wirszubski, C. 1954. "Cicero's *cum dignitate otium*: A Reconsideration." *Journal of Roman Studies* 44: 1–13.
Wiseman, T. P. 1974. *Cinna the Poet and Other Roman Essays.* Leicester.
Wiseman, T. P. 1984. "Cybele, Virgil, and Augustus." In T. Woodman and D. West eds. *Poetry and Politics in the Age of Augustus.* Cambridge. 117–128.
Wiseman, T. P. 1985. *Catullus and His World.* Cambridge.
Wiseman, T. P. 1998. "The Publication of *De Bello Gallico*." In K. Welch and A. Powell eds. *Julius Caesar as Artful Reporter: The War Commentaries as Political Instruments.* London. 1–9.
Wissowa, G. 1884–1937a. "Saturnus." In Roscher 4: 427–444.
Wissowa, G. 1884–1937b. "Vesta." In Roscher 6: 241–273.
Wissowa, G. 1912. *Religion und Kultus der Römer.* 2nd ed. Munich.
Wolf, F. 1801. *M. Tulli Ciceronis quae vulgo feruntur Orationes quatuor: I. Post Reditum in Senatu; II. Ad Quirites post Reditum; III. Pro Domo Sua ad Pontifices; IV. De Haruspicum Responsis.* Berlin.
Wölfflin, E. 1881 [1933]. "Zur Alliteration." *Sitzungsberichte der Königlich-Bayerischen Akademie der Wissenschaften* 2: 1–94 = *Ausgewählte Schriften*, ed. G. Meyer. Leipzig 1933. 225–281.
Wölfflin, E. 1885. "Genetiv mit Ellipse des regierenden Substantivs." *Archiv für lateinische Lexicographie und Grammatik* 2: 365–371.
Wölfflin, E. 1896. "*Sescenti, mille, centum, trecenti*, als unbestimmte und runde Zahlen." *Archiv für lateinische Lexikographie und Grammatik* 9: 177–190.
Wolters, X. F. M. G. 1935. *Notes on Antique Folklore on the Basis of Pliny's "Natural History" (28.22–9).* Amsterdam.
Woodcock, E. C. 1959. *A New Latin Syntax.* London.
Woodman, A. J. 1977. *Velleius Paterculus: The Tiberian Narrative (2.94–131).* Cambridge.
Woodman, A. J. 1980. "The Craft of Horace in Odes 1.14." *Classical Philology* 75: 60–67.
Woodman, A. J. 1998. *Tacitus Reviewed.* Oxford.
Woodman, A. J. 2008. *The Annals of Tacitus. Book 4.* Cambridge.

Woodman, A. J. 2014. *Tacitus: Agricola*. Cambridge.
Wright, F. 1931. *Cicero and the Theater*. Northampton, Mass. Smith College Classical Studies 11.
Wuilleumier, P., and A.-M. Tupet. 1966. *Cicéron: Discours. Tome XIII, 2, "Sur la réponse des haruspices."* Paris.
Wülker, L. 1903. *Die geschichtliche Entwicklung des Prodigienwesens bei den Römern. Studien zur Geschichte und Überlieferung der Staatsprodigien*. Diss. Leipzig.
Yaron, R. 1967. "Reflections on *usucapio*." *Revue d'histoire du droit (Tijdschrift voor Rechtsgeschiedenis)* 35: 191–229.
Zanker, P. 1979. "Zur Funktion und Bedeutung griechischer Skulptur in der Römerzeit." In H. Flashar ed. *Le classicisme à Rome aux I^{ers} siècles avant et après J.-C.* Vandoeuvres-Geneva. 283–306. Entretiens sur l'antiquitè classique 25.
Zetzel, J. 1995. *Cicero: De Re Publica. Selections*. Cambridge.
Zevi, F. 1996–1997. "Costruttori eccellenti per le mura di Ostia. Cicerone, Clodio e l'iscrizione della Porta Romana." *Rivista dell'Istituto Nazionale d'Archeologia e Storia dell'Arte* 19–20: 61–112.
Zevi, F., and I. Manzini. 2008. "Le iscrizioni della Porta Romana ad Ostia: un riesame." In M. L. Caldelli ed. *Epigrafia 2006: Atti della XIVe Rencontre sur l'épigraphie in onore di Silvio Panciera*. 187–206.
Zevi, F., and P. Fedeli. 2013. "*Fam.* 1, 9, 15 e il *monumentum* di Cicerone." *Rivista di filologia e di istruzione classica* 141: 137–160.
Ziegler, K. 1969. "*Mater Magna* oder *Magna Mater*?" In J. Bibauw ed. *Hommages à Marcel Renard*. Brussels. 2: 845–855.
Zielinski, T. 1904. *Das Clauselgesetz in Ciceros Reden: Grundzüge einer oratorischen Rhythmik*. Leipzig.
Zielinski, T. 1912. *Cicero im Wandel der Jahrhunderte*. 3rd ed. Leipzig and Berlin.
Zwierlein-Diehl, E. 1980. "*Simpuvium Numae*." In H. A. Cahn and E. Simon eds. *Tainia: Roland Hampe zum 70. Geburtstag am 2. Dezember 1978*. Mainz. 1: 405–422.

Index of Latin Terms

(for Latin names of rhetorical figures, see *General Index*)

aetatula 244
amicitia 83
an 161, 267
atque (ac) xli, 175, 195, 323
    before a consonant 64, 102, 104, 129–130

bacchor 228
belua 76
boni 74

caelestis 151, 302
caerimoniae 90
cavea 173–174, 177
comprimo 54
concido 57
concordia 321
configo 94
coniectura 288
consecratio 100–101
contio 88
corrumpo 77
credo 58, 217
creo xli, 232
cunctus 119
curriculum 154

dare, alicui senatum dare 49
decido 247
dedicatio 100–101
deteriores 297, 322
devotio 78–79
di immortales 170–171, 200, 229–230, 242
dignitas 73
divinitus 137–138, 232–233
dolor 61–62, 67, 251–252

emitto 256
et xli
examen 175
expiare 103

fas 95, 208, 249
fax 66
foedus (adj.) 203, 223, 273–274
foedus ferire 251
fornix 159
fremitus 97–98, 145–147, 165
frequens 115–116

furia 66–67
furor 58–59, 72, 102, 227

Gallograecus 185
glans 77

haud 101, 119, 158
heri 47
hesterno die 47–48
hodie 47
hodierno die 48
homo 50–51, 95, 265, 278
honos 286, 298

ille 56, 80
imperium 233
imprudens 95
impudens (impudicus) 49
impurus 106, 126, 206, 287
in ius vocatio 53
incestum 69
inimicitiae 83
inquam 66–67, 70, 91, 165, 318
intendo 51
interdico 108
ira (iracundia) 61
ius 208
    auctoritatis 119–120
    civile 121, 200
    gentium 200, 207
    hereditarium 119
    mancipi 120
    nexi 120
    optimum 120
    publicum 120, 124
    sacrum 120
iustitium 294–295

labes 264
ludius 162
lues 169

magmentarium 196–199
miraculum 101
mobilis 71–72
monstrum 67, 101, 175
mortalis 200

Index of Latin Terms

natio 299
-ne 271
nefas xii, 274
nisi forte 220, 224, 295
nominis delatio 52
numen 137
nuntio 101, 164, 325

obligo 183-184
odium 68, 73, 291-292
opinor 127
optimates 231-232, 285
orator xli, 207
os 106-7
ostentum 101
otium 72-73

paene 57-58, 67
pater 48, 232
pax deorum xxxii
pecunia 233-234
pecus 76-77
penates 110, 216-217
poenio 123
polluo 216
portentum 67, 101
postilio 150, 199
praecentio 154
praeda 65
princeps 116, 232, 259
prodigium 67, 101
profanus 100
publicani 50
pudor (pudicitia) 49, 249-250
purus 104

quasi 81
-que xli, 95, 156
quid ergo 119
quidem 192, 212, 299, 324

recito 98-99
refertus 187-188
reicio 118
relatio 99, 105, 118, 325
religio xlv, 89-90, 103-104, 115, 117, 183-184
religiosus 69, 90, 100, 105, 117, 159, 203, 287
repulsi 297-299
responsum xxviii, 109, 128, 155-156
rideo 92

sacer 89-90, 99-100, 105, 117-118
sanctus 117
satis superque 132
scaena 172-174
scelus (sceleratus) 74, 102, 212, 274, 313
senati (genitive) 94, 121
servare, de caelo 271
severitas 73
stipes 75-76
strepitus 145-147, 165
stuprare xxvi, 205
stuprum 69, 94, 205, 223, 255, 296
superstitio 90, 109

tandem 103, 280
tantus 103-104
tensa 154, 163

ubertas 241
unus (+ superlative) 188-189, 262, 276, 300
usucapio 200-201

vaecor 57, 138
vel 192, 241
vendito 50, 269, 284
verba facere 117
verum 118
violo 74, 91
vir 51, 95
voluto 245-246, 315

General Index

Ab urbe condita construction 102, 114, 123, 234
Abstract nouns,
   concrete nouns, coupled with 48–49, 51,
      69, 97, 143, 160, 171, 187, 213,
      249, 255
   to describe persons 48, 171, 219, 245
   in plural 231, 233, 328
Acilius Glabrio, Manius 112
Aemilius Lepidus, M. 112–113
Aemilius Scaurus, M. 113
Ager Latiniensis 145, 325
Ager Picenus 326
Albinovanus, P. 113
Alcmaeon 65, 225–226
Allegory xxi–xxii, 293
Alliteration 63, 113, 198, 203, 204, 221, 222,
      239, 265
Ambassadors (*oratores*), murder of
      207–209, 211
Anacoluthon 63, 322, 324
Anaphora 57, 62, 260, 269, 279–280, 287
Annius Milo, T. *See* Milo, T. Annius
Anticipatio 61
Appuleius Saturninus, L. 237–238, 239–240,
      242, 252
Archaisms xx, xl–xlii, 64, 91, 94, 121, 151,
      207, 232
Arnobius of Sicca xxviii, 89, 100, 150,
      152–153, 162–163, 219
Asconius Pedianus, Q. xxvii, 121, 168–169
Asicius, P. xvi, 208
Asyndeton xli, 48, 71, 89, 91, 151, 159, 183,
      247, 249, 262–263, 269, 287,
      307, 312
   Asyndeton bimembre 105–106, 160,
      171, 192
Athamas 225
Athenion 177
Atilius Serranus, Sex. 199, 202–203
Augury and auspices xxxviii, 133–134, 262,
      271–272, 309–310

Bacchus, suppression of worship of xxxvi
Bona Dea. *See* Clodius Pulcher, P.
Brogitarus 179, 184–187, 189–190,
      310, 316

Caecilius Metellus Creticus, Q. 112
Caecilius Metellus Nepos, Q. 116, 122, 279

Caecilius Metellus Pius Scipio Nasica, Q. 112
Caecilius Metellus Celer, Q. 258–259
Caecilius Rufus, L. 311
Calpurnius Bibulus, M. 270–271
Calpurnius Piso Caesoninus, L. 55–56,
      58, 62–67, 77, 201, 211–213, 269, 310
Carthaginians 141
Catilina, L. Sergius 74–75, 247
Catilinarian conspiracy xiii–xiv, xxxix, 136,
      249, 273, 307–308
   See too Catilina, L. Sergius
Cato the Elder. *See* Porcius Cato, M. (the
   Elder)
Charybdis 315–317
Chiasmus 85, 139, 152, 171, 183, 235,
      256, 264
Cicero, M. Tullius, *passim*
   boasting of 124–127, 273–274
   and Bona Dea. *See* Clodius Pulcher, P.
   De domo sua xi, xiv–xv, xxxviii, xxxix,
      passim in commentary
   De haruspicum responsis,
      date of xxix–xxxi
      title of xxvii–xxix
      rhetorical strategy in xvii–xix
      style in xix–xxv and *passim* in
      commentary
      See also *various literary devices listed
      in* General Index
   deniability in 50, 54, 77, 81, 245
   exile and recall of xi, xiii, 107–108,
      263–264, 268–269, 277, 298
   house on Palatine xiii, xvi, xxxvii–xxxviii,
      107, 121
   location of 193, 206–207
   myth, use of 65, 95, 149–150, 224–226,
      315–317, 318–319
   Post reditum orations, common motifs
      in xiv–xv, xix–xx, xxv–xxvii, 48,
      55–56, 61, 62–63, 69, 82
   provincial origins of, mockery of 126–127
   Roman state, identifies self with 48, 56,
      62–63, 67, 73, 122–123, 299, 328
   Tellus, curator of temple of 197–198
   wit of 56, 75–76, 91–92, 96–97, 100, 124,
      190, 207, 214, 221, 227–228, 248,
      253, 304, 307, 317
Claudia Quinta 180–183
Claudius, L. 112

General Index

Claudius Caecus, Appius 179, 182, 221–222
Claudius Pulcher, Appius (father of Clodius) 60, 176, 183
Claudius Pulcher, Appius (brother of Clodius) 196–200, 205
Claudius Pulcher, C. (uncle of Clodius) 176, 183
Clodia (sister of Clodius) 58, 69, 106, 158, 182–183, 222–223, 258–259
Clodius Pulcher, P., *passim*
  adoption as plebeian 126, 257, 261, 270–271, 303–304
  as aedile in 56 BCE xvii, xxx, 50, 53–54, 88, 158–159, 170, 172, 183, 205, 279, 295
  as animal 58, 76–77, 82, 83–84, 256, 285–286, 301
  biography of xii, 176
    according to Cicero 243–278
  and Bona Dea festival xii, xvii–xix, 69–70, 92–95, 97, 111, 113, 118, 179, 186, 214–224, 246, 249, 254–256, 305–306
  bribes and illicit payments 268, 299
    accused of dispensing 214, 221, 261
    accused of receiving 50, 185–186, 189–191, 248, 264–265, 284, 316, 320
  buildings, attacking public and private 66, 81–82, 204–205, 223, 227, 306, 310–311
  and Cicero's house xiv–xv, xxx, 90, 107, 121, 122, *passim*
  contio De haruspicum responsis of xv–xvii, 87–101, 129, 132, 153, 176–177, 207, 208, 220, 283–284, 294–295
  death of 78–79, 107
  followers of xiii, 159, 170–179, 185–186, 210–211, 227, 285–286, 316–317
  and Furies xxii, 65–66, 227, 262
  house on Palatine of 193, 206–207
  legislation of 106–107, 184
    censorship, elimination of 309–310
    Cicero, exile of xi, xiii–xiv, 56, 113, *passim*
    on grain distribution 312
    kings, on appointing 186, 189, 310
    leges Aelia et Fufia, elimination of 309
    provinces, on assigning 310
    Ptolemy of Cyprus, on 310, 316
    veto and auspices, elimination of 310
  madness of 51, 55–59, 65, 204, 224–229, 236, 240, 256, 270, 278, 282, 308–309
  masculinity. *See* Invective, motifs of; masculinity, lack of
  as a prodigy 306
  as *quindecimvir sacris faciundis* xvi, 100, 135, 178, 183
Cloelius, Sex. 106–107, 316–317
Conduplicatio 67, 91
Cornelius, Q. 113
Cornelius Cinna, L. 136, 290–291
Cornelius Lentulus Crus, L. 217–218
Cornelius Lentulus Marcellinus, Cn. xxix–xxx, 53, 54–55, 57, 58, 105, 152–153, 169
Cornelius Lentulus Niger, L. 112
Cornelius Lentulus Spinther, P. 111–112, 116, 122
Cornelius Scipio Aemilianus, P. 80–81
Cornelius Scipio Africanus the Elder, P. 168, 238
Cornelius Scipio Nasica, P. 157, 169, 181
Cornelius Scipio Nasica Serapio, P. 160, 169
Cornelius Sulla Felix, L. 136, 290–291
Correctio 220, 283, 319

Deiotarus I of Galatia 184, 187, 188–191, 310, 313
Dilemma 78, 324
Dio (philosopher) 208

Elision 139, 164, 292
Exile in ancient Rome xxxviii–xxxix
  See too Cicero, M. Tullius; exile and recall of

Families, private rites of (*sacra privata*) 90, 118, 202, 206–207, 303–304
Fannius, C. 112
Figura etymologica 84, 134, 160, 163, 214–215, 241, 248, 290
First Triumvirate xxx, 112, 235, 260, 266–267, 269–270, 287, 289, 293–294, 318, 323
  See also Julius Caesar, C.; Pompeius Magnus, Cn.; Licinius Crassus, M.
Florilegium Gallicum xxvii–xxviii, xliii, 228, 289
Fonteius, P. (adoptive father of Clodius) 126, 202, 303–304
Furies 65–66, 225–226, 227–228, 262
  See too Clodius Pulcher, P.; and Furies

Gabinius, Aulus xxx, 50, 54–56, 58, 62–67, 72, 75, 77, 201, 244, 269, 310
Gauls 140–141
Gellius (follower of Clodius) 316, 317
Gemination xx, 70, 157, 159, 274
Gracchi. *See* Sempronius Gracchus, C. *and* Tib.
Grammatical gender, play on xxiii, 80, 81, 169, 219, 242, 244, 255, 262, 264, 280, 314, 316

General Index

Haruspices xi, xxxii–xxxiii, xxxiv–xxxviii, 133, 135–136, *passim*
   and brontoscopic calendar 145, 147–148, 230–231, 233, 288, 297
   and extispicy xxxiv, 151
   and *Libri Etrusci* xxviii–xxix, 98, 136, 148, 218, 286
   response of (65 and 63 BCE) 136, 231, 294
   response of (56 BCE) xvi–xix, xxx, xxxix–xlii, *passim*
   training and method for compiling responses xxviii–xxix, xxxiv–xxxix, 97–99, 105, 191, 192, 207, 297, 318
   and prophecy of Vegoia xli, 231
Hendiadys 86, 129–130, 159, 163, 188, 213, 246, 255, 279, 285–286
   See also Abstract nouns; concrete nouns, coupled with
Hermarchus of Chios 210
Hispani 140
Homoioteleuton 57, 63, 64–65, 73, 80, 81, 110, 123, 146–147, 165, 204, 212, 265, 271, 279
Hostilius Mancinus, C. 251–252
Hyperbaton 52, 58, 68, 70, 81, 87, 93–94, 101, 107, 131, 144, 158–159, 197, 224, 235, 300, 313
   conjunct ("brave men and true") 56, 185, 218, 265, 327

Infinitive, historic 269–270
Instauratio 155, 161–164
Invective, motifs of xviii
   ancestors, not living up to 60, 176–177, 222, 304
   biography, contrived 176, 243–248
   excessive erudition 130–132, 137
   gladiators 54, 121
   legacy hunting 247–248
   masculinity, lack of xix, 69, 77, 127–128, 242–243, 246, 254–255, 280
   non-Roman origins 50, 126
   rhetorical ineptitude 92, 128
   sexual deviance 50, 54, 295–296, 314–315
      incest 95, 96–97, 126, 222–223, 227–228, 245–246, 315
      prostituting oneself 50, 244–245, 314–315
Isocolon 63, 110, 123, 134
Itali 141–143

Julius Caesar, C. xxxi, 109, 111, 258–262, 267–268, 269–272, 293
   and Bona Dea festival xii, 70, 223, 305
   See also First Triumvirate

Julius Caesar, Sex. 113
Julius Caesar Strabo Vopiscus, C. 253
Julius Obsequens xxxiv
Jupiter Optimus Maximus 102, 104, 145, 151, 153, 155, 327

Lactantius 218–219
Latini 141–143
Libertas (goddess) xi, xiii, xvi, 90, 99, 104, 111, 205–206, 308
Licinius Crassus, M. (triumvir) 113, 177, 214, 268–269
   See also First Triumvirate
Licinius Lucullus, L. 246, 313
Licinius Murena, L. xii, 247
Luca, conference at xxx, 294, 318
Lucullus. *See* Licinius Lucullus, L.
Ludi Romani 153–155, 161–162, 168–169
Lutatius Catulus, Q. *See* Porticus Catuli

Marcius Philippus, L. 54–55, 105, 165
Marius, C. 136, 282, 290–291
Markland, Jeremiah xxv–xxvii
Mater Magna 156–161, 164–192
   name of 165
   priests of (*Galli*) 157, 167–168
Megalesia xvii, xxx, 152, 156–161, 164–179, 182–184, 227
Metaphor xxi–xxii, 59, 60, 66–67, 68, 70, 72, 77, 78–79, 83, 87, 106, 175, 262–263, 269, 293, 296, 302
Milo, T. Annius xxiii, 78–87, 250, 279, 311

Naming conventions 49, 50, 68, 84–85, 105, 112, 157, 220, 303
Neptune (god) 151
Nigidius Figulus, P. 147–148, 234
Numa Pompilius 114

Octavius, Cn. 291
Oracles xxxi–xxxii
   See too Quindecimviri sacris faciundis
Orestes 65–66, 225–226

Peroratio 286, 321–322
Philoctetes 224–225
Pinarius Natta, L. 111, 198
Plator 211–212
Poets and poetry, references to 142, 149–150, 315–316, 319
   of tragedy 65–66, 138, 224–226, 228–229, 300–301, 323, 324–325
Polyptoton 117, 167, 204, 223, 328–329
Polysyndeton 183, 301
Pompeia (wife of Pompey) xii, 223, 305

General Index

Pompeius Magnus, Cn. (Pompey) xiii, xvii, xxxi, 82, 189, 223, 258–268 and 272–285 *passim*, 292, 313
    Cicero, compared with 273–274, 276, 282, 310
    as grain commissioner xv, 116, 158, 166, 198–199, 306
    See also First Triumvirate
Pontifex maximus 69–70, 109, 111, 305
Pontifices xi–xii, xxxiii, xxxvi–xxxix, 99, 104, 108–113, 133–134, 155, 192
    judges, as equivalent to 111, 113–115, 118
Porcius Cato, M. (the Elder) xxxiv, 141–142
Porticus Catuli 193, 205–206, 277, 311, 313
Postumius Albinus, Sp. xxxvi
Priamel 140
Prodigies and the prodigy process xi, xxxi–xxxiv, 67, 105, 149, *passim*
    as metaphor 66–67
    of bees 174–175
    of earthquakes xi, 143, 145–147, 151, 325–326
    as word of the gods 102, 129, 144–145, 257, 324, 327
    See also Haruspices
Prose rhythm xxiii–xxv, 57, 60–61, 62, 71, 73, 96, 101, 110, 114, 123, 124, 134, 136, 139, 143, 167, 171, 227, 242, 264, 313, 326–327, 328
    with *atque* plus consonant 64, 102, 129–130
    internal 47, 106, 151, 159, 217
    heroic clausula 79–80, 124
    and textual criticism xxvi, 86, 194–195, 288, 289
    unusual instance of 207
Publicani (tax collectors) 49–50, 320

Quindecimviri (decemviri) sacris faciundis xxxiii, xxxviii, 133–135, 178, 179–180, 183
    See also Clodius Pulcher, P.; as *quindecimvir sacris faciundis*
Quintilianus, M. Fabius xxvii, 61

Redundancy 104, 118, 143, 144, 155, 156, 171, 184–185, 230, 241, 284
Relative clause, preposed 64
Ring composition 87, 97, 156, 242, 313, 320, 321

Saturn (god) 151
Scribonius Curio, C. 113
Scylla 315–318
Seius Postumus, Q. 192–195, 313
Sempronius Gracchus, C. 238–239, 242, 252
Sempronius Gracchus, Tib. 160, 236–239, 242, 251–252
Sempronius Gracchus, Tib. (father of Gracchi) 238

Septemviri epulones 153, 155
Servilius Atia Isauricus, P. 59–60, 109, 112
Servilius Glaucia, C. 239, 282
Sibylline Books. *See* Quindecimviri sacris faciundis
Sound play xxiii, 146–147, 149, 159–160, 164, 169, 193, 239, 291–292, 325
    See also alliteration, grammatical gender, homoioteleuton, prose rhythm
Spartacus 177
Subiectio 204
Sulla. *See* Cornelius Sulla Felix, L
Sulpicius Galba, P. 112
Sulpicius Rufus, P. 238, 240–242, 253–254
Synchysis 300–301

Tages xxviii, 102, 148
Tellus (god) xvi–xvii, 151, 165–166, 196–198, 200
Temple,
    of Castor and Pollux 185–186, 274–275
    of Concordia 321
    of Diana (*sacellum*) 201
    of Mater Magna in Rome 157, 165, 166–167, 182
    of Mater Magna in Phrygia (shrine) 179–181, 184
    of Nymphae 227, 304–307
    of Tellus 151, 197–198
Terentius Culleo, Q. 113
Terentius Varro, M. *See* Varro, M. Terentius
Terentius Varro Lucullus, M. 109, 112, 114
Tettius Damio 311
Theodosius of Chios 210
Titius (follower of Clodius) 317
Tricolon xx–xxi, 62–64, 71, 81, 106, 110, 113, 118, 129–130, 136, 139, 161, 179, 184, 192, 198, 202, 227, 239, 242–243, 272, 302
    capped by a fourth colon 184, 190, 203, 264, 265, 269, 284
    descending 57, 73, 123, 172, 183–184
    single words, consisting of 89, 91, 167
Tullius Cicero, M. *See* Cicero, M. Tullius
Tullius Cicero, Q. 197–198, 311
Tullius Nisyrus, P. 50

Valerius Maximus xxxiv, 133, 135, 188
Valerius Messala Niger, M. 112
Valerius Publicola, P. 123
Varro, M. Terentius 149
Vatinius, P. 298–299
Vegetius Renatus 144
Vestal virgins and cult of Vesta xii, 68–69, 110, 114–115, 220

Wolf, Friedrich xxvi–xxvii